4TH CANADIAN EDITION

LanguageArts

CONTENT AND TEACHING STRATEGIES

Gail E. Tompkins
California State University, Fresno

Robin M. Bright
University of Lethbridge

Michael J. Pollard
University of Lethbridge

Pamela J.T. Winsor
University of Lethbridge

PEARSON

Prentice
Hall

Toronto

Library and Archives Canada Cataloguing in Publication

Language arts : content and teaching strategies / Gail E. Tompkins . . . [et al.].—4th Canadian ed.

Includes bibliographical references and index.
ISBN 978-0-13-198880-4

1. Language arts (Elementary).   2. English language—Study and teaching (Elementary)
I. Tompkins, Gail E.   II. Title.

LB1576.L297 2008   372.6'044   C2006-905299-9

ISBN-13: 978-0-13-198880-4
ISBN-10:   0-13-198880-8

Editor-in-Chief, Vice-President of Sales: Kelly Shaw
Acquisitions Editor: Christine Cozens/Kathleen McGill
Marketing Manager: Toivo Pajo
Developmental Editor: Jody Yvonne
Production Editor: Tara Tovell/Amanda Wesson
Copy Editor: Joe Zingrone
Proofreader: Tara Tovell
Production Coordinator: Avinash Chandra
Composition: Integra
Photo Research: Amanda McCormick
Permissions Research: Amanda McCormick
Art Director: Julia Hall
Cover Design: Miguel Acevedo
Interior Design: Miguel Acevedo
Cover Image: Getty Images/Digital Vision/Rayman

For permission to reproduce copyrighted material, the publisher gratefully acknowledges the copyright holders listed on page 542, which is considered an extension of this copyright page.

3 4 5   12 11 10 09 08

Printed and bound in the United States of America.

*To Linda and John Cooke, who are always there
for me—Gail E. Tompkins*

*To the children in classrooms, the teachers, and the student teachers
who inspire and challenge us to write, research, and teach
—Robin M. Bright, Michael J. Pollard, Pamela J. T. Winsor*

Brief Contents

Contents

Special Features

Profiles

Teacher's Notebook

Step by Step

Minilessons

Adapting

Preface

Teachers who help students learn to communicate effectively are challenged by the cultural and linguistic diversity the students present in their classrooms. Further, technological advances both enhance and complicate the nature of language learning and teaching.

It is our intent with this fourth Canadian edition of *Language Arts: Content and Teaching Strategies* to provide a useful resource to teachers as they accept and meet these challenges. Both preservice and inservice teachers will find this text a valuable addition to their professional libraries. For preservice teachers who will work with students in kindergarten through grade 8, the text offers a consistent model of instruction that will help them become knowledgeable about language learning and guide the many instructional decisions they will make. For experienced inservice teachers, the text provides a rich array of strategies and ideas that they can adapt to suit their personal instructional styles.

The fourth Canadian edition of *Language Arts* is a significant revision of a popular core text designed for elementary- and middle-school language arts methods courses and language and literacy courses.

Philosophy of the Text

The philosophy of *Language Arts* reflects a constructivist approach to teaching and learning. The processes of reading and writing provide the foundation for the instructional approaches presented: resource-based units, thematic units, inquiry-based units, and readers and writers workshops. Such timeless, research-based approaches to teaching share these important features:

- Establishing a community of learners
- Using exemplary children's and young adult literature
- Involving students in meaningful, functional, and genuine activities and decision making
- Teaching skills and strategies in context
- Connecting instruction and assessment

Goal of the Text

The goal of *Language Arts* is to present the nature of language and language learning together with the most effective strategies for teaching the language arts. The text is organized in three parts. The first two chapters present an overview of learning and teaching the language arts. The middle chapters describe the content and teaching strategies that represent research-based best practices. The final chapter demonstrates how to create a variety of field-tested language arts units.

The fourth edition continues to recognize the importance visual literacy plays in communication and extends discussion of new literacies and technology. Visual literacy is demonstrated through viewing and visually representing. Viewing, like listening and reading, is receptive. Students are viewing when they compare video versions of stories to the print versions; examine illustrations in books they are reading; and analyze webpages, maps, and charts classmates have constructed. Visually representing, like talking and writing, is productive. Students are visually representing when they create story quilts, dramatize a story, or synthesize information in a chart or diagram.

Highlights and Features of the Fourth Canadian Edition

- New content on the reading process and how children learn to read.
- New literacies and critical literacy are included in Chapter 1.
- New content on viewing and visually representing strengthens the visual literacy component of the book. Teaching and learning activities relating to these specific paired skills have also been added.
- New Canadian research and new culturally diverse Canadian literature and resources have been added.
- New resources have been added in the area of integrating the fine arts into literacy programs.
- Content is drawn from across Canada. Urban and rural schools are featured in chapter-opening profile boxes, and more diverse instructional strategies are presented.
- New and extended ideas are offered for differentiating instruction to meet the needs of every student.
- Extended information is included on organizing readers and writers workshop within instructional units.
- More information on integrating communication technology into English language arts has been incorporated throughout the book.
- The Glossary at the back of the book includes definitions of important terms and concepts.

Supplements

The following instructor supplements are available for downloading from a password-protected section of Pearson Education Canada's online catalogue (vig.pearsoned.ca). Navigate to your book's catalogue page to view a list of those supplements that are available. See your local sales representative for details and access.

- **Instructor's Manual**
  The Instructor's Manual contains a wealth of resources for instructors, including chapter overviews, outlines, teaching suggestions, and further readings. A very practical resource, the Instructor's Manual will help teachers create engaging lesson plans and an environment of literacy for their students.
- **Test Item File**
  The Test Item File to accompany this textbook contains a complete series of fill-in-the-blank, true/false, multiple choice, short-answer, and application questions, which will enable teachers to create interesting and meaningful student assessments.
- **Transparency Masters**
  Teachers can use the transparency masters to create overheads for classroom use. The transparency masters highlight the key concepts in each chapter and will enhance classroom activities and discussion.

Acknowledgments

We would like to acknowledge the following individuals who willingly shared their time and expertise. First, we thank Margaret Rodermond from the University of Lethbridge Curriculum Laboratory, whose knowledge of children's and teachers' resources continues to amaze and delight us. She was instrumental in helping us identify quality literature to include in this text.

Second, we would like to thank the following instructors who wrote detailed reviews of various portions of the fourth Canadian edition manuscript: Anne Murray Orr, Antigonish, Nova

Scotia; Catherine Cornford, Carp, Ontario; Elizabeth Lee, Queen's University; Kathryn Noel, London, Ontario; Mary Clare Courtland, Lakehead University; Martha Gabriel, Cornwall, Prince Edward Island; Jeanie Bellamy, Niagara Falls, Ontario; Sharon Abbey, St. Catharines, Ontario; and Linda Doody, Clarenville, Newfoundland and Labrador.

Furthermore, we want to thank the teachers spotlighted in the chapter-opening profiles:

Sally Bender, Brandon, Manitoba

Kathy Chody, Winnipeg, Manitoba

Paul Comeau, Mount Pearl, Newfoundland and Labrador

Karen Dicks, Yellowknife, Northwest Territories

Dawn King-Hunter, Lethbridge, Alberta

Diana McCabe, Fredericton, New Brunswick

Cheryl Ann Miles, Fredericton, New Brunswick

Linda Pierce Picciotto, Victoria, British Columbia

Jann Porritt, Regina, Saskatchewan

Samantha Schultz, Stirling, Alberta

Heidi Jardine-Stoddart, Waterloo, Ontario

Our appreciation is also extended to the children who provided writing samples, pictures, and photographs that appear in this edition of the text. Finally, thanks go to Christine Cozens, Jody Yvonne, and Toivo Pajo from Pearson Education Canada, and to production editor Tara Tovell and copy editor Joe Zingrone. They have worked diligently with us to make this fourth Canadian edition of *Language Arts: Content and Teaching Strategies* a reality.

About the Authors

Gail E. Tompkins is a professor at California State University, Fresno, in the Department of Literacy and Early Education, where she teaches courses in the language arts, reading, and writing for preservice and inservice teachers. She directs the San Joaquin Valley Writing Project and works regularly with teachers, both by teaching model lessons in classrooms and by leading inservice workshops. Previously, Dr. Tompkins taught at Miami University in Ohio and at the University of Oklahoma, where she received the prestigious Regent's Award for Superior Teaching. She was also an elementary school teacher in Manassas, Virginia, for eight years.

Several years ago, Dr. Tompkins took a course in quilting offered by a local fabric store, and she's been buying fabric, piecing scraps of fabric together, and quilting ever since. Dr. Tompkins says that she has enjoyed combining her two hobbies—quilting and writing.

Dr. Tompkins is the author of the U.S. edition of this text, *Language Arts: Patterns of Practice* (6th ed., 2005), one of the six texts she authors for Merrill Education/Prentice Hall, and is a contributing author for three other Merrill/Prentice Hall texts. She has also written numerous articles related to the language arts that have appeared in *Language Arts*, *The Reading Teacher*, *Journal of Adolescent and Adult Literacy*, and other professional journals. She currently serves on the Editorial Review Board of *The Reading Teacher* and was recently honoured with an induction to the California Reading Association's Reading Hall of Fame.

Robin M. Bright is a professor in the University of Lethbridge's Faculty of Education. She teaches courses to undergraduate and graduate students in the areas of the language arts, reading, writing, and gender. Previously, Dr. Bright taught elementary school for ten years. She is the author of *Writing Instruction in the Intermediate Grades: What Is Said, What Is Done, What Is Understood* (International Reading Association, 1995); *Write from the Start: Writers Workshop in the Primary Grades* (Portage & Main, 2001); the co-author of *From Your Child's Teacher: Helping a Child Learn to Read, Write and Speak* (FP Hendriks, 1998); and has written numerous articles on learning to read and write. Her work has appeared in the *Journal of Reading Education*, *Canadian Children*, the *Canadian Journal of English Language Arts*, *Alberta English*, *The Writing Teacher*, *English Quarterly*, and the *Journal of Teacher Education*. Robin enjoys working with student teachers and teachers through professional development activities related to meeting the varied literacy needs and interests of Canadian children. She and her family enjoy reading and travelling together.

Michael J. Pollard is an associate professor in the Faculty of Education at the University of Lethbridge. His interests include children's literature, writing, the role of story in the learning process, learning styles, and holistic approaches to education.

He teaches language arts methods courses and supervises students in various levels of practica. A firm believer in integrating theory and practice, Michael has twice returned to teach in public schools in southern Alberta in the past ten years.

He is a certified mediator in private practice in southern Alberta. He also conducts workshops in alternative approaches to dispute resolution.

Michael is a certified yoga instructor teaching both at the university and in the community. He is also an avid golfer.

Pamela J. T. Winsor is an associate professor in the Faculty of Education at the University of Lethbridge. She teaches graduate and undergraduate courses in language education, including courses concerning children experiencing learning difficulties. She is also a supervisor and mentor of student teachers at both beginning and advanced levels of their field experiences.

Pamela regularly presents at local, national, and international conferences and leads professional development workshops on topics related to early literacy development and associated classroom practice. Her work concerning literacy and teacher education has extended internationally through participation in projects in Belize, South Africa, the Republic of the Maldives, Kosovo, and the Kingdom of Jordan.

A strong believer in a symbiotic relationship between research and teaching practice, she is currently exploring the benefits of revised Language Experience Approach for children learning English and developing English literacy. She has written several articles related to phonemic awareness development, beginning reading, learning difficulties, and professional portfolio development. Her work has appeared in *The Reading Teacher*, *Journal of Reading*, *Alberta English*, *Teaching Exceptional Children*, and the *Journal of Teacher Education*.

chapter one

Learning and the Language Arts

Procedure

As a teacher/librarian, I see my job as one of collaboration and design. The teachers and I meet to discuss a theme or integrated unit that fits their curricular needs. Together we make decisions about literature to be used, connections to be made, ways to integrate subjects, and means to assess learning.

In many grade 2 classrooms, the themes of "change" and "family" are studied. Grandparents are often involved in school activities related to these themes. The grandparents are asked to share stories of their own and those of older relatives. These are easily connected with quilts. To begin, I have two baby quilts made by my aunt for my children—two of more than fifty she has made in her lifetime. Everyone gets a chance to tell his or her own "quilt story." These stories help us learn about each other. They connect us as a community.

To introduce the children to the history of quilt patterns and design, we begin with literature. Our reading builds on previous knowledge and encourages us to try designing our own paper quilts. *Selina and the Bear Paw Quilt* (Smucker, 1995) links us to our Canadian heritage. A lovely story of a young girl and her grandmother, it makes connections in social studies (pioneers/Mennonites),

> *"The quilt is a perfect metaphor for the classroom—begin with small pieces and, through hard work and creative design, achieve a masterpiece of unity."*

Sally Bender
Teacher/Librarian
George Fitton School and Harrison
Middle School, Brandon, Manitoba

health (family/change), art (design), and mathematics (pattern/repetition). Janet Wilson's exquisite borders encourage us to begin our own paper designs.

As we explore the literature, we are made aware of issues of slavery (*Sweet Clara and the Freedom Quilt*), poverty (*The Rag Coat*), equal rights (*Sam Johnson and the Blue Ribbon Quilt*), displacement (*Dia's Story Cloth*), and pioneer life (*The Quilt-Block History of Pioneer Days*). The reading continues, projects for learning are

Kid watching is our most effective way of evaluating students' learning. Fully integrated units allow us to design projects to meet the needs of all children. As they work together in cooperative groups, we focus on their individual ways of using language, unique problem-solving abilities, willingness to connect past and present ways of life, and mathematical and artistic genius at designing intricate and elaborate patterns. We also see the range of abilities within our classroom, and accommodate to the needs of our learners.

As we share the growing array of children's literature, students become excited about what they are learning and bring that new knowledge to the quilts they design and the stories they create.

Adaptations

By using quilts as a starting block for learning, we are able to link the beauty of the craftsmanship to family history, earlier times, designs in nature, other cultures, recycling, and even electronic communication. Greater access to computers in the classroom makes it easier to connect with classrooms that share our interest in quilts.

In the future, we hope to design a webpage to show others what we do with quilts in our classroom.

Reflections

The quilt is a perfect metaphor for the classroom—begin with small pieces and, through hard work and creative design, achieve a masterpiece of unity. Since quilts are a part of many children's lives, the threads of a quilt unit can be woven through the entire year. A quilting postcard welcomes your students to a new year and invites them to bring their own quilt (and story) on the first day of school. A draw on the last day allows one student to take a class quilt home. We hope students remember this "year of quilts." Maybe one or two will even "have a go" at quilting in later years.

chosen, and class quilts are created with the help of volunteer parents, grandparents, and seniors.

There are so many projects—we cannot wait to begin! Some ideas: profile quilts for Open House (black silhouettes on white background with black edges), a community quilt (white hand prints on coloured squares), or buddy quilts that tell something about our reading partners. The list is endless!

Here are a few titles of the wonderful books we use:

With Needle and Thread (Bial, 1996)

Dia's Story Cloth (Cha, 1998)

The Quilt-Block History of Pioneer Days (Cobb, 1995)

Sam Johnson and the Blue Ribbon Quilt (Ernst, 1983)

The Patchwork Quilt (Flournoy, 1985)

Luka's Quilt (Guback, 1994)

Sweet Clara and the Freedom Quilt (Hopkinson, 1995)

The Rag Coat (Mills, 1991)

Eight Hands Round (Paul, 1996)

The Keeping Quilt (Polacco, 1993)

Tar Beach (Ringgold, 1996)

The Whispering Cloth (Shea, 1995)

Selina and the Bear Paw Quilt (Smucker, 1995)

Bringing the Farmhouse Home (Whelan, 1992)

Assessment

It is important for our students to know how they will be assessed as the study of quilts progresses, and to help determine the value of the various projects. We encourage their thoughts and ideas, and value them.

Two students examine a poster created by grade 5 teacher Robin Wevers depicting the life and times of well-known Canadian children's author Jean Little. The poster includes photos of Little, biographical information, book titles, and excerpts from some of her many books. This type of teaching strategy introduces exemplary literature to students and encourages them to engage in one or more of the language arts: listening, speaking, reading, writing, viewing, and visually representing.

Understanding how children learn and, particularly, how they learn language influences how we teach the language arts. The instructional program should never be construed as a smorgasbord of materials and activities; instead, teachers design instruction based on what they know about how children learn. The teacher's role in the elementary and middle-school classroom has adapted to changes in the teaching environment. For example, elementary classrooms may be organized into team-teaching pods or combination classrooms where two or more grades, such as grades 1 and 2, work together. As well, middle schools (often characterized by grades 5 to 8) have emerged as flexible and responsive organizational structures for pre-adolescent and adolescent learning needs. In these environments, teachers are now decision makers, empowered with both the obligation and the responsibility to make curricular decisions. In the language arts program, these curricular decisions have an impact on the content (information being taught) and the teaching strategies (techniques for teaching content).

Our approach in this textbook incorporates both the sociolinguistic theory of Lev Vygotsky and the constructivist theory of learning proposed by Jean Piaget.

How Children Learn

Language acquisition theorists emphasize the importance of language in learning and view learning as a reflection of the culture and community in which students live (Heath, 1983b; Vygotsky, 1978, 1986). According to Russian psychologist Lev Vygotsky (1896–1934), language helps organize thought, and children use language to learn as well as to communicate and share experiences with others. Understanding that children use language for social purposes, teachers plan instructional activities that incorporate a social component, such as having

To Guide Your Reading

As you read this chapter, prepare to

Explain how children learn

•

Explain the roles of language and culture in learning

•

Describe how critical literacy affects our understanding of learning language and learning through language

•

List and define the language arts

•

Explain how children learn the language arts

students share their writing with classmates. And, because children's language and concepts of literacy reflect their cultures and home communities, teachers must respect students' language and appreciate cultural differences in their attitudes toward learning—and toward learning the language arts in particular.

Swiss psychologist Jean Piaget (1896–1980) developed a theory of learning that radically changed our conceptions of child development. His constructivist framework (1969) differs substantially from behavioural theories that had influenced education for decades. Piaget described learning as the modification of students' cognitive structures as they interact with and adapt to their environment. He believed that children construct their own knowledge from their experiences. This view of learning requires a re-examination of the teacher's role. Instead of being primarily dispensers of knowledge, teachers provide students with reading and writing experiences and opportunities to manipulate objects such as storyboards, magnetic letters, and objects in book boxes in order for students to construct their own knowledge (Pearson, 1993).

THE COGNITIVE STRUCTURE

Children's knowledge is not just a collection of isolated bits of information; it is organized in the brain, and this organization becomes increasingly integrated and interrelated as their knowledge grows. The organization of knowledge is the cognitive structure, and knowledge is arranged in category systems called *schemata* (a single category is called a *schema*). Within the schemata are three components: categories of knowledge, the features or rules for determining what constitutes a category and what will be included in each category, and a network of interrelationships among the categories.

These schemata may be likened to a conceptual filing system in which children and adults organize and store the information derived from their past experiences. Taking this analogy further, information is filed in the brain in "file folders." As children learn, they add file folders to their filing system, and as they study a topic, that file folder becomes thicker.

As children learn, they invent new categories, and while different people have many similar categories, schemata are personalized according to individual experiences and interests. Some people, for example, may have only one general category, *bugs*, into which they lump their knowledge of ants, butterflies, spiders, and bees, while other people distinguish between insects and spiders and develop a category for each. Those who distinguish between insects and spiders also develop a set of rules based on the distinctive characteristics of these animals for classifying them into one category or the other. In addition to *insect* or *spider* categories, a network of interrelationships connects these categories to other categories. Networks, too, are individualized, depending on each person's unique knowledge and experiences. The category of *spiders* might be networked as a subcategory of *arachnids*, and the class relationship between scorpions and spiders might be made. Other networks, such as a connection to a *poisonous animals* category or a *webs and nests* category, could have been made. The networks that link categories, characteristics, and examples with other categories, characteristics, and examples are extremely complex. As children adapt to their environment, they add new information about their experiences that requires them to enlarge existing categories or to construct new ones.

According to Piaget (1969), two processes make this change possible. *Assimilation* is the cognitive process by which new information in the environment is integrated into existing schemata. In contrast, *accommodation* is the cognitive process by which existing schemata are modified or new schemata are restructured to adapt to the environment. Through assimilation, children add new information to their picture of the world; through accommodation, they change that picture on the basis of new information.

THE PROCESS OF LEARNING

Piaget recognized that children are naturally curious about their world and are active and motivated learners. New experiences are necessary for learning. Children experiment with the objects they encounter and try to make sense out of their experiences; that is to say, they construct their own knowledge from interactions and experiences rather than through passively receiving environmental stimulation. Oral and written language work the same way. Children interact with language just as they experiment with bicycles they ride.

Learning occurs through the process of equilibration (Piaget, 1975). When a child encounters something he or she does not understand or cannot assimilate, disequilibrium, or cognitive conflict, results. This disequilibrium typically produces confusion and agitation, feelings that impel children to seek equilibrium or a comfortable balance with the environment. In other words, when confronted with new or discrepant information, children (as well as adults) are intrinsically motivated to try to make sense of it. If the child's schemata can accommodate the new information, then the disequilibrium caused by the new experience will motivate the child to learn. Equilibrium is thus regained at a higher developmental level. These are the steps of this process:

1. Equilibrium is disrupted by the introduction of new or discrepant information.
2. Disequilibrium occurs, and the dual processes of assimilation and accommodation function.
3. Equilibrium is attained at a higher developmental level.

The process of equilibration happens to us again and again during the course of a day. In fact, it is occurring right now as you are reading this chapter. If you are already familiar with the constructivist learning theory and have learned about Piaget in other education courses, your mental filing cabinet has been activated and you are assimilating the information you are reading into the folder on "Piaget" or "learning theories" already in your files. If, however, you're not familiar with constructivist learning theories, your mind is actively creating a new file folder in which to put the information you are reading.

Learning doesn't always occur when we are presented with new information, however. If the new information is too difficult and we cannot relate it to what we already know, we do not learn. This is true for both children and adults. The important implication for teachers is that new information must be puzzling, challenging, or, in Piaget's words, "moderately novel." Information that is too familiar is quickly assimilated, and information that is too unfamiliar cannot be accommodated and will not be learned.

LEARNING STRATEGIES

We all have skills that we use automatically, as well as self-regulated strategies for things that we do well—driving defensively, playing volleyball, training a new pet, or maintaining classroom discipline. We apply skills we have learned unconsciously and choose among skills as we think strategically. The strategies we use in these activities are problem-solving mechanisms that involve complex thinking processes. When we are first learning how to drive a car, for example, we learn both skills and strategies. Some of the first skills we learn are how to start the engine, make left turns, and parallel park. With practice, these skills become automatic. Some of the first strategies we learn are how to pass another car and how to stay a safe distance behind the vehicles ahead of us. At first we have only a small repertoire of strategies, and we don't always use them effectively. That's one reason why we take lessons from a driving instructor and have a learner's permit that requires a more experienced driver to ride along with us. A seasoned driver teaches us defensive driving strategies. We learn strategies for driving on superhighways, on slippery roads, and at night. With practice and guidance, we become more successful drivers, able to anticipate driving problems and take defensive actions.

During the elementary grades, children develop a number of learning strategies or methods for learning. Rehearsal—repeating information over and over—is one learning strategy or cognitive process that children can use to remember something. Other learning strategies include

- **P**redicting: anticipating what will happen
- **O**rganizing: grouping information into categories
- **E**laborating: expanding on the information presented
- **M**onitoring: regulating or keeping track of progress

Reciprocal teaching theory suggests that as children grow older, their use of learning strategies improves (Palinscar, 1985).

As they acquire more effective methods for learning and remembering information, children also become more aware of their own cognitive processes and better able to regulate them. Elementary and middle-school students can reflect on their literacy processes and talk about themselves as readers and writers. For example, grade 2 student Trisha describes her writing: "That's the writing we do for 'Kids in the News.' 'Kids in the News' is where we write to somebody. We can write to anybody . . . and then they have to write back to us something about what we did. I like to write to my mom, my dad, my auntie, my cousin, my brother, my sister, or Miss W. [her classroom teacher], or Janie" (McKay & Kendrick, 2001, p. 14). Fifth grader Hobbes reports that "the pictures in my head help me when I write stuff down 'cause then I can get ideas from my pictures" (Cleary, 1993, p. 142). Eighth grader Chandra talks about poetry: "Poetry is a fine activity, and it can get you in tune with yourself. . . . I think that my favourite person who does poetry is Maya Angelou" (Steinbergh, 1993, p. 212).

Students become more realistic about the limitations of their memories and more knowledgeable about which learning strategies are most effective in particular situations. They also become increasingly aware of what they know and don't know. The term *metacognition* refers to this knowledge children acquire about their own cognitive processes and to children's regulation of their cognitive processes to maximize learning.

Students in grade 1 use organizing and elaborating strategies as they retell the story, "I Know an Old Lady Who Swallowed a Fly."

Teachers play an important role in developing children's metacognitive abilities. During large-group activities, teachers introduce and *model* learning strategies. In small-group lessons, teachers provide *guided practice*, talk with children about learning strategies, and ask students *to reflect* on their own use of these cognitive processes. Teachers also guide students about when to use particular strategies and which strategies are more effective with various activities.

SOCIAL CONTEXTS OF LEARNING

Children's cognitive development is enhanced through social interaction. In his social development theory, known as sociolinguistics, Lev Vygotsky asserted that children learn through socially meaningful interactions, and that language is both social and an important facilitator of learning. Children's experiences are organized and shaped by society, but rather than merely absorbing these experiences, children negotiate and transform them as a dynamic part of culture. They learn to talk through social interactions and to read and write through interactions with literate children and adults (Dyson, 1993; Harste, 1990). Community is important for both readers and writers. Students talk about books they are reading with classmates, and they turn to classmates for feedback about their writing (Zebroski, 1994).

Through interactions with adults and collaboration with other children, children learn things they could not learn on their own. Adults guide and support children as they move from their current level of knowledge toward a more advanced level. Vygotsky (1978) described these two levels as, first, the actual developmental level, at which children can perform a task independently; and second, the level of potential development, at which children can perform a task with assistance. Children can typically do more difficult things in collaboration than they can on their own, and this is why teachers are important models for their students and why children often work with partners and in small groups.

A child's "zone of proximal development" (Vygotsky, 1978) is the range of tasks that the child can perform with guidance from others but cannot yet perform independently. Vygotsky believed that children learn best when what they are attempting to learn is within this zone. He felt that children learn little by performing tasks they can already do independently—tasks at their actual developmental level—or by attempting tasks that are too difficult or beyond their zone of proximal development.

Vygotsky and Jerome Bruner (1986) both used the term *scaffold* as a metaphor to describe adults' contributions to children's learning. Scaffolds are support mechanisms that teachers, parents, or other more competent individuals provide to help children successfully perform a task within their zone of proximal development. Teachers serve as scaffolds when they model or demonstrate a procedure, guide children through a task, ask questions, break complex tasks into smaller steps, and supply pieces of information. As children gain knowledge and experience about how to perform a task, teachers gradually withdraw their support so that children make the transition from social interaction to internalized, independent functioning.

The teacher's role in guiding students' learning within the zone of proximal development includes three components, according to Dixon-Krauss (1996):

1. Teachers mediate or augment children's learning through social interaction.
2. Teachers are flexible and provide support based on feedback from the children as they are engaged in the learning task.
3. Teachers vary the amount of support from very explicit to vague, according to children's needs.

Language, according to Vygotsky, can be used for purposes other than social. Piaget (1975) described how young children engage in egocentric speech—talking aloud to themselves as they pursue activities, such as building with blocks. Vygotsky (1986) noticed that older children and adults sometimes talk to themselves while performing a difficult or frustrating task, and he noted that this talking aloud seemed to guide or direct their thinking. From these observations, Vygotsky concluded that language is a mechanism for thought and that children's egocentric speech (which he called *self-talk*) gradually becomes inner speech, whereby children talk to themselves mentally rather than orally. Self-talk is the link between talk used for social purposes and for intellectual purposes. According to Vygotsky, children use both self-talk and inner speech to guide their learning.

IMPLICATIONS FOR LEARNING THE LANGUAGE ARTS

Students interact with their environment and actively construct knowledge using the processes of assimilation and accommodation. Students learn when their existing schemata are enlarged because of assimilated information and when their schemata are restructured to account for new experiences being acted on and accommodated.

As students engage in learning activities, they are faced with learning and discovering some new element in an otherwise known or familiar system of information. Students recognize or seek out the information embedded in a situation that makes sense and is moderately novel. When students are forced to contend with the novel part of the information, their schemata are disrupted, or put in a state of disequilibrium. Accommodation of the novel information causes a reorganization of the schemata, resulting in students' having more complex schemata and being able to apply more complex information than was previously possible.

Vygotsky's (1978) concept of the zone of proximal development emphasizes the importance of talk, and explains how children learn through social interactions with adults. Adults use scaffolds to help children move from their current stage of development toward their potential, and teachers provide a similar type of assistance as they support students in learning the language arts (Applebee & Langer, 1983).

In the lessons they prepare for their students, teachers can create optimal conditions for learning. When students do not have the schemata for predicting and interpreting the new information, teachers must help students relate what they know to what they do not know. Therefore, the new information must appear in a situation that makes sense and must be moderately novel; it must not be too difficult for students to accommodate it.

How children learn has important implications for how students learn the language arts in school and how teachers teach the language arts. Contributions from the constructivist and sociolinguistic learning theories include the following:

- Students are active participants in learning.
- Students learn by relating the new information to prior knowledge.
- Students organize their knowledge in schemata.
- Students use skills automatically and strategies consciously as they learn.
- Students learn through social interactions with classmates and the teacher.
- Teachers provide scaffolds for students.

Language Learning and the Language Arts

Psychology has largely defined our views on language arts learning and instruction. Behaviourists have focused on the language arts as skill development while cognitive psychologists have focused on language learning processes and more recently we've begun to recognize the importance of the social aspects of the process (Bainbridge & Malicky, 2004).

A skill acquisition orientation to the language arts suggests that language is learned from part to whole and that the learning of lower-level skills such as letter and word identification in learning to read must precede the learning of higher-level skills such as comprehension. In this approach, lower-level skills are taught and mastered before moving on to more complex, higher-level skills. In learning to read, for example, children are taught letter- and then word-identification skills as a prerequisite to combining words into sentences, paragraphs, and whole texts, leading eventually to comprehension.

An interactive approach to language arts views the learner as a maker of meaning who, when reading, discovers the meaning of text through a complex process; and a creator of meaning through a similarly complex process when writing. The focus is on understanding, and skills are used to the extent that they help clarify meaning. In reading, the language and thought process of the reader interacts with that of the writer. Understanding is achieved when the two come together in what Goodman (1969) called "a psycholinguistic guessing game." The more the reader is familiar with the language and thought of the writer, the easier it will be to achieve understanding. In this sense, meaning is the interaction between the reader and the text and language arts is seen as a cognitive process of discovery.

Language is a complex system for creating meaning through socially shared conventions (Halliday, 1978). Before children enter elementary school, they learn the language of their community. They understand what community members say to them, and they share their ideas with others through that language. In an amazingly short period of three or four years, children master the exceedingly complex system of their native language, allowing them to understand sentences they have never heard before and to create sentences they have never said before. Young children are not "taught" how to talk; this knowledge about language develops tacitly, or unconsciously.

THE FOUR CUEING SYSTEMS

Language involves four cueing systems, and together these systems make oral and written communication possible. The four cueing systems are

- The phonological, or sound, system of language
- The syntactic, or structural, system of language
- The semantic, or meaning, system of language
- The pragmatic, or social and cultural use, system of language

As children learn oral language by listening and speaking, they develop an implicit understanding of the systems, and they apply their knowledge of the four systems whenever they use words—whether for listening or talking, reading or writing, or viewing or visually representing. Students integrate information simultaneously from these four cueing systems in order to communicate. No one system is more important than any other one, although at different stages of literacy development, one system may require more attention than another. As children begin learning to read, their attention will necessarily gravitate to the phonological system as they try to appreciate and understand the new task that reading our written language presents, namely associating written symbols with their familiar oral language counterparts.

The Phonological System. There are approximately forty-four speech sounds in English. Children learn to pronounce these sounds as they learn to talk, and they learn to associate the sounds with letters as they learn to read and write. Sounds are called *phonemes*, and they are presented in print between slashes to differentiate them from *graphemes*, or letter combinations that represent sounds. Thus, the first letter in *mother* is written *m*, while the phoneme is written /m/; the phoneme in *soap* represented by the grapheme *oa* is written /ō/.

The phonological system is important in both oral and written language. Regional and cultural differences exist in the way people pronounce phonemes. For instance, the English spoken in different regions of Canada varies. It is common to hear differences in the pronunciation of words like *out* and *about*, and *Newfoundland* and *Quebec* across Canada. Children who are learning English as a second language (ESL) must learn to pronounce English sounds, and new sounds not found in their native language are particularly difficult for children to learn. Younger children usually learn to pronounce the difficult sounds more easily than older children and adults.

For more information on phonics, see Chapter 3, "Emergent Literacy," pages 97–101.

Children use their knowledge of the phonological system as they learn to read and write. In a phonetically regular language, with a one-to-one correspondence between letters and sounds, teaching students to sound out words would be a simple process. But English is not a phonetically regular language, since there are 26 letters and 44 sounds and many ways to combine the letters to spell some of the sounds, especially vowels. Consider these ways to spell long *e*: *sea, green, Pete, me,* and *people*. And sometimes the patterns used to spell long *e* don't work, as in *head* and *great*. Phonics, which describes the phoneme–grapheme correspondences and related spelling rules, is an important part of reading instruction, since students use phonics information to decode words. However, because not all words can easily be decoded, and because good readers do much more than just decode words when they read, phonics instruction has limited utility for a beginning reader. Early readers' knowledge of the various ways phonemes are spelled (the ways their familiar and known speech sounds are represented in print) may require that they give more attention to the phonological system until they are able to make sense of the various sound–symbol correspondences and appreciate the role knowledge of phonics plays in their ability to learn to read words.

Students in the primary grades also use their understanding of the phonological system to create invented or temporary spellings. First graders might, for example, spell *home* as *hm* or *hom*, and second graders might spell *school* as *skule*, based on their knowledge of phoneme–grapheme relationships and spelling patterns. As students learn more phonics and gain more experience in reading and writing, their spellings become more sophisticated and finally conventional. For students who are learning English as a second language, their spellings often reflect their pronunciations of words (Nathenson-Mejia, 1989).

For more information on invented spelling, see Chapter 9, "Words and the Language Tools to Use Them: Spelling, Grammar, and Handwriting," pages 373–375.

The Syntactic System. The syntactic system is the structural organization of a language. English is both a positional and reflexive language. The position a word occupies in a sentence conveys part of the meaning. In the sentence, "The girl kicked the ball," we know *girl* is a noun because of its position in the sentence and because other words like *the* mark or tell us that a noun follows. Similarly *kicked* occupies the position of verb in this sentence. We also convey meaning by adding to words in sentences. For example, another indicator that *kicked* is a verb is the addition of *ed* to *kick*. This system that describes how words go together to form meaning and the rules about how we add affixes to words to change meaning is the grammar that regulates how words are combined into sentences. Children use the syntactic system as they combine words to form sentences. Word order is important in English, and speakers of the language must arrange words into a sequence that makes sense. Children also learn to comprehend and produce statements, questions, and other types of sentences during the preschool years.

Students use their knowledge of the syntactic system as they read. They anticipate that the words they are reading have been strung together into sentences. When they come to an unfamiliar word, they recognize its role in the sentence even if they don't know the terms for parts of speech. In the sentence, "The horses galloped through the gate and out into the field," students may not be able to decode the word *through*, but they can easily substitute a reasonable word or phrase, such as *out of* or *past*. Many of the capitalization and punctuation rules that elementary students learn reflect the syntactic system of language. Similarly, when students study simple, compound, and complex sentences, they are learning about the syntactic system.

Another component of syntax is word forms. Words such as *dog* and *play* are *morphemes*, the smallest meaningful units of language. Word parts that change the meaning of a word are also morphemes. When the plural marker *-s* is added to *dog* to make *dogs*, for instance, or the past-tense marker *-ed* is added to *play* to make *played*, these words are now comprised of two morphemes because the inflectional endings change the meaning of the words. The words *dog* and *play* are free morphemes because they convey meaning while standing alone. The endings *-s* and *-ed* are bound morphemes because they must be attached to a free morpheme to convey meaning. As they learn to talk, children quickly become adept at learning to combine words and word parts, such as

For more information on teaching grammar in the elementary grades, see Chapter 9, "Words and the Language Tools to Use Them: Spelling, Grammar, and Handwriting," pages 363–371.

adding -s to *cookie* to create a plural, and adding -er to *big* to indicate a comparison. They also learn to combine two or more free morphemes to form compound words. *Birthday*, for example, is a compound word created by combining two free morphemes.

For more information on root words and affixes, see Chapter 9, "Words and the Language Tools to Use Them: Spelling, Grammar, and Handwriting," pages 343–345.

During the elementary grades, students learn to add affixes to words. Affixes added at the beginning of a word are *prefixes*, and affixes added at the end are *suffixes*. Both kinds of affixes are bound morphemes. For example, the prefix *un-* in *unhappy* is a bound morpheme, whereas *happy* is a free morpheme because it can stand alone as a word.

The Semantic System. The third cueing system is the semantic, or meaning, system. Vocabulary is the key component of this system. As children learn to talk, they acquire a vocabulary that is continually increasing through the preschool years and the elementary grades. Researchers estimate that children have a vocabulary of 5000 words by the time they enter school, and they continue to acquire 3000 words each year during the elementary grades (Lindfors, 1987; Nagy, 1988). Considering how many words students learn each year, it is unreasonable to assume that they learn words only through formal instruction. Students learn many, many words informally via reading and through social studies, science, and other curricular areas. Students probably learn eight to ten words a day—a remarkable achievement!

At the same time that children are learning new words, they are also learning that many words have more than one meaning. Meaning is usually based on the context, or the surrounding words. The common word *run*, for instance, has more than thirty meanings listed in *The Random House Dictionary of the English Language* (Flexner, 1993). Read these sentences to see how the meaning of the word *run* is tied to the context in which it is used:

Will the mayor run for re-election?

The bus runs between Montreal and Ottawa.

The advertisement will run for three days.

Did you run in the 50-metre dash?

The plane made a crop-dusting run.

Will you run to the store and get a loaf of bread for me?

The dogs are out in the run.

Oh, no! I've got a run in my new pair of pantyhose!

Children often don't have the full, adult meaning of many words; rather, they learn meanings through a process of refinement. They add "features," or layers of meaning.

For more information on vocabulary, see Chapter 9, "Words and the Language Tools to Use Them: Spelling, Grammar, and Handwriting," pages 352–360.

For more information on wordplay, see Chapter 6, "Reading and Writing Stories and Poetry," pages 235–239.

Children learn other sophisticated concepts about words as well. They learn about shades of meaning—for example, the differences among these *sad* words: *unhappy, crushed, desolate, miserable, disappointed, cheerless, down,* and *grief-stricken.* They also learn about synonyms and antonyms, wordplay, and figurative language, including idioms.

The Pragmatic System. The fourth cueing system is the pragmatic system, which deals with the social and cultural aspects of language use. People use language for many different purposes, and how they talk or write varies according to purpose and audience.

Language variety is also part of the pragmatic system. Language use varies among social classes, cultural and ethnic groups, and geographic regions. These varieties are known as dialects. School is one cultural community, and the language of school is Standard English. This register, or style, is formal—the one used in textbooks, newspapers, and magazines, and by television newscasters. Nonstandard forms of English are alternatives in which the phonology, syntax, and semantics differ from those of Standard English, but they are neither inferior nor substandard. They reflect the communities of the speakers, and the speakers communicate as effectively as those who use Standard English in their communities. The goal is for students to add Standard English to their repertoire of language registers, not to replace their home dialect with Standard English.

As students who speak nonstandard English read texts written in Standard English, they often translate what they read into their own dialect. Sometimes this occurs when they are reading aloud. For example, a sentence that is written "they are going to school" might be read aloud this way: "they's goin' to school." Emergent or beginning readers are not usually corrected when they translate words into nonstandard dialects without changing the meaning, but older, more fluent readers should be directed to read the words as they are printed in the book.

System	Description	Terms	Uses in the Elementary Grades
Phonological System	The sound system of English with approximately 44 sounds	• Phoneme (the smallest identifiable unit of sound) • Grapheme (the written representation of a phoneme using one or more letters)	• Pronouncing words • Detecting regional and other dialects • Decoding words when reading • Using invented spelling • Reading and writing alliterations and onomatopoeia
Syntactic System	The structural system of English that governs how words are combined into sentences	• Syntax (the structure, or grammar, of a sentence) • Morpheme (the smallest meaningful unit of language) • Free morpheme (a morpheme that can stand alone as a word) • Bound morpheme (a morpheme that must be attached to a free morpheme to convey meaning)	• Adding inflectional endings to words • Combining words to form compound words • Adding prefixes and suffixes to root words • Using capitalization and punctuation to indicate beginnings and ends of sentences • Writing simple, compound, and complex sentences • Combining sentences
Semantic System	The meaning system of English that focuses on vocabulary	• Semantics (meaning)	• Learning the meanings of words • Discovering that some words have multiple meanings • Studying synonyms, antonyms, and homonyms • Using a dictionary and thesaurus • Reading and writing comparisons (metaphors and similes)
Pragmatic System	The system of English that varies language according to social and cultural uses	• Function (the purpose for which a person uses language) • Standard English (the form of English used in textbooks and by television newscasters) • Nonstandard English (other forms of English)	• Varying language to fit specific purposes • Reading and writing dialogue in dialects • Comparing standard and nonstandard forms of English

Figure 1–1 Overview of the Four Cueing Systems

The four cueing systems and their terminology are reviewed in Figure 1–1 on page 13. Both children and adults use the four cueing systems as they communicate through oral and written language. Their knowledge of, and dependence upon, the cueing systems varies with age and experience, with greater emphasis needed at appropriate times.

The New Literacies

Literacy, in its traditional sense, is characterized by "the ability to create written text and then to decode and comprehend this text according to certain internalized linguistic rules" (Cammack, 2002, p. 51). Today, technology and the social, economic, political, and cultural contents surrounding it are challenging this view of literacy, encouraging researchers and teachers to develop a more thorough and complete understanding of what it means to be literate. According to Chandler-Olcott and Mahar (2003), part of being a literate member of society is understanding how information and communications technologies change peoples' lives. Bruce (2002) points out that new technologies challenge the educational system by throwing into question traditional ways of teaching and learning. However, these same technologies support an expanded view of learning, and this has caused researchers to declare that there is already a "fundamental transformation visible in the literacy practices of young people" (Alvermann, 2002, p. 3).

Moreover, the rapid changes in technology and society are both the cause and result of our changing views of literacy (Leu, 2000). In order to broaden the definitions of literacy, a new emphasis is placed on teaching students to engage in reading and writing, not only in traditional print media such as books and newspapers, but also in multiple formats such as software, music, video, dance, and art. Kist (2005) and Watts Pailliotet (2000) indicate "new literacies"—sometimes referred to as critical media literacy, multiple ways of knowing, and multiliteracies—involve visual, auditory, and print information and allow us to understand literacy contexts in and out of school. Kist further suggests that new literacy classrooms are characterized by specific features such as student choice and collaboration; work centred around projects; ongoing, continuous use of multiple forms of representation (e.g., art, sculpture, and drama); and the breakdown of traditional teacher and student roles.

Pahl and Rowsell (2005) assert that the literacy students facing the teacher today are "intelligent, imaginative, and linguistically talented." As such, their use of technology is best understood as social and cultural practice. Pahl and Rowsell suggest that the notion of new literacies more accurately describes what children, adolescents, and teenagers do as literate beings when they play computer games, text-message, use email and instant messaging, surf the Internet, and create and consume webpages and weblogs (or blogs). Accordingly, these activities are seen to be sophisticated literacy practices.

For students today, being literate is much more than reading traditional school-based texts, books, and periodicals. Literacy encompasses "the multiple ways that people use language." (Rowsell, 2005). Therefore, technology's role helps teachers redefine literacy beyond developing skills in using email and word processing. It points to the need for educators to understand the social and cultural impact of technology use in today's society.

LITERACY AND TECHNOLOGY

There has always been a relationship between literacy and technology. Our conceptions of literacy have continuously evolved since the development of book technologies in the sixteenth century. Today, this is evident through the advent of many new technologies—these include word processors, email, podcasts, digital video, cell phones, and the Internet (Teale, Leu, Labbo, & Kinzer, 2002). The current climate demands that teachers respond by acknowledging the emergence of new literacies needed to effectively understand, manage, and evaluate available technology. Preparing students in the new literacies means helping them learn to use word processors and computer spell and grammar check features; manage email and communications technology; and choose search engines to locate and evaluate information from the Internet (Watts-Taffe, Gwinn, Johnson, and Horn, 2003). Learning these types of skills is important for both scholastic and workforce/lifestyle technology use.

In school, students are encouraged to use word processing, PowerPoint, Web reference tools, visual media, and the Internet. Out of school, students are using email, instant messaging, electronic games, chat rooms, and blogs. In an instant, students are able to log on to the Internet and engage in near-synchronous conversation with another person virtually anywhere in the world. They can also access a wealth of information on virtually any topic. It is up to teachers and parents to ensure students engage in a variety of ways to learn about the world, express themselves in new ways, and communicate well with others. As students are exposed to multiple technologies, they require thoughtful education about selecting, using, and evaluating these tools.

Wepner, Valmont, and Thurlow point out that, "learning should drive the technology, not vice versa" (2000, p. 620). In other words, technology is a tool that facilitates learning. There are many classroom examples of teachers and students using technology to develop literacy skills. These include using alphabet-related websites to teach letter recognition for beginners' reading (Duffelmeyer, 2002); finding desktop-publishing programs that incorporate text and pictures to write a book review and make a recommendation for reading (Maslin & Nelson, 2002); and writing with technological applications such as brainstorming software, databases and spreadsheets, CD-ROMs, and the Internet (Roberts, 2002). In addition, teachers use assistive technology and well-researched websites to help students with special learning needs to better meet curriculum objectives. Educators have much to learn about literacy and learning at all levels as research into technology use in the classroom continues.

THE LANGUAGE ARTS AND TECHNOLOGY

The language arts include the following: reading, writing, listening, speaking, viewing, and visually representing. These are the cornerstone activities of what it means to be literate. However, as technology use has increased, these activities have also changed. Students of all ages are as likely to be exposed to digital texts on the computer as they are to hard copies in the form of books, newspapers, textbooks, comics, and magazines. Technology clearly affects the reading process. For example, Henry (2006) reports on the activities of two grade 6 students in a social studies class. The students are working on a project related to the topic of the Second World War. They decide to focus their report on navy battles in the Pacific Ocean. They are seated at a computer and proceed to go to Google (**www.google.ca**), their favourite search engine. At first, in response to having typed in "Second World War," six million possible websites are displayed. The students begin clicking on the links in the order in which they appear. They examine the sites but do not find the kind of information they are looking for. They continue doing this for the remainder of the period.

While it is evident that the students are on task, Henry suggests that the reason these two students lack success in locating useful information for their report is that they do not have the new literacies required to sift through huge amounts of information. According to Henry, they are unable to locate, read, and comprehend the information they have accessed. The skills needed to read and comprehend conventional texts are not the same as those needed for digital texts: "Students require new reading comprehension strategies to effectively use the Internet and other information technologies" (Henry, p. 2).

Eagleton and Guinee (2002) indicate that many new literacy skills are needed for obtaining and comprehending information on the Internet. Students need to be taught to narrow the focus of their search, use the words or phrase that they hope to find, search for one focus at a time (and not repeat their focus), eliminate unnecessary words, and select words for a search in a careful and mindful manner.

Technology can also be a motivation factor for some students. Hagood, Stevens, and Reinking (2002) present one student's comments about the role of the computer in reading. Although Tee, a thirteen-year-old, says, "I don't really like reading," he adds that it's "because I can never find a good book. But computers are good because I like to create cards and other things on the computer" (p. 72). In the educational milieu, it is paramount that the term *literacy* encompass a wide range of experiences and interpretations; otherwise, as Buckingham and Sefton-Green indicate, "schools run the risk of becoming anti-educational sites" (1998, p. 81).

Changes in writing technology have also affected literacy in important ways. For instance, word processors and built-in editing techniques have changed the ways in which students write. As students create more and more digital texts, they learn how to organize, store, index, and retrieve their writing. This is "an epochal shift in the ways we write and the ways we think about the importance of writing" (Burbules & Bruce, 1995, p. 107).

Another important way in which writing has changed is in its convergence with other activities such as Web browsing, instant messaging, finding and listening to music, adding images and video, and using Web reference tools. These activities are divergent from the conventional image of the solitary writer. Bruce (2002) observes, "the student doing his/her own work may soon be seen as the anomalous case for writing" (p. 7).

Student writing, once shared only with the teacher and perhaps classmates, can now be posted for a global community and promote feelings of connection among fledgling writers. Also, new technologies make it easier to access, use, and modify photographs and visual images to accompany writing or to demonstrate understanding through visual representation.

Books about technology can also inspire students to learn more about its usefulness in their own lives and beyond. For instance, *Galileo's Treasure Box* (Brighton, 1987), features Virginia, Galileo's nine-year-old daughter and her experiences being immersed in her father's scientific world. *Steven Spielberg: Crazy for Movies* (Rubin, 2001) and *Meltdown: A Race Against Nuclear Disaster at Three Mile Island: A Reporter's Story* (Hampton, 2001) show how advancements in technology open up possibilities, but not always in a positive manner. Books such as these inform students about the ways technology simplifies and enhances our lives on one level, with a reminder that its greater complexity must also be understood. It is important to recognize that all the language arts are affected by technology in subtle ways.

TEACHING AND LEARNING THE NEW LITERACIES

To become fully literate, students must be proficient in the new literacies. In response to a growing need, the International Reading Association (2003) provides a position statement for integrating literacy and technology in the curriculum. The statement says students have the right to have

- teachers who are skilled in the effective use of information and communication technology (ICT) for teaching and learning;
- a literacy curriculum that integrates the new literacies of ICT into instructional programs;
- instruction that develops the critical literacies essential to effective information use;
- assessment practices in literacy that include reading and writing with technology tools;
- opportunities to learn safe and responsible use of information and ICT; and
- equal access to ICT.

These principles help guide teachers as they provide effective integration of computer technologies into the classroom. Today's teachers are prepared to embrace an expanded view of literacy in a number of ways:

- They explore instructional strategies and resources developed by other teachers on technology use.
- They stay up to date on technology research to improve students' literacy skills.
- They ensure students stay safe as they use a variety of technological tools.
- They join professional groups to exchange insights about effective instructional strategies.

As noted above, technology continues to have a substantial impact on our views of literacy. Gurak (2001) and Chandler-Olcott and Mahar (2003) respectively offer the terms "critical technological literacy" and "multiliteracy" to describe the many and varied ways that technology and literacy support each other. Part of being literate in the Internet age entails understanding how information and communications technologies can change people's lives. As teachers, our goal is to develop a strong background in effective literacy instruction in order to make sound decisions about selecting, using, and critically understanding technology (Watts-Taffe, Gwinn, Johnson, & Horn, 2003). Students and teachers benefit from literacy instruction that permits effective technology use and its critical examination.

CULTURALLY AND LINGUISTICALLY DIVERSE STUDENTS

North America is a culturally pluralistic society, and the ethnic, racial, and socio-economic diversity is being reflected increasingly in elementary school classrooms. According to the *2003 Canadian Sourcebook*, English and French (Canada's official languages) have retained their positions as the two predominant languages in Canada. However, the number of Canadians reporting a non-official language as their mother tongue fluctuated between 11.4 and 13.8 percent over the ten years leading up to the *Sourcebook*'s publication. Such languages include Italian, Chinese, and German. It is also worth noting that in the United States, 27 percent of the population classify themselves as non-European Americans (the *World Almanac and Book of Facts 1997*, 1996, p. 377).

These changing demographic realities will have a significant impact on elementary classrooms, as more and more students come from linguistically and culturally diverse backgrounds. More than ever before, today's students will live in a global society, and they need the skills and knowledge to live harmoniously with other cultural groups.

Children of diverse cultures come to school with a broad range of language and literacy experiences, even if those experiences are not the same as those of mainstream or European-heritage children. Linguistically diverse children have already learned to communicate in at least one language, and, if they don't speak English, they want to learn English in order to make friends, learn, and communicate just like their classmates. Teachers of culturally and linguistically diverse students must implement a language arts program that is sensitive to, and reflective of, these students' backgrounds and needs. In fact, all teachers must be prepared to work with this ever-growing population, and teachers who have no linguistically diverse students in their classrooms still need to incorporate a multicultural perspective in their curriculum in order to prepare their students to interact effectively in Canada's increasingly multicultural society.

We take the perspective that cultural and linguistic diversity is not a problem for teachers to overcome; instead, it provides an opportunity to enhance and enrich the learning of all students. Teachers need to provide literacy experiences that reflect the multitude of backgrounds from which their students come, and multicultural literature plays an important role in filling that need (Yokota, 1993).

BILINGUAL STUDENTS AND STUDENTS WHO SPEAK ENGLISH AS A SECOND LANGUAGE (ESL)

Students whose first language is not English are referred to as English as a second language (ESL) students. The first language spoken as a child and still understood is often referred to as the *mother tongue*, or *native language*. Children who converse in their native language at home but also speak English fluently at school are bilingual speakers.

Students learning English as a second language are a diverse group. Some are fluent in both English and their native language, while others know little or no English. Some learn to speak English quickly, and others learn more slowly. It often takes four to seven years to become a proficient speaker of English, and the more similar the first language is to English, the easier it will be to learn English (Allen, 1991).

In Canada, 2001 census figures indicate that English was reported as the mother tongue for 60 percent of the population, while French was 23 percent. As well, 18 percent of the population of Canada reported speaking a mother tongue other than English or French, up from 16.6 percent in 1996. Chinese was the third most common mother tongue in Canada at 2.9 percent. Other common mother tongue languages include Italian, German, Punjabi, and Spanish. Cree was the most common Aboriginal language reported as a mother tongue, followed by Inuktitut and Ojibway.

Valuing Students' First Language. Until recently, most non–English-speaking students were submerged into English-speaking classrooms and left to "sink or swim" (Spangenberg-Urbschat & Pritchard, 1994). Unfortunately, many students sank and dropped out before graduating from high school. To better meet the needs of linguistically diverse students, teachers now value students' first language and help their students develop a high level of proficiency in their first language as well as in English as a second language. Instruction in students' first language is effective and equitable for large groups of language-minority students (Faltis, 1993).

Whether language arts instruction is in English or in students' first language, teachers can support and value students' first language (Freeman & Freeman, 1993). A list of suggestions for supporting and valuing students' first language is presented in the Teacher's Notebook on page 20. Even teachers who do not speak or write students' first language themselves can follow most of these guidelines using a foreign-language dictionary. For example, they can use a foreign-language dictionary to post signs in the classroom and encourage students to read and write books in their first language. The activities also help students expand their first-language proficiency, develop greater self-confidence, and value their own language.

Learning a Second Language. Learning a second language is a constructive process, just as learning a first language is, and children develop language in a predictable way through interactions with children and adults. Research suggests that second-language acquisition is similar to first-language acquisition (Spangenberg-Urbschat & Pritchard, 1994). Urzua (1980) lists three principles culled from the research:

1. People use many similar language-learning strategies, whether they are small children learning their first language or older children or adults learning a second language.
2. Just as children learning to speak their first language move through a series of developmental stages, second-language learners move through several stages as they learn a new language.
3. First- or second-language learning takes place only when learners have the opportunity to use language for meaningful, functional, and genuine purposes.

When linguistically diverse children and adults first arrive in Canada, they generally go through a silent period (Krashen, 1982) of several months during which they observe others communicating prior to talking or writing in English themselves. Then they begin tentatively to use language to communicate, and through listening, talking, reading, and writing, their language use becomes more cognitively and linguistically complex. The English spoken by newcomers is syntactically less complex; in addition, they enunciate words clearly, speak more slowly, and avoid using idiomatic expressions.

New English speakers use very short sentences, often with two or three keywords, much like the telegraphic speech of young children. For example, a newcomer might say "no pencil" for "I don't have a pencil," or "book table" for "the book is on the table." They may also overgeneralize and call all adults in the school "teachers." As second-language learners acquire labels for more concepts and more sophisticated syntactic structures, they progressively use longer and more complex sentences. They move out of here-and-now, present-tense verb constructions to past and future constructions; however, many ESL students have difficulty adding the -*ed* past-tense marker to verbs, as in "yesterday I play ball."

When parents talk with preschool children learning to speak their first language, they scaffold and extend the children's language. Parents also understand their children's special words for things. These adaptations are called *motherese*. There are striking parallels between the adaptations made by people who interact effectively with ESL students and those described for motherese.

Many ESL Students learning English as a second language often mix English with their first language, shifting back and forth even within sentences. This often-misunderstood phenomenon is called *code-switching* (Lara, 1989; Troika, 1981). Sometimes students read the text in English, but mentally translate it into their first language in order to understand it. This takes a little more time than first speakers need, so teachers must allow more time for ESL students to translate teachers' and classmates' questions and comments from English into their first language and translate their ideas from their first language into English. Too often, teachers assume that students have not understood or do not know the answer when they do not respond immediately. Code-switching is a special linguistic and social skill; it is not a confusion between languages or a corruption of students' first language.

After approximately two years, many second-language learners are fluent enough in English to carry on everyday conversations, but it can take these students as many as five, six, or seven years to achieve the same level of fluency in English as their mainstream classmates (Cummins, 1989). Interestingly, Wong-Fillmore (1985) has found that ESL students learn English in class from teachers and classmates who speak fluent English rather than from their cultural peer group. Moreover, school may be the only place where students speak English!

CRITICAL LITERACY

Understanding how children learn, and particularly how they learn language, allows teachers to select the strategies and provide instruction that will develop a deep and critical understanding of the world. It is in this context that critical literacy is important for the teacher and the student. Critical literacy is not an "add-on" activity; it is a deeper, active approach to understanding language and making meaning.

Critical literacy goes beyond the informative *what* of language to its *how, why,* and *so what?* It goes beyond the reader's competency and comprehension to require a capacity for reflective insight. It asks the reader to "read" a text's symbolism in a philosophical and political context and discern its cultural influences and the writer's craft. Critical literacy enables not only the comprehension of text, but also its implications for our own lives (Shor, 2003, p. 1).

This understanding of critical literacy is based on Paulo Freire's pedagogy. Freire's (1970) premise is that oppression occurs wherever the powerless are excluded from economic and political life. They can more easily be kept powerless if they are also kept uninformed and unaware. Freire sees literacy as an emancipatory process of self-awareness and self-determination that ultimately makes social transformation possible. "Reading the world always precedes reading the word, and reading the word implies continually reading the world" (Freire and Macedo, 1987, p. 25). Freire views critical literacy as one of the ways in which teachers and students learn to read the world.

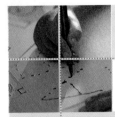

Teacher's Notebook

Guidelines for Supporting and Valuing Students' First Language

1. Use Environmental Print in the Students' First Language

Teachers can post signs and other environmental print written in the students' first language in the classroom. Environmental print refers to signs students frequently encounter in their environment such as names of restaurants, supermarkets, shopping stores, and stop and yield signs. It also includes household items they learn to identify even before learning to read (e.g., McDonald's, Coca-Cola, and Campbell's). In a primary-grade classroom, posters with colour words, numbers, and the days of the week should be written both in English and in the students' first language. Bulletin board titles and captions in posters can also be translated into the students' first language.

2. Add Reading Materials in the Students' First Language to the Classroom Library

Teachers can add books, magazines, and other reading materials written in the students' first language to the library centre. Quality books for children written in a variety of languages are becoming increasingly available in Canada. Also, award-winning books of children's literature are being translated into other languages, especially French and Chinese. Books such as *Where the Wild Things Are* (Sendak, 1963) have been translated for younger children, and *Tuck Everlasting* (Babbitt, 1975) for older children. Sometimes parents and other members of the community are willing to lend books written in a child's first language for the child to use in school. Or, sometimes parents can translate a book being used in class for their child.

3. Encourage Students to Write Books in Their First Language

Linguistically diverse students can write and publish books in their first language. They use the writing process just as English-speaking students do, and they can share their published books with classmates and place them in the classroom library.

4. Use Bilingual Tutors

Linguistically diverse students can read and write with tutors, older students, classmates, and parents who speak their first language. Some classrooms have first-language aides who read and write with students in their first language. Other times parents or older students come into the classroom to work with students.

5. View Videos in the Students' First Language

Teachers can use videos of students reading and dramatizing stories in their first language. In addition, students can dramatize events in history or demonstrate how to do something in their first language. Creating and viewing these videos is useful for building students' proficiency in their first language.

Source: Adapted from Freeman & Freeman, 1993.

Pedagogy and Critical Literacy. Children who are encouraged to focus on the craft of a text (how it is produced) and reflect on their responses to it (how it has affected them) develop active, critical, and metacognitive reading strategies.

The teacher's knowledge of how and why children learn the language arts directs how the curriculum unfolds. This means that the teacher's familiarity with and commitment to critical literacy determines the degree to which students learn critical literacy skills. For example, a teacher brings attention to the place of language in relations of power. She examines how these relations are shaped by the social and cultural contexts of the text and of the student. The teacher understands that her own language comes from a particular social and cultural location. She realizes that no language-learning process is neutral and understands that teaching style and instructional choices and decisions influence how students understand themselves.

Teachers who provide learning opportunities that invite students to develop as reflective citizens will help to critique the status quo, and aid students in imagining and planning for an alternative world. Activities such as writing (e.g., journal writing and collaborative writing) and portfolio assessment across the curriculum encourage critical thinking. Also, exposure to techniques of parody and comparison, such as those in Robert Munsch's *The Paper Bag Princess* (1980), can lead to an understanding of stereotyped roles and questioning of the dominant, or popular, culture. Studying how advertisements, music videos, junk food wrappers, fashion magazines, and history texts are produced also provides tools that enable students to critique the existing social culture and to envision a different kind of society.

Teachers may find this approach daunting, and unpredictable. For example, a critical reading of *Anne of Green Gables* (Montgomery, 1908/1999) shows a setting that rests on the exploitation of child labour. Matthew and Marilla were initially acquiring an orphan as a source of free labour, a common practice of the times. Critically literate teachers may read *Little House on the Prairie* (Wilder, 1953) and its sequels by pointing out the racism and colonization on which the Wilder family's migrations depended. And when Laura is whipped, it is almost always because of disobedience to her father's authority.

A critical reading of the classic *The Secret Garden* (Burnett, 1911) highlights that era's assumptions about class and gender. In the book's fairytale ending, the invalid boy Colin is healed by the garden's magic and reunited with his father. He returns to the world of privilege to which he is heir. The women and servants who have helped him fade away.

Culture, Gender, and Critical Literacy. Each child's family demonstrates the nature of culture and gender roles for that child. In choosing literature for children, teachers should keep in mind that children need to find validation and reflection of their own lives, and they also need to expand their understanding of culture and gender roles beyond their own experience. Literature that satisfies these needs helps children assimilate and accommodate new information. In Vygotsky's terms, well-chosen and challenging literature puts students in a zone of proximal development (see page 8), and their learning is maximized in a way they might not have managed independently.

Contemporary Canadian literature offers a rich selection of finely written and illustrated books whose images, phrases, and experiences are sufficiently novel, as Piaget would put it, to construct scaffolding that enhances students' critical reading of the world. Here are a few examples:

Tomson Highway's *Caribou Song* (2001), the first of a trilogy of northern Aboriginal tales of childhood, presents two small brothers who live a close family life with their nomadic parents. They travel by dogsled across the north, moving with the seasons.

SkySisters (Waboose & Deines, 2000) presents a vast and varied northern landscape that dictates the patterns of life and experience. The Ojibway children of this luminous picture book are intimately linked to the beauty of seasonal rhythms, which they learn to read in the context of their rich Aboriginal traditions.

Waiting for the Whales (McFarlane & Lightburn, 1998) focuses on the family of a daughter, mother, and grandfather. This small family is aware of, and connected to, nature. On the forested West Coast, with its vivid seasonal changes, the daughter gradually understands that her grandfather's autumn death and the subsequent spring's whale migration are part of the cycle of life.

How Smudge Came (Gregory & Lightburn, 1995) is the story of Cindy, a young girl with Down's syndrome, who lives in a group home with house parents. Her life is urban. So is

Khyber's in *Looking for X* (Ellis, 2002). An inner-city child, she lives with her struggling mother and autistic twin brothers.

The Breadwinner (Ellis, 2000), set in contemporary Afghanistan, centres on a young girl who disguises herself as a boy in order to support her family when her father is imprisoned by the Taliban. This novel was written prior to September 11, 2001, but a sequel, *Parvana's Journey* (2002), follows her odyssey across a bomb-strewn landscape of violence and danger to search for scattered family members. On her way, she constructs an alternate "family" of other orphaned and traumatized children. *Mud City* (2003), the third book of this trilogy, follows the children through refugee camps and across the Pakistan border. This is a book by a writer who has lived in that culture, and offers a description of family life that is difficult, dangerous, and unpredictable.

These stories might lead students to look critically at the media, which may present a different account of the same settings and those in them. For example, students who read *Looking for X*, with its first unforgettable sentence, "Mom used to be a stripper," might be asked to examine and critique stereotypes of the welfare family in literature and the media. Khyber and her mother strive for meaning and dignity in a culture of urban poverty. Khyber is not, at first glance, an appealing child. She is stringy-haired, dressed in welfare hand-me-downs, and abrasive at school. Sleep-deprived, she nods off in class. She has an "attitude." But Khyber is also imaginative, creative, resourceful, loving, and loyal. None of these qualities is recognized by her teachers, who are unresponsive, judgmental, and punitive. Khyber does receive nurturing and inspiration from her struggling mother, and from their tough waitress friend. Friendship and acceptance come from X, a schizophrenic street person. As well, Khyber's creative imagination is fed by the public library.

Through books as varied as those discussed above, students come to understand that a variety of families exist. They discover that daily lives, activities, and values are structured by geographical location, family relationships, and cultural inheritance. Students in culturally diverse environments may be exposed to greater cultural variety than those from homogeneous neighbourhoods, but all need that reassuring and stimulating mix of the familiar and the new: traditional, two-parent families; multi-generational families; single-parent families; same-sex parent families; biracial families; adoptive families; large and small families; families with talent and opportunities; families struggling with challenges and deprivation; urban families; and rural families.

As students develop a repertoire of experiences from literature and from life, they develop more schemata and a deeper understanding of themselves and the world. The experiences of family, friendship, and death are universal ones, but the cultural contexts in which they occur demand critical awareness from the reader. Critical literacy helps students understand a diverse and increasingly complex world.

Aesthetics and Critical Literacy. Critical literacy also has an aesthetic dimension. By taking into account the creative skill with which language and images are created, students can deepen their understanding of text. Both *Charlotte's Web* (White, 1980) and *Sunwing* (Oppel, 1999) are examples in which language images are vibrant and real to the reader. In the opening passage of Chapter XI in *Charlotte's Web*, Charlotte first weaves the words that will save Wilbur's life:

> The next day was foggy. Everything on the farm was dripping wet. The grass looked like a magic carpet. The asparagus looked like a silver forest. On foggy mornings, Charlotte's web was truly a thing of beauty. This morning each thin strand was decorated with dozens of tiny beads of water. The web glistened in the light and made a pattern of loveliness and mystery, like a delicate veil. (p. 77)

This opening, with its visual appeal, creates a mysterious mood and a sense of Charlotte's impending "miracle" for the student. The language seems simple, but its aesthetic impact is rich with meaning. The image suggests something precious as well as mysterious.

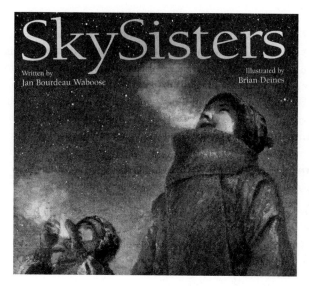

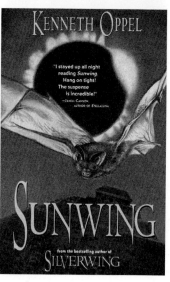

Compare this passage with the final reference to Charlotte's death as she is left to die alone on the trash-littered fairground: "No one was with her when she died." (p. 171). Even young students sense the poignancy of the unsentimental treatment of Charlotte's death, and respond to the language and feeling. Older students recognize that it is the inevitability of loss and death that makes friendship and life so precious. It is the aesthetic quality of E. B. White's language that make *Charlotte's Web* a perennial classic.

Cindy of *How Smudge Came* has Down's syndrome, lives in a group home, and works in an AIDS hospice. The nameless little girl of *Waiting for the Whales* loses her beloved grandfather and experiences loss, grief, and, finally, acceptance. Both stories convey difficult situations through exquisite language and pictures that, when considered, enhance the young student's capacity for understanding and critical literacy.

Teachers nervous about presenting such "difficult" subject matter to children can be reassured that beautifully produced texts written for young readers offer them enriched worlds. Many children already live with the encumbrances of poverty, discrimination, disability, or bereavement. They find their lives and experiences validated through storylines they recognize. At the same time, other children have the opportunity to empathize and expand their own horizons of understanding.

IMPLICATIONS FOR LEARNING THE LANGUAGE ARTS

Children come to school with an intuitive understanding of the four cueing systems based on having learned to speak their first language. Listening to parents tell and read aloud stories also contributes to this knowledge. During the elementary grades, students learn more about the phonological system as they learn phonics and spelling; the semantic system as their vocabularies expand; the syntactic system through grammar instruction; and the pragmatic system as they learn to vary the language they use according to purpose and audience.

Think about writing and how the four cueing systems work together as writers express ideas through words. Writers gather and organize ideas and choose specific words and phrases to express their ideas. They use the semantic system as they choose words to express their ideas, and the syntactic system to organize the words into sentences, paragraphs, and various writing forms, such as letters, reports, and stories. The pragmatic system comes into play as writers consider

their audience and purpose for writing. They decide whether to craft longer or shorter sentences, and consider the impact of informal or more formal word choices, jargon, nonstandard English, or technical vocabulary on their readers. They consider the style of their composition, and decide whether to state facts objectively, use persuasive language, or create wordplays, rhymes, or poetic images to express their ideas. As they transcribe their ideas into words and sentences, writers use their knowledge of the phonological system to spell words. Without any one of the cueing systems, writers would be hampered in their attempt to use language to express ideas.

Culture affects the way people think and how they use language. In her study of three culturally different communities, Shirley Brice Heath (1983b) found that because of different lifestyles and child-rearing practices, children come to school with radically different literacy experiences and expectations about learning. Since the families in her study had dramatically different experiences with written language in their English-speaking homes, the diversity of experiences of children from homes where English is not the primary language would be even greater.

Children from each cultural group bring their unique backgrounds of experience to the process of learning, and they have difficulty understanding concepts outside their backgrounds of experience. This difficulty is greater for students who are learning English as a second language. Think, for example, of the different experiences and language knowledge that children of Vietnamese refugees, Aboriginal children, and children of Hispanic immigrants bring to school. No matter what ethnic group they belong to or what language they speak, all students use the same cognitive and linguistic processes to learn.

Children of diverse ethnic groups have met with varying degrees of success in schools, depending on their previous cultural experiences, the expectations students and their parents have, and the expectations teachers have for them. Often a discrepancy exists between the way classrooms operate and the ways students from various ethnic groups behave (Law & Eckes, 1990). Four common cultural behaviours that differ from mainstream ones are:

1. *No eye contact.* In some Asian and Aboriginal cultures, avoiding eye contact is polite and respectful behaviour. Mainstream teachers sometimes mistakenly assume that when students avoid eye contact, they are not paying attention or are sullen and uncooperative.

2. *Cooperation.* Students from many Southeast Asian, Polynesian, and Aboriginal cultures are taught to cooperate and help each other, and in school they often assist classmates with their work. In contrast, many mainstream students are more competitive than cooperative, and sometimes mainstream teachers view cooperating on assignments as cheating.

3. *Fear of making mistakes.* Teachers encourage students to take risks and view making mistakes as a natural part of the learning process. In some cultures, especially Japan's, correctness is valued above all else, and students are taught not to guess or take risks.

4. *Informal classroom environment.* In some cultures, including those of Europe and Asia, the school environment is much more formal than it is in North America. Students from Europe or Asia often view North American schools as chaotic, and they interpret the informality as permission to misbehave.

For more information on grand conversations, see Chapter 5, "Listening and Speaking in the Classroom," pages 198–200.

Many Asian-heritage students have been taught to keep a social distance between the teacher and themselves. For example, out of respect for the teacher, they look down when they are spoken to and feel more comfortable remaining in their assigned seats. Literature discussions, called *grand conversations*, and other informal activities can make these students feel uncomfortable because the lack of structure appears to indicate disrespect for the teacher. Some research indicates Asian parents typically equate learning and knowledge with memorizing factual information, and they expect a great deal of homework (Cheng, 1987).

McGrath (1991) suggests that "it is impossible to . . . introduce all of our country's children of different cultural backgrounds to one another, but the next best alternative is to introduce them

Elementary-aged students are exposed to print in both of Canada's official languages.

to each other through their own popular literature" (p. 153). In this way, children learn to take pride in their own heritage, and to develop an understanding of other cultures. Such books include *Billy's World* (Weber-Pillwax, 1989), the story of a small boy who lives on a northern Cree reserve with his family, and *Mina's Spring of Colors* (Gilmore, 2000), a story about an 11-year-old girl whose grandfather, Nanaji, has moved to Canada from India to live with his daughter's family.

Aboriginal students also have unique needs. For too long, schools have neglected and failed these students. Teachers understand and build on these students' abilities, appreciate their varied backgrounds, and nurture their potential for learning. Teachers must also take into account historical, economic, psychological, and linguistic barriers that have led to oppression and low expectations. One way to help raise children's self-esteem and build pride in their cultural groups is to incorporate literature about, for example, Japanese-Canadian and Aboriginal cultures, into their instructional programs. One powerful title, *Storm Child* (Bellingham, 1985), is historically based fiction "telling of the trauma, all too often experienced by families abandoned by father-traders who left them behind on their return to Europe" (McGrath, 1991, p. 156).

Language and culture have important implications for the ways in which schoolchildren learn, and teachers teach, the language arts. Some implications:

- Children use the four cueing systems simultaneously as they communicate.
- Children from each cultural group bring their unique backgrounds of experience to the process of learning.
- Children's cultural and linguistic diversity provides an opportunity to enhance and enrich the learning of all students.
- Literature offers a rich selection of well-written and illustrated books to enhance children's critical understanding of the world.

Guidelines for teaching linguistically diverse students are presented in the Teacher's Notebook on page 27.

Critical literacy is an important part of language learning. Through a critical literacy approach, teachers and students develop an understanding of how the language arts—listening, speaking, reading, writing, viewing, visually representing—can be used to understand and change our world. Students learn to critique the existing social culture and work toward a new and perhaps better kind of society.

How Children Learn the Language Arts

Language arts instruction is changing to reflect the greater oral, written, and visual communication needs as we move through the twenty-first century (*Standards*, 1996). The Steering Committee of the Elementary Section of the National Council of Teachers of English (NCTE, 1996) has identified these characteristics of competent language users:

1. *Personal expression.* Students use language to express themselves, to make connections between their own experiences and their social world, to choose books they want to read and topics they want to write about, and to create a personal voice.

2. *Aesthetic appreciation.* Students use language aesthetically to read literature, talk with others, and enrich their lives.

3. *Collaborative exploration.* Students use language as a learning tool as they investigate concepts and issues in collaboration with classmates.

4. *Strategic language use.* Students use strategies as they create and share meaning through language.

5. *Creative communication.* Students use text forms and genres creatively as they share ideas through language.

6. *Reflective interpretation.* Students use language to organize and evaluate learning experiences, question personal and social values, and think critically.

7. *Thoughtful application.* Students use language to solve problems, persuade, and take action.

Students exemplify these characteristics of competent and critical language users as they

- compare the video and book versions of the same story;
- interview community resource persons with special knowledge, interests, or talents in connection with resource-based units and social studies/science thematic units;
- examine propaganda techniques used in print advertisements and television commercials;
- assume the role of a character while reading a story, and write simulated journal entries as that character;
- use the writing process to write stories, and share the stories with classmates;
- analyze an author's writing style during an author unit, or an artist's drawing style during an illustrator unit; and
- critique stereotypes of characters in books they are reading.

These activities exhibit the four characteristics of all worthwhile experiences with language. First, they use language in meaningful instead of contrived situations. Second, they are functional, or real-life, activities. Third, they are genuine, not artificial (e.g., filling in worksheets), activities, because they communicate ideas. And fourth, they ask students to critically examine and question what they are reading and writing.

THE LANGUAGE ARTS

Traditionally, language arts educators have defined the language arts as the study of the four modes of language: listening, speaking, reading, and writing. However, the National Council of Teachers of English and the International Reading Association (*Standards*, 1996) proposed two additional language arts—viewing and visually representing. These new language arts reflect the growing importance of visual literacy (Ernst, 1983; Whitin, 1996b). Also, *thinking* is sometimes referred to as an additional language art, but, more accurately, it permeates all of the language arts.

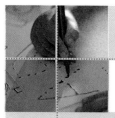

Teacher's Notebook

Guidelines for Teaching Linguistically Diverse Students

1. **Provide a Comprehensible Environment**
   - Use language that is neither too hard nor too easy for students.
   - Embed language in context-rich activities.
   - Speak more slowly, and rarely use idioms.
   - Highlight keywords.
   - Expand the two- and three-word sentences that students produce.

2. **Create an Environment with Minimal Stress**
   - Show genuine interest in students, their language, and their culture.
   - Allow students to speak and write their own language.
   - Avoid forcing students to speak.
   - Encourage risk-taking.
   - Don't correct grammatical errors.
   - Understand that diverse students are caught between two cultures.

3. **Provide Opportunities to Use English**
   - Provide many opportunities for students to speak and listen to English and to read and write English in low-risk situations.
   - Have students work together with buddies and in cooperative groups.
   - Promote friendships among students.

4. **Examine Your Attitude**
   - Avoid stereotyping any linguistic or cultural group.
   - Do not lower your expectations for certain groups of students.
   - Encourage bilingualism.
   - Consider your tolerance for nonstandard English and code-switching.

5. **Alleviate Home–School Mismatches**
   - Consider the contrast between how children use language in home communities and at school.
   - Smooth the transition between home and school.
   - Expect students to be uncomfortable in unfamiliar activities.

6. **Involve Linguistically Diverse Parents**
   - Make home visits and phone calls to parents.
   - Encourage parents to participate in school activities.
   - Translate letters, information sheets, and memos into first languages.
   - Have translators available for school meetings and conferences.
   - Plan parent–child and home-school activities.

Source: Gibbons, 1991; Faltis, 1993; Law & Eckes, 1990; Scarcella, 1990.

For more information on strategies for teaching listening, see Chapter 5, "Listening and Speaking in the Classroom," pages 174–185.

Listening. Beginning at birth, a child's first contact with language is through listening. Listening instruction is often neglected in elementary classrooms because teachers feel that students have already learned how to listen, and that instructional time should be devoted to reading and writing. We present an alternative view of listening and its instruction, and focus on these key concepts:

● Listening is a process of which hearing is only one part.

● Students listen differently according to their purpose.

● Students listen aesthetically to stories, efferently to learn information as part of across-the-curriculum thematic units, and critically to persuasive appeals.

● Students use listening strategies and monitor their comprehension in order to listen more effectively.

For more information on speaking activities, see Chapter 5, "Listening and Speaking in the Classroom," pages 192–196 and pages 201–212.

Speaking. As with listening, teachers often neglect instruction in speaking during the elementary grades because they feel students already know how to speak. Recent research emphasizes the importance of speaking in the learning process (Dwyer, 1991; Newkirk & McLure, 1992). For example, students use talk to respond to literature, provide feedback about classmates' compositions in writing groups, and present oral reports during social studies and science thematic units. The key concepts about speaking are

● Speaking is an essential part of the language arts curriculum.

● Students use speaking for both aesthetic and efferent purposes.

● Students participate in grand conversations as they respond to literature.

● Students give presentations, including oral reports and debates.

● Drama, including storytelling and role-playing, provides a valuable method of learning and a powerful way of communicating.

For more information on the reading process, see Chapter 4, "The Reading and Writing Processes," page 131.

Reading. Reading is a process, and students use skills and strategies in order to decode words and comprehend what they are reading. Students vary the way they read according to their purpose. They read for pleasure differently than they read to locate and remember information (Rosenblatt, 1991). The key concepts about reading are

● Reading is a strategic process.

● The goal of reading instruction is comprehension, or meaning-making.

● Students read differently for different purposes.

● Students participate in five types of reading: independent reading, shared reading, guided reading, buddy reading, and reading aloud to students.

For more information on writing stories, journals, and poetry, see Chapter 6, "Reading and Writing Narrative Text," pages 216–229 and pages 235–239.

Writing. Like reading, writing is a strategic process. Students use the writing process as they write stories, reports, poems, and other types of writing. Students also do informal writing, such as writing in reading logs and making clusters. As you continue reading, you will learn about these key concepts about writing:

● Writing is a process in which students cycle recursively through prewriting, drafting, revising, editing, and publishing stages.

● Students experiment with many written language forms.

● Informal writing is used to develop writing fluency and as a learning tool.

● Spelling and handwriting are tools for writers.

Viewing. Visual media include film and videos, print advertisements, television commercials, photographs and book illustrations, PowerPoint presentations, and CD-ROMs. Because visual media are commonplace in Canadian life today, children need to learn how to comprehend them and to integrate visual knowledge with other literacy knowledge. The key concepts about viewing are

- Viewing is an important component of literacy.
- Students view visual media for a variety of purposes.
- Viewing is much like reading, and students use comprehension strategies in both reading and viewing.
- Students use storyboards to examine the illustrations in picture books.
- Students learn about propaganda techniques in order to critically analyze commercials and advertisements.

Visually Representing. Students create meaning through multiple sign systems such as video and music productions; hypertext and other computer programs; improvisation role-playing; readers' theatre; story quilts; and illustrations for charts, posters, and books they are writing. According to Harste, "seeing something familiar in a new way is often a process of gaining new insights" (1993, p. 4). Projects involving visual texts are often completed as part of resource-based and thematic units. A couple of key concepts about visually representing are presented in this book:

- Students consider audience, purpose, and form as they create visual texts.
- Visual texts, like writing, can be created to share information learned during resource-based units and thematic units.

Relationships among the Language Arts. Discussing the language arts one by one suggests a division among them, as though they could be used separately. In reality, they are used simultaneously and reciprocally. Almost any activity in this area involves more than one of the language arts. In a seminal study, researcher Walter Loban (1976) documented the language growth and development of a group of 338 students from kindergarten through grade 12 (ages 5 to 18). Two purposes of his longitudinal study were, first, to examine differences between students who used language effectively and those who did not, and second, to identify predictable stages of language development. Three of Loban's conclusions are especially noteworthy for our discussion of the language arts. First, he reported positive correlations among listening, speaking, reading, and writing. Second, he found that students with less effective oral language abilities tended to have less effective written language abilities. And third, he found a strong relationship between students' oral language ability and their overall academic ability. Loban's study demonstrates clear relationships among the language arts and emphasizes the need to teach listening and talking during the elementary grades.

Resource-based units, readers and writers workshops, and across-the-curriculum thematic units are three ways to make language arts instruction meaningful. Students use all six language strands as they read and respond to literature in focus units. For example, as fifth graders read and respond to *Number the Stars* (Lowry, 1989), a story about friendship between a Christian girl and a Jewish girl set in Denmark during the Second World War, they use listening, speaking, reading, writing, viewing, and visual representing in some of the ways shown in Figure 1–2 on page 30. Across-the-curriculum connections are also possible given the historical setting of the story.

1. Listening
   Students listen to *Number the Stars* as it is read aloud, and they listen to classmates' comments during literature discussions. They listen and watch as classmates dramatize events from the story and as classmates share reports of information or projects.

2. Speaking
   Students speak as they make predictions about what will happen in upcoming chapters and as they share their responses to the story during literature discussions. They may share the results of their research into World War II, or report on the geography of Denmark and trace the trip the girls took from Copenhagen to the seacoast. Students also use speaking as they dramatize story events and share projects they create after reading the story.

3. Reading
   Students read *Number the Stars* aloud, with a buddy or independently. They may reread brief excerpts from the story during discussions or read-arounds and read other books by the author, Lois Lowry, or other books about World War II and the Holocaust. Students read aloud their journal entries and quickwrites to share them with classmates. During writing groups students read aloud sequels, poems, reports, or other projects they are writing.

4. Writing
   Students write their predictions about and reactions to each chapter in reading logs or keep simulated journals written from the viewpoint of one of the characters. Students write quickwrites on topics related to the story. They also make notes during presentations by the teacher about World War II and the Holocaust. Students also use the writing process as they write sequels, poems, reports, and other compositions after reading *Number the Stars*.

5. Viewing
   Students observe as classmates dramatize scenes from the story. They examine large black-and-white photos of war scenes that the teacher has collected, and talk about the impact of the black-and-white photos. They consider how the impact would differ if they were in colour. They also watch videotapes about World War II and take notes after viewing and talk about the video in grand conversations.

6. Visually Representing
   Students make setting maps of Denmark and include sites mentioned in the story, and they make a story quilt to celebrate students' favourite quotes from the story. They also make open-mind portraits of the main characters. For these portraits, students draw a large picture of the character's face and cut it out. Then they cut a second piece of paper the same size and glue it on a piece of construction paper. They draw pictures and write words on this piece of paper to represent the character's thoughts. Then they staple the character's face paper on top so that it flips open to reveal the character's thoughts.

Figure 1–2 Ways Grade 5 Students Use the Six Language Strands in a Resource-Based Unit on *Number the Stars*

Similarly, students use the six language arts as they learn and share their learning in social studies and science thematic units. As second graders learn about dinosaurs in a thematic unit, they use the six strands to explore the concepts they are learning as well as to share what they have learned. See Figure 1–3 for some of these across-the-curriculum connections for a thematic unit on dinosaurs.

1. Listening

   Students listen to the teacher read books about dinosaurs. They listen to *Dinosaurs Before Dark* (Osborne, 1992), a fictional story and easy reader about a magic tree house and dinosaurs. They look at informational books like *Inside Dinosaurs and Other Prehistoric Creatures* (Dewar, 1993) and picture books such as *Creatures of Long Ago* (National Geographic, 1996). Students also listen as the teacher presents information about dinosaurs.

2. Speaking

   Students talk about dinosaurs and about what they are learning in the thematic unit. After reading or listening to the teacher read a book, they participate in grand conversations in which they share their responses to the book. They also create their own riddles after listening to the teacher read the riddles in *Two Dozen Dinosaurs: A First Book of Dinosaurs Facts, Mysteries, Games and Fun* (Ripley, 1991). Later, students will write their riddles and add them to a dinosaur mural they are creating.

3. Reading

   Students read informational books about dinosaurs in small groups and then make a timeline in their learning logs of the dinosaurs' time on earth. Students record interesting facts in their learning logs. Also, using books from the classroom library, students read and reread other stories, informational books, and poems about dinosaurs.

4. Writing

   Students write in learning logs and make clusters, diagrams, and other charts in the logs, too. Then they use the writing process to research and write reports about dinosaurs. They post their finished reports next to the large papier-mâché mountain they create. Some students work together to write an alphabet book about dinosaurs. Each student chooses a letter and writes one page, and then the pages are compiled and bound into a book. Other students write a cumulative book following the pattern in *One More Dinosaur* (Demers, 1989). Each student prepares one page for the book, and then the pages are compiled and bound into a book.

5. Viewing

   Students view videos and films about dinosaurs and examine posters about dinosaurs.

6. Visually Representing

   As they learn about dinosaurs, students take notes and draw pictures and diagrams to help them remember important information. Students make Plasticine models of dinosaurs and place these on or next to a large papier-mâché display of the dinosaurs' habitat. They hang their reports next to this display.

Figure 1–3 Ways Grade 2 Students Use the Six Language Arts in a Thematic Unit on Dinosaurs

A PARADIGM FOR LANGUAGE ARTS INSTRUCTION

Language arts instruction should be based on how children learn, the impact of language and culture on learning, and society's goals for its children's literacy development. Teachers create a community of learners in their classrooms in order to facilitate students' learning, they support students as they learn skills and strategies related to the language arts, and they teach lessons that allow students to apply what they are learning in listening, speaking, reading, writing, viewing, and visually representing activities.

A Community of Learners. Language arts classrooms are social settings. Together, students and their teacher create the classroom community, and the type of community they create strongly influences students' learning. Effective teachers establish a community of learners in which students are motivated to learn and are actively involved in language arts activities. The teacher and students work collaboratively and purposefully. Perhaps the most striking quality of classroom communities is the partnership that the teacher and students create. Students are a "family" in which all the members respect one another and support each other's learning. Students value culturally and linguistically diverse classmates and recognize that all students can make important contributions to the classroom (Wells & Chang-Wells, 1992).

Students and the teacher work together for the common good of the community. Consider the differences between renting and owning a home. In a classroom community, students and the teacher are joint owners of the classroom. Students assume responsibility for their own learning and behaviour, work collaboratively with classmates, complete assignments, and care for the classroom. In contrast, in traditional classrooms, the classroom is the teacher's, and students are simply renters for the school year. This doesn't mean that in a classroom community teachers abdicate their responsibility to students. Teachers retain their roles as organizer, facilitator, participant, instructor, model, manager, diagnostician, evaluator, coordinator, and communicator. These roles are often shared with students, but the ultimate responsibility remains with teachers.

Researchers have identified ten characteristics of classroom communities (Cambourne & Turbill, 1987). These characteristics, which are described in Figure 1–4, show how the learning theories presented at the beginning of this chapter are translated into practice.

Susan Hepler writes, "the real challenge to teachers . . . is to set up the kind of classroom community where children pick their own ways to literacy and continue to learn to read" (1991, p. 179). Frank Smith (1988) calls these classrooms "literacy clubs" in which all students feel a sense of acceptance and belonging and no one is left out because he or she doesn't read or write as well as others. All students are welcomed and treated with respect, and teachers expect excellence. Donald Graves (1994) identifies five characteristics for writing classrooms: opportunities, demonstrations, choice, time, and engagement.

Motivation for Learning. Motivation is intrinsic and internal—a driving force within us. Often students' motivation for the language arts diminishes as they reach the upper grades. Penny Oldfather (1995) conducted a four-year study to examine the factors influencing students' motivation, and she found that when students had opportunities for authentic self-expression as part of language arts activities, they were more highly motivated. Students she interviewed reported that they were more highly motivated when they had ownership of the learning activities. Specific activities that they mentioned included opportunities to

- express their own ideas and opinions;
- choose topics for writing and books for reading;
- talk about books they are reading;
- share their writings with classmates; and
- pursue "authentic" activities—not worksheets—using the language arts.

Some students are not strongly motivated for the language arts, and they adopt strategies for avoiding failure rather than for making meaning. These strategies are defensive tactics (Dweck, 1986; Paris, Wasik, & Turner, 1991). Unmotivated students often give up or remain passive, uninvolved in reading and other language arts activities (Johnston & Winograd, 1985).

1. Responsibility

   Students are responsible for their learning, their behaviour, and the contributions they make in the classroom. They see themselves as valued and contributing members of the classroom community. Students become more self-reliant when they make choices about the language arts activities in which they are involved.

2. Opportunities

   Students have opportunities to participate in language arts activities that are meaningful, functional, and genuine. They read real books and write books for real audiences—their classmates, their parents and grandparents, and other members of their community. They rarely use workbooks or drill-and-practice sheets.

3. Engagement

   Students are motivated to learn and to be actively involved in language arts activities. In a student-centred classroom, the activities are interesting, and students sometimes choose which books to read, how they will respond to a book, topics for writing, and the writing form they will use.

4. Demonstration

   Students learn procedures, concepts, skills, and strategies through demonstrations—with modelling and scaffolding—that teachers provide.

5. Risk-taking

   Students are encouraged to explore topics, make guesses, and take risks. Rather than having students focus on correct answers, teachers promote students' experimentation with new skills and strategies.

6. Instruction

   Teachers are expert language users, and they provide instruction through minilessons son procedures, skills, strategies, and other concepts related to the language arts. These minilessons are planned and taught to small groups, the whole class, or individual students so that students can apply what they are learning in meaningful literacy projects.

7. Response

   Students have opportunities to respond after reading and viewing and to share their interpretations of stories. Through writing in reading logs and participating in discussions called grand conversations, students share personal connections to the story, make predictions, ask questions, and deepen their comprehension. When they write, students share their rough drafts in writing groups to get feedback on how well they are communicating, and they celebrate their published books by sharing them with classmates and other "real" audiences.

8. Choice

   Students often make choices about the language arts activities in which they are involved. They choose what books they will read and what projects they will create after reading. Students make choices within the parameters set by the teacher. When they are given the opportunity to make choices, students are often more highly motivated to do the activity, and they value their learning experience more. It is more meaningful to them.

(continued)

Figure 1–4 Ten Characteristics of Classroom Communities

9. Time

Students need large chunks of time to pursue language arts activities. It doesn't work well for teachers to break the classroom schedule into many small time blocks for phonics, reading, spelling, handwriting, grammar, and writing. Students need two or three hours of uninterrupted time each day for language arts instruction. It is important to minimize disruptions during the time set aside, and administrators should schedule computer, music, art, and other pull-out programs so that they do not interfere. This is especially important in the primary grades.

10. Assessment

Teachers and students work together to establish guidelines for assessment, and students monitor their own work and participate in the evaluation. Rather than imposing assessment on students, teachers share with their students the responsibility for monitoring and evaluating their progress.

Figure 1–4 Ten Characteristics of Classroom Communities (*continued*)
Source: Adapted from Cambourne & Turbill, 1987.

Some students feign interest or pretend to be involved even though they are not. Others don't think language arts are important, and they choose to focus on other curricular areas—math or sports, for instance. Some students complain about feeling ill or that other students are bothering them.

Other students avoid the language arts entirely. They just don't do them. There are also students who read books that are too easy for them or write short pieces so that they don't have to exert much effort. Even though these strategies are self-serving, students use them because they lead to short-term success. The long-term result, however, is devastating because these students fail to learn to read and write competently.

Language Arts Strategies and Skills. Students learn both strategies and skills through language arts instruction. *Strategies* are problem-solving methods or behaviours. Students develop and use both general learning strategies and specific strategies related to the language arts. While there is no definitive list of language arts strategies, researchers have identified a number of strategies that capable readers and writers use (Paris & Jacobs, 1984; Schmitt, 1990). We will focus on twelve of these strategies in this text:

tapping prior knowledge	applying fix-up strategies
predicting	revising meaning
organizing ideas	monitoring
figuring out unknown words	playing with language
visualizing	generalizing
making connections	evaluating

These strategies are described in Figure 1–5. Students often use more than one of these strategies for a language arts activity, but they rarely, if ever, use all them for a single activity. Students choose the appropriate strategies to accomplish the activities in which they are engaged.

1. Tapping Prior Knowledge

   Students think about what they already know about the topic as they listen, read, view, or write. This knowledge includes information and vocabulary about content-area topics such as whales or the solar system, as well as language arts information about authors, types of literature, and literal and figurative meanings.

2. Predicting

   Students make predictions about what will happen as they read or view. These guesses are based on students' knowledge about the topic and the type of literature, or what they have read or viewed thus far. Students also make predictions as they speak, write, and visually represent. They make plans and set purposes.

3. Organizing Ideas

   Students organize ideas and sequence story events when they read, write, view, or listen to stories read aloud. Students organize ideas for writing using clusters and demonstrate comprehension after reading or viewing using other graphic organizers. Students organize ideas differently depending on whether they are exploring stories, informational books, or poetry.

4. Figuring Out Unknown Words

   Students figure out unknown words as they read, listen, and view. Depending on the particular situation, students choose whether to use word attack skills, context clues, or skip over a word. Writers use "sound it out" and "think it out" strategies to spell unfamiliar words.

5. Visualizing

   Students draw pictures in their minds of what they are listening to, reading, or writing. Often film versions of stories are disappointing because they don't match students' visualizations.

6. Making Connections

   Students relate what they are listening, reading, or viewing to their own lives and to books they have read. Similarly, students make connections between their writing or oral presentations and books they have read and experiences they have had.

7. Applying Fix-up Strategies

   When students are listening, speaking, reading, writing, viewing, or visually representing and something doesn't make sense, they apply fix-up strategies. They may assume that things will make sense soon and continue with the activity, or they may ask a question, go back, or skip ahead when reading or viewing, or speak with a classmate.

8. Revising Meaning

   Students continuously revise meaning as they proceed with a language arts activity. When reading, for example, students reread for more information or because something doesn't make sense, they study the illustrations, or they get ideas from classmates during discussions. Writers meet in writing groups to get feedback on their rough drafts in order to revise their writing and make it stronger. Students also get feedback when they create visual representations.

9. Monitoring

   Students ask themselves questions to monitor their understanding as they participate in language arts activities. They monitor their comprehension as they read,

(continued)

Figure 1–5 Language Arts Strategies

view, and listen. They recognize when comprehension breaks down and use other strategies to regain comprehension. When they give oral presentations or participate in discussions, students monitor what they are saying and the reactions of classmates.

10. Playing with Language
Students notice figurative and novel uses of language as they listen, read, and view. When they give oral presentations and write, students incorporate interesting language in their presentations and compositions.

11. Generalizing
When students read, view, and listen, they note ideas and put them together to draw conclusions. Generalizing is important because big ideas are easier to remember than lots of details. Writers often state their big ideas at the beginning of a paragraph and then support them with facts. They want their readers to be able to make generalizations. When students give oral presentations and create visual representations, they emphasize generalizations, too.

12. Evaluating
Students make judgments about, reflect on, and value the language arts activities in which they participate. They also think about themselves as language users and reflect on what they do as listeners, speakers, readers, and writers.

Figure 1–5 Language Arts Strategies (*continued*)

These strategies are applied in all six language arts. Consider revising meaning, for example. Probably the best-known application is in writing. Students revise meaning as they add, substitute, delete, and move information in their rough drafts. Revising meaning in visual representations works the same way. But students also revise meaning as they listen to a speaker, view a video, or read a book. They revise their understanding as they continue listening, viewing, or reading and get more information. And, students revise meaning while they are talking on the basis of feedback from the audience.

Skills, in contrast, are information-processing techniques that students use automatically and unconsciously as they construct meaning. Many skills focus at the word level, but some require students to attend to larger chunks of text. For example, readers use skills such as decoding unfamiliar words, noting details, and sequencing events, and writers employ skills such as forming contractions, using punctuation marks, and capitalizing people's names. Skills and strategies are not the same thing, since strategies are problem-solving tactics selected deliberately to achieve particular goals (Paris et al., 1991). The important difference between skills and strategies is how they are used.

During the elementary and middle-school grades, students learn to use and refine five types of skills. While many of the skills are oriented to reading and writing, some are used for listening, speaking, viewing, and visually representing. The five types of skills are

1. *Meaning-making skills.* These include summarizing, separating facts and opinions, comparing and contrasting, and recognizing literary genres and structures. Students use these skills as they create meaning using all six language arts.

2. *Decoding and spelling skills.* These include sounding out words, noticing word families, using root words and affixes to decode and spell words, and using abbreviations. Students use these skills as they decode words when reading and as they spell words when writing.

3. *Study skills.* These include skimming and scanning, taking notes, making clusters, and previewing a book before reading. Students use study skills during across-the-curriculum thematic units, while reading informational books, and while collecting information to use in writing reports.

4. *Language skills.* These include identifying and inferring meanings of words, noticing idioms, dividing words into syllables, and choosing synonyms. Students are continuously interacting with language as they use the language arts, and they use these skills to analyze words when they are listening and reading, and to choose more precise language when they are speaking and writing.

5. *Reference skills.* These include alphabetizing a list of words, using a dictionary, and reading and making graphs and other diagrams. Elementary and middle-school students learn to use reference skills in order to read newspaper articles, locate information in encyclopedias and other informational books, and use library resources.

Examples of each of the five types of skills are presented in Figure 1–6 on page 38. Students use these skills for various language arts activities. For example, students use some of the skills when giving an oral report and others when making a poster advertising a book they have read or comparing several versions of a folktale. It is unlikely that students use every skill listed in Figure 1–6 for any particular language arts activity, but capable students are familiar with most of these skills and can use them automatically whenever they are needed.

Teachers often wonder when they should teach the skills listed in Figure 1–6. Provincial education departments and school districts often prepare curriculum guides that list the skills to be taught at each grade level, and skills are usually listed on scope-and-sequence charts that accompany language arts series and programs. On scope-and-sequence charts, series and program writers identify the grade level at which a skill should be introduced and the grade levels at which it is practised and tested. These resources provide guidelines, but teachers decide which skills to teach based on their students' level of development and the activities in which their students are involved.

Teachers use both direct and indirect instruction to provide information that students need to know about skills and strategies. Both types of instruction are presented in context so that students see a reason to learn them and are able to apply what they learn in meaningful ways (Calkins, 1980; Routman, 1996). When teachers model how to do something, scaffold a student's use of a strategy or skill, or respond to a student's question, they are using indirect instruction. In contrast, direct instruction is planned. Teachers often teach minilessons, brief 10- to 30-minute lessons in which teachers explicitly explain a particular skill or strategy, model its use, and provide examples and opportunities for practice. Then students apply what they have learned using meaningful, functional, and genuine activities.

A Teaching Strategy. Learning theories can be applied in designing a strategy or lesson format to be used in teaching strategies, skills, concepts, procedures, and other types of information. Piaget's concepts of assimilation and accommodation are important because they describe how children learn concepts and add information to their cognitive structures. Similarly, Vygotsky's concept of the zone of proximal development is useful because it explains that teachers can support students and assist them in learning things that they cannot learn by themselves. The six-step teaching strategy in the Step by Step box on page 39 establishes a sequence of instruction for minilessons, and it can be adapted for teaching almost any language arts procedure, concept, strategy, or skill.

Students do not, of course, learn in such neat little steps. Rather, learning is a process of ebb and flow in which the assimilating and accommodating processes move back and forth as the student grasps pieces of information. Students may grasp a new concept in any of the steps of the teaching strategy; some students may not learn it at all. Teachers will plan additional lessons for the students who do not learn. Whether or not they learn depends on the closeness of the fit between their schemata and the information being presented. Information that does not in someway relate to an existing schema is almost impossible to learn. Information must be moderately novel to fit students' existing cognitive structures.

Meaning-Making Skills

Sequence
Summarize
Categorize
Classify
Identify the author's purpose
Separate facts and opinions
Note details
Draw conclusions
Identify cause and effect
Compare and contrast
Determine problem and solution
Use context clues
Notice organizational patterns of poetry, plays, business and friendly letters, stories, essays, and reports
Recognize literary genres (traditional stories, fantasies, speculative fiction, realistic fiction, historical fiction, biography, autobiography, and poetry)
Identify mood
Recognize persuasion and propaganda

Decoding and Spelling Skills

Sound out words using knowledge of phonics
Notice word families
Look for picture cues
Ask a classmate or the teacher
Consult a dictionary or glossary
Apply spelling rules
Write plurals
Use root words and affixes
Use structural clues
Capitalize proper nouns and adjectives
Use abbreviations

Study Skills

Adjust rate of reading
Skim
Scan
Preview
Follow directions
Make outlines and clusters
Take notes
Paraphrase

Language Skills

Choose among multiple meanings of words
Notice compound words
Use contractions
Divide words into syllables
Use possessives
Notice figurative language
Use similes and metaphors
Notice idioms and slang
Use comparatives and superlatives
Choose synonyms
Recognize antonyms
Differentiate among homonyms
Appreciate rhyme, imagery, and other poetic devices
Use punctuation marks (period, question mark, exclamation mark, quotation marks, comma, colon, semicolon, and hyphen)
Use simple, compound, and complex sentences
Use declarative, interrogative, exclamatory, and imperative sentences
Combine sentences
Recognize parts of sentences
Avoid sentence fragments
Recognize parts of speech (nouns, pronouns, verbs, adjectives, adverbs, conjunctions, prepositions, and interjections)

Reference Skills

Sort in alphabetical order
Use a glossary or dictionary
Locate etymologies in the dictionary
Use the pronunciation guide in the dictionary
Locate synonyms in a thesaurus
Locate information in an encyclopedia, atlas, or almanac
Compare information from more than one source
Use a table of contents
Use an index
Use a card catalogue
Read and make graphs, tables, and diagrams
Read and make timelines
Read newspapers and magazines
Use bibliographic forms

Figure 1–6 Language Arts Skills

This teaching strategy will be adapted for minilessons in just about every chapter of this book. Some lessons may not lend themselves readily to this six-step sequence of instruction; for certain concepts, one or more of the steps may not be appropriate, and some adjustments may be necessary.

Two applications to illustrate how the teaching strategy can be used with almost any language arts topic are presented in Figure 1–7 on page 40. The first is a minilesson on *fables*—brief stories that teach a lesson. Some of the best-known fables were compiled by Aesop, a Greek slave who lived in the sixth century BCE, but many other civilizations have contributed fables as well. A number of fables have been

Step by Step

Sequence of Instruction for Minilessons

1. **Initiating.**
   The teacher introduces the strategy, skill, concept, or procedure. The initiating step includes questions, statements, examples, and activities for stimulating interest in the lesson and engaging students' participation.

2. **Structuring.**
   The teacher presents information and relates it to what students already know so that students can begin to overcome the cognitive conflict they experienced in the first step. To overcome cognitive conflict, students begin to enlarge or restructure an existing schema to fit the information, or they begin to develop a new schema to organize the information.

3. **Conceptualizing.**
   Students experiment with and analyze the information presented in the second step in order to make connections to related information. This step furthers the process of accommodation begun earlier. When the accommodation process is completed, the existing schemata have been enlarged or a new schema has been developed that fits the new information.

4. **Summarizing.**
   The teacher and students review the major points of the lesson. The information and examples presented in the structuring step and the relationships established during the conceptualizing step are organized and summarized. This step allows students to make any necessary adjustments in the schema and in the new interrelationships established within their cognitive structures. For students who have not understood the information being presented, summarizing presents another opportunity to accommodate the information.

5. **Generalizing.**
   The teacher presents new examples or variations of the information introduced in the first step. This step is a check on students' understanding, and students demonstrate their understanding by generalizing from the first example to this new example.

6. **Applying.**
   Students incorporate the information in an activity that allows them to demonstrate their knowledge by using the concept in a novel or unique way.

retold for children, and children's authors such as Arnold Lobel (1980) have written their own books of fables. The goal of this minilesson is for students to examine the genre of fables and learn the characteristics of a fable. This minilesson might be taught as part of a resource-based unit on fables in which students read and respond to fables and then tell and write some of their own. The minilesson is organized around the six steps of the teaching strategy we have presented. For the sake of brevity, other activities that would be part of this two-week unit for a grade 4 class are not included in this plan.

The second application presented in Figure 1–7 focuses on rhyming words. This minilesson might be taught after students read Dr. Seuss's *The Cat in the Hat* (1985). The goal of this lesson is for students to create words that rhyme with *cat*, including *bat, fat, hat, mat, pat, rat,* and *sat*. Other *-at* words requiring consonant digraphs and blends include *flat, chat, splat,* and *that*. This plan is also organized around the six steps of the teaching strategy. This minilesson is a part of a two-week author study on Dr. Seuss, planned for a grade 1 class.

Step	Fables Lesson	Rhyming Words Lesson
Initiating	The teacher rereads "The Hare and the Tortoise" and "The Lion and the Mouse" from Hague's *Aesop's Fables* (1985) and explains that these short stories that teach a moral are called *fables*.	The teacher sets out a large hat and passes out a variety of small objects, including a bat puppet, a block, a toy cat, a place mat, a fork, a plastic rat, and a toy horse. Students place the objects with rhyming names in the hat. The teacher explains that rhyming words sound the same at the end: *cat, hat, mat, bat,* and *rat.*
Structuring	Students and the teacher develop a chart listing the characteristics of fables. The list may include these characteristics: • Fables are short. • The characters are usually animals. • The setting is usually rural and not important to the story. • Fables involve only one event. • The moral is usually stated at the end of the story.	The teacher distributes word cards with these -*at* words written on them: *bat, cat, fat, hat, mat, pat, rat, sat, flat, chat, that,* and *splat.* Students read the words and place them in the hat. They also suggest any other -*at* words they can think of, and the teacher writes these words on word cards.
Conceptualizing	The teacher then reads one or two other fables, and the students check that their lists of the characteristics of fables are complete.	The teacher passes out white eraseboards, and students write -*at* family words as the teacher holds up objects from the hat and reads words on the word cards. Students can invent other -*at* words, such as *dat* and *zat.*
Summarizing	The teacher asks students to make a chart in their language arts notebooks explaining what a fable is. Students share their explanations and compare them to the list of characteristics.	Students brainstorm a list of words that rhyme with *hat* and write them on a chart. Students take turns circling the -*at* pattern at the end of each word.
Generalizing ✸	Students read other fables, such as Lobel's *Fables* (1980) or Mollel's *Rhinos for Lunch and Elephants for Supper! A Maasai Tale* (1991). It is important to include some fables that state the moral implicitly rather than explicitly. Students explain why these stories are or are not fables. The teacher also points out that these fables were created—not retold—by Arnold Lobel and Tololwa Mollel.	Students create a rhyming -*at* book. They draw pictures of four rhyming words and write the words beside each picture. After students compile their books, they share them with classmates.
Applying	Students apply what they have learned when they write their own fables. Students may explicitly state the moral at the end of the story or imply it in the story.	Students apply what they have learned about rhyming words with other rhyming patterns. The teacher sets out a pan, a hen, a toy car, and a nail, and students match rhyming objects with these objects: pan: can, man, fan, tan crayon hen: pen, ten, men car: candy bar, jar, star nail: mail, pail, sail (on a boat), snail

Figure 1–7 Using the Teaching Strategy

Review

Language arts instruction should be based on theories and research about how children learn. Language and culture also have an impact on how elementary students learn the language arts. The goal of language arts instruction is for students to develop communicative competence in the six language arts—listening, speaking, reading, writing, viewing, and visually representing.

The following key concepts are presented in this chapter:

1. Language arts instruction should be based on how children learn.
2. Students learn through active involvement in listening, speaking, reading, writing, viewing, and visually representing activities.
3. Teachers should provide instruction within children's zone of proximal development.
4. Teachers scaffold or support children's learning.
5. Students use all four cueing systems: phonological, syntactic, semantic, and pragmatic.
6. New technology is challenging our view of literacy and these technologies demand that teachers respond by acknowledging the emergence of new literacies needed to effectively understand, manage, and evaluate Web reference tools, visual media, and the Internet.
7. Seven characteristics of competent language users are personal expression, aesthetic appreciation, collaborative exploration, strategic language use, creative communication, reflective interpretation, and thoughtful application.
8. Students need opportunities to participate in language arts activities that are meaningful, functional, and genuine.
9. Teachers create a community of learners in their classrooms.
10. Students learn and use language arts strategies and skills.
11. A teaching strategy should include initiating, structuring, conceptualizing, summarizing, generalizing, and applying components.

Extensions

1. Observe a language arts lesson being taught in an elementary or middle-school classroom. Try to determine if the components of the language-learning paradigm presented in this chapter are operational in the classroom. What conclusions can you draw about students' learning?
2. Observe and record several students' talk. Analyze their phonological, syntactic, semantic, and pragmatic cueing systems. If possible, compare primary-grade students' language with that of middle- and upper-grade students.
3. Interview a language arts teacher and ask how he or she teaches the six language arts—listening, speaking, reading, writing, viewing, and visually representing. Compare the teacher's comments with the information in this chapter.
4. Observe in an elementary classroom. Has the teacher created a community of learners? If yes, how did the teacher create the community? If not, how might the teacher create such a community?
5. Observe a student participating in language arts activities. What skills and strategies from those listed in Figures 1–5 and 1–6 does this student demonstrate? What other skills and strategies should the teacher introduce to that student?
6. Examine a popular piece of children's literature and consider it in the context of critical literacy. Imagine how you might teach children about how the text has been produced, by whom, and for what purposes.

chapter two

Teaching the Language Arts

PROFILE

A Medieval
History Unit

Procedure

Nearing the completion of a medieval history unit, I asked my grade 6 class to do a piece of writing to follow this social studies theme. When Mandy told me she didn't know what to write about, I suggested she ask Peter if he would like to write collaboratively with her, since Peter always had an abundance of writing ideas. Peter enthusiastically agreed to be her partner. Mandy volunteered to be the recorder and together they quickly got started.

After about 15 minutes of "topic" discussion, Peter and Mandy decided to create a conversation between a king and his servant about the kingdom having run out of food. Although Mandy had trouble writing, she joined in the brainstorming activity and contributed to the final topic. Peter provided the support Mandy needed to get started, and once started, Mandy had a variety of ideas to offer.

Peter: What do you want to do the story about?
Mandy: I don't know. Do you want to do it? You can pick who the story is gonna be about cuz I'm not very good at that.
Peter: Well, let's just list a bunch of ideas first and then pick one that we both like.
Mandy: Okay, that's a good idea.
Peter: Let's do a joker. No, let's do a jester and an executioner, the executioner is going to kill the jester.
Mandy: That's kinda violent.
Peter: Okay, then how about . . .
Mandy: We could do the jester part but maybe instead of a jester, we could use someone else who's like a jester, a . . .
Peter: . . . the king and a fool.

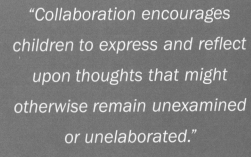

"Collaboration encourages children to express and reflect upon thoughts that might otherwise remain unexamined or unelaborated."

Jann Porritt
Grade 6 Teacher
W. S. Hawrylak School
Regina, Saskatchewan

If the major purpose of using collaborative writing was to motivate reluctant writers to write, then this becomes the major focus of my evaluation.

I evaluate the product holistically, and then focus on our target skill or strategy. I then watch the students' individual writing to check for transfer of the skill or strategy. For me, this is the true picture of evaluation.

Adaptations

Collaborative writing partnerships or groups should fluctuate throughout the year to expose students to a variety of writers. Often, the teacher should select groups according to need, choosing partners who have different strengths to offer. In this way, students, and especially reluctant writers, can feel good about themselves as writers by drawing on the strengths of their peers and by feeling needed.

Balancing collaborative and individual writing sessions gives students a chance to integrate and incorporate what they have learned from collaborative writing.

Reflections

The collaborative alternative offers more opportunities for success. Collaboration encourages children to express and reflect upon thoughts that might otherwise remain unexamined or unelaborated. All writers have strengths and skills to share. As writers come up against their individual limits, they can look to each other for support.

Mandy:	Yeah, that's like a jester.
Peter:	What else?
Mandy:	I don't know, what do you think?
Peter:	Where should it take place?
Mandy:	In a castle?
Peter:	Or maybe in a dungeon.
Mandy:	Why would a king be down in a dungeon?
Peter:	Because he's gonna kill somebody.
Mandy:	That's violent again.
Peter:	Just put it down, it's just an idea.
Mandy:	A courtyard?
Peter:	Not in a courtyard.
Mandy:	How about a ballroom?
Peter:	All right, put both ideas down.

The step in which writers get ideas is perhaps the most important phase, and often the most neglected, of the writing process. This stage can take a large amount of time, but is always time well spent. If you can't get a student past the point of generating topics and ideas, there is little hope of helping a reluctant writer. It can be a difficult and frustrating task to help an unwilling writer find a topic. Providing the topic may get them writing. Most often, it just gets the assignment done. Partnering these students with others who are very creative in this area provides them with many ideas and also a role model. They can see how another person comes up with a topic and ideas for writing.

Assessment

When evaluating collaborative writing, I emphasize process as much as product. As students work through writing stages, I keep records of their progress, noting strengths and weaknesses. Evaluation begins during the first stage of the writing process and continues through the finished product.

As part of the language-rich classroom and multi-grade program in which she worked, student teacher Lindsay Smith read to small groups of students daily. Together, they shared fiction and non-fiction texts, often choosing to link their reading to the thematic and inquiry-based units of their program.

To Guide Your Reading

As you read this chapter, prepare to

Describe the components of a language-rich classroom

•

Describe the three organizational structures for learning: resource-based units, thematic units, and inquiry-based units

•

Define readers workshops and writers workshops

•

Explain how technology influences teaching and learning in the language arts

•

Describe how teachers assess students' learning in the language arts

Language arts instruction should be based on how children learn. Donald Graves (1991) encourages teachers to build a literate environment that facilitates the development of lifelong readers and writers. Certainly, the classroom environment reflects teachers' goals for their students. Classrooms with libraries filled with books; laptop computers with word-processing, drawing/paint programs, and presentation software; and publishing centres reflect teachers' expectations for their students to use all six language arts effectively.

Three popular organizational structures involve students in meaningful, functional, and genuine language-learning activities in a balanced way. These three structures are *resource-based units*, *thematic units*, and *inquiry-based units*. Within these organizational structures, many teachers use readers and writers workshops as ways of organizing a large part of their instruction. Although teachers may use prescribed textbooks as a foundation for their programs, effective language arts instruction, regardless of organizational structure, involves engagement with a variety of texts both narrative and expository—print and other media—and multiple opportunities to explore language and communicate with others.

Assessment is also a component of the instructional program. By *assessment*, we specify the ongoing collection of information about students' learning as they read, write, and use all of the language arts to construct meaning and communicate effectively. Teachers use assessment information to guide their instruction to help them meet students' needs. This information should be authentic and reflect how children learn. Teachers and students collaborate to document students' learning and to collect artifacts in portfolios. The assessment information contributes to summative evaluation and the assigning of grades. Assigning grades is a fact of life in most classrooms, and teachers must use innovative ways to determine grades and involve students in assessing their own learning.

Language-Rich Classrooms

Elementary classrooms should be authentic language environments that encourage students to listen, speak, read, write, view, and visually represent; that is, they should be language-rich. As Susan Hepler explains, "the real challenge to teachers . . . is to set up the kind of classroom community where children pick their own ways to literacy" (1991, p. 179). The physical arrangement and materials provided in the classroom play an important role in setting the stage for language arts instruction (Morrow, 1996).

In the past, prescribed readers, or basal reading programs, were the primary instructional material, and students sat in desks arranged in rows facing the teacher. Now a wide variety of instructional materials are available in addition to textbooks, including trade books and multimedia materials. Students' desks are arranged in small groups, materials are set out in centres, and classrooms are made visually stimulating with signs, posters, charts, and other teacher- and student-made displays often related to the literature being read. These are frequently observed components of a language-rich classroom:

- Desks arranged in groups to facilitate cooperative learning
- Classroom libraries stocked with a variety of reading materials
- Posted messages about the current day
- Displays of student work and projects
- A chair designated as the author's chair
- Displayed signs, labels for items, and quotations
- Posted directions for activities or use of equipment
- Abundant supply of materials for recording language, including pencils, pens, paper, journals and logs, books, and computers
- Centres for reading and writing activities
- Reference materials for group and individual use
- A listening centre plus multimedia equipment and software
- A puppet stage or an area for presenting plays and storytelling
- Charts for recording information (e.g., writing-group charts, or sign-in charts for attendance)
- World-related print (e.g., newspapers, maps, and calendars)
- Reading and writing materials in young children's dramatic play centres

Figure 2–1 on pages 46–47 elaborates on these components of a language-rich classroom.

THE PHYSICAL ARRANGEMENT

Any classroom can be configured to include many language-rich characteristics. You can group desks or tables to encourage students to talk, share, and work cooperatively. Designate areas for reading and writing—ideally, these will include accessible computers, a classroom library, a listening and viewing station, areas for materials related to content-area topics that facilitate inquiry-based learning, and a dramatic play centre. Some variations obviously occur across grade levels. For example, kindergarten classes need dramatic play centres. Older students need space for more independent research than do younger ones. The diagram in Figure 2–2 on page 48 suggests ways to make the layout for a grade 3 classroom more language-rich.

CENTRES

Canadian elementary schools extensively use a *centres* approach to instruction in kindergarten and grade 1 and then increasingly less in the higher grade levels. Many classrooms, however, are physically arranged in centres to facilitate ready access to materials and promote a rich language

1. Classroom Organization
- Desks are arranged in groups.
- The arrangement facilitates group interaction.
- The arrangement facilitates teacher working with whole class, small groups, and individuals.
- Other parts of the classroom are organized into centres such as the library centre, writing centre, and theme centre.

2. Classroom Library Centre
- There are at least four times as many books as there are students in the classroom.
- Stories, informational books, and poetry are included.
- Multicultural books and other reading materials are included.
- Information about authors and illustrators is displayed.
- Some of the books were written by students.
- Books related to resource-based units and thematic units are highlighted.
- Students monitor the centre.

3. Message Centre
- Schedules and announcements about the current day are posted.
- Some of the announcements are student-initiated.
- There are mailboxes and/or a message board for students to use.
- Students are encouraged to write notes to classmates.
- Messages concerning school, community, and world events of interest are posted.

4. Display of Student Work and Projects
- All students have work displayed in the classroom.
- Student work reflects a variety of curricular areas.
- Students' projects and other student-made displays are exhibited in the classroom.
- There is an area where students can display their own work.
- Other student work is stored in portfolios accessible to students and teacher.

5. Author's Chair
- One chair in the classroom has been designated as the author's chair for students to use when sharing their writing.
- The author's chair is labelled and considered a special place of honour.

6. Signs, Labels, and Quotations
- Equipment and other classroom items are labelled.
- Words, phrases, and sentences are posted in the classroom.
- Some signs, labels, and quotations are written by students.
- Displays of words, phrases, and quotations are relevant to units of study and change frequently.

7. Routines and Directions
- Routines are established and followed so students know what to expect and learning time is maximized.
- Directions are provided in the classroom so that students can work independently.
- Some of the directions are written and posted by students.

(continued)

Figure 2–1 Characteristics of a Language-Rich Classroom

8. Materials for Writing

- Pencils, pens, paper, journals, books, computers, and other materials are available for recording language.
- Materials are clearly organized and students shown how to care for them.
- Students have easy access to these materials and monitor their use.

9. Places for Reading and Writing

- There are special places in the classroom for reading and writing activities.
- These areas are quiet and separated from other areas.
- These areas are welcoming and kept in order.

10. Reference Materials

- Word walls list important words related to study units.
- Lists, clusters, pictures, charts, books, models, CD-ROMs, and other reference materials are available for content-area study.
- Artifacts and other items related to study units are labelled and displayed.
- Students use these materials as they work on projects related to study units.

11. Multimedia Technology

- A listening centre with audio tapes of stories read during resource-based units is available for students to use.
- Computers with word-processing, illustration, and presentation software, a CD-ROM, DVD player, a modem, a scanner, and other related technology are available.
- Multimedia materials—such as CD-ROMs, films, videos, and DVDs—related to resource-based units and thematic units and the corresponding equipment are available.
- A camcorder, digital camera, and VCR playback system are available for student use.

12. Dramatic Play Centre

- A puppet stage is set up in the classroom.
- Art materials are available for making puppets and other props.
- An area in the classroom is accessible for presenting plays and telling stories.
- Props are available in the classroom.
- Primary-grade classrooms have dramatic play centres, including reading and writing materials.

Figure 2–1 Characteristics of a Language-Rich Classroom (*continued*)

environment by encouraging and supporting small group interaction among students (again, see Figure 2–1).

Typically, classrooms include three centres: a library centre to support reading, a listening centre to make recorded stories and information available, and a writing centre to support writing and publishing. In addition to the specific centres, most classrooms have computers available to facilitate the students' learning. Having ready access to technology and the Internet can make a significant contribution to creating a language-rich classroom.

Stock library centres with trade books that are attractively displayed and available to students. Often, many of these books relate to units of study, and are changed as new units are

GRADE 3 CLASSROOM

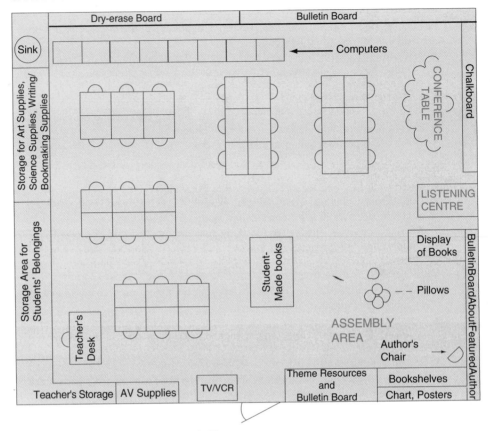

Figure 2–2 Diagram of a Language-Rich Classroom

introduced. After studying library centres in classrooms, Leslie Morrow (1989) makes these recommendations:

1. Make the library centre inviting.
2. Define the library centre with shelves, carpets, benches, sofas, or other partitions.
3. Make the centre large enough to accommodate five or six students comfortably at a time.
4. Use two kinds of bookshelves. Most of the collection should be shelved with the spines facing outward, but some books should be set so that the front covers are displayed.
5. Shelve books by category and colour-code them by type.
6. Display books written by one author or related to a theme being studied, and change the displays regularly.
7. Cover the floor with a rug and furnish the area with pillows, beanbag chairs, or comfortable furniture.
8. Stock the centre with at least four times as many books as there are students in the classroom.
9. Include a variety of types of reading materials, such as books, newspapers, magazines, posters, and charts, in the centre.
10. Display posters that encourage reading in the library centre.

Equip listening centres with tape and CD players, computers, and headphones. Students listen to audiotapes of stories, watch CD-ROMs, or access full-text stories and literature on the Internet, and sometimes follow along in accompanying books. Many commercially prepared recordings of children's books are available as interactive stories that children can read and respond to with a variety of activities. Teachers can also record their own reading of books so that students can reread books and listen again and again. Too often, teachers think of listening centres as equipment for primary-grade classrooms and do not realize the possibilities for older students.

Store supplies of writing and art materials for students to use as they write books and respond in writing centres to titles they've read. Supply materials include the following:

- A variety of pens, pencils, crayons, markers, and other writing and drawing instruments
- Lined and unlined paper of varied sizes and colours
- Materials for making and binding books
- Computers with word-processing, graphic, and multimedia programs; CD-ROMs; DVD players; scanners; and printers
- A digital camera for taking illustration photos and photos of students for their "About the Author" pages
- Scrap-art materials for illustrations and covers

In primary-grade classrooms, a table is included in the writing centre so that students can gather to write and share their writing. In middle- and upper-grade classrooms, however, writing materials are usually stored on shelves or in cabinets, and students write at their own desks. Students gather in small groups to revise their writing wherever there is space in the classroom, and they meet with the teacher at a conference table to edit their writing.

Teachers also set up centres that are directly related to a unit or particular skills for students to work at independently or in small groups to apply skills and explore literacy concepts. These centres are available for short periods of time and often employ baskets or folders that keep the materials organized and easily accessible to students. Activities are self-directed and can be completed with little teacher involvement, freeing the teacher to work with students on other tasks. Typical activities in these centres for primary-grade students who are just beginning to read include sorting sets of small pictures according to beginning sounds, using flannel-board pictures or puppets to retell stories, using magnetic letters to spell words from class word lists, or playing simple card games that require reading or writing. In classrooms where students are capable of more reading and writing, activities might include collaboratively writing a story or a poem following a pattern from a minilesson presented to the whole class, playing computer games that offer practice in using writing conventions, and completing word puzzles. Other centres might encourage exploratory activities such as reading brochures or magazines to learn more about a unit theme, or reinforcement activities focused on spelling or vocabulary building.

LANGUAGE ARTS PROGRAMS

Teachers are not on their own when it comes to preparing their language arts programs. Many publishers offer packaged programs of resources for teachers and students. Typically, a program includes a teacher's resource book and student reading materials, together with supplementary materials such as student activity books; resources concerning assessment; and other instructional supports such as videos, CD-ROMs, puppets, or posters. Historically, prepared programs were referred to as *basal reading programs*. Basal reading programs, however, were more limited than current programs. Most basal programs included a teacher's guide, one reader in which the selections were often written to a formula and were tightly controlled in regard to the level of difficulty, and a student workbook. Informed by research, basal reading programs have evolved over the past twenty-five years to be comprehensive programs that offer teachers a wide base of support. In particular, programs in this country have evolved from straightforward Canadianized versions of US programs to being packages designed especially to help teachers meet the expectations of provincial curricula. One significant characteristic is the inclusion of

Canadian literature, either as selections within an anthology or as individual texts. Recently published programs offer a wide variety of resources, including multimedia texts, that support a balanced approach to instruction for teaching all of the six language arts.

Decisions to select language arts programs are made at both provincial and local school levels. Teachers involved in decision making should consider the program characteristics identified by Shanahan and Knight (1991):

1. Centre on children's own language.
2. Emphasize the social uses of language.
3. Integrate the six language arts.
4. Recognize the developmental aspects of students' learning.
5. Assist teachers in assessing students' learning.
6. Develop students' creative and critical thinking.
7. Respect cultural and linguistic diversity.
8. Emphasize the language arts as tools for learning across the curriculum.

Teachers should not assume that packaged programs are equivalent to the total language arts program. Student teachers and beginning teachers, however, may rely heavily on their programs when they begin teaching. Recently published programs approved for Canadian schools have much credibility and can form a solid foundation for language arts instruction. Teachers must be sure that their programs include extensive reading (time and variety of literature) and extensive writing opportunities. Published programs sometimes fall short in these areas.

Teachers choose how to use the materials in a program and do not necessarily use all materials. For example, teachers choose materials for use in thematic units or inquiry-based units using some selections for shared reading and others for independent reading. They also use selected pages from skillbooks as resources for minilessons in readers and writers workshops rather than ask students to complete the skillbooks in consecutive order. Other materials might be used as resources for centre activities or as guides to collaborative work.

TRADE BOOKS

Books written for children that are not textbooks are called *trade books*. These are formatted as either picture books or chapter books. They include stories, informational books, and poetry books.

Picture Books. In picture books, text and illustrations combine to tell a story, present information, or illustrate a poem. The text is minimal, and striking illustrations often supplement the sparse text. Many picture books, such as *Something from Nothing* (Gilman, 1992) are appropriate for young children, but others, such as *Smoky Night* (Bunting, 1994b), were written with middle-grade students in mind. Fairy tales, myths, and legends have also been retold beautifully as picture books, and new versions of these traditional tales have also been created. Examples include three Cinderella tales, *The Tender Tale of Cinderella Penguin* (Perlman, 1993), *The Gift of the Crocodile: A Cinderella Story* (Sierra, 2000), and *Cendrillon: A Caribbean Cinderella* (San Souci, 1998); *The Three Little Javelinas* (Lowell, 1992), a Southwestern adaptation of *The Three Little Pigs*; *The True Story of the 3 Little Pigs!* (Scieszka, 1989), the hilarious wolf's version of the story; and *The Girl Who Spun Gold* (Hamilton, 2000), a West Indian version of *Rumpelstiltskin*.

Many informational books, such as *Who Eats What? Food Chains and Food Webs* (Lauber, 1995), are published in picture book format. Single poems and collections of poems are also published as picture books. Robert Service's *The Cremation of Sam McGee* (1986) is both a poem and a picture book with Ted Harrison's brilliant paintings on each page, and Nancy Larrick's collection of cat poems, *Cats Are Cats* (1988), is sensitively illustrated by Ed Young. The coveted Caldecott

Medal, given annually for the best illustrations in a children's book published during the preceding year, has honoured many books over the years. *Kitten's First Full Moon* (2004), by Kevin Henkes, was a winner in 2005.

Wordless picture books contain no text. The pictures tell the story, which makes this type of book particularly useful when working with children who are learning English as a second language or are novice readers. Books such as *The Snowman* (Briggs, 1980) and *Tabby: A Story in Pictures* (Aliki, 1995) are popular with primary-grade students. Other books, such as *Anno's Britain* (Anno, 1982) and *The Story of a Castle* (Goodall, 1986), appeal to middle- and upper-grade students because they connect to social studies and science themes.

Chapter Books. Chapter books are longer story and informational books, written in chapter format, for elementary students. Most are written for middle- and upper-grade students, but easy-to-read chapter books are also available for those young readers who are gaining independence and who want to read "grown-up" chapter books. Patricia Reilly Giff has written stories, including *Ronald Morgan Goes to Camp* (1995), for students reading at the grade 2 level. Celia Barker-Lottridge also writes for children growing into novel reading with such enticing stories as *Berta: A Remarkable Dog* (2002). Children will also enjoy Tim Wynne-Jones's engaging story, *Ned Mouse Breaks Away* (2003).

A variety of chapter books are available for middle-grade students. Linda Bailey, a Canadian author, has written a series of detective stories including *How Can a Frozen Detective Stay Hot on the Trail?* (1996) and *How Come the Best Clues are Always in the Garbage?* (1992). Other chapter books are *The Several Lives of Orphan Jack* (2003) by Deborah Ellis, *Nobody's Child* (2003) by Marsha Skrypuch, and *Mary Ann Alice* (2001) by Brian Doyle. Two acclaimed chapter books for upper-grade students are the Governor General's Award–winning *Stitches* (2003) by Glen Huser, and *The Giver* (Lowry, 1993), about a "perfect" society. Chapter books have only a few illustrations, if any, and the illustrations do not play an integral role in the book.

Some informational books are also written in the chapter book format. *The Riddle of the Rosetta Stone* (Giblin, 1990) and *Toilets, Bathtubs, Sinks, and Sewers: A History of the Bathroom* (Colman, 1994), are two examples. In informational books, illustrations (often photographs and diagrams) are used to support the text, but are not as integral as in picture books. Informational books usually include a table of contents, a glossary, and an index.

Other chapter books, directed toward readers in upper elementary grades, include information as part of their stories and contexts. Three examples are *Ticket to Curlew* (Lottridge, 1992) and *A Prairie as Wide as the Sea: An Immigrant Diary of Ivy Weatherall* (Ellis, 2001), stories of early settlers, and *Irish Chain* (Haworth-Attard, 2002), the story of the Halifax explosion.

A number of chapter books, such as *Sarah, Plain and Tall* (MacLachlan, 1985), *The Giver*, and *Crispin: The Cross of Lead* (Avi, 2002), have received the Newbery Medal for distinguished children's literature. In contrast to the Caldecott Medal (awarded for outstanding illustrations), the Newbery is given for distinguished prose.

Stories. Most stories for younger children, such as *Sylvester and the Magic Pebble* (Steig, 1969) and *Officer Buckle and Gloria* (Rathmann, 1995), are picture books, and many stories for older children, including Natalie Babbitt's *Tuck Everlasting* (1975) and Gary Paulsen's *Hatchet* (1987), are chapter books. There are, however, a number of picture book stories that appeal to older students, such as Chris Van Allsburg's *The Polar Express* (1985), David Macaulay's *Black and White* (1990), and other fantasies. Many stories feature multicultural characters and themes, including *The Secret of the White Buffalo* (Taylor, 1997) in which a white buffalo woman teaches the Sioux to work together and smoke the peace pipe; *A Wilderness Passover* (Cook-Waldron, 1994), a touching story about friendship and good neighbours, and the customs associated with the Jewish holiday; *Obasan* (Kogawa, 1982), about a Japanese-Canadian family's experience of relocation and internment during the Second World War; and *The Buffalo Jump* (Roop, 1996), a colourfully illustrated story of Blackfoot traditions.

Informational Books. Informational books provide information on a wide variety of topics, including those related to social studies, science, math, art, and music. Some are written in a story format, such as *The Magic School Bus Inside a Hurricane* (Cole, 1995), *Secrets of the Mummies: Uncovering the Bodies of Ancient Egyptians* (Tanaka, 1999), and *The Buried City of Pompeii* (Tanaka, 2000). Others are written in a more traditional informational style, with a table of contents, an index, and a glossary. Examples of traditional informational books are *A Kid's Guide to the Brain* (Funston & Ingram, 1994) and *Hands On, Thumbs Up* (Gryski, 1994). Some informational books are written for young children, with a phrase or sentence of text presented on each page along with a photograph or illustration. *Giant Sequoia Trees* (Wadsworth, 1995) is an easy-to-read description of the life cycle of this giant tree, and is illustrated with colour photographs on every page. In *I See Animals Hiding* (1995), Jim Arnosky explains camouflage using watercolour illustrations of wild animals in natural settings and simple sentences about animals that blend in with their environment.

Another type of informational book presents language arts concepts, including opposites, homonyms, and parts of speech. One example is Burningham's *Opposites* (1985), which presents pairs of opposites illustrated on each two-page spread. Another example is Ruth Heller's *Up, Up and Away: A Book about Adverbs* (1998). Alphabet books are informational books, too. Although many alphabet books are designed for very young children, others are appropriate for elementary students, such as *Aardvarks, Disembark!* (Jonas, 1990).

Biographies are another type of informational book. Most biographies are chapter books, such as *The Man Who Created Narnia: The Story of C. S. Lewis* (Coren, 1994), but several authors have written shorter biographies that resemble picture books. Perhaps the best-known biographer for younger children is David Adler, who has written *A Picture Book of Helen Keller* (1990) and other biographies of important historical figures. A few autobiographies have also been written for children, such as *Born Naked* (1995), the story of Farley Mowat's childhood years in Ontario and Saskatchewan, and *The Beet Fields: Memories of a Sixteenth Summer* (2000), the story of Gary Paulsen's life.

Poetry Books. There are many delightful poetry books written especially for children. Some are collections of poems on a single topic written by one poet, such as *There's a Mouse in My House* (Fitch, 1997) and *Joyful Noise: Poems for Two Voices* (Fleischman, 1988), which is about insects. Other collections of poetry include *Til All The Stars Have Fallen: Canadian Poems For Children* (Booth, 1989), *The New Wind Has Wings: Poems From Canada* (Downey & Robertson, 1987), and *Nothing Beats a Pizza* (Lesynski, 2001). An excellent anthology (a collection of poems written by different poets on a variety of topics) is *The Random House Book of Poetry for Children* (Prelutsky, 1983).

All three genres—stories, informational books, and poetry books—can be used in teaching the language arts or any content area. By using all three types, students learn more about a topic than they could if they read only stories or only informational books or poetry books. Figure 2–3 on page 53 presents three text sets (or collections) of books. One text set is for a primary-grade unit on insects, the second is for a middle-grade unit on oceans, and the third is for an upper-grade unit on the Middle Ages. Trade books are not sequenced and prepackaged as textbooks are, so teachers must make choices and design activities to accompany the books. Similar text sets of trade books can be collected for almost any topic.

MULTIMEDIA TECHNOLOGY

Multimedia technology is changing the face of language arts instruction. Computers with word-processing programs, and other multimedia software as well as digital cameras, scanners, and projection equipment, are commonplace in many Canadian classrooms. And if not consistently available in the classroom, such equipment is available in the school. Further, schools and classrooms are rapidly becoming linked to the Internet. How does, and how should, technology influence instruction in a language-rich classroom?

Text Set on Insects

Stories

Brinckloe, J. (1985). *Fireflies!* New York: Aladdin.

Carle, E. (1969). *The Very Hungry Caterpillar.* New York: Philomel.

Carle, E. (1986). *The Grouchy Ladybug.* New York: Crowell.

Carle, E. (1990). *The Very Quiet Cricket.* New York: Philomel.

Carle, E. (1995). *The Very Lonely Firefly.* New York: Philomel.

Informational Books

Facklam, M. (1996). *Creepy, Crawly Caterpillars.* Boston: Little, Brown.

Fowler, A. (1990). *It's a Good Thing There Are Insects.* Chicago: Children's Press.

Gibbons, G. (1989). *Monarch Butterfly.* New York: Holiday House.

Godkin, C. (1995). *What about Ladybugs?* New York: Sierra.

Heiligman, D. (1996). *From Caterpillar to Butterfly.* New York: HarperCollins.

Heller, R. (1985). *How to Hide a Butterfly and Other Insects.* New York: Grosset & Dunlap.

Micucci, C. (1995). *The Life and Times of the Honeybee.* New York: Ticknor.

Poetry Books

Moses, A. (1992). *If I Were an Ant.* Chicago: Children's Press.

Ryder, J. (1989). *Where Butterflies Grow.* New York: Lodestar.

Walton, R. (1995). *What to Do When a Bug Climbs in Your Mouth: And Other Poems to Drive You Buggy.* New York: Lothrop & Lee.

Text Set on Oceans

Stories

Andrews, J. (1985). *Very Last First Time.* Vancouver: Douglas & McIntyre. ❧

Butler, G. (1995). *The Killik: A Newfoundland Story.* Montreal: Tundra Books. ❧

Creech, S. (2000). *The Wanderer.* London: Macmillan Children's Books.

Harlow, J. (2000). *Star in the Storm.* Toronto: Aladdin Paperbacks. ❧

McFarlane, S. (1998). *Waiting for the Whales.* Vancouver: Orca Book Publishers. ❧

Mills, J. (1995). *The Stonehook Schooner.* Toronto: Key Porter Kids. ❧

Van Allsburg, C. (1983). *The Wreck of the Zephyr.* Boston: Houghton Mifflin.

Informational Books

Cole, J. (1992). *The Magic Schoolbus on the Ocean Floor.* New York: Scholastic.

Earle, S. (2000). *Sea Critters.* Washington: National Geographic Society.

Morris, N. (1996). *Oceans.* New York: Crabtree Publishing.

Simon, S. (1990). *Oceans.* New York: Morrow Junior Books.

Simon, S. (2002). *Under the Ice: A Canadian Museum of Nature Book.* Toronto: Kids Can Press. ❧

Poetry Books

Bouchard, D. (1997). *If Sarah Will Take Me.* Victoria: Orca Book Publishers. ❧

Heard, G. (2003). *Creatures of Earth, Sea, and Sky Animal Poems.* Honesdale, PA: Boyds Mill Press.

Text Set on the Middle Ages

Stories

Cushman, K. (1994). *Catherine, Called Birdy.* New York: HarperCollins.

Cushman, K. (1995). *The Mid-wife's Apprentice.* New York: Clarion.

Ellis, D. (2002). *The Company of Fools.* Markham: Fitzhenry and Whiteside.

Mayer, M. (1987). *The Pied Piper of Hamelin.* New York: Macmillan.

Morpurgo, M. (1995). *Arthur, High King of Britain.* San Diego: Harcourt Brace.

Shannon, M. (1994). *Gawain and the Green Knight.* New York: Putnam.

Vaes, A. (1994). *Reynard the Fox.* New York: Turner.

Informational Books

Aliki. (1983). *A Medieval Feast.* New York: Crowell.

Bailey, L. (2000). *Adventures in the Middle Ages.* Toronto: Kids Can Press. ❧

Gibbons, G. (1995). *Knights in Shining Armor.* Boston: Little, Brown.

Howarth, S. (1993). *The Middle Ages.* New York: Viking.

Howe, J. (1995). *Knights.* New York: Orchard.

Hunt, J. (1989). *Illuminations.* New York: Bradbury Press.

Lasker, J. (1976). *Merry Ever After.* New York: Viking.

Steele, P. (1995). *Castles.* New York: Kingfisher.

Poetry Books

Yolen, J. (1994). *Here there be unicorns.* San Diego: Harcourt Brace.

Figure 2–3 Three Text Sets

For the past thousand years, print has been the pre-eminent technology, but the technology of today and the future is digital media (Rose & Meyer, 1994). Digital information—text, sounds, images, recorded language, movie clips, and animations—can be manipulated, transformed, customized, and copied. In contrast, print is fixed, not malleable. With digital media, students read books on CD-ROMs and write using word-processing programs. They view dramatizations of stories or other films on CD-ROMs, DVDs, and on selected Internet sites. Students can create visual representations using HyperCard and other software programs and scan their drawings to add them to books they are writing on the computer. Through digitized sound, students add their own voice to projects they create and listen to stories or other texts that they or other students have written. Further, they can view videos and movie clips from the Internet that let them do such things as listen to authors talk about their books, listen to the speeches of historical figures, or read accounts of the daily activities of extreme travellers and space missions. Clearly, computers and related technologies give students new powers and incentives (Marcus, 1990) and contribute to redefining what it means to be literate. Redefining literacy is the subject of much current research. "The definition of literacy has expanded from traditional notions of reading and writing to include the ability to learn, comprehend, and interact with technology in a meaningful way" (C. L. Selfe cited in Pianfetti, 2001, p. 256).

Perhaps the word processor is the technology most often used in language arts classrooms. Although studies comparing the quantity and quality of computer writing with traditional writing have yielded inconclusive results (Sharp, 1999), it is clear that computers have a positive motivational effect (Hatfield, 1996). Young children who use word processors for writing have shown more focus on content and editing of text as well as increased metacognitive awareness (Schrader, 1990). Atwell (1998) observes that word processing helps older students not only produce more writing, but also experiment with their text through rearranging, adding, deleting, and correcting. All this leads to writing that is ready for a wide audience. Children must learn the procedures of word processing such as keyboarding, moving and deleting text, and using a spell checker before computer use will result in improved writing. When and how to teach keyboarding can be controversial, but most teachers agree that children can be taught by software designed for that purpose or by traditional methods of teaching typing. We recommend that children be taught as soon as they have regular access to word processors. We have observed that children in grade 3 can learn efficient keyboarding and avoid inefficient hunt-and-peck methods of typing.

Because of the limited number of computers available in many classrooms, students often work collaboratively, talking about ideas, planning their writing projects, deciding how to spell words and use writing formats, and rereading to check what they have written. When students compose collaboratively, they work longer at the computer and write longer compositions than they do with paper and pencil.

For more information on taking students' dictation, read about the language experience approach (LEA) in Chapter 3, "Emergent Literacy," pages 113–114.

Teachers also use computers to take young children's dictation (Grabe & Grabe, 2001). Teachers take children's dictation as they do in traditional language experience activities, using a computer rather than paper and pencil. Text dictated by a class or group of children is easily projected for rereading and editing as a group. The text can be printed and copied for each child. Copies can be illustrated by the children and later used for independent reading in the classroom or at home. The computer simplifies the process of taking children's dictation—teachers can record dictation more quickly than they can write, the dictation can be revised without any trouble, and copies of the text are easily made available.

Language-rich classrooms make far greater use of technology than simple word processing. Multimedia production capabilities enable students to express themselves and represent their thinking in dynamic ways. The term *multimedia* is used to refer to the integration of sound, graphics, animation, video, and text. HyperCard, HyperStudio, PowerPoint, and Kids Pix are computer applications that students can use to create presentations with text, sound, and graphics (see Figure 2–4 on page 56 for an example of a student's use of Hyper Card). Information from the

These grade 4 and 5 students use the Internet as a resource for their writing.

Internet, CD-ROMs, and digitized pictures and photos can be added to create interactive presentations. Elementary students can create reports, biographies, files on favourite authors, and other types of writing projects using these software packages. Where facilities are available, they can also create and post webpages as a way of demonstrating and sharing their learning.

Technology not only supports the creation of text, but also promotes meaningful reading. Electronic reading programs written in hypertext—a system that allows extensive cross-referencing—make it possible for students to link to related information as they read, such as meanings of unfamiliar words, information about the author, and details on literary elements. When they use electronic reading programs, students apply special reading skills and strategies, such as noticing a selection's structure and organization, engaging with the selection in order to comprehend, and making choices as they move through the selection. Electronic reading programs show students that reading is more than a linear, once-through-the-text process.

Interactive electronic books, available on CD-ROM, use hypertext to organize information and provide reading options to students. The text and illustrations are displayed page by page on the computer screen. With this technology, a teacher can read aloud a selection to students, with each word or phrase highlighted onscreen as it is read; students can read the electronic book themselves and ask the computer to identify unfamiliar words; or students can read along with the computer to develop reading fluency. Music and sound effects accompany each electronic book. Many electronic books include reading logs, word-identification exercises, and other reading and writing activities.

Electronic encyclopedias provide students with learning opportunities in ways that book encyclopedias cannot. For example, *Compton's Multimedia Encyclopedia* (twenty-six volumes in book format) is contained on a single CD-ROM, which makes searching for information quick and easy. Many Canadian schools now rely almost exclusively on online encyclopedias to provide students with the most current information available. Popular ones include *The Canadian Encyclopedia* online (**www.thecanadianencyclopedia.com**) and *World Book Online* (**www.worldbookonline.com**). Students can use electronic encyclopedias to

- Search for information on a particular topic
- Ask the computer to pronounce or define unfamiliar words

Dr. Roberta Bondar

Dr. Bondar flew aboard the space shuttle Discovery in January 1992. When she was a child she wanted to become an astronaut. She used to build plastic models, rockets, space stations and satellites when she was eight years old. She would look up on at the stars and want to see what Earth and other other planets looked like from space.

CANADIAN ASTRONAUT

NEXT

Figure 2–4 A Frame from an Upper-Grade Student's HyperCard Report

- View colour photographs, diagrams, and animated illustrations
- Listen to sounds related to the topic
- View film clips
- Locate related articles in the encyclopedia
- Print hard copies of the information

Because of the format and search capabilities of electronic encyclopedias, students explore topics in more depth than they can in book encyclopedias. Electronic books, including encyclopedias, have the potential to improve comprehension and promote in-depth learning (Anderson-Inman & Horney, 1999).

THE INTERNET

The Internet (also called *the Net*) is a global network of computers that are connected to each other. The World Wide Web (also called *the Web*) is a means of linking documents, graphics, animation, video, and sound across the computers that are on the Internet. Together, the Internet and the Web are the most powerful tools and resources that have ever been available to teachers and students.

The Internet is redefining what it means to be literate (Kinzer & Leu, 1997). As access increases, teachers have a responsibility to use its power to support literacy learning and to teach learning skills. Students must learn to search the Internet to locate information, to compose text and multimedia messages, and to post those messages. More important, teachers must teach the reading skills needed to use the Internet. Students must be able to read Internet sources critically, evaluating information, synthesizing it, and making connections with what is already known. As there is little control over the information posted to the Internet, even very young readers need to develop critical reading skills to use it wisely. Further, students must be able to structure information as they read, view, and listen to what is presented on a particular website. Information presented in hypertext format gives the reader choices of what links to make, and it is incumbent upon the reader to construct a meaningful whole. Just as students need special reading, listening, and viewing skills to interpret information on the Internet, so too do they need special composing skills to add information to the Internet. Producing an informative and effective webpage, for example, requires writers to compose for wide audiences, to write informatively, and to enhance their text with graphics and sound, all in addition to such writing fundamentals as clarity, appropriate word choice, fluency, and accurate use of punctuation.

Teachers often introduce students to the Internet through what Leu and Leu (1998) refer to as an *Internet activity*. An Internet activity is an excellent way to introduce students to sites that relate to a thematic unit or a collaborative unit of inquiry. Although there may be many variations, an Internet activity generally includes the following steps:

1. Locate a site, or several sites, on the Internet with content related to a unit of instruction, and set a bookmark for the location(s).
2. Develop an activity requiring children to use the site(s).
3. Assign this activity requiring children to use the site(s).

Another popular form of learning with the Internet, especially during inquiry-based units, is called a *WebQuest*. A WebQuest is an inquiry-oriented activity in which some or all of the information students interact with comes from resources on the Internet. There are two basic types of WebQuests—short term and longer term. A short-term WebQuest usually lasts one to three class periods. When doing short-term WebQuests, students learn new information and begin to make sense of it. In contrast, longer-term WebQuests typically span one week to one month and involve students in extending and refining their knowledge. Students doing longer-term WebQuests analyze their new knowledge and represent their new understanding in ways that others can respond to online or offline. WebQuests in elementary classrooms are most likely to be group activities.

When teachers organize WebQuests for elementary students, they introduce the students to the topic by providing some background knowledge then explain to students the task and how to proceed to collect information from the Internet. Teachers bookmark the appropriate sites to guide the students' search for information. Often students are given printed outlines on which to record their information. WebQuests conclude with an activity that reminds students of all they have learned and allows them to share their work, questions, and new insights. Two excellent websites on WebQuests are **http://webquest.sdsu.edu** and **http://tommarch.com/learning**.

Another way to use the Internet to support students' learning is through Internet projects (Leu & Kinzer, 1999). An Internet project is a collaborative learning experience among two or more classrooms that takes place over the Internet. Such projects involve communication and sharing of information, often across cultures, providing unique opportunities to learn about other cultural contexts and gain appreciation for cultural differences. A central website for Internet projects does not exist yet, but project descriptions can be posted at the following sites to attract interested teachers and classes:

SchoolNet's Grassroots Project Centre (Canada)
www.schoolnet.ca/grassroots/e/project.centre/index.asp

Global SchoolNet's Internet Project Registry (United States)
www.gsn.org/pr/index.cfm

A simple way to start students in online communication is through email. In many Canadian schools, every student has an email address. Through email, students can communicate with each other, in the same school and in other schools across the province and beyond, with authors, or with sources from which they seek information on their instructional units. We are familiar with two successful projects in which elementary students and student teachers communicate by email. The first is a project in which students in an elementary school and student teachers at the local university are reading buddies. Sometimes they read the same books and sometimes they read different ones. Their email messages form electronic reading response dialogue journals. The second is a modified pen-pal project in which a letter exchange was enhanced by Internet use. The students of one intern teacher working in Belize communicated with the students of another intern teacher working in Alberta. The school in Central America is not connected to the Internet, so traditional letters were written, but by going to their town's only public computers in the community centre, the Belizean students were able to see their pen pals' city website. Similarly, the Canadian pen pals were able to visit Belize through their Internet search. Although the students exchanged traditional letters by mail, the teachers communicated by email. These are good examples of teachers using technology as a resource.

New multimedia technology expands the range of language arts materials and the tools students have available for learning. The traditional language arts—listening, speaking, reading, and writing—have not been abandoned, but technology provides new tools for learning and using these language arts, as well as for redefining what the language arts are. The recent addition of viewing and visually representing as the fifth and sixth language arts illustrates the changes brought by technology. Technology is a powerful learning tool. Children adapt easily to using hardware, software, and the Internet. They use them for valuable language-learning activities across the curriculum. Teachers must find ways to use the technology to support their programs rather than supplant them with technology (Lapp, Flood, & Lungren, 1995). Furthermore, research concerning the use of technology in the language arts is highly dependent on classroom teachers. It is the opinion of Leu, Karchner, and Leu (1999) that, "Our understanding of effective literacy instruction may be informed more often by teachers who use continuously changing technologies on a daily basis and less often on traditional forms of research." The exchange among teachers as they share discoveries of useful sites, teaching strategies, methods of evaluation, and reflections on student learning while using technology is a valued and needed form of research.

Balanced Instructional Frameworks

Many instructional programs in Canadian schools focus on a balanced approach to literacy. These programs recognize that all areas of the language arts need systematic attention with continuity from grade to grade (Brailsford and Coles, 2004). Listening, speaking, reading, writing, viewing, and visually representing are developed in ways that enhance appropriate skill development. Balanced approaches often include shared reading of common texts, class lessons on key reading-comprehension strategies, guided reading and literature circles, reading aloud, and independent reading. Phonics and other word-recognition skills are developed in conjunction with daily writing and the reading of quality literature. The skills and strategies for reading information are developed in appropriate content areas and children learn a variety of ways to respond to text, including writing and visually representing their experiences. All aspects of the language arts are developed in a balanced and integrated way.

Three frameworks for organizing balanced language arts instruction are resource-based units, thematic units, and inquiry-based units. All three approaches embody the characteristics of learning described in Chapter 1, "Learning and the Language Arts," and provide opportunities for students to be involved in meaningful, functional, and genuine activities. Giving students opportunities to participate in all three types of units during each school year is strongly recommended; that is, both teacher-led and student-selected instructional programs provide valuable language-learning opportunities, and neither type of program alone provides all the opportunities that students need (see Figure 2–5 on page 60).

RESOURCE-BASED UNITS

In resource-based units, instruction and learning are organized around a featured selection or several related books or other print or non-print media texts, such as newspapers or videos. Students read, view, or listen to the featured selection using a five-step reading process in which they prepare, read (listen or view), respond, explore, and extend their study of the text. Because students are working together in groups or as a class, they share their interpretations of the text and become a community of language learners. One popular example of resource-based units is the novel study. There are four components of resource-based units:

For more information on the reading process, see Chapter 4, "The Reading and Writing Processes," pages 127–147.

1. ***Reading, listening, viewing texts.*** Students read, listen to, or view texts together as a class or in small groups. Students may work independently or together with a partner, or if using print literature, they may read along as the teacher reads the book aloud or guides their reading.

2. ***Responding.*** Students respond to the selection to record their initial impressions of it and to develop their comprehension. Typically, students write in response logs and participate in discussions called *grand conversations*.

3. ***Teaching minilessons.*** Teachers teach minilessons on language arts procedures, concepts, strategies, and skills, and connect the lesson to books students are reading or compositions they are writing (Atwell, 1987). Similarly, minilessons may pertain to other types of texts such as those on video, film, or CD-ROMs. While minilessons are best known in relation to reading and writing, they may relate to any of the six language arts. They are brief, usually lasting roughly 10 minutes. Some topics may require several minilessons taught over several succeeding days. The six steps in teaching a minilesson are

   a. Introduce the language arts procedure, concept, strategy, or skill.
   b. Share examples of the topic or technique using children's writing or trade books written for children.
   c. Provide information about the topic and make connections to trade books or to children's writing.
   d. Have students make notes about the topic or create a classroom poster to remind students about the concept or strategy.
   e. Have students practise the procedure, concept, strategy, or skill being taught.
   f. Ask students to reflect or speculate on how they can use this information in their reading and writing.

   The purpose of minilessons is to highlight the topic and teach it in the context of authentic literacy activities, not to isolate it or provide drill and practice. Worksheets are rarely used in minilessons; instead, students apply the lesson to their own language arts activities. Minilessons can be conducted with the whole class, with small groups of students who have indicated that they need to learn more about a particular topic, and with individual students. Teachers can also plan minilessons on a regular basis to introduce or review topics.

4. ***Creating projects.*** Students create projects to extend their engagement with, and understanding of, the selection (literature, film, etc.). Projects may involve any of the language arts, but students usually choose the projects they create based on their interests and the opportunities the selection presents to them. For example, after reading *Jumanji* (Van Allsburg, 1981), students often choose to write sequels; and after reading *Sylvester and the Magic Pebble* (Steig, 1969), students may work together as a small group to dramatize the story, or they may choose to read other books by William Steig.

	Time	Purpose	Typical Activities
Teacher Sharing	5 minutes	• Shows teacher as reader and writer, member of learning community	• Sharing of personal writing • Sharing of literature reading for pleasure • Sharing of news article related to classroom reading, e.g., film review or obituary of a writer
Minilesson	10–15 minutes	• Instruction relates to specific concept or skill or workshop procedure	• Teacher-directed lesson on specific skill using literature as example of a writing technique • Teacher modelling of particular reading skill • Teacher and student demonstration of procedure, such as responding to peer writing
State-of-Class	2–5 minutes	• Teacher determines intended activities for each student and identifies need for teacher assistance	• Students tell teacher what they will be doing, e.g., will be peer editing draft or will be reading chapter 2 of novel
Reading/Writing/ Responding	30–45 minutes	• Time for uninterrupted reading and/or writing • Time for organized response to literature or student writing	• Reading of selected literature independently or in groups • Conversations about literature • Sustained writing • Conferencing with teacher about literature read or about writing
Student Sharing	10–20 minutes	• Sharing of reading to invite conversation • Sharing of student writing to attain peer feedback • Sharing of writing for celebration of accomplishments	• Students reading from "author's chair" • Students giving book talks • Students reading each other's writings from classroom library

Figure 2–5 Components of Readers and Writers Workshops

THEMATIC UNITS

Thematic units are a type of interdisciplinary unit that integrates language arts with one or more of social studies, science, math, and other curricular areas (Altwerger & Flores, 1994; Gamberg et al., 1988). In primary grades, they often extend across most or all of the school day. Students are sometimes involved in planning the direction for the theme, especially in upper grades. Topics for thematic units should be broad and encompass many possible directions for exploration. Example topics include holidays and celebrations, people who make a difference, our green earth, humour in our lives, natural disasters, and civilizations.

Students use all of the language arts as they explore, experiment, synthesize, question, and extend learning during thematic units. They also use language arts to demonstrate their new learning at the end of the theme. Four types of language arts activities are usually included in thematic units:

1. **Reading books and other print and nonprint texts.** Students read a range of material, including stories and informational text. Many teachers choose theme-related text sets as core materials for a thematic unit.

2. **Writing.** Various types of writing are done according to the theme. For example, an environmental theme might include making conservation posters or writing letters to the local press.

3. **Oral language activities.** Oral language activities are focused on one or more aspects of the theme. These include interviewing, listening to guest speakers, debating issues, or dramatizing theme-related literature or events.

4. **Creative projects.** Students engage in creative projects using all six language arts to deepen their understanding of the theme, to extend their learning, and to demonstrate their new knowledge. Theme-related projects often involve working in more than one area of the curriculum. Many projects involve use of technology to enhance and share learning. For example, an environmental theme might include creation of a webpage to show what the students' community does to reduce waste.

INQUIRY-BASED UNITS

In inquiry-based units, students and teachers learn together. Both grapple with issues out of genuine interest and curiosity. Teachers who facilitate inquiry-based learning believe that shared inquiry is inherently motivating, and they provide time and resources for students to pursue learning individually, in small groups, or as a class. The Internet is becoming a primary source of information for students engaged in inquiry-based learning.

Topics for inquiry-based language arts units develop from students' interests, but often grow from shared experiences with literature or nonprint media texts. As partners in inquiry, teachers and students share the control and responsibility for learning. Students take active roles in planning and implementing classroom experiences (Thomas & Oldfather, 1995).

Inquiry-based units follow a recursive cycle of activities, including

1. **Identifying inquiry focus.** Teachers read aloud to students, students read widely and browse informational texts, teachers and students engage in dialogue, do quickwrites, and ask questions to identify the focus.

2. **Exploring multiple data sources.** Resources for inquiry units must be abundant and diverse. Students need access to fiction and nonfiction, knowledgeable human resources, related Internet sites, and other nonprint sources to increase their knowledge, skills, and understanding of the focus.

3. **Sharing what is learned.** All of the language arts can be used to share learning. Students can use writing, drama, music, art, oral presentations, and multimedia to represent their learning.

4. **Reflecting and planning.** Inquiry is a never-ending process. Students need time to reflect on new learning, make connections to what is already known, and begin planning further inquiry.

READERS AND WRITERS WORKSHOPS

Readers and writers workshops are ways of structuring classroom reading and writing that facilitates both student-centred and teacher-directed learning. Initially made popular by the research and writings of Nancie Atwell, *workshop* now has many interpretations. Nevertheless, the components outlined in Figure 2–5 are the mainstay of workshops as an approach to instruction. Workshops can be implemented within all three of the instructional frameworks presented in this chapter.

Readers Workshop. In a readers workshop, students read self-selected books independently or in small groups and respond to books by writing in reading logs and by discussing the book, if a small group of students is reading the same book (Atwell, 1987, 1998; Hornsby, Sukarna, & Parry, 1986; Mackenzie, 1992). Through readers workshop, students become more fluent readers and deepen their appreciation of books and reading. They develop lifelong reading habits, are introduced to different genres, and choose favourite authors. Most important, students come to think of themselves as readers (Daniels, 1994). The primary components of readers workshop are

1. *Reading and responding.* Students spend 30 to 45 minutes independently reading books and other reading materials. They also keep reading logs to write responses to their reading and participate in conferences with the teacher or in small discussion groups to extend their understanding of books read. They may also engage in other interpretive responses designed to extend their understandings. Responses might include dramatic interpretations or visual images such as posters, collages, or sketches.

2. *Sharing.* For the last 10 to 20 minutes of the readers workshop, the class gathers together to share books and response projects.

3. *Minilessons.* The teacher spends approximately 10 to 15 minutes teaching lessons on readers workshop procedures, literary concepts, or reading strategies and skills.

Writers Workshop. The writers workshop is a way of implementing the writing process (Atwell, 1987, 1998; Calkins, 1994; Graves, 1983; Parry & Hornsby, 1985). Students usually write on topics they choose themselves or those related to their language arts unit, and they assume ownership of their learning. The classroom becomes a community of writers in which students come to see themselves as writers (Samway et al., 1991). They develop and apply writing skills and strategies and perhaps most important, they see first-hand the power of writing to entertain, inform, and persuade.

In a writers workshop classroom, students have writing folders in which they keep all papers related to the writing project they are working on. They also keep writing notebooks in which they jot down images, impressions, dialogue, and experiences that they can build on for writing projects (Calkins, 1991).

The physical arrangement of the classroom for a writers workshop usually includes space for students to write individually or in small groups, a space for students to conference with the teacher, a place for reference aids such as dictionaries, and facilities for publishing writing. The classroom atmosphere is one of support and encouragement for students to share quietly with each other, solving problems within their writing and making suggestions when writers need assistance.

Writers workshop is a 60- to 90-minute period scheduled each day. During this time the teacher and the students are involved in three primary activities:

For more information on the writing process, see Chapter 4, "The Reading and Writing Processes," pages 147–164.

1. *Writing.* Students spend 30 to 45 minutes working independently on writing projects. They move through all stages of the writing process—prewriting, drafting, revising, editing, and publishing—at their own pace. When students reach the publishing stage, they often compile their final copies to make books, but sometimes they attach their writing to artwork, make posters, write letters that are mailed, or perform scripts as skits or puppet shows.

2. *Sharing.* The class gathers together for 10 to 15 minutes to share their writing, sometimes to seek help with drafts and often to share new publications and make related announcements of forthcoming publications. If an author's chair is available, each student sits in the special chair to read his or her composition. After the reading, classmates offer compliments, ask questions, and make suggestions. When incomplete works are shared, the emphasis is on problem solving and encouragement. When completed works are shared, the focus is on celebrating, not on revising the composition to make it better.

3. *Minilessons.* During a 10- to 15-minute period, teachers provide brief lessons on writing workshop procedures, literary concepts, and writing skills and strategies. They often talk about authors of children's trade books and the writing strategies and skills they use.

Sometimes teachers add a fourth component to writers workshops in which they read literature aloud to share examples of good writing with students. Often, teachers choose to read literature that provides a model for the kind of writing that their students are doing. Sometimes, teachers choose to read examples from literature as part of a minilesson. For example, recently one of our former student teachers read from Jon Scieszka's *The True Story of the 3 Little Pigs!* (1989) to illustrate point of view. Hearing the wolf's declaration that he would tell readers the way things "really" happened made very clear to her grade 6 students that writers make choices regarding perspective. Sharing literature in this way helps students to feel part of the community of writers. Teachers often connect readers workshop with writers workshop and, as a consequence, they engage their students in extended literate activities involving all six language arts.

For more information on readers and writers workshops, see Chapter 11, "Putting It All Together," pages 461–471.

THE TEACHER'S ROLE

As may be gleaned from the preceding descriptions of classrooms and instruction, the teacher's role in a language arts classroom is complex and multidimensional. No longer are teachers simply providers of knowledge. Nor do teachers assign an endless series of worksheets and "busy work." Instead, teachers understand that children's literacy develops most effectively through purposeful and meaningful social contexts. These teachers create the classroom environment and a community of learners. They plan the language arts curriculum to meet the needs of their increasingly diverse classes of students. Their goal is to help students develop communicative competence and to excite students about literacy. They are instructors, coaches, facilitators, and managers. Figure 2–6 on page 64 presents a list of some of the roles teachers assume.

Establishing a Community of Learners. Teachers begin the process of establishing a community of learners when they make deliberate decisions about the kinds of classroom culture they want to create (Sumara & Walker, 1991). School is "real" life for students, and they learn best when they see a purpose for learning to read and write. The social contexts that teachers create are key. Teachers must make conscientious decisions about their roles and the kind of language arts instruction they want in their classrooms.

Teachers are more successful when they take the first two weeks of the school year to establish the classroom environment (Sumara & Walker, 1991). Teachers can't assume that students will be familiar with the procedures and routines used in language arts, or that students will instinctively be cooperative, responsible, and respectful of classmates. During this time, teachers explain classroom routines, such as how to get supplies out and put them away and how to work with classmates in a cooperative group, and set the expectation that students will adhere to the routines. They demonstrate literacy procedures, such as how to choose a book from the classroom library, how to provide feedback in a writing group, and how to participate in a grand conversation or discussion about a book. Also, teachers model ways of interacting with students, responding to literature, respecting classmates, and assisting classmates with reading and writing projects.

Teachers are classroom managers or administrators. They clearly explain to students what is expected of them and what is valued in the classroom. Teachers model classroom rules themselves, as they interact with students. According to Sumara and Walker, the process of socialization at the beginning of the school year is planned, deliberate, and crucial to the success of the language arts program.

Throughout the year, teachers continue to reinforce classroom routines and teach additional literacy procedures as students are involved in new types of activities; that is, the classroom community evolves during the school year, but the foundation is laid during the first two weeks.

When teachers develop a predictable classroom environment with familiar routines and procedures, students feel comfortable, safe, and more willing to take risks and to experiment. This is especially true for students from varied cultures, students learning English as a second language, and less capable readers and writers.

Role	Description
Organizer	• Creates a language-rich environment • Plans the language arts program • Sets time schedules • Develops resource-based units and thematic units • Schedules readers and writers workshops • Uses the language arts as tools for learning across the curriculum
Facilitator	• Develops a community of learners • Stimulates students' interest in language and literacy • Allows students to choose books to read and topics for projects • Provides opportunities for students to use language for meaningful, functional, and genuine activities • Invites parents to become involved in classroom activities
Participant	• Reads and writes with students • Learns along with students • Asks questions and seeks answers to questions
Instructor	• Provides information about books, authors, and illustrators • Explains language arts procedures • Teaches minilessons on concepts, skills, and strategies • Provides background knowledge before reading, writing, and viewing • Groups students flexibly for instruction
Model	• Demonstrates procedures, skills, and strategies • Reads aloud to students every day
Manager	• Sets expectations and responsibilities • Tracks students' progress during resource-based units • Monitors students' work during readers and writers workshop • Keeps records • Arranges the classroom to facilitate learning • Provides technology hardware and software to support language arts activities
Diagnostician	• Conferences with students • Observes students participating in language arts activities • Assesses students' strengths and weaknesses • Plans instruction based on students' needs
Evaluator	• Assesses students' progress in the language arts • Helps students self-assess their learning • Assigns grades • Examines the effectiveness of the language arts program
Coordinator	• Works with librarians, aides, and parent volunteers • Works with other teachers on grade-level projects, pen pal programs, and cross-age reading programs
Communicator	• Expects students to do their best • Encourages students to become lifelong readers • Communicates the language arts program to parents and administrators • Shares language arts goals and activities with parents and the community • Encourages parents to support the language arts program

Figure 2–6 Roles Teachers Assume

What about Teaching? We could say that everything a teacher does, by one definition or another, is teaching. However, at this time, we want to look at two contrasting kinds of teaching that are significant within the role of language arts teaching. One kind is called *direct instruction*. In this kind of teaching, teachers provide systematic, planned lessons in which they explicitly present information, provide an opportunity for supervised practice, and then have students apply what they have learned through authentic reading and writing activities (Slaughter, 1988). Teachers often use direct instruction during minilessons in which they teach students about reading and writing procedures, skills, and strategies. Direct instruction has been associated with skill-and-drill activities, but it doesn't have to be. This kind of teaching is necessary to provide information and opportunities for students to apply what they are learning with guidance from the teacher. Examples of direct-instruction lessons include the following:

- Presenting a biographical sketch of poet Dennis Lee during a unit featuring the author and his humorous verse
- Highlighting important vocabulary from *Sarah, Plain and Tall* (MacLachlan, 1985) on the classroom word-wall
- Teaching a word-processing lesson on using columns to write for the class newspaper
- Demonstrating how to proofread a piece of writing to identify spelling, punctuation, and capitalization errors

The second kind of teaching is *indirect instruction* (Slaughter, 1988). Teachers use indirect instruction for brief on-the-spot lessons as they respond to students' questions or when students demonstrate the need to know something. These lessons take place during whole-class activities, during conferences with students, and while working with small groups. Teachers also do indirect instruction as they model reading when reading aloud to the class and as they model writing when students are writing in a class collaboration. Other examples include the following:

- Demonstrating how to use an index when a student says he or she can't find anything about scorpions in the informational book *Desert Life* (Taylor, 1992)
- Teaching a student how to use quotation marks while editing the student's piece of writing
- Explaining what a prologue and an epilogue are during a conference with a child who is reading *Tuck Everlasting* (Babbitt, 1975)
- Explaining the spelling rule that *y* at the end of a word is usually changed to *i* before adding *-es* if a child asks for help when using a spell checker

While direct instruction is planned, teachers seize the teachable moment for indirect instruction. Both kinds of teaching are valuable. Because teachable moments may not present themselves for some important language arts strategies and skills, there needs to be both planned and unplanned instruction (Baumann, 1987).

Sometimes teachers ask how they should balance the two types of teaching. It is important to remember that most of the instructional time should be devoted to real reading and writing and teacher-led instruction offered as needed to meet students' needs.

ADAPTING TO MEET THE NEEDS OF EVERY STUDENT

In Canadian schools, it is usual that policies regarding special-needs students call for integration and inclusion; that is, most classes include students of diverse learning abilities and styles. Teachers are expected to meet all students' instructional needs. To do this, teachers must provide flexibly structured programs that can be modified as needed to ensure that all students enjoy success. It is particularly important that the language-learning needs of special-needs students be met in classrooms because language development is a significant factor in learning in all curricular areas.

It is our position in this text that students with special learning needs benefit from the same language arts content and teaching strategies that are generally recommended for elementary classrooms, but that adaptations are needed to maximize each student's learning. The most common adaptations of instruction involve choosing resources that are appropriate to the student, changing the nature of teacher–student interaction to offer the assistance needed for success, and altering assignments so that successful completion is possible. For example, teachers must choose reading materials suited to the students' reading level, must offer individualized instruction when needed, and must tailor expectations in regard to such things as the length of written assignments and the time available for assignment completion. While it is beyond the scope of this text to provide extensive description, what follows is an overview of the needs of some special-needs students together with suggestions for adapting language arts instruction.

Students with Specific Learning Disabilities. Many children who experience significant learning problems have specific learning disabilities. Although there is no universally agreed-upon definition of *learning disability*, educators in Canada generally conceptualize a learning disability as any one of a mixed group of long-lasting disorders that may be the result of a central nervous system dysfunction. These disorders may be evidenced by difficulties in one or more processes such as attention, concentration, perception, memory, reasoning, organization, planning, and problem solving (Andrews & Lupart, 1993). Children with specific learning disabilities are of average or above-average intelligence and can be very able learners when adequate instruction is provided.

In language arts classrooms, specific learning disabilities are evidenced by such behaviours as students' difficulties in learning word-recognition skills such as phonics, difficulties in spelling, underdeveloped vocabulary, poor comprehension skills (such as sequencing material read or heard), and poor organization skills in written work. Further, specific learning disabilities may negatively affect students' self-esteem and consequently their social interactions, especially with peers.

Instruction for students with specific learning disabilities must be clearly structured, and the structure made apparent to the students. Such students do well when routines are followed and when guidelines for tasks are presented sequentially and in writing as well as orally. These students benefit from modifications to length and time of writing and independent reading assignments. Peer and cross-age tutoring also provide advantages, especially as opportunities for reinforcement of concept learning.

Students with Delayed Cognitive Skills. Historically, children with delayed cognitive skills (mental retardation) were described as intellectually subnormal individuals who were incurable (Doll, 1941). Currently, it is widely recognized that children who are considered to have delayed cognitive skills or mental retardation meet three criteria: subaverage intellectual functioning, deficits in adaptive behaviour, and delays observed between conception and 18 years of age (Andrews & Lupart, 1993). Delays and limitations are exhibited in such areas as communication, self-care, social skills, functional academics, and gross and fine motor development. Although included in many Canadian classrooms for at least part of each school day, students with delayed cognitive skills need individualized instruction to ensure continuous conceptual and skill development. Most often, their instruction is planned by a team of teachers and comprises an *individual education plan* (or IEP). In general, the focus of instruction should be on helping students develop the functional skills considered essential to living independently. In the language arts classroom, the focus is on communication (oral, written, and visual) and enjoyment of literature.

Students with Behaviour Disorders. Students whose behaviour interferes with learning are characterized as having behaviour disorders. They often exhibit inappropriate behaviour and feelings under normal circumstances; they may be either aggressive and disruptive or anxious and withdrawn. These students have difficulty in developing satisfactory relationships with classmates and the teacher. Often, they are unhappy or depressed, and they may develop physical symptoms or fears associated with personal or school problems. Although any student can exhibit one of these behaviours for a brief period, students with behaviour disorders exhibit more than one of these behaviours to a marked degree and consistently over time.

Students with behaviour disorders need a structured and positive classroom environment in order to be successful. For that reason, it is important that all teachers who work with such a student collaborate to set behavioural expectations and consequences. In the language arts classroom, open-ended activities such as literature circle discussions may require explicit rule-setting and careful teacher coaching. Similarly, it may be necessary to set time limits for writing and keep periods of independent reading relatively short.

Students with Language Disorders. Students who have grown up in an English-speaking community, but have difficulty understanding or expressing language, are classified as having a language disorder. Often these children talk very little, speak in childlike phrases, and lack the language to understand basic concepts. This is a very serious problem because a student's limited ability to communicate has a negative impact on learning as well as on social interaction with classmates and the teacher. Such students may require extensive language therapy and specialized programming. It is important to note that students who speak their first language fluently and are learning English as a second language do not have a language disorder.

Students with Attention-Deficit/Hyperactivity Disorder. Students with attention-deficit disorder (ADD) have great difficulty attending to tasks and activities. While there is much discussion about definition, it is widely accepted that there are at least two types of attention-deficit disorder—with and without hyperactivity. All students with ADD display distractibility, inattention, and mood fluctuations. Their inattention is not wilful as is sometimes mistakenly thought. In addition to these behaviours, some students are also highly impulsive and physically active. These students are diagnosed as having attention-deficit hyperactivity disorder (ADHD). Some students are helped by stimulant drugs, but medication must be accompanied by well-structured instruction and efforts to help the students learn to focus on tasks at hand. While success is important for all students, it is crucial that students with ADD and ADHD be successful in the classroom, and that teachers structure their environment to minimize their distractibility (Weaver, 1994b). In the language arts classroom, it is frequently necessary to modify programs in ways such as arranging for a distraction-free area for writing, shortening independent reading expectations, and encouraging oral contributions rather than written.

Students Who Are Learning English as a Second Language. Many children in Canadian classrooms come from linguistic and cultural backgrounds beyond the official languages of English and French. Many of these children are fluent in one or more languages when they come to school, where they are immersed in English. For children learning English as a second language (ESL), or a third language, language arts as a curricular subject is especially challenging, and instructional provisions must be made for them. Students learn a second language in much the way they learned to speak their native language. It is now widely recognized that effective ESL classroom instruction includes sharing the students' first language and culture with classmates. Teachers must include culturally relevant literature in the selections available in their classrooms. Such literature facilitates the sharing of culture that is beneficial to language learning among ESL students.

In Canada, particular consideration must be given to students for whom English is a second dialect (ESD), such as Aboriginal students who have grown up in a mixed linguistic setting, speaking English and an Aboriginal language. The risk is that when languages become confused with one another during development, children may not achieve fluency in either. There is a growing consensus among educators in Canada and elsewhere that a secure grasp of one language provides the optimal basis for all subsequent cognitive development (Piper, 1993).

Students Who Are Gifted. Gifted students are academically advanced, but giftedness is more than a high IQ score. Gifted students are curious, have unusually good memories, express themselves well, enjoy working independently, have a well-developed sense of humour, and are often perfectionists. However, some gifted students are underachievers who do not work up to their potential because of a lack of motivation, peer pressure, or fear of success. Gifted students require special adaptations to meet their needs. Typical adaptations for gifted students include allowance for student choice and design of assignments, often involving independent research and experimentation, increased level of complexity of resource materials, involvement in cross-age study groups, and flexibility in grading criteria.

The material in this book capitalizes on the natural ways children learn, and it can be used effectively with almost all learners, given some adaptations. Special educators continue to point out that there is no one way to teach students with special needs that is different from how other students are taught. Moreover, educators recommend an integrated approach as especially valuable for learning-disabled and remedial learners (Rhodes & Dudley-Marling, 1988; Stires, 1991b) and for students learning English as a second language (Freeman & Freeman, 1993; Kucer, Silva, & Delgado-Larocco, 1995).

Assessing Students' Learning

Assessing students' learning in the language arts is a complex task. Although it may seem fairly easy to develop and administer a criterion-referenced test, tests measure language skills rather than students' ability to use language in authentic ways. Further, such tests do not measure listening, speaking, viewing, and representing very well. A test on punctuation marks, for example, does not indicate students' ability to use punctuation marks correctly in their own writing. Instead, such a test typically evaluates students' ability to add punctuation marks to a set of sentences created by someone else, or to proofread and spot punctuation errors in someone else's writing.

Traditional assessment reflects outdated views of how students learn to read and write. Tests, particularly written tests, focus on only a few aspects of what readers and writers do as they work. Assessment should resemble real language use (Valencia, Hiebert, & Afflerbach, 1994). Therefore, a better approach is *authentic assessment*, in which teachers examine both the processes that students use as they listen, speak, read, write, view, and visually represent, and the artifacts or products that students produce, such as projects and reading logs. Students, too, participate in reflecting on, and self-assessing, their learning. Authentic assessment has five purposes:

- To document progress in students' language and literacy development
- To identify students' strengths in order to plan for instruction
- To document students' language arts activities and projects
- To determine grades
- To help teachers learn more about how students become strategic readers and writers

Assessment is more than testing; it is an integral part of teaching and learning (K. S. Goodman, Goodman, & Hood, 1989). The purpose of classroom assessment is to inform and influence instruction. According to Valencia and Pearson,

> The best possible assessment of reading would seem to occur when teachers observe and interact with students as they read authentic texts for genuine purposes. As teachers interact with students, they evaluate the way in which the students orchestrate resources to construct meaning, intervening to provide support or suggestions when the students appear on the verge of faltering in their attempt to build a reasonable model of the meaning of the text. (1986, p. 6)

Although it seems increasing attention is given to high stakes, standardized assessment and test results, authentic assessment is the key to effective instruction. Through authentic assessment, teachers learn about their students, about themselves as teachers, and about the impact of the instructional program. Similarly, when students reflect on their learning and use self-assessment, they learn about themselves as learners and also about their learning. The following Teacher's Notebook presents guidelines for authentic assessment and describes how teachers use authentic assessment tools in their classrooms.

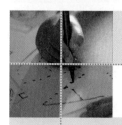

Teacher's Notebook

Guidelines for Authentic Assessment

1. **Choose Appropriate Assessment Tools**
   Teachers identify their purpose for assessment and choose an appropriate assessment tool. To judge students' spelling development, for example, teachers examine students' spelling in stories they write and their use of proofreading, as well as their performance on spelling tests.

2. **Use a Variety of Assessment Tools**
   Teachers regularly use a variety of authentic assessment tools that reflect current theories about how children learn, including anecdotal notes and reading logs. Using a variety of tools increases the likelihood of identifying growth and instructional needs.

3. **Integrate Instruction and Assessment**
   Teachers use the results of assessment to inform their teaching. They observe and conference with students as they teach and supervise students during language arts activities. When teachers observe that students do not understand, they need to try other instructional procedures.

4. **Keep a Positive Focus**
   Teachers focus on what students can do, not what they can't do. They should focus on how to facilitate students' continuous development as readers, writers, and users of language.

5. **Consider Both Processes and Products**
   Teachers examine both the language processes students use and the products they create. Teachers notice the strategies students use for language activities as well as assess the quality of students' visual representations, oral reading, compositions, and other products.

6. **Consider Multiple Contexts**
   Teachers assess students' language arts development in a variety of contexts, including specific language arts activities and across-the-curriculum learning activities. Multiple contexts are important because students often demonstrate different competencies in one context than in another.

7. **Focus on Individual Students**
   In addition to whole-class assessments, teachers make time to observe, conference, and do other assessment procedures, such as running records with individual students to develop a clear understanding of a student's development.

8. **Teach Students to Self-Assess Their Learning**
   Self-assessment is an integral part of assessment. Students need to learn to judiciously reflect on their progress and to recognize their strengths and areas that need further development.

Teachers monitor students' progress through conferences during writers workshops.

MONITORING STUDENTS' PROGRESS

Teachers monitor students' progress as they are involved in language arts and across-the-curriculum activities during resource-based units, thematic units, and inquiry-based units. They use the results of their monitoring to inform their teaching (Baskwill & Whitman, 1988; Goodman et al., 1989). Six ways to monitor students' progress are classroom observations, anecdotal notes, conferences, checklists, miscue analyses, and running records. In addition to these informal and teacher-designed classroom assessments, provincial departments of education administer standardized assessments. Teachers and students also engage in portfolio development to monitor progress over time. To determine students' progress and especially to identify reading difficulties that impede progress, teachers conduct miscue analysis as they complete informal reading inventories.

Classroom Observations. Language arts teachers engage in "kid watching," a term that Yetta Goodman coined and defined as "direct and informal observation of students" (1978, p. 37). To be an effective kid watcher, teachers must understand how children develop language and the role of errors in language learning. Teachers engage in kid watching spontaneously when they interact with children and are attentive to their behaviour and comments. Other observation times should be planned when the teacher focuses on particular students and makes anecdotal notes about the students' involvement in literacy events and other language arts activities. The focus is on what students do as they use oral and written language, and the effects on the students' language use of any intervention offered by the teacher.

Anecdotal Notes. Teachers write brief notes as they observe students, and the most useful notes describe specific events, report rather than evaluate, and relate the events to other information about the student (Rhodes & Nathenson-Mejia, 1992). Teachers make notes about students' performance in listening, speaking, reading, writing, viewing, and visually representing activities; the questions students ask; and the strategies and skills they use fluently or indicate confusion about. These records document students' growth and pinpoint problem areas for future minilessons and conferences. A year-long collection of anecdotal notes provides a comprehensive picture of a student's learning in the language arts. An excerpt from a fifth-grade teacher's anecdotal notes about one student's progress during a unit on Canada in the early 1900s is shown in Figure 2–7.

Several organizational schemes for anecdotal notes are possible, and teachers should use the format that is most comfortable for them. Some teachers make a card file with dividers for each child and write anecdotes on note cards. They feel comfortable jotting notes on these small cards or even carrying around a set of cards in a pocket. Other teachers divide a spiral-bound notebook into sections for each child and write anecdotes in the notebook, which they

---

Notes about Matthew

March 5	Matthew selected Prime Minister William Lyon Mackenzie King as historical figure for Canada in the early 1900s.
March 11	Matthew fascinated with information he has found about M. K. Brought several sources from home. Is completing M. K.'s lifeline with many details.
March 18	Simulated journal. Four entries in four days! Interesting how he picked up language style of the period in his journal. Volunteers to share daily. I think he enjoys the oral sharing more than the writing.
March 25	Nine simulated journal entries, all illustrated. High level of enthusiasm.
March 29	Conferenced about cluster for M. K. biography. Well-developed with five rays, many details. Matthew will work on "contributions" ray. He recognized it as the least-developed one.
April 2	Three chapters of biography drafted. Talked about "working titles" for chapters and choosing more interesting titles after writing that reflects the content of the chapters.
April 7	Drafting conference. Matthew has completed all five chapters. He and Dustin are competitive, both writing on M. K. They are reading each other's chapters and checking the accuracy of information.
April 12	Writers group. Chapters longer and more complete since drafting conference. Compared with autobiography project, writing is more sophisticated. Longer, too. Reading is influencing writing style—e.g., "I have a great future." He is still somewhat defensive about accepting suggestions except from me. He will make 3 revisions—agreed in writers group.
April 15	Revisions: (1) eliminated "he" (substitute), (2) re-sequenced Chapter 3 (move), and (3) added sentences in Chapter 5 (add).
April 19	Proofread with Dustin. Working hard.
April 23	Editing conference—no major problems. Discussed use of commas within sentences, capitalizing proper nouns. Matthew and Dustin more task-oriented on this project; I see more motivation and commitment.
April 29	Final copy of biography completed and shared with class.

Figure 2–7 Anecdotal Notes about One Student's Learning During a Thematic Unit on Canada in the Early 1900s

keep on their desk. Some teachers write anecdotes on sheets of paper and clip the sheets into students' assessment folders or file them in loose-leaf binders organized with a section for each student. Still others maintain computer word-processed files that allow for easy access and additions.

Conferences. Teachers talk with students to monitor their progress in language arts activities as well as to set goals and help students solve problems. Seven types of conferences are described in the accompanying Teacher's Notebook. The type of conference selected by the teacher is dependent on the purpose for conferring with the student. Some conferences are brief and impromptu, held at students' desks as the teacher moves around the classroom, whereas at other times the conferences are planned and students meet with the teacher at a designated conference table.

The teacher's role is to be listener and guide. Teachers can learn a great deal about students and their learning if they listen as students talk about their reading, writing, or other activities. When students explain a problem they are having, the teacher is often able to decide on a way to work through it. Graves (1994) suggests that teachers balance the amount of their talk with the student's talk during the conference and, at the end, reflect on what the student has taught them, what responsibilities the student can take, and whether the student understands what to do next.

Checklists. Teachers use checklists as they observe students; they track students' progress during instructional units by documenting use of language arts skills, strategies, procedures, and concepts. For example, when students participate in writing conferences in which they read their compositions to small groups of classmates and ask for suggestions for improving their writing, teachers can note whether students participate fully in the group, share their writing with classmates, gracefully accept suggestions about improving their writing, and make substantive changes in their writing based on some of their classmates' suggestions. Students, too, can use checklists to monitor their performance and progress. Experienced teachers recommend that students participate in constructing checklists so that they understand what is expected of them.

Middle-grade students might complete the sample checklist in Figure 2–8 on page 74 to monitor their work during readers and writers workshops. Notice that students are directed to write a letter to the teacher on the back of the sheet, reflecting on their work.

Miscue Analyses. Teachers often need to assess students' reading in a focused way to help determine instructional needs, particularly when students are struggling to read fluently and with understanding. One way that teachers can do such assessment is through miscue analysis. *Miscue analysis* involves working individually with one student at a time. The term *miscue*, coined by Goodman (1969), refers to oral reading errors. Goodman proposed that readers make the errors because they attend to the wrong cues. Miscues occur when what the reader says does not match the printed text.

Miscue analysis is a system for analyzing reader errors in an attempt to identify what cues the reader is and is not using adequately. It can help teachers identify what strategies the reader is using and point to the areas where instruction is needed. Miscue analysis can also help teachers determine whether a reader is attending to letters and sounds, to meaning, or to both. In addition, it can point out when the reader is making substitutions, mispronunciations, and omissions. Miscue analysis helps teachers answer two questions: Is the reader attending to print at the word or within word level? Is the reader attending to meaning? There are many versions of miscue analyses, but all serve generally the same purposes and follow similar procedures.

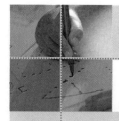

Teacher's Notebook

Seven Types of Conferences

1. On-the-Spot Conferences
Teachers visit briefly with students to monitor some aspect of the students' work or to check on progress. These conferences are brief; the teacher may spend less than a minute with each student.

2. Prereading or Prewriting Conferences
The teacher and student make plans for reading or writing at the conference. At a prereading conference, they may talk about information related to the book, difficult concepts or vocabulary words related to the reading, or the reading log the student will keep. At a prewriting conference, they may discuss possible writing topics or how to narrow a broad topic.

3. Revising Conferences
A small group of students and the teacher meet to provide writers with specific suggestions for revising their compositions. These conferences offer student writers an audience to provide feedback on how well they have communicated.

4. Book Discussion Conferences
Students and the teacher meet to discuss the book they have read. They may share reading log entries, discuss plot or characters, compare the story with others they have read, or make plans to extend their reading.

5. Editing Conferences
The teacher reviews students' proofread compositions and helps them correct spelling, punctuation, capitalization, and other mechanical errors.

6. Minilesson Conferences
The teacher meets with students to explain a procedure, strategy, or skill (e.g., writing a table of contents, using the visualization strategy when reading, or capitalizing proper nouns).

7. Assessment Conferences
The teacher meets with students after they have completed an assignment or project to talk about their growth as readers or writers. Students reflect on their competencies and set goals.

Miscue analysis involves teacher preparation, student oral reading, and teacher recording and analysis of reading errors. To prepare, the teacher needs to select one or more short passages to be read by the student. Two copies of the text are needed, one from which the student reads and one on which the teacher writes. Choosing the level of text can be challenging, but a rule of thumb is to choose a text with which the teacher anticipates the student will have some success. Additional selections may include more challenging texts as the teacher and student work together to determine the student's skills and instructional needs.

The teacher asks the student to read aloud. While the student reads, the teacher records the student's reading errors on the second copy of the text. The teacher uses a system of symbols as shown in Figure 2–9 on page 75 that facilitate quick recording. Some teachers record the oral reading so that it can be reviewed.

Following the reading, the teacher reviews the reading errors, observing the types of errors made and looking for patterns in those errors. By observing reading errors, the teacher can

Readers–Writers Workshop Activity Sheet

Name_____   Week _____

Read independently	M T W Th F	Made a cluster	M T W Th F
Wrote in a reading log	M T W Th F	Wrote a rough draft	M T W Th F
Listened to the teacher read aloud	M T W Th F	Went to a writing group	M T W Th F
Read with a classmate	M T W Th F	Made revisions	M T W Th F
Read at the listening centre	M T W Th F	Proofread my own writing	M T W Th F
Had a reading conference	M T W Th F	Had a writing conference	M T W Th F
Shared a book with classmates	M T W Th F	Shared my writing with classmates	M T W Th F
Other		Other	
Interesting words read this week		Spelling words needed this week	
Titles of books read		Titles of writings	

Write a letter on the back, thinking about the week and your reading and writing.

Figure 2–8 Assessment Checklist

hypothesize which cues from the text the student uses and what instruction is needed to improve the student's reading. Figure 2–9 shows miscue analysis of Christopher's reading and the teacher's interpretation.

Miscue analysis is a component of two other forms of assessment that are popular in Canadian schools: running records and Informal Reading Inventories (IRIs). Each has unique characteristics, but both are forms of individual assessment.

Running Records. A running record (Clay, 1985) is similar to miscue analysis in that it is a way to record what students do while reading a text aloud. Teachers record the reading to see the strengths and weaknesses in the use of cues and strategies. The primary purpose is to determine whether a text is easy, appropriate, or difficult for a student. Teachers use running records to aid them in choosing appropriate materials for students and to monitor student reading progress, especially progress of beginning readers.

Taking a running record differs from miscue analysis in that teachers record on a simple recording sheet or plain piece of paper rather than on a copy of the text. Although the teacher needs to be able to see the text, it is not necessary to have two copies. In this way, it is more flexible than miscue analysis. While it is possible to take running records of older students reading

Little Bear's First Snow

because T
It began to snow.

T
care T
/ha/hap/haping/
Little Bear <u>did not</u> know what was happening.

He <u>put out his paw.</u>

Snow fell <u>on his paw.</u>

SC
loded
He licked his paw.

no-thing
He could taste nothing.

it
"What is this?" he asked.

SC
mom
"Snow" said his <u>mother.</u>

's
"<u>It is</u> time for (us) to sleep."

Teacher's comments:

Seems to overuse first letter cues.
Uses repetition excessively.
Reads with expression indicating recoginition of speech.
Offer minilesson on combining first letter and semantic cues.

Symbols used

Substitution	*it* this
Omission	(the)
Attempt to decode	/ /
Repetition	═══
Teacher correction	T
Self-correction	SC

Figure 2–9 Miscue Analysis: Christopher's Reading and the Teacher's Interpretation

comprehensive text, it is most often used with beginning readers and simple text. A running record involves the teacher choosing a passage (or simple book) of approximately one hundred words, the student reading aloud, followed by the teacher's analysis of the miscues and determination of the student's progress. While the student reads, the teacher records reading and miscues as follows:

- Reads word correctly: Write a check mark (✓).
- Misreads word: Write the word with the error above it.
- Omits word: Write the word and circle or draw a line and write the word above.
- Self-corrects: Write the word with *SC* above it.
- Teacher tells the word: Write the word with *T* above it.

Text: At the Seashore
               I can build a sandcastle.
               The castle is white and pink.
               I can dig a clam.
               The clam is small and round.
               I can see the waves
               I cannot catch the waves.

Student: At the Seashore
               I can make a sandcastle.
               The castle is white and pink.
               I can big a car.
               The car is small, is small, and red.
               I can see the waves
               I can catch the waves.

Running Record: ✔   ✔   ✔
                 ✔   ✔   make   ✔   ✔
                         build

                 ✔   ✔   ✔   ✔   ✔   ✔
                 ✔   ✔   dig   ✔   car   ✔
                         big   clam

                 ✔   car   R   R   ✔   red
                     clam   ✔   ✔   ✔   round
                 ✔   ✔   ✔   ✔   ✔   ✔
                 ✔   can   ✔   ✔   ✔
                     cannot

Teacher's Analysis:

Attends to meaning and seems to use picture cues. Tends to focus only on first letter cues.

$$\frac{29\ correct}{35\ words} \times 100 = 85\%$$ *Needs more practice at this level.*

Figure 2–10 Running Record: Sarah's Reading of *At the Seashore*

Figure 2–10 shows a running record of Sarah's reading of *At the Seashore*. Her teacher determined that she was making good progress. Progress is often determined using the following formula. Ninety percent accuracy or higher is considered good progress.

$$\frac{\text{Total Words Read Correctly*}}{\text{Number of Words in Passage/Book}} \times 100 = \underline{\quad}\%$$

Self-corrections are counted as correct.

Running records form a significant part of the assessment and evaluation in the Reading Recovery Program (Clay, 1985; Pinnell, Fried, & Estice, 1990). To learn more about taking running records, refer to Clay (1985).

Informal Reading Inventories. An informal reading inventory (IRI) consists of materials organized by increasing difficulty for the purpose of individual assessment. Most published IRIs include graded word lists, graded passages with questions to assess comprehension, and graded passages to assess listening comprehension. When administering an IRI with a student, teachers ask the student to first read orally from the graded word lists. This reading gives the teacher an indication of which passages to present for oral reading. When the student reads the selected passage orally, the teacher conducts a miscue analysis of the reading. Following the reading, the teacher asks the student comprehension questions, expecting the student to respond orally. When the miscue analysis is complete, the teacher reviews the information to determine the cues the student is using or not using and what instruction is needed. If listening comprehension is included in the analysis, the teacher reads passages to the student and follows the reading with oral questioning.

Despite controversy regarding best practices in reading assessment, IRIs remain popular because they provide information needed for teachers to plan instruction. When administered in their complete form, they give teachers a clear indication of the levels of text with which students will be frustrated, will be able to read with assistance, and those they can read independently. Many published IRIs are available, but teachers can also create their own using classroom reading materials. One criticism often raised is that using published IRIs means asking students to read inauthentic texts—that is, to read the texts prepared especially for testing, as opposed to literature texts in regular use in classrooms. To overcome this potential weakness, yet maintain the strength of IRIs as diagnostic tools, some teachers with whom we work include reading of both test materials and literature selections when they assess their students. Published IRIs include administration guidelines, but teachers can also find a full description of the procedures and use of IRIs in Cooper and Kiger (2003) and Pikulski (1990).

IMPLEMENTING PORTFOLIOS IN THE CLASSROOM

Portfolios are systematic and meaningful collections of artifacts documenting students' language arts learning and development over a period of time (De Fina, 1992; Graves & Sunstein, 1992; Porter & Cleland, 1995). These collections are dynamic and reflect students' day-to-day learning activities in the language arts and across the curriculum. Students' work samples provide "windows" on the strategies that students employ as language users—listeners, speakers, readers, writers, viewers, and visual representers.

There are many reasons why portfolio assessment complements language arts instruction. The most important one is that students become involved in the assessment of their work and are reflective about the quality of their reading, writing, and other language use. Other benefits include the following:

- Students feel ownership of their work.
- Students accept responsibility for their work.
- Students set goals and are motivated to work toward accomplishing them.
- Students reflect on their accomplishments.
- Students make connections between learning and assessing.
- Students' self-esteem is enhanced.
- Students recognize the connection between process and product.

In addition, portfolios eliminate the need to grade all student work. Portfolios are useful in student and parent conferences and complement the information provided in report cards.

Collecting Work in Portfolios. Portfolios are folders, large envelopes, binders, or boxes that hold students' work. Teachers often have students label and decorate large folders and then store them in plastic crates or large cardboard boxes. One teacher with whom we work uses presentation binders for portfolios in her classroom. At the beginning of the school year, she takes and prints digital photographs of each child for the portfolio cover. Students date and label items as they place them in their portfolios, and they attach notes to the items to explain the context of the activity and why they selected that particular item for inclusion in the portfolio. Students' portfolios should be stored in the classroom in a place readily accessible to students. Students review their portfolios periodically and add new pieces to them.

Students usually choose the items to place in their portfolios within the guidelines provided by their teacher. However, teachers may require that particular items be included. Guidelines should take into account all of the six language arts. In addition to the writing and art samples, students also record oral language and drama samples on audiotapes and videos to place in their portfolios. Large-size art and writing projects can be photographed, and the photographs placed in the portfolio. Figure 2–11 lists examples of what might be placed in a portfolio.

Not all work that is placed in a student's portfolio needs to be graded in the same manner that tests are graded. It may be appropriate on some occasions to simply indicate that a piece is "complete" or "satisfactory." Teachers should encourage inclusion of pieces that show process and improvement as well as finished products and "best work."

Many teachers collect students' work in folders, and they assume that portfolios are basically the same as work folders; however, the two types of collections differ in several important ways. Portfolios are student-oriented, whereas work folders are usually teachers' collections. Students choose which samples will be placed in portfolios, while teachers often place all completed assignments in work folders (Clemmons, Lasse, Cooper, Areglado, & Dill, 1993). Next, portfolios focus on students' strengths and growth, not their weaknesses. Because students choose items for portfolios, they choose samples they feel best represent their language development. Finally, the most significant difference is that portfolios involve reflection (D'Aoust, 1992). Through reflection, students become aware of their strengths as readers, writers, and language users. They use their work samples to identify the language arts skills, strategies, procedures, and concepts they already know, and the ones they need to focus on. (Students include written reflections in their portfolios). That is, they become metacognitively aware: They understand not only what they know, but also how they learn and what they need to learn.

Involving Students in Self-Assessment. Portfolios are a useful vehicle for engaging students in self-reflection and goal setting (Clemmons et al., 1993). Students can learn to reflect on and assess their own reading and writing activities, and their development as readers and writers (Stires, 1991a).

Teachers use minilessons and conferences to talk with students about the characteristics of good language users—listeners, readers, writers, storytellers, viewers, and visual representers. For example, they discuss such topics as what good readers do when they encounter unfamiliar words, and what good listeners do to understand what is said. They also discuss such topics as

- How to view a video or CD-ROM or surf a website for information
- What fluent reading is
- How to prepare to give an oral report
- How to locate information when doing research
- How students demonstrate comprehension
- What makes a good project to extend student reading
- How students decide what to write in journals
- How students adapt their writing to their audience
- How students visually represent important concepts

As students learn about what it means to be effective language users, they acquire the tools they need to reflect on and evaluate their own language development. They also acquire the vocabulary to use in their reflections—terms such as *goal*, *strategy*, and *rubric*.

Students write notes on items they choose to put into their portfolios. In these notes, students explain their reasons for the selection and identify strengths and accomplishments in their work. Their notes constitute self-assessment. In some classrooms, students write their reflections and other comments on index cards, while in other classrooms students design special comment sheets that they attach to the items in their portfolios. A grade 5 student chose to put his reading

Listening
- picture or other interpretation of music
- notes of information presented orally
- pictures showing audience for peer report
- drawings or log entries to represent stories listened to on tape
- pictures showing listening at listening station

Speaking
- puppet show (on video)
- oral reports (on audio tape or video)
- cue cards and audio tape of speech or debate

Reading
- reading logs
- oral reading (on audio tape or video)
- readers theatre (on audio tape or video)

Writing
- journal entries
- letters
- poems
- reports
- stories

Viewing
- Venn diagrams comparing stories and film versions
- clusters or semantic maps of information, or story of video
- pictures to interpret video watched
- notes comparing paintings viewed

Visually Representing
- multimedia reports on disc
- Venn diagrams of information read
- timelines or lifelines
- drawings to communicate information
- illustrations to interpret stories

Figure 2–11 Examples of Portfolio Artifacts

All items should be accompanied by a brief explanation of what the artifact represents for student learning and the date it was placed in the portfolio.

log for *Shiloh* (Naylor, 1991) in his portfolio. He wrote this reflection: "I put my journal on the computer. It looks good! I used the SPELCHEK. I put this reading log in my portfolio to show that I can write lots of details like Mrs. Naylor."

Showcasing Students' Portfolios. Sharing students' portfolios has many benefits. In particular, portfolios are valuable to show learning progress to students' families. In many schools, students present their portfolios in three-way conferences—teacher, student, and parents—as part of the regular reporting procedures. Parents examine samples of daily work accompanied by the students' self-assessment to see their strengths and areas of need as language users. Portfolios provide evidence to support the grades and teachers' comments on report cards.

Another use of portfolios concerns a wider audience. At the end of the school year, many teachers organize Portfolio Share Days to celebrate students' accomplishments and to provide an opportunity for students to share their portfolios with classmates and the wider community (Porter & Cleland, 1995). Family members, local business people and politicians, school administrators, student teachers, and others are often invited to attend. Students and community members form small groups, and students share their portfolios, pointing out their accomplishments and strengths. This activity involves community members in the school and shows them how students participate in the language arts as they become effective readers, writers, and language users.

ASSIGNING GRADES

Assigning grades is one of the most difficult responsibilities placed on teachers. "Grading is a fact of life," according to Donald Graves (1983, p. 93), but he adds that teachers should use grades to encourage students, not to hinder their achievement. The authentic assessment procedures described in this chapter are meaningful and encourage students because they document how students are using the language arts in authentic ways. Reviewing and translating this documentation into grades is the difficult part.

Assignment Checklists. Students can keep track of assignments by using checklists. Teachers create assignment checklists as they plan a unit, giving students a copy of the checklist at the beginning of the unit to keep in their unit folder. Then, as they complete the assignments, students check them off, sometimes adding notes of their reflections about their learning while doing the assignment. Checklists help both students and teachers make periodic checks of student progress toward completion of unit activities and assignments.

A checklist for a grade 2 thematic unit on hermit crabs is presented in Figure 2–12. Eight assignments included on the checklist include both science and language arts activities. Students put a check in the boxes in the "Student's Check" column when they complete each assignment, and the teacher adds the grade in the right-hand column. Some assignments will be graded as simply "completed" and others will be graded for quality. When teachers grade for quality, they explain the criteria to students and provide them with a written description of the criteria such as in the rubrics discussed below. The checklists in Figure 2–12 refer only to completion of projects and assignments.

Teachers of middle- and upper-grade students often assign points to each activity in the unit checklist so that the total point value for the unit is 100 points. Activities that involve more time and effort and relate directly to unit goals earn more points. The second checklist in Figure 2–12 is for a grade 5 resource-based unit on *Number the Stars* (Lowry, 1989). The point value for each activity is listed in parentheses. Students write check marks on the lines on the left side of the grading sheet, and the teacher marks the numerical grades on the right side.

Rubrics. Teachers and students develop rubrics, or scoring guides, to assess students' growth as writers (Farr & Tone, 1994). Rubrics make the analysis of writing simpler and the assessment process more reliable and consistent. Rubrics may have three, four, five, or six levels, with descriptors related to ideas, organization, language, and mechanics at each level. Some rubrics are general and appropriate for almost any writing project, while others are designed for a specific writing assignment. Figure 2–13 on pages 82–83 presents two rubrics. One is a general five-level writing rubric for middle-grade students, and the other is a four-level rubric for assessing grade 6 students' reports on ancient Egypt. In contrast to the general rubric, the report rubric includes specific components that students were to include in their reports. Many websites offer helpful assistance with creating rubrics tailored to your goals and projects. One such website, which classroom teachers we know find easy to use, is **http://teach-nology.com/web_tools/rubrics**.

Teachers and students can assess writing with rubrics. They read the composition and highlight words or check statements in the rubric that best describe the composition. It is important to note that rarely are all the highlighted words or checked statements at the same level. Examine the

---

Checklist for Thematic Unit on Hermit Crabs

Name _____   Begin _____
                                   End _____

	Student's Check	Teacher's Check

1. Keep an observation log on the hermit crab on your table for 10 days. ☐ ____
2. Make a chart of a hermit crab and label the parts. ☐ ____
3. Make a map of the hermit crab's habitat. ☐ ____
4. Read three books about hermit crabs and do quickwrites about them. ☐ ____
   _____ Hermit Crabs
   _____ A House for Hermit Crab
   _____ Is This a House for Hermit Crab?
5. Do two science experiments and write lab reports. ☐ ____
   _____ Wet–Dry Experiment
   _____ Light–Dark Experiment
6. Write about hermit crabs. Do one: ☐ ____
   _____ All About Hermit Crabs book
   _____ A poem about hermit crabs
   _____ A story about hermit crabs
7. Do a project about hermit crabs. Share it. ☐ ____
8. Keep everything neatly in your hermit crab folder. ☐

Number the Stars Grading Sheet

Name _____   Date _____

____ 1. Read *Number the Stars*. ____
____ 2. Write 5 entries in a reading log or simulated journal. (25) ____
____ 3. Talk about your reading in five grand conversations. (25) ____
____ 4. Make a Venn diagram to compare characters. Summarize what you learned from the diagram in an essay. (10)
____ 5. Make a cluster about one word on the word wall. (5) ____
____ 6. Make a square with a favourite quote for the story quilt. (10) ____
____ 7. Do a response project. (25) ____
Total (100) ____

Figure 2–12 Two Assignment Checklists

highlighted words or checked statements to determine the score and which level best represents the quality of the composition.

To assess students' learning fairly and systematically, teachers should use at least three assessment approaches. Approaching evaluation from three viewpoints is called *triangulation*. Triangulation of assessment data fosters accurate and reliable evaluation. Using a variety of

Middle-Grade Writing Rubric
5 EXCEPTIONAL ACHIEVEMENT
• Creative and original • Clear organization • Precise word choice and figurative language • Sophisticated sentences • Essentially free of mechanical errors
4 EXCELLENT ACHIEVEMENT
• Some creativity, but more predictable than an exceptional paper • Definite organization • Good word choice but not figurative language • Varied sentences • Only a few mechanical errors
3 ADEQUATE ACHIEVEMENT
• Predictable paper • Some organization • Adequate word choice • Little variety of sentences and some run-on sentences • Some mechanical errors
2 LIMITED ACHIEVEMENT
• Brief and superficial • Lacks organization • Imprecise language • Incomplete and run-on sentences • Many mechanical errors
1 MINIMAL ACHIEVEMENT
• No ideas communicated • No organization • Inadequate word choice • Sentence fragments • Overwhelming mechanical errors *(continued)*

Figure 2–13 Two Rubrics

techniques enables students to show their strengths and increases the likelihood of the evaluation accurately representing the students' learning, performance, and skills.

Standardized Assessment. Although it is beyond the scope of this text to describe standardized assessment and discuss the topic of setting standards, we would be remiss not to note that most provinces and territories engage in annual assessment of student achievement in the language arts, in particular, reading and writing. Students are required to read narrative and informational text and to respond in both structured and creative ways. They also compose more than one form of writing, showing both their process and their written products.

Rubric for Assessing Reports on Ancient Egypt

4 EXCELLENT REPORT

_____ Three or more chapters with titles
_____ Main idea clearly developed in each chapter
_____ Three or more illustrations
_____ Effective use of Egypt-related words in text and illustrations
_____ Very interesting to read
_____ Very few mechanical errors
_____ Table of contents

3 GOOD REPORT

_____ Three chapters with titles
_____ Main idea somewhat developed in each chapter
_____ Three illustrations
_____ Some Egypt-related words used
_____ Interesting to read
_____ A few mechanical errors
_____ Table of contents

2 AVERAGE REPORT

_____ Three chapters
_____ Main idea identified in each chapter
_____ One or two illustrations
_____ A few Egypt-related words used
_____ Some mechanical errors
_____ Sort of interesting to read
_____ Table of contents

1 POOR REPORT

_____ One or two chapters
_____ Information in each chapter rambles
_____ No illustrations
_____ Very few Egypt-related words used
_____ Many mechanical errors
_____ Hard to read and understand
_____ No table of contents

Figure 2–13 Two Rubrics (_continued_)

The goal of provincial testing is to provide a means of assessing student performance against a standard and to improve student learning. For example, in Alberta reading and writing are assessed in grades 3, 6, and 9; while in Newfoundland and Labrador reading and language skills are assessed in grades 4, 7, 10, and 12. Although policies and practices regarding use and distribution of assessment results vary from province to province, they are generally studied carefully by schools and school jurisdictions to plan their programs. Results are usually shared with parents on the basis of overall grade achievement—not on a per-pupil basis. Standardized tests assess cumulative growth and achievement, not just learning in the grade assessed. It is important, therefore, for teachers of all grades to be guided by their students' results, not just those of the students that write the standardized tests.

Review

This chapter focused on how teachers teach and assess the language arts. Creating a language-rich classroom is an important prerequisite. Teachers plan language arts instruction using three instructional approaches: resource-based units, thematic units, and inquiry-based units. Many teachers implement readers and writers workshops as a way of organizing instruction within these units. Assessment is an integral part of instruction, and should be authentic.

The following key concepts are presented in this chapter:

1. Classrooms should be authentic learning environments that encourage students to use all six language arts.
2. Basal reading programs should not constitute the total language arts program.
3. Teachers collect and use five types of trade books—picture books, chapter books, stories, informational books, and poetry books—related to instructional units.
4. Resource-based focus units include four components: reading, listening, or viewing texts; minilessons; responding; and creative projects.
5. Thematic units are interdisciplinary and integrate language arts with one or more of social studies, science, math, and other curricular areas.
6. Inquiry-based units are based on students' genuine curiosity and include using all of the language arts to discover answers to their questions.
7. Readers workshop components are reading and responding, sharing, and minilessons. Writers workshop components are writing, sharing, and minilessons.
8. Teachers play many roles during language arts instruction, including organizer, facilitator, participant, instructor, model, manager, diagnostician, evaluator, coordinator, and communicator.
9. Students with special learning needs benefit to greater and lesser extents from the same language arts program that other students do, but some adaptations are always necessary.
10. Teachers use authentic assessment procedures, including classroom observations, anecdotal notes, conferences, checklists, portfolios, and rubrics.
11. Teachers assess individual students' use of reading cues and strategies by conducting miscue analysis.
12. Running records and informal reading inventories (IRIs) include miscue analysis procedures.

Extensions

1. Visit an elementary classroom and note which characteristics of a language-rich classroom it exemplifies. What might be changed in the classroom to incorporate other characteristics?
2. Form a literature-sharing club with your peers. For each meeting of the club, choose as your focus one of the following categories of children's literature that were discussed in this chapter: picture books, chapter books, stories, informational books, and poetry books. Hold lively book talks, and take turns presenting to one another examples of Canadian and other award-winning selections.
3. Create an elementary school text set of at least ten books on a social studies or science topic similar to the text sets presented in Figure 2–3 on page 53. Include stories, informational books, and poetry books, if possible.

4. Reflect on the advantages and disadvantages of the three ways to organize for language arts instruction—resource-based units, thematic units, and inquiry-based units—and how you plan to organize your classroom. Write a brief paper about your reflections and your plans.

5. Interview an elementary teacher and ask about the kinds of assessment he or she uses.

6. Through your provincial department of education website, research the practices related to standardized testing of the language arts.

Emergent Literacy

Reading and Writing Connections

Procedure

To teach writing is also to teach reading. When I teach children to write, they also learn skills necessary for both efficient writing and reading.

Perhaps the most important thing I do during the day is writing the "daily message" on the blackboard. Usually we decide together what sentences we want to write, for children are more attentive when they have a say in the content, and when they write about things that interest them. Sometimes we compose a poem, write a thank-you letter, or write about a book I've read to them. As I write words of our chosen sentences on the board, I encourage my students to spell along with me and to answer my questions aloud. Not all are ready to respond orally, but everyone listens and watches. As the younger students gain experience, I'll be hearing their voices too. As we work through our sentences, I explain how our language works: rules of phonics, punctuation, rhyming words, irregular spellings, formation of the letters, and the like. I even throw in the word *derivation* when I think they'll find it interesting. (Remember the French word *beau*? Here it is in *beautiful*!)

"It is a challenge to plan activities for students who are at many levels of development, activities that will help each child achieve success and grow in skills and self-confidence. Group writing followed by individual practice, writing conferences, and sharing with classmates meets this challenge."

Linda Pierce Picciotto
Primary Teacher
South Park School, Victoria, British Columbia

Students learn different things from this collaborative writing, depending upon their readiness. Jamie is learning the names of the letters and to be aware of spaces between words. Some of the things I talk about have no meaning for him at this point, but he won't be required to do a too-difficult worksheet afterwards, and

in certain words I pronounce carefully for them. I always make some positive remarks about their writing progress and I suggest—or ask them to suggest—things to remember the next time they write. Some students need a little encouragement to write more or with more care.

It is easy to see where each child is in his or her writing development when I conference with each one after a writers workshop. By working with individuals, I can help them with exactly the skills they need and make mental notes about certain concepts to emphasize during group writing time.

Often students share their writing with a partner, group, or the entire class. I make sure they are supportive of one another when they make their observations. I teach them that different children develop skills at varying rates and in many ways. All students encourage each other without insults or comparisons. We celebrate our differences and our progress!

hearing about compound words and apostrophes may make them less mysterious later on. Nicky is learning the concept of root words, how to form contractions, spell irregular words, add suffixes to words, and compose interesting and varied sentences.

When we're finished, we read our message as a group. Some days we do a little editing so they can learn that skill and become aware of more descriptive language.

After the group writing process, students have the chance to practise their writing on special "writing workshop" paper. While drawing their pictures, they think about what sentences to print below. If they have trouble coming up with ideas, I ask them to tell me about their drawing. It's easy to develop sentences with this information. I encourage them to start with something other than "this is . . ." to make their message more interesting. I do not help them with the writing process, for I want them to think carefully about the words, to say them quietly, to listen to the sounds, and "feel the letters in their mouths." In the beginning, some only do "pretend writing," or draw strings of letters that have no relationship to sounds. With experience and maturity, they begin to include correct or "good guess" consonants and vowels, start separating words, use more interesting words, write using lowercase letters, and write longer and more complex sentences. Each child works at the level exactly appropriate to his or her own developmental level.

Assessment

When students complete their work, we have a short conference. They read the sentences to me, and we talk a bit about the content. Then I write the sentence in Standard English on the facing page while the students look on and listen as I talk about their use of correct or good guess letters and punctuation. I ask them what additional letters they can hear

Reflections

It is a challenge to plan activities for students who are at many levels of development, activities that will help each child achieve success and grow in skills and self-confidence. Group writing followed by individual practice, writing conferences, and sharing with classmates meets this challenge. It provides the teacher with a wealth of information about the needs of his or her students. In addition, most students enjoy the writers workshop and come to be able to talk about their own growth, and to articulate what they need to focus on to continue their progress, a skill that will help them throughout their years in school and beyond.

Books published by Linda Pierce Picciotto: *Evaluation: A Team Effort.* Toronto: Scholastic Canada, Ltd. 1992. *Learning Together: A Whole Year in a Primary Classroom.* Toronto: Scholastic Canada, Ltd., 1993. *Student-Led Parent Conferences*, New York, NY: Scholastic Inc., 1996.

In a combination grade 2/3 classroom, school-based family literacy activities invite parents to collaborate in learning with their children. Nicholas Armstrong and his mom, Haja, look through Nicholas's portfolio together. The portfolio was developed and maintained in school. During their portfolio conference, parent and child review work in progress, discuss completed assignments, and talk about successes and future learning goals. Portfolios also give parents access to materials that allow them to share in their child's development and performance.

The process of becoming literate begins well before the elementary grades and continues into adulthood, if not throughout life. It used to be that five-year-old children came to kindergarten to be "readied" for reading and writing instruction, which would formally begin in grade 1. The implication was that there was a point in children's development when it was time to begin teaching them to read and write. For those not ready, a variety of "readiness" activities would prepare them for reading and writing. Since the 1970s this view has been discredited by teachers' and researchers' observations (Clay, 1991; Chapman, 2002). The children themselves demonstrated that they could recognize signs and other environmental print, retell stories, scribble letters, invent print-like writing, and listen to stories read aloud to them. Some children even taught themselves to read.

This perspective on how children become literate is known as *emergent literacy*. New Zealand educator Marie Clay is credited with coining the term. Studies from 1966 onward have shaped the current outlook (Clay, 1967; Durkin, 1966; Holdaway, 1979; Snow, Burns, & Griffin (2005); Taylor, 1983; Teale, 1982; Teale & Sulzby, 1989). Now, researchers look at literacy learning from the child's point of view. The age range has been extended to include children as young as 12 or 14 months of age who listen to stories being read aloud, notice labels and signs in their environment, and experiment with a variety of writing tools, such as pencils, crayons, and chalk. The concept of literacy has been broadened to include the cultural and social aspects of language learning, and children's experiences with and understanding of written language are included as part of emergent literacy.

Teale and Sulzby (1989) point out that

- Children begin to learn to read and write very early in life.
- Young children learn the functions of literacy through observing and participating in real-life settings in which reading and writing are used.

To Guide Your Reading

As you read this chapter, prepare to

Describe how teachers can foster young children's interest in literacy

•

Describe how young children develop as readers and writers

•

Explain the teaching strategies teachers use to teach reading and writing to beginning readers and writers

- Young children's reading and writing abilities develop concurrently and interrelatedly through experiences in reading and writing.

- Young children learn through active involvement with literacy materials, by constructing their understanding of reading and writing.

Bainbridge and Malicky (2000) describe young children as active learners who construct their own knowledge about reading and writing with the assistance of parents and other literate persons. These caregivers demonstrate literacy as they read and write (for example, grocery lists), by supplying materials, and by structuring opportunities for children to be involved in reading and writing. The environment is positive, with children experiencing reading and writing in many facets of their everyday lives and observing others engaged in literacy activities.

Fostering Young Children's Interest in Literacy

Most children are introduced to written language before they come to school. Parents and other caregivers read to young children, and the children observe adults reading. They learn to read signs and other environmental print in their community. Children experiment with writing and have adults write for them. They also observe adults writing. When young children come to kindergarten, their knowledge about written language expands quickly as they participate in meaningful, functional, and genuine experiences with reading and writing. Their literacy development depends on an enthusiastic and knowledgeable teacher who shares a love for reading and writing.

Students also grow in their ability to reflect on language. The ability to talk about concepts of language is called *metalinguistics* (Chapman, 2002). Children's ability to think metalinguistically is developed by their experiences with reading and writing (Read, 2005; Templeton & Spivey, 1980).

CONCEPTS ABOUT WRITTEN LANGUAGE

Through experiences in their homes and communities, young children learn that print carries meaning and that reading and writing are used for a variety of purposes. They read menus, write and receive letters, and read (and listen to) stories for enjoyment. Children also learn as they observe parents and teachers using written language.

While reading and writing are part of daily life for almost every household, families use written language for different purposes in different communities (Heath, 1983b). It is important to realize that children have a wide range of literacy experiences in both middle- and working-class families, even though those experiences might be different (Taylor, 1983; Taylor & Dorsey-Gaines, 1987). Wells's (1986) extensive study of language development showed that, contrary to previous research findings, children from working-class families did not show impoverished language use. In some communities written language is used mainly as a tool for practical purposes such as paying bills, and in some communities reading and writing are also used for leisure-time activities. In other communities, written language serves wider functions, such as debating social and political issues.

Teachers demonstrate the purposes of written language and provide opportunities for students to experiment with reading and writing by

- Posting signs in the classroom
- Making a list of classroom rules
- Using literacy materials in dramatic play centres
- Writing notes to students in the class
- Exchanging messages with classmates
- Reading and writing stories

- Making posters about favourite books
- Labelling classroom items
- Drawing and writing in journals
- Writing morning messages
- Recording questions and information on charts
- Writing notes to parents
- Reading and writing letters to pen pals
- Reading and writing charts and maps

Yet, Bainbridge and Malicky (2000) note that there is a problem with oral language in classrooms when teachers dominate the conversation. In addition, they note that students' classroom talk often lacks the purpose and spontaneity found in language used outside the classroom. This occurs when language is separated from its normal usage by being put on white boards, in worksheets, and in workbooks. In some classrooms, the focus is on students' role to learn language at the expense of their actually using it. (Hall, 1998).

Concept of a Word. Children's understanding of the concept of a "word" is an important part of becoming literate. Young children have only vague notions of language terms, such as *word, letter, sound,* and *sentence* (Downing, 1971–1972). Researchers have found that young children move through several levels of awareness and understanding about this terminology during the primary grades (Downing & Oliver, 1973–1974).

Preschoolers equate words with the objects they represent. As they are introduced to reading and writing experiences, children begin to differentiate between objects and words, and finally come to appreciate that words have meanings of their own. Templeton (1980) explains children's development with these two examples:

> When asked if "dog" were a word, a four-year-old acquaintance of mine jumped up from the floor, began barking ferociously, and charged through the house, alternatively panting and woofing. Confronted with the same question, an eight-year-old friend responded "of course 'dog' is a word," and went on to explain how the spelling represented spoken sounds and how the word dog stood for a particular type of animal. (p. 454)

Papandropoulou and Sinclair (1974) identified four stages of word consciousness. At the first level, young children do not differentiate between words and things. At the next level, children describe words as labels for things. They consider words that stand for objects as words, but do not classify articles and prepositions as words because they cannot be represented by objects. At the third level, children understand that words carry meaning and that stories are built from words. At the fourth level, more fluent readers and writers describe words as autonomous elements having meanings of their own with definite semantic and syntactic relationships. Children might say, "You make words with letters." Also, at this level children understand that words can be spoken, listened to, read, and written.

Environmental Print. In reading, children move from recognizing environmental print to reading decontextualized words in books. Many young children begin reading by recognizing logos on fast-food restaurants, department stores, supermarkets, and commonly used household items within familiar contexts (Harste, Woodward, & Burke, 1984b). They recognize the golden arches of McDonald's and say "McDonald's," but when they are shown the word *McDonald's* written on a sheet of paper without the familiar sign and restaurant setting, they cannot read the word. Researchers have found that young emergent readers depend on context to read familiar words and memorized texts (Dyson, 1984; Sulzby, 1985b). Slowly, children develop relationships linking form and meaning as they learn concepts about written language.

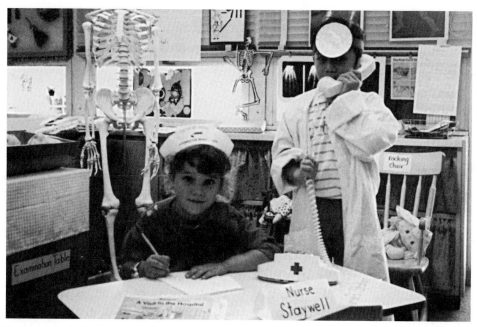

Kindergarten students use reading and writing in this doctor's office dramatic play centre.

When children begin writing, they use scribbles or single letters to represent complex ideas (Clay, 1991; Schickedanz, 1990). As they learn about letter names and phoneme–grapheme correspondences, they use one, two, or three letters to stand for a word. At first they run their writing together, but they slowly learn to segment words and leave spaces between words. They sometimes add dots or lines as markers between words, or they draw circles around words. They also move from capitalizing words randomly to using a capital letter at the beginning of a sentence and to mark proper nouns. Similarly, children move from using periods at the end of each line of writing to marking the ends of sentences with periods. Then they learn about other end-of-sentence markers and, finally, punctuation marks that are embedded in sentences.

Dramatic Play Centres. Young children learn about the functions of reading and writing as they use written language in their play. As they construct block buildings, children write signs and tape them on the buildings; as they play doctor, they write prescriptions on slips of paper; and as they play teacher, they read stories aloud to friends who are pretending to be students or to doll and stuffed-animal "students." Hall (1998) describes a garage centre set up in a kindergarten to coordinate with the school theme of transportation. The students engaged in a variety of literacy experiences throughout their play in the garage, including composing thank-you letters, writing lists of things needed in the garage, reading and writing rules for play in the garage centre, writing estimates for repairs, filling out application forms to work in the garage, and writing invitations for the grand opening of the garage centre.

For more information on the power of drama as a learning tool in the language arts, see Chapter 10, "The Language Arts and the Fine Arts," pages 412–425.

Housekeeping centres are probably the most common play centres in primary classrooms, but these centres can be easily transformed into a grocery store, a post office, or a medical centre by changing the props. Materials for reading and writing are included in each of these play centres. Food packages, price stickers, and money are props in grocery store centres; letters, stamps, and mailboxes in post office centres; and appointment books, prescription pads, and folders for patient records in medical centres. A variety of dramatic play centres can be set up in classrooms to coordinate with units and themes. Ideas for five dramatic play centres and related props are offered in Figure 3–1 on page 92. Each centre includes authentic literacy materials.

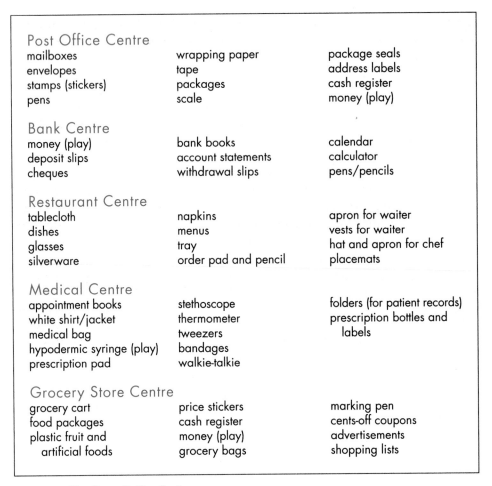

Post Office Centre

mailboxes	wrapping paper	package seals
envelopes	tape	address labels
stamps (stickers)	packages	cash register
pens	scale	money (play)

Bank Centre

money (play)	bank books	calendar
deposit slips	account statements	calculator
cheques	withdrawal slips	pens/pencils

Restaurant Centre

tablecloth	napkins	apron for waiter
dishes	menus	vests for waiter
glasses	tray	hat and apron for chef
silverware	order pad and pencil	placemats

Medical Centre

appointment books	stethoscope	folders (for patient records)
white shirt/jacket	thermometer	prescription bottles and
medical bag	tweezers	labels
hypodermic syringe (play)	bandages	
prescription pad	walkie-talkie	

Grocery Store Centre

grocery cart	price stickers	marking pen
food packages	cash register	cents-off coupons
plastic fruit and	money (play)	advertisements
artificial foods	grocery bags	shopping lists

Figure 3–1 Five Dramatic Play Centres

CONCEPTS ABOUT THE ALPHABET

Young children develop concepts about the alphabet and how letters are used to represent phonemes, referred to as *phonemic awareness* (Adams, 1994; Chapman, 2002). Children use phonemic awareness to decode unfamiliar words as they read and to create spellings for words as they write. Effective primary teachers foster phonemic awareness development using "play" activities such as singing, playing rhyming games and reading rhyming books by authors like Phoebe Gilman and Shel Silverstein, clapping out syllables of names and words, and doing finger plays (Stewart, 2004). Often it is assumed that phonemic awareness instruction is the most important component of the reading program for young children, but phonology is only one of the four language systems. Emergent readers and writers use all four language systems as well as their knowledge about written language concepts as they read and write.

For more information on the four language systems, see Chapter 1, "Learning and the Language Arts," pages 10–14.

The Alphabetic Principle. The one-to-one correspondence between the phonemes (or sounds) and graphemes (or letters), such that each letter consistently represents one sound, is known as the *alphabetic principle*. In phonetic languages, there is a one-to-one correspondence; however, English is not a purely phonetic language. The 26 letters represent approximately 44 phonemes, and three letters—*c*, *q*, and *x*—are superfluous because they do not represent unique phonemes. The letter *c*, for example, can represent either /k/ as in *cat* or /s/ as in *city*, and it can be joined with *h* for the digraph /ch/. To further complicate matters, there are more than 500 spellings to represent the 44 phonemes. Consonants are more consistent and predictable than vowels. Long *e*, for instance, is spelled 14 different ways in common words (Horn, 1957).

Researchers estimate that words are spelled phonetically approximately half the time (Hanna, Hanna, Hodges, & Rudorf, 1966). The nonphonetic spellings of many words reflect morphological information. The word *sign*, for example, is a shortened form of *signature*, and the spelling shows this relationship. Spelling the word phonetically (e.g., *sine*) might seem simpler, but the phonetic spelling lacks semantic information (Venezky, 1970).

Letter Names. The most basic information that children learn about the alphabet is how to identify and form the letters in handwriting (Stanovich, 1998). They notice letters in environmental print and they often learn to sing the ABC song. By the time children enter kindergarten, they usually recognize some letters, especially those in their own names, and in common words in their homes and communities. Children can also write some of these familiar letters.

Young children associate letters with meaningful contexts—names, signs, T-shirts, and cereal boxes. Baghban (1984) notes that the letter *M* was the first letter her daughter noticed. She pointed to *m* in the word *Kmart* and called it "McDonald's." Even though the child confused a store and a restaurant, this account demonstrates how young children make associations with letters. Research suggests that children do not learn alphabet letter names in any particular order or by isolating letters from meaningful written language. Stanovich (1998) points out that while "many children come to kindergarten already knowing letter names, many others do not" (p. 38).

Children become aware that words are composed of letters by reading environmental print and by seeing their own name and the names of family members written. Even when children know the names of several letters and use mock letters as well as real letters in their writing, they have different concepts about letters. For example, Anne Haas Dyson reports that 5-year-old Dexter said, "N spell my grandmama" when his grandmother's name was Helen (1984, p. 262). Emergent readers do not have the same concepts about letters that more accomplished readers have, but they are developing their understanding of the form, the structure and the communicative power of written language (Snow, 2005).

Being able to name the letters of the alphabet is a good predictor of beginning reading achievement, even though being able to cite the alphabet does not directly affect a child's ability to read (Adams, 1994). The speed with which a child can name the letters is also important. The faster the ability to recognize letters, the better (Stanovich, 1998). Children who have been actively involved in reading and writing activities before entering grade 1 know the names of the letters, and are more likely to emerge quickly into reading, if they have not already done so. Teaching children to name the letters without accompanying reading and writing experiences does not have this effect.

Phonemic Awareness. Phonemic awareness (Adams, 1994) is considered to be one cueing system that children use when making sense of text. While it is important to help children understand how language works, such instruction should not lead to isolated skill instruction, separate from meaningful reading and writing experiences. Rather, "Reading is not a decoding activity; it is making sense of written language" (Smith, 1988, p. 2).

In this context, phonemic awareness is children's basic understanding that speech is composed of a series of individual sounds, and it provides the foundation for phonics (Yopp, 1992; Cameron, 1998). When children can choose a duck as the animal that begins with /d/ from a collection of toy animals; identify *duck* and *luck* as two words in a song that rhyme; or blend the sounds /d/, /ŭ/, and /k/ to pronounce *duck*; they are phonemically aware. (Note that the emphasis is on the sounds of spoken words, not reading letters or pronouncing letter names.) Developing phonemic awareness enables children to use sound–symbol correspondences to read and spell words. Phonemic awareness is not sounding out words for reading, nor is it using spelling patterns to write words; rather, it is the foundation for phonics.

Understanding that words are composed of smaller sound units—phonemes—is a significant achievement for young children. Phonemes carry no meaning, and children think of words according to their meanings, not their linguistic characteristics (Griffith & Olson, 1992). When children think about ducks, they think of animals covered with feathers that swim in ponds and make noises we describe as "quacks." They don't think of *duck* as a word with three phonemes or four graphemes, as a word beginning with /d/ and rhyming with *luck*. Phonemic awareness requires that children treat speech as an object and that they shift attention away from the meaning of words to the linguistic features of speech. This focus on phonemes is even more complicated because phonemes are not discrete units in speech. Often they are blended or slurred together in speech. Think about the blended initial sound in *tree* and the ending sound in *eating*.

Children develop phonemic awareness as they sing songs, play with words, interact with word walls, chant rhymes, and listen to parents and teachers read wordplay books to them (Griffith & Olson, 1992). Yopp (1995) recommends that teachers read books with wordplay aloud and encourage students to talk about the books' language. Teachers ask questions and make comments such as, "Did you notice how _____ and _____ rhyme?" and "This book is fun because of all the words beginning with the /m/ sound." Once students are very familiar with the book, they can create new verses or make other variations. Books such as *Mabel Murple* (Fitch, 1995) and *It's Raining Pigs and Noodles* (Prelutsky, 2000) stimulate children to experiment with sounds, create nonsense words, and become enthusiastic about reading. When teachers read books with alliterative or assonant patterns, such as *Zigzag: Zoems for Zindergartens*, children attend to the smaller units of language.

Teachers also teach lessons to help students understand that their speech is composed of sounds (Ball & Blachman, 1991; Lundberg, Frost, & Petersen, 1988; Snow, Dickinson, & Tabors, 2002).

The goal of phonemic awareness activities is to break down and manipulate spoken words. Students who have developed phonemic awareness can

- Match words by sounds
- Isolate a sound in a word
- Blend individual sounds to form a word
- Substitute sounds in a word
- Segment a word into its constituent sounds (Stanovich, 1998)

Teachers teach minilessons focusing on each of these tasks using familiar songs with improvised lyrics, riddles, and guessing games, and wordplay books. These activities should be playful and game-like, and they should be connected to resource-based units and thematic units whenever possible. Five types of phonemic awareness activities are

1. *Sound matching.* Children choose one of several words beginning with a particular sound or say a word that begins with a particular sound (Yopp, 1992). For these games, teachers use familiar objects (e.g., feather, toothbrush, book) and toys (e.g., small plastic animals, toy trucks, artificial fruits and vegetables) as well as pictures of familiar objects. Children also identify rhyming words as part of sound-matching activities. Students name a word that rhymes with a given word and identify rhyming words from familiar songs and stories. As children listen to Jack Prelutsky books such as *For Laughing Out Loud: Poems to Tickle Your Funny Bone* (2001) and other wordplay books, students refine their understanding of rhyme.

2. **Sound isolation.** Students are given a word and are asked to identify the sounds at the beginning, middle, or end of the word. Yopp (1992) created new verses to the tune of "Old MacDonald Had a Farm":

> What's the sound that starts these words:
> Chicken, chin, and cheek?
> (wait for response)
> /ch/ is the sound that starts these words:
> Chicken, chin, and cheek.
> With a /ch/, /ch/ here, and a /ch/, /ch/ there,
> Here a /ch/, there a /ch/, everywhere a /ch/, /ch/.
> /ch/ is the sound that starts these words:
> Chicken, chin, and cheek. (p. 700)

Teachers change the question at the beginning of the verse to focus on medial and final sounds. For example:

> What's the sound in the middle of these words?
> Whale, game, and rain. (p. 700)

And for final sounds:

> What's the sound at the end of these words?
> Leaf, cough, and beef. (p. 700)

Teachers can also set out a tray of objects and ask students to choose the one object that doesn't belong because it doesn't begin with the sound. For example, from a tray with a toy pig, a puppet, a teddy bear, and a pen, the teddy bear doesn't belong.

3. **Sound blending.** Children blend sounds in order to combine them to form a word. For example, children blend the sounds /d/, /ŭ/, and /k/ to form the word *duck*. Teachers can play the "What am I thinking of?" guessing game with children by identifying several characteristics of the item and then saying its name, articulating each of the sounds separately (Yopp, 1992). Then children blend the sounds and identify the word using both the phonological and semantic information that the teacher provided. For example:

> We're studying about the pond, and I am thinking of an animal that lives in the pond when it is young. When it is an adult, it can live on land and it is called a /f/, /r/, /o/, /g/. What is it?

The children blend the sounds to pronounce the word *frog*. In this example, the teacher connects the game with a thematic unit, thereby making the game more meaningful for students.

4. **Sound addition or substitution.** Students play with words and create nonsense words as they add or substitute sounds in words in songs they sing or in books that are read aloud to them. Teachers read wordplay books such as Hutchins's *Don't Forget the Bacon!* (1976), in which a boy leaves for the store with a mental list of four items to buy. As he walks, he repeats his list, substituting words each time. "A cake for tea" changes to "a cape for me" and then to "a rake for leaves." Children suggest other substitutions, such as "a pail for maple sugar trees."

Students can substitute sounds in refrains of songs (Yopp, 1992). For example, students can change the "Ee-igh, ee-igh, oh!" refrain in "Old MacDonald Had a Farm" to "Bee-bigh, bee-bigh, boh!" to focus on the initial /b/ sound. Teachers can choose one sound, such as /sh/, and have children substitute this sound for the beginning sound in their names and in words for items in the classroom. For example, *Jimmy* becomes *Shimmy*, *José* becomes *Shosé*, and the *clock* becomes the *shock*.

5. **Segmentation.** One of the more difficult phonemic awareness activities is segmentation, in which children isolate the sounds in a spoken word (Yopp, 1988). An introductory segmentation

activity is to draw out the beginning sound in words. Children enjoy exaggerating the initial sound in their own names and other familiar words.

Yopp (1992) suggests singing a song to the tune of "Twinkle, Twinkle, Little Star" in which children segment entire words. Here is one example:

Listen, listen
To my word
Then tell me all the sounds you heard: coat
(slowly)
/k/ is one sound
/o/ is two
/t/ is last in coat
It's true. (p. 702)

After several repetitions of the verse segmenting other words, the song ends this way:

Thanks for listening
To my words
And telling all the sounds you heard! (p. 702)

Using the story, the *Three Billy Goats Gruff* (Galdone, 1973b), Winsor and Pearson (1992) suggest a game in which children help animals to cross the ugly troll's bridge by paying a penny for each phoneme in the animals' names. Using toy animals of two, three, and four phonemes and a plastic bridge, children dramatize paying the troll while orally segmenting the words. The child who assists the dog says "d/o/g" and pays three pennies.

Teachers also use Elkonin boxes to teach students to segment words. This activity comes from the work of Russian psychologist D. B. Elkonin (Clay, 1985). As shown in Figure 3–2, the teacher shows an object or picture of an object and draws a series of boxes, with one box for each sound in the name of the object or picture. Then the teacher or a child moves a marker into each box as the sound is pronounced. Children can move small markers onto cards on their desks, or the teacher can draw the boxes on the chalkboard and use tape or small magnets to hold the larger markers in place. Elkonin boxes can also be used for spelling activities. When a child is trying to spell a word, such as *duck*, the teacher can draw three boxes, do the segmenting activity, and then have the child write the letters representing each sound. Spelling boxes for *duck* and other words with two, three, and four sounds are also shown in Figure 3–2.

In all of these activities, students are engaged in experimenting with oral language. During phonemic awareness activities the focus is on speech. However, once children begin reading and writing, these activities reinforce the segmentation and blending activities they have learned. The phonemic awareness activities stimulate children's interest in language and provide valuable experiences with books and words. Some educators have argued that a child must develop phonemic awareness before learning to read; there is strong evidence that phonemic awareness develops as a consequence of learning to read and write (Chapman, 2002).

The relationship among oral language, phonemic awareness, learning to read, and later reading achievement is extremely important. Researchers have concluded that at least some level of phonemic awareness is a prerequisite for learning to read (Tunmer & Nesdale, 1985) and a consequence of learning to read (Stanovich, 1980; Perfetti, Beck, Bell, & Hughes, 1987). As they become phonemically aware, children recognize that speech can be segmented into smaller units, and they use this knowledge to learn about sound–symbol correspondences and spelling patterns. Moreover, research evidence suggests that lack of this knowledge is associated with reading difficulties and reading failure (Busink, 1997).

Furthermore, phonemic awareness has been shown to be the most powerful predictor of later reading achievement (Juel, Griffith, & Gough, 1986; Lomax & McGee, 1987; Snider, 1997; Stanovich, 1998). Klesius, Griffith, and Zielonka (1991) found that children who began first grade

1. The teacher shows students an object or the picture of an object, such as a duck, a bed, a game, a bee, a cup, or a cat.

2. The teacher prepares a diagram with a series of boxes, corresponding to the number of sounds heard in the name of the object. For example, the teacher draws three boxes side by side to represent the three sounds heard in the word *duck*. The teacher can draw the boxes on the chalkboard or on small cards for each child to use. The teacher also prepares markers to place on the boxes.

3. The teacher or students say the word slowly and move markers onto the boxes as each sound is pronounced.

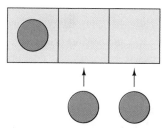

4. Elkonin boxes can also be used when spelling words. The teacher draws a series of boxes corresponding to the number of sounds heard in the word, and then the child and teacher pronounce the word, pointing to each box or sliding markers into each box. Then the child writes the letters representing each sound or spelling pattern in the boxes.

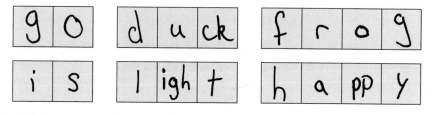

Figure 3–2 How to Use Elkonin Boxes for Segmentation Activities

with strong phonemic awareness did well regardless of the kind of reading instruction they received. No type of instruction was better for children who were low in phonemic awareness at the beginning of grade 1.

Phonics. Phonics is the set of relationships between phonology (the sounds in speech) and orthography (the spelling patterns of written language). Sounds are spelled in different ways. One reason is that the sounds, especially vowels, vary according to their location in a word (e.g., *go, got*). Adjacent letters often influence how letters are pronounced (e.g., *bed, bead*), as do vowel markers such as the final *e* (e.g., *bit, bite*) (Shefelbine, 1995).

Phonics is still a controversial topic. Ken Goodman called it "the most widely misunderstood aspect" of reading instruction (1993, p. 1). Some believe that most of the educational ills concerning reading could be solved if children were taught to read using phonics. A few argue that phonics is a complete reading program, but that view ignores what we know about the interrelatedness of the four language systems. Reading is a complex process, and the phonological system works in conjunction with the semantic, syntactic, and pragmatic systems—not in isolation. Snow, Griffin, and Burns (2005) point out that reading instruction "calls for lessons that model and practice decoding, teaching blending and sound-symbol links, promote generalization, integrate skills in context, and aim toward fluent application to reading connected text" (p. 79).

The controversy centres on how to teach phonics. Marilyn Adams (1994) recommends that phonics be taught within a balanced approach that integrates instruction in reading skills and strategies with meaningful opportunities for reading and writing. Gordon and Donnon (2003) report that a balanced literacy program includes emphasis on phonemic awareness, together with guided and independent literacy activities, shared reading and reading aloud, oral language activities, and modelled/directed independent writing. Phonics instruction should focus on the most useful information for identifying words and be systematic, intensive, and completed by grade 3.

Teachers teach sound–symbol correspondences, how to blend sounds to decode words, how to segment sounds to spell, and the most useful phonics generalizations or "rules." Phonics concepts build on phonemic awareness. The most important concepts that primary-grade students learn are

1. ***Consonants.*** Letters are classified as either consonants or vowels. The consonants are *b, c, d, f, g, h, j, k, l, m, n, p, q, r, s, t, v, w, x, y,* and *z*. Most consonants represent a single sound consistently, but there are some exceptions. For example, *c* does not represent a sound of its own. When it is followed by *a, o,* or *u,* it is pronounced /k/ (e.g., *castle, coffee, cut*) and when it is followed by *e, i,* or *y,* it is pronounced /s/ (e.g., *cell, city, cycle*). *G* represents two sounds, as the word *garage* illustrates. It is usually pronounced /g/ (e.g., *glass, go, green, guppy*), but when *g* is followed by *e* or *i,* it is pronounced /j/, as in *giant. X* is also pronounced differently according to its location in a word. When *x* is at the beginning of a word, it is often pronounced /z/, as in *xylophone,* but sometimes the letter name is used, as in *X-ray.* At the end of a word, *x* is pronounced /ks/, as in *box.*

   The letters *w* and *y* are particularly interesting. At the beginning of a word or a syllable they are consonants (e.g., *wind, yard*), but when they are in the middle or at the end they are vowels (e.g., *saw, flown, day, by*).

   Two kinds of combination consonants are blends and digraphs. Consonant blends are two or three consonants that appear next to each other in words, and their individual sounds are blended together, such as *grass, belt,* and *spring.* Consonant digraphs are letter combinations that represent single sounds. The four most common are *ch* as in *chair* and *each, sh* as in *shell* and *wish, th* as in *father* and *both,* and *wh* as in *whale.* Another consonant digraph is *ph,* as in *graph* and *photo.*

2. ***Vowels.*** The remaining five letters—*a, e, i, o,* and *u*—are vowels, and *w* and *y* are vowels when used in the middle and at the end of syllables and words. Vowels represent several sounds. Short-vowel sounds are /ă/ as in *cat,* /ĕ/ as in *bed,* /ĭ/ as in *win,* /ŏ/ as in *hot,* and /ŭ/ as in *cup.* Long-vowel sounds are the same as the letter names, and they are illustrated in the words *make, feet, bike, coal,* and *mule.* Long vowels are usually spelled with two vowels, except when *y* is used at the end of a word.

   When *y* is a vowel at the end of a word, it is pronounced as long *e* or long *i,* depending on the length of the word. In one-syllable words such as *by* and *try,* the *y* is pronounced as long *i,* but in longer words such as *baby* and *happy,* the *y* is pronounced as long *e.*

When the letter *r* follows one or more vowels in a word, it influences the pronunciation of the vowel sound, as in *car, air, are, ear, bear, first, for, more, murder,* and *pure.* Vowel sounds are more complicated than consonant sounds, and there are additional vowel combinations representing other sounds. These vowel combinations often represent more than one sound and are used in only a few words:

> *au* as in *laugh* and *caught*
> *aw* as in *saw*
> *ew* as in *sew* and *few*
> *oi* as in *oil*
> *oo* as in *cook* and *moon*
> *ou* as in *about* and *through*
> *ow* as in *now*
> *oy* as in *toy*

3. **Rimes and rhymes.** One-syllable words and syllables in longer words can be divided into two parts: the onset and the rime. The *onset* is the consonant sound that precedes the vowel, and the *rime* is the vowel and any consonant sounds that follow it. For example, in *show, sh* is the onset and *ow* is the rime, and in *ball, b* is the onset and *all* is the rime. For *at* and *up,* there is no onset—the entire word is the rime. Research has shown that children make more errors decoding and spelling final consonants than initial consonants and that they make more errors on vowels than on consonants (Treiman, 1985). These problem areas correspond to rimes, and educators now speculate that onsets and rimes could provide the key to unlocking phonemic awareness. This is partly because both the sound and spelling of rimes tend to be fairly predictable (Snow et. al., 2005).

Children can focus their attention on a rime (sometimes referred to as a *word family*), such as *ay,* and create rhyming words, including *bay, day, lay, may, ray, say,* and *way.* These words can be read and spelled by analogy because the vowel sounds are consistent in rimes. Wylie and Durrell (1970) identified thirty-seven rimes that can be used to produce nearly five hundred words that primary-grade students read and write. These rimes and some common words using them are presented in the Teacher's Notebook on page 100.

4. **Blending into words.** Readers "blend," or combine, sounds in order to decode words. Even though children may identify the sounds in a word one by one, they must be able to blend them into a word. For example, in order to read the short-vowel word *best,* children identify /b/, /ĕ/, /s/, and /t/ and then combine them to form the word. For long-vowel words, children must identify the vowel pattern as well as the surrounding letters. In *lake,* for example, children identify /l/, /ā/, and /k/ and recognize that the *e* at the end of the word is silent and marks the preceding vowel as long. Shefelbine (1995) emphasized the importance of blending, and suggested that students who have difficulty decoding words usually know the sound–symbol correspondences but cannot blend the sounds into recognizable words. The ability to blend sounds into words is part of phonemic awareness, and students who have not had practice blending speech sounds into words are likely to have trouble identifying unfamiliar written words.

5. **Phonics generalizations.** Because English does not have a one-to-one correspondence between sounds and letters, both linguists and educators have tried to create rules or generalizations to clarify English spelling patterns. One rule is that *q* is followed by *u* and pronounced /kw/ (e.g., *queen, quick,* and *earthquake*). Another generalization relates to *r*-controlled vowels: *r* influences the preceding vowel so that the sound is neither long nor short (e.g., *car, market, birth,* and *four*). There are exceptions, however, and one example is *fire.* Many generalizations aren't very useful because there are many exceptions to the rule (Clymer, 1996). A good example is this long-vowel rule: when there are two vowels side by side, the long-vowel sound of the first one is pronounced and the second is silent. Teachers

sometimes refer to this as the "when two vowels go walking, the first one does the talking" rule. Examples of words conforming to this rule are *meat*, *soap*, and *each*. There are many exceptions, however, including *food*, *said*, *head*, *chief*, *bread*, *look*, *soup*, *does*, *too*, *again*, and *believe*.

Only a few phonics generalizations have a high degree of utility for readers. Generalizations that work most of the time are the most useful (Adams, 1994). Eight high-utility generalizations are listed in the Teacher's Notebook on page 101. Even though these rules are fairly reliable, very few approach 100 percent utility. The *r*-controlled vowel rule mentioned above has 78 percent utility (Adams, 1990). Other useful rules have even lower percentages of utility. The CVC pattern rule—when a one-syllable word has only one vowel between two consonants, the vowel is usually short, as in *bat*, *land*, and *cup*—is estimated to work 62 percent of the time. Exceptions include *told*, *fall*, *fork*, and *birth*. The CVCe pattern rule—when there are two vowels in a one-syllable word and one vowel is an *e* at the end of the word, the first vowel is long and the final *e* is silent—is estimated to work in 63 percent of CVCe words. Examples of conforming words are *came*, *hole*, and *pipe*, and two common exceptions are *have* and *love*.

Students learn phonics as a natural part of reading and writing activities, and teachers teach minilessons about phonics directly and systematically as part of resource-based units and readers workshop. Teachers often explain phonics concepts as they engage children in authentic literacy activities using children's names, titles of books, and environmental print in the classroom. Teachers answer students' questions about words, and they model using phonics knowledge to decode and spell words, and students share the strategies they use for reading and writing (Mills, O'Keefe, & Stephens, 1992). For example, as part of a resource-based unit on *The Very Hungry Caterpillar*

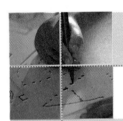

Teacher's Notebook

Thirty-Seven Rimes and Some Common Words Using Them

Rime	Words	Rime	Words
-ack	black, pack, quack, stack	-ide	bride, hide, ride, side
-ail	mail, nail, sail, tail	-ight	bright, fight, light, might
-ain	brain, chain, plain, rain	-ill	fill, hill, kill, will
-ake	cake, shake, take, wake	-in	chin, grin, pin, win
-ale	male, sale, tale, whale	-ine	fine, line, mine, nine
-ame	came, flame, game, name	-ing	king, sing, thing, wing
-an	can, man, pan, than	-ink	pink, sink, think, wink
-ank	bank, drank, sank, thank	-ip	drip, hip, lip, ship
-ap	cap, clap, map, slap	-ir	fir, sir, stir
-ash	cash, dash, flash, trash	-ock	block, clock, knock, sock
-at	bat, cat, rat, that	-oke	choke, joke, poke, woke
-ate	gate, hate, late, plate	-op	chop, drop, hop, shop
-awc	law, draw, jaw, saw	-ore	chore, more, shore, store
-ay	day, play, say, way	-or	for, or
-eat	beat, heat, meat, wheat	-uck	duck, luck, suck, truck
-ell	bell, sell, shell, well	-ug	bug, drug, hug, rug
-est	best, chest, nest, west	-ump	bump, dump, hump, lump
-ice	ice, mice, nice, rice	-unk	bunk, dunk, junk, sunk
-ick	brick, pick, sick, thick		

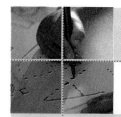

Teacher's Notebook

The Most Useful Phonics Generalizations

Pattern	Description	Examples	
1. Two sounds of c	The letter c can be pronounced as /k/ or /s/. When c is followed by a, o, or u, it is pronounced /k/—the hard c sound. When c is followed by e, i, or y, it is pronounced /s/—the soft c sound.	cat cough cut	cent city cycle
2. Two sounds of g	The sound associated with the letter g depends on the letter following it. When g is followed by a, o, or u, it is pronounced as /g/—the hard g sound. When g is followed by e, i, or y, it is usually /j/—the soft g sound. Exceptions include get and give.	gate go guess	gentle giant gypsy
3. CVC pattern	When a one-syllable word has only one vowel and the vowel comes between two consonants, it is usually short. One exception is told.	bat cup land	
4. Final e or CVCe pattern	When there are two vowels in a one-syllable word and one of them is an e at the end of the word, the first vowel is long and the final e is silent. Two exceptions are have and love.	home safe cute	
5. CV pattern	When a vowel follows a consonant in a one-syllable word, the vowel is long. Exceptions include the, to, and do.	go be	
6. R-controlled vowels	Vowels that are followed by the letter r are overpowered and are neither short nor long. One exception is fire.	car for birthday	
7. -igh	When gh follows i, the i is long and the gh is silent. One exception is neighbour.	high night	
8. Kn- and wr-	In words beginning with kn- and wr-, the first letter is not pronounced.	knee write	

Source: Adapted from Clymer, 1996.

(Carle, 1969), teachers might point out that *Very* begins with *v* but that not many words start with *v*. The teacher and children might list other *v* words, such as *valentine*, on the chalkboard, looking closely at spelling patterns as they are written. Teachers also demonstrate how to segment words and apply phonics information as they read big books with the class and do interactive writing.

Young Children Emerge as Readers

Children move through three stages as they learn to read: emergent reading, beginning reading, and fluent reading (Juel, 1991). In emergent reading, also known as the *selective-cue stage*, children gain an understanding of the communicative purpose of print. They notice environmental print, dictate stories for the teacher to record, and reread predictable books after they have memorized the pattern. From this foundation, children move into the beginning reading stage, known as the *spelling–sound stage*. In this stage, children learn phoneme–grapheme correspondences and begin to decode words. In the fluent reading stage, children have learned how to read, recognize most words automatically, and decode unfamiliar words quickly. They are fluent readers who concentrate their cognitive energy on comprehension.

Primary-grade teachers organize language arts instruction into resource-based units and readers and writers workshops, making special adaptations to accommodate young children's developing literacy abilities. Children in kindergarten, and children in grades 1 and 2, need to listen to books read aloud and to read aloud with classmates through shared reading and other reading approaches.

Children also need opportunities to read some books themselves—independently. Young children often begin by reading books with predictable refrains and repetition of events, and then move on to easy-to-read books to practise decoding and to develop reading fluency. Through a multi-faceted language arts program of literature; daily reading and writing experiences; and instruction in phonics, skills, and strategies; young children develop into fluent readers and writers.

ADAPTING RESOURCE-BASED UNITS FOR EMERGENT READERS

For more information on the five stages of the reading process, see Chapter 4, "The Reading and Writing Processes," pages 127–144.

Kindergarten, grade 1, and grade 2 teachers plan and teach resource-based units using quality books of children's literature, including *Officer Buckle and Gloria* (Rathmann, 1995), *Two by Two* (Reid, 1992), and *If You Give a Mouse a Cookie* (Numeroff, 1985). Teachers use the same five-stage reading process for teaching resource-based units in kindergarten and the primary grades, adapting the stages to make them developmentally appropriate for young children. Teachers involve students in hands-on activities, use shared reading and other strategies, and include minilessons on phonics. Figure 3–3 on page 104 presents an outline for a resource-based unit on Laura Numeroff's *If You Give a Mouse a Cookie*.

Shared Reading. In shared reading, teachers read a book aloud as children follow along in individual books or look at an enlarged version of a picture book, called a *big book*. Teachers use this approach to share with students the enjoyment of high-quality literature when students cannot read the books independently (Holdaway, 1979). Teachers use the big book to read with children rather than to children (Bainbridge & Malicky, 2000; Morrow, 2005). Through shared reading, teachers demonstrate how print works, provide opportunities for students to use the prediction strategy, and increase children's confidence in their ability to read. Teachers also use shared reading with older students who cannot read the shared book independently. The steps in shared reading are explained in the accompanying Step by Step box.

Predictable Books. The stories and other books used for shared reading with young children often have repeated words and sentences, rhyme, or other patterns. Books that use these patterns, known as *predictable books*, make a valuable tool for emergent readers because the repetition enables children to predict the next sentence or episode in the story (Heald-Taylor, 1987; Tompkins & Webeler, 1983). Four characteristics of predictable books are

1. **Repetition.** In some books, phrases and sentences are repeated over and over. Examples include *The Doorbell Rang* (Hutchins, 1986), *Barnyard Banter* (Fleming, 1994), and *Polar Bear, Polar Bear, What Do You Hear?* (Martin, 1992). Sometimes, each episode or section of the text ends with the same words or a refrain; other times, the same statement or question is repeated. For example, in *The Little Red Hen* (Galdone, 1973a), the animals repeat "Not I" when the Little Red Hen asks them to help her plant the seeds, harvest the wheat, and bake the bread. After their refusals, the hen each time says, "Then I will."

2. **Cumulative sequence.** In some books, phrases or sentences are repeated and expanded in each episode. In *The Gingerbread Boy* (Galdone, 1975), for example, the Gingerbread Boy repeats and expands his boast as he meets each character. Other examples include *We're Going on a Picnic* (Hutchins, 2002) and *Jump, Frog, Jump* (Kalan, 1995).

Step by Step

Shared Reading

1. *Introduce the book.*   The teacher introduces the book by activating children's prior knowledge about the topic or by presenting new information on a topic related to the book, and then by showing the cover of the book and reading the title and author. Then children make predictions about the book. The purpose of these introductory activities is to involve children in the reading activity and to build their anticipation.

2. *Read the book.*   The teacher reads the book aloud while children follow along in individual copies of the book or on a big book positioned on a chart stand beside the teacher. The teacher models fluent reading and uses a dramatic style to keep the children's attention. The teacher encourages children to chime in on words they can predict and for phrases, sentences, and refrains that are repeated. Periodically, the teacher stops to ask the children to make predictions about the story or to redirect their attention to the text.

3. *Have children respond to the book.*   Children respond to the book by drawing and writing in reading logs and by sharing their responses in a grand conversation. Whenever children read books, enjoyment is the first and foremost goal. Afterwards, they use the book to learn more about written language.

4. *Reread the book.*   Children and the teacher read the book again together in a group, and children reread the book independently or with partners. Children need to read the book several times in order to become comfortable with the text.

5. *Teach minilessons.*   The teacher uses the book as the basis for minilessons to explore letters, words, and sentences in the text. Minilessons may also focus on rhyme, word-identification strategies, and reading procedures, concepts, strategies, and skills.

6. *Create projects.*   Children extend their understanding of the book through other reading and talking activities and through drama, technology, and writing projects.

3. **Rhyme and rhythm.** Rhyme and rhythm are important devices in some books. Sentences have a strong beat, and rhyme is used at the end of each line or in another poetic scheme. Some books have an internal rhyme within lines. Books in this category include Dr. Seuss's *Hop on Pop* (1963), *Row, Row, Row Your Boat* (Muller, 1993), and *Sarah Saw a Blue Macaw* (Bogart, 1991).

4. **Sequential patterns.** Some books use a familiar sequence—such as months of the year, days of the week, numbers 1 to 10, or letters of the alphabet—to structure the text. For example, *The Very Hungry Caterpillar* (Carle, 1969) combines number and day-of-the-week sequences as the caterpillar eats through an amazing array of foods. Laura Numeroff's *If You Give a Mouse a Cookie* (1985) and Martyn Godfrey's *Is It OK If This Monster Stays for Lunch?* (1992) are two other examples.

A list of predictable books illustrating each of these patterns is presented in Figure 3–4 on pages 105–106.

Big Books. Teachers use enlarged picture books called *big books* in shared reading, most commonly with primary-grade students. In this approach, developed in New Zealand, teachers use a big book placed on an easel or chart stand where all children can see it; the teacher reads the big book with

1. Preparing
- The teacher brings in several types of cookies for children to sample. Students talk about their favourite cookies, and they create a graph and chart their favourite cookies.
- The teacher introduces the book using a big book version of the story.
- The teacher shares a book box of objects mentioned in the story (cookie, glass of milk, straw, napkin, mirror, scissors, broom, etc.), and children talk about how some of the items might be used in the story.
- Students and the teacher begin making a word wall with cookie and mouse.

2. Reading
- The teacher reads the big book version of *If You Give a Mouse a Cookie* using shared reading.
- The teacher rereads the book, and students join in reading and use echo reading to repeat each sentence after the teacher reads it.

3. Responding
- The students and teacher participate in a grand conversation about the book.
- Students dramatize the story using objects in the book box.
- Students draw pictures in reading logs and add words (using invented spelling) to record their reactions to the book.

4. Exploring
- Students and teacher add interesting and important words to the word wall.
- Students buddy-read small-size versions of the book with partners and reread the book independently.
- The teacher teaches minilessons on the /m/ sound or other phonemic awareness or phonics concepts.
- The teacher explains the concept of a circle story, and students sequence picture cards of the events in the story to make a circle diagram.
- The teacher presents a minilesson about the author, Laura Numeroff, and reads other books by the author.
- Students make word posters of words on the word wall.
- The teacher teaches a minilesson on irregular plurals (e.g., *mouse–mice, child–children*).
- The teacher sets up centres for students to sort objects related to the phonics lesson, and gives students opportunities to listen to a tape recorded version of *If You Give a Moose a Muffin* (Numeroff, 1991), write books about cookies, and use cards to sequence story events.

5. Extending
- Students write their own versions of the story or original stories.
- Students create other projects.
- Students share their complete projects from the author's chair.

Figure 3–3 Outline for a Resource-Based Unit on *If You Give a Mouse a Cookie*

small groups of children or with the whole class (Holdaway, 1979). Trachtenburg and Ferruggia (1989) found that making and reading big books dramatically improved children's reading scores on standardized achievement tests. Children's self-concepts as readers were decidedly improved as well.

Many popular picture books, including *Red Is Best* (Stinson, 1984), *The New Baby Calf* (Chase & Reid, 1984), *Wilfrid Gordon McDonald Partridge* (Fox, 1988), *The Mitten* (Brett, 1989), *Rosie's Walk* (Hutchins, 1987), and *Eating the Alphabet: Fruits and Vegetables From A to Z* (Ehlert, 1994), are available in big book editions. Teachers can also make big books themselves by printing the text of a picture book on large sheets of posterboard and adding illustrations. The steps in making a big book are shown in Figure 3–5 on pages 107–108.

Repetitive Sentences

Bennett, J. (1985). *Teeny Tiny*. New York: Putnam.

Bennett, J. (2000). *Jason Mason Middleton-Tap.* Vancouver: Raincoast. 🍁

Carle, E. (1973). *Have You Seen My Cat?* New York: Philomel.

Carle, E. (1984). *The Very Busy Spider*. New York: Philomel.

Carle, E. (1990). *The Very Quiet Cricket*. New York: Philomel.

Carle, E. (1995). *The Very Lonely Firefly*. New York: Philomel.

Cohen, C. L. (1996). *Where's the Fly?* New York: Greenwillow.

Fleming, D. (1994). *Barnyard Banter*. New York: Henry Holt.

Galdone, P. (1973). *The Little Red Hen*. New York: Seabury.

Guarino, D. (1989). *Is Your Mama a Llama?* New York: Scholastic.

Hill, E. (1980). *Where's Spot?* New York: Putnam.

Hutchins, P. (1972). *Good-night, Owl!* New York: Macmillan.

Hutchins, P. (1986). *The Doorbell Rang.* New York: Morrow.

Kovalski, M. (1987). *The Wheels on the Bus.* Boston: Little, Brown.

Lyon, G. E. (1989). *Together*. New York: Orchard.

Martin, B., Jr. (1983). *Brown Bear, Brown Bear, What Do You See?* New York: Holt, Rinehart & Winston.

Martin, B., Jr. (1992). *Polar Bear, Polar Bear, What Do You Hear?* New York: Holt, Rinehart & Winston.

Peek, M. (1985). *Mary Wore Her Red Dress*. New York: Clarion.

Rosen, M. (1989). *We're Going on a Bear Hunt*. New York: Macmillan.

Souhami, J. (1996). *Old MacDonald*. New York: Orchard.

Stinson, K. (1984). *Red Is Best*. Toronto: Annick Press. 🍁

Stinson, K. (1985). *Those Green Things*. Toronto: Annick Press. 🍁

Stinson, K. (1991). *Who Is Sleeping in Aunty's Bed?* Toronto: Oxford University Press. 🍁

Viorst, J. (1972). *Alexander and the Terrible, Horrible, No Good, Very Bad Day*. New York: Atheneum.

Weiss, N. (1987). *If You're Happy and You Know It.* New York: Greenwillow.

Weiss, N. (1989). *Where Does the Brown Bear Go?* New York: Viking.

Westcott, N. B. (1988). *The Lady with the Alligator Purse*. Boston: Little, Brown.

Williams, S. (1989). *I Went Walking*. San Diego: Harcourt Brace Jovanovich.

Repetitive Sentences in a Cumulative Sequence

Beck, A. (2002). *Elliot Gets Stuck*. Toronto: Kids Can Press. 🍁

Brett, J. (1989). *The Mitten*. New York: Putnam.

Fox, H. (1986). *Hattie and the Fox*. New York: Bradbury.

Galdone, P. (1975). *The Gingerbread Boy*. New York: Seabury.

Kalan, R. (1995). *Jump, Frog, Jump!* New York: Greenwillow.

Litzinger, R. (1993). *The Old Woman and Her Pig*. New York: Harcourt Brace Jovanovich.

Neitzel, S. (1989). *The Jacket That I Wear in the Snow*. New York: Greenwillow.

Thomas, S. M. (1995). *Putting the World to Sleep*. Boston: Houghton Mifflin.

West, C. (1996). *"I Don't Care!" Said the Bear*. Cambridge, MA: Candlewick.

Westcott, N. B. (1980). *I Know an Old Lady Who Swallowed a Fly*. Boston: Little, Brown.

Westcott, N. B. (1990). *There's a Hole in the Bucket*. New York: HarperCollins.

Zemach, M. (1983). *The Little Red Hen*. New York: Farrar, Straus & Giroux.

(continued)

Figure 3–4 Books with Predictable Patterns

Rhyme and Rhythm

de Paola, T. (1985). *Hey Diddle Diddle and Other Mother Goose Rhymes*. New York: Putnam.

Fitch, S. (1992). *There Were Monkeys in My Kitchen*. Toronto: Doubleday Canada. ✦

Gilman, P. (1994). *Jillian Jiggs to the Rescue*. Richmond Hill: Scholastic Canada. ✦

Lee, D. (2001). *The Cat and the Wizard*. Toronto: Key Porter Books. ✦

Muller, R. (1992). *Hickory, Dickory, Dock*. Richmond Hill: Scholastic Canada. ✦

Sendak, M. (1962). *Chicken Soup with Rice*. New York: Harper & Row.

Seuss, Dr. (1963). *Hop on Pop*. New York: Random House.

Sequential Patterns

Carle, E. (1969). *The Very Hungry Caterpillar*. Cleveland: Collins-World.

Carle, E. (1987). *A House for a Hermit Crab*. Saxonville, MA: Picture Book Studio.

Galdone, P. (1986). *Over in the Meadow*. New York: Simon & Schuster.

Godfrey, M. (1992). *Is It OK If This Monster Stays for Lunch?* Toronto: Oxford University Press. ✦

Keats, E. J. (1972). *Over in the Meadow*. New York: Scholastic.

Kingsley, C. (2001). *Ten Little Puppies*. Toronto: Fitzhenry & Whiteside. ✦

Martin, B., Jr. (1970). *Monday, Monday, I Like Monday*. New York: Holt, Rinehart & Winston.

Numeroff, L. J. (1985). *If You Give a Mouse a Cookie*. New York: HarperCollins.

Numeroff, L. J. (1991). *If you Give a Moose a Muffin*. New York: HarperCollins.

Sendak, M. (1975). *Seven Little Monsters*. New York: Harper & Row.

Wood, A. (1984). *The Napping House*. San Diego: Harcourt Brace Jovanovich.

Figure 3–4 Books with Predictable Patterns (*continued*)

Almost any type of picture book can be turned into a big book, but predictable books, nursery rhymes, songs, and poems are most popular. Heald-Taylor (1987) lists types of big books that teachers can make:

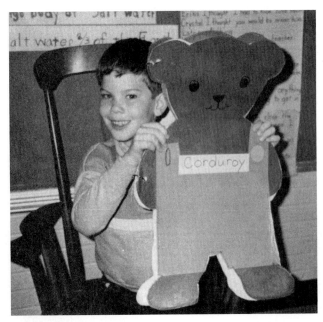

A grade 1 student holds up a class big book to retell the story of *Corduroy*.

- Replica book—an exact copy of a picture book
- Newly illustrated book—a familiar book with new illustrations
- Adapted book—a new version of a familiar picture book
- Original book—an original book composed by students or the teacher

With the big book on a chart stand or an easel, the teacher reads it aloud, pointing to every word. Before long, students join in the reading. Then the teacher rereads the book, inviting students to help with the reading. The next time the book is read, the teacher reads to the point that the text becomes predictable, such as the last word of a sentence or the beginning of a refrain, and the students supply the missing text. Having students supply missing text is important because it leads to independent reading. Once students have become familiar with the text, they read the big book independently or to each other.

Following the same steps as teachers use, students can also make big books. They can make big books of favourite stories, of retellings of stories they know, or of stories they create. Young children will need assistance. They can dictate their stories to older students or classroom assistants. The story texts can be word-processed and printed using a large-point-size font. The children can illustrate each page. Finally, a title page can be added and the book bound, ready for classroom use.

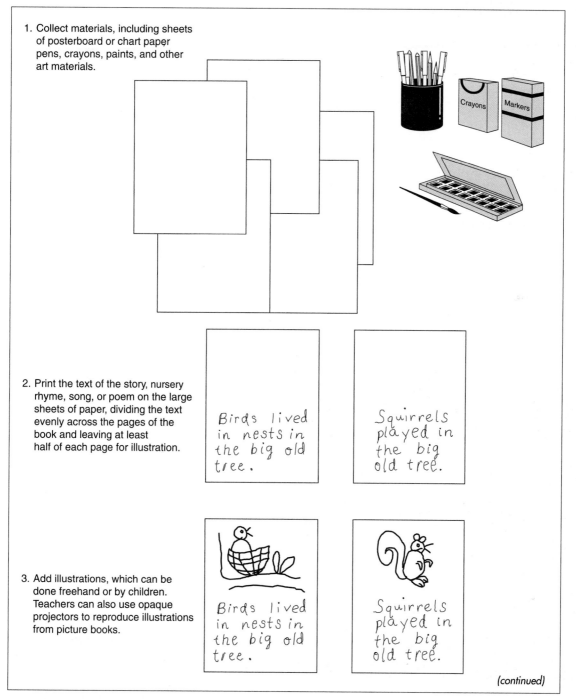

1. Collect materials, including sheets of posterboard or chart paper pens, crayons, paints, and other art materials.

2. Print the text of the story, nursery rhyme, song, or poem on the large sheets of paper, dividing the text evenly across the pages of the book and leaving at least half of each page for illustration.

Birds lived in nests in the big old tree.

Squirrels played in the big old tree.

3. Add illustrations, which can be done freehand or by children. Teachers can also use opaque projectors to reproduce illustrations from picture books.

Birds lived in nests in the big old tree.

Squirrels played in the big old tree.

(continued)

Figure 3–5 Steps in Constructing a Big Book

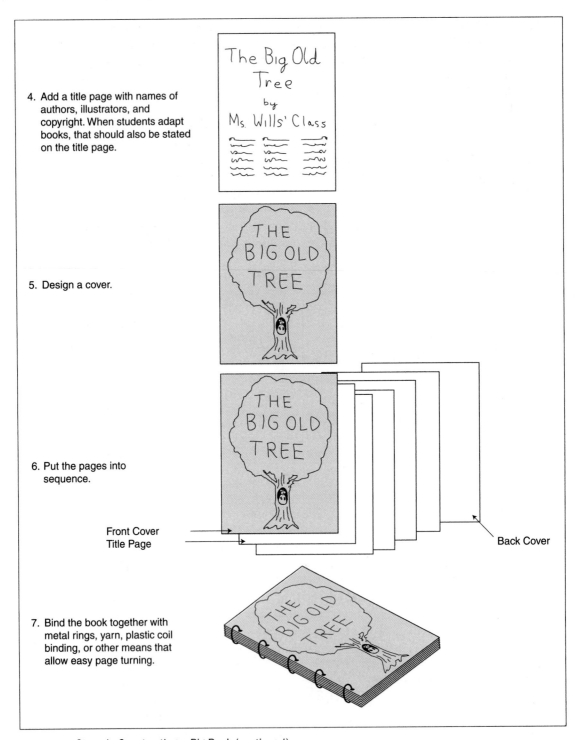

4. Add a title page with names of authors, illustrators, and copyright. When students adapt books, that should also be stated on the title page.

5. Design a cover.

6. Put the pages into sequence.

Front Cover
Title Page

Back Cover

7. Bind the book together with metal rings, yarn, plastic coil binding, or other means that allow easy page turning.

Figure 3–5 Steps in Constructing a Big Book *(continued)*

ADAPTING READERS WORKSHOP FOR EMERGENT READERS

Even emergent readers can participate in a readers workshop. Like all students, young children need opportunities to look at books, reread favourite stories, and explore new texts. Young children read and reread many predictable books and read easy-to-read books with decodable words and familiar sight words, such as *Row, Row, Row Your Boat* (Muller, 1993), *Red Is Best* (Stinson,

1982), and *The Josefina Story Quilt* (Coerr, 1986). As they read and reread books, children gain valuable experience, develop concepts about print, and practise decoding words. Providing daily opportunities for children to practise reading and rereading books they have chosen themselves is an essential part of literacy development.

Children in kindergarten and others who are not yet reading can look at books, too. Teachers begin by demonstrating how to look at both familiar and unfamiliar books. For familiar books, teachers demonstrate how to think about the book, and how to remember the title, characters, or plot. Then teachers model how to turn the pages and think aloud about the story, recreating it in their minds. For unfamiliar books, teachers show children how to carefully examine the illustrations and create a probable text for the books. Without this training, young children often flip through a book without looking at each page and developing an appreciation for the book.

Researchers Fountas and Pinnell (2000) advocate the use of guided reading in small groups during readers workshops. Guided reading helps students develop as individual readers; it helps students use reading strategies that enable them to read at progressing levels of difficulty.

OTHER TEACHING STRATEGIES

Two other strategies teachers use with young children are assisted reading and the language experience approach. These teaching strategies are more personal, based on children's own experience and language, and more closely approximate the literacy activities that go on at home. They are both useful for older nonreaders, too.

Assisted Reading. Assisted reading extends the familiar routine of parents reading to their children (Bright, McMullin, & Platt, 1999). In this approach, a child and a teacher (or another fluent reader) sit together to read a book. As the teacher reads aloud, the child listens and looks at the illustrations in the book. Gradually the child assumes more and more of the reading until the child does most of the reading and the teacher fills in the difficult words. The three stages in assisted reading are

1. *Reading to children.* Teachers read to children and have them repeat each phrase or sentence. At first, most children's attention will not be on the lines of print as they repeat the words. To direct their attention to the lines of print, the teacher points to the words on each line as they are read. This allows children to see that lines of print are read from left to right, not randomly. Many different books are read and reread during this stage.

    Rereading is important because the visual images of the words must be seen and read many times to ensure their recognition in other books. Later, one repetition of a word may be sufficient for subsequent recognition of the word in context.

2. *Shared reading.* When children begin to notice that some words occur repeatedly from book to book, they enter the second stage of assisted reading. In this stage the teacher reads and children repeat or echo the words; however, the teacher omits the words the children seem to recognize, and the children fill them in. The fluency, or flow, of the reading should not be interrupted. If fluency is not maintained during this stage, children will not grasp the meaning of the passage, because the syntactic and semantic cues that come from a smooth flow of language will not be evident to them.

3. *Becoming independent readers.* The transition to the third stage occurs when children begin to ask the teacher to let them read the words themselves. Stage three may be initiated by the child, or may be introduced by the teacher. When children know enough words to do the initial reading themselves, they read and the teacher willingly supplies any unknown words. It is important to assist children so that the fluency of the reading is not disrupted. In this stage, children do the major portion of the reading, but they tire more easily because

they are struggling to use all the information they have acquired about written language. Children at this stage need constant encouragement; they must not feel a sense of frustration, because moving to independent reading is a gradual process.

Figure 3–6 presents a list of easy-to-read books that are written at approximately the grade 2 level. These books include humorous stories such as *Amelia Bedelia* (Parish, 1963) and informational books such as *Canadian Police Officers* (Bourgeois, 1992). The titles given represent a transition between picture books and chapter books. They have more text on each page and are sized more like a chapter book than a picture book; most pages include a picture. Young children developing confidence as readers enjoy reading these books, as do older students who are less successful readers.

Teachers use assisted reading whenever they read with individual children during readers workshop and resource-based units. They sense the child's familiarity with the book and his or her comfort level, and then support the child by doing most of the reading or supplying only the words the child does not seem to know. Parents, aides, and cross-age reading buddies also need to understand the three stages of assisted reading and learn how to use assisted reading to support young children as they emerge into reading.

One way to use assisted reading in a kindergarten or first-grade classroom is with cross-age reading buddies. A class of upper-grade students can be paired with a class of primary-grade children to become reading buddies. Older students read books aloud to younger children, and they

Stories

Abramson, B. (2006). *Off We Go!* Toronto: Tundra Books. 🍁

Benchley, N. (1979). *Running Owl the Hunter.* New York: Harper & Row.

Blume, J. (1971). *Freckle Juice.* New York: Dell.

Blume, J. (1981). *The One in the Middle Is the Green Kangaroo.* New York: Dell.

Brown, M. (1984). *There's No Place Like Home.* New York: Parents Magazine Press.

Calmenson, S. (1994). *Merigold and Grandma on the Town.* New York: HarperCollins.

Chataway, C. (2002). *The Perfect Pet.* Toronto: Kids Can Press. 🍁

Delton, J. (1992). *Lights, Action, Land-ho!* New York: Dell. (And other books in the series)

Eastman, P. D. (1960). *Are You My Mother?* New York: Random House.

Edwards, F. (1997). *Downtown Lost and Found.* Toronto: Firefly Books. 🍁

Gay, M.-L. (2002). *Stella, Fairy of the Forest.* Vancouver: Groundwood Books/Douglas & McIntyre. 🍁

Giff, P. R. (1984). *The Beast in Ms. Rooney's Room.* New York: Dell. (And other books by this author.)

Helmer, M. (2002). *Three Barnyard Tales: The Little Red Hen; the Ugly Duckling; Chicken Little* (Once-Upon-a-Time series). Toronto: Kids Can Press. 🍁

Krensky, S. (1994). *Lionel in the Winter.* New York: Dial.

Lewison, W. C. (1992). *"Buzz," Said the Bee.* New York: Scholastic.

Lobel, A. (1970). *Frog and Toad Are Friends.* New York: Harper & Row. (And other books in the series.)

Marzollo, J., & Marzollo, C. (1987). *Jed and the Space Bandits.* New York: Dial.

Northey, L. (2002). *I'm a Hop Hop Hoppity Frog.* Don Mills, ON: Stoddart Kids. 🍁

Parish, P. (1963). *Amelia Bedelia.* New York: Harper & Row. (And other books in the series)

Pomerantz, C. (1993). *The Outside Dog.* New York: HarperCollins.

Rylant, C. (1995). *Mr. Putter and Tabby Pick the Pears.* Orlando, FL: Harcourt Brace. (And other books by this author)

Schwartz, A. (1982). *There Is a Carrot in My Ear and Other Noodle Tales.* New York: Harper & Row.

Schwartz, A. (1984). *In a Dark, Dark Room.* New York: Scholastic.

Scrimger, R. (2002). *Princess Bun Bun.* Toronto: Tundra Books. 🍁

Sharmat, M. W. (1995). *Nate the Great and the Tardy Tortoise.* New York: Dell.

Smith, J. (1991). *But No Elephants.* New York: Parents Magazine Press.

(continued)

Figure 3–6 Easy-to-Read Books

Van Leeuwen, J. (1995). *Oliver and Amanda and the Big Snow*. New York: Dial.

Yolen, J. (1980). *Commander Toad in Space*. New York: Coward-McCann. (And other books in the series.)

Ziefert, H. (1983). *Small Potatoes Club*. New York: Dell. (And other books in the series.)

Easy Novel Series

Bates, C. (2001). *Shooting Star*. (Sports Stories Series). Halifax, NS: James Lorimer & Co. 🍁

Hughes, M. (2001). *Jan's Awesome Party*. (First Novels Series). Halifax, NS: Formac Publishing. 🍁

Leblanc, L. (1993). *Maddie Goes to Paris*. Halifax, NS: Formac Publishing. 🍁

Leblanc, L. (1993). *Maddie Wants Music*. Halifax, NS: Formac Publishing. 🍁

Little, J. (2001). *Orphan at My Door: The Home Child Diary of Victoria Cape*. (Dear Canada Series). Toronto: Scholastic Canada. 🍁

Park, B. (2003). *Junie B., First Grader: Toothless Wonder*. New York: Random House Children's Books. 🍁

Staunton, T. (2001). *Great Play, Morgan*. (First Novels Series). Halifax, NS: Formac Publishing. 🍁

Poetry

Florian, D. (1994). *Beast Feast*. New York: Harcourt Brace.

Hopkins, L. B. (1995). *Blast Off! Poems about Space*. New York: HarperCollins.

Muller, R. (1992). *Hickory, Dickory, Dock*. Toronto: North Winds Press. 🍁

Yolen, J. (2000). *Color Me a Rhyme: Nature Poems for Young People*. Honesdale, PA: Boyds Mills Press.

Social Studies

Bailey, D. (1992). *Canada*. Austin, TX: Steck-Vaughn.

Bourgeois, P. (1991). *Canadian Fire Fighters*. Toronto: Kids Can Press. 🍁

Bourgeois, P. (1991). *Canadian Garbage Collectors*. Toronto: Kids Can Press. 🍁

Bourgeois, P. (1992). *Canadian Police Officers*. Toronto: Kids Can Press. 🍁

Bourgeois, P. (1991). *Canadian Postal Workers*. Toronto: Kids Can Press. 🍁

Day, M. (2002). *Edward the "Crazy Man."* Toronto: Annick Press. 🍁

Sorenson, L. (1995). *Canada: The Land*. Vero Beach, FL: Rourke Book Co. (And other books in the series.)

Science

Cole, J. (1986). *Hungry, Hungry Sharks*. New York: Random House.

Fowler, A. (1990). *It's a Good Thing There Are Insects*. Chicago: Children's Press.

Keir, B. (1990). *Diary of a Honeybee*. Auckland: Shortland Publications.

Mason, A. (2005). *Move It! Motion, Forces, and You*. Toronto: Kids Can Press. 🍁

Smith, M. (1991). *A Snake Mistake*. New York: HarperCollins.

Swanson, D. (2001). *Burp! The Most Interesting Book You'll Ever Read about Eating*. Toronto: Kids Can Press. 🍁

Vaughan, M. (1990). *Clouds*. Auckland: Shortland Publications.

Wilson, B. (2005). *Trongate Fury* (Izzie: Book Two of the Our Canadian Girl series). Toronto: Penguin Books. 🍁

Ziefert, H. (1991). *Bob and Shirley: A Tale of Two Lobsters*. New York: HarperCollins.

Figure 3–6 Easy-to-Read Books (*continued*)

also read with the children using assisted reading. The effectiveness of cross-age tutoring is supported by research, and teachers report that students' reading fluency increases and their attitudes toward school and learning become more positive (Caserta-Henry, 1996; Labbo & Teale, 1990; Morrice & Simmons, 1991).

Teachers arranging a buddy reading program decide when the students will get together, how long each session will last, and what the reading schedule will be. Primary-grade teachers explain the program to their students and talk about activities the buddies will be doing together. Primary-grade students may want to draw pictures in advance to give to their buddies. Upper-grade teachers teach a series of minilessons about how to work with young children, read aloud and encourage children to make predictions, use assisted reading, select books to appeal to younger children, and help them respond to books. Older students choose books to read aloud and practise reading them until they can read the books fluently.

At the first meeting, the students pair off, get acquainted, and read together. They also talk about the books they have read and perhaps write in special reading logs. Buddies may want to go to the library and choose the books they will read at the next session.

There are significant social benefits to cross-age tutoring programs. Children get acquainted with other children they might otherwise not meet, and learn to work with older or younger children. As they talk about books they have read, they share personal experiences and interpretations. They also talk about reading strategies, how to choose books, and their favourite authors or illustration styles. Sometimes reading buddies write notes or email messages back and forth, or the two classrooms plan holiday celebrations together, and these activities strengthen the social connections between the children.

For more information on LIFT, see Chapter 5's opening profile on pages 170–171.

A second way to encourage more one-on-one reading is to involve families in literacy activities at home through travelling bags of books. Carla and Samantha, teachers of grades 2 and 3, respectively, organized a LIFT (Literacy is a Family Thing) program for their students. They created thematically organized bags of books and activities for their students to take home and enjoy with their families. Most bags contained three books, including both narrative and informational texts. Bags also included suggestions for family literary activities and the materials needed for each. For example, in addition to *Grandma and the Pirates* (Gilman, 1990), *Tough Boris* (Fox, 1994), and *The Time Warp Trio: The Not-So-Jolly Roger* (Scieszka, 1991), the pirate bag included a pirate puppet for role play. The weather bag included a thermometer and graph paper for recording daily temperatures. Others included audiotapes and videos. Parents and children shared their responses to the literature and activities with one another and with the teachers by writing in a journal kept in the bag. Text sets for ten travelling bags of books are listed in Figure 3–7.

Books about Airplanes

Barton, R. (1982). *Airport.* New York: Harper & Row.

Maynard, C. (1995). *Airplane.* New York: Dorling Kindersley.

McPhail, D. (1987). *First Flight.* Boston: Little, Brown.

Ziegler, S. (1988). *A Visit to the Airport.* Chicago: Children's Press.

Books about Dogs

Barracca, D., & Barracca, S. (1990). *The Adventures of Taxi Dog.* New York: Dial.

Bridwell, N. (1963). *Clifford the Big Red Dog.* New York: Greenwillow.

Cole, J. (1991). *My Puppy Is Born.* New York: Morrow.

Derrickson, J. (2001). *Bomo and the Beef Snacks.* Markham, ON: North Winds Press. ❦

Gregory, N. (1995). *How Smudge Came.* Red Deer, AB: Red Deer College Press. ❦

Kingsley, C. (2001). *Ten Little Puppies.* Toronto: Fitzhenry & Whiteside. ❦

Reiser, L. (1992). *Any Kind of Dog.* New York: Greenwillow.

Walsh, A. (2001). *Heroes of Isle aux Morts.* Toronto: Tundra Books. ❦

Books by Paulette Bourgeois

Bourgeois, P. (1986). *Franklin in the Dark.* Toronto: Kids Can Press. ❦

Bourgeois, P. (1993). *Franklin Is Bossy.* Toronto: Kids Can Press. ❦

Bourgeois, P. (1994). *Franklin Is Messy.* Toronto: Kids Can Press. ❦

Bourgeois, P. (1994). *The Many Hats of Mr. Minches.* Don Mills: Stoddart. ❦

Bourgeois, P. (1995). *Franklin Plays the Game.* Toronto: Kids Can Press. ❦

Books about Frogs and Toads

Clarke, B. (1990). *Amazing Frogs and Toads.* Toronto: Stoddart Publishing. ❦

Lobel, A. (1970). *Frog and Toad Are Friends.* New York: Harper & Row.

Mayer, M. (1974). *Frog Goes to Dinner.* New York: Dial.

Pallotta, J. (1990). *The Frog Alphabet Book: And Other Awesome Amphibians.* Watertown, MA: Charlesbridge.

Watts, B. (1991). *Frog.* New York: Lodestar.

Yolen, J. (1980). *Commander Toad in Space.* New York: Coward-McCann.

(continued)

Figure 3–7 Text Sets for Travelling Bags of Books

Books about Mice

Cauley, L. B. (1984). *The Town Mouse and the Country Mouse*. New York: Putnam.

Fitch, S. (1997). *There's a Mouse in My House*. Toronto: Doubleday Canada. 🍁

Henkes, K. (1991). *Chrysanthemum*. New York: Greenwillow.

Lionni, L. (1969). *Alexander and the Wind-up Mouse*. New York: Pantheon.

Lobel, A. (1977). *Mouse Soup*. New York: Harper & Row.

Numeroff, L. J. (1985). *If You Give a Mouse a Cookie*. New York: Harper & Row.

Books about the Alphabet

Major, K. (2000). *Eh? To Zed: A Canadian AbeCedarium*. Red Deer, AB: Red Deer Press. 🍁

Moak, A. (2002). *A Big City ABC*. Toronto: Tundra Books. 🍁

Ruurs, M. (2001). *A Pacific Alphabet*. Toronto: Whitecap Books. 🍁

Books about Plants

Bunting, E. (1994). *Flower Garden*. San Diego: Harcourt Brace.

Ehlert, L. (1987). *Growing Vegetable Soup*. San Diego: Harcourt Brace Jovanovich.

Ford, M. (1995). *Sunflower*. New York: Greenwillow.

Hickman, P. (1996). *The Kids Canadian Tree Book*. Toronto: Kids Can Press. 🍁

Lobel, A. (1990). *Alison's Zinnia*. New York: Greenwillow.

McCormick, R. (2002). *Plants and Art Activities*. St. Catharines, ON: Crabtree Publishing. 🍁

Silsbe, B. (2001). *A Tree Is Just a Tree?* Vancouver: Raincoast. 🍁

Books about Pirates

Gilman, P. (1990). *Grandma and the Pirates*. Richmond Hill: Scholastic Canada. 🍁

Fox, M. (1994). *Tough Boris*. San Diego: Harcourt Brace.Lawson, J. (1996). *Whatever You Do, Don't Go Near That Canoe*. Richmond Hill: Scholastic Canada. 🍁

Scieszka. J. (1991). *The Time-warp Trio: The Not-So-Jolly Roger*. New York: Penguin.

Thompson, J., & Macintosh, B. (1996). *A Pirate's Life for Me!* Watertown: Charlesbridge.

Books about the Three Bears

Cauley, L. B. (1981). *Goldilocks and the Three Bears*. New York: Putnam.

Galdone, P. (1972). *The Three Bears*. New York: Clarion Books.

Tolhurst, M. (1990). *Somebody and the Three Blairs*. New York: Orchard Books.

Turkle, B. (1976). *Deep in the Forest*. New York: Dutton.

Books about Trucks

Crews, D. (1980). *Truck*. New York: Greenwillow.

Hundal, N. (2001). *Number 21*. Toronto: Fitzhenry & Whiteside. 🍁

Llewellyn, C. (1995). *Truck*. New York: Dorling Kindersley.

Rockwell, A. (1984). *Trucks*. New York: Dutton.

Rotner, S. (1995). *Wheels Around*. Boston: Houghton Mifflin.

Siebert, D. (1984). *Truck Song*. New York: Harper & Row.

Figure 3–7 Text Sets for Travelling Bags of Books (*continued*)

Teachers, like Carla and Samantha, introduce programs like LIFT at a special meeting or open-house get-together at which they explain the purpose of the travelling bags of books in facilitating family literacy and how to use the books and materials with the children. It is important that families understand that their children are not expected to read all of the books independently. Teachers also encourage parents to share their families' responses through writing in the response journal in each bag by showing sample journal entries.

Language Experience Approach. The language experience approach (LEA) is based on children's language and experiences (Ashton-Warner, 1965; Stauffer, 1970). In this approach, stories are usually composed as a group. Children dictate sentences about their experiences to their teacher, who records their language on a large chart. The text they develop becomes their reading material. Because the content is familiar, and because the text is their language, children can usually read the chart stories easily. Collaboratively composing, dictating, and then rereading demonstrates to the children the connections between reading and writing. The steps in LEA are laid out in the Step by Step box on page 114.

Step by Step

Language Experience Approach (LEA)

1. *Provide an experience.*   A meaningful experience is identified to serve as the stimulus for the writing. For group writing, it can be an experience shared in school, a book read aloud, a field trip, or some other experience—such as having a pet or playing in the snow—familiar to all children. For individual writing, the stimulus can be any experience that is important for the particular child.

2. *Talk about the experience.*   The children and teacher discuss the experience prior to writing. The purpose of the talk is to generate thoughts and words and to review the experience so that the children's dictation will be more interesting and complete. The teacher often begins with an open-ended question, such as, "What do you want to say about _____?" As children talk about their experiences, they clarify and organize ideas, use more specific vocabulary, and extend their understanding.

3. *Record the dictation.*   The teacher writes the children's dictation. Texts for individual children are written on sheets of writing paper or in small booklets. Group texts are written on chart paper. The teacher prints neatly, spells words correctly, and preserves children's language as much as possible. It can be a great temptation to change the children's language, but editing should be kept to a minimum so that children do not get the impression that their language is inferior or inadequate.

    For individual texts, the teacher continues to take the child's dictation and write until the child finishes or hesitates. If the child hesitates, the teacher rereads what has been written and encourages the child to continue. For group texts, the teacher leads children to collaboratively formulate sentences to include the ideas they want to record. The children then take turns dictating sentences. As the teachers take dictation and write, they encourage talk about the words, the spelling patterns, and the punctuation being used. After writing each sentence, the teacher leads children in choral reading of the sentence. As the chart story progresses, the teacher engages children in choral rereading of all that has been written so far.

    As children become familiar with dictating to the teacher to create chart stories, they can be engaged in orally spelling individual words. With experience, children become very observant of the features of written language.

4. *Read the text.*   After the text has been written, the teacher leads the children in choral reading of the whole text, running a hand under each line to encourage fluent reading. This reading reminds children of the content of the text and demonstrates how to read it aloud with appropriate intonation. Then children join in the reading. After reading group texts together, individual children can take turns rereading. Group texts can also be copied so that each child has a copy to read independently.

The language experience approach is an effective way to help children emerge as readers. Even students who have not been successful with other types of reading activities can read what they have dictated. There is a drawback, however: Teachers provide a "perfect" model when they take children's dictation—they write neatly and spell all words correctly. After language experience activities, some young children are not eager to do their own writing, because they prefer their teacher's "perfect" writing to their own childlike writing. To avoid this problem, teachers have young children do their own writing in personal journals and other writing activities at the same time they are participating in language experience activities. In this way, children learn that sometimes they do their own writing and at other times the teacher takes their dictation.

Young Children Emerge as Writers

Many young children become writers before entering kindergarten; others are introduced to writing during their first year of school (Bright, 2002; Harste et al., 1984b; Temple, Nathan, Burris, & Temple, 1988). Young children's writing development follows a pattern of stages similar to their reading development: emergent writing, beginning writing, and fluent writing. In the initial emergent writing stage, children make scribbles to represent writing. At first, the scribbles may appear randomly on a page, but with experience children line up the letters or scribbles from left to right and from top to bottom. Children also begin to "read," or tell what their writing says. The next stage is beginning writing, and it marks children's growing awareness of the alphabetic principle. Children use invented spelling to represent words, and as they learn more about phoneme–grapheme correspondences, their writing approximates conventional spelling. The third stage is fluent writing, in which children use conventional spelling and other conventions of written language, including capital letters and punctuation marks.

Opportunities for writing begin on the first day of kindergarten and continue on a daily basis throughout the primary grades, regardless of whether children have already learned to read or write letters and words. Children often begin using a combination of art and scribbles or letter-like forms to express themselves. Their writing moves toward conventional forms as they apply concepts they are learning about written language.

Four samples of young children's writing are shown in Figure 3–8 on page 116. The first sample is a kindergartner's letter to the Great Pumpkin. The child wrote using scribbles, much like cursive writing, and followed the left-to-right, top-to-bottom orientation. The Great Pumpkin's comment, "I love you all," can be deciphered. The second sample is a page from a grade 1 student's dinosaur book. The text reads, "No one ever saw a real dinosaur." The third sample is from a grade 1 writer's reading log. The child used invented spelling to list the animal characters that appear in *The Mitten* (Brett, 1989). The fifth animal from the top is a badger. The fourth sample is also a list. A kindergartner wrote this list of favourite foods as part of a resource-based unit on *The Very Hungry Caterpillar* (Carle, 1969). The list reads, "orange, strawberry, apple, pizza, birthday cake."

INTRODUCING YOUNG CHILDREN TO WRITING

Teachers help children emerge into writing as they show them how to use kid writing, model adult writing for children, teach minilessons about written language, and involve them in writing activities. It is important to contrast teachers' writing—adult writing—with the "kid" writing that children can do.

Kid Writing. Kid writing takes many different forms. It can be scribbles or a collection of random marks on paper. Sometimes children imitate adults' cursive writing as they scribble. Children can string together letters that have no phoneme–grapheme correspondences, or they can use one or two letters to represent entire words. Children who have more experience with written language can invent spellings that represent more sound features of words, and they can apply spelling rules. A child's progressive spellings of "Abbie is my dog. I love her very much," beginning at five years old and over a period of eighteen months, are presented in Figure 3–9 on page 117. The child moves from using scribbles to single letters to represent words (top two entries), to spelling phonetically and misapplying a few spelling rules (third and fourth entries). Note that in the fourth example, the child is experimenting with using periods to mark spaces between words.

Kid writing is important for young children to understand because it gives them permission to experiment with written language when they draw and write. Too often, children assume that they should write and spell like adults do, and they cannot. Without this ability, children do not want to write, or they ask teachers to spell every word or copy text out of books or from charts. Kid writing offers students several strategies for writing and gives them permission to invent spellings that reflect their knowledge of written language.

Figure 3–8 Four Samples of Young Children's Writing

Young children's writing grows out of talking and drawing. As they begin to write, their writing is literally their talk written down, and children can usually express in writing the ideas they talk about. At the same time, children's letter-like marks develop from their drawing. With

Scribble Writing

One-Letter Labelling

Invented Spelling without Spacing

More Sophisticated Invented Spelling with Spacing

Invented Spelling with Application of Rules

Figure 3–9 Kid Writing

experience, children differentiate between drawing and writing. Some kindergarten teachers explain to children that they should use crayons when they draw and use pencils when they write. Teachers can also differentiate where children should write and draw on a page. The writing might go at the top or bottom of a page, or children can use paper with space for drawing at the top and lines for writing at the bottom.

Sign-In Sheets. Teachers use sign-in sheets to provide opportunities for children to practise writing their names for genuine purposes. To take attendance, they can set out a piece of paper each day with writing instruments, and children write their names as they arrive in the classroom (Harste et al., 1984b). These sign-in sheets document children's progress in learning to print their names and their understanding of concepts about written language.

Bobbi Fisher (1991), a kindergarten teacher, makes a T-chart with a question written at the top of the chart and two answer columns, and the children write their names in the answer columns in response to the question. For example, after she brought a green pumpkin to class, she wrote, "Will this pumpkin turn orange?" Students answered the question by writing their names in either the Yes or the No column.

For an example of a T-chart, see Chapter 5, "Listening and Speaking in the Classroom," page 186.

Children in kindergarten learn about the alphabetic principle as they collect classmates' autographs at the writing centre.

Teachers can develop other types of sign-in charts that ask students to make choices or offer opinions. For example, students can choose favourite books during an author study, or they can report information during a thematic unit on nutrition, such as what they eat for breakfast. Other grade 1 and 2 teachers have sign-up sheets for students to make books, work at a computer, or air a problem during a class meeting.

Interactive Writing. Teachers use interactive writing to model adult or conventional writing (Button, Johnson, & Furgerson, 1996; Picciotto, 1993; McCarrier, Pinnell, & Fountas, 2000). Interactive writing grew out of the language experience approach. One difference is that in interactive writing, the children are involved in the writing. Another is that conventional writing forms are always used. Also in interactive writing, teachers reinforce concepts about written language, provide opportunities to create texts, and focus students' attention on individual words and sounds within words. In many Canadian classrooms, the two strategies are combined, pending the writing experience of the children.

Topics for interactive writing can come from stories the class has read, classroom news, and information learned during thematic units. Children take turns holding the marking pen and doing the writing themselves. They usually sit in a circle on the carpet and write the text that they construct on chart paper that is displayed on an easel. While individual students take turns writing at the easel, other students are writing on small chalkboards or whiteboards in their laps. The steps in interactive writing are presented in the accompanying Step by Step box.

Interactive writing can be used for many types of writing projects in many areas of the curriculum. Examples include lists, clusters and other diagrams, collaborative books, classroom newspapers, stories, science experiment reports, and poems.

Minilessons on Reading and Writing. Teachers teach minilessons about written language concepts and other reading and writing topics to young children in kindergarten and the primary grades. Children learn about how reading and writing are used to convey messages, and how children behave as readers and writers. For example, the teacher shows children how to hold a book, how to examine the pictures, how to predict what will happen next, and how to track print when they are ready to do so. A list of topics for minilessons on emergent literacy is presented on page 120. These minilessons can be taught during readers workshop and resource-based units and through other activities.

ADAPTING WRITERS WORKSHOPS FOR EMERGENT WRITERS

Young children gain valuable writing experience through writers workshops. Kindergartners and first graders often work at a writing centre with the teacher or an aide, making books and working on other writing projects. For these emergent writers, teachers often abbreviate

Step by Step

Interactive Writing

1. **Construct the text.** Children and the teacher choose the topic and brainstorm ideas for the text. Children suggest sentences to write, and the group reaches consensus on each sentence.

2. **Identify the words in the first sentence.** The teacher repeats the first sentence and asks the children to identify or "count" the words in the sentence on their fingers as they repeat the sentence, articulating each word distinctly.

3. **Write the sentence.** Children take turns coming to the easel to write sentences. Depending on the children's experience with writing, they take turns writing each word or sentence. As the sentence is written, the teacher asks questions and provides information to focus children's attention on concepts about written language, phoneme–grapheme correspondences, spelling rules, and other conventions of print, depending on children's level of literacy development. Children and the teacher watch as children write words and sentences, and the teacher helps children write accurately and legibly.

4. **Read the sentence.** After children write each sentence, the class reads what has been written and prepares to write the next sentence.

5. **Repeat steps.** Children and the teacher repeat steps 2, 3, and 4 for each sentence.

6. **Reread the completed text.** Children and the teacher reread the completed text, and individual children take turns reading sentences.

the revising and editing stages of the writing process. At first, children's revising is limited to reading the text to themselves or to the teacher to check that they have written all that they want to say. Revising becomes more formal as children learn about audience and start to want to "add more" or "fix" their writing to make it appeal to their classmates. Some emergent writers ignore editing altogether. Others change a spelling, fix a poorly written letter, or add a period to the end of the text as they read over their writings. When children begin writing, teachers accept their writing as it is written and focus on the message. As children gain experience with writing, teachers encourage them to "fix" one or two errors. Guidelines for using the writing process with emergent writers are presented in the Teacher's Notebook on page 121.

For more information on the five stages of the writing process, see Chapter 4, "The Reading and Writing Processes," pages 147–164.

Writing Centres. Writing centres can be set up in kindergarten and primary classrooms so that children have a special place to write. The centre should be located at a table with chairs, and a box of supplies—including pencils, crayons, a date stamp, different kinds of paper, journal notebooks, a stapler, blank books, notepaper, and envelopes—should be stored nearby. The alphabet, printed in upper- and lowercase letters, should be available on the table for children to refer to as they write. In addition, there should be a place for children to file their work.

When children come to the writing centre, they draw and write in journals, compile books, and write messages to classmates. Teachers, aides, or parent volunteers should be available to

Minilessons

Emergent Literacy

Procedures	Concepts	Strategies and Skills
Hold a book correctly	Purposes for reading	Locate familiar words and signs
Turn pages correctly	Purposes for writing	Sing ABC song to identify a letter
Separate words into onsets and rimes	Direction of print	Identify letter names
Match each word as it is read aloud with the word on the page	A word	Match upper- and lowercase letters
	A sentence	Notice letters in words
	Uppercase letters	Identify phoneme–grapheme correspondences
Do assisted reading	Lowercase letters	"Stretch" words
Do buddy reading	Alphabetic principle	Blend phonemes to decode
Do shared reading	Rhyming words	Read environmental print
Dictate language experience stories	Repetition of words, phrases, and sentences	Match printed words with words read aloud
Do interactive writing	Big books	Make predictions
Write name on sign-in sheets	Audience awareness	Notice repetition
Use writing in play activities	The author's chair	Notice rhyme patterns
Exchange messages with classmates	Kid writing	Notice sequential patterns
Share writing in the author's chair	Adult spelling	Identify familiar words
	Invented spelling	Use scribbles and random letters for writing
		Write own name
		Copy familiar words and environmental print
		Space between words
		Use capital letters to begin sentences
		Use punctuation marks to end sentences
		Use invented spelling
		Use sentence patterns for writing

encourage and assist children at the centre. They can observe children as they invent spellings and can provide information about letters, words, and sentences as needed.

The Author's Chair. In primary-grade classrooms, a special chair should be designated as the author's chair (Graves & Hansen, 1983). This chair might be a rocking chair, a lawn chair with a padded seat, a wooden stool, or a director's chair, and it should be labelled "Author's Chair." Children and the teacher sit in the chair to share books they have read and other books they have written, and this is the only time anyone sits in the chair.

When teachers sit in the chair to read books aloud to children, they name the author(s) of the book and, if possible, tell something about the person(s). In this way, children can gain an awareness of who authors are. Children also sit in the author's chair to share books and other compositions they have written. Sitting in the special author's chair helps children gradually realize that they are authors. Graves and Hansen describe children's growing awareness of authors and of themselves as authors in three phases

1. ***Authors write books.*** After hearing many books read to them and reading books themselves, children develop the concept that authors are the people who write books.

Teacher's Notebook

Guidelines for Using the Writing Process with Emergent Writers

Prewriting

Prewriting is as important to young children as it is to other writers. Children write about topics they know well and have the vocabulary to express ideas about. Topics include personal experiences, classroom activities, stories children have listened to or have read independently, and thematic unit topics. Children use drawing to gather and organize ideas before writing. Children often talk about the topic or dramatize it before beginning to write.

Drafting

Young children usually write single-draft compositions. They add words to accompany drawings they have already made. The emphasis is on expressing ideas, not on handwriting skills or conventional spelling. Often children write in small booklets of paper, beginning on unlined paper and later moving to lined paper.

Revising

Teachers play down this stage until children have learned the importance of revising to meet the needs of their readers. At first children reread their writings to see that they have included every-thing they wanted to say, and they make very few changes. As they recognize the importance of audi-ence, they begin to make changes to make their writing clearer, and add more information to make their writing more complete.

Editing

Like revising, this stage is de-emphasized until children have learned conventional spellings for some words and have gained control over rules for capitalizing words and adding punctuation marks. To intro-duce editing, teachers help children make one or two corrections by crossing out the error and writing the correction in pencil on the child's writing. Teachers do not circle errors on a child's paper with a red pen. As young children become more fluent writers, teachers help them make more corrections.

Publishing

Children read their writings to their classmates and share their drawings. Through sharing, children develop a concept of audience and learn new ways of writing from their classmates. Children in kindergarten and grade 1 students usually do not recopy their writings, but sometimes the teacher or an assistant inputs the final copy, changing the child's writing into conventional form. Before adults recopy children's writing, children must be helped to understand that their published writing is being made "book-like," ready to share. This will avoid perceptions of inadequacy.

2. *I am an author.* Sharing the books they have written with classmates from the author's chair helps children view themselves as authors.

3. *If I wrote this published book now, I would make some changes.* Children learn that they have options when they write, and this awareness grows after they have experimented with various writing functions, forms, and audiences. When children reach this phase, they are more receptive to the idea of revising.

When children share their writings, one child sits in the author's chair and a group of children sit on the floor or in chairs in front of the author's chair (Karelitz, 1993). The child sitting in the author's chair reads the book or other piece of writing aloud and shows the accompanying illustrations. Then children who want to make a comment raise their hands, and the author chooses several children to ask questions, give compliments, and make comments. Then the author chooses another child to share and takes a seat in the audience.

Review

Emergent literacy is the accepted perspective on how children learn to read and write (Hayden & Kendrick, 2002). Young children learn concepts about written language as they experiment with reading and writing, and teachers demonstrate reading and writing through assisted reading, shared reading, interactive writing, and other teaching strategies. Children emerge into writing as they learn to use graphic symbols to represent their thoughts, and they refine their kid writing as they learn about phoneme–grapheme correspondences.

The following key concepts are presented in this chapter:

1. Emergent literacy, the concept that young children move into reading and writing through experiences with written language, has replaced the traditional "readiness" approach.
2. As children learn about words, they move from recognizing environmental print to reading contextualized words in books.
3. Children use phonics as well as information from the other three language systems as they learn to read.
4. Both reading and writing development have three stages: emergent, beginning, and fluent.
5. Two ways to read books with young children are assisted reading and shared reading.
6. Emergent readers read predictable books, big books, and easy-to-read books.
7. Children are introduced to writing as they watch adults at home and school write and as they experiment with writing.
8. Children use kid writing to experiment with written language concepts and invented spelling.
9. Young children begin writing books and other compositions using an abbreviated form of the writing process that emphasizes prewriting, drafting, and publishing.
10. Young children learn about audience as they share their writing from the author's chair.

Extensions

1. Observe in a kindergarten or grade 1 classroom to see how children are learning concepts about written language. Examine reading materials available in the classroom, including predictable books and big books, and opportunities for writing, such as sign-in sheets, dramatic play and writing centres, a message centre, and an author's chair.
2. Establish and monitor a buddy reading program between a primary-grade class and an upper-grade class.
3. Collect books and other materials for two travelling bags of books, and share them with a small group of grade 1 and 2 students.
4. Plan a resource-based unit using a big book, and teach the unit in a kindergarten, grade 1, or grade 2 classroom.

5. Construct a big book version of a predictable book, or compose a big book for a favourite story with a group of young children.

6. Create a dramatic play centre that incorporates authentic reading and writing materials, and observe as children use the materials for a week or two.

7. Set up a writing centre in a kindergarten classroom, and work with children for several weeks. Keep track of the types of writing that children engage in and note their growth as writers.

chapter four

The Reading and Writing Processes

Student Authors at Work

Procedure

"Reading and writing are inter-related: what is learned in one area makes it easier to learn in the other" (Fountas & Pinnell, 1996, p. 13).

Many, if not most of my beginning grade 3 students choose to and are able to read chapter books independently. They were particularly interested in reading books from a variety of series and were always on the lookout for new additions to our collections.

In order to help my students extend their understanding of the conventions and features found in chapter books—series, genres, elements of literature, and the author's writing style—we embarked on an extended reading and writing project based on the Nate the Great series by Marjorie Weinman Sharmat. I chose this series for three reasons. First, the series contained the features I wanted to explore with my students. Second,

the majority of students in my class were able to read text at this level independently. This was important because my students were able to focus their learning on book conventions rather than on decoding text. Third, this series provided a clear, consistent structure from which my students could successfully model the writing of their own stories.

The end result of this project was the creation of our class collection of Nate the Great stories authored and illustrated by each one of our students. Activities throughout this project were designed to allow students the opportunity to interact with texts from the series, their classmates, and adults in a variety of ways. This meaningful interaction was important to help students construct and consolidate their learning. In my planning, I was careful to scaffold their learning. Responsibility for task completion began with me and, after guided practice and the gradual release of responsibility, shifted to my students.

The following activities illustrate our project:

- *The whole class studies the first Nate the Great book in the series.* I read the story aloud to introduce the students to the genre and author, and to model and encourage interest in the story. We examine the cover, identify various features within the book itself, and discuss the story. Students are then asked to reread the story with a partner and to identify the characters, setting, problem, and solution. We come back together as a whole group and record the information on one large, chart-size story map. (In order for students to be successful, the same story map format is used throughout the project.)

- *The whole class discusses and explores book conventions.* We talk about titles, reading levels,

Assessment

My observations of students at work and during conferences provided a wide range of information that I recorded using checklists and anecdotal notes (e.g., oral reading skills, comprehension, cooperative group work skills, participation, writing skills, etc.). I also looked at their work samples for evidence. During the writing process in particular, I undertook assessment according to the criteria we set prior to the writing assignment. I also provided opportunities for student self-assessment and for parents to assess their child's published work by using the "two stars and a wish" format.

Adaptations

You might choose a different genre or author to study based on the age, needs, and/or interests of your students. Studying the work of Robert Munsch is one possibility. Structure groups to support learners who struggle with reading and/or writing.

publishing information, series information, the summary on the back cover, and the About the Authors page. What purpose do they serve? What information do they provide to the reader?

- *Small groups share reading.* Each group reads a different version from the Nate the Great series and completes one story map together.
- *Debriefing takes place with the whole class.* We discuss and record similarities and differences among books in the series. We also discuss and look for evidence of book conventions, elements of literature, and the author's writing style (e.g., each story has a mystery to solve; Nate always writes a note to his mother; each story reads, "I, Nate the Great . . ." etc.).
- *Students undertake independent reading.* We have a - variety of Nate the Great books available for independent reading. Students are encouraged to read more than one other book from the series.
- *Each student writes his or her own Nate the Great story.* We set criteria for the writing project as a class by referring back to our charts of similarities and differences and by using the elements from our story maps.
- *Student work is published.* I make coil-bound books for students to publish their stories. After some class discussion, they decide on an appropriate reading level for their book, a name for our publishing company, and a list of other books from this series using our class story titles. We also write summaries for the back cover and an About the Author page.
- It's time to share and celebrate!

> *"Students need time to read, write, and talk to one another in order to process and consolidate their learning."*

Kathy Chody
Early Years Consultant
River East Transcona School Division,
Winnipeg, Manitoba

Reflections

When implementing this type of extended project, it is important to remember not to rush the process. Students need time to read, write, and talk to one another in order to process and consolidate their learning. It is equally important to take the time to set criteria with your class so that they are clear about what is expected of them. Setting criteria for group work expectations and story writing are two such examples.

It was wonderful watching the growth demonstrated by each of my students throughout this project. They were extremely proud of their work and eagerly shared their stories with their grade 3 partners, the principal, and their parents.

As part of their pre-service course work in language arts instruction, student teachers learn about the reading and writing processes by researching children's literature titles and sharing their favourite books with peers in class. Ryan Gash, a social studies major, shares one of his favourite books, *Sacred Places* (1996) by author Jane Yolen. After reading, student teachers maintain a journal of the books they have enjoyed, providing a resource for them to use while teaching.

In the past twenty years there has been a significant shift in thinking about what people do as they read and write. Reading and writing are now viewed as transactive processes in which readers and writers create meaning through the lived-through experience of reading or writing (Graves, 1994; Harste, Woodward, & Burke, 1984a; Rosenblatt, 1978; Weaver, 1994a).

Both reading and writing are meaning-making processes. According to constructivist and sociolinguistic learning theories, readers create meaning through negotiation with the texts they are reading, and, similarly, writers create meaning through negotiation with the texts they are writing. Readers use their life and literature experiences and knowledge of written language as they read, and writers bring similar knowledge and experiences to writing. It is quite common for two people to read the same text and come away with different interpretations, and for two writers to write different accounts of the same event. Meaning does not exist within the text that a reader is reading or in the words of the composition that a writer is writing; instead, meaning is created through the transaction between readers and what they are reading, or between writers and what they are writing.

The reading process involves a series of stages during which readers construct interpretations—known as *comprehension*—as they read and then respond to the text they have read. Cognitive theorists have created models of the reading process as it occurs in the reader's mind. Other scholars have focused on the stages readers go through to read with understanding. Teachers provide instruction to assist students in moving through the stages when reading text. Text comprises all reading materials—paper and electronic—including stories, maps, newspapers, graphs, cereal boxes, textbooks, and so on.

To Guide Your Reading

As you read this chapter, prepare to

•

Describe key characteristics of four models of the cognitive reading process

•

Describe five stages of reading text

•

Describe the stages in the writing process

•

Explain how reading and writing are alike

•

Explain how teachers' knowledge of reading and writing processes affects their teaching of language arts

The writing process is a similar recursive process involving a variety of activities as students gather and organize their ideas, draft their compositions, revise and edit the drafts, and, finally, publish their writings.

Reading and writing have long been thought of as the flip sides of a coin, as opposites: readers decoded or deciphered written language, and writers encoded or produced written language. Then researchers began to note similarities between reading and writing and talked of both of them as processes. Now reading and writing are viewed as parallel processes of meaning construction, and readers and writers use similar strategies for making meaning with text.

The Reading Process

As noted in Chapter 1, "Learning and the Language Arts," psychology has largely defined our knowledge of the cognitive process of reading and subsequently influenced our understanding of how children and adults learn to read. While understanding of the cognitive process is not yet complete, much is known about how what begins as a flutter of patterns on the retina and ends (when successful) with a definite idea about the author's intended message (Rumelhart, 1994).

Several models of the reading process have been developed. The purpose for developing models is to summarize available knowledge, which will hopefully lead to developing new knowledge through predicting. While the models can be categorized in many ways, one of interest to teachers is to categorize according to the aspect of the process, such as word identification, that each emphasizes. A sampling of four models demonstrates this way of categorizing.

Gough's original model (1972) attempted to describe the flow of information during the reading process. It emphasized letter and word recognition. In this model, the process is described as linear with letters being processed left to right, first by a visual system and then transferred to a sound (phonetic) system for recognition. The information about each letter is held in memory until the next letter is similarly processed. When words are processed, they are held in working memory until they are processed for meaning identification in the mental lexicon and ultimately understood as sentences and whole texts. Briefly, Gough's model was characterized by letter-by-letter processing followed by phonological recoding, and the implication that all words are processed in this manner.

Two aspects of this model are almost certainly wrong (Gough, 1985). Although letters may mediate word recognition, serial letter-by-letter processing is a false notion. Similarly, there is consensus that skilled readers have direct or visual access to high-frequency words (McCusker, Hillinger, & Bias, 1981), negating Gough's contention that all words are phonologically recoded. Gough (1985) maintains that readers recognize the majority of words through phonological recoding, even if they have direct access to high-frequency words. The changes in Gough's theory, made necessary by further research, are an example of the intended dynamic nature of models.

LaBerge and Samuels' (1974) model is like Gough's in that word identification is primary, but adds the concept of *automaticity* of word recognition as essential to comprehension. Laberge and Samuels explain that automaticity is necessary because limited cognitive attention is available at any one moment and if all attention is consumed with decoding, readers cannot simultaneously attend to comprehension. Hence, the need for word recognition to be automatic to make sure cognitive attention is available for understanding, associating, comparing, evaluating, and other comprehension processes. Some criticism of this model (Logan, 1988; Stanovich, 1990) has raised questions regarding the precise role of automaticity in skillful reading, but, nevertheless, the Laberge and Samuels model has aided teachers in understanding readers' processing, gaining insights when their processing is unsuccessful, and determining the benefits of such instructional practices as repeated readings.

A third model stands in contrast to Gough's and LaBerge and Samuels' models. In Kenneth Goodman's model, comprehension is emphasized. Decoding is not perceived as preceding comprehension. Goodman (1993) claims that skilled readers do not process letter-by-letter, but rather process words as wholes, relying heavily on context to predict each word. Readers, in his view, bring all of their experiences and background knowledge to the text. They expect meaning from the text and they coordinate all the language cues (pragmatic, syntactic, semantic, and graphophonic) to get that meaning. Using the information available from the systems, they engage in a cycle of predicting and confirming as they process text. When breaks in meaning are detected, they go back and correct using different information as needed. Goodman initially referred to his theory as *psycholinguistic* to reflect its language-processing nature, but more recently uses the term *transactional socio-psycholinguistic* to reflect the interaction of readers with the text as they construct meaning.

A fourth model, Rumelhart's (1994) interactive model of reading, has characteristics in common with each of the previously described models. Rumelhart contends that multiple sources of information appear to interact in complex ways during the process of reading. Readers focus on comprehension and on letter features at roughly the same time, with the reading beginning in response to the graphic stimulus. To understand, readers must make use of sensory, syntactic, semantic, and pragmatic information. Although a linear model of the process as described by Rumelhart would be somewhat inaccurate because it could not capture the complexity of the interactions of the pieces of information, it is possible to perceive the process in three stages: perception of the visual input, extraction of the visual features to determine patterns, and synthesis of the patterns using the four sources of information listed above. During the synthesis, words are identified and meaning is developed. This interactive model sees the reader as processing the letters and words, but acknowledges that comprehension is influenced by the additional available information including context and meaning.

All of these models offer pieces of information that help teachers and researchers understand the complex process of reading. Differences in the models give rise to differences in beliefs about how children should be taught. For example, teachers whose beliefs align with LaBerge and Samuels' theory of automaticity are likely to see recognition of letters and words as primary for their students, while those who align with Goodman's model are likely to emphasize dealing with whole texts. One thing is clear: the process is complex.

During reading, the meaning does not go simply from the page to the reader. Instead, reading involves a complex negotiation, referred to as a transaction (Rosenblatt, 1978), between the text and the reader. The transaction is shaped by many factors: the reader's knowledge about the topic; the reader's purpose for reading; the language community the reader belongs to, and how closely that language matches the language used in the text; the reader's culturally based expectations about reading; and the reader's expectations about reading based on his or her previous experiences (Weaver, 1994a).

AESTHETIC AND EFFERENT READING

Readers read for different purposes, and the way they approach the reading process varies according to their purpose. Often they read for enjoyment, but at other times they read to carry away information. When reading for enjoyment or to be entertained, readers assume an *aesthetic stance* and focus on the lived-through experience of reading. They concentrate on the thoughts, images, feelings, and associations evoked during reading. Readers also respond to these thoughts, images, feelings, and associations. For example, as children read Barbara Reid's story *The Party* (1997), they may relate the events in the book to a time when they visited relatives for a celebration; as they read Jane Yolen's *Owl Moon* (1987), they may respond to the language of the text; or as they read *The Breadwinner* (Ellis, 2000), they may imagine the determination, fear, and struggle for survival that Parvana and her family experienced in war-torn Afghanistan.

When reading to carry away information, readers assume an *efferent stance*. They concentrate on the public, common referents of the words and symbols in the text. For example, as children read Roberta Bondar's *Touching the Earth* (1994), with its breathtaking photographs of the earth taken by satellites, their focus is on the information in the text and illustrations, not on the experience of reading.

Almost every reading experience calls for a balance between aesthetic and efferent reading (Rosenblatt, 1978, 1991; Langer, 1995). Readers do not simply read stories and poems aesthetically and informational books efferently. As they progress through a text, readers move back and forth between the aesthetic and efferent stances.

Teachers help students to engage in both aesthetic and efferent reading by guiding them through five stages of reading: preparing, reading, responding, exploring, and extending through fine arts and technology. The key features of each stage are presented in the Teacher's Notebook on page 131. Many of the features are characteristic of both aesthetic and efferent reading, but a few features exemplify one stance or the other.

To compare aesthetic and efferent reading with similar stances for listening, see Chapter 5, "Listening and Speaking in the Classroom," pages 176–178.

STAGE 1: PREPARING

Reading begins before students open a book. The first stage is preparing. Students undertake the following activities in the preparing stage:

- Choosing books
- Activating background knowledge
- Setting purposes
- Planning for reading

Choosing Books. Readers often begin the reading process by choosing the book they will read. Choosing an appropriate book is not easy. First of all, students need to know about themselves as readers: What types of books do they like? Who are their favourite authors? As they become readers, students learn the answers to these questions. They can also point to books they have read and can tell about them and explain why they enjoyed reading them.

Students need to learn to choose books they can read. Ohlhausen and Jepsen (1992) developed a strategy for choosing books called the "Goldilocks Strategy." These teachers developed three categories of books—"Too Easy," "Too Hard," and "Just Right"—using "The Three Bears" folktale as their model. The books in the Too Easy category were ones they had read before or could read fluently. Too Hard books were unfamiliar and confusing, and books in the Just Right category were interesting and had just a few unfamiliar words. The books in each category vary according to the students' reading levels. This strategy was developed with a grade 2 class, but the categorization scheme can work at any grade level. Figure 4–1 on page 130 presents a chart on choosing books using the Goldilocks Strategy with a grade 3 class.

Sometimes teachers choose books for students, but it is important that readers have many opportunities to select the books they are interested in reading.

Activating Background Knowledge. Readers activate their background knowledge, or schemata, about the book (or other selection) before beginning to read. The topic of the book, the title, the author(s), the genre, the cover illustration, a comment someone makes about the book, or something else may trigger this activation. When students are reading independently—during readers workshop, for example—they choose the books they will read and activate their background knowledge themselves. For example, readers who love horses often choose horse books to read, such as *How the Pinto Got Her Colour* (Buchholz, 1995).

At other times, such as during resource-based units, teachers teach minilessons to help students activate and build their background knowledge. They share information on a topic related to the book or introduce a book box with a collection of objects related to the book. Or, they show a video or film, tell about the author, read the first paragraph aloud, or ask students to make a prediction about the book. For instance, before reading Kate Di Camillo's *Because of*

How to Choose the Best Books for YOU

"Too Easy" Books

1. The book is short.
2. The print is big.
3. You have read the book before.
4. You know all the words in the book.
5. The book has a lot of pictures.
6. You are an expert on this topic.

"Just Right" Books

1. The book looks interesting.
2. You can decode most of the words in the book.
3. Mrs. Donnelly has read this book aloud to you.
4. You have read other books by this author.
5. There's someone to give you help if you need it.
6. You know something about this topic.

"Too Hard" Books

1. The book is long.
2. The print is small.
3. There aren't many pictures in the book.
4. There are a lot of words that you can't decode.
5. There's no one to help you read this book.
6. You don't know much about this topic.

Figure 4–1 A Grade 3 Chart Applying the Goldilocks Strategy

Winn-Dixie (2000), teachers talk about missing friends when they move away; before reading Jan Brett's *The Mitten* (1989), teachers show students a white mitten and several stuffed animals representing characters in the story—a bear, a fox, a rabbit, and an owl—and ask students whether they think these animals could fit into the mitten.

In order for readers to make meaning from the selection they are reading, their schemata must be activated. When students are preparing to read a book on an unfamiliar topic, they need to build background knowledge. By building a new schema before reading and being introduced to key vocabulary, students are more likely to be successful when they read. For example, teachers show a video on hermit crabs before reading *A House for Hermit Crab* (Carle, 1987a), or before reading *The Giver* (Lowry, 1993), they build a concept of what a "perfect" society might be like by having students brainstorm a list of problems in today's world and think of possible remedies.

Another part of activating knowledge before reading is to make connections with personal experiences and with literary experiences. The more connections students make between the book they are about to read and personal experiences, the better. Students who have observed a hermit crab at the seashore, for instance, will be better prepared to read *A House for Hermit Crab* than students who have never seen one. Similarly, students who are familiar with other books by Eric Carle and know about his fabulous collage illustrations will be better prepared for *A House for Hermit Crab* than those who have not experienced Carle's work.

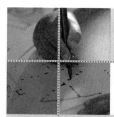

Teacher's Notebook

Key Features of the Stages of Reading

Stage 1: Preparing

- Choose a book.
- Activate prior knowledge.
- Connect to prior personal and literary experiences.
- Connect to thematic units or special interests.
- Set purposes for reading.
- Make predictions.
- Preview the text.
- Consult the index to locate information.

Stage 2: Reading

- Make predictions.
- Apply skills and strategies.
- Read independently, with a buddy using shared reading, through guided reading, or listen to the text read aloud.
- Read the illustrations, charts, and diagrams.
- Read the entire text from beginning to end.
- Read one or more sections of the text to learn specific information.
- Take notes.

Stage 3: Responding

- Write in a reading journal.
- Participate in a grand conversation.

Stage 4: Exploring

- Reread and think more deeply about the text.
- Make connections with personal experiences.
- Make connections with other literary experiences.
- Examine the author's craft.
- Identify memorable quotes.
- Learn new vocabulary words.
- Participate in minilessons.

Stage 5: Extending (through Fine Arts and Technology)

- Construct projects (develop multimedia projects using video, CD-ROM, and PowerPoint).
- Use information in thematic units.
- Connect with related books.
- Reflect on their interpretations.
- Engage in role-playing, storytelling, improvisation, and readers theatre.

Setting Purposes. The two overarching purposes for reading are pleasure and information. When students read for pleasure or enjoyment, they read aesthetically, to be carried into the world of the text; when they read to locate and remember information or for directions about how to do something, they read efferently (Rosenblatt, 1978). Often readers use elements of both purposes as they read, but usually one purpose is more primary to the reading experience than the other. For example, when students pick up *The Sweetest Fig* (1993) or *Bad Day at Riverbend* (1995), two Chris Van Allsburg picture book fantasies, their primary purpose is enjoyment. They want to experience the story, but at the same time, they search for the white dog—a trademark that Van Allsburg includes in all of his books—and compare these books with other Van Allsburg titles that they have read. As students search for the white dog or make comparisons, they add efferent purposes to their primarily aesthetic reading experience.

Readers are more successful when they have a single purpose for reading the entire selection. Purpose-setting is usually directed by the teacher during resource-based units, but in readers workshop students set their own purposes because everyone is reading different self-selected books. For teacher-directed purpose-setting, teachers explain how students are expected to read and what they will do after reading. The goal of teacher-directed purpose-setting is to help students learn how to set personally relevant purposes when they are reading independently (Blanton, Wood, & Moorman, 1990). Students should always have a purpose for reading, whether they are reading aesthetically or efferently, whether they are reading a selection for the first time or the tenth.

When readers have a purpose for reading, comprehension of the selection they are reading is enhanced in three ways (Blanton et al., 1990). First, the purpose guides the reading process that students use. Having a purpose provides motivation and direction for reading as well as a mechanism that students use for monitoring their reading. As they monitor their reading, students ask themselves whether or not they are fulfilling their purpose. Second, purpose-setting activates a plan for teachers to use in teaching reading. They help students draw on background knowledge as they set purposes, consider strategies they might use as they read, and think about the structure of the text they are reading. Third, students are better able to sort out important from unimportant information as they read when they have a purpose for reading. Teachers direct students' attention to relevant concepts as they set purposes for reading and show them how to connect the concepts they are reading about to their background knowledge.

Planning for Reading. Students often preview the reading selection as they prepare to read. They look through the selection and check its length, the reading difficulty of the selection, and the illustrations in order to judge the general suitability of the selection for them as readers. Previewing serves an important function as students connect with their background knowledge, identify their purpose for reading, and take their first look at the selection.

Teachers set the guidelines for the reading experience. They explain how the book will be read—independently, in small groups, or as a class—and set the schedule for reading. Setting the schedule is especially important when students are reading a chapter book. Often teachers and students work together to create a two- or three-week schedule for reading and responding and then write the schedule on a calendar to which students can refer.

When students are preparing to read informational books, they preview the selection noting section headings, illustrations, diagrams, and other charts. Sometimes they examine the table of contents to see how the text is organized, or consult the index to locate specific information. They may also notice unfamiliar terminology and other words they can check in the glossary, ask a classmate or the teacher about, or look up in a dictionary. Teachers also use the SQ4R study strategy (in which students survey, question, read, recite, review, and reflect to remember information), anticipation guides, and other teaching strategies as they work with informational books and content-area textbooks.

STAGE 2: READING

In the second stage, students read the book or other selection. They use their knowledge of word identification, sight words, reading strategies and skills, and vocabulary while they read. Fluent readers are better able to understand what they are reading because they identify most words automatically and use decoding skills when necessary (Mason, Herman, & Au, 1991). They also apply their knowledge of the structure of text as they create meaning. They continue reading as long as what they are reading fits the meaning they are constructing. When something doesn't make sense, fluent readers slow down, back up, and reread until they are making meaning again. Applying strategies to reinstate meaning is sometimes referred to as using "fix-up" strategies.

Students may read the entire selection or only read sections. When students are reading aesthetically, they usually read the entire selection, but when they are reading efferently, they may be searching for specific information and read only until they locate that information. It is unrealistic to assume that students will always read entire selections or finish reading every book they begin, even when reading for aesthetic purposes.

Outside of school, readers usually read silently and independently. Sometimes, however, people listen as someone else reads. Young children often sit in a parent's lap and look at the illustrations as the parent reads a picture book aloud. Adults read and listen in group settings such as church services and listen to stories read aloud on CDs, DVDs, and podcasts. In the classroom, teachers and students use five types of reading:

- Shared reading
- Guided reading
- Independent reading
- Buddy reading
- Reading aloud to students

Shared Reading. Teachers use shared reading to introduce a book or another reading selection to students before the students read the selection with partners or individually (Pappas & Brown, 1987; Sulzby, 1985a). In this type of reading, students follow along as the teacher reads the selection aloud. Kindergarten teachers and other primary-grade teachers often use big books— enlarged versions of the selection—for shared reading (Sampson, Rasinski, & Sampson, 2003). Students sit so that they can see the book, and they either listen to the teacher read aloud or join in and read along. The teacher or a student points to each line of text as it is read to draw students' attention to the words, to show the direction of print on a page, and to highlight important concepts about letters, words, and sentences.

For more information on big books, see Chapter 3, "Emergent Literacy," pages 103–107.

Teachers also use shared reading when students have individual copies of the reading selection. Students follow along in their copies as the teacher or another fluent reader reads aloud. This "first" reading is preparation for students so that they become familiar enough with the storyline and the vocabulary that they can read the selection independently later.

For more information on using shared reading with young children, see Chapter 3, "Emergent Literacy," pages 102–103.

When students are reading chapter books, shared reading is used as the main reading approach if some students can't read the selection independently. The teacher and other fluent readers take turns reading aloud as students follow along in their copies of the selection. To ensure that all the students are following along in their copies of the book, teachers sometimes ask all students or a group of students to read aloud very softly or "mumble" along as they read aloud. Sometimes teachers read the first chapter or two of a chapter book together as a class using shared reading, and then students use other types of reading as they read the rest of the book. Only students for whom the book is too difficult continue to use shared reading and read along with the teacher.

There are several variations of shared reading (Slaughter, 1993). One is *choral reading*, when students divide into groups to read poems aloud. Another is *readers theatre*, in which students read play scripts aloud. A third type of shared reading is the *listening centre*, where students can listen to a book read aloud as they follow along in the book. Listening centres are a good way to provide

For more information on choral reading, see Chapter 6, "Reading and Writing Stories and Poetry," pages 242–246.

These grade 5 students used the reading process during a resource-based unit featuring *Bridge to Terabithia* (Paterson, 1987).

models of fluent reading and additional reading practice to help students become fluent readers.

Guided Reading. Teachers scaffold students' reading to enable them to develop and use reading skills and strategies in guided reading (Clay, 1991; Fountas & Pinnell, 1996). This type of reading is teacher-directed and usually done in small groups with students who read at the same level or use similar reading skills and strategies. Teachers often group and regroup students for guided reading so that the book that teachers select is appropriate for all students in a group. Selections used for guided reading should be written at students' instructional reading levels; that is, slightly beyond their ability to read the text independently or at their level of proximal development.

Guided Reading as described by Fountas and Pinnell (1996) and outlined here is a popular practice with beginning readers in Canadian classrooms. A Guided Reading program is one way to help meet the varied needs of all students. Although Guided Reading may take different forms, most involve working with small groups of students at similar levels of development, using texts that are carefully matched to their needs, providing instructional support to build reading strategies and increase independence (Rog, 2003). As the following Step by Step box shows, there are six steps in Guided Reading, according to Fountas and Pinnell (1996):

Step by Step

Guided Reading

1. *Choose a book.* The teacher chooses a book or other selection for the group to read based on knowledge of students' reading levels and ability to use reading skills and strategies.

2. *Introduce the selection.* The teacher briefly introduces the selection by activating background knowledge, introducing characters, and setting a purpose for reading. The teacher may also ask students to make predictions about what they think will happen in the selection.

3. *Observe students as they read.* Students read silently and the teacher observes them as they read. The teacher notices the reading skills and strategies that students exhibit as they read and makes anecdotal notes about these observations. The teacher also notes any words students ask for help with or any questions that students ask.

4. *Provide assistance.* If students require assistance, the teacher assists them one-on-one with word identification and supports their efforts to comprehend the selection, trying not to interrupt students while they are reading.

5. **Talk about the selection.**   The teacher encourages students to briefly share their responses to the book. Students talk about the selection, ask questions to clarify misconceptions, and relate the reading to their own lives.

6. **Teach minilessons.**   The teacher introduces, practises, or reviews one or two skills or strategies after reading. The teacher may select topics for minilessons in advance or respond to students' observed needs. In these lessons, the teacher asks students to return to the text to practise word-identification or comprehension skills or strategies. The teacher also has students focus their attention on elements of story structure and the language patterns used in the selection.

Source: Adapted from Fountas and Pinnell (1996).

A modified form of Guided Reading is often used when teachers read with students during resource-based and thematic units. When teachers read a featured selection with students they have opportunities to demonstrate reading strategies, clarify misconceptions as students construct meaning, point out key vocabulary words, and take advantage of many teachable moments. When the reading takes place in a small-group arrangement, and each student has a copy of the text, teachers have the opportunity to observe individual students as they read, monitor their comprehension, and informally assess their reading progress.

Independent Reading. Independent reading is an important part of language arts instruction because it is the most authentic type of reading. This is the type of reading that most people do, and this is the way students develop a love of reading and come to think of themselves as readers.

When students read independently, they read silently by themselves and at their own pace (Hornsby, Sukarna, & Parry, 1986; Taylor, 1993). In order for students to read independently, the selections must be at their reading level or very familiar to them. For beginning readers, independent reading often follows the teacher's reading of the book one or more times during shared reading experiences. It is essential for students to have access to many texts with which they can be successful. Access to books has been repeatedly shown to encourage more frequent reading (Krashen, 1998; Morrow, 2003).

Buddy Reading. In buddy reading, students read or reread a selection with another student. Sometimes students read with buddies because it is an enjoyable social activity, and sometimes they read together to help each other. Often students can read selections together that neither one could read individually. By working together, they are often able to figure out unfamiliar words and talk out comprehension problems. Buddy reading is a good alternative to independent reading because it gives students reading practice and opportunity to talk about reading selections of interest to them.

Teachers sometimes choose to pair older and younger students for buddy reading. For example, upper-elementary- and middle-school students can be reading buddies with kindergarten and grade one. Both buddies benefit. Older students develop their oral reading skills and serve as tutors to give their younger compatriots reading practice.

As teachers introduce buddy reading, they show students how to read with buddies and how to support each other as they read. Unless the teacher has explained and modelled the approach and taught students how to work collaboratively, buddy reading often deteriorates into the better reader reading aloud to the other student, and that is not the intention of this type of reading. Students need to take turns reading aloud to each other or read in unison. They often stop and help each other identify an unfamiliar word or take a minute or two at the end of each page to talk about what they have read. Buddy reading is a valuable way of providing the practice that beginning readers need to become fluent readers, and it is also an effective way to work with students who have special learning needs and those who are learning English.

Reading Aloud to Students. Research and current practice support the use of teacher read-alouds as a significant component of instruction across grade levels (Dreher, 2003; Sipe, 2000). Teachers read aloud to students for a variety of purposes each day. Sometimes, they do this to give students an opportunity to experience a text solely from an aesthetic, or efferent, stance. Sometimes, teachers read aloud featured selections that are appropriate for students' interest level but too difficult for students to read by themselves. Teachers also read aloud featured selections during thematic and resource-based units if they have only one copy of the book available. Sometimes it is also appropriate to read the featured selection aloud before distributing copies of the selection for students to read with buddies or independently. When they read aloud, teachers model expressive reading, show what good readers do and how good readers use reading strategies, and invite listeners to be readers (Cochran-Smith, 1984; Richardson, 2000).

During readers workshop, teachers also read aloud stories and other books to introduce students to literature they might not choose to read on their own. The reading-aloud component of a readers workshop provides students with a shared social experience and an opportunity to talk about literature and reading. In addition, teachers also read aloud books related to science, social studies, and other across-the-curriculum themes.

Reading aloud to students is not the same as "round-robin" reading, in which students take turns reading paragraphs aloud as the rest of the class listens. Round-robin reading has been used for reading chapter books aloud, but it is more commonly used for reading chapters in content-area textbooks, even though there are more effective ways both to teach content-area information and to read textbooks.

Round-robin reading is no longer recommended for several reasons (Durkin, 1993). First, if students are going to read aloud, they should read fluently. When less capable readers read, their reading is often difficult to listen to and embarrassing to them personally. Less capable readers need reading practice, but performing in front of the entire class is not the most productive way for them to practise. They can read with buddies and in small groups during guided reading. Second, if the selection is appropriate for students to read aloud, they should be reading independently, not hindered in their reading by the differences in reading rate that naturally occur in group reading. During round-robin reading, students often follow along only just before it is their turn to read. Third, round-robin reading is often tedious and boring, and students lose interest in reading.

The advantages and drawbacks of each type of reading are outlined in Figure 4–2.

STAGE 3: RESPONDING

During the third stage, readers respond to their reading and continue to negotiate meaning in order to deepen their comprehension. Two ways that students make tentative and exploratory comments immediately after reading are as follows:

- Writing in reading response journals
- Participating in grand conversations

Writing in Reading Logs. Students write and draw thoughts and feelings about what they have read in reading response journals. Rosenblatt (1978) explains that as students write about what they have read, they unravel their thinking and, at the same time, elaborate on and clarify their responses. When students read informational books, they sometimes write in reading logs just as they do after reading stories and poems, but at other times they make notes of important information or draw charts and diagrams to use in thematic units.

Type	Advantages	Drawbacks
Shared Reading Teacher reads aloud while students follow along using individual copies of book, a class chart, or a big book.	• Students access books they could not read themselves • Teacher models fluent reading • Opportunities given to model reading strategies • Students practise fluent reading • It develops a community of readers	• Multiple copies, a class chart, or a big book needed. • Text may not be appropriate for all students • Students may not be interested in the text
Guided Reading Teachers support students as they read texts at their reading levels. Students are grouped homogeneously.	• Teacher provides direction and scaffolding • Opportunities given to practise reading strategies and skills • Students read silently • Students practise the prediction cycle	• Multiple copies of text needed • Teacher controls the reading experience • Some students may not be interested in the text
Independent Reading Students read a text independently and often choose the text themselves.	• Students develops responsibility and ownership • Texts are self-selected • Experience is more authentic	• Students may need assistance to read the text • Teacher has little involvement and control
Buddy Reading Two students read or reread a text together.	• Collaboration takes place between students • Students assist each other • It is used to reread familiar texts • It develops reading fluency • Students talk and share interpretations	• Teacher has limited involvement • Teacher has less control
Reading Aloud to Students Teacher or other fluent reader reads aloud to students.	• Students access books they could not read themselves • Teacher models fluent reading • Opportunities given to model reading strategies • It develops a community of readers • It is used when only one copy of text is available	• No opportunity given for students themselves to read • Text may not be appropriate for all students • Students may not be interested in the text • It does not require students to take turns reading

Figure 4–2 Advantages and Drawbacks of the Five Types of Reading

Students sometimes make reading journals by stapling together several sheets of paper at the beginning of a unit. They decorate the covers in keeping with the topic of the unit, write entries related to their reading, and make notes related to what they are learning in minilessons.

Students usually choose their own topics for reading journal entries, but at other times teachers offer a list of prompts from which students choose. Students are never expected to respond to all prompts. Many teachers display a list of prompts in the classroom or give the list to students to place in their language arts notebooks. Possible prompts include the following:

I really don't understand . . .

I like/dislike (character) because . . .

This book reminds me of . . .

(Character) reminds me of myself because . . .

I think (character) is feeling . . .

I wonder why . . .

(Event) makes me think about the time I . . .

I like this quote because . . .

If I were (character), I'd . . .

I noticed that (the author) is . . .

I predict that . . .

These prompts are open-ended and allow students to make connections with their own lives. At other times, teachers ask a specific question to direct students' attention to some aspect of a book. For example, as upper-grade students are reading Lois Lowry's Newbery Medal–winning book *The Giver*, teachers often ask questions like these:

After Chapter 2: Does Jonas's community seem more perfect than ours?

After Chapter 6: What assignment do you think Jonas will get?

After Chapter 11: Would you like to have Jonas's assignment?

After Chapter 19: What does *release* mean?

After Chapter 23: What happened to Jonas and Gabe?

These questions, like the prompts listed above, are open-ended and ask for students' interpretations—even the questions for Chapters 19 and 23, which may at first seem like literal questions.

Teachers monitor students' entries, often reading and responding to those entries. Because these journals are learning tools, teachers rarely correct students' spellings. They focus their responses on the students' ideas At the end of the unit, teachers review students' work and often grade the journals based on whether students completed all the entries and on the quality of the ideas in their entries.

Participating in Grand Conversations. Students also talk about the text in discussions called *grand conversations* or *literature circles* (Daniels, 1994). Peterson and Eeds (1990) explain that in this type of discussion, students share their personal responses and tell what they liked about the selection. After sharing personal reactions, they shift the focus to "puzzle over what the author has written and . . . share what it is they find revealed" (p. 61). Often students make connections between the selection and their own lives or other literature they have read. If they are reading a chapter book, they also make predictions about what will happen in the next chapter.

Martinez and Roser (1995) have researched students' grand conversations and found that often students talk about story events or characters and explore the themes of the story, while less often they delve into the author's craft to explore the way the author structured the book, the arrangement of text and illustrations on the page, or the author's use of figurative or repetitive language. The researchers call these three conversation directions *experience*, *message*, and *object*. They suggest that stories help to shape students' talk about books, and that some books lend themselves to talk about message and others to talk about experience or object. Stories with dramatic plots or ones that present a problem students can relate to, such as *Chrysanthemum* (Henkes, 1991), *One on One* (Aker, 2005), and *Breath of a Ghost* (Horrocks, 1996), focus the conversation on the book as experience. Multi-layered stories or books in which main characters deal with dilemmas, such as *One Thing That's True* (Foggo, 1997), *Sarah, Plain and Tall* (MacLachlan, 1985), and *What They Don't Know* (Horrocks, 1998), focus the conversation on the message. Books with distinctive structures or language features, such as *Black and White* (Macaulay, 1990), *Tuesday* (Wiesner, 1991), and *Being with Henry* (Brooks, 1999), focus the conversation on the object.

Teachers often participate in grand conversations, but they act as interested participants, not leaders. The discussion is primarily among students, but teachers ask open-ended questions regarding things they are genuinely interested in learning more about and share information in response to questions students ask. Open-ended questions teachers might ask during grand conversations include (Daniels, 1994) the following:

> Which character is most like you?
> What would you have done if ...?
> What did that make you think of?

In the past, many discussions have been "gentle inquisitions" during which students recited answers to factual questions teachers asked about books students were reading (Eeds & Wells, 1989). Teachers dominated the talk and asked these questions in order to determine whether or not students read the assignment; in contrast, the focus in grand conversations is on clarifying and deepening students' understanding or comprehension of the selection they have read.

Grand conversations can be held with the whole class or in small groups. Young children usually meet together as a class, while older students often prefer to talk with classmates in small groups. When students meet together as a class, there is a shared feeling of community, and the teacher can be part of the group. When students meet in small groups, students have more opportunities to participate in the discussion and share their responses, but fewer viewpoints are expressed in each group and teachers must move around, spending only a few minutes with each group. Some teachers compromise and have students begin their discussions in small groups and then come together as a class and have each group share what their group discussed.

For more information on grand conversations, see Chapter 5, "Listening and Speaking in the Classroom," pages 192–200.

STAGE 4: EXPLORING

During this stage, students go back into the text to explore it more analytically. They participate in some of these activities:

- Rereading the text
- Examining the author's craft
- Focusing on new vocabulary words
- Minilessons

Rereading the Text. Through repeated readings, students reread the text and think again about what they have read. Each time they reread, students benefit in specific ways (Yaden, 1988). They enrich their comprehension and make further connections between the text and their own lives or between the text and other literature they have read. Students often reread a text several times. If the teacher used shared reading to read the text with students in the reading stage, students might reread it with a buddy once or twice, read it with their parents, and after these experiences, read it independently.

Examining the Author's Craft. Teachers plan exploring activities to focus students' attention on the structure of the text and the literary language that authors use (Eeds & Peterson, 1995). Students notice opposites in the story, use storyboards to sequence the events in the story, and make story maps to visually represent the plot, characters, and other story elements (Bromley, 1996). Older students also examine closely the writing devices used by authors and explore their use in their own writing. They can use technology to do these same activities and create PowerPoint or other multimedia presentations. Another way students learn about the structure of stories is by writing books based on the text they have read. Students write sequels, telling what happened to the characters after the story ends. Some stories, such as *Jumanji* (Van Allsburg, 1981), end in a way that seems to invite students to create a sequel. Students also write innovations, or new versions, for the selection by following the sentence pattern. First graders often write innovations for Bill Martin, Jr.'s *Brown Bear, Brown Bear, What Do You See?* (1983) and *Polar Bear, Polar Bear, What Do You Hear?* (1992), and older students write innovations for *Alexander and the Terrible, Horrible, No Good, Very Bad Day* (Viorst, 1977).

Teachers share information about the author of the featured selection and introduce other books by that author. Sometimes teachers have students compare several books written by a particular author. They use technological resources such as the Internet, CD-ROM, videos, and videodiscs to find information about authors and their books.

When students read picture books, they also learn about illustration and the illustrator's craft. Students can learn about the media and techniques the artist used and experiment with the media themselves. They can examine the illustrations to find out about the illustrator's stylistic choices and think more deeply about how they affect interpretation of the text.

Focusing on New Vocabulary Words. Teachers and students add "important" words to word walls after reading and post these word walls in the classroom. Students refer to the word walls when they write, using these words for a variety of activities during the exploring stage. Researchers emphasize the importance of immersing students in words, teaching strategies for learning words, and personalizing word learning (Blachowicz & Fisher, 1996). Students make word clusters and posters to highlight particular words. They also make word chains, sort words, create a semantic feature analysis to analyze related words, and play word games.

For more information on word walls and vocabulary instruction, see Chapter 9, "Words and the Language Tools to Use Them: Spelling, Grammar, and Handwriting," pages 352–354.

Teachers choose words from word walls to use in minilessons, too. Words are used to teach phonics skills, such as beginning sounds, rhyming words, vowel patterns, *r*-controlled vowels, and syllabication (Bear, Templeton, Invernizzi, & Johnston, 1996). Other concepts such as root words and affixes, compound words, and metaphors can also be taught using examples from word walls. Teachers often teach a minilesson on a particular concept, such as the *-ly* suffix, because five or six words representing the concept are listed on the word wall.

Minilessons. Teachers present minilessons on reading concepts, procedures, strategies, and skills during the exploring stage. A list of topics for minilessons on the reading process is presented on page 143. In a reading minilesson, teachers introduce the topic and make connections between the lesson topic and reading of the featured selection. In this way students are better able to connect the information teachers are presenting with their own reading process. Students need to learn about the process approach to reading—both aesthetic and efferent—and about ways to develop interpretations.

STAGE 5: EXTENDING (THROUGH FINE ARTS AND TECHNOLOGY)

During the extending stage, readers move beyond comprehension to broaden and deepen their interpretations, reflect on their understanding, and value the reading experience. Students build on their reading, the responses they made immediately after reading, and the exploring activities as they engage in projects. These projects can involve reading, writing, speaking and drama, viewing, visually representing, or research, and are often interactive with other readers. They may take many forms, including murals, readers' theatre scripts, oral presentations, and written texts, as well as reading other books by the same author. A list of extending projects is presented in Figure 4–3. The wide variety of project options offers students choices and takes into account Howard Gardner's (1993a) theory of multiple intelligences, that students have preferred ways of learning and showing knowledge. Usually students choose which projects they will do rather than work as a class on the same project. Sometimes, however, the class decides to work together on a project.

TEACHING THE STAGES OF READING

For more information on creating a community of learners and arranging the classroom, see Chapter 2, "Teaching the Language Arts," pages 45–49.

Teachers apply a five-stage reading process in the reading lessons they teach, whether they organize instruction into resource-based units, thematic units, or inquiry units. Successful language arts instruction doesn't just happen (Hickman, 1995). Teachers bring students together as a community of learners and teach them the procedures for various language arts activities. Each unit requires that teachers carefully structure activities, provide appropriate books and other materials, and create time and space for students to work. Teachers, too, must be prepared to assume a variety of roles.

Writing Projects

Note that many of these writing projects are completed using various forms of technology to enhance both the process and the products.

1. Write a review of a favourite book for a class review file.
2. Write a postcard or letter about a book to a classmate, friend, or pen pal.
3. Dictate or write another episode or sequel for a book.
4. Create a newspaper with news stories and advertisements based on characters and episodes from a book.
5. Make a five-senses cluster about the book.
6. Write and mail a letter to a favourite author (or participate in a class collaboration letter).
7. Write a simulated letter from one book character to another.
8. Copy five "quotable quotes" from a book and list them on a poster.
9. Make a scrapbook about the book. Label all items in the scrapbook and write a short description of the most interesting ones.
10. Write a poem related to the book. Some types of poems to choose from are acrostics, concrete poems, colour poems, "I wish" or "I am" poems, haiku, or found poems.
11. Write a lifeline related to the book, the era, the character, or the author.
12. Write a business letter to a company or organization requesting information on a topic related to the book.
13. Keep a simulated journal from the perspective of one character from the book.
14. Write a dictionary defining specialized vocabulary in a book.
15. Write the story from another point of view (e.g., write the story of the Little Red Hen from the perspective of the lazy characters).
16. Make a class collaboration book. Each child dictates or writes one page.
17. Write a letter to a famous person from a character in a book.
18. Create an alphabet book on a topic related to the book.
19. Make a cube with information about the book or a related topic.

Reading Projects

20. Read another book by the same author.
21. Read another book by the same illustrator.
22. Read another book on the same theme.
23. Read another book in the same genre.
24. Read another book about the same character.
25. Read and compare two versions of the same story.
26. Read a biography about the author or illustrator of the book.

Speaking and Drama Projects

27. Record a book or an excerpt from it to place in the listening centre.
28. Read a poem that complements the book aloud to the class. Place a copy of the poem in the book.
29. Give a readers theatre presentation of a book.
30. Create a song about a book or choose a tune for a poem and sing the song for the class.
31. Write a script and present a play about a book.
32. Make puppets and use them in retelling a book.
33. Dress as a character from the book and answer questions from classmates about the character.
34. Write and present a rap about the book.
35. Record on video a commercial for a book.

Research Projects

36. Interview someone in the community who is knowledgeable about a topic related to the book.
37. Research the author or illustrator of the book and compile information in a chart or summary. Post the chart or summary in the library centre.
38. Research a topic related to the book. Present the information in an oral or written report.
39. Research the setting or context of the book and share findings with other readers.
40. Conduct a poll among readers of a book (or readers of several sources concerning the same topic). Record and share poll results.

Figure 4–3 Extending Projects

In Resource-Based Units. In resource-based units, students might read a single book, such as *Bunnicula: A Rabbit-Tale of Mystery* (Howe & Howe, 1979), and as they read they will move through the five stages of the reading process. Or, they might read a collection of books on the same theme (e.g., about dogs), in the same genre (e.g., folktales), or by the same author (e.g., books by Carol Matas). When students read several books together, they move back and forth among the second, third, and fourth stages as they read, respond to, and explore each book before moving on to the extending stage.

Figure 4–4 shows one way to organize a resource-based unit on *Bunnicula: A Rabbit-Tale of Mystery*. In this unit, grade 5 students work through all five stages of the reading process. The

---

Stage 1: Preparing
The teacher shares a book box of objects related to the book with students. Objects include a stuffed rabbit dressed in a vampire costume, plastic vegetables that have been painted white and marked with two small pinpricks, and a children's version of the Dracula story. The teacher shares the objects, and students make predictions about the book.

Stage 2: Reading
The teacher uses the shared reading approach to read the chapter book. Each student has a copy of the book and follows along as the teacher reads the book aloud. One or two chapters are read aloud each day.

Stage 3: Responding
After reading a chapter or two, students write responses in reading logs and share these logs with classmates. Students also participate in grand conversations and make connections between the story and their own lives and other experiences with literature.

Stage 4: Exploring
Students write interesting and important words from the book on a word wall (chart paper hanging on the wall) and use the words in a variety of vocabulary activities, including word sorts. The teacher shares information about the authors, Deborah and James Howe, and a text set of other books by James Howe. The teacher teaches several minilessons on characterization and the meaning-making strategy of identifying with a character. The teacher asks students to choose the character they identify with the most (Harold the dog, Chester the cat, or Bunnicula the rabbit) and explain why they chose that character. Students make an open-mind portrait of one character. Other minilessons include portmanteau words (e.g., *bunny + dracula = Bunnicula*) and homonyms.

Stage 5: Extending (Through Fine Arts and Technology)
Each student chooses a project from a list of choices posted in the classroom. A number of students choose to read one of the sequels and other stories about Bunnicula: *Howliday Inn* (1982), *The Celery Stalks at Midnight* (1983), *Nighty-Nightmare* (1987), *Return to Howliday Inn* (1992), *Scared Silly* (1989), *The Fright Before Christmas* (1989), and *Hot Fudge* (1990). Other students choose these projects:

- Write and/or e-mail a letter to authors Deborah and James Howe.
- Perform a play about an episode of the book.
- Make a book box and place five items related to the book with explanations in the box.
- Write a sequel to the book.
- Make a tabletop display of the Monroes' house.
- Research Dracula and vampires using the Internet and CD-ROM.

Figure 4–4 A Plan for Teaching a Resource-Based Unit on *Bunnicula: A Rabbit-Tale of Mystery*

teacher uses a book box with a stuffed rabbit dressed like a vampire, plastic vegetables that have been painted white, and a children's version of the Dracula story. Students use shared reading to read the chapter book; then they respond to their reading and participate in exploration activities. The teacher presents minilessons on homophones (e.g., *steak*, *stake*) and portmanteau words (*bunny + dracula = Bunnicula; smoke + fog = smog*), and shares information about the authors, Deborah and James Howe. Students also construct projects and engage in dramatizations to extend their study of the book.

In Thematic Units. Teachers coordinate the books and other materials students are reading with what they are studying during thematic units. Thematic units usually include study across curriculum subject areas. For example, during a thematic unit on insects in a grade 2 classroom, students might read *It's a Good Thing There Are Insects* (Fowler, 1990) at the beginning of the theme. Students move through all five stages of the reading process. First they read the easy-to-read informational book using shared reading; then they read it a second time with reading buddies; and then they read it a third time independently. During the grand conversation held after students read the book the first time, they brainstorm a list of reasons why it's a good thing there are

Minilessons

The Reading and Writing Processes

	Procedures	Concepts	Strategies and Skills
The Reading Process	Choose books to read	The reading process	Decode words
	Use the Goldilocks Strategy	Aesthetic reading	Predict
	Listen to books read aloud	Efferent reading	Confirm
	Do shared reading	Interpretation	Visualize
	Do buddy reading		Retell
	Do independent reading		Connect to literature
	Respond in reading logs		Connect to life
	Participate in grand conversations		Empathize
			Identify with characters
	Reread a book		Monitor
	Create projects		
	Participate in readers workshop		
The Writing Process	Choose a topic	The writing process	Gather ideas
	Cluster	Functions of writing	Organize ideas
	Quickwrite	Writing forms	Draft
	Participate in writing groups	Audience	Revise
	Proofread	Focus on content	Edit
	Make hardcover books	Focus on mechanics	Identify and correct spelling errors
	Write About the Author pages	Proofreaders' marks	Use capital letters correctly
	Share published writing	Publish writing	Use punctuation marks correctly
			Value the composition

insects. Later they can write their own books about insects. Teachers can also use this book to teach minilessons about the differences between stories and informational books. *It's a Good Thing There Are Insects* is an excellent example of an informational book because the illustrations are photos, and a glossary and index are included.

Later in the thematic unit the teacher might pair two books about ladybugs for the students to read: *The Grouchy Ladybug* (Carle, 1986), a repetitive story about an unfriendly ladybug who is looking for a fight, and *Ladybug* (Watts, 1987), an informational book with one line of large-sized type on each page for students to read and additional information in smaller-sized type that students or the teacher can read. If the teacher has enough copies of each book for half the class, the students divide into two groups. One group reads one book and the other group reads the other book; then the two groups trade books. As the students read these two books, the teacher has many opportunities to continue comparing stories and informational books. After reading, students might talk about which book they liked better, and they work on projects to extend their understanding of ladybugs and other insects.

In Readers Workshop. Students also work through the stages of reading during readers workshop. In readers workshop, students focus on the prereading, reading, and responding stages of the reading process, but the remaining stages are also involved. Students choose books (often using the Goldilocks Strategy), activate background knowledge, set purposes, and make plans as they begin to read (stage 1). Next, they read the book independently (stage 2). After reading, they may write in reading logs and talk about the books they are reading in conferences with the teacher (stage 3). Sometimes students read three or four books and then choose one book for a project (stage 5). Students also talk about the books they read and show their completed projects to classmates during sharing time (stages 3 and 5). In readers workshop, teachers also teach minilessons, and during these lessons students learn reading concepts, procedures, strategies, and skills (stage 4).

ADAPTING TO MEET THE NEEDS OF EVERY STUDENT

Reading instructional activities are flexible and can be adapted to help every student, whether talented or struggling, become a more successful reader. For students with limited experiences or for those who are learning English as a second or third language, more time should be spent in the preparing stage. During reading, teachers often read books aloud or use shared reading when working with students who are not yet fluent readers. Many easy-to-read stories and informational books that are well-written and enticing to students are currently available, so it is possible to have several books at different reading levels on almost any topic. During the responding stage, students can draw or dramatize rather than write their responses in reading journals, and grand conversations take on an even greater importance for students who need to clarify misconceptions about their reading. Students can reread the text with a buddy or listen to the audiobook version during the exploring stage. The fifth stage is important for all students, and many students who find reading difficult are very successful in creating art projects and dramatic productions. Suggestions for adapting reading instruction to meet the needs of every student are presented in the accompanying Adapting box.

LANGER'S PROCESS OF TEXT INTERPRETATION FOR MIDDLE-GRADE STUDENTS

Langer (1995) proposes using a four-stance process of text interpretation for students. "Through literature, students learn to explore possibilities and consider options for themselves and humankind. They come to find themselves, imagine others, value difference, and search for justice. They gain connectedness and seek vision. They become the literate thinkers we need to

Adapting

The Reading Process to Meet the Needs of Every Student

Stage 1: Preparing

- Spend more time activating and constructing background knowledge.
- Use concrete experiences, multimedia presentations, and photos.
- Introduce important vocabulary related to the topic, but not limited to the vocabulary in the text. Use independent reading and research skills to develop background knowledge. Share background knowledge with other readers

Stage 2: Reading

- Read books aloud.
- Use shared reading or buddy reading.
- Listen to a recorded version of the book.
- Break the reading time into smaller chunks.
- Provide easier-to-read or more challenging alternative texts.

Stage 3: Responding

- Have students draw or dramatize responses instead of writing in reading journals.
- Take time in grand conversations to clarify misconceptions. Engage students in critical thinking followed by oral or written presentations.

Stage 4: Exploring

- Role-play important events in the book.
- Reread the text with a buddy.
- Teach minilessons to individual students and small groups of students. Engage students in comparisons of texts and views of authors.

Stage 5: Extending (through Fine Arts and Technology)

- Encourage students to create art projects.
- Encourage students to produce dramatic productions.
- Set out clear expectations for the projects students develop.
- Encourage students to pursue projects that they are interested in and that challenge them.

shape the decisions of tomorrow" (p. 1). As students mature in their ability to interpret and respond to text, we can extend their understanding by helping them to use their literary skills to think and rethink their understandings of texts. Langer's stances provide a framework that allows students to explore their understandings in greater depth as they learn to "move" through texts with their teacher's guidance.

In the first stance, "Being Out and Stepping In," readers interpret the genre, structure, and language of the text by using their prior knowledge and the surface features of the text; after this initial contact, students have sufficient information to build an "envisionment." *Envisionment* refers to the world of understanding a person has at any given point in time. As Langer states, "Envisionments are dynamic sets of related ideas, images, questions, disagreements, anticipations, arguments, and hunches that fill the mind during every reading, writing, speaking, or other experience when one gains, expresses, and shares thoughts and understandings" (1995, p. 9). Stepping into a text or story requires that the teacher engage students in an exploration of both their individual envisionment of the text and the collective envisionment of a group as it listens to, speaks about, reads, and writes about the text.

In the second stance, "Being In and Moving Through" the text, readers are immersed in the text and use their background knowledge in conjunction with the text knowledge to develop meaning. Here, the teacher helps students move beyond what they already know by asking questions about motives, feelings, causes, interrelationships, and implications. At this stage, the teacher invites students to speculate about what things *might* mean.

In the third stance, "Being In and Stepping Out," readers are involved in developing understandings, or "text worlds," to add to their own knowledge and experiences. The teacher engages students in the process of connecting the text to their own lives; reflecting on their personal knowledge; and reflecting on their individual lives, the lives of others, or on the human condition generally.

In the fourth stance, "Stepping Out and Objectifying the Experience," readers are asked to distance themselves from the text world, reflecting and reacting to both the content and the experience of having engaged with the text. Students judge the text, either relating it to other stories they have read or to their own experiences. By seeing the text at a distance, students review it analytically.

Langer suggests that the four stances do not occur in a linear sequence. They can occur and recur at any time during the taking up of a text, during the later discussion of the text, or in later reflection on the text. The stances lead teachers and students to consider the meanings of a text in a number of different ways: "Our envisionments develop through the shifting relationships between self and text that occur from stance to stance. The stances offer variety to the kinds of meaning we consider, filtering our thoughts through slightly different vectors as we develop our understandings of the text, our envisionment, and life" (p. 19).

An Example of Langer's Four-Stance Process of Text Interpretation. Linda Iagallo's grade 5 class is working on a mythology unit and is about to read the Northwest Coast Aboriginal myth *How the Loon Lost Her Voice* (Cameron, 1985). Ms. Iagallo begins by exploring possibilities with her students, giving them a sense of literary orientation and helping them build an initial envisionment (Being Out and Stepping In). They begin with the title of the story and by listening to a Naturescape CD of bird calls, including the plaintive call of the loon. The students write about the loon calls, describing what they hear and comparing it with the sounds of other songbirds, especially the western meadowlark, which is one of the bird calls they've studied and is familiar to them as a sign that spring has returned to the prairie. They've been waiting for the first report in their class of a western meadowlark song so that they can record the day and time the meadowlarks returned to their community from their winter journey south. The discussion focuses on the unusual call of the loon.

The discussion then shifts to what the students know about myths. The students talk about how myths often contain gods or heroes and explain ordinary events in our lives. Ms. Iagallo explains that the story they are about to read is a myth from the West Coast of Canada, an Aboriginal myth that explains why some animals behave the way they do. She also explains that there are several versions of this myth and in some traditions this story is called "Raven Steals the Light."

Ms. Iagallo reads the opening of the story: "There was a time when Loon was the most beautiful singer of all the birds on the island. She would float on the surface of the waves and pour her joy out in clear golden notes." The students wonder about the title, "How the Loon Lost Her Voice," and what event or circumstance might have caused Loon to lose her beautiful voice. The students are developing their envisionments as they explore possibilities. They use their imaginations to create scenarios as ways to help them try out possible understandings of the story.

Before Ms. Iagallo continues to read the story, she asks the students to consider the story in the light of their speculations and what they know about myths (Being In and Moving Through). The students keep track of the animals and their adventures in the story: Raven, Osprey, Deer, Bear, Mole. Before she reads the end of the story, Ms. Iagallo asks the students to speculate on how the behaviour of each animal might be explained from their actions in the story (Being In and Stepping Out). The students write and share their writing in small groups before bringing their responses to the entire class.

The students gather and share their predictions with Ms. Iagallo before she reads the end of the story. They move beyond the story when Ms. Iagallo asks them to choose other animals from their experience and write a myth explaining some aspect of the animal's behaviour or appearance. Students also discuss and write about the effectiveness of the myth in explaining our experience (Stepping Out and Objectifying the Experience).

The Writing Process

The focus in the writing process is on what students think and do as they write. The five stages are prewriting, drafting, revising, editing, and publishing, and the key features of each stage are shown in the Teacher's Notebook on page 148. The labelling and numbering of the stages does not mean, however, that the writing process is a linear series of neatly packaged categories. Research has shown that the process involves recurring cycles, and labelling is only an aid to identifying and discussing writing activities (Graves, 1994; Perl, 1994). In the classroom, the stages merge and recur as students write.

STAGE 1: PREWRITING

Prewriting is the getting-ready-to-write stage. The traditional notion that writers must have a topic completely thought out and ready to flow onto the page is generally not reasonable. If writers wait for ideas to fully develop, they may wait forever. Instead, writers begin tentatively—talking, reading, writing—to discover what they know and decide what direction they want to take (Flower & Hayes, 1994). Prewriting has probably been the most neglected stage in the writing process; however, it is as crucial to writers as a warm-up is to athletes. Calkins (1994) believes that a significant amount of writing time should be spent in prewriting. Students undertake the following activities in the prewriting stage:

- Choosing a topic
- Considering purpose, audience, and form
- Generating and organizing ideas for writing

Choosing a Topic. Choosing a topic for writing can be a stumbling block for students who have become dependent on teachers to supply topics. For years teachers have supplied topics by suggesting gimmicky story starters and relieving students of the "burden" of topic selection. Often, these "creative" topics stymied students, who were forced to write on topics they knew little about or had no interest in. Graves (1976) calls this "writing welfare." Instead, students need to choose their own writing topics.

Some students complain that they do not know what to write about, but teachers can help them brainstorm a list of three, four, or five topics, and then identify the one topic they are most interested in and know the most about. Students who feel they cannot generate any writing topics

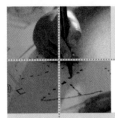

Teacher's Notebook

Key Features of the Writing Process

Stage 1: Prewriting
- Students write on topics based on their own experiences.
- Students engage in rehearsal activities before writing.
- Students identify the audience for whom they will write.
- Students identify the function of the writing activity.
- Students choose an appropriate form for their compositions based on audience and purpose.
- Students gather and organize information.

Stage 2: Drafting
- Students write a rough draft.
- Students emphasize content rather than mechanics.

Stage 3: Revising
- Students reread their own writing.
- Students share their writing in writers groups.
- Students participate constructively in discussions about classmates' writing.
- Students make changes in their compositions to reflect the reactions and comments of both teacher and classmates.
- Between the first and final drafts, students make substantive rather than only minor changes.

Stage 4: Editing
- Students proofread their own compositions.
- Students help proofread classmates' compositions.
- Students increasingly identify and correct their own mechanical errors.
- Students meet with the teacher for a final editing.

Stage 5: Publishing
- Students publish their writing in an appropriate form.
- Students share their finished writing with an appropriate audience.

are often surprised that they have so many options. Then, through prewriting activities, students talk, draw, read, and even write to develop information about their topics.

Asking students to choose their own topics for writing doesn't mean that teachers never give writing assignments; teachers do provide general guidelines. Sometimes they may specify the writing form, and at other times they may establish the function, but students should choose their own specific content.

Considering Purpose. As students prepare to write, they need to think about their purpose for writing. Are they writing to entertain? To inform? To persuade? Understanding the purpose of a piece of writing is important because it influences other decisions students make about audience and form.

Considering Audience. Students may write primarily for themselves—to express and clarify their ideas and feelings—or they may write for others. Possible audiences include classmates, younger children, parents, foster grandparents, children's authors, and pen pals. Other audiences are more distant and less well known. For example, students write letters to businesses to request information, submit articles to the local newspaper, and compose stories and poems for publication in literary magazines.

Children's writing is influenced by their sense of audience. Bright (1995) defines audience as "internal," meaning the writer him- or herself, or "external," meaning any individual or group, however distant, outside the writer.

Considering Form. One of the most important considerations is the form the writing will take: A story? A letter? A poem? A journal entry? As part of a thematic unit on hermit crabs, for example, students might write a story about a hermit crab, draw a picture and label body parts, explain how hermit crabs obtain shells to live in, write poems about the crustacean, or keep a log of observations about the pet hermit crabs in the classroom. There is an almost endless variety of forms that children's writing may take. A list of these forms is presented in the Teacher's Notebook on page 150. Students need to experiment with a wide variety of writing forms and explore the potential of these functions and formats.

Through reading and writing, students develop a strong sense of these forms and how they are structured. Langer (1985) found that by grade 3, students responded in distinctly different ways to story- and report-writing assignments; they organized the writing differently and included varied kinds of information and elaboration. Similarly, Hidi and Hildyard (1983) found that elementary students could differentiate between stories and persuasive essays. Because children are clarifying the distinctions between various writing forms during the elementary grades, it is important that teachers use the correct terminology and not label all children's writing "stories."

Decisions about purpose, audience, and form influence each other. For example, if the function is to entertain, an appropriate form might be a story, poem, or script, and these three forms look very different on a piece of paper. Whereas a story is written in the traditional block format, scripts and poems have unique page arrangements. Scripts are written with the character's name and a colon, and the dialogue is set off. Action and dialogue, rather than description, carry the storyline in a script. In contrast, poems have unique formatting considerations, and each word and phrase is chosen to convey a maximum amount of information.

Generating and Organizing Ideas for Writing. Students engage in activities to gather and organize ideas for writing. Graves (1994) calls what writers do to prepare for writing "rehearsal" activities. Through these activities, students activate background knowledge and make plans for writing. Rehearsal activities can take many forms:

1. *Drawing.* Drawing is the way young children gather and organize ideas for writing. Primary-grade teachers notice that children often draw before they write, and, thinking that the students are eating dessert before the meat and vegetables, the teachers insist that they write first. But many young children cannot because they don't know what to write until they see what they draw (Dyson, 1986).

2. *Clustering.* Students make clusters—web-like diagrams—in which they write the topic in a centre circle and draw out rays for each main idea (Rico, 1983). Then they add details and other information on rays drawn out from each main idea. Through clustering, students organize their ideas for writing. Clustering is a successful prewriting strategy that has the advantage over outlining of being nonlinear.

3. *Talking.* Students talk with each other to share ideas about possible writing topics, try out ways to express an idea, and ask questions. Too often, teachers don't recognize the power of talk as a prewriting activity. When students cannot talk about a topic, it is unlikely that they will be able to write about it.

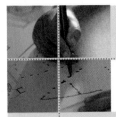

Teacher's Notebook

Writing Forms

acrostics
advertisements
"all about . . ." books
"about the author"
alphabet books
announcements
anthologies
apologies
applications
autobiographies
awards
bibliographies
biographies
book jackets
books
brochures
captions
cartoons
catalogues
certificates
character sketches
charts
cinquain poems
clusters
comics
comparisons
complaints
computer programs
concrete poems
crossword puzzles
cubes
definitions
descriptions
diagrams
dialogue
dialogue journals

diamante poems
dictionaries
directions
double-entry journals
editorials
email
essays
evaluations
explanations
fables
fairy tales
folk tales
formula poems
found poems
greeting cards
haiku poems
hink-pinks
"I am" poems
instructions
interviews
invitations
jokes
lab reports
learning logs
letters
life lines
limericks
lists
lyrics
maps
menus
mysteries
myths
newspapers
notes
obituaries

oral histories
personal narratives
postcards
posters
puzzles
questionnaires
questions
quickwrites
reading logs
recipes
reflections
reports
reviews
riddles
schedules
scripts
sentences
signs
simulated journals
stories
storyboards
study guides
tall tales
telegrams
telephone directories
thank-you notes
thumbnail sketches
timelines
tongue twisters
valentines
Venn diagrams
word-finds
wordless picture books
word posters
word walls

4. ***Reading.*** Students gather ideas for writing and investigate the structure of various written forms through reading. They may retell on paper a favourite story; write new adventures for favourite story characters; or experiment with repetition, onomatopoeia, or another poetic device used in a poem they have read. Informational books also provide raw material for writing. For example, if students are studying polar bears, they read to gather information about the animal, its habitat, and its predators, which they may use in writing a report.

5. ***Drama and Role-playing.*** Students discover and shape ideas they will use in their writing through role-playing. During thematic units and after reading stories, students can re-enact events to bring an experience to life. Heathcote (Wagner, 1983) suggests that teachers choose a dramatic focus or a particular critical moment for students to re-enact. For example, after reading *Sarah, Plain and Tall* (MacLachlan, 1985), children might re-enact the day Sarah took the wagon to town. This is a critical moment: does Sarah like them and their prairie home well enough to stay?

6. ***Quickwriting.*** Students do a quickwrite to brainstorm ideas or explore a topic. Through this informal writing activity, they gather and organize ideas they will be able to use as they draft their compositions. Quickwrites may be combined with other strategies such as clustering to organize ideas.

STAGE 2: DRAFTING

Students write and refine their compositions through a series of drafts. During the drafting stage, students focus on getting their ideas down on paper or on the computer. Because writers do not begin writing with their compositions already composed in their minds, students begin with tentative ideas developed through prewriting activities. The drafting stage is the time to pour out ideas, with little concern about spelling, punctuation, and other mechanical aspects of writing.

When students write their drafts, they may write on only one side of the page and on every other line to leave space for revisions (Lane, 1993). When writing on notepaper, they may use arrows to move sections of text, cross-outs to delete sections, and scissors and tape to cut apart and rearrange text. When facilities are available, they learn to revise and cut and paste using the computer.

Teachers teach students to label their drafts by writing the date and "Draft #1" in ink at the top of the paper, by stamping them with a DRAFT stamp or including "draft" in their electronic file name. This label indicates to the writer, other students, and parents that the composition is a draft in which the emphasis is on content, not mechanics. It also explains why the teacher has not graded the paper or marked mechanical errors.

During drafting, students may need to modify their earlier decisions about purpose, audience, and, especially, the form their writing will take. For example, a composition that began as a story may be transformed into a report, a letter, or a poem if the new format allows the student to communicate more effectively. The process of modifying earlier decisions continues into the revising stage.

As students write drafts, it is important not to emphasize correct spelling and format. In fact, pointing out mechanical errors during the drafting stage sends students a message that mechanical correctness is more important than content (Sommers, 1994). Later, during editing, students can clean up mechanical errors and put their composition into a neat, final form.

STAGE 3: REVISING

During the revising stage, writers refine ideas in their compositions. Students often break the writing process cycle as soon as they complete a draft, believing that once they have jotted down their ideas, the writing task is complete. Experienced writers, however, know that they must turn to others for reactions and revise on the basis of these comments (Sommers, 1994). Revision is not just polishing; it is meeting the needs of readers by adding, substituting, deleting, and rearranging material. The word *revision* means "seeing again," and in this stage writers see their compositions again with the help of their classmates and teacher. Students undertake the following activities in the revising stage:

- Rereading the draft
- Sharing the draft in writers groups
- Revising on the basis of feedback
- Conferencing with the teacher

Rereading the Draft. After finishing the first draft, writers need to distance themselves from the draft for a day or two, then reread it from a fresh perspective, as a reader might. As they reread, students make changes—adding, substituting, deleting, and moving—and place question marks by sections that need work. It is these trouble spots that students ask for help with in their writers groups.

Sharing the Draft in Writers Groups. Students meet in writers groups to share their compositions with classmates. Because writing must meet the needs of readers, feedback is crucial. Mohr (1984) identifies four general functions of writers groups: to offer the writer choices; to provide the writer with group members' responses, feelings, and thoughts; to show different possibilities in revising; and to speed up revising. Writers groups provide a scaffold in which teachers and classmates talk about plans and strategies for writing and revising (Calkins, 1994).

Writers groups can form spontaneously when several students have completed drafts and are ready to share their compositions, or they can be formal groupings with identified leaders. In some classrooms writers groups form when four or five students finish writing their drafts. Students gather around a conference table or in a corner of the classroom and work as authors, sometimes without the teacher. They take turns reading their drafts aloud, and classmates in the group listen and respond, offering compliments and suggestions for revision (Gere & Abbott, 1985). Regardless of how the groups are formed, students need instruction, demonstrations, reminders, and time to learn to conference well and support each other as writers (Atwell, 1998).

In other classrooms the writers group membership is established, usually by the teacher, and maintained for a period of time. Students get together when all students in a group have completed rough drafts and are ready to share their writing. Sometimes the teacher participates in these groups, providing feedback along with the students. At other times, the writers groups can function independently. Four or five students are assigned to each group, and a list of groups and their members is posted in the classroom. The teacher puts a star by one student's name, and that student serves as group leader. The leader changes intermittently to give all group members the opportunity to be leader.

In writers groups, students share their writing through the activities listed in the following Step by Step box:

Step by Step

Writers Groups

1. *The writer reads.*   Students take turns reading their compositions aloud to the group. All the students listen politely, thinking about compliments and suggestions they will make after the writer finishes reading. Only the writer looks at the composition, because when classmates and teacher look at it, they quickly notice and comment on mechanical errors, even though the emphasis during revising is on content. Listening to the composition read aloud keeps the focus on content.

2. *Listeners offer compliments.*   Next, writers group members say what they liked about the writing. These positive comments should be specific, focusing on strengths, rather than the often heard "I liked it" or "It was good." Even though these are positive comments, they do not provide

effective feedback. When teachers introduce revision, they should model appropriate responses because students may not know how to offer specific and meaningful comments. The teacher and students can brainstorm a list of appropriate comments and post it in the classroom for students to refer to. Comments may focus on organization, leads, word choice, voice, sequence, dialogue, theme, and so on. Possible comments are

I like the part where . . .

I'd like to know more about . . .

I like the way you described . . .

Your writing made me feel . . .

I like the order you used in your writing because . . .

3. *The writer asks questions.* After a round of positive comments, writers ask for assistance with trouble spots they identified earlier when rereading their writing, or they may ask questions that reflect more general concerns about how well they are communicating. Admitting that they need help from their classmates is a major step in students' learning to revise. Possible questions to classmates are

What do you want to know more about?

Is there a part that I should throw away?

What details can I add?

What do you think the best part of my writing is?

Are there some words I need to change?

4. *Listeners offer suggestions.* Members of the writers group ask questions about things that were unclear to them, and they make suggestions about how to revise the composition. Almost any writer resists constructive criticism, and it is especially difficult for elementary students to appreciate suggestions. It is important to teach students what kinds of comments and suggestions are acceptable so that they will word what they say in helpful rather than hurtful ways. Possible comments and suggestions that students can offer are

I got confused in the part about . . .

Do you need a closing?

Could you add more about . . .?

I wonder if your paragraphs are in the right order because . . .

Could you combine some sentences?

5. *The process is repeated.* The first four steps are repeated for each student's composition. This is the appropriate time for the teacher to provide input as well. The teacher should react to the piece of writing as any other listener would—not error-hunting with red pen in hand (Sommers, 1994). In fact, most teachers prefer to listen to students read their compositions aloud, since teachers may become frustrated by having to contend with the numerous misspelled words and nearly illegible handwriting common in handwritten and unedited drafts.

6. *Writers plan for revision.* At the end of the writers group session, all students make a commitment to revise their writing based on the comments and suggestions of the group members. The final decisions on what to revise always rest with the writers themselves, but with the understanding that their rough drafts are not perfect comes the realization that some revision will be necessary. When students verbalize their planned revisions, they are more likely to complete the revision stage. Some students also make notes for themselves about their revision plans. After the group disbands, students make the revisions.

Revising on the Basis of Feedback. Students make four types of changes: additions, substitutions, deletions, and moves (Faigley & Witte, 1981). As they revise, students might add words, substitute sentences, delete paragraphs, and move phrases. Students often use a blue or red pen to cross out, draw arrows, and write in the space left between the double-spaced lines of their rough drafts so that revisions will show clearly. When using a computer for writing, students can print a copy of their rough drafts before making revisions. That way, teachers can examine the types of revisions students make by examining their revised rough drafts. Revisions are another gauge of students' growth as writers.

Conferencing with the Teacher. Conferences play an important role in all aspects of literacy learning (Calkins, 1994). In writing conferences, the focus is on the student as writer. The particular piece of writing being addressed is the vehicle for coaching the writer. The teacher's role during conferences is to help students make choices and define directions for revision. Barry Lane (1993) offers these suggestions for talking with students about their papers:

- Have students come to a conference prepared to begin talking about their concerns. Students should talk first in a conference.
- Ask questions rather than give answers. Ask students what is working well for them, what problems they are having, and what questions they have.
- React to students' writing as a reader, not as a teacher. Offer compliments first; give suggestions later.
- Keep the conference short and recognize that not all problem areas or concerns can be discussed.
- Limit the number of revision suggestions and make all suggestions specific.
- Have students meet in writers groups before they conference with the teacher. Then students can share the feedback they received from classmates.
- To conclude the conference, ask students to identify the revisions they plan to make.
- Take notes during conferences and summarize students' revision plans. These notes are a record of the conference, and the revision plans can be used in assessing students' revisions.

It is time-consuming to meet with every student, but many teachers believe it to be worthwhile (Calkins, 1994; Graves, 1994). In a short 5-minute conference, teachers listen to students talk about their writing processes, guide students as they make revision plans, and offer feedback during the writing process when it is most usable.

STAGE 4: EDITING

Editing is putting the piece of writing into its final form. Until this stage, the focus has been primarily on the content of students' writing. Once the focus changes to mechanics, students polish their writing by correcting misspellings and other mechanical errors. The goal here is to make the writing "optimally readable" (Smith, 1982). Writers who write for readers understand that if their compositions are not readable, they have written in vain because their ideas will never be read.

Mechanics are the commonly accepted conventions of written Standard English. They include capitalization, punctuation, spelling, sentence structure, usage, and formatting considerations specific to poems, scripts, letters, and other writing forms. The use of these commonly accepted conventions is a courtesy to those who will read the composition.

Mechanical skills are best taught during the editing stage, not through workbook exercises. When editing a composition that will be shared with a genuine audience, students are more interested in using mechanical skills correctly so that they can communicate effectively. In a study of two third-grade classes, Calkins (1980) found that the students in the class who learned punctuation marks as a part of editing could define or explain more marks than the students in the other class who were taught punctuation skills in a traditional manner, with instruction and practice exercises on each punctuation mark. In other words, the results of this research, as well as other studies (Graves, 1994; Routman, 1996; Weaver, 1996), suggest that students learn mechanical skills better as part of the writing process than through practice exercises.

Students move through three activities in the editing stage:

- Getting distance from the composition
- Proofreading to locate errors
- Correcting errors

Getting Distance from the Composition. Students are more efficient editors if they set the composition aside for a few days before beginning to edit. After working so closely with a piece of writing during drafting and revising, they are too familiar with it to be able to locate many mechanical errors. With the distance gained by waiting a few days, children are better able to approach editing with a fresh perspective and gather the enthusiasm necessary to finish the writing process by making the paper optimally readable.

Proofreading to Locate Errors. Students proofread their compositions to locate and mark possible errors. Proofreading is a unique type of reading in which students read slowly, word by word, hunting for errors rather than reading quickly for meaning (King, 1985). Concentrating on mechanics is difficult because our natural inclination is to read for meaning. Even experienced proofreaders often find themselves reading for meaning and thus overlooking errors that do not inhibit meaning. It is important, therefore, to take time to explain proofreading and demonstrate how it differs from regular reading.

To demonstrate proofreading, a teacher copies a piece of student writing onto the chalkboard or displays it on a screen using a computer and projector. The teacher reads it several times, each time hunting for a particular type of error. During each reading, the teacher reads the composition slowly, softly pronouncing each word and pointing to focus attention on it. The teacher marks possible errors as they are located.

Errors are marked or corrected with special proofreaders' marks. Students enjoy using these marks, the same ones that adult authors and editors use. Proofreaders' marks that elementary students can learn to use in editing their writing are presented in Figure 4–5 on page 156. Editing checklists help students focus on particular types of errors. Teachers can develop checklists with two to six items appropriate for the grade level. A grade 1 checklist, for example, might include only two items—perhaps one about capital letters at the beginning of sentences and a second about periods at the end of sentences. In contrast, a middle-grade checklist might include items such as using commas in a series, indenting paragraphs, capitalizing proper nouns, and spelling homonyms correctly. Teachers can revise the checklist during the school year to focus attention on skills that have recently been taught.

A sample grade 3 editing checklist is presented in Figure 4–6 on page 156. First, students proofread their own compositions, searching for errors in each category on the checklist; after proofreading, they check off each item. Then, after completing the checklist, students sign their names and trade checklists and compositions. Now they become editors and complete each other's checklist. Having both author and editor sign the checklist helps them to take the activity seriously.

For students in the intermediate grades, the focus shifts even more to the content of the writing while still requiring rereading for errors in spelling and punctuation. "Children need to know that editing involves not only correcting errors but also tightening and linking, smoothing out language, ordering thoughts, and listening to the poetry of one's sentences" (Calkins, 1994, p. 301). An example of an editing checklist for grade 6 writers is presented in Figure 4–7 on page 157.

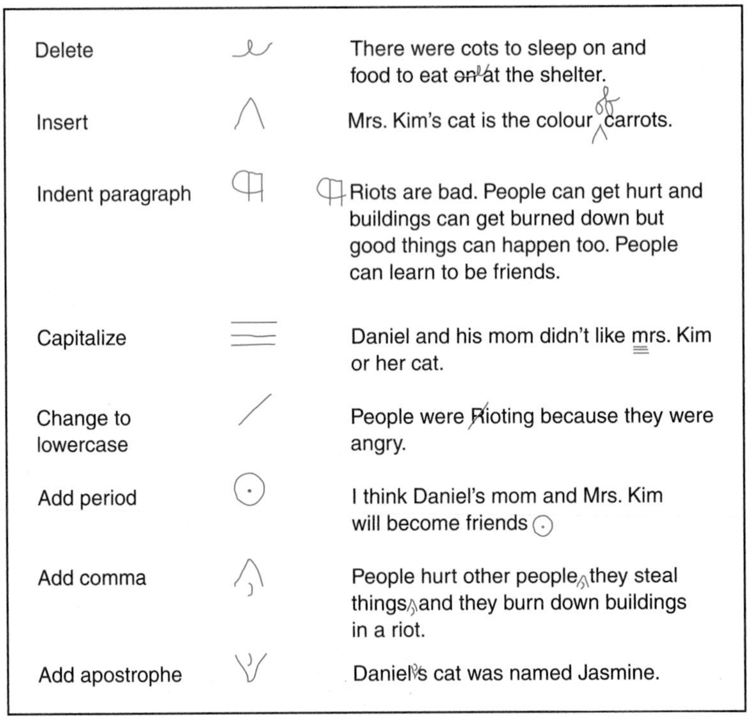

Delete	ℒ	There were cots to sleep on and food to eat on at the shelter.
Insert	∧	Mrs. Kim's cat is the colour carrots.
Indent paragraph	⊄	⊄ Riots are bad. People can get hurt and buildings can get burned down but good things can happen too. People can learn to be friends.
Capitalize	≡	Daniel and his mom didn't like mrs. Kim or her cat.
Change to lowercase	/	People were Rioting because they were angry.
Add period	⊙	I think Daniel's mom and Mrs. Kim will become friends ⊙
Add comma	⋀	People hurt other people they steal things and they burn down buildings in a riot.
Add apostrophe	⋁	Daniels cat was named Jasmine.

Figure 4–5 Proofreaders' Marks

Editing Checklist

Author	Editor	
☐	☐	1. I have circled the words that might be misspelled.
☐	☐	2. I have checked that all sentences begin with capital letters.
☐	☐	3. I have checked that all sentences end with punctuation marks.
☐	☐	4. I have checked that all proper nouns begin with a capital letter.

Signatures:

Author: _____   *Editor:* _____

Figure 4–6 A Grade 3 Editing Checklist

Title:

Date Began: Date Finished:

Editor: Peer Editor:

- Have you reread your writing carefully, noting the places where it seems particularly strong and clear?

- Have you reread it carefully, trying to imagine places where readers might be confused?

- Have you underlined words that look as if they may not be spelled correctly and tried to get some help on those words?

- Have you reread your piece aloud, paying attention to the punctuation?

- Have you tried to cut your piece, taking out the extra words that don't add much?

- Have you tried adding to your piece or changing your writing where there is confusion?

- What new risks have you taken with the conventions of written language?

- What questions do you have? What are the issues around which you want help?

Figure 4–7 A Grade 6 Editing Checklist
Source: Adapted from Calkins, 1994.

Correcting Errors. After students proofread their compositions and locate the errors, they correct the errors individually or with an editor's assistance. Some errors are easy to correct, some require use of a dictionary, and others involve instruction from the teacher. It is unrealistic to expect students to locate and correct every mechanical error in their compositions.

When mechanical correctness is crucial, students can meet with the teacher for a final editing conference. Teachers proofread the composition with the student, and they identify and make the remaining corrections together, or the teacher makes check marks in the margin to note errors for the student to correct independently. Error correction is an important step in the writing process, one that is significantly simplified by word processing.

STAGE 5: PUBLISHING

In this stage students bring their compositions to life by publishing them or sharing them orally with an appropriate audience. When they share their writing with real audiences of classmates, other students, parents, and the community, students come to think of themselves as authors. Students undertake activities such as the following in the publishing stage:

- Making books of stories and poetry
- Producing pamphlets, newspapers, and newsletters
- Sharing writing orally and electronically
- Producing illustrated, informational reports

Making Books. One of the most popular ways for children to publish their writing is by making books (L. King & Stovall, 1992). Simple booklets can be made by folding a sheet of paper into quarters, like a greeting card. Students write the title on the front and use the three remaining sides for their compositions. They can also construct booklets by stapling sheets of writing paper together and adding construction paper covers. Sheets of wallpaper cut from old sample books also make sturdy covers. These stapled booklets can be cut into various shapes, too. Students can also produce formatted manuscripts using computer software that allows integration of text and illustrations. Students can make more sophisticated books by covering cardboard covers with contact paper, wallpaper samples, or cloth. Pages are sewn or stapled together, and the first and last pages (endpapers) are glued to the cardboard covers to hold the book together. Directions for making one type of hardcover book are shown in Figure 4–8.

Sharing Writing. Students read their writing to classmates or share it with larger audiences through hardcover books placed in the class or school library, plays performed for classmates, or letters sent to authors, businesses, and other correspondents. Computer programs and websites can be helpful for publishing student writing as well. Other ways students might share writing are as follows:

- Read it aloud in class and to other classes
- Submit it to writing contests
- Display it as a mobile
- Contribute it to a class anthology
- Contribute it to the local newspaper or literary magazine
- Make a shape book
- Make an audio recording
- Read it at a school assembly
- Share it at a read-aloud party
- Share it with parents, siblings, or grandparents
- Produce a video of it
- Display poetry on a "poet-tree"
- Send it to a pen pal
- Make a hardbound book
- Produce it as a roller movie
- Display it on a bulletin board
- Make a big book
- Design a poster about it
- Share it as a puppet show
- Create a PowerPoint presentation of it
- Publish it on the Internet

Through this sharing, students communicate with genuine audiences who respond to their writing in meaningful ways.

Sharing writing is a social activity that helps children develop sensitivity to audiences and confidence in themselves as authors. Dyson (1985) advises that teachers consider the social interpretations of sharing—students' behaviour, teacher's behaviour, and interaction between students and teacher—within the classroom context. Individual students interpret sharing differently. More than just providing the opportunity for students to share writing, teachers need to teach students how to respond to their classmates. Teachers themselves serve as a model for responding to students' writing without dominating the sharing.

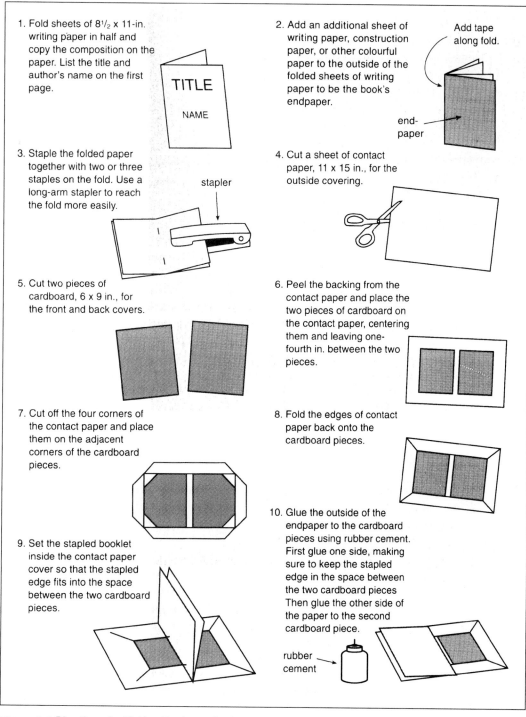

1. Fold sheets of 8½ x 11-in. writing paper in half and copy the composition on the paper. List the title and author's name on the first page.

2. Add an additional sheet of writing paper, construction paper, or other colourful paper to the outside of the folded sheets of writing paper to be the book's endpaper.

3. Staple the folded paper together with two or three staples on the fold. Use a long-arm stapler to reach the fold more easily.

4. Cut a sheet of contact paper, 11 x 15 in., for the outside covering.

5. Cut two pieces of cardboard, 6 x 9 in., for the front and back covers.

6. Peel the backing from the contact paper and place the two pieces of cardboard on the contact paper, centering them and leaving one-fourth in. between the two pieces.

7. Cut off the four corners of the contact paper and place them on the adjacent corners of the cardboard pieces.

8. Fold the edges of contact paper back onto the cardboard pieces.

9. Set the stapled booklet inside the contact paper cover so that the stapled edge fits into the space between the two cardboard pieces.

10. Glue the outside of the endpaper to the cardboard pieces using rubber cement. First glue one side, making sure to keep the stapled edge in the space between the two cardboard pieces Then glue the other side of the paper to the second cardboard piece.

Figure 4–8 Directions for Making Hardcover Books

TEACHING THE WRITING PROCESS

Learning to use the writing process is more important than any particular writing project students might be involved in because the writing process is a tool. Students need many opportunities to learn to use the writing process. Teachers model the writing process by writing class collaborations, and they teach minilessons on the writing process that look at the procedures, concepts, strategies, and skills writers use.

Writing Class Collaborations. One way to introduce the writing process is to write a collaborative or group composition. The teacher models the writing process and provides an opportunity for students to practise the process approach to writing in a supportive environment. As students and the teacher write a composition together, they move through the five stages of the writing process just as writers do when they work independently. The teacher demonstrates the strategies that writers use and clarifies misconceptions during the group composition, and students offer ideas for writing as well as suggestions for tackling common writing problems. With young students, the whole composition may be written collaboratively, whereas with older students, the teacher may choose to write a particular part of the composition or writing project.

For more information on writing a class collaborative story, see the profile in this chapter, "Student Authors at Work," on pages 124–125.

The teacher begins by introducing the idea of writing a group composition and by reviewing the project. Students dictate a rough draft, which the teacher records on the chalkboard, on chart paper, or on the computer. The teacher notes any misunderstandings students have about the writing assignment or process and, when necessary, reviews concepts and offers suggestions. Then the teacher and students read the composition and identify ways to revise it. Some parts of the composition will need reworking, and other parts may be deleted or moved. More specific words will be substituted for less specific ones, and redundant words and sentences will be deleted. Students may also want to add new parts to the composition. After making the necessary content changes, students proofread the composition, checking for mechanical errors, paragraph breaks, and sentences to combine. They correct errors and make changes. Then the teacher or a student copies the completed composition to chart paper, to a sheet of notebook paper, or onto the computer. Copies can be made and given to each student.

Collaborative compositions are an essential part of many writing experiences, especially when students are learning to use the writing process or a new writing form. Group compositions serve as a "dry run" during which students' questions and misconceptions can be clarified.

Minilessons on the Writing Process. Students need to learn how to move through the five stages of the writing process, how to gather and organize ideas for writing, how to participate in writers groups, how to proofread, and how to share their writing. Teachers teach these procedures, concepts, and strategies and skills during minilessons.

Minilessons can be taught as part of class collaborations, during resource-based units and thematic units, and in writers workshop. A list of topics for minilessons on the writing process is presented on page 143. Many teachers use the editing stage as a time to informally assess students' spelling, capitalization, punctuation, and other mechanical skills, and to give minilessons on a skill that a student or several students are having trouble with. The teacher notes which students are having difficulty with a particular skill—paragraphing, capitalizing proper nouns, or using the apostrophe in possessives, for example—and conducts an impromptu minilesson using the students' writing as the basis of the lesson. In this brief, 5-minute lesson, the teacher reviews the particular skill, and students practise it as they correct their own writing and help to correct their classmates' writing. This procedure individualizes instruction and teaches the skill when learning it matters and is relevant to students.

For more information on minilessons, see Chapter 2, "Teaching the Language Arts," page 65.

In Resource-Based Units. Students use the writing process as they create projects during the extending stage of the reading process. Sometimes the class works together to write a class collaboration; sometimes students work in small groups on the same writing project; and at other times students work on a variety of writing projects. Here are three examples:

- After reading Freeman's teddy bear story *Corduroy* (1968), a class of grade 1 students worked together to write a retelling of the story, which they published as a big book.

- During an author unit on Chris Van Allsburg, grade 5 students each chose an illustration from *The Mysteries of Harris Burdick* (1984) and wrote a description or story about it.

- As part of a unit on point of view, grade 7 students each rewrote familiar folktales from the viewpoint of one character after reading *The True Story of the 3 Little Pigs!* (Scieszka, 1989), which is told from the wolf's viewpoint.

In each of these projects, students used the writing process and moved through all five stages as they prewrote, drafted, revised, edited, and published their compositions.

In Thematic Units. Teachers often plan writing projects in connection with thematic units. Frequently, the projects involve writing forms and information from more than one area of the curriculum. For example, a thematic unit concerning protecting the environment might include persuasive writing when students write letters of protest to government officials. A unit concerning historical figures might involve biography writing. In these cases, teachers review the writing forms required in minilessons and draw upon information learned in other subject areas.

Sometimes all students in the classroom work together on a single project, such as making an alphabet book about the ocean as part of a theme on the oceans, or writing a collection of animal poems to display with the animal sculptures they made in art. At other times, however, students choose projects and work independently. For example, during a thematic unit on pioneers, students might choose one of the following projects:

- Write a simulated journal from the viewpoint of a pioneer.
- Write a story about a pioneer family.
- Write an informational book about covered wagons.
- Write an explanation to accompany a relief map of the pioneer trails across Canada.
- Make a timeline for westward expansion in Canada, with notes about important dates and events.
- Make posters about pioneer legends (e.g., Alexander Mackenzie, Peter Pond, and Jerry Potts).

For each of these projects, students use the writing process to develop their compositions. They meet in writers groups to share their drafts and revise their compositions using feedback from peers and their teacher. They also edit their compositions to correct as many mechanical errors as possible. Then they make final copies of their compositions and share them with classmates or other audiences.

In Inquiry-Based Units. Students use the writing process in inquiry-based units in same way they do in resource-based and thematic units. They select topics, gather information, compose drafts, revise, edit, and publish. Students often choose topics in which they have particular interest. Teachers make it possible for students to pursue interests by designing writing projects that are flexible and open-ended, yet linked to whole class studies.

Students sit in the author's chair to share writing with classmates.

In a grade 7 class, students became interested in genealogy after one student reported that his family was able to trace roots to early settlers in Nova Scotia. Several students in the class read Sheree Fitch's *The Gravesavers* (2005) and were intrigued by 12-year-old Minn's fight to save the eroding maritime graves of shipwrecked victims who had hoped to be settlers. The teacher asked the students to create a piece of writing that demonstrated their ability to combine fact and fiction. As writers of historical fiction they were to demonstrate knowledge of family and social history. Students wrote letters, diary entries, newspaper articles, ballads, and short stories using the writing process. By using a process approach they learned from each other as writers and historians.

About Writers Workshop and Writing Process. Sometimes *writers workshop* and *writing process* are confused or mistakenly used interchangeably. We use *writers workshop* to refer to a way of organizing writing instruction that facilitates the writing process. The *writing process* refers to the stages through which writers move a composition from idea generation to publication. It would be convenient if the writing process were equated with an instructional framework that included prewriting on Monday, drafting on Tuesday, revising on Wednesday, editing on Thursday, and publishing on Friday, but it does not. Writers move back and forth through the stages as they develop, refine, and polish their compositions, and they participate in some activities, such as revising, throughout the writing process (Flower & Hayes, 1994). The process for a particular piece often ends during a special time set aside for students to share their published writing projects with an interested audience. Sharing is a social experience, and when students share their writing with real audiences, they feel the satisfaction of a job well done.

Responding to Student Writing. The teacher's role should not be restricted to that of evaluator. Again and again, researchers report that although teachers are the most common audience for student writing, they are also one of the worst audiences, because they read with a red pen in hand. Teachers should instead read their students' writing for information, enjoyment, and all the reasons that other readers do. Much of students' writing does not need to be assessed; it should simply be shared with the teacher as a "trusted adult" (Calkins, 1994).

For more information on how to adapt the writing process for young children, see Chapter 3, "Emergent Literacy," pages 119–122.

When students use a process approach to writing, there is less chance they will plagiarize because they will have developed their compositions step-by-step—from prewriting and drafting to revising and editing. Nonetheless, at some time or other and increasingly with Internet access, most teachers fear that a composition they are reading is not the student's own work. Jackson, Tway, and Frager (1987) cite several reasons why students might plagiarize. First, some students may simply internalize a piece of writing through repeated readings so that, months or years later, they do not realize that it is not their own work. Second, some students may plagiarize because of competition to succeed. Third, students can plagiarize by accident, not realizing the consequences of their actions. A final reason some students plagiarize is that they have not been taught to write by means of a process approach, so they may not know how to synthesize information for a report from published sources. The two best ways to avoid having students copy work from another source and pass it off as their own are to teach the writing process and to have students write mostly at school rather than at home. Students who work at school and move through the various writing process activities know how to complete the writing project.

ADAPTING TO MEET THE NEEDS OF EVERY STUDENT

Teachers adapt the activities involved in each stage of the writing process to make writing a successful experience for all students. Teachers often shorten the writing process to three stages—prewriting, drafting, and publishing—for young children and for students with few

Adapting

The Writing Process to Meet the Needs of Every Student

Stage 1: Prewriting
- Use drawing as a rehearsal activity.
- Have students "talk out" their compositions before beginning to write.
- Draw a cluster with students, using the ideas and words they suggest.
- Make available multiple sources of topical information.

Stage 2: Drafting
- Have students dictate their drafts.
- Mark students' papers so that they write on every other line to allow space for revision.
- Reassure students that spelling and other mechanical skills are not important in this stage.
- Have older students act as "scribes" for younger children.
- Have students draft using a computer if handwriting/printing is too difficult.
- Encourage students to explore more than one form of writing to carry their message.

Stage 3: Revising
- Participate in writers groups with older, more capable students.
- Focus on compliments rather than on suggestions for revisions when students begin writers groups.
- Expect students to make only one or two revisions at first.
- Expect talented writers to be astutely aware of audience.

Stage 4: Editing
- Teach students how to proofread.
- Have students mark possible errors; then correct errors with them.
- Have students identify and correct errors on the first page of their compositions; then correct remaining errors for students when edited copy is required.
- Encourage self- and peer-editing among talented writers.

Stage 5: Publishing
- Use a word processor for final copies.
- Input the final copy for students.
- Provide opportunities for students to share their writing with a trusted group of classmates.
- Do not correct any remaining errors on the final copy.
- Ensure a wide audience for talented writers products.

For more information on how to teach students to write reports without plagiarizing, see Chapter 9, "Reading and Writing Expository Text," pages 297–305.

successful writing experiences. Then, as students become more fluent writers and develop audience awareness, teachers add the revising and editing stages. Teachers also pair students with special needs with older students who act as scribes, recording the story as their partners tell it. When working with talented student writers, teachers extend the scope of writing projects and encourage elaboration at all stages of the process.

Teachers can develop checklists with activities for each stage of the writing process listed so that students with short attention spans or students who have trouble completing an assignment can stay on task. Other suggestions for adapting each stage are listed on page 163.

Connections between Reading and Writing

Reading and writing are both meaning-making processes, and readers and writers are involved in many similar activities. It is important that teachers plan literacy activities so that students can connect reading and writing.

COMPARING THE TWO PROCESSES

The reading and writing processes have comparable activities at each stage (Butler & Turbill, 1984). In both reading and writing the goal is to construct meaning, and, as shown in Figure 4–9, reading and writing activities at each stage are similar. For example, notice the similarities between the activities listed for responding and revising—the third stage in reading and writing, respectively. Fitzgerald (1989) analyzed these two activities and concluded that they draw on similar processes of author–reader–text interactions. Similar analyses can be made for other activities, as well.

Tierney (1983) explains that reading and writing are multidimensional and involve concurrent, complex transactions between writers, between writers as readers, between readers, and between readers as writers. Writers participate in several types of reading activities. They read other authors' works to obtain ideas and to learn about the structure of stories, but they also read and reread their own work in order to problem-solve, discover, monitor, and clarify. That is, readers are involved in many of the same activities that writers use—generating ideas, organizing, monitoring, problem solving, and revising. Smith (1982) believes that reading influences writing skills because readers unconsciously "read like writers":

> To read like a writer we engage with the author in what the author is writing. We can anticipate what the author will say, so that the author is in effect writing on our behalf, not showing how something is done but doing it with us. . . . Bit by bit, one thing at a time, but enormous numbers of things over the passage of time, the learner learns through reading like a writer to write like a writer. (pp. 563–564)

Also, both reading and writing are recursive, cycling back through various parts of the process; and, just as writers compose text, readers compose their meaning.

CLASSROOM CONNECTIONS

Teachers can help students appreciate the similarities between reading and writing in many ways. Tierney explains: "What we need are reading teachers who act as if their students were developing writers and writing teachers who act as if their students were readers" (1983, p. 151). These are some ways to point out the relationships between reading and writing:

1. Help writers assume alternative points of view as potential readers.
2. Help readers consider the writer's purpose and viewpoint.

	What Readers Do	**What Writers Do**
Stage 1	*Preparing*	*Prewriting*
	Readers use knowledge about • the topic • reading • literature • language systems	Writers use knowledge about • the topic • writing • literature • language systems
	Readers' expectations are cued by • previous reading/writing experiences • format of the text • purpose for reading • audience for reading	Writers' expectations are cued by • previous reading/writing experiences • format of the text • purpose for writing • audience for writing
	Readers make predictions.	Writers gather and organize ideas.
Stage 2	*Reading*	*Drafting*
	Readers • use word identification strategies • use meaning-making strategies • monitor reading • create meaning	Writers • use transcription strategies • use meaning-making strategies • monitor writing • create meaning
Stage 3	*Responding*	*Revising*
	Readers • respond to the text • interpret meaning • clarify misunderstandings • expand ideas	Writers • respond to the text • interpret meaning • clarify misunderstandings • expand ideas
Stage 4	*Exploring*	*Editing*
	Readers • examine the impact of words and literary language • explore structural elements • compare the text to others	Writers • identify and correct mechanical errors • review paragraph and sentence structure
Stage 5	*Extending*	*Publishing*
	Readers • go beyond the text to extend their interpretations • share projects with classmates • reflect on the reading process • make connections to life and literature • value the piece of literature • feel success • want to read again	Writers • produce the finished copy of their compositions • share their compositions with genuine audiences • reflect on the writing process • value the composition • feel success • want to write again

Figure 4–9 A Comparison of the Reading and Writing Processes
Source: Adapted from Butler & Turbill, 1984.

3. Point out that reading is much like composing, so that students will view reading as a process, much like the writing process.

4. Talk with students about the similarities between the reading and writing processes.

5. Talk with students about similarities and linkages between reading and writing strategies.

For more information on reading and writing strategies, see Chapter 1, "Learning and the Language Arts," pages 35–36.

Readers and writers use similar strategies for constructing meaning as they interact with print. As readers, we use a variety of problem-solving strategies to make decisions about an author's meaning and to construct meaning for ourselves. As writers, we also use problem-solving strategies to decide what our readers need as we construct meaning for them and for ourselves. Comparing reading to writing, Tierney and Pearson (1983) described reading as a composing process because readers compose and refine meaning through reading much as writers do. Connecting reading and writing is not a new idea. Researchers have consistently supported integration of the language arts for many years (Dahl & Farnan, 1998; Durkin, 1989; Loban, 1963).

There are practical benefits to connecting reading and writing. Reading contributes to students' writing development, and writing contributes to students' reading development. Shanahan (1988) has outlined seven instructional principles for relating reading and writing so that students develop a clear concept of literacy:

1. Involve students in reading and writing experiences every day.
2. Introduce reading and writing processes in kindergarten.
3. Plan instruction that reflects the developmental nature of the reading–writing relationship.
4. Make the reading–writing connection explicit to students.
5. Emphasize both the processes and the products of reading and writing.
6. Emphasize the purposes for which students use reading and writing.
7. Teach reading and writing through meaningful, functional, and genuine literacy experiences.

OTHER CONSIDERATIONS IN TEACHING READING AND WRITING PROCESSES

A Balanced Approach. It is important to consider and maintain balance when teaching students to read and write. In a balanced language arts program, teachers devote attention to each component in accordance with its importance to literacy development and students' needs. Our responsibility as teachers is to discern the level and intensity of instruction required for individuals or small groups and modify our instruction accordingly. Likewise, students learn at different rates. In a balanced language arts program, the teacher makes adjustments for these and other variables.

Balanced instruction guides a teacher's instructional decision making. Teachers wishing to achieve the highest rate of reading and writing success for their students will continuously seek balance in the following areas:

- Teaching students and facilitating their learning; that is, balancing teacher-directed explicit instruction and learner-centred discovery learning
- Employing instructional approaches to reading and writing and open activity time; that is, balancing sequenced, prescribed instruction and curriculum based on learner needs
- Using code and meaning methodologies; that is, balancing isolated skill emphasis with meaning emphasis methods
- Teaching intervention strategies incidentally to individual students and teaching direct lessons based on core curriculum standards; that is, balancing unplanned and planned instruction

- Using trade books and published teaching materials; that is, balancing student- and teacher-selected materials

- Using informal observations and formal assessment; that is, balancing authentic assessment and norm-referenced standardized tests

- Teaching use and awareness of language; that is, balancing and integrating the processes of all the language arts within the context (Blair-Larsen & Williams, 1999)

Gender Differences in Reading and Writing. As early as kindergarten and grade 1, the difference between the reading and writing preferences of girls and boys is evident. In writing, stereotypical gender roles and relationships are reflected in the characters, plots, and styles of children's stories (Peterson, 2001). In reading, research also shows that boys resist aesthetic reading of fictional texts and have difficulty expressing their feelings in peer groups about what they have read. It is important to consider gender differences when teaching reading and writing to children and young adults (Cole, 1997).

The following examples illustrate these differences. In their writing, grade 1 girls tend to choose domesticated animals (e.g., cats, horses), while boys choose animals that are dangerous and wild (e.g., cougars, monsters). Grade 2 girls choose "primary territory" as the focus of their writing (e.g., home, school, parents, friends), while boys choose secondary territory (e.g., professions) or extended territory (e.g., wars, space) as the focus of their writing (Newkirk, 2000).

Grade 2 boys write stories that tend to focus on contests, physical and social, in which the protagonists act alone. Success is determined by winning or losing. By contrast, grade 2 girls write stories that tend to focus more on joint action and protagonists who struggle to remain connected to the community (Trepanier-Street, Romatowski, & McNair, 1990).

Boys read far less than girls at all age levels. By adolescence, 85 percent of girls read for pleasure compared with only 65 percent of boys (Moffitt & Wartella, 1992). And the choices of what they read differ significantly. Girls are interested in stories that emphasize personal feelings and relationships, and boys prefer scary stories, sports books, adventure stories, comics, and magazines. By adolescence, boys will have spent countless hours reading code books for video games.

Male students often perceive school-defined literacy as excluding or even dismissing their preferences (Newkirk, 2000). They generally conclude that reading and writing is more "natural" for girls. For boys generally, literacy gets in the way of the need to move, to talk, to play, to live with and in one's own body. There is a perception in young readers and writers of both genders that literacy entails solitude, isolation from peers, and loneliness (Newkirk, 2000).

It is imperative for teachers to consider these gender differences when teaching the reading and writing processes to children of all ages. For example, teachers who are sensitive to these needs use strategies that encourage boys in reading and writing what is of interest to them (Young & Brozo, 2001). Reading aloud to boys from texts that reflect their interests will help them continue to develop as competent readers. As well, by introducing texts that reflect the choices and preferences of both genders, teachers help broaden boys' and girls' interests and their appreciation for each other.

We must also reconsider literacy practices, which are often viewed as universally good, and their effects on girls' and boys' reading and writing development. In particular, the personal growth model advocated by Dixon (1967), and implicitly endorsed by many teachers, requires re-examination. This model, which stresses personal relationships; "expressive" writing; directness of feeling and sensory awareness; and realistic, introspective fiction; is often valued over comedy, science fiction, crime novels, and nonfiction—all genres which may appeal more to boys and could be the models for their own future writing. As such, boys may feel that their preferences aren't validated in reading and writing.

A balanced approach to gender issues in reading and writing focuses on what is of interest to students, with activities that students find personally meaningful (Au, 1997). The idea that children learn to read by reading and to write by writing remains true. However, we need to accommodate gender differences by expanding our notions of what is of interest to boys and girls and by valuing those differences as boys and girls grow and develop into mature readers and writers.

Review

Reading and writing are similar processes of constructing meaning. Teachers organize reading and writing instruction using the five stages of the reading and writing processes. Students learn to use the reading and writing processes through resource-based, thematic, and inquiry-based units as well as readers and writers workshops.

The following key concepts are presented in this chapter:

1. The cognitive process of reading is complex and not yet fully understood. Understandings have been captured in models of the flow of information from the eye to meaningful message.

2. The five stages of reading are preparing, reading, responding, exploring, and extending.

3. Students use aesthetic reading when they read for enjoyment and efferent reading when they read for information.

4. Students use the Goldilocks Strategy or a modified version of it to choose books at their reading level.

5. Five ways to read a selection are shared reading, guided reading, independent reading, buddy reading, and reading aloud.

6. The five stages of the writing process are prewriting, drafting, revising, editing, and publishing.

7. Purpose, form, and audience are three considerations that influence students' compositions.

8. Teachers present minilessons on procedures, concepts, skills, and strategies in the reading and writing processes.

9. There are gender differences in reading and writing that influence effective learning and teaching.

10. The goal of both reading and writing is to construct meaning, and both processes have comparable activities at each stage.

Extensions

1. Observe students using the reading and writing processes in an elementary or middle school classroom. In what types of preparing, reading, responding, exploring, and extending activities are they involved?

2. Observe students using the writing process. What minilessons would be beneficial to them?

3. Plan a resource-based unit or thematic unit and include a variety of activities on the reading and writing processes.

4. Sit in on a writers group in which students share their writing and ask peers for feedback in revising their compositions. Make a list of the students' questions and comments. What conclusions can you draw about their interactions with each other?

5. Reflect on your own reading and writing processes. Are you conscious of moving through the stages when you are engaged in reading and writing? What strategies do you use at each stage? How do you vary your reading when you read aesthetically and efferently?

6. Observe students composing using a computer. How do they engage in the writing process as they work?

chapter five

Listening and Speaking in the Classroom

Grade 3 Makes Literacy a Family Thing

Procedure

Since I began teaching four years ago, I have experimented with ways to motivate children to read for enjoyment. Giving extrinsic rewards in the form of stickers and treats has been somewhat effective, but it also sends a message that reading is something you do to earn points or prizes. That is not the message I want to deliver. Literacy is a Family Thing (LIFT), the family literacy program that I started this year with my grade 3 class, sends a different message. It says clearly that reading is a pleasurable activity that you anticipate and do with people you love.

LIFT is based on sharing book bags, and is similar to other "backpack" programs that support reading and writing by providing families with books and materials. I put together fifteen colourful book bags that the children take home on alternating weeks. Each book bag is centred on a theme, and contains a novel (chapter book), a picture book, and an informational book. A few book bags include theme-related videos. Each bag also contains a letter to adult family members giving suggestions for response activities and materials needed for the suggested activities. Most response activities are designed to require family members' interaction, and include such things as retelling stories using puppets or felt board characters, following a recipe, doing simple crafts, and writing stories, postcards, or letters.

> "The LIFT program has generated genuine enthusiasm for reading and writing at school and at home. I feel strongly that this is a way to lead children to develop a lasting love of reading."
>
> Samantha Schultz
> Stirling School
> Stirling, Alberta

The children take the book bags home on Thursday afternoons and bring them back to school the following Thursday morning. When book bags come back to

to develop a lasting love of reading. This early literary experience within their families sends a message I want to endorse. I can't imagine teaching without LIFT.

Guidelines for LIFT Book Bags

1. When a new book bag arrives in your home, check to see that it contains the materials listed on the contents card. If something is missing, please notify your child's teacher.
2. Plan time for your family to read and complete the activities during the next week. You need not do all activities. Rather, review the books and activities, and choose which ones you will do.
3. Please return the book bags on Thursday mornings. Returning bags on time is very important. Another child and family are anxiously waiting.
4. Encourage all family members to handle books, materials, and bags with care. Care is essential if the book bags are to be a lasting addition to our program. Parents are asked to reimburse the costs of any lost or damaged books.
5. Talk about the books before, during, and after reading with your children. Introduce the books to your children, or let the children introduce them to you by examining the covers, talking about the titles, and making predictions about the contents.
6. Encourage your children to ask questions about the books and ask questions of your children, especially questions with more than one possible response and that require children to think about and reflect upon what is being read.
7. Share the reading with your children. Some books require that you or an older child read to your children, others can be read by grade 3 students. When possible, take turns reading among several family members.
8. Read the books more than once if your child asks to repeat the reading. Each time the book is read, there are new things to notice or talk about.
9. Keep a playful tone to all of your activities. The book bags are intended to support you and your family in having literary fun together. Enjoy!

school, the children are always anxious to tell their classmates and me about their reading and to show us the activities they did with their families. They proudly share their stories, crafts, and artwork. I display their products in the classroom as a way of celebrating their family activities. Early Thursday afternoons, I check that all of the books are in place and restock each bag.

Assessment

LIFT is a source of much pleasure and satisfaction for all participants. The parents of my children report that not only my students, but also other children in their family look forward to the bags. A recent survey indicates that the time families spend in literary activities has increased since the implementation of LIFT. In describing LIFT to classroom visitors, the children claim, "I like reading with my family. My mom really likes the pig books," and "I don't like it when it is not my week to have a bag."

Adaptations

The success of the LIFT program has been contagious. Another teacher started along with me; but now several more are interested. Some changes are needed to expand to other grade levels. For example, grade 1 book bags need to include both easy readers and picture books to be read to children, whereas upper-grade-level bags might focus on novels and such response activities as visiting particular Internet sites.

Reflections

The LIFT program has generated genuine enthusiasm for reading and writing at school and at home. For children, receiving a book bag is like opening a present and finding surprises. I feel strongly that this is a way to lead children

The children in kindergarten and grade 1 in Linda Boroski's class created several small fox quilts after reading *Rosie's Walk* (Hutchins, 1968), the story of a hen who outwits a fox that is following her. After reading the book, students asked many questions about foxes, and Ms. Borowski read aloud several books to provide some answers. The children decided to make a fox quilt to share what they had learned. Pictures of a fox were cut from fabric and glued to each quilt square. The children wrote or dictated a sentence about foxes to accompany their pictures.

To Guide Your Reading

As you read this chapter, prepare to

Describe the listening process

•

Explain how students listen aesthetically and efferently

•

Explain why speaking is important in the learning process

•

Explain how students learn to conduct conversations in the classroom

•

Identify the types of aesthetic talk activities that are appropriate for elementary students

•

Identify the types of efferent talk activities that are appropriate for elementary students

•

Explain how listening and speaking can be taught as part of language arts units

Listening and speaking (talking) are the basic communication tools in most human lives. That is, we use oral language to relate to family and friends, to negotiate our work, and to express ourselves. In school, students learn to use their listening and speaking skills to clarify and understand the ideas, thoughts, and perceptions of others and themselves, and to integrate the two to make sense of their world. Teachers who provide time for and instruction in listening and speaking find that their students learn to engage in meaningful talk and responsive listening. The terms *speaking* and *talking* are often used interchangeably to describe aspects of oral language. In this chapter, *speaking* is used to denote formal aspects of oral language and *talking* is used to denote informal aspects.

Listening in the Classroom

Listening has been called the "neglected language art" for almost 50 years because it is rarely taught in elementary classrooms. Rather, students are asked to listen, and admonished if it appears that they are not engaged in the process, yet they are not regularly taught how to improve their listening strategies and skills. Despite this seeming gap in instruction, most teachers agree that students need to know how to listen because listening is "the most used and perhaps the most important of the language (and learning) arts" (Devine, 1982, p. 1).

Listening is the first language mode that children acquire, and it is the basis for the other language arts. When children are read to, they begin to see the connection between what they hear and what they see on the printed page. The processes of reading and listening, and the strategies and skills used during reading and listening are similar in many ways (Sticht & James, 1984).

Researchers have found that children and adults spend as much time listening as they do in reading, writing, and talking combined (Rankin, 1926; Werner, 1975; Wilt, 1950). Figure 5–1 illustrates the amount of time we communicate in each language mode. Both children and adults spend approximately 50 percent of their communication time listening.

The Listening Process

Listening is a complex, multistep process "by which spoken language is converted to meaning in the mind" (Lundsteen, 1979, p. 1). As this description suggests, listening is more than just hearing, even though children and adults often use the terms *hearing* and *listening* synonymously. Rather, hearing is an integral component, but only one component, of the listening process. The crucial part is thinking, or converting to meaning what one has heard.

STEPS IN THE LISTENING PROCESS

The listening process involves three steps: receiving, attending, and assigning meaning (Wolvin & Coakley, 1985). In the first step, listeners receive the aural stimuli or the combined aural and visual stimuli presented by the speaker. Next, listeners focus on selected stimuli while ignoring other, distracting, stimuli. In the third step, listeners assign meaning to, or understand, the speaker's message. Listeners assign meaning using assimilation and accommodation to fit the message into their existing cognitive structures or to create new structures if necessary. Responding or reacting to the message is not considered part of the listening process.

The second step of Wolvin and Coakley's listening process model may be called the "paying attention" component. Learning to attend to the speaker's message is especially important because researchers have learned that students can listen to 250 words per minute—two to three times the normal rate of speaking (Foulke, 1968). This differential allows listeners time to tune in and out as well as to become distracted during listening.

Furthermore, the intensity of students' need to attend to the speaker's message varies with the purpose for listening. Some types of listening require more attentiveness than others. Effective listeners, for example, listen differently to directions on how to reach a friend's home than they do to a poem or story being read aloud.

For more information on Piaget's equilibration process, see Chapter 1, "Learning and the Language Arts," pages 5–6.

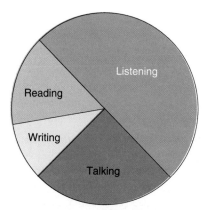

Figure 5–1 Percentage of Communication Time in Each Language Mode
Sources: Data from Rankin, 1926; Werner, 1975; Wilt, 1950.

PURPOSES FOR LISTENING

In and beyond classrooms, people have many purposes for listening. Pending their reasons for listening, they engage in different types of listening. Wolvin and Coakley (1979, 1985) delineate five broad types of listening:

- Discriminative listening
- Aesthetic listening
- Efferent listening
- Critical listening
- Therapeutic listening

We have applied Louise Rosenblatt's (1985b, 1991) terms *aesthetic reading*, meaning "reading for pleasure," and *efferent reading*, meaning "reading to carry away information," for the listening categories. These terms can be applied because reading and listening are similar language modes, except that one is written and the other is oral.

Discriminative Listening. People use discriminative listening to distinguish sounds and to develop a sensitivity to nonverbal communication. Teaching discriminative listening involves one sort of activity in the primary grades and a different activity for older students. Having kindergartners listen to recorded animal sounds and common household or outdoor noises is one discriminative listening activity. Most children are able to discriminate among sounds by the time they reach age five or six. Primary-grade students also use discriminative listening as they develop *phonemic awareness*, the ability to blend and segment the sounds in spoken words. Older students use discriminative listening to sound out spellings of words and divide words into syllables.

For more information on phonemic awareness, see Chapter 3, "Emergent Literacy," pages 93–97.

Students at all levels also learn to "listen" to the nonverbal messages that people communicate. Young children quickly recognize the unspoken message when a parent's expression changes from a smile to a frown or when a teacher expresses puzzlement. Older students learn the meanings of more sophisticated forms of body language, such as folding your arms over your chest, and the ways that teachers emphasize that something is important, such as speaking more loudly, or repeating what was said.

When teachers read aloud books such as Sheree Fitch's *There's a Mouse in My House* (1997) and Nancy Shaw's *Sheep Out to Eat* (1992) (and other books in the series about the cavorting sheep), they provide opportunities for young children to develop their discriminative listening abilities. Middle- and upper-grade students develop more sophisticated knowledge about the sounds of language when they read such books as *Zin! Zin! Zin! A Violin* (Moss, 1995) and *The Night the Stars Flew* (Bogart, 2001).

Aesthetic Listening. People listen aesthetically when they listen for enjoyment. Teachers encourage children's aesthetic listening by reading aloud and teaching students how to visualize characters and episodes and notice figurative language. West Coast author Sheryl McFarlane's *Tides of Change* (1995) and Nancy Hundal's *Melted Star Journey* (1999) offer strong verbal images for teacher and students to talk about. Hundal writes, "Now come the dozing skyscrapers. Boxes of yellow light and mute machines. Down a quiet street, a darker street, where an old man with a blank face leans in a doorway, not going in, not going out." Viewing video or CD-ROM versions of stories and listening to classmates converse, or talk about literature they have read or listened to someone else read aloud are other examples of aesthetic listening. Ensure CD-ROM versions of stories are thoughtful reproductions as these can sometimes over-simplify a story and its illustrations.

As students listen to the teacher read aloud well-crafted stories and poems such as *Heartbeat* (Creech, 2004), *A Prairie as Wide as the Sea* (Ellis, 2001), *Airborn* (Oppel, 2004), and *Welcome to the Green House* (Yolen, 1993), they engage with the text and step into the secondary world it creates. In *Heartbeat*, they feel the friendship between Annie and Max who is sometimes inexplicably moody.

In *A Prairie as Wide as the Sea*, they experience Ivy Doris Weatherall's immigration to the Canadian prairies in 1926 and the joys and challenges of finding a home in a new country. In *Airborn*, they feel the exhilaration of flying in an airship with Matt and Kate through an imaginary past. And in *Welcome to the Green House*, a book-length poem about the rain forest, they recognize the ecological treasures of the rain forest and appreciate the contribution of rhythmic language to meaning.

Efferent Listening. People listen efferently to understand a message. This is the type of listening required in many classroom instructional activities. Students determine the speaker's purpose, identify the main ideas, and then organize the information they are listening to in order to remember it. Elementary students usually receive little instruction in efferent listening; rather, teachers assume that students simply know how to listen. Note-taking and web creation are two efferent listening strategies taught in the elementary grades.

Students often use efferent listening as they listen to teachers read aloud informational books or view video or CD-ROM versions of books. As they listen to the teacher read from *Take Action! A Guide to Active Citizenship* (Kielburger, 2002), they learn tips, strategies, and examples to become more socially aware and involved, and while listening to *Where Does a Tiger-Heron Spend the Night?* (Carney, 2002), they find out about a wider range of birds than we see in our backyards. Even though these books are informational books, students don't necessarily listen to them only efferently. Louise Rosenblatt (1991) explains that aesthetic and efferent approaches to reading represent two ends of a continuum and that students rarely use one type of reading exclusively. The same is true of listening.

Critical Listening. People listen critically to evaluate a message. Critical listening is an extension of efferent listening. As in efferent listening, listeners seek to understand a message, but must filter the message to detect propaganda devices, persuasive language, and emotional appeals. Critical listening is used when people listen to debates, commercials, political speeches, and other arguments.

For more information on critical viewing and listening, see Chapter 8, "Viewing and Visually Representing," pages 325–329.

When students listen to teachers read aloud stories such as *The True Story of the 3 Little Pigs!* (Scieszka, 1989) and *Nothing But the Truth* (Avi, 1991), they critically analyze the characters' claims, and when they read informational books such as *Antarctica* (Cowcher, 1990) and biographies such as *My Hiroshima* (Morimoto, 1987), they evaluate the authors' warnings about destroying the environment and nuclear war.

Therapeutic Listening. In therapeutic listening, people listen to allow a speaker to talk through a problem. Children, as well as adults, serve as sympathetic listeners for friends and family members. Although this type of listening is important, it is less appropriate for elementary students, so we will not discuss it in this chapter.

Students rarely use these types of listening in isolation. As students listen to stories such as *Catherine, Called Birdy* (Cushman, 1994), set in the Middle Ages, or *Naomi's Road* (Kogawa, 1986), set during the Second World War, for instance, they often use several types of listening simultaneously. They step back into history and imagine they are Birdy or Naomi and feel what the characters feel as they listen aesthetically. Students use efferent listening as they think about geographic locations, historical events, historical figures, and other information that authors have carefully researched and included in the story. They use discriminative listening as they notice rhyme, alliteration, and other types of wordplay. Critical listening plays a role, too, as students consider the author's viewpoint, assess emotional appeals, and think about the theme. The five types of listening are reviewed in Figure 5–2 on page 176.

TEACHING LISTENING STRATEGIES

Activities involving listening go on in every elementary classroom. Students listen to the teacher give directions and instruction, to recorded stories at listening centres, to classmates during discussions, and to someone reading stories and poetry aloud. However, although

Type	Characteristics	Example
Discriminative	Distinguish among sounds	Participate in phonemic awareness activities Notice rhyming words in poems and songs Recognize alliteration and onomatopoeia Experiment with tongue twisters Listen to stories and poems read aloud View video or CD-ROM versions of stories
Aesthetic	Listen for pleasure or enjoyment	Listen to stories at a listening centre Watch students perform a play or readers theatre reading Participate in grand conversations Participate in tea party activities
Efferent	Listen to understand a message	Listen to informational books read aloud or at a listening centre Listen to oral reports View informational videos or CD-ROMs Listen to book talks Participate in writers groups Listen during minilessons Listen to students share projects
Critical	Evaluate messages	Listen to debates and political speeches View commercials and other advertisements Evaluate themes and arguments in books read aloud
Therapeutic	Listen sympathetically	Very few language arts activities focus on this type of listening, even though children use therapeutic listening when they listen to a friend talk out a problem.

Figure 5–2 Overview of the Five Types of Listening

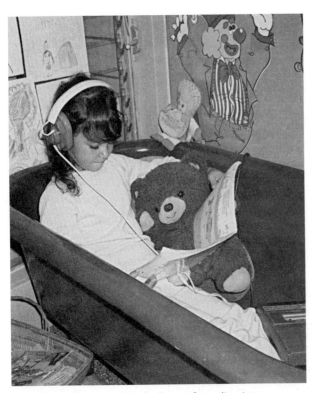

This student listens aesthetically to a favourite story.

these activities provide opportunities for students to practise listening strategies and skills they already possess, they do not teach students how to become more effective listeners.

Language arts educators have repeatedly cited the need to teach listening strategies (Brent & Anderson, 1993; Devine, 1982; Lundsteen, 1979; Pearson & Fielding, 1982; Wolvin & Coakley, 1985). Rather than just have practice opportunities, students need to learn to vary how they listen to fit the purpose for listening, and they need to develop specific strategies to use when listening (Brent & Anderson, 1993; Jalongo, 1991). Teachers must teach specific strategies and guide students in their use of strategies to match their purposes for listening.

Aesthetic Listening

Louise Rosenblatt (1978, 1983, 1991) coined the term *aesthetic reading* to describe one stance readers take. During aesthetic reading, the focus is on the readers' experience during reading, not on the information they will carry away from the experience. The term *aesthetic listening* can be used to describe the type of listening children and adults do as they listen to storytellers tell stories, poets recite poems, actors perform plays, and singers sing songs. The focus of this type of listening is on the listeners' experience and the connections the listeners are making to the literature they are listening to.

STRATEGIES FOR AESTHETIC LISTENING

Students use many of the same strategies for aesthetic listening that they use for reading and writing (Pinnell & Jaggar, 1991). Six strategies that are especially important for aesthetic listening are

1. *Predicting.* As students listen to a story read aloud, they are predicting or making guesses about what will happen next. They revise their predictions as they continue listening to the story. When they read aloud, teachers help students develop the predicting strategy by asking them what they think will happen in the story before reading and stopping several times while reading to have students predict again.

2. *Visualizing.* Students create an image or picture in their minds while listening to a story that has strong visual images, details, or descriptive words. Students practise this strategy by closing their eyes and trying to draw mental pictures while they listen to a story, and then reproducing these pictures on paper after reading.

3. *Making connections.* Students make personal connections between the story they are listening to and experiences in their own lives. Students might share these connections in reading log entries and in grand conversations. They also make connections between the story they are listening to and other ones they have listened to or read themselves. Students make connections between the story they are listening to and another story with the same theme, or a character or episode in this story and a character or episode in another story. Teachers help students use this strategy by asking them to talk about any connections they are making as the story is discussed or by having them make entries in their reading logs. These literary connections are known as *intertextuality*.

4. *Revising meaning.* Students begin to formulate meaning as soon as they see the cover or hear the title of the book. As students listen to the story read aloud, their comprehension, or understanding, of the story expands and deepens. Comprehension doesn't occur all at once, but it happens in layers as students listen to the story. Sometimes students misunderstand a word or phrase, don't see a character's motivations, or miss some important information when they are distracted, and their understanding of the story goes awry. As they continue to listen, students realize that what they are listening to doesn't make sense, and they make corrections.

5. *Playing with language.* As they are listening, students should be sensitive to the author's choice of language, to the way sentences are phrased, and to the author's use of comparisons or wordplay. Children take over the language they hear and make it part of their own (Cullinan, 1987). Teachers comment on examples of powerful and beautiful language as they are reading or after reading, and students can collect examples in their reading logs, on charts, or in story quilts.

6. *Organizing ideas.* As they listen to a story read aloud, students apply their knowledge of plot, characters, setting, theme, and point of view in order to anticipate what will happen next and how the problem introduced in the beginning of the story will be resolved at the end. They also apply their knowledge of various genres (e.g., fantasy, historical fiction, contemporary realistic fiction) in order to understand stories they are listening to.

Students also use these strategies as they listen aesthetically to poems or informational books read aloud. They create mental images and make connections among what they are listening to, other literature they know, and their own lives. Instead of using story structure to help them organize what they are listening to, students use their knowledge about how poetry or informational books are organized. Similarly, as they think about the powerful figurative language of poems, they consider the impact that alliteration and metaphors have on listeners. When listening to informational books such as Shelley Tanaka's book *The Buried City of Pompeii* (2000), they think about how the author's use of factual information, examples, diagrams, and photographs help students to create mental images.

Since reading and listening involve many of the same strategies, teachers can teach strategies through listening and then have students use the strategies during reading (Pearson & Fielding, 1982). As they read aloud, teachers model how to use these strategies, and after listening, students can reflect on how they used the strategies. It is easier for students to focus on strategy use during listening than during reading because students don't have to decode written words when listening.

READING ALOUD TO STUDENTS

For more information on intertextuality, see Chapter 6, "Reading and Writing Narrative Text," pages 231–233.

For more information on the elements of story structure, see Chapter 6, "Reading and Writing Narrative Text," pages 217–226.

Sharing stories, poems, and informational books orally with students is a wonderful way to develop an appreciation of literature, model fluent reading, encourage interest in reading, and create a community of learners in the classroom. Sharing literature with students also creates an excellent opportunity to teach listening skills. Strategies such as setting a purpose for listening, asking students to make predictions, and discussing the outcome of their predictions after reading help students develop active listening skills. Reading stories to children is an important component in most kindergarten and first-grade classrooms. Unfortunately, teachers often think they need to read to children only until they learn to read for themselves; however, reading aloud and sharing the excitement of books, language, and reading should remain an important part of the classroom learning at all grade levels. Good literature often provides rich vocabulary and access to ideas and places not experienced by young readers. David Bouchard's *If You're Not From the Prairie . . .* (1995) is a wonderful example of a book that shares new language and images with its readers that can be shared with all ages of learners.

A common complaint is that there is not enough time in the school day to read to children. Many educators, such as Jim Trelease (1995) and Ron Jobe and Mary Dayton-Sakari (1999), point out the necessity of finding time to read aloud so as to take advantage of its many benefits:

- Stimulating children's interest in books and in reading
- Broadening children's reading interests and developing their taste for quality literature
- Introducing children to the sounds of written language and expanding their vocabulary and sentence patterns
- Sharing with children books that are "too good to miss"
- Allowing children to listen to books that would be too difficult for them to read on their own or books that are "hard to get into"
- Expanding children's background of experiences
- Introducing children to concepts about written language, different genres of literature, poetry, and elements of story structure
- Providing a pleasurable, shared experience
- Modelling to children that adults read and enjoy reading, to increase the likelihood that children will become lifelong readers

Guidelines for choosing literature to read aloud are simple: choose books that you like and think will appeal to your students. Trelease (1995) suggests four additional criteria for good read-aloud books. They should be fast-paced to hook children's interest as quickly as possible; contain

Books

Bishop, R. S. (Ed.). (1994). *Kaleidoscope: A Multi-Cultural Booklist for Grades K–8*. Urbana, IL: National Council of Teachers of English.

Devers, W., & Cipielewski, J. (1993). *Every Teacher's Thematic booklist*. Toronto: Scholastic. ❧

Gertridge, A. (1994). *Meet Canadian Authors and Illustrators*. Richmond Hill, ON: Scholastic. ❧

Greenwood, B. (Ed.) (1994). *The CANSCAIP Companion: A Biographical Record of Canadian Children's Authors, Illustrators and Performers*. Markham, ON: Pembroke. ❧

Jobe, R., & Hart, P. (1991). *Canadian Connection: Experiencing Literature with Children*. Markham, ON: Pembroke. ❧

Jobe R., & Dayton-Sakari, M. (1999). *Reluctant Readers: Connecting Students and Books for Successful Reading Experiences*. Markham, ON: Pembroke Publishers. ❧

McTeague, F. (1992). *Shared Reading in the Middle and High School Years*. Markham, ON: Pembroke. ❧

Trelease, J. (1995). *The New Read-Aloud Handbook* (4th ed.). New York: Penguin. ❧

Journals and Newsletters

CBC Features. The Children's Book Council, 67 Irving Place, New York, NY 10003. ❧

Children's Book News, Canadian Children's Book Centre, Toronto, ON M4R 1B9. ❧

The Horn Book. Park Square Building, 31 St. James Avenue, Boston, MA 02116.

Language Arts. National Council of Teachers of English, 1111 Kenyon Road, Urbana, IL 61801.

The New Advocate. Christopher-Gordon Publishers, P.O. Box 809, Needham Heights, MA 02194.

The Reading Teacher. International Reading Association, P.O. Box 8139, Newark, DE 19711.

Online Journals

Canadian Children's Literature/Literature canadienne pour la jeunesse. ❧
http://ccl.uwinnipeg.ca

The Looking Glass. ❧
www.the-looking-glass.net

Children's Literature—Electronic Journal and Book Reviews. ❧
www.ucalgary.ca/~dkbrown/journals.html

Figure 5–3 Guides for Choosing Literature to Read Aloud to Students

well-developed characters; include easy-to-read dialogue; and keep long descriptive passages to a minimum. There are a number of annotated guidebooks, journals, and online journals that are useful to teachers to guide their selection of books for reading aloud and independent reading. Figure 5–3 lists these books and journals. Information prepared and published by the Canadian Children's Book Centre is also helpful.

Books that have received awards or other acclaim from teachers, librarians, and children make good choices. Two of the most prestigious awards are the Caldecott Medal and the Newbery Medal. Other awards include the Canadian Library Association's (CLA) Book of the Year for Children and CLA's Young Adult Canadian Book Award, and the Children's Literature Roundtables of Canada Information Book Award. Several other regional awards are given to celebrate diversity and excellence in Canadian writing for children and young adults. Lists of outstanding books are published annually to publicize the choices of children, young adults, teachers, and librarians. *Our Choice* is published by the Canadian Children's Book Centre and is posted on the centre's website. Three lists, *Children's Choices*, *Young Adults' Choices*, and *Teachers' Choices*, are published by the International Reading Association in *The Reading Teacher*.

Teachers in many primary-grade classrooms read one story aloud daily as part of language arts instruction, and later during the day they read informational books aloud as part of social studies or science lessons. Poems, too, are read aloud in connection with content-area themes. It is not unusual for primary-grade students to listen to their teacher read aloud three or more stories and other books during the school day. Students in middle and upper grades should also listen to chapter books, picture books and poems read aloud as part of language arts units, along with reading and listening to informational books, magazines, and newspaper articles in content-area lessons.

Students—especially kindergartners and primary-grade students—often beg to have a familiar book reread. Although it is important to share a wide variety of books with children, researchers have found that children benefit in specific ways from repeated readings (Yaden, 1988). Through repetition, students gain control over the parts of a story and are better able to synthesize those parts into a whole, gaining greater understanding.

Also, Martinez and Roser (1985) found that children's comments after repeated readings were more probing and more specific, suggesting that they had greater insight into the story. Researchers investigating the value of repeated readings have focused mainly on preschool and primary-grade students, but rereading favourite stories may have similar benefits for older students as well.

TEACHING AESTHETIC LISTENING

Students must listen aesthetically in many situations both in and out of the classroom to learn simply to enjoy stories and new information. Teachers can help students become effective listeners by making them aware of what they are doing when they are listening. Teachers can speak with students about listening behaviours. They can ask such questions as, "What do you think about when a friend tells you about his birthday present?" "How do you let your friend know that you are interested in what he is saying?" Listening is a social skill as well as a learning skill.

Teachers also teach aesthetic listening when they read aloud a variety of children's literature to students. Before and during reading aloud, minilessons help students develop and use aesthetic listening strategies.

Steps in Reading Aloud to Students. Sometimes teachers simply pick up a book and start reading aloud to students, but for the most meaningful experience, teachers use the five-stage reading process described in Chapter 4, even though one or more stages might be abbreviated. It is important that teachers help students activate their background knowledge before reading and provide opportunities for students to respond to the book after reading (Pinnell & Jaggar, 1991). The steps in reading aloud are presented in the following Step by Step box:

Step by Step

Reading Aloud

1. *Prepare to share the story.*   The teacher activates background knowledge or provides necessary concepts or experiences so that students can understand the story. The teacher may also set the purpose for listening.

2. *Read aloud to students.*   The teacher reads the story aloud to students or plays a pre-recorded version of the story. One procedure teachers can use to read the story aloud is the Directed Listening–Thinking Approach (DLTA), in which the teacher asks students to make predictions about the story and then listen to confirm or reject their predictions. DLTA is described in Figure 5–4 on pages 181–182.

3. *Capture an initial response.*   Immediately after reading, students reflect on the story (or a chapter of a longer book) by talking about the story or writing in a reading log. In these initial

responses, students focus on voicing their personal feelings, making connections to their own lives, articulating questions and confusions, and identifying favourite characters, events, and quotations. Students need an opportunity to talk about a story after reading. They may talk about it with a partner, in small groups, or with the entire class. The focus is on interpreting the story, not answering the teacher's questions about the story.

Students also capture initial responses to a story by writing entries in a reading log. Primary- grade students keep a reading log by writing the title and author of the story and drawing a picture related to the story. They can also add a few words or a sentence. Figure 5–5 on pages 182–183 presents three entries from a grade 3 student's reading log written during an author study on Eve Bunting. Very young children compose and dictate log entries indirectly or collaboratively. Older students sometimes write an entry after each chapter. After drawing and writing, students often share their reading logs with classmates, and this sharing provides another opportunity for classmates to listen aesthetically.

4. *Explore the story.*   Students explore the text by examining the vocabulary, collecting notable language samples, learning about story structure and authors, and participating in other word-study activities. The teacher also teaches minilessons related to aesthetic listening. This stage is often abbreviated when teachers are reading aloud stories for enjoyment, as they often do after lunch or at the end of the day. Even so, the teacher often needs to clarify difficult words, discuss the structure of the story, or share information about the author or topics related to the book.

5. *Extend the response.*   Students expand their responses through reading, writing, speaking, drama, research, and other projects. Students choose projects they are interested in pursuing to extend their enjoyment and interpretation of a book. These projects include making puppets to use in retelling a favourite story, writing letters to authors, creating a mobile for a favourite story, doing a short presentation as a book character and reading other books by the same author or on a similar theme, to name only a few possibilities.

The Directed Listening–Thinking Approach (DLTA) is based on the Directed Reading–Thinking Activity, a procedure developed by Russell Stauffer (1975). In DLTA the teacher reads the story or other piece of literature aloud to students, who are actively listening by making predictions and listening to confirm their predictions. After reading, students discuss their predictions and give reasons to support them. The three steps are:

1. Prepare to Read
Teachers provide necessary information related to the story or the author, thereby stimulating students' interest in the story. Teachers might discuss the topic or theme, show pictures, or share objects related to the story to draw on prior knowledge or to create new experiences. For example, teachers might talk about students' knowledge of animal habitats before reading Carl Hiaasen's adventure story, *Hoot* (2004). Then the teacher shows students the cover of the book and reads the title and asks them to make a prediction about the story using questions like these:

For a list of extending projects, see Chapter 4, "The Reading and Writing Processes," pages 140–141.

- What do you think a story with a title like this might be about?
- What do you think might happen in this story?
- Does this picture give you any ideas about what might happen in this story?

(continued)

Figure 5–4 The Directed Listening–Thinking Approach

If necessary, the teacher reads the first paragraph or two to provide more information for students to use in making their predictions. After a brief discussion in which all students commit themselves to one or another of the alternatives presented, the teacher asks these questions:

- Which of these ideas do you think would be the likely one?
- Why do you think that idea is a good one?

2. Read Aloud to Students

After students set their purposes for listening, the teacher reads part of the story aloud and then asks students to confirm or reject their predictions by answering questions such as the following:

- What do you think now?
- What do you think will happen next?
- What would happen if . . . ?

The teacher continues reading the story aloud, stopping at several key points to repeat this step.

3. Reflect on Students' Predictions

Students talk about the story, expressing their feelings and making connections to their own lives and experiences with literature. Then students reflect on the predictions they made as they listened to the story being read aloud, and they provide reasons to support their predictions. Teachers ask these questions to help students think about their predictions:

- What predictions did you make?
- What in the story made you think of that prediction?
- What in the story supports that idea?

DLTA is useful only when students are reading or listening to an unfamilar story so that the prediction actively involves them in the story. This strategy can be used both when students are listening to the teacher read literature aloud and when they are doing the reading themselves.

Figure 5–4 The Directed Listening–Thinking Approach (*continued*)

<u>Fly Away Home</u> by Eve Bunting

This book was so sad I stareted crying. Its sad to be homeless but Andrew has a lot of hope and hes going to get out just like the bird. Hes going to get a home again. I think everone shold have a home to live in.

(continued)

Figure 5–5 Three Entries from a Grade 3 Student's Reading Log

A Day's Work by Eve Bunting

I liked this book alot. Francesco said his Abuelo was a fine gardner but he didn't know what to do. But they got to keep the jobs because they were honest. Weeds and flowers can look the same if your not a gardner.

| weed | flower | weed |

The Man Who Could Call Down Owls by Eve Bunting

This was a scary story. The man who could call down owls was a good person who loved the owls and cared for them. Then, an evil man killed him and took his beautiful coat so he could call down the owls. I am glad the owls weren't fooled by him. The little boy was given the power to call the owls instead.

Figure 5–5 Three Entries from a Grade 3 Student's Reading Log (*continued*)

Minilessons on Aesthetic Listening. Teachers also teach minilessons to introduce, practise, and review procedures, concepts, and skills related to aesthetic listening. A list of topics for minilessons on aesthetic listening and the other types of listening is presented on page 185. The steps in teaching a minilesson on aesthetic listening strategies are presented in the following Step by Step box:

Step by Step

A Minilesson on Aesthetic Listening

1. *Introduce the strategy.*   The teacher explains the listening strategy, the way it is used, and the types of listening activities for which it is most effective. The teacher develops a chart with the students to list the characteristics or steps of the strategy. For example, after introducing visualizing, the teacher can list the following steps in creating a mind picture on a chart:

   ● Close your eyes.
   ● Draw a picture of a scene or character in your mind.

- Listen for details and add them to your picture.
- Add colours to your mind picture.

2. *Demonstrate the strategy.*   The teacher demonstrates the strategy while reading a story aloud or as students listen to an audiotape of a story. The teacher stops the presentation periodically to talk about what she is doing or how she is using the strategy. After completing the activity, the teacher discusses the use of the strategy with students. For example, the teacher might demonstrate how to create mind pictures of the characters and story events while reading aloud the first four or five chapters of Tim Wynne-Jones's *The Boy in the Burning House* (2000).

3. *Practise the strategy.*   The teacher provides students with opportunities to practise the strategy as she reads aloud several other stories. The teacher stops reading periodically to ask students to describe how they are using the strategy to listen aesthetically. For example, the teacher might provide opportunities for students to practise creating mind pictures as they continue listening to the last chapters of *The Boy in the Burning House*.

4. *Review the strategy.*   After using an aesthetic listening strategy, the teacher asks a student to summarize the strategy and explain how he or she used it. Students can also write about how they used what they have learned, or they can draw pictures. For example, after listening to the first chapter of *The Boy in the Burning House* read aloud, one fourth grader explained his visualization strategy:

> I made a picture in my mind of Jim's farm. He lives there with his mom and I can tell they are both pretty sad that Jim's dad died a while ago. I can see the yellow '65 Chevy Malibu car that used to be the Dad's, and now it has to be sold. I see Gladys the scarecrow, too, that Jim's taking with him to try and scare away the beavers. I had a new picture in my mind when Jim was remembering the day his dad disappeared and how they found some yarn from his sweater on the fence, but nothing else. It made me feel sad for Jim.

5. *Apply the strategy.*   After students develop a repertoire of the aesthetic listening strategies, they practise the strategies as they listen to stories and other types of literature read aloud.

ASSESSING STUDENTS' AESTHETIC LISTENING

For more information on critical viewing and listening, see Chapter 8, "Viewing and Visually Representing," pages 325–329.

Students need to learn how to listen aesthetically so that they can engage more fully with the experience of literature. Teachers assess whether students are listening aesthetically in several ways. They can listen to the comments students make during grand conversations and read entries in students' reading logs to see if they are

- Making predictions
- Visualizing
- Connecting to personal experience and to literature
- Revising meaning
- Playing with language from the story
- Applying knowledge of story structure

Teachers can also convert the list of aesthetic listening procedures, concepts, and strategies and skills presented in the list of minilessons on page 185 into a checklist and keep track of each topic as it is introduced, practised, and reviewed.

Minilessons

Listening

	Procedures	Concepts	Strategies and Skills
Aesthetic Listening	Listen to a story read aloud Respond to classmates' comments Listen to a poem read aloud Write a response in a reading log Choose favourite quotations from a story Work on projects	Aesthetic listening Difference between aesthetic and efferent listening Concept of story	Predict Confirm Visualize Connect to personal experiences Connect to other stories Notice the power and beauty of language Apply knowledge of text structure
Efferent Listening	Take notes Do note-taking/note-making Use graphic organizers	The listening process Efferent listening Organizational patterns of informational texts	Categorize ideas Generalize Monitor Ask questions of the speaker Ask self questions Note cue words Get clues from the speaker
Critical Listening	Write advertisements Make storyboards Film commercials	Critical listening Three types of persuasion Propaganda Persuasion compared to propaganda Deceptive language Propaganda devices	Evaluate the message Determine the speaker's purpose Recognize appeals Recognize deceptive language Identify propaganda devices

Efferent Listening

Efferent listening is practical listening to understand a message. The term *efferent*, first applied to language arts by Louise Rosenblatt (1978, 1983), means "to carry away." It is the most common type of listening students do in school. Students use efferent listening to identify and remember important pieces of information.

Whether students comprehend and remember the message is determined by many factors. Some of these factors are operative before listening, others during and after. First, students need a background of knowledge about the content they are listening to. They must be able to relate what they are about to hear to what they already know. Speakers can help provide some of these links. Second, as they listen, students use a strategy to help them remember. They organize and "chunk" the information they receive, and may want to take notes to help them remember. Then, after listening, students should somehow apply what they have heard so that there is a reason to remember the information.

STRATEGIES FOR EFFERENT LISTENING

Students use a variety of strategies as they listen efferently; some of the strategies are the same as for reading and writing, and others are unique to efferent listening. The purpose of each strategy is to help students organize and remember the information they are listening to. Elementary students use six strategies for efferent listening:

1. ***Organizing ideas.*** Informational presentations are usually organized in special ways called *expository text structures.* The five most common patterns are description, sequence, comparison, cause and effect, and problem and solution. Students learn to recognize these patterns and use them to understand and remember a speaker's message more easily. Speakers often use certain words to signal the organizational structures they are following. Signal words include *first, second, third, next, in contrast,* and *in summary.* Students learn to attend to these signals to identify the organizational pattern the speaker is using.

   Students often use graphic organizers to visualize the organization of oral presentations, informational videos, CD-ROMs, or informational books (Yopp & Yopp, 1996). When students listen to a presentation comparing amphibians and reptiles, for example, they make T-charts or Venn diagrams to organize the information. Students can draw a two-column T-chart, labelling one column "Amphibians" and the other "Reptiles." Then students write notes in the columns while they listen to the presentation or immediately after listening. A grade 6 student's T-chart comparing amphibians and reptiles is shown in Figure 5–6.

   When students are listening to a presentation or hearing an informational book being read that contains information on more than two or three categories, they can make a cluster diagram, write each category on a ray, and then add descriptive information. For example, when students are listening to a presentation on simple machines, they can make a cluster with five

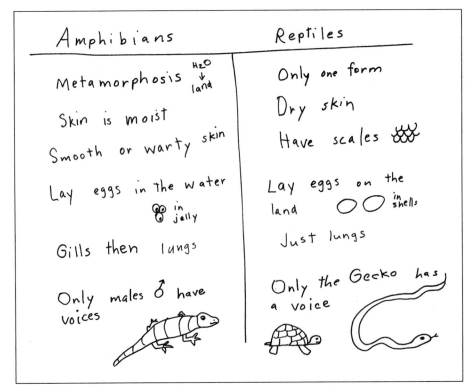

Figure 5–6 A Grade 6 Student's T-Chart Comparing Amphibians and Reptiles

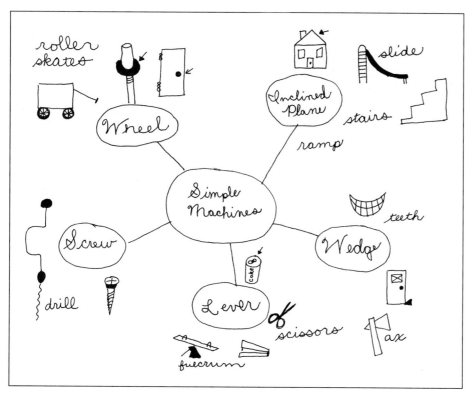

Figure 5–7 A Grade 5 Student's Cluster Diagram on Simple Machines

rays, one for each type of simple machine. Then students add words and drawings to take notes about each type of simple machine. A grade 5 student's cluster diagram is shown in Figure 5–7.

2. ***Generalizing.*** Speakers present several main ideas and many details during oral presentations, and students need to learn to generalize or focus on the main ideas. Otherwise, they try to remember everything and quickly feel overwhelmed. Once students can identify the main ideas, they can then chunk the details to the main idea.

When teachers introduce the generalizing strategy, they ask students to listen for two or three main ideas. They write these ideas on the chalkboard and draw boxes around them. Then, as they give an oral presentation, teachers ask students to raise their hands when they hear the first main idea stated. Students raise their hands when they hear the second main idea, and again for the third main idea. Once students gain practice in detecting already-stated main ideas, teachers give a very brief presentation with one main idea and ask students to identify it. Once students can identify the main idea, teachers give longer oral presentations and ask students to identify two or three main ideas. A grade 5 teacher might make these points when giving an oral presentation on simple machines:

1. There are five kinds of simple machines.
2. Simple machines are combined in specialized machines.
3. Machines make work easier.
4. Almost everything we do involves machines.

Once students can identify the main ideas during an oral presentation, they can chunk details to the main ideas. This hierarchical organization is the most economical way to remember information, and students need to understand that they can remember more information when they use the generalization strategy.

3. *Note-taking.* Note-taking helps students become more active listeners. Devine describes note-taking as "responding-with-pen-in-hand" (1982, p. 156). Students' interest in note-taking begins with the realization that they cannot store unlimited amounts of information in their minds; they need some kind of external storage system. Many listening strategies require listeners to make written notes about what they are hearing. Note-taking is often thought of as a listing or an outline, but notes can also be written in clusters and other diagrams.

Teachers introduce note-taking by taking notes with the class on the chalkboard. During an oral presentation, the teacher stops periodically, asks students to identify what important information was presented, and lists their responses on the chalkboard. Teachers often begin by writing notes in a list format, but notes can also be written in outline or cluster formats. Similarly, the teacher can use keywords, phrases, or sentences in recording notes. After an introduction to various note-taking strategies, students develop personal note-taking systems in which they write notes in their own words and use a consistent format.

Upper-grade students might try a special kind of note-taking in which they divide their papers into two columns, labelling the left column "Take Notes" and the right column "Make Notes." They take notes in the left column, but more importantly, they think about the notes, make connections, and personalize the notes in the right column (Berthoff, 1981). Students can use this strategy when listening to oral presentations as well as when reading a content-area textbook or an informational book. A sample note-taking and note-making sheet is presented in Figure 5–8. In this figure, a grade 5 student is taking notes as she reads about illegal drugs.

The information students should include in the notes they take depends on their purpose for listening. Thus, it is essential that students understand the purpose for listening before they begin to take notes. Some listening tasks require noting main ideas or details; others require noting sequence, cause and effect, or comparisons.

Students can also take notes from informational books and from reference materials; however, taking notes from a speaker is a more complex task. When they are taking notes from a speaker, students cannot control the speed at which information is presented. They usually cannot listen more than once to a speaker in order to complete their notes, and the structure of oral presentations is often not as formal as that of printed materials. Students need to become aware of these differences so that they can adapt their note-taking system to the presentation mode.

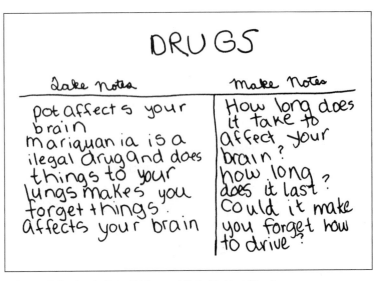

Figure 5–8 A Grade 5 Student's Note-Taking and Note-Making Sheet

4. *Monitoring*. Students need to monitor their listening to make sure they are understanding. Monitoring is important so that students know when they are not listening successfully, when a listening strategy is not working, or when they need to ask a question. Students can use these self-questions to monitor their understanding:

- What is the purpose of listening to this message?
- Do I know what _____ means?
- Does this information make sense to me?

5. *Applying fix-up strategies*. When students are listening and something doesn't make sense, they must take action in order to resolve the problem. Otherwise, they are likely to become confused and frustrated. Often students ask a question to clarify information or eliminate confusion.

Asking questions is only one fix-up strategy. Other ways to fix comprehension problems include the following:

- Continue listening because the speaker may clarify, summarize, or review the point.
- Check any visual displays the speaker has presented.
- Make connections to what the listener already knows about the topic.
- Write down questions to ask later.

Students need to learn how to manage comprehension problems during listening rather than becoming confused and frustrated. When readers don't understand something, they often turn back a page or two and reread, but listeners can't turn back unless they are listening to an audiotape or video presentation.

6. *Getting clues from the speaker*. Speakers use both visual and verbal cues to convey their messages and direct their listeners' attention. Visual cues include gesturing, writing or underlining important information on the chalkboard, and changing facial expressions. Verbal cues include pausing, raising or lowering the voice, slowing down speech to stress key points, and repeating important information. Surprisingly, many students are not aware of these attention-directing behaviours, so teachers must point them out. Once students are aware of these cues, they can use them to increase their understanding of a message.

TEACHING EFFERENT LISTENING

Learning to listen efferently helps students efficiently remember information and better understand the message they are listening to. Teachers need to explain the differences between aesthetic and efferent listening and teach students to use efferent listening strategies. Teachers also need to teach minilessons related to efferent listening.

Minilessons on Efferent Listening. Teachers teach minilessons to introduce, practise, and review procedures, concepts, and strategies and skills related to efferent listening. The list of topics for minilessons presented on page 185 includes topics related to efferent listening. The teaching strategy discussed in the previous section on aesthetic listening can be used to teach minilessons on efferent listening.

Students need to learn to select appropriate strategies for specific listening purposes. The choice depends on both the listener's and the speaker's purpose. Although students must decide which strategy to use before they begin to listen, they need to continue to monitor their selection during and after listening. Students can generate a list of questions to guide their selection of strategies and monitor their effectiveness. Asking themselves questions like these before listening will help them select a strategy *before* listening:

- What is the speaker's purpose?
- What is my purpose for listening?
- What am I going to do with what I listen to?

For more information on expository text structures, see Chapter 7, "Reading and Writing Expository Text," pages 284–287.

For other examples of double-entry journals written in two columns, see Chapter 6, "Reading and Writing Narrative Text," pages 259–260.

To review the steps in teaching a minilesson on aesthetic listening, see "Step by Step: A Minilesson on Aesthetic Listening" in this chapter on pages 183–184.

- Will I need to take notes?
- Which strategies could I use?
- Which strategy will I select?

These are possible questions to use *during* listening:

- Is my strategy still working?
- Am I organizing the information effectively?
- Is the speaker giving me cues about the organization of the message?
- Is the speaker giving me nonverbal cues, such as gestures and facial expressions?
- Is the speaker's voice giving me other cues?

These questions are appropriate *after* listening:

- Do I have questions for the speaker?
- Is any part of the message unclear?
- Are my notes complete?
- Did I make a good choice of strategies? Why or why not? (Tompkins, Friend, & Smith, 1987, p. 39)

Presenting Information So It Is Understood. Just as students need to use efferent listening to remember the important information that teachers present, teachers need to present information in ways that facilitate learning. The way teachers present information often determines whether students understand the presentation. The steps in presenting information are described in the following Step by Step box:

Step by Step

Presenting Information

1. *Build students' background knowledge.*   Before beginning the presentation, the teacher makes sure that students have the necessary background knowledge; then, when the teacher presents the new information, she links it to students' background knowledge. The teacher explains the purposes of the listening activity and reviews one or more strategies students can use to facilitate their understanding. The teacher may also draw a graphic organizer on the chalkboard or give students copies of one to use in taking notes.

2. *Present the information.*   While students listen, the teacher can draw a graphic organizer on the chalkboard and add keywords to help students organize the information being presented. This information can also be the basis for the notes students take either as they are listening or immediately after they have listened. The teacher can also pass out sheets with skeleton notes that students complete while they are listening or after they have listened. The teacher uses both visual and verbal cues—writing notes on the chalkboard, repeating key concepts, raising the voice to highlight conclusions—to direct students' attention to the important information being presented. As the teacher draws the presentation to a close, he summarizes the important points or draws conclusions.

3. *Provide application opportunities.*   After students listen to the presentation, the teacher provides opportunities to apply the new information in a meaningful way.

As part of a thematic unit on explorers, for example, a grade 6 teacher might give a presentation on Hudson Bay. First, the teacher builds background knowledge by locating Hudson Bay on a large map of Canada, and then asking students to trace the routes of early explorers on their smaller, individual maps. Then the teacher explains that she will speak about four early explorers related to Hudson Bay: Munk, Radisson, Hudson, and Frobisher. Students divide a sheet of paper into four sections to take notes as each explorer is discussed.

The teacher gives the first part of the presentation, speaking briefly about the water route around Canada that led the explorers to Hudson Bay and the vast numbers of fur-bearing animals that were found there. She writes keywords on the chalkboard as she describes the routes taken by each explorer. She stops for students to take notes using the keywords she has written. She also asks students to monitor their listening, think about what she has said, and ask themselves if they have understood. The teacher repeats this process as she speaks briefly about each topic.

After this presentation, students review their notes with a classmate and add any important information they have not included. Later, during the unit, students will divide into small groups to teach their classmates about other Canadian explorers using the same procedure.

ASSESSING STUDENTS' EFFERENT LISTENING

Teachers often use objective tests to measure students' efferent listening. For example, if teachers have provided information about planets, they can ask which is nearest to earth. From students' responses, they can check the students' understanding of the information and infer whether students listened. Teachers should also assess students' listening habits and strategies. Specifically, they should check how well students understand efferent listening procedures, strategies, and skills and how they apply them in listening activities. Asking students to reflect on and talk about the strategies they use and what they do before, during, and after listening provides insights into children's thinking in a way that objective tests cannot.

ADAPTING TO MEET THE NEEDS OF EVERY STUDENT

Because listening is the language mode used most often, it is especially important that all students be effective listeners. To become effective listeners, students need to learn how to vary the way they listen for different purposes and how to use the listening strategies presented in this chapter. The following Adapting box presents a list of ways to adapt listening instruction to meet the needs of all students.

For more information on critical viewing and listening, see Chapter 8, "Viewing and Visually Representing," pages 325–329.

Adapting

Listening Instruction to Meet the Needs of Every Student

1. Identify a Purpose for Listening
Whenever students listen to a lesson or an oral presentation, they need to have a specific purpose for listening and to know what they will be expected to do after listening.

2. Use the Directed Listening–Thinking Approach
The Directed Listening–Thinking Approach is a good way to introduce the aesthetic listening strategies. Many teachers use DLTA when they read aloud to involve their students actively in listening.

3. **Teach Students to Take Notes**

   Many students have difficulty identifying the key concepts in order to take useful notes. Teachers demonstrate note-taking by writing notes on chart paper as they present lessons and give oral presentations, and afterwards they talk about why some points were more important than others.

4. **Teach Students to Monitor Their Listening**

   Often students don't realize that listeners are actively involved in the listening process. It is important for students to learn to monitor themselves as they listen and to ask themselves if they are understanding what they are listening to and whether or not the listening strategies they are using are working.

5. **Make the Listening Process Visible**

   Listening is an invisible process, but students can make it more visible by speaking, drawing, and writing about what they do when they listen. Teachers encourage students to think about how they vary the way they listen for different purposes and to think about the strategies they use.

Speaking in the Classroom

Talk is the primary expressive language mode. Both children and adults use it more frequently than writing, and children learn to speak before they learn to read and write. Talk is also the communication mode that all peoples around the world develop. Of the nearly three thousand languages spoken today, only a fraction of them—fewer than two hundred—have developed written forms. A recent snapshot of Canadian populations indicates that "in the metropolitan area of Vancouver alone, students for whom English is a second language represent close to half of the elementary and secondary population" (Dagenais & Day, 1998, p. 376).

When they come to school, most children are fluent oral language users. They have had four or five years of extensive practice talking and listening. Because students have acquired basic oral language competencies, teachers often assume that they don't need to emphasize talk in the elementary school curriculum. Research shows, however, that students benefit from participating in talk activities throughout the school day and that talk is a necessary ingredient for learning (Cazden, 1988; Heath, 1983a; Wells & Chang-Wells, 1992).

Heath (1983a) concluded that children's talk is an essential part of language arts and is necessary for academic success in all content areas. Research now suggests that talk is a necessary ingredient for learning. Shuy (1987) says talk is often thwarted in elementary classrooms because of class size and the assumption that silence facilitates learning. Furthermore, Swain (1988) documented that sustained language use by grade 3 and 6 students occupies a minute 14 percent of classroom time. According to the researcher, "sustained talk provides both opportunities for variety and complexity of language use" (p. 70). Teachers must make an extra effort to provide opportunities for socialization and talk.

Conversations

Brief, informal conversations are common occurrences in the social environment of school. Students converse with classmates as they work on a mural, as they sort books in the class library centre, and after they listen to a story at the listening centre. Students use talk for different purposes (Wilkinson, 1984). They try to control the behaviour of classmates, maintain social relationships, convey information, and share personal experiences and opinions. Teachers use conversations with students for socialization. Conversations with students are essential to creating a climate of trust in the classroom. Ketch indicates, "[conversation] helps to build empathy, understanding, respect for different opinions, and ownership of the learning process" (2005, p. 8).

Other conversations serve instructional purposes. Students meet in small groups to react to literature they have read, respond to each other's writing, work on projects, and explore concepts in resource-based units and thematic units. Students use talk for both aesthetic and efferent purposes, and the most important feature of small-group conversations is that they promote thinking. Teachers take students' ideas seriously, and Nystrand, Gamoran, and Heck (1993) point out that students are validated as thinkers, not just "rememberers," in these conversations. As students work in groups, they become engaged in the learning process and feel ownership of the knowledge they produce.

Researchers have found that students' learning is enhanced when they relate what they are learning to their own experiences—especially when they do so in their own words (Wittrock & Alesandrini, 1990). Pressley (1992) reported that students' learning was promoted when they had opportunities to elaborate on ideas through talk.

For more information on aesthetic and efferent stances, see Chapter 4, "The Reading and Writing Processes," pages 128–129.

Students use talk to work out problems, accomplish a goal, or generate an interpretation or new knowledge in small-group conversations. These conversations can be used at all grade levels. For example, children in kindergarten might work together in a small group to experiment with objects and sort them according to whether or not they float. Middle-school students might work in a small group to plan a dramatization of a story they have read. Cross-age conversations allow students of different ages talk together when they meet as book buddies.

Students' talk is spontaneous and reflects their thinking. Group members extend and expand on each other's comments as the conversation grows. They disagree, ask questions, and seek clarification for comments they do not understand. In the conversation, students' talk determines the direction of the activity because students are not hunting for predetermined correct answers. For example, in a small-group conversation during a thematic unit on weather, students might brainstorm a list of ways weather has an impact on their lives, but they would not talk about weather in order to recall the four types of clouds they had studied. Characteristics of small-group conversations are listed in Figure 5–9.

Teachers play an important role in planning activities for small-group conversations. The activities and projects should be interesting to students, and teachers should ask authentic questions—questions without obvious answers—that require students to interpret or think critically.

---

1. Each group has three to six members. These groups may be permanent, or they may be established for specific activities. It is important that the group be cohesive and courteous to and supportive of each other. Students in established groups often choose names for their groups.
2. The purpose of the small-group conversation or work session is to develop interpretations and create knowledge.
3. Students' talk is meaningful, functional, and genuine. They use talk to solve problems and discover answers to authentic questions—questions that require interpretation and critical thinking.
4. The teacher clearly defines the goal of the group work and outlines the activities to be completed. Activities should require cooperation and collaboration and could not be done as effectively through independent work.
5. Group members have assigned jobs. Sometimes students keep the same jobs over a period of time, and at other times specific jobs are identified for a particular purpose.
6. Students use strategies to begin the conversation, keep it moving forward and on task, and end it.
7. Students feel ownership of and responsibility for the activities they are involved in and the projects they create.

Figure 5–9 Characteristics of Small-Group Conversations
Source: Adapted from Cintorino, 1993; Nystrand, Gamoran, & Heck, 1993; Shafer, 1993.

As students work in small groups, teachers assist and make suggestions, but they do not impose their ideas on students. Teachers are confident of students' ability to create knowledge, respect their ideas, and take their comments and questions seriously.

GUIDELINES FOR CONDUCTING CONVERSATIONS

Students learn and refine their strategies and skills for socializing and conversing with classmates as they participate in small-group conversations (Cintorino, 1993; Routman, 2000). Toohey (1996) documents how young children develop both identity and social participation in complex and dynamic ways through conversation. Students learn how to begin the conversation, take turns, keep the conversation moving forward, support comments and questions that group members make, deal with conflicts, and bring the conversation to a close. And, they learn how powerful talk is in making meaning and creating knowledge.

Beginning the Conversation. To begin the conversation, a student volunteers or someone is appointed. Sometimes teachers provide an authentic question to be discussed. The teacher or a student begins the conversation by repeating or reading the question, and a group member offers a response or subdivides the question into manageable parts. If students have written quickwrites or journal entries, one student might begin by reading his or her writing aloud to the group.

Keeping the Conversation Going. Students take turns making comments and asking questions, support other group members, and elaborate on and expand their comments. The tone is exploratory, and throughout the conversation the group is progressing toward a common goal (Cintorino, 1993). The goal may be creating a project, developing an interpretation to a book, or responding to the teacher's question. From time to time the conversation slows down and there may be a few minutes of silence (Sorenson, 1993). Then a group member asks a question or makes a comment that sends the conversation in a new direction.

Students are courteous, and receive group members' comments attentively and respectfully. Students support one another in groups by calling each other by name. They cultivate a climate of trust in the group by expressing agreement, sharing feelings, voicing approval, and referring to group members' comments.

Conflict in small-group conversations is inevitable, but students need to learn how to deal with it so that it doesn't get out of control. Students need to accept that they will have differing viewpoints and interpretations, and learn to respect each other's ideas and make compromises. Cintorino (1993) reported that her grade 8 students used humour to defuse disagreements in small-group conversations.

Ending the Conversation. At the end of a conversation, students reach consensus, conclude that they have explored all dimensions of a question, or complete a project. Sometimes students have a product from the conversation—a brainstormed list, collection of notes, or project. Group members may be responsible for collecting and storing materials or for reporting on the group's work.

TYPES OF CONVERSATIONS

Students participate in many types of small-group conversations, and they use talk for both aesthetic and efferent purposes. Here are ten examples of conversation-based activities:

- Analyze propaganda in commercials and advertisements.
- Compare characters in book and video versions of a story.
- Brainstorm questions for an interview.
- Design a mural or bulletin board display.
- Assess the effectiveness of a cross-age reading buddy program.
- Share writing in writers groups and get feedback from classmates about how to revise rough drafts.

- Write a script for a puppet show, design puppets, and plan for the puppet show performance.
- Discuss reactions and develop comprehension as students read a chapter book.
- Make a cluster diagram or other graphic organizer about information presented in a video.
- Plan a storytelling project.

These sample activities create opportunities to talk with classmates and to listen, argue, and agree. They are authentic and integrate talking with listening, reading, writing, viewing and visually representing. Students do not hunt for correct answers; they talk to develop interpretations and create knowledge.

TEACHING STUDENTS TO SPEAK IN SMALL GROUPS

For small-group conversations to be successful, teachers need to demonstrate that they trust students and their ability to learn. Similarly, students learn to socialize with classmates and to trust each other as they work together in small groups. For primary and middle-school students, reading Diane Stanley's *The Conversation Club* (1983) is a good way to introduce the climate of trust and to explain the roles of speakers and listeners during conversations.

Sorenson (1993) begins the school year by telling her grade 8 students that they will participate in a different type of discussion in her classroom. She hangs a sign in the classroom that says "Teach Each Other," and tells them that it is a quote from one of her students about why this different kind of discussion works. The students learn that what they say is as important as what the teacher says and that through conversations, students teach each other.

The teacher models working in small groups and discusses how students can begin conversations, sustain them, and bring them to a close. Together the teacher and students summarize what they have learned and develop guidelines for small-group conversations. The teacher observes students as they work in small groups and teaches minilessons on needed procedures, concepts, and strategies and skills.

Students participate in a grand conversation about *The Giver*.

For more information on the teaching strategy on which these minilessons are based, see Chapter 1, "Learning and the Language Arts," pp. 37–40.

Minilessons on Speaking. Even though most children come to school speaking fluently, they need to learn new ways to use talk. Small-group conversations provide one of these new ways. Students know how to talk, but they may not know how to work in small groups, tell stories, participate in debates, and use talk in other ways. Teachers need to explain and demonstrate various types of talk and teach minilessons on procedures, concepts, and strategies and skills for different types of talk. A list of minilesson topics on talk is presented on page 197. Teachers use the procedure developed in Chapter 1, "Learning and the Language Arts," for these minilessons so that students are introduced to the topic and have opportunities to use talk in meaningful ways.

ADAPTING TO MEET THE NEEDS OF EVERY STUDENT

Talk is a useful learning tool, and it is important that activities be adapted so that every student can speak effectively to learn and get along with others. Small-group conversations and the other talk activities can be adapted in many ways to meet students' needs. Perhaps the most basic way to meet the needs of students who are uncomfortable speaking in a large group, or who are hesitant to speak because they are learning English as a second language, or have other language disabilities, is to have them work in a small, comfortable group and to keep the language use informal. It is much easier to work in a small group to accomplish a project than to give an oral report in front of the class or participate in a debate.

Dagenais and Day (1998) suggest the following classroom activities that appear beneficial to ESL students: story reading, question-and-answer periods, role-playing, detective games with words and sentences, the use of visual aids, making predictions, referring to personal experiences, and drawing on background knowledge as it relates to a particular topic. The authors suggest that, in addition to using these effective teaching practices, it is the teacher's orientation to language that enhances or inhibits an ESL student's language development. Teachers who view a child's first language as a resource see multilingualism as beneficial and enriching to that child and to other children in the classroom. These and other ways to adapt talk activities to meet the needs of every student are presented in the Adapting box on page 198.

ASSESSING STUDENTS' SPEAKING ABILITIES

Because students and their parents often value what can be assessed, it is important to assess talk, and all of the types of talk discussed in this chapter can be assessed. In small-group conversations, teachers can simply note whether or not students are contributing members of their groups, or they can observe students' behaviour and assess how students contribute to their groups. Teachers can "listen in" on students' conversations to learn about their language competencies and their abilities to work in small groups. Teachers of primary-grade students might assess whether students

- Contribute to the conversation
- Share ideas and feelings
- Are courteous
- Listen carefully to classmates' comments
- Call group members by name
- Look at classmates when talking to them

Middle- and upper-level students learn more sophisticated procedures, strategies, and skills, and in addition to the six behaviours listed above, teachers of older students might assess whether students

- Volunteer to begin the conversation
- Perform their assigned jobs in the group
- Extend and expand classmates' comments

- Ask questions and seek clarifications
- Invite other group members to contribute
- Stay on task
- Take turns
- Deal with conflict within the group
- Help to end the conversation
- Assume a leadership role in the group

Teachers can create a self-assessment checklist so that students can assess their own contributions to small-group conversations. It is important that students know what is expected of them during conversations and that they reflect on their behaviour and contributions.

Minilessons

Talk

	Procedures	Concepts	Strategies and Skills
Conversations	Begin a conversation Take turns Expand or extend a classmate's comment Sustain a conversation Deal with conflicts End a conversation	Small-group conversations Climate of trust Roles of speakers and listeners	Share ideas and feelings Refer to previous comments Call group members by name Look at classmates Ask questions Extend and expand classmates' comments Seek clarification
Aesthetic talk	Participate in literature conversations Choose a story to tell Prepare and tell a story Make props Select a script for readers theatre	Aesthetic talk Storytelling Readers theatre Parts of a script	Include the beginning, middle, and end Incorporate interesting or repeated phrases Use dialogue Use props Use facial expressions or gestures
Efferent talk	Participate in thematic unit conversations Do a show-and-tell presentation Prepare and present an oral report Do a book talk and/or a book review Conduct an interview Participate in a debate	Efferent talk Thematic unit conversations Facts and opinions Guidelines for speakers and listeners Persuasion	Present information Vary points of view Support opinions Ask clarifying questions Choose a topic Gather information Organize information Use visuals Rehearse Speak loudly Use note cards Look at the audience

Aesthetic Speaking

Aesthetic speaking, like aesthetic listening, deals with having experiences with literature and creating interpretations. Students use aesthetic speaking in discussing literature, telling stories, and participating in interviews, debates, oral reports, and show and tell.

CONVERSATIONS ABOUT LITERATURE

Students talk about literature they are reading in order to clarify understanding and develop their interpretations of a story. In these conversations, often called *grand conversations* (Eeds & Wells, 1989; Peterson & Eeds, 1990) or *literature circles* (Daniels, 1994), students voice their opinions and support their views with examples from the literature. Through these conversations, students take responsibility for learning. They talk about what puzzles them, what they find interesting, their personal connections to the story, and the connections between this story and others they have read. Students also encourage their classmates to contribute to the discussion. Teachers often sit in on conversations about literature as a participant, not as a judge; the talk is primarily among the students. Ketch (2005) points out that it is important for the classroom to be a place where students feel comfortable enough to think out loud.

Adapting

Talk Activities to Meet the Needs of Every Student

1. Include All Students in Conversations
Conversations have social as well as instructional purposes. As students learn ways to talk with classmates—how to ask questions, share information, and keep the conversation moving—they build a sense of community and a climate of trust.

2. Use Small Groups
Some students may feel more comfortable working with a partner or in small groups of classmates they know well or in the same cultural group. These students might be more successful in small-group conversations, or they might be more articulate in giving book talks to a small group than to the whole class.

3. Give Group Presentations
Instead of preparing oral presentations individually, students can work in pairs or small groups to interview, tell stories, and give oral reports and book talks. When students work with a partner or in a small group, they share the responsibility and the talking. Students also learn important socialization skills and develop friendships.

4. Use Manipulatives
Many students find it easier to talk in front of a group when they are talking about an object they are holding. Young children bring photographs and objects for show and tell, and students can make charts, posters, projection slides, or technological displays to support or enhance oral reports. Older students feel more comfortable speaking in front of others if they have an opportunity to write down their thoughts and ideas first.

5. Encourage Students to Relate Personal Experiences
Students are encouraged to share their own personal experiences as these relate to a text being read or written. This strategy provides students with concrete ideas to use when making sense of a story.

Literature conversations can be held with the whole class or in small groups. Young children usually meet together as a class, while older students often talk in small groups. When students meet together as a class, there is a shared feeling of community, and the teacher can be a part of the group. Both younger and older students meet together when they are learning literature conversation procedures or when they are listening to the teacher read a book aloud. Both younger and older students meet in small groups when they are reading different books and when they want more opportunities to talk. When the entire class meets together, students have few opportunities to talk, but in small groups they have many more opportunities to share their interpretations.

Steps in Literature Conversations. Literature conversations often have two parts. The first part is open-ended: Students talk about their reactions to the book, and the direction of the conversation is determined by students' comments. Teachers share their responses, ask questions, and provide information. In the second part the teacher focuses students' attention on one or two aspects of the book not talked about in the first part of the conversation. The steps in literature conversations are presented in the following Step by Step box:

Step by Step

Literature Conversations

1. *Meet in groups.* Students meet together as a class or in small groups to talk about a book or a section of a book. When students meet together as a class, they sit in a circle in order to see each other; when they meet in a small group, they sit close together so that they can talk without disturbing their classmates.

2. *Share responses.* Students share their reactions to the book. To begin the conversation, a student or the teacher asks, "Who would like to begin? What did you think of the story? Who would like to share a reaction?" Students comment on the events in the story, the literary elements, characters they have encountered, or the author's language, and they might make connections to their own lives and to other literature they have read. Each student participates and may build on classmates' comments and ask for clarifications. In order that everyone may participate, teachers often ask students to make no more than three comments until everyone has spoken at least once. Students may refer to the book or read a short piece to make a point, but there is no round-robin reading. Usually students don't raise their hands and are not called on by the teacher or a group leader. Instead, students take turns and speak when no else is speaking, much like adults do when they talk with friends. Pauses and brief silences may occur, and when students indicate they have run out of things to say, the discussion may end or continue on to the next part.

3. *Ask questions.* The teacher asks open-ended questions to focus students' attention on one or two aspects of the book that have been missed. Four possible directions are

● Focus on illustrations. After reading *Eagle Dreams* (McFarlane, 1994), the teacher might ask, "Did you like the illustrations in *Eagle Dreams*? How did the illustrations show mood during the book? Why do you think the illustrator, Ron Lightburn, did that?"

- Focus on authors. During a resource-based unit on J. K. Rowling, the teacher might say, "This is the sixth book in the Harry Potter series we've read by J. K. Rowling. What is so special about her books? Why do we like her books so much? Is there something they all share?"
- Focus on comparison. The teacher asks students to make a comparison: "How did this book compare with _____? Did you like the book or the film version better? Why? Which of Beverly Cleary's characters is your favourite?"
- Focus on literary elements, stylistic devices, and/or genres. After reading *The White Archer: An Eskimo Legend* (Houston, 1967) and *Swamp Angel* (Isaacs, 1994), the teacher might ask, "Is *The White Archer* a legend? Is *Swamp Angel* a legend? What are the characteristics of legends? Which of these characteristics did you notice in these two books? What was the theme of the books? How did the authors tell us the theme?"

4. *Retell the story.*   In small groups, students can learn and practise storytelling skills by retelling the story, or parts of it, to interested classmates or even to younger students. Students love to retell the events of Phoebe Gilman's (1992) *Something From Nothing*. They especially enjoy retelling the picture story of the mice who live beneath the floorboards in this exceptional picture book.

After the literature conversation, students often write (or draw) in their reading response journals, or write again if they wrote before the literature conversation. Then they continue reading the book. Participating in literature conversations and writing entries in reading journals help students think about and respond to what they have read.

The most useful questions about literature cannot be answered with *yes* or *no*, and require students to give personal opinions. After reading *Amber Brown Is Not a Crayon* (Danziger, 1994), a group of grade 3 students wrote their own questions, and spent the first few minutes considering them and deciding which ones to use. Their questions included the following:

- Why do you think Amber and Justin are best friends?
- Do you think Mr. Cohn is sort of like Ms. Frizzle [in the Magic School Bus series]?
- Do you think Mr. Cohn is a good teacher?
- Did you know from the beginning that Justin was going to move away?
- How can best friends fight and still be best friends?
- Is Justin happy or sad about moving to Alabama?
- Why is Amber so mean to Justin?
- What do you think will happen to Amber and Justin after he [Justin] moves away?
- Can they still be best friends after Justin moves away?

Benefits of Conversations about Literature. Eeds and Wells (1989) found that, through talk, students extend their individual interpretations of their reading and create a better understanding of it. Students talk about their understanding of the story and can change their opinions after listening to classmates' alternative views. They share personal stories related to their reading in poignant ways that trigger other students to identify with them. Students also gain insights about how authors use the elements of story structure to develop their message. Ketch (2005) shares three classroom examples in which student comprehension of reading material is enhanced and deepened through conversation rather than by teachers telling students what they should know.

When students talk in depth about literature, their writing shows the same level of interpretation (Sorenson, 1993). Students are more successful in literature conversations if they have written in journals first, and are more successful in writing journal entries if they have participated in literature conversations first.

Efferent Speaking

Students use efferent talk to inform and persuade. They use efferent talk in conversations during thematic units and four other types of efferent talk: show and tell, oral reports, interviews, and debates. These activities are more formal, and students prepare and rehearse their talks before giving them in front of an audience.

CONVERSATIONS DURING THEMATIC UNITS

Conversations are an important part of thematic units. Students talk about concepts they are learning and about issues such as pollution, immigration, nuclear energy, and human rights. These conversations can take place in small groups or as a class. In contrast to literature conversations, in which students use primarily aesthetic talk to create and deepen their interpretations, students use primarily efferent talk to create knowledge and understand relationships among concepts. Students gather information for the conversation through giving or listening to oral presentations, reading informational books and newspapers, researching related websites, and watching television news reports, videos, and films. As they participate in conversations—offering information, considering other points of view, searching for additional information to support opinions, and listening to alternative viewpoints—students learn social skills as well as content-area information.

Questioning Strategies. Teachers often use questions to initiate conversations during thematic units, and the questions teachers ask go beyond knowledge-level thinking (with single correct answers) to authentic questions in which students analyze and synthesize information and make connections to their own lives. Here are some examples for a thematic unit on pioneers:

- As part of a conversation introducing a thematic unit on pioneers, teachers ask if there are pioneers today. After students conclude that there are, teachers ask where modern-day pioneers go, what they do, and why they are pioneers.
- After making a list of the reasons why people moved west, teachers ask students which reason seems most important to them.
- After sharing a map of the westward trails that pioneers travelled, teachers ask students to choose a destination and plan their travel along one of the trails.
- Together as a class, students brainstorm a list of the possessions pioneers carried with them, and then students work in small groups to choose the five most important possessions for pioneers travelling to and settling in particular areas.

Wilen (1986) offers these suggestions:

- Ask carefully planned questions to organize and direct the lesson.
- Ask clearly phrased questions rather than vaguely worded or multiple questions.
- Sequence questions to move from factual-level to higher-level questions that require critical thinking.
- Ask questions to follow up on students' responses.

Students need sufficient time to think about questions and plan their responses. Sometimes the most effective way to do this is to have students talk about the question in small groups and then report back to the class. It is important to encourage wide participation and interaction among students and to draw in students who do not volunteer contributions. Seating students in a circle or a horseshoe formation is one technique, and having students work in small groups is another. Other ways to promote student involvement are to have class memberscreate questions, lead the conversation, and follow up on ideas developed during the conversation. The emphasis in these conversations is on creating knowledge and making connections with information students are learning. Students also use persuasive language as they try to convince classmates of the importance of the points they make and the issues they discuss.

K-W-L Charts. K-W-L charts are a good way to help students take an active role in talking about what they are learning in thematic units (Ogle, 1986, 1989). The letters *K*, *W*, and *L* stand for "What We *K*now," "What We *W*ant to Learn," and "What We *L*earned." Ogle (1986) suggests that students include two types of information in the Learned column, both "What we learned" and "What we still need to learn." We prefer a variation of the traditional chart as proposed by Sippola (1995) that adds an *S* column for "What We *S*till Want to Know" as shown in Figure 5–10. Teachers use these charts at the beginning of thematic units to help students think and ask questions about what they will study during the theme.

To begin, the teacher asks students to brainstorm what they know about a topic. The teacher records the information in the "K" column—"What We Know"—on a class chart, as shown in the Teacher's Notebook on page 204. As students suggest information and as questions arise, the teacher adds questions in the "W" column—"What We Want to Learn." Students also suggest questions they would like to explore during the thematic unit. Brainstorming information in the "K" column helps students activate prior knowledge, and developing questions in the "W" column provides students with specific purposes for learning.

Figure 5–10 A Middle-Grade Student's K-W-L-S Chart on Spiders

Next, students look for ways to categorize the information they brainstormed, and use the categories to organize information they are reading or learning from a video presentation. For example, grade 2 students making a K-W-L chart on penguins might identify these categories: what they look like, where they live, how they move, and what their families are like. Older students might use categories such as appearance, habitat, diet, and enemies.

After categorizing, students participate in activities related to the thematic unit, looking for new information and for answers to questions in the "W" column. Later, students reflect on what they have learned and complete the "L" column—"What We Learned." The questions that remain after completing the "L" column can be recorded in the "S" column. Answers can then be sought through research by the whole class, small groups, or individuals, as a way of extending or completing the thematic unit. The K-W-L-S chart helps prepare students to learn, helps them organize their learning, clarifies their misconceptions, and helps them appreciate their learning.

Teachers can make class K-W-L-S charts on chart paper or a bulletin board. Class charts are best for primary-grade students or for older students who have not made K-W-L-S charts before. Older students can also work in small groups to make charts on chart paper, or they can make individual K-W-L-S charts. Students make individual K-W-L-S charts by folding a sheet of paper in half vertically. Then students cut four flaps and label them K, W, L, and S as shown in the top drawing in Figure 5–10. Students flip up the flaps to write on the chart as shown in Figure 5–10's lower picture.

SHOW AND TELL

Daily sharing time is a familiar ritual in many kindergarten and primary-grade classrooms. Children bring favourite objects to school and talk about them. Show and tell is a nice bridge between home and school, and a good introduction to speaking in front of a group.

Guidelines for Speakers and Listeners. If sharing time becomes repetitive, children can lose interest, so teachers must play an active role. Teachers can discuss the roles and responsibilities of both speakers and listeners. A grade 2 class developed the list of responsibilities for speakers and listeners shown in Figure 5–11. This list, with minor variations, has been used with students in upper grades as well.

Some children need prompting even if they have been advised to plan in advance to say two or three things about the object they have brought to school. It is tempting for teachers to speed

---

Our Rules for Show-and-Tell

What a Speaker Does
Brings something interesting to talk about.
Brings each thing only one time.
Thinks of three things to say about it.
Speaks loudly so everyone can hear.
Passes what he or she brought around so everyone can see it.

What Listeners Do
Show interest.
Pay attention.
Listen.
Ask a question.
Say something nice.

Figure 5–11 A Grade 2 Class List of Responsibilities of Speakers and Listeners

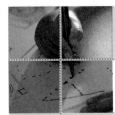

Teacher's Notebook

A "K-W-L-S" Chart

K What We Know	W What We Want to Learn	L What We Learned	S What We Still Want to Know

Categories of information we expect to use

A.

B.

C.

D.

Source: Ogle, 1986, p. 565, and revised as proposed by Sippola, 1995.

things up by asking questions and, without realizing it, to answer their own questions, especially for a very quiet child. Show and tell could go like this:

Teacher:	Jerry, what did you bring today?
Jerry:	(Holds up a stuffed bear.)
Teacher:	Is that a teddy bear?
Jerry:	Yeah.
Teacher:	Is it new?
Jerry:	(Nods head yes.)
Teacher:	Can you tell us about your bear?
Jerry:	(Silence.)
Teacher:	Jerry, why don't you walk around and show your bear to everyone?

Jerry needed prompting, but the teacher in this example dominated the conversation and Jerry said only one word—"Yeah." Two strategies may help. First, talk with children like Jerry and help them plan something to say. Second, invite listeners to ask the speakers questions using the "5 *W*s plus one" questions (*who, what, where, when, why,* and *how*).

Classmates are the audience for show-and-tell activities, but often teachers become the focus (Cazden, 1988). To avoid this, teachers join the audience rather than direct the activity. They also limit their comments and allow the student who is sharing to assume responsibility for the activity and the discussion that follows. Students can ask three or four classmates for comments and then choose which student will share next. It is difficult for teachers to share control of their classrooms, but young students are capable of handling the activity themselves.

Assessing Show-and-Tell Presentations. Students can discuss the effectiveness of their presentations using the guidelines in Figure 5–11. These guidelines can be converted into a checklist that both speakers and listeners can complete for each presentation. Through the checklists and discussion, students learn to give interesting presentations and gain confidence in speaking in front of a group.

Show and tell can evolve into an informal type of oral report for middle-grade students. When this method is used effectively, older students gain valuable practice talking in an informal and non-threatening situation. For example, to begin a sharing activity, students can talk about a collection of hockey cards, a program from an Ice Capades show, a recently found snakeskin, or snapshots of a vacation at Banff National Park. Such show-and-tell presentations can lead to informal dramatics, and reading and writing activities. One student may act out routines recalled from the Ice Capades show; another student may point out the location of Banff National Park on a map or check an almanac for more information about the park. A third student may write about a prized collection of hockey cards. Experience plus oral rehearsal helps students gear up for other language activities.

ORAL REPORTS

Learning how to prepare and present an oral report is an important efferent talk activity for middle- and upper-grade students. But students are often assigned an oral report without any guidance about how to prepare and give one. Too many students simply copy the report verbatim from an encyclopedia, book, or website and then read it aloud. The result is that students learn to fear speaking in front of a group rather than build confidence in their oral language abilities. Even young children can be encouraged to read and write informational reports. Read (2005) documents a study of twenty-four grade 1 and 2 students in a multi-age classroom. The students show

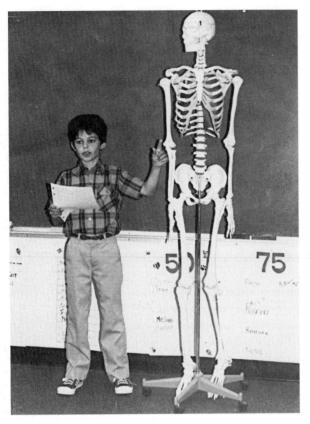

Students present oral reports to share what they learn during thematic units.

they are interested in the content of the report, the form and organization of the report, and finally in rereading and reflecting on how the work was done.

We will focus on the steps in teaching students how to prepare and present two types of oral reports. The first type is reports of information—these include reports on social studies or science topics such as the Laurentian Shield, the solar system, or rain forests. The second type comprises book talks and reviews of television shows and films. Oral reports have genuine language functions—to inform or to persuade—and are often done as projects during thematic units.

Reports of Information. Students prepare and give reports of information about topics they are studying in social studies and science. Giving a report orally helps students learn about specific content areas as well as develop their speaking abilities. Students need more than just an assignment to prepare a report for presentation on a particular date; they need to learn how to prepare and present research reports. The four steps in preparing reports, as explained in the following Step by Step box, are choosing a topic, gathering and organizing information, creating visuals, and giving the presentation.

Step by Step

Preparing and Presenting Reports of Information

1. *Choose a topic.*   The class begins with each student choosing a topic for a report. For example, if a grade 2 class is studying the human body, each student might select a different part of the body for a report. When students can choose their own topics to research and present, they are more likely to be engaged in the process. After students have chosen a topic, they need to inventory, or think over, what they know about the topic and decide what they need to learn about it. They can learn to focus on the key points for their reports in several ways. One strategy is to create a cluster diagram with the topic written and circled in the centre of a piece of paper; the key points are drawn out from the topic like rays from the sun. Then students write the details on rays drawn from each main idea.

   Another strategy is a data chart, in which the teacher provides a chart listing three or more key points to guide students as they gather information for their reports (McKenzie, 1979). Figure 5–12 shows a cluster diagram and a data chart for a report on the human body. A third strategy is brainstorming ideas for possible key points by asking questions about the topic prefaced with the 5 Ws plus one question words. The number and complexity of the key points depend on the students' ages or levels of experience.

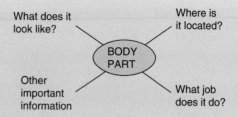

HUMAN BODY REPORT DATA CHART				
Source of information	What does it look like?	Where is it located?	What job does it do?	Other important information

Figure 5–12 A Cluster Diagram and a Data Chart for a Report on the Human Body

2. *Gather and organize information.*   Students gather information using a variety of reference materials, including, but not limited to, informational books, magazines, newspapers, encyclopedias, almanacs, and atlases. Encyclopedias (book form and CD-ROM) are a valuable resource, but they are only one possible source, and other reference materials must be available. In addition to print sources, students can view filmstrips, films, and videos; visit websites; or interview people in the community who have special expertise on the topic. In the beginning, students read information that they find interesting. They can tell a peer about what they read as a way to paraphrase the resource and put the knowledge into their own words. From there, they make notes or use point form to record the information.

   The preliminary organization—deciding on the key points—completed in the first step gives direction for gathering the information. Now students review the information they have gathered and decide how best to present it so that the report will be both interesting and well organized. Students can transfer the "notes" they want to use for their reports from the cluster diagram or data chart onto note cards. Only keywords—not sentences or paragraphs—should be written on the cards. This helps guard against copying down information verbatim from research sources.

3. Create visuals.   Students may develop visuals such as charts, diagrams, maps, projection slides, pictures, models, and timelines. For example, the grade 2 students who gave reports on parts of the body made drawings and clay models of the parts and used a large skeleton hanging in the classroom to show the location of the organ in the body. Visuals provide a "crutch" for the speaker and add an element of interest for the listeners.

4. Give the presentation.   The final step is to rehearse and then give the presentation. Students can rehearse several times by reviewing key points and reading over their note cards. They should not, however, read the report directly from the note cards. Students might want to choose a particularly interesting fact to begin the presentation. The teacher can record presentations on video so that the presenter can assess his or her own performance at a later time.

Before the presentations begin, teachers teach minilessons on the characteristics of successful presentations. For example, speakers should talk loudly enough for all to hear, look at the audience, keep to the key points, refer to note cards for important facts, and use the visuals they have prepared.

Students are usually the audience for the oral reports, and members of the audience have responsibilities. They should be attentive, listen to the speaker, ask questions, and applaud the speaker's work. Sometimes students give presentations to the whole class, but it is possible to divide the class into groups so that students can present reports in each group simultaneously.

Book Talks and Other Reviews. Students give oral reports to review books they have read or television shows and films they have viewed. These book talks and reviews are one type of project students create in resource-based units, readers workshops, and thematic units. The steps in preparing and presenting book talks and other reviews are similar to those for reports of information, as shown in the following Step by Step box:

Step by Step

Preparing and Presenting Book Talks and Other Reviews

1. *Gather information.*   Students select information for the report, including a brief summary of the selection and bibliographic information; comparisons to other selections (e.g., with similar themes, written by the same author, starring the same actor); strengths and weaknesses; and opinions and conclusions. They also choose a brief excerpt from the book to read or an excerpt from a video to show.

2. *Organize information.*   Students record and organize the information on a cluster diagram and then copy keywords onto note cards.

3. *Create visuals.*   Students locate or create props to show during the review. Students may show the book in a book talk or show a poster for the film. Or, they may collect a box or bag of objects related to the book/film to show during the presentation.

4. *Give the presentation.*   Students briefly rehearse the review, and then they give the presentation, referring to the note cards but not reading them, and sharing the props.

Assessing Students' Oral Reports. Teachers can assess students' oral reports according to the steps students move through in developing their reports as well as the presentations of their reports in front of the class. Students can also assess their own presentations, considering each of the four steps involved in developing the oral report. These points might be used in developing an assessment checklist:

- Did you choose a narrow topic?
- Did you collect and organize information in a cluster diagram or a data chart?
- Did you prepare a chart or other visual(s) to use in the presentation?
- Did you rehearse the presentation?

Students can reflect on the presentation and respond to questions such as,

- Did you present the report as you planned?
- Did you speak loudly enough to be heard?

- Did you look at the audience?
- Did you use your visual(s)?
- Did you make your key points?
- How did the audience respond to your presentation?
- What are you most pleased with about your presentation?
- What will you change or do differently when you give another report?

Students should also be asked to comment on what they learned through the process of researching, writing, and presenting the report.

INTERVIEWS

Almost all children see interviews on television news programs and are familiar with the interviewing techniques reporters use. Interviewing is an exciting language arts activity that helps students refine questioning skills and use oral and written language for authentic purposes (Haley-James & Hobson, 1980).

Interviewing is an important language tool that can be integrated effectively in resource-based and thematic units. As part of a thematic unit on school, for example, a grade 1 class invited the local high school principal to visit their class to be interviewed. The principal, who is blind, brought his guide dog with him. The children asked him questions about how visually impaired people manage everyday tasks, as well as how he performed his job as a principal. They also asked questions about his guide dog. After the interview, students drew pictures and wrote summaries of the interview. One grade 1 student's report is shown in Figure 5–13.

Figure 5–13 A Grade 1 Student's Interview Report

Or, during a resource-based unit on *Naomi's Road* (Kogawa, 1986), grade 5 students can interview grandparents and great-grandparents about their memories of the Second World War. After reading excerpts from Eva Marques's book *100 Jobs for Kids and Young Adults: A Self-Empowerment Tool* (1997), a grade 8 class interviewed people in the community to learn about their jobs. To begin, students brainstormed a list of twenty-five questions to ask people about their jobs. Then they interviewed people and shared the answers with the class. Afterwards, students wrote reports of their interviews, either in first person or in third person (Bowser, 1993). In small groups, students brainstormed questions before the interviews, and met again in small gatherings to revise and edit their compositions. The papers were both informative and insightful, as this excerpt from one student's report about being a real estate agent shows:

> Long and unpredictable hours are what she hates most about her job. You never know how much time you'll be spending with a customer. . . . She does not have close friends at work because the business is so competitive. (Bowser, 1993, p. 40)

One way to introduce interviewing is to watch interviews conducted on a television newscast and discuss what the purpose of the interview is, what a reporter does before and after an interview, and what types of questions are asked. Interviewers use a variety of questions, some to elicit facts, others to probe for feelings and opinions, but all questions are open-ended. Rarely do interviewers ask questions that require only a yes or no answer.

Steps in Conducting Interviews. There are three steps in the interview process: planning the interview, conducting the interview, and sharing the results, as shown in the following Step by Step box:

Step by Step

Conducting Interviews

1. *Plan the interview.* In the planning step, students arrange for the interview and brainstorm questions to ask the person being interviewed. From this list, students choose which questions they will ask, making sure to avoid questions that require only *yes* or *no* answers. Students often write the questions on note cards. Then they sequence the cards in a reasonable order.

2. *Conduct the interview.* The second step is conducting the actual interview. Students greet the interviewee and conduct the interview by asking questions they have prepared in advance. They take notes or record the answers on audio. They ask follow-up questions about points that are not clear, and if the answer to one question elicits an impromptu, unscripted query, students ask it anyway. Students are polite and respectful of the answers and opinions of the interviewee. Before finishing, students thank the person for participating in the interview.

3. *Share the results.* Students share the results of the interview by presenting an oral report, writing a report or newspaper article, or making a poster.

Assessing Students' Interviews. Teachers assess students' interviews by checking that they followed the three steps of the interview process and by examining the quality of their final products. Similarly, students can assess their own use of the interview process and their reports, much like they assess other types of efferent talk projects. One way is through writing reflective journal entries.

DEBATES

Debates are useful when the whole class is excited about an issue and most or all of the students have taken supporting or opposing positions. As they participate in debates, students learn to use language to persuade their classmates and to articulate their viewpoints. Two types of debates are impromptu debates and formal debates.

Impromptu Debates. The class decides on an issue, clarifies it, and identifies positions that support or oppose the issue. Then students who wish to speak in favour of the issue move to the side of the room designated for supporters, and students who wish to speak against the issue move to the other side. Class members who have not formulated a position sit in the middle.

A lectern is set up in front of the classroom, and the teacher initiates the debate by asking a student from the supporting side to state the position on the issue. After this opening statement, the opposing side counters with a statement. Students take turns going to the lectern and speaking in support of or in opposition to the issue. Students who wish to participate go to the side of the room for the position they support and wait in line for their opportunity to speak. After hearing arguments, students may change their minds and move to the opposite side of the room; if they are no longer certain what side they are on, they take a seat in the middle.

Students who have just made a statement may be asked a question before a student for the other side makes a return statement.

Formal Debates. A more formal type of debate is appropriate for students in the upper-elementary and middle-school grades. Debates take the form of arguments between opposing sides of a proposition. A proposition is a subject that can be discussed from opposing points of view, such as the following:

> *Resolved, that students should have a role in setting standards of behaviour in classes and in disciplining those students who disrupt classes.*

After the proposition has been determined, teams of three or four students are designated to support the proposition (the affirmative team) or oppose it (the negative team).

Depending on the number of members on each team, the debate proceeds in this order:

1. The first student from the affirmative team makes a statement.
2. The first student from the negative team makes a statement.
3. The second student from the affirmative team makes a statement.
4. The second student from the negative team makes a statement.
5. The third student from the affirmative team makes a rebuttal statement.
6. The third student from the negative team makes a rebuttal statement.
7. The fourth student from the affirmative team makes a rebuttal statement.
8. The fourth student from the negative team makes a rebuttal statement.

Sometimes three or four statements are made by each team before beginning to make rebuttal statements rather than just two for each team (steps 1 to 4). Normally there are as many rebuttal statements as there are statements about the position, but teachers may vary the procedure to fit the class and their purposes.

Students can also choose judges to determine the winning team and decide the criteria for judging. They brainstorm questions that form the basis for their criteria and then develop a rubric. The rubric used in one grade 6 class is shown in Figure 5–14 on page 212. Questions similar to the following might initiate the brainstorming sessions:

- Did the speakers communicate their ideas to the listeners?
- Was a mastery of information evident in the presentations and rebuttals?

DEBATE RUBRIC

Resolved: There should be more sports for students at Lakeview Middle School.

Rating Code: 1–5;
5 = highest,
1 = lowest

	Appearance	Delivery	Factual information	Keeping to the point	Persuasiveness	Teamwork	Participation in rebuttal	Total
Pro								
Kristen Auch	____	____	____	____	____	____	____	____
James Wilson	____	____	____	____	____	____	____	____
Jeremy Fox	____	____	____	____	____	____	____	____
							Total	____
Con								
Rene LeBlanc	____	____	____	____	____	____	____	____
Whitney Lawson	____	____	____	____	____	____	____	____
Kim Lee	____	____	____	____	____	____	____	____
							Total	____

Figure 5–14 Debate Scoring Rubric

- Was the team courteous?
- Did the team work cooperatively?
- Did the second speaker on each team pick up and extend the statement of the first team member?

Review

Listening is the most basic and most used of the language modes. Despite its importance, listening instruction has been neglected in elementary classrooms. Students vary the way they listen for different purposes, and they use different procedures, strategies, and skills for each type of listening. In addition, teachers sustain talk in the elementary classroom because speaking has definite benefits for elementary students. Too often teachers assume that students already know how to speak effectively, so they concentrate on reading and writing. The four types of talk activities—conversations, aesthetic talk, efferent talk, and dramatic activities—are important for developing children's talk, and they also complement students' written language development.

The following key concepts are presented in this chapter:

1. Listening is the neglected language art because it is rarely taught; instead, teachers merely provide practice activities.
2. Students need to learn to use listening strategies to enhance their listening abilities.
3. Listening is a three-step process: receiving, attending, and assigning meaning.
4. There are five types of listening: discriminative, aesthetic, efferent, critical, and therapeutic.
5. Students listen aesthetically as teachers read stories aloud and while viewing puppet shows, plays, and video/CD-ROM versions of stories.
6. The Directed Listening–Thinking Approach (DLTA) is one way to actively involve students in aesthetic listening.

7. Students use efferent listening to remember information.

8. Talk is a necessary ingredient for learning.

9. Students talk in informal conversations as part of resource-based units and thematic units.

10. Students participate in many types of small-group conversations, and they use talk for both aesthetic and efferent purposes.

11. In conversations about literature, students use aesthetic talk to respond to a book and develop interpretations.

12. In storytelling and readers theatre activities, students use aesthetic talk to present stories.

13. K-W-L-S charts are a good way to help students talk about what they are learning in a thematic unit.

14. In show and tell, oral reports, interviews, and debates, students use efferent talk to inform and persuade listeners.

Extensions

1. Visit a classroom and observe how listening is taught or practised. Consider how practice activities might be changed into instructional activities.

2. Interview primary-, middle-, and upper-grade students about strategies they use while listening. Ask questions such as these:

   - What is listening?
   - Why do people listen? Why else?
   - What do you do to help you remember what you are listening to?
   - Do you always listen in the same way, or do you listen differently to stories read aloud and to information your teacher is telling you?
   - How do you know what is important in the message you are listening to?
   - What is the hardest thing about listening?
   - Are you a good listener? Why? Why not?
   - Compare students' responses across grade levels. Are older students more aware of the listening process than younger students are? Can older students identify a greater variety of listening strategies than younger students can?

3. Plan and teach a minilesson on one of the aesthetic listening strategies and on one of the efferent listening strategies discussed in this chapter. Reflect on the lessons and on the differences between aesthetic and efferent listening.

4. Read Stanley's *The Conversation Club* (1983) to a group of primary-grade students to introduce conversation activities. Then organize a conversation club with the students and plan several activities with the group.

5. Teach students how to participate in conversations about literature. Then, as you read a chapter book or a collection of picture books with a group of students, have the students participate in a series of literature conversations. Observe students as they talk about the book, and notice how they interact with their classmates as well as how they develop their interpretations.

6. Plan and conduct a debate with a group of upper-grade students. Help them choose a topic from current events, school and community issues, or a thematic unit.

7. In a small group, share several photos of yourself growing up. Notice how the photos serve as a catalyst for you to talk about yourself as you share stories and anecdotes.

8. Have upper-elementary or middle-school students create a list of interesting questions to use to interview a variety of individuals in the school such as the librarian, a parent, the school custodian, the school secretary, a classroom aide, or an administrator. Share the interviews with the class.

chapter six

Reading and Writing Narrative Text

PROFILE

Readers Workshop in a Grade 6 Classroom

Procedure

My grade 6 classroom bulges with children's literature, purposefully displayed to attract readers. Throughout the year, the children and I read extensively, and engage in many forms of response to the literature. Our responses regularly include extended talk, writing, and dramatization.

At the beginning of each school year, I ask the children to design our room to make reading inviting. We instill warmth in our classroom climate by including comfortable chairs, reading lamps that provide soft lighting, and colourful baskets of books arranged by authors, themes, and specific interests designated by the children. Casual book displays celebrating new authors appear often throughout the year.

Silent sustained reading begins quietly each morning at 8:30 a.m. I find a spot somewhere in the classroom and begin reading. The children, like quiet mice, model me. We read for 20 minutes at the beginning of the year, and progress to 30 minutes by year's end. Reading materials, fiction and nonfiction, are of the children's choice, but I monitor closely to see that all children read a balanced menu of genres.

Each child has a red readers workshop Duo-Tang folder that contains the child's reading logs, reading responses, and presentation sheets concerning the books that have been read or are being read. The journal entries confirm the child's understanding of her or his reading.

> "Literature circles and book talks within readers workshop provide favourite moments for the children . . . Observing the children's focused engagement with literature affirms my confidence in their learning and provides favourite moments for me."

Diana McCabe
Assistant Principal and Teacher
Liverpool Street School
Fredericton, New Brunswick

Minilessons are a part our readers workshop. At this time, we may discuss a piece of literature I have read aloud to the class, a favourite author, or a literary element I wish to introduce or reinforce. For example, we did a jigsaw cooperative lesson in which groups of three children each read from their choice of novel for 15 minutes. After the reading, I asked them to find three examples of text rich in imagery. They put their chosen images together cooperatively. I asked them to decide which one was the best. It was recorded, and then shared with the whole class by a reporter from the group. Quickly, the children realized that some books in the classroom, especially serial books, did not contain the richness of language typical of those written by some of their favourite authors, such as Roald Dahl, Wilson Rawls, and Chris Van Allsburg.

Assessment

Formative assessment is a regular and integral part of my interaction with the students during readers workshop. At 9:00 a.m. it is time for "Day at a Glance." At this time, my flowered clipboard (so I can find it easily each morning) accompanies me throughout the room as I do a quick check to see where the children are in their reading, and what instruction might be necessary. The names of the children are arranged alphabetically on the Day at a Glance sheet. Beside each name is a block, which is large enough to make anecdotal notes on each child's progress. These notes provide me with much of the information I need to plan instruction, effectively guide my children's literary growth, and communicate meaningfully with parents regarding their children's learning.

Adaptations

During Storyfest Week at our school we shared and compared old and new versions of fairy tales. One of our activities to celebrate our responses to literature was the creation of a wax museum. We invited our grade 1 reading buddies to tour the museum.

The children in my class worked individually or in pairs. Through discussion, the children chose a fairy tale and agreed upon a particular scene or action-filled event in the story to be depicted in their "still" pose. On a large sheet of mural paper, they designed and painted a backdrop of a scene or set for their story. They donned costumes and gathered simple props. Each child was responsible for a descriptive, postcard-length summary of the scene or event she/he had chosen.

Our room was darkened for the event, with only spotlights illuminating each set. When all was ready, student docents led visitors through the museum. It was an exciting response to literature. Both the participants and the observers gained understanding from the dramatic and oral interpretations of the literature, traditional and new.

Reflections

Literature circles and book talks within readers workshop provide favourite moments for the children. Sharing their thoughts orally about text not only affirms readers' understanding, but also contributes to new and extended understanding. Observing the children's focused engagement with literature affirms my confidence in their learning and provides favourite moments for me.

Given choices of topics for their combined social studies and language arts project, these students chose to first read from printed texts. When they discovered that at least some of the information printed was outdated, they turned to the Internet for more recent statistics. Later, with all of their information in place, they chose to present it to their classmates through realistic fiction.

Stories and poetry give meaning to the human experience, and are a powerful way of knowing and learning. Preschool children who listen to family members tell and read stories aloud develop a concept about stories by the time they come to school. Students use and refine this knowledge as they read and write stories during the elementary grades. They also learn to write their own stories through journal work they do in response to other stories and events. Many educators, including Jerome Bruner (1986), recommend using stories as a way into literacy.

Students tell and write stories about events in their lives, such as a birthday party, fishing trip, or car accident; retell familiar stories, including "The Gingerbread Man"; and write sequels for stories such as *Jumanji* (Van Allsburg, 1981). The stories students write reflect the ones they have read. When students read stories, their writing reflects the more sophisticated language structures and literary style. Dressel (1990) found that the quality of grade 5 students' writing was dependent on the quality of the stories they read or listened to, regardless of the students' reading levels.

Developing Students' Concept of Story

Young children have a rudimentary awareness about what makes a story. Children's concept of story includes information about the elements of story structure, such as characters, plot, and setting, as well as information about the conventions authors use. Children are usually not conscious of what they know. Golden describes children's concept of story as "a mental representation of story structure, essentially an outline of the basic story elements and their organization" (1984, p. 578).

Children's concept of story begins in the preschool years. Children as young as two years old have a rudimentary sense of story (Applebee, 1978; Pitcher & Prelinger, 1963). Children acquire this concept of story gradually, by listening to

To Guide Your Reading

As you read this chapter, prepare to

Explain how students develop a concept of story

•

Explain how teachers teach students about story structure

•

Explain how knowledge of stories affects comprehension

•

Explain how students read and respond to poems

•

Explain how students read and write stories during language arts instruction

•

Describe the types of journals elementary students write

•

stories, reading stories, and telling and writing stories. Older children have a better understanding of story structure than younger children. The stories older children tell and write are increasingly more complex, the plot structures more tightly organized, the characters more fully developed. Applebee found that kindergarten children have already developed a basic concept of what a story is, and these expectations guide them in responding to, and telling their own, stories. He found that kindergartners could use three story markers: "Once upon a time . . ." to begin; the past tense in telling a story; and formal endings such as "The End" or ". . . and they lived happily ever after."

Students' concept of story plays an important role in interpreting stories they read (Mandler & Johnson, 1977; Rumelhart, 1975; Stein & Glenn, 1979), and is just as important in writing (Golden, 1984). Students grow in their understanding of stories through reading and writing experiences (Golden, Meiners, & Lewis, 1992). As they explore and respond to stories, students learn about elements of story structure and genre. Golden and her colleagues say that story meaning is dynamic, growing continuously in the reader's mind.

> Explain how students use journals as tools for learning in the language arts and across the curriculum
>
> •
>
> Identify the kinds of poems students write
>
> •
>
> Explain how teachers encourage students to play with words and express ideas using figurative language
>
> •
>
> Explain how teachers incorporate poetry activities in resource-based units, readers and writers workshops, and thematic units

ELEMENTS OF STORY STRUCTURE

Stories have unique structural elements that are quite complex—plot, characters, setting, and other elements interact to produce a story. Authors manipulate the elements to make their stories complex and interesting. We will focus on five elements of story structure—plot, characters, setting, point of view, and theme—and illustrate each element using familiar and award- winning books.

Plot. The sequence of events involving characters in conflict situations is the *plot*. It is based on the goals of one or more characters and the processes they go through to attain these goals (Lukens, 1995). The main characters want to achieve a goal, and other characters are introduced to oppose them. The story events are put in motion by characters as they attempt to overcome conflict, reach their goals, and solve their problems.

In the beginning, the author introduces the characters, describes the setting, and presents a problem. Together, the characters, setting, and events develop the plot and sustain the theme throughout the story. In the middle, the author adds new events, each preparing readers for what will follow. Conflict heightens as the characters face roadblocks that keep them from solving their problems. Seeing how the characters tackle these problems adds suspense. In the end, the author reconciles all that has happened in the story, and readers learn whether the characters' struggles are successful.

Conflict, the tension or opposition between forces in the plot, motivates readers to continue reading. Conflict usually occurs (Lukens, 1995)

- Between a character and nature
- Between a character and society
- Between characters
- Within a character

Conflict between a character and nature occurs in stories in which severe weather plays an important role, such as *Stormbound* (Fairbridge, 1995) in which a snowstorm forces school to close and Loren becomes embroiled in a terrifying confrontation, and in stories set in isolated geographic locations, such as *Hatchet* (Paulsen, 1987), in which 13-year-old Brian struggles to survive after an airplane crash in the wilderness. In some stories, a character's activities and beliefs differ from those of other members of the society, and the differences cause conflict. One example of this type of conflict is *The Quarter-Pie Window* (Brandis, 1985) in which the orphaned

Emma Anderson moves to the town of York, Upper Canada, in 1830 to live under the guardianship of stern Mrs. McPhail whose hotel business exposes Emma to folks of all ranks of society.

Conflict between characters is common in children's literature. In *The Maestro* (Wynne-Jones, 1995), the young boy must deal with his strong negative feelings toward his father to learn to appreciate the gift from the maestro. Conflict within a character occurs in stories such as *Ira Sleeps Over* (Waber, 1972) and *Chrysanthemum* (Henkes, 1991). In *Ira Sleeps Over*, six-year-old Ira must decide whether to take his teddy bear when he spends the night with a friend, and in *Chrysanthemum*, classmates tease a young, eponymous mouse of the tale about her name. Chrysanthemum learns to appreciate her name with the support of an understanding teacher. Figure 6–1 lists stories representing the four types of conflict.

Conflict between a Character and Nature

Bunting, E. (1991). *Fly Away Home.* New York: Clarion. (P–M)

George, J. C. (1972). *Julie of the Wolves.* New York: Harper & Row. (M–U)

Loyie, L. (2005). *As Long as the River Flows.* Toronto: HarperCollins. 🍁

MacLachlan, P. (1994). *Skylark.* New York: HarperCollins. (M)

O'Dell, S. (1960). *Island of the Blue Dolphins.* Boston: Houghton Mifflin. (M–U)

Paulsen, G. (1987). *Hatchet.* New York: Bradbury Press. (M–U)

Poulsen, D. (1996). *Billy and the Bearman.* Toronto: Napoleon Publishing. (M–U) 🍁

Steward, S. (2003). *Raven Quest.* Toronto: Scholastic. (M-U) 🍁

Conflict between a Character and Society

Brandis, M. (1985/2003). *The Quarter-Pie Window.* Toronto: Tundra Books. (U) 🍁

Ellis, D. (2002). *A Company of Fools.* Markham, Ontario: Fitzhenry & Whiteside. (M–U) 🍁

Langston, L. (2003). *Lesia's Dream.* Toronto: HarperTrophy. (M–U) 🍁

Lowry, L. (1993). *The Giver.* Boston: Houghton Mifflin. (U)

O'Brien, R. C. (1971). *Mrs. Frisby and the Rats of NIMH.* New York: Atheneum. (M)

Polacco, P. (1994). *Pink and Say.* New York: Philomel. (M–U)

Taylor, C. (1994). *Summer of the Mad Monk.* Toronto: Greystone Books. (M–U) 🍁

Uchida, Y. (1993). *The Bracelet.* New York: Philomel. (P–M)

Conflict between Characters

Citra, B. (1999). *Ellie's New Home.* Victoria, B.C.: Orca Books. (M) 🍁

Ghent, N. (2003). *No Small Thing.* Toronto: HarperCollins. (M) 🍁

Little, J. (1984). *Mama's Going to Buy You a Mockingbird.* Toronto: Penguin Canada. (U) 🍁

Little, J. (1991). *Jess Was the Brave One.* Toronto: Viking. (P) 🍁

Naylor, P. R. (1991). *Shiloh.* New York: Atheneum. (M–U)

Paterson, K. (1994). *Flip-flop Girl.* New York: Lodestar. (U)

Rathmann, P. (1995). *Officer Buckle and Gloria.* New York: Putnam. (P)

Wynne-Jones, T. (1995). *The Maestro.* Toronto: Groundwood Books. (M–U) 🍁

Zelinsky, P. O. (1986). *Rumpelstiltskin.* New York: Dutton. (P–M)

Conflict within a Character

Byars, B. (1970). *The Summer of the Swans.* New York: Viking. (M)

Cumyn, A. (2002). *The Secret Life of Owen Skye.* Toronto: Douglas & McIntyre. (M-U) 🍁

Ellis, S. (1986). *The Baby Project.* Toronto: Groundwood Books. (M) 🍁

Henkes, K. (1991). *Chrysanthemum.* New York: Greenwillow. (P)

Hudson, J. (1984). *Sweetgrass.* Edmonton: Tree Frog Press. (U) 🍁

Matas, C. (1995). *The Primrose Path.* Winnipeg: Blizzard Publishing. (U) 🍁

Skrypuch, M. (2001). *Hope's War.* Toronto: Boardwalk Books. (U) 🍁

Waber, B. (1972). *Ira Sleeps Over.* Boston: Houghton Mifflin. (P)

P = primary grades (K–2); M = middle grades (3–5); U = upper grades (6–8).

Figure 6–1 Stories That Illustrate the Four Types of Conflict

Plot is developed through conflict introduced in the beginning of a story, expanded in the middle, and resolved at the end. Plot development involves four components:

1. *A problem.* A problem that introduces conflict is presented at the beginning of a story.
2. *Roadblocks.* In the middle of the story, characters face roadblocks in attempting to solve the problem.
3. *The high point.* The high point in the action occurs when the problem is about to be solved. This high point separates the middle and end of the story.
4. *The solution.* The problem is solved and roadblocks are overcome at the end of the story.

The problem, introduced at the beginning of the story, determines the conflict. In *The Ugly Duckling* (Mayer, 1987), the big, grey duckling does not fit in with the other ducklings. This is an example of conflict between characters.

After the problem has been introduced, authors use conflict to throw roadblocks in the way of an easy solution. As characters remove one roadblock, the author devises another to thwart the characters. Postponing the solution by introducing roadblocks is the core of plot development. Many children's stories contain three, four, or five roadblocks.

In *The Ugly Duckling*, the first conflict occurs when the ducks, other animals, and the woman who feeds the ducks make fun of the main character. The conflict is so great that the duckling goes out alone into the world. Next, conflict comes from the wild ducks and other animals that scorn him. Third, the duckling spends a miserable, cold winter in the marsh.

The high point of the action occurs when the solution to the problem hangs in the balance. Tension is high, and readers continue reading to learn whether the main characters solve the problem. Readers are relieved that the ugly duckling has survived the winter, but tension continues because he is still an outcast. Then he flies to a pond and sees three beautiful swans.

As the story ends, the problem is solved and the goal achieved. The other swans welcome him. He sees his reflection in the water and realizes he is no longer an ugly duckling. Children praise the new swan's beauty. The newly arrived swan is happy at last.

Characters. Characters are often the most important element of story structure because many stories are centred on a character or group of characters. In *Anne of Green Gables* (Montgomery, 1908/1999), for example, the story focuses on Anne's struggles to settle into her new life in Avonlea, her antics with Diana, the trials she presents to Marilla, and ultimately, her devotion to both Matthew and Marilla.

Usually, one or two well-rounded characters and several supporting characters are involved in a story. Fully developed main characters have many traits, both good and bad. By understanding or inferring a character's traits we get to know that figure well, and the character seems to come alive. Figure 6–2 on page 220 presents a list of stories with fully developed main characters.

Supporting characters may be individualized but portrayed less vividly than the main character. The extent to which supporting characters are developed depends on the author's purpose and the needs of the story.

Anne is the main character in *Anne of Green Gables*, and readers get to know her as a real person. She is a bright young woman with a vivid imagination and a tremendous desire to live a life filled with adventure and excitement. Her day-to-day existence in the village of Avonlea pales in comparison to the magical poetic land of her imagination. L. M. Montgomery takes readers into Anne's world through monologues in which the young woman transforms her natural surroundings of the Cuthbert place into inviting places of some mystique. Through dialogue and reports of Anne's antics at home and at school, readers come to know her quick wit, mischievous scheming, and quick temper. Readers come to know the supporting characters through their contrasts to Anne.

Character	Story
Jolene	Beveridge, C.(2003). *Shadows of Disaster*. Vancouver: Ronsdale Press. (M–U) 🍁
Mary	Blades, A. (1971). *Mary of Mile 18*. Montreal: Tundra Books. (P) 🍁
Ramona	Cleary, B. (1981). *Ramona Quimby, Age 8*. New York: Morrow. (M)
Birdy	Cushman, K. (1994). *Catherine, Called Birdy*. New York: HarperCollins. (U)
Mary Ann Alice	Doyle, B. (2001). *Mary Ann Alice*. Van: Douglas & McIntyre. (M–U) 🍁
Little Willy	Gardiner, J. R. (1980). *Stone Fox*. New York: Harper & Row. (M–U)
Chrysanthemum	Henkes, K. (1991). *Chrysanthemum*. New York: Greenwillow. (P)
Travis	Huser, G. (2003). *Stitches*. Toronto: Douglas & McIntyre. (M) 🍁
Swamp Angel	Isaacs, A. (1994). *Swamp Angel*. New York: Dutton. (P–M)
Jeremy	Little, J. (1984). *Mama's Going To Buy You a Mockingbird*. Toronto: Puffin Books. (M-U) Harper & Row. (M) 🍁
Sarah	MacLachlan, P. (1985). *Sarah, Plain and Tall*. New York:
Marty	Naylor, P. R. (1991). *Shiloh*. New York: Atheneum. (M–U)
Brian	Paulsen, G. (1987). *Hatchet*. New York: Viking. (U)
Matthew	Slade, A. (2001). *Dust*. Toronto: HarperCollins.(U) 🍁
Miriam	Skrypuch, M. (2003). *Nobody's Child*. Toronto: Dundurn Press (M–U) 🍁
Maria	Soto, G. (1993). *Too Many Tamales*. New York: Putnam. (P)
Maniac	Spinelli, J. (1990). *Maniac Magee*. New York: Scholastic. (U)
Cassie	Taylor, M. (1976). *Roll of Thunder, Hear My Cry*. New York: Dial. (U)
Winston	Walters, E. (2003). *Run*. Toronto: Viking. (M) 🍁

P = primary grades (K–2); M = middle grades (3–5); U = upper grades (6–8).

Figure 6–2 Stories with Fully Developed Main Characters

Characters are developed in four ways—via appearance, action, dialogue, and monologue. Readers notice these four types of information as they read in order to understand the characters.

Authors generally provide some physical description of the characters—their facial features, body shapes, habits of dress, mannerisms, and gestures. Early in the story, much emphasis is placed on Anne's appearance, especially her long braids of flaming red hair and her forlorn, worried expression as she waits at the train station's platform to be collected to go to her new home.

What a character does is often the best way to know about that character. Readers are endeared to Anne through her actions. As she ventures to the ice cream social, dyes her hair, studies diligently, and cracks her slate over Gilbert's head when he calls her "Carrots," readers come to know her vivaciousness.

Dialogue is the third way character is developed. What characters say is important, but so is the manner in which they speak. A character might speak less formally with friends than with respected elders or characters in positions of authority. The geographic location of the story, the historical period, and the characters' socio-economic status also determine how characters speak. Anne's incessant talking frequently provides readers with a social commentary on life in Avonlea, including a glimpse of current fashion when Anne describes her Christmas gift:

> I'd rather feast my eyes on that dress. I'm so glad that puffed sleeves are still fashionable. It did seem to me that I'd never get over it if they went out before I had a dress with them. I'd never have felt quite satisfied, you see. (p. 214)

Authors provide insight into characters by revealing their thoughts, or inner dialogue. Anne does not need an audience to share her thoughts. With no apparent listeners, she chatters on in metaphoric discourse about such things as how she is invigorated by the arrival of mornings, her pleasure in knowing that there is a lively brook at Green Gables, and how utterly humiliated she feels having been reprimanded at school.

Students can draw open-mind portraits to examine characters and reflect on story events from the character's viewpoint. These portraits have two parts: the face of the character is on one page, and the mind of the character is on the second page. The two pages are stapled together, with the "mind" page under the "face" page. A grade 7 student's open-mind portrait of Anne is shown in Figure 6–3. The student divided Anne's thinking into two groups, Anne's likes and dislikes. In each picture she has shown some of the things and people that Anne repeatedly tells the reader she likes and dislikes.

Setting. In some stories the settings are merely backdrops. Many folktales, for example, simply use the convention, "Once upon a time . . ." to set the stage. In other stories, the setting is elaborate and integral (Lukens, 1995).

Location is an important dimension in many stories. For example, the Boston Commons in *Make Way for Ducklings* (McCloskey, 1969) and the Alaskan North Slope in *Julie of the Wolves* (George, 1972) are integral to the stories' effectiveness. The settings are artfully described and

Figure 6–3 An Open-Mind Portrait of Anne in *Anne of Green Gables*

Andrews, J. (1985). *Very Last First Time*. Toronto: Groundwood Books. (M–U) 🍁

Babbitt, N. (1975). *Tuck Everlasting*. New York: Farrar, Straus & Giroux. (M–U)

Brandis, M. (1985/2003). *The Quarter-Pie Window*. Toronto: Tundra Books. (P–M) 🍁

Bunting, E. (1994). *Smoky Night*. Orlando, FL: Harcourt Brace. (P–M)

Cauley, L. B. (1984). *The City Mouse and the Country Mouse*. New York: Putnam. (P–M)

Choi, S. N. (1991). *Year of Impossible Goodbyes*. Boston: Houghton Mifflin. (U)

George, J. C. (1972). *Julie of the Wolves*. New York: Harper & Row. (M–U)

Harvey, B. (1988). *Cassie's Journey: Going West in the 1860s*. New York: Holiday House. (M)

Johnston, T. (1994). *Amber on the Mountain*. New York: Dial. (P)

Konigsburg, E. L. (1983). *From the Mixed-Up Files of Mrs. Basil E. Frankweiler*. New York: Atheneum. (M)

L'Engle, M. (1962). *A Wrinkle in Time*. New York: Farrar, Straus & Giroux. (M)

Lowry, L. (1989). *Number the Stars*. Boston: Houghton Mifflin. (M–U)

MacLachlan, P. (1983). *Sarah, Plain and Tall*. New York: Harper & Row. (M)

McCloskey, R. (1969). *Make Way for Ducklings*. New York: Viking. (P)

Myers, W. D. (1988). *Scorpions*. New York: Harper & Row. (U)

Ness, E. (1966). *Sam, Bangs, and Moonshine*. New York: Holt, Rinehart & Winston. (P)

Paterson, K. (1977). *Bridge to Terabithia*. New York: Crowell. (M–U)

Paulsen, G. (1987). *Hatchet*. New York: Viking. (U)

Polacco, P. (1988). *The Keeping Quilt*. New York: Simon & Schuster. (M)

Ringgold, F. (1991). *Tar Beach*. New York: Crown. (P–M)

Say, A. (1993). *Grandfather's Journey*. Boston: Houghton Mifflin. (P–M)

Speare, E. G. (1983). *The Sign of the Beaver*. Boston: Houghton Mifflin. (M–U)

Steig, W. (1986). *Brave Irene*. New York: Farrar, Straus & Giroux. (P–M)

Torres, L. (1993). *Subway Sparrow*. New York: Farrar, Straus & Giroux. (P–M)

Tregebov, R. (1993). *The Big Storm*. New York: Hyperion. (P)

Uchida, Y. (1993). *The Bracelet*. New York: Philomel. (P–M)

Wilder, L. I. (1971). *The Long Winter*. New York: Harper & Row. (M)

P = primary grades (K–2); M = middle grades (3–5); U = upper grades (6–8).

Figure 6–4 Stories with Integral Settings

add something unique to the story. Other stories take place in predictable settings that do not contribute to the story's effectiveness.

The time period is an important element in stories set in the past or future. If *The Quarter-Pie Window* (Brandis, 1985/2003) and *Number the Stars* (Lowry, 1989) were set in different eras, for example, they would lose much of their impact. Today, few people would believe that Jewish people are the focus of government persecution. In stories that take place in the future, such as *A Wrinkle in Time* (L'Engle, 1962), things are possible that are not possible today. Figure 6–4 presents a list of stories with integral settings.

The fourth dimension, time, includes both time of day and the passage of time. Most stories ignore time of day, except for scary stories that take place after dark. In stories such as *The Ghost-Eye Tree* (Martin & Archambault, 1985), a story of two children who must walk past a scary tree at night, time is important because night makes things scarier.

Many short stories span a brief period of time. In *Jumanji* (Van Allsburg, 1981), Peter and Judy's bizarre adventure, during which their house is overtaken by exotic jungle creatures, lasts only the several hours their parents are at the opera. Other stories, such as *Charlotte's Web* (White, 1952/1980) and *The Ugly Duckling* (Mayer, 1987), span a long enough period for the main character to grow to maturity.

Students can draw maps to show the setting of a story. These maps may show the path a character travelled or the passage of time.

Point of View. Stories are written from a particular viewpoint, and this focus determines to a great extent readers' understanding of the characters and the events of the story. The four points of view are first-person viewpoint, omniscient viewpoint, limited omniscient viewpoint, and objective viewpoint (Lukens, 1995). Figure 6–5 presents a list of stories written from each viewpoint.

The first-person viewpoint tells a story through the eyes of one character using the first-person pronoun "I." The reader experiences the story as the protagonist/narrator tells it. The protagonist/narrator speaks as an eyewitness to, and participant in, the events. For example, in *Shiloh* (Naylor, 1991), Marty tells how he works for Judd Travers in order to buy the puppy Travers has mistreated, and in *That Scatterbrain Booky* (Hunter, 1981), young Booky describes her family's troubled life during the Great Depression of the 1930s. Many children's books are written from the first-person viewpoint. One limitation is that the narrator must remain an eyewitness in all scenes of the story.

First-Person Viewpoint

Howe, D., & Howe, J. (1979). *Bunnicula: A Rabbit-Tale of Mystery*. New York: Atheneum. (M)

MacLachlan, P. (1985). Sarah, *Plain and Tall*. New York: Harper & Row. (M)

Naylor, P. R. (1991). *Shiloh*. New York: Atheneum. (M–U)

Say, A. (1993). *Grandfather's Journey*. Boston: Houghton Mifflin. (M)

Stinson, K. (1982) *Red Is Best*. Toronto: Annick Press. (P) ❧

Tanaka. S. (1996). *I Was There: On Board the Titanic*. Toronto: Scholastic. (M–U) ❧

Omniscient Viewpoint

Andrews, J. (1996). *Keri*. Toronto: Groundwood Books. (U) ❧

Babbitt, N. (1975). *Tuck Everlasting*. New York: Farrar, Straus & Giroux. (M–U)

Grahame, K. (1961). *The Wind in the Willows*. New York: Scribner. (M)

Lewis, C. S. (1981). *The Lion, the Witch and the Wardrobe*. New York: Macmillan. (M–U)

Steig, W. (1982). *Doctor De Soto*. New York: Farrar, Straus & Giroux. (P)

Limited Omniscient Viewpoint

Bunting, E. (1994). *A Day's Work*. New York: Clarion. (P–M)

Cleary, B. (1981). *Ramona Quimby, Age 8*. New York: Morrow. (M)

Gardiner, J. R. (1980). *Stone Fox*. New York: Harper & Row. (M)

Levine, G. (1996). *Ella Enchanted*. Toronto: Harper Collins. (M–U) ❧

Lionni, L. (1969). *Alexander and the Wind-Up Mouse*. New York: Pantheon. (P)

Lowry, L. (1993). *The Giver*. Boston: Houghton Mifflin. (U)

Objective Viewpoint

Brett, J. (1987). *Goldilocks and the Three Bears*. New York: Putnam. (P)

Cauley, L. B. (1988). *The Pancake Boy*. New York: Putnam. (P)

Conrad, P. (1989). *The Tub People*. New York: Harper & Row. (P–M)

Galdone, P. (1978). *Cinderella*. New York: McGraw-Hill. (P–M)

Lunn, J. & Gal, L. (1979). *The Twelve Dancing Princesses*. Toronto: Methuen. ❧

Mollel, T. (1990). *The Orphan Boy*. Don Mills: Stoddart/Oxford University Press. ❧

Zemach, M. (1983). *The Little Red Hen*. New York: Farrar, Straus & Giroux. (P)

Multiple and Alternating Viewpoints

Avi. (1991). *Nothing But the Truth*: A Documentary Novel. New York: Orchard. (U)

Dorris, M. (1992). *Morning Girl*. New York: Hyperion. (U)

Fleischman, P. (1991). *Bull Run*. New York: HarperCollins. (U)

Gray, N. (1988). *A Country Far Away*. New York: Orchard. (P–M)

Laker, J. (1976). *Merry Ever After*. New York: Viking. (M)

Rowland, D. (1991). *Little Red Riding Hood/The Wolf's Tale*. New York: Birch Lane Press. (P–M)

P = primary grades (K–2); M = middle grades (3–5); U = upper grades (6–8).

Figure 6–5 Stories That Illustrate the Four Points of View

In the omniscient viewpoint, the author is godlike, seeing and knowing all about the characters in the story. Using the third-person viewpoint, the author tells readers about the thought processes of each character without worrying how the information is obtained. Most stories told from the omniscient viewpoint are chapter books. Examples of chapter books written from the omniscient viewpoint are *Tuck Everlasting* (Babbitt, 1975) and *Keri* (Andrews, 1996).

The limited omniscient viewpoint is used to reveal the thoughts of one character. The story is told in the third person, and the author concentrates on the thoughts, feelings, and significant past experiences of the main character or another important character. Many picture book– and chapter book–stories are told from this viewpoint. Lois Lowry uses the limited omniscient viewpoint in *The Giver* (1993), concentrating on the main character, Jonas, using his thoughts to explain Jonas's "perfect" community to readers. Later, Jonas's thoughts reveal his growing dissatisfaction with the community and his decision to escape to Elsewhere with the baby Gabriel.

In the objective viewpoint, readers are eyewitnesses to the story and are confined to the immediate scene. They learn only what is visible and audible, without knowing what any character thinks. Many folktales, such as *Cinderella* (Galdone, 1978) and *The Little Red Hen* (Zemach, 1983), are told from the objective viewpoint. Other picture book stories, such as *The Tub People* (Conrad, 1989) and *The Orphan Boy* (Mollel, 1990), are told from this eyewitness viewpoint. The focus is on recounting events, not on developing the personalities of the characters.

Younger children can experiment with point of view to understand how the author's viewpoint affects a story. One way to demonstrate point of view is to contrast *The Three Little Pigs* (Galdone, 1970), the traditional version of the story told from an objective viewpoint, with *The True Story of the 3 Little Pigs!* (Scieszka, 1989), a self-serving narrative told by Mr. A. Wolf from a first-person viewpoint. In this unusual and satirical retelling, the wolf tries to explain away his bad image. Even first graders are struck by how different the two versions are and how the narrator filters the information.

Another way to demonstrate the impact of different viewpoints is for students to retell or rewrite a familiar story, such as *Little Red Riding Hood* (Hyman, 1983), from specific points of view—through the eyes of Little Red Riding Hood; her sick, old grandmother; the hungry wolf; or the hunter. As they shift the point of view, students learn they can change some aspects of a story but not others. To help them appreciate how these changes affect a story, take a story such as *The Lion, the Witch and the Wardrobe* (Lewis, 1950), told from the omniscient viewpoint, and retell short episodes from the viewpoints of different characters. As students shift to other points of view, they must decide what to leave out.

A few stories are written from multiple viewpoints. In flip picture books, one version of the story begins at the front of the book, and another begins at the back of the book. In Rowland's *Little Red Riding Hood/The Wolf's Tale* (1991), the traditional version begins on one side of the book, the wolf's version on the other. In some chapter books, such as *Bull Run* (Fleischman, 1991), alternating chapters are written from different characters' perspectives. Other stories written from multiple or alternating viewpoints are also listed in Figure 6–5.

Theme. The underlying meaning of a story, the theme, embodies general truths about human nature (Lehr, 1991). It usually deals with the characters' emotions and values. Explicit themes are stated openly and clearly in the story. Lukens (1995) uses *Charlotte's Web* to point out how one theme of friendship—the giving of oneself for a friend—is expressed as an explicit theme:

> Charlotte has encouraged, protected, and mothered Wilbur, bargained and sacrificed for him, and Wilbur, the grateful receiver, realizes that "friendship is one of the most satisfying things in the world." And Charlotte says later, "by helping you perhaps I was trying to lift up my life a little. Anyone's life can stand a little of that." Because these quoted sentences are exact statements from the text they are called explicit themes. (p. 94)

Implicit themes are implied rather than explicitly stated, emerging through the thoughts, speech, and actions of the characters as they seek to resolve their conflicts. Lukens also uses *Charlotte's Web* to illustrate implicit themes:

> Charlotte's selflessness—working late at night to finish a new word, expending her last energies for her friend—is evidence that friendship is giving oneself. Wilbur's protection of Charlotte's egg sac, his sacrifice of first turn at the slops, and his devotion to Charlotte's babies—giving without any need to stay even or to pay back—leads us to another theme: true friendship is naturally reciprocal. As the two become fond of each other, still another theme emerges: one's best friend can do no wrong. In fact, a best friend is sensational! Both Charlotte and Wilbur believe in these ideas; their experiences verify them. (p. 95)

Charlotte's Web has several friendship themes, one explicitly stated and others inferred from the text. Stories usually have more than one theme that cannot be articulated with a single word. Friendship is a multidimensional theme. Teachers can ask questions to guide students' thinking as they work to construct a theme (Au, 1992). Students must go beyond one-word labels in describing and constructing their ideas about a theme.

Sketch-to-stretch activities (see Figure 6–6) are used to help students better understand the plot, characters, theme, or other elements of a story (Harste, Short, & Burke, 1988; Whitin, 1994, 1996a). Many teachers use sketch-to-stretch activities as responses to texts they read to students, asking the students to sketch as they listen. When the reading is finished, students explain their drawings to one or more peers. Through drawing and explaining, the students can transform or extend meanings, discover new insights, clarify misunderstandings, or construct new meanings about the text. Students may also include short sentences or captions as part of their drawings. In sketch-to-stretch, the emphasis is on representing the students' ideas and feelings, not on artistic technique. Sketch-to-stretch can also be used across curricula to respond to nonfiction information texts. The steps in sketch-to-stretch are presented in the following Step by Step box:

Figure 6–6 A Grade 6 Student's Sketch-to-Stretch Drawing for *The Very Last First Time*

Step by Step

Sketch-to-Stretch

1. *Read and respond to a story.* Students read a story or several chapters of a longer book and respond to the story in a grand conversation about literature or in reading logs.

2. *Talk about the themes in the story and ways to symbolize meanings.* The teacher reminds students that there are many ways to represent the meaning of an experience, and that students

can use lines, colours, shapes, symbols, and words to visually represent what a story means to them. Students and the teacher talk about possible meanings and ways they might visually represent these meanings.

3. *Have students draw sketches.*   Students work in small groups to draw sketches that reflect what the story means to them. The teacher emphasizes that students should focus on the meaning of the story, not their favourite episode, and that there is no single correct interpretation of the story.

4. *Have students share their sketches with classmates.*   Students meet in small groups to share their sketches and talk about the symbols they used. The teacher encourages classmates to study each student's sketch and tell what they think the student is trying to convey.

5. *Have some students share with the class.*   Each group chooses one sketch from their group to share with the class.

6. *Revise sketches and make final copies.*   Some students will want to revise and add to their sketches based on feedback they received and ideas from classmates. Also, students make final copies if the sketches are being used as projects (Whitin, 1994, 1996a).

TEACHING STUDENTS ABOUT STORIES

Teachers help students expand their concepts of story through minilessons that focus on particular story elements. Minilessons are usually taught during the exploring stage of the reading process, after students have had an opportunity to read and respond to a story and share their reactions.

Minilessons on Stories. Teachers adapt the teaching strategy set out in Chapter 1 to teach minilessons on the elements of story structure and other procedures, concepts, and strategies and skills related to stories. The steps in teaching a minilesson on stories are presented in the following Step by Step box:

Step by Step

A Minilesson on Stories

1. *Introduce the element.*   The teacher introduces the element of story structure using a chart to define and list the characteristics of the element. Figure 6–7 on pages 227–228 shows examples of charts that can be developed for some story elements. Next, students think about stories they have read recently that exemplify the element, and talk about how these stories were organized.

2. *Analyze the element in stories.*   Students read or listen to one or more stories that illustrate the element. Students analyze how the author used the element in the story and tie their analyses to the information about the element presented in the first step. Students can write the information from the chart in their reading logs.

3. **Explore the story**. Students participate in exploring activities to investigate how authors use the element in particular stories. Activities include

- Retell a story.
- Write a retelling of a story in book format.
- Dramatize a story.
- Present a puppet show of a story.
- Draw clusters or other diagrams to visually represent the structure of a story.
- Make a class book of the story, with each student contributing one page.

Chart 1

Stories

Stories have three parts:

1. A beginning
2. A middle
3. An end

Chart 2

Beginnings of Stories

Writers put these things in the beginning of a story:

1. The characters are introduced.
2. The setting is described.
3. A problem is established.
4. Readers get interested in the story.

Chart 3

Middles of Stories

Writers put these things in the middle of a story:

1. The problem gets worse.
2. Roadblocks thwart the main character.
3. More information is provided about the characters.
4. The middle is the longest part.
5. Readers become engaged with the story and empathize with the characters.

Chart 4

Ends of Stories

Writers put these things in the end of a story:

1. The problem is resolved.
2. The loose ends are tied up.
3. Readers feel a release of emotions that were built up in the middle.

Chart 5

Conflict

Conflict is the problem that characters face in the story. There are four kinds of conflict:

1. Conflict between a character and nature
2. Conflict between a character and society
3. Conflict between characters
4. Conflict within a character

(continued)

Figure 6–7 Charts for the Elements of Story Structure

As students participate in these activities, the teacher draws their attention to the element being studied.

4. Review the element.   The teacher reviews the information about the element, using the charts introduced in the first step. Students explain the element in their own words, using one story they have read as an example.

Chart 6

Plot

Plot is the sequence of events in a story. It has four parts:

1. A Problem: The problem introduces conflict at the beginning of the story.
2. Roadblocks: Characters face roadblocks as they try to solve the problem in the middle of the story.
3. The High Point: The high point in the action occurs when the problem is about to be solved. It separates the middle and the end.
4. The Solution: The problem is solved and the roadblocks are overcome at the end of the story.

Chart 7

Setting

The setting is where and when the story takes place.

1. Location: Stories can take place anywhere.
2. Weather: Stories take place in different kinds of weather.
3. Time of Day: Stories take place during the day or at night.
4. Time Period: Stories take place in the past, at the current time, or in the future.

Chart 8

Characters

Writers develop characters in four ways:

1. Appearance: How characters look
2. Action: What characters do
3. Dialogue: What characters say
4. Monologue: What characters think

Chart 9

Theme

Theme is the underlying meaning of a story.

1. Explicit Themes: The meaning is stated clearly in the story.
2. Implicit Themes: The meaning is suggested by the characters, action, and monologue.

Chart 10

Point of View

Writers tell the story according to one of four viewpoints:

1. First-Person Viewpoint: The writer tells the story through the eyes of one character using "I."
2. Omniscient Viewpoint: The writer sees all and knows all about each character.
3. Limited Omniscient Viewpoint: The writer focuses on one character and tells that character's thoughts and feelings.
4. Objective Viewpoint: The writer focuses on the events of the story without telling what the characters are thinking and feeling.

Figure 6–7 Charts for the Elements of Story Structure *(continued)*

A list of topics for minilessons about stories is presented on page 230. These topics include procedures, concepts, and strategies and skills for reading and writing stories.

ADAPTING TO MEET THE NEEDS OF EVERY STUDENT

Teachers must find ways to involve all students in successful reading and writing experiences with stories. A list of suggestions for adapting the information presented in this chapter to meet the needs of every student is presented on page 231. These suggestions emphasize the importance of allowing students to respond to stories before exploring them, and of finding ways to support students as they read and write.

ASSESSING STUDENTS' CONCEPT OF STORY

Teachers assess students' concept of story in many ways. They observe students as they read and respond to stories. They can note whether or not students are sensitive to story elements as they talk during grand conversations. Some students talk about the character who is most like them, or compare two stories. Teachers note whether students use terminology related to story elements. Do they talk about conflict, or the way a story ends? If they are talking about point of view, do they use that term? Teachers also ask questions about story elements during grand conversations and note students' responses. Students' reading logs also provide evidence of the same sorts of comments and reactions.

Students can demonstrate their understanding of story elements by making cluster diagrams, charts, and other diagrams. These activities are a natural outgrowth of students' responses to a story, not the reason students read stories (Urzua, 1992). Teachers document students' understanding of story elements by examining stories they write to see how they apply their knowledge.

Reading Stories

Students read stories aesthetically, and their concept of story informs and supports their reading. They read popular and award-winning stories together during resource-based units, stories they choose themselves in readers workshop, and other stories as part of thematic units. Students use the reading process to read, respond to, explore, and extend their reading. Reading stories with students is more than simply a pleasurable way to spend an hour; it is how classroom communities are created (Cairney, 1992). Reading, writing, and talking about stories are natural extensions of the relationships that students have built together. Students share stories with classmates and work together on projects to extend their interpretations.

AESTHETIC READING

According to Louise Rosenblatt (1978), reading is a personal experience during which readers connect the story they are reading to their own lives and previous experiences with literature. The goal of aesthetic reading is comprehension, the negotiation of meaning between the reader and the text (Rosenblatt, 1978, 1985a). Readers do not search for the author's "correct" meaning; instead, they create a personal meaning for themselves. A story evokes different meanings from different readers, or even from the same reader at different times in his or her life.

Students use a number of strategies to respond to stories. Our role as teachers is to enhance students' repertoire of responses over time so that they develop a range of possibilities. Students might use the following strategies to respond to stories:

- *Visualizing.* Students create images or pictures of the story in their minds.
- *Predicting.* Students anticipate or make predictions about what will happen in the story. Students consider the impact of what they have read on what they are reading.

Minilessons

Reading and Writing Stories

Procedures	Concepts	Strategies and Skills
Make a beginning-middle-end cluster diagram	Concept of story	Visualize
	Beginning-middle-end	Predict and confirm
Make a setting map	Plot	Engage with text
Make a plot profile	Characters	Empathize with characters
Make an open-mind portrait	Setting	Identify with characters
	Theme	Write dialogue for characters
Do a sketch-to-stretch drawing	Point of view	Elaborate on the plot
Design a story quilt	Genre of story	Notice opposites in the story
Use storyboards	Aesthetic reading	Retell the story
Make a chart to compare versions of a folktale	Comprehension	Monitor understanding
	Authors	Connect to one's own life
Make a class collaboration book	Illustrators	Connect to previously read literature
Write an innovation on a text	Types of illustrations	Extend the story
Write a sequel	Sequels	Value the story
Assess effectiveness of a story		Evaluate the story
Assess use of reading/ writing strategies		Analyze the story

- *Engaging.* Students become so involved they feel transported through time and space into the story.
- *Empathizing.* Students respond with their feelings as they read.
- *Identifying.* Students make connections between a character and themselves.
- *Elaborating.* Students make inferences and add information to what they read.
- *Noticing opposites.* Students note tensions or contrasts in the story.
- *Monitoring.* Students make sure that what they are reading makes sense to them.
- *Connecting to life.* Students make connections between events, characters, and other aspects of the story with their own lives.
- *Connecting to literature.* Students make connections between the story they are reading and other stories they have read.
- *Evaluating.* Students make judgments about why they liked a story or whether it was worth reading.
- *Analyzing.* Students analyze the author's use of the elements of story structure (Corcoran, 1987; Cox & Many, 1992; Tompkins & McGee, 1993).

With practice and guidance, students learn to use these strategies as they read aesthetically and participate in response activities.

Comprehension develops gradually. As students pick up a book by a favourite author or look at the cover of a book, they call to mind past experiences and make predictions. Comprehension continues to develop as students read, respond to, and explore the story, and it deepens as they

Adapting

Reading and Writing Stories to Meet the Needs of Every Student

1. Read Aloud to Students

Teachers can make accessible stories that students cannot read independently by reading aloud to students or by having them read to by older students or classroom volunteers. Engagement in active listening can be fostered by clarifying unfamiliar vocabulary and by having students make predictions as the reading proceeds. When students listen together in a class or small group, they become an interpretive community and develop strong bonds as readers, providing support for less able readers.

2. Make Stories Available at a Listening Centre

Stories and other written materials can be made available to students through a listening centre. Make the text available so listeners can read along as they listen. The audio tapes should be available for frequent rereading.

3. Encourage Students to Choose Stories to Read

Teachers should regularly schedule time for sustained reading. Classroom libraries should be well stocked with a variety of books at various reading levels. Teachers should introduce books and entice readers to read a wide range of literature through book talks.

4. Dramatize Stories

Drama is an effective technique that students can use to understand stories they are reading and to create stories they will write. When students are reading a complex story, they can role-play important scenes in order to better understand the characters and events.

5. Write Retellings of Stories

Students can write retellings of favourite stories or retell the story from a particular character's viewpoint. Writing retellings of favourite stories provides the support that some writers need to write successfully. Retellings can involve writing new settings, new endings, changes to characters, and changes of perspective.

6. Work in Collaborative Readers and Writers Groups

Students can work together in pairs or in small groups to support each other as they read and write.

---

discuss the story and write responses in reading logs. Students move beyond the actual text as they work on projects and extend their comprehension further.

Students use the aesthetic stance when reading stories. The stance that readers take indicates their focus of attention. Joyce Many found that students who read aesthetically have higher levels of comprehension (1991).

Teachers encourage aesthetic reading and comprehension by sharing stories, teaching mini-lessons, and planning response and exploring activities. Guidelines for enhancing comprehension in the classroom are presented in the Teacher's Notebook on page 232.

Intertextuality. As students comprehend and create interpretations, they make connections to books read previously. These connections are called *intertextuality* (de Beaugrande, 1980). Students use intertextuality as they respond to books by recognizing similarities between characters, plots, and themes, and incorporate ideas and structures from the stories they have read into the stories they are writing. Intertextuality has five characteristics (Cairney, 1990, 1992):

1. *Individual and unique.* Students' literary experiences and the connections they make among them are different.

2. *Dependent on literary experiences.* Intertextuality is dependent on the types of books students have read, their purpose for and interest in reading, and the literary communities to which they belong.

3. *Metacognitive awareness.* Most students are aware of intertextuality and consciously make connections among texts.

4. *Links to concept of story.* Students' connections among stories are linked to their knowledge about literature.

5. *Reading–writing connections.* Students make connections between stories they read and stories they write.

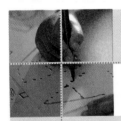

Teacher's Notebook

Guidelines for Enhancing Comprehension

1. Encourage Aesthetic Reading
Students learn about the aesthetic and efferent stances and the differences between them. Students are encouraged to read stories aesthetically for the lived-through experience of reading.

2. Group Books into Text Sets
Students read a wide variety of literature, including stories, poems, and informational books. Often, the teacher should group the literature into text sets, or students can make their own text sets.

3. Make Initial Responses
Students make initial responses to stories through grand conversations, writing in reading logs, and participating in role-playing activities.

4. Explore the Story
Students explore the story through activities such as creating word walls, rereading the story, sequencing the events using storyboards, making diagrams, looking for opposites, and noting examples of literary style.

5. Teach Reading Strategies
The teacher teaches minilessons on reading strategies, including imaging, predicting, engaging, connecting to life and literature, valuing, and evaluating.

6. Expand the Concept of Story
The teacher teaches minilessons about the elements of story structure, genre, authors and illustrators, and illustration to help students expand their concept of story.

7. Develop Intertextuality
Students make connections from the story to their own lives and to other literature they have read.

8. Create Projects
Students extend comprehension through reading, writing, talk, drama, and research projects. It is important that students choose the projects they pursue.

The sum of students' experiences with literature—including the stories parents have read and told to young children, the books/audiobooks students have read or listened to, film versions they have viewed, their concepts of story and knowledge about authors and illustrators, and the books students have written—constitute their intertextual histories (Cairney, 1992). Cairney's research indicates that elementary students are aware of their past experiences with literature and use this knowledge as they read and write.

One way teachers encourage students to make intertextual links is by grouping literature into text sets—collections of three or more books that are related in some way. Possible text sets include

- Stories written by the same author
- Stories featuring the same character
- Stories illustrating the same theme
- Different versions of a folktale
- Stories in the same genre
- Stories and other books related to a thematic unit

As students read and discuss these books, they make connections and share these connections, allowing classmates to gain insights about literature and build on classmates' ideas. Teachers can prompt students and ask them to describe commonalities among the books. Students can make charts and other diagrams to compare authors, characters, and other aspects of stories.

TEACHING STORIES

Students move through the five stages of the reading process as they read and respond to stories. Some of the activities in each stage are

1. *Preparing.* Teachers introduce the story and activate students' background knowledge.
2. *Reading.* Students read the story in one of several ways: they listen to the teacher read the book, read independently or with a buddy, or read through shared reading.
3. *Responding.* Students respond to the story through grand conversations, by dramatizing events from the story, and by writing in reading logs.
4. *Exploring.* Students participate in a variety of exploring activities to dig more deeply into the story. A list of exploring activities is presented in the Teacher's Notebook on page 234. Students also add interesting and important words from the story to a word wall. Teachers teach minilessons about story elements, aesthetic reading, comprehension, reading strategies, and other topics during this stage.
5. *Extending.* Students do projects to extend their interpretations of the story and share completed projects with classmates.

Teachers plan resource-based units featuring award-winning stories for children and adolescents. Some resource-based units feature a single book, others a text set of books. Students may focus on the story or they might learn about a particular genre, or category, of literature by reading stories illustrating the genre. They might also be involved in an author study where they read and respond to stories written by a particular author.

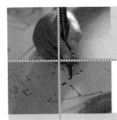

Teacher's Notebook

Activities to Explore Stories

Storyboards

The teacher cuts apart two copies of a picture book, backs each page with a sheet of posterboard, and laminates each page. Students read storyboards and identify important words for the word wall, memorable quotes, and so on. Students can also create storyboards for a chapter book. After reading the book, each student chooses a chapter, rereads it, draws a picture about it, and writes a summary of it. Then the pictures and summaries are backed with posterboard and laminated.

Story Boxes

Students and the teacher collect items related to a story and place them in a box. The box cover is decorated with the title and author, pictures of scenes from the story, pictures of the characters, and memorable quotes. Making the box is a good way to focus students' attention on what is important about the story, and students can examine the items in a box prepared by students in a previous class as they talk about the story and what it means to them.

Open-Mind Portraits

In order to probe a character, students draw portraits of the character and cut around the face so that the head flips up. Next they back the page with another sheet of paper. Then they write words and draw pictures in the "open mind" behind the face that reflect the character's thoughts.

Setting Maps

Students draw setting maps to illustrate a character's journey in a story. Other types of maps are beginning–middle–end cluster diagrams, Venn diagrams to compare characters, and plot profiles. For more information about maps, see *Responses to Literature, Grades K–8* (Macon, Bewell, & Vogt, 1991).

Sketch-to-Stretch

Students make sketch-to-stretch drawings to represent the theme of a story. These drawings are not illustrations of particular events in the story, but they symbolize the story's message. After making their sketches, students share them with classmates and talk about the symbols and messages they have included in the drawings.

Story Quilts

Students create paper or cloth quilts with pictures to represent the story and memorable quotes. Students design the quilt to emphasize the theme of the book and choose colours to symbolize the story. Students work individually or in small groups to make each square, and then the squares are placed side by side to complete the quilt.

For more information on readers workshops, see Chapter 4, "The Reading and Writing Processes," page 144.

Readers workshop is another way of organizing instruction that provides time for students to engage in independent or shared reading, to respond through conversation and writing, and for teachers to offer instruction. In a typical setting, students choose what they read from literature introduced by their teachers or recommended by their classmates. Students are encouraged to respond freely and to make connections between their lives and the literature they read. Readers workshop simulates reading outside of school.

Students often read stories as part of thematic units or inquiry-based units. Stories are useful because they give life to information and make it more memorable than many informational texts. For example, those that are historical fiction personalize history in a way that informational books cannot (Fennessey, 1995; Tunnell & Ammon, 1993). Many stories have been written to describe life on the Prairies and to show how living on the dusty, wind-swept, open plains is distinctive from living elsewhere. Here is a sampling:

- Poetic description of prairie life—*If You're Not From the Prairie* ... (Bouchard, 1995)
- Ruination of fertile soil—*Grandpa's Alkali* (Bannatayne-Cugnet, 1993)
- Travel across the prairies—*Dandelions* (Bunting, 1995)
- Family life on the prairies—*A Prairie Year* (Bannatayne-Cugnet, 1994)
- Immigrating to live on the prairies—*The New Land* (Reynolds, 1997)
- Unusual weather for a prairie Christmas—*Chinook Christmas* (Wiebe, 1992)
- Sale of family farm—*The Auction* (Andrews, 1990)
- Friendship and an immigrant child's struggle to begin again—*Josepha: A Prairie Boy's Story* (McGugan, 1994)
- Summer work and play—*A Prairie Boy's Summer* (Kurelek, 1975)
- Prairie nature and activities in winter—*A Prairie Boy's Winter* (Kurelek, 1973)
- Drought on the prairies—*The Dust Bowl* (Booth, 1996)

ASSESSING STUDENTS' UNDERSTANDING OF STORIES

Students' interpretations are unique and personal. Having students answer comprehension questions or fill in the blanks on worksheets is not an effective assessment technique. Teachers can better assess students' interpretation in these ways (Cairney, 1990):

- Listen to students as they talk about stories during grand conversations and other literature discussions.
- Read students' entries in reading logs.
- Note students' use of reading strategies.
- Observe students' participation in exploring activities.
- Examine the projects that students do.

Teachers also ask students to reflect on their interpretations during reading conferences or in reading log entries.

Teachers expect students to go beyond literal recall to critique the stories through making connections and comparisons among texts, identifying personal meanings of text, and recognizing story structure and the writing techniques used.

Developing Students' Concept of Poetry—Playing with Words

Poetry "brings sound and sense together in words and lines," according to Donald Graves, "ordering them on the page in such a way that both the writer and reader get a different view of life" (1992, p. 3). Children are natural poets, and poetry surrounds them as they chant jump-rope rhymes on the playground, clap out the rhythm of favourite poems, and dance in response to songs. Larrick (1991) believes that we enjoy poetry because of the physical involvement that the words evoke. Also, people play with words as they invent rhymes and ditties, create new words, and craft powerful comparisons.

Georgia Heard calls language "the poet's paint" (1989, p. 65). As students experiment with words, they learn to create images, play with words, and evoke feelings. They laugh with language, experiment with rhyme, and invent new words. These activities provide students with a rich background of experiences for reading and writing poetry, and they gain confidence in choosing the "right" word to express an idea, emphasizing the sounds of words, and expressing familiar ideas with fresh comparisons. Figure 6–8 lists wordplay books that elementary students enjoy.

CHANTING

Alligator pie, alligator pie.
If I don't get some I think I'm gonna die.
Give away the green grass, give away the sky,
But don't give away my alligator pie.

Children need to hear the rhythms and patterns of English over and over, until the regular syntactic patterns are as familiar to them as their everyday language. Poetry is an excellent way to allow children that repeated practice, especially if it begins with music and chanting. Children love to chant the poems in Dennis Lee's *Alligator Pie* (1974) because the rhythm of the language evokes a response that is compelling to them. They enjoy the sounds and the humour in the title poem. Similarly, the songs of Sharon, Lois, and Bram, or Raffi engage children at that same level of rhythmic response that allows these speech patterns to become part of their syntactic repertoire.

Alligator soup, alligator soup,
If I don't get some I think I'm gonna droop.
Give away my hockey stick, give away my hoop,
But don't give away my alligator soup.

In a grade 2 class, children begin each morning with songs such as Sharon, Lois, and Bram's "The Smile on the Crocodile," which combines music with actions, or "Good Day, Good Day to You," which includes clapping rhythms with the words and music. These activities introduce children to a variety of language patterns, and give them the practice they need while engaging in an enjoyable activity. They learn patterns and rhythms with words that are essential for their future development as readers and writers.

From songs, children can proceed to chanting favourite poems for their own enjoyment, moving eventually to chanting with expression that reflects a public performance standard. Children need to chant frequently and repetitively.

EXPERIMENTING WITH RHYME

Because of their experience with Dr. Seuss and Robert Munsch stories, finger plays, and nursery rhymes, kindergartners and grade 1 students enjoy creating rhymes naturally, but when it is equated with poetry, it can get in the way of wordplay and vivid images. The following three-line poem shows a grade 5 student's effective use of rhyme:

Thoughts After a 40-Mile Bike Ride

My feet
And seat
Are beat.

Agee, J. (1992). *Go Hang a Salami! I'm a Lasagna Hog! and Other Palindromes*. New York: Farrar Straus & Giroux. (U)

Bierhorst, J. (Ed.). (1992). *Lightning Inside You: And Other Native American Riddles*. New York: Morrow. (M–U)

Booth, D. (1993). *Doctor Knickerbocker*. Toronto: Kids Can Press. (P–M) 🍁

Brown, M. (1983). *What Do You Call a Dumb Bunny? And Other Rabbit Riddles, Games, Jokes, and Cartoons*. Boston: Little, Brown. (P–M) 🍁

Cole, J., & Calmenson, S. (1995). *Yours Till Banana Splits: 201 Autograph Rhymes*. New York: Morrow. (M–U)

Degen, B. (1996). *Sailaway Home*. New York: Scholastic. (P)

Esbensen, B. J. (1986). *Words with Wrinkled Knees*. New York: Crowell. (M–U)

Fitch, S. (1994). *I Am Small*. Toronto: Doubleday. (P–M) 🍁

Fitch, S. (1997). *If You Could Wear My Sneakers*. Toronto: Doubleday. (M) 🍁

Fitch, S. (1999). *If I Were the Moon*. Toronto: Doubleday. (P) 🍁

Gilman, P. (1985). *Jillian Jiggs*. Richmond Hill: Scholastic. (P–M) 🍁

Gwynne, F. (1976). *A Chocolate Moose for Dinner*. New York: Dutton. (M–U)

Gwynne, F. (1980). *The Sixteen Hand Horse*. New York: Prentice-Hall. (M–U)

Gwynne, F. (1988). *A Little Pigeon Toad*. New York: Simon & Schuster. (M–U)

Hall, R. (1985). *Sniglets for Kids*. Yellow Springs, OH: Antioch. (M–U)

Hall, K., & Eisenberg, L. (1992). *Spacey Riddles*. New York: Dial. (P)

Hanson, J. (1972). *Homographic Homophones. Fly and Fly and Other Words That Look and Sound the Same But Are As Different in Meaning As Bat and Bat*. Minneapolis: Lerner. (M)

Hartman, V. (1992). *Westward Ho Ho Ho! Jokes from the Wild West*. New York: Viking. (M–U)

Keats, E. J. (1972). *Over in the Meadow*. New York: Scholastic. (P)

Kellogg, S. (1987). *Aster Aardvark's Alphabet Adventures*. New York: Morrow. (P–M)

Lee, D. (1974). *Alligator Pie*. Toronto: Macmillan. (P–M) 🍁

Lee, D. (1977). *Garbage Delight*. Toronto: Macmillan. (M–U) 🍁

Lee, D. (1983). *Jelly Belly*. Toronto: Macmillan. (M–U) 🍁

Lee, D. (2000). *Bubblegum Delicious: Poems*. Toronto: Key Porter Books. (M–U) 🍁

Lesynski, L. (1999). *Dirty Dog Boogie*. Toronto: Annick Press. (M) 🍁

Lewis, J. P. (1996). *Riddle-icious*. New York: Knopf. (M)

McMillan, B. (1990). *One Sun: A Book of Terse Verse*. New York: Holiday House. (M)

Merriam, E. (1992). *Fighting Words*. New York: Morrow. (P–M)

Most, B. (1992). *Zoodles*. San Diego: Harcourt Brace Jovanovich. (M)

New, W. (1998). *Vanilla Gorilla: Poems*. Vancouver: Ronsdale Press. (P–M) 🍁

Perl, L. (1988). *Don't Sing Before Breakfast, Don't Sing in the Moonlight*. New York: Random House. (M–U)

Rees, E. (1995). *Fast Freddie Frog and Other Tongue Twister Rhymes*. Honesdale, PA: Wordsong. (P)

Schwartz, A. (1973). *Tomfoolery: Trickery and Foolery with Words*. Philadelphia: Lippincott. (M–U)

Schwartz, A. (1982). *The Cat's Elbow and Other Secret Languages*. New York: Farrar, Straus & Giroux. (M–U)

Schwartz, A. (1992). *Busy Buzzing Bumblebees and Other Tongue Twisters*. New York: HarperCollins. (P–M)

Simmie, L. (1986). *An Armadillo Is Not a Pillow*. Saskatoon: Western Producer Prairie Books. (M–U) 🍁

Smith, W. J., & Ra, C. (1992). *Behind the King's Kitchen: A Roster of Rhyming Riddles*. Honesdale, PA: Wordsong. (M–U)

Steig, J. (1992). *Alpha Beta Chowder*. New York: HarperCollins. (P–M)

Sterne, N. (1979). *Tyrannosaurus Wrecks: A Book of Dinosaur Riddles*. New York: Crowell. (M)

Terban, M. (1985). *Too Hot to Hoot: Funny Palindrome Riddles*. New York: Clarion. (M–U)

Terban, M. (1992). *Funny You Should Ask: How to Make Up Jokes and Riddles with Wordplay*. New York: Clarion. (M–U)

Terban, M. (1995). *Time to Rhyme: A Rhyming Dictionary*. Honesdale, PA: Wordsong. (M)

Van Allsburg, C. (1987). *The Z Was Zapped*. Boston: Houghton Mifflin. (M)

Wilbur, R. (1995). *Runaway Opposites*. San Diego: Harcourt Brace. (P)

Zalben, J. B. (1992). *Lewis Carroll's Jabberwocky*.

P = primary grades (K–2); M = middle grades (3–5); U = upper grades (6–8).

Figure 6–8 Wordplay Books for Elementary Students

A small group of grade 1 students wrote their own version of *Oh, A-Hunting We Will Go* (Langstaff, 1974):

> Oh, a-hunting we will go,
> a-hunting we will go.
> We'll catch a little bear
> and curl his hair,
> and never let him go.
> Oh, a-hunting we will go,
> a-hunting we will go.
> We'll catch a little mole
> and put him in a hole,
> and never let him go.
> Oh, a-hunting we will go,
> a-hunting we will go.
> We'll catch a little bug
> and give him a big hug
> and never let him go.
> Oh, a-hunting we will go,
> a-hunting we will go.
> We'll catch a little bunny
> and fill her full of honey,
> and never let her go.
> Oh, we'll put them in a ring
> and listen to them sing
> and then we'll let them go.

The grade 1 students wrote this collaboration with the teacher taking dictation. After the rough draft was written, students reread it, checking the rhymes and changing a word here or there. Then each student chose one stanza to copy and illustrate. The pages were collected and compiled to make a book. Students shared the book with their classmates, with each student reading his or her "own" page.

OTHER POETIC DEVICES

Poets choose words carefully. They craft powerful images when they use unexpected comparisons, repeat sounds within a line or stanza, imitate sounds, and repeat words and phrases. These techniques are called *poetic devices*. Students learn to appreciate the poet's ability to manipulate devices in poems, and to apply the devices in their own writing (Cullinan, Scala, & Schroder, 1995). The terminology is also helpful in response groups when students talk about poems, and in writers groups.

Comparison. One way to describe something is to compare it to something else. Students can compare images, feelings, and actions to other things using two types of comparison—similes and metaphors. A *simile* is an explicit comparison of one thing to another—that one thing is like something else. Similes are signalled by the use of *like* or *as*. In contrast, a *metaphor* compares two things by implying that one is something else, without using *like* or *as*. Differentiating between the two terms is less important than using comparisons to make writing more vivid; for example, children can compare anger to a thunderstorm. Using a simile, they might say, "Anger is like a thunderstorm, screaming with thunder-feelings and lightning-words." Or, as a metaphor, they might say, "Anger is a volcano, erupting with poisonous words and hot-lava actions."

Alliteration. *Alliteration* is the repetition of the initial consonant sound in consecutive words or in words in close proximity. Alliteration makes poetry fun, and children enjoy reading and reciting alliterative verses like *A My Name Is Alice* (Bayer, 1984) and *The Z Was Zapped* (Van Allsburg, 1987). After reading one of these books, children can create their own versions.

Onomatopoeia. *Onomatopoeia* is a device in which poets use "sound words" to make their writing more sensory and vivid. These words (e.g., *crash, slurp, varoom, me-e-e-ow*) sound like their meanings. Students can compile a list of sound words to refer to when they write their own poems.

Spier has compiled two books of sound words—*Gobble Growl Grunt* (1971), about animal sounds, and *Crash! Bang! Boom!* (1972), about the sounds people and machines make. Students can use these books to select sound words for their writing. Comic strips are another good source of sound words.

In *Wishes, Lies, and Dreams* (1980), Koch recommends having children write noise poems that include a noise or sound word in each line. These first poems often sound contrived (e.g., "A dog barks bow-wow"), but the experience helps children learn to use onomatopoeia, as this poem dictated by a kindergartner illustrates:

> **Elephant Noses**
>
> Elephant noses
> Elephant noses
> Elephants have big noses
> Big noses
> Big noses
> Elephants have big noses
> through which they drink
> SCHLURRP

Repetition. Repetition is another device used to structure writing as well as to add interest. Edgar Allan Poe's use of the word *nevermore* in "The Raven" is one example, as is the gingerbread boy's boastful refrain in "The Gingerbread Boy."

Reading Poetry

Children grow rather naturally into poetry. Opie and Opie (1959) conclude that children have a natural affinity to verse, songs, riddles, jokes, chants, and puns. Preschoolers are introduced to poetry when their parents repeat Mother Goose rhymes, read *The House at Pooh Corner* (Milne, 1956) and the Dr. Seuss stories, and sing songs to them. During the elementary grades, youngsters often create jump-rope rhymes and other ditties.

TYPES OF POEMS CHILDREN READ

Poems for children assume many different forms. The most common type of poetry is rhymed verse, such as Robert Louis Stevenson's "Where Go the Boats?" Vachel Lindsay's "The Little Turtle," and John Ciardi's "Mummy Slept Late and Daddy Fixed Breakfast." Narrative poems tell a story; examples are Clement Moore's "The Night Before Christmas," Robert Browning's "The Pied Piper of Hamelin," Robert W. Service's "The Cremation of Sam McGee," and Sheree Fitch's "There's a Mouse in My House." A Japanese form, haiku, is a three-line poem that contains seventeen syllables. Because of its brevity, it has been considered an appropriate form of poetry for children. Free verse has lines that don't rhyme, and rhythm is less important than in other types of poetry. Images take on greater importance in free-form verse. Langston Hughes's "Subway Rush Hour" and William Carlos Williams's "This Is Just to Say" are two examples. Other forms of poetry include limericks, a short, five-line rhymed verse form popularized by Edward Lear (1995), and concrete poems, which are arranged on the page to create a picture or an image.

Poetry books published for children include picture book versions of single poems such as Alfred Noyes' *The Highwayman*, illustrated by Charles Keeping; specialized collections of poems written by a single poet or related to a single theme, such as dinosaurs or Halloween; and comprehensive anthologies featuring 50 to 500 or more poems arranged by category. One of the best anthologies is *The Random House Book of Poetry for Children* (Prelutsky, 1983). A list of poetry books written for children is presented in Figure 6–9 on page 240.

Picture Book Versions of Single Poems

Carroll, L. (1992). (Ill. by J. B. Zalben). *Lewis Carroll's Jabberwocky*. Honesdale, PA: Wordsong. (M–U)

Cohen, L. (1995). *Dance Me to the End of Love*. New York: Welcome Enterprises. (U) 🍁

Frost, R. (1988). (Ill. by E. Young). *Birches*. New York: Henry Holt. (U)

Harrison, T. (2002). *O Canada*. Toronto: Kids Can Press. (P–M–U) 🍁

Lear, E. (1986). (Ill. by L. B. Cauley). *The Owl and the Pussycat*. New York: Putnam. (P–M)

Moore, C. (1995). *The Night Before Christmas*. New York: North-South. (P–M)

Noyes, A. (1981). (Ill. by C. Keeping). *The Highwayman*. Oxford, England: Oxford University Press. (U)

Service, R. (Ill. by T. Harrison) (1986). *The Cremation of Sam McGee*. Toronto: Kids Can Press. (M–U) 🍁

Service, R. (Ill. by T. Harrison) (1988). *The Shooting of Dan McGrew*. Toronto: Kids Can Press. (U) 🍁

Thayer, E. L. (1988). (Ill. by P. Polacco). *Casey at the Bat: A Ballad of the Republic, Sung in the Year 1888*. New York: Putnam. (M–U)

Specialized Collections

Adoff, A. (1995). *Street Music: City Poems*. New York: HarperCollins. (P)

Carle, E. (1989). *Animals, Animals*. New York: Philomel. (P–M)

Dickinson, E. (1978). *I'm Nobody! Who Are You? Poems of Emily Dickinson for Children*. Owing Mills, MD: Stemmer House. (M–U)

Fleischman, P. (1985). *I am Phoenix: Poems for Two Voices*. New York: Harper & Row. (M–U)

Fleischman, P. (1988). *Joyful Noise: Poems for Two Voices*. New York: Harper & Row. (M–U)

Frost, R. (1982). *A Swinger of Birches: Poems of Robert Frost for Young People*. Owing Mills, MD: Stemmer House. (U)

Glaser, I. J. (1995). *Dreams of Glory: Poems Starring Girls*. New York: Atheneum. (M–U)

Greenfield, E. (1988). *Under the Sunday Tree*. New York: Harper & Row. (M)

Hopkins, L. B. (1995). *Blast Off! Poems About Space*. New York: HarperCollins. (P)

Janeczko, P. B. (Sel.). (1993). *Looking for Your Name: A Collection of Contemporary Poems*. New York: Orchard Books. (U)

Jones, H. (Ed.). (1993). *The Trees Stand Shining: Poetry of the North American Indians*. New York: Dial. (M–U)

Kuskin, K. (1980). *Dogs and Dragons, Trees and Dreams*. New York: Harper & Row. (P–M)

Lewis, J. P. (1995). *Black Swan/White Crow*. New York: Atheneum. (Haiku) (M–U)

Livingston, M. C. (1985). *Celebrations*. New York: Holiday House. (M)

Livingston, M. C. (1986). *Earth Songs*. New York: Holiday House. (See also Sea Songs and Space Songs.) (M–U)

Livingston, M. C. (Sel.). (1991). *Lots of Limericks*. New York: McElderry Books. (M–U)

Lobel, A. (1983). *The Book of Pigericks*. New York: Harper & Row. (limericks) (P–M)

McCord, D. (1974). *One at a Time*. Boston: Little, Brown. (M–U)

Pomerantz, C. (1982). *If I Had a Paka: Poems in 11 Languages*. New York: Greenwillow. (M–U)

Prelutsky, J. (1984). *The New Kid on the Block*. New York: Greenwillow. (P–M)

Prelutsky, J. (1989). *Poems of A. Nonny Mouse*. New York: Knopf. (P–M)

Prelutsky, J. (1990). *Something Big Has Been Here*. New York: Greenwillow. (P–M)

Prelutsky, J. (1993). *A. Nonny Mouse Writes Again!* New York: Knopf. (M–U)

Siebert, D. (1984). *Truck Song*. New York: Harper & Row. (P–M)

Silverstein, S. (1996). *Falling Up*. New York: HarperCollins. (P–M)

Yolen, J. (1990). *Bird Watch: A Book of Poetry*. New York: Philomel. (M–U)

Comprehensive Anthologies

Booth, D. (Ed.) (1989). *Til All the Stars Have Fallen: Canadian Poems for Children*. Toronto: Kids Can Press. (P–M–U) 🍁

Booth, D. (Ed.) (1990). *Voices on the Wind: Poems for All Seasons*. Toronto: Kids Can Press. (P–M–U) 🍁

de Paola, T. (Compiler). (1988). *Tomie de Paola's Book of Poems*. New York: Putnam. (P–M)

Dunning, S., Leuders, E., & Smith, H. (Compilers). (1967). *Reflections on a Gift of Watermelon Pickle, and Other Modern Verse*. New York: Lothrop, Lee & Shepard. (U)

Kennedy, X. J. (Compiler). (1985). *The Forgetful Wishing Well: Poems for Young People*. New York: McElderry Books. (U)

Prelutsky, J. (Compiler). (1983). *The Random House Book of Poetry for Children*. New York: Random House. (P–M–U)

P = primary grades (K–2); M = middle grades (3–5); U = upper grades (6–8).

Figure 6–9 Poetry Books Written for Children

Some poetry written for adults can be used effectively with elementary students, especially at upper-grade levels. Apseloff (1979) explains that poems written for adults use more sophisticated language and imagery and provide children with an early introduction to poems and poets they will study later. For example, upper-grade students enjoy Shakespeare's "The Witches' Song" from *Macbeth* and Robert W. Service's "The Shooting of Dan McGrew." A list of poems written for adults that may be appropriate with upper-grade students is presented in Figure 6–10.

Children's Favourite Poems. Children have definite preferences about poems, just as adults do. Fisher and Natarella (1982) surveyed the poetry preferences of grade 1, 2, and 3 students; Terry (1974) investigated grade 4, 5, and 6 students' preferences; and Kutiper (1985) researched grade 7, 8, and 9 students' preferences. The most popular forms of poetry were limericks and narrative poems; the least popular were haiku and free verse. Children preferred funny poems, poems about animals, and poems about familiar experiences; they disliked poems with visual imagery and figurative language. The most important elements were rhyme, rhythm, and sound. Primary-grade students preferred traditional poetry, middle-grade students preferred modern poetry, and upper-grade students preferred rhyming verse. Children in all three studies liked

Poet	Poems and/or Books of Poetry
William Blake	"The Lamb," "The Tyger," "The Piper," and other selections from *Songs of Experience and Songs of Innocence*. Compare with Nancy Willard's *A Visit to William Blake's Inn: Poems for Innocent and Experienced Travelers* (1981).
Emily Dickinson	"I'm Nobody! Who Are You?," "There Is No Frigate Like a Book," and other favourite poems from *I'm Nobody! Who Are You? Poems of Emily Dickinson for Children* (1978) and *A Brighter Garden* (1990).
T. S. Eliot	Poems about cats from *Old Possum's Book of Practical Cats* (1967).
Robert Frost	"The Pasture," "Birches," "Fire and Ice," "Stopping by Woods on a Snowy Evening," and other favourites are included in *A Swinger of Birches: Poems of Robert Frost for Young People* (1982). *Stopping by Woods on a Snowy Evening*, illustrated by Susan Jeffers (1978), and *Birches* (1988) are picture book versions of individual poems.
Langston Hughes	Two new editions of Langston Hughes's poems are *The Dream Keeper and Other Poems* (1994) and *The Book of Rhythms* (1995).
Alfred Noyes	Charles Keeping's stunning black and white illustrations of *The Highwayman* (1981) capture the beauty and tragedy of this classic poem.
Robert W. Service	Ted Harrison's beautiful paintings illuminate *The Cremation of Sam McGee* (1986) and capture the mood of the arctic in this cherished classic.
Walt Whitman	Lee Bennett Hopkins has compiled *Voyages: Poems of Walt Whitman* (1988), and Robert Sabuda has illustrated a picture book version of *I Hear America Singing* (1991).

Figure 6–10 Adult Poems Appropriate for Upper-Grade Students

poetry, enjoyed listening to poetry read aloud, and could give reasons why they liked or disliked particular poems.

Kutiper and Wilson (1993) found that the humorous poetry of Shel Silverstein and Jack Prelutsky was the most popular. The three most widely circulated books in school libraries were *The New Kid on the Block* (Prelutsky, 1984), *Where the Sidewalk Ends* (Silverstein, 1974), and *A Light in the Attic* (Silverstein, 1981). Fourteen of the thirty most popular books in the study were written by these two poets. Both Silverstein and Prelutsky use rhyme and rhythm effectively in their poems and write humorous narrative poems about familiar, everyday occurrences.

Poets Who Write for Children. Many poets write for children today, among them Arnold Adoff, Byrd Baylor, Gwendolyn Brooks, David Day, Sheree Fitch, Lee Bennett Hopkins, Karla Kuskin, Lilian Moore, Mary O'Neill, and Jack Prelutsky. Children are interested in learning about favourite poets. When children view poets and other writers as real people, people whom they can relate to and who enjoy the same things they do, they begin to see themselves as poets—a necessary criterion for successful writing. Information about poets is available in *Speaking of Poets: Interviews with Poets Who Write for Children and Young Adults* (Copeland, 1993), *Speaking of Poets 2: More Interviews with Poets Who Write for Children and Young Adults* (Copeland & Copeland, 1994), and *A Jar of Tiny Stars: Poems by NCTE Award-Winning Poets* (Cullinan, 1996).

For more information on poets, see Appendix B, "Resources about Authors and Illustrators."

TEACHING STUDENTS TO READ POEMS

The focus in reading poems with students is on enjoyment. Students should have many opportunities to read and listen to poems read aloud, and should learn a variety of approaches for sharing poetry. Teachers should share poems they especially like with students. Students are not expected to analyze them; instead, they read poems they enjoy and share their favourite ones with classmates. Students use the reading process as they read and respond to poems, and they often read poems during readers workshop and in connection with resource-based and thematic units.

During an author unit, these grade 6 students read many of Jack Prelutsky's poems, including "Mean Maxine," "I'm Thankful," and "The New Kid on the Block."

Introducing Students to Poetry. In her poem "How to Eat a Poem," Eve Merriam (1966) provides useful advice to students: reading a poem is like eating a piece of fruit, so bite right in and let the juice run down your chin. Because poems can be shared quickly, they can be tied in with almost any activity, and are often coordinated with resource-based and thematic units.

When teachers and students read poems aloud, they enhance their reading using these four elements (Stewig, 1981):

- Tempo—how fast or slowly to read the lines
- Rhythm—which words to stress or say loudest
- Pitch—when to raise or lower the voice
- Juncture—when and how long to pause

Students experiment with these elements during minilessons and learn how to vary them to make their reading of poetry more interpretive. Students also learn that in some poems one element may be more important than another. During rehearsal, students experiment with tempo, rhythm, pitch, and juncture in order to read the poem effectively.

Teachers begin by reading favourite poems aloud to students and hanging charts with the poems written on them in the classroom. After several days, teachers point out a collection of poetry books in the classroom library and invite students to compose a poem to share with the class. Before long, students eagerly volunteer to read poems to the class. Guidelines for reading poems with children are presented in the Teacher's Notebook on page 244.

In Readers Workshop. Students sometimes choose collections of poetry to read during readers workshop, or teachers can plan a special poetry workshop. Poetry workshop can have the same components as regular readers workshop, or it can integrate both readers and writers workshops (Tompkins & McGee, 1993).

During a poetry workshop, the reading time is often divided into two parts. During the first part, students spend time browsing in collections of poetry and selecting poems they want to share with classmates. During the second part of reading time, students read poems aloud to partners or small groups of classmates. Students need to have the opportunity to read poems aloud. They also write responses to poems in reading logs and do projects to extend their poetry experience.

In Resource-Based Units. Teachers often share poems with students in conjunction with stories and other books they read aloud. For example, they might read Langston Hughes's poem "Dreams" (Prelutsky, 1983) together with *Number the Stars* (Lowry, 1989), or read Lee Bennett Hopkins's "Night Bear" (1984) before or after reading *Ira Sleeps Over* (Waber, 1972). Sometimes, teachers read a poem as a preparing activity; other times, as an exploring activity. Students may also locate a poem related to a story or other book and share it with the class as a project during the extending stage.

Teachers can teach a unit on poetry. During the unit, students read and respond to a collection of poems. In this unit, poetry is at the centre. Teachers choose some poems that all students will read and respond to; students select others.

Teachers read many poems to students, and students read other poems themselves. One way for students to read poems is choral reading, in which students take turns reading a poem together. Students need multiple copies of the poem for choral reading, or the poem must be displayed on a chart or overhead projector so that everyone can read it. Students may read the poem aloud together or in small groups, or individual students can read particular lines or stanzas. Four possible approaches to reading poems (Stewig, 1981) are as follows:

1. *Echo reading.* The leader reads each line, and the group repeats it.
2. *Leader and chorus reading.* The leader reads the main part of the poem, and the group reads the refrain or chorus in unison.

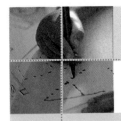

Teacher's Notebook

Guidelines for Reading Poems with Children

1. Read Aloud
Children and teachers read poetry aloud, not silently. Even if students are reading independently, they should speak each word, albeit softly or in an undertone.

2. Read with Expression
The teacher teaches students how to read a poem with expression, how to emphasize the rhythm and feel of the words, and where to pause.

3. Sing Poems to Familiar Tunes
Children sing poems to familiar tunes such as "Twinkle, Twinkle Little Star" or "I've Been Working on the Railroad." Children experiment to find a tune that fits the line structure of the poem and then sing the poem to the tune.

4. Rehearse
Readers rehearse poems several times before reading aloud so that they can read fluently and with expression. The teacher encourages students to read "poetically."

5. Include Poetry Books in the Classroom
A collection of poetry books should be included in the classroom library for children to read during readers workshop and other independent reading times.

6. Avoid Requiring Memorization
Children should not be assigned to memorize a particular poem; rather, children who are interested in learning a favourite poem should be encouraged to do so and share it with class members.

7. Avoid Analysis
Children do not analyze the meaning of a poem or its rhyme scheme; instead, they talk about poems they like and why they like them.

8. Teach Units on a Poet
The teacher teaches author units to focus on a poet, such as Dr. Seuss, Jack Prelutsky, Sheree Fitch, Dennis Lee, or Gary Soto.

3. Small-group reading. The class divides into two or more groups, and each group reads one part of the poem.

4. Cumulative reading. One student or one group reads the first line or stanza, and another student or group joins in as each line or stanza is read so that a cumulative effect is created.

Choral reading makes students active participants in the poetry experience, and helps them learn to appreciate its sounds, feelings, and magic. Two books of award-winning poems written specifically for choral reading are *I Am Phoenix* (Fleischman, 1985) and *Joyful Noise* (Fleischman, 1988). Many other poems can be used for choral reading; try, for example, Shel Silverstein's "Boa Constrictor," Karla Kuskin's "Full of the Moon," Laura E. Richards's "Eletelephony," and Eve Merriam's "Catch a Little Rhyme."

Students respond to the poem they have read or listened to. Sometimes students talk informally about the poem, sharing connections to their own lives or expressing whether they liked it.

They might write responses in reading logs or quickwrites. Or, students may explore the poem, choose favourite lines, or illustrate it. A list of ways students respond to poems is presented in the Teacher's Notebook on page 246.

One way students explore familiar poems is to sequence the lines of the poem. Teachers copy the lines of the poem on sentence strips (long strips of chart paper), and students sequence the lines in a pocket chart or by lining up around the classroom. Teachers can enlarge the text of the poem using a photocopier and then cut the lines apart. Students arrange the lines in order on a tray and read the familiar poem. As students sequence the poem, they check a copy of it posted in the classroom, if necessary. For a more challenging activity, teachers can cut apart the words on each line so that students "build" the poem word by word. Through these sequencing activities, students have opportunities to practise word-identification skills and experiment with the syntactic structure of poems.

During poetry units, students often create projects, using drama, art, and music activities to extend their interpretations. For example, students can role-play Kuskin's "I Woke Up This Morning" or construct monster puppets for the Lurpp creature in Prelutsky's "The Lurpp Is on the Loose." Students may compile picture book versions of narrative poems with one line or stanza on each page, adding an illustration for each page. A page from a grade 3 class book illustrating Shel Silverstein's "Hug O' War" (1974) is shown in Figure 6–11.

Some students enjoy compiling anthologies of their favourite poems. They copy favourite poems to keep, and staple their collections together to make books. Copying poems can also be a worthwhile handwriting activity because students are copying something meaningful to them, not just words and sentences in a workbook. In *Pass the Poetry, Please!* poet and anthologist Lee Bennett Hopkins (1987) suggests setting up a tree branch or an artificial Christmas tree in the classroom as a "poetree" on which students can hang copies of their favourite poems.

In Thematic Units. Teachers often share poems in connection with thematic units. They read poems from *Dinosaurs* (Hopkins, 1987) and *Tyrannosaurus Was a Beast* (Prelutsky, 1988) during a theme on dinosaurs, and from *Mojave* (Siebert, 1988) and *Desert Voices* (Baylor & Parnall, 1981)

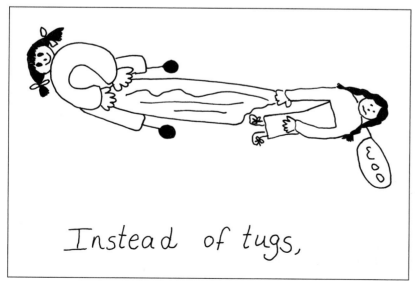

Figure 6–11 An Excerpt from a Grade 3 Class Book Illustrating Shel Silverstein's Poem "Hug O' War"

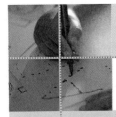

Teacher's Notebook

Ways to Respond to a Poem

1. Students read the poem aloud to classmates.
2. Students perform the poem using puppets or pantomime as a tape recording is played aloud.
3. Students write a reading log entry, discussing what the poem brings to mind or why they like it.
4. Students arrange the poem for choral reading, and with classmates present it to the class.
5. Students identify a favourite line in a poem and explain why they like it, either by talking to a classmate or in a reading log entry.
6. Students draw or paint a picture of an image the poem brings to mind and write a favourite line or two from the poem on the picture. Or, students can write the favourite line on a sentence strip (long strip of chart paper). Then the line is read aloud during sharing time and added to a bulletin board of favourite lines.
7. Students make a picture book with lines or a stanza of the poem written on each page and illustrated.
8. Students make a mobile with stanzas cut apart and hung together with pictures.
9. Students "can" or "box" a poem by decorating a container and inserting a copy of the poem and two items related to the poem.
10. Students or the teacher write the poem on word cards, and then students "build" the poem, sequencing the cards in a pocket chart. Older students can enlarge a copy of the poem using a photocopier and then cut apart the words and sequence them on their desks. Sometimes students decide to arrange the words differently than the way the poet wrote them because they like their arrangement better!
11. Students read other poems written by the same author.
12. Students investigate the poet and, perhaps, write a letter to the poet.
13. Students make a cluster diagram on a topic related to the poem.
14. Students write a poem on the same topic or following the format of the poem they have read.
15. Students dramatize the poem with a group of classmates.
16. Students make a filmstrip of the poem.
17. Students make a poster to illustrate the poem and attach a copy of the poem to it.
18. Students add the poem to a personal notebook of favourite poems.

during a thematic unit on the desert. Text sets of books for thematic units should include poetry books or copies of poems written on charts. A list of poetry collections that can be coordinated with thematic units and holiday celebrations is presented in Figure 6–12. Including poems in thematic units is important because poetry gives students a different perspective on social studies and science concepts.

Both teachers and students can share poems during thematic units. Teachers read poems aloud to students, or duplicate copies of a poem for students to read. Students can add these poems to their learning logs. Teachers can display poems related to a theme on a bulletin board. Students can select poems to share as projects, or write a favourite poem related to a theme.

Amon, A. (Sel.). (1981). *The Earth Is Sore: Native Americans on Nature.* New York: Atheneum. (M–U)

Bauer, C. F. (Sel.). (1986). Snowy Day: Stories and Poems. New York: Lippincott. (See other books of weather stories and poems by the same selector.) (P–M)

Baylor, B. (1981). *Desert Voices.* New York: Scribner's. (P–M)

Bouchard, D. (1994). *The Colours of British Columbia.* Vancouver: Raincoast Books. (M–U) 🍁

Bouchard, D. (1996). *Voices from the Wild: An Animal Sensgoria.* Vancouver: Raincoast Books. (M–U) 🍁

Bouchard, D. (1997). *If Sarah Will Take Me.* Victoria, B.C.: Orca Books. (M–U) 🍁

Carle, E. (Sel.). (1989). *Eric Carle's Animals, Animals.* New York: Philomel. (P–M)

Cassedy, S. (1993). *Zoomrimes: Poems About Things That Go.* New York: HarperCollins. (P)

Downie, M.A. & Robertson, B. (1984). *The New Wind Has Wings: Poems from Canada.* Toronto: Oxford. (M–U) 🍁

Esbensen, B. J. (1984). *Cold Stars and Fireflies: Poems of the Four Seasons.* New York: Crowell. (U)

Fisher, A. (1988). *The House of a Mouse.* New York: Harper & Row. (Poems about mice) (P–M)

Fitch, S. (1997). *There's a Mouse in My House.* Toronto: Doubleday Canada. (P–M) 🍁

Fleischman, P. (1985). *I Am Phoenix: Poems for Two Voices.* New York: Harper & Row. (Poems about birds) (M–U)

George, D. (1974). *My Heart Soars.* Saanichton, B.C.: Hancock House. (U) 🍁

Goldstein, B. S. (Sel.). (1989). *Bear in Mind: A Book of Bear Poems.* New York: Puffin. (P–M)

Goldstein, B. S. (Sel.). (1992). *What's on the Menu?* New York: Viking. (Poems about food) (P–M)

Harvey, A. (Sel.). (1992). *Shades of Green.* New York: Greenwillow. (Poems about ecology) (U)

Hopkins, L. B. (Sel.). (1983). *The Sky Is Full of Song.* New York: Harper & Row. (Poems about the seasons) (P–M)

Hopkins, L. B. (Sel.). (1985). *Munching: Poems About Eating.* Boston: Little, Brown. (M–U)

Hopkins, L. B. (Sel.). (1987). *Dinosaurs.* San Diego: Harcourt Brace Jovanovich. (M–U)

Hopkins, L. B. (Sel.). (1991). *On the Farm.* Boston: Little, Brown. (P–M)

Hopkins, L. B. (Sel.). (1992). *To the Zoo: Animal Poems.* Boston: Little, Brown. (P–M)

Hopkins, L. B. (Sel.). (1993). *Extra Innings: Baseball Poems.* San Diego: Harcourt Brace. (M–U)

Janeczko, P. B. (Sel.). (1984). *Strings: A Gathering of Family Poems.* New York: Bradbury Press. (U)

Larrick, N. (Sel.). (1988). *Cats Are Cats.* New York: Philomel. (M–U)

Larrick, N. (Sel.). (1990). *Mice Are Nice.* New York: Philomel. (M)

Livingston, M. C. (Sel.). (1984). *Sky Songs.* New York: Holiday House. (M–U)

Livingston, M. C. (Sel.). (1986). *Earth Songs.* New York: Holiday House. (M–U)

Livingston, M. C. (Sel.). (1986). *Sea Songs.* New York: Holiday House. (M–U)

Livingston, M. C. (Sel.). (1987). *New Year's Poems.* New York: Holiday House. (See other collections of holiday poems by the same selector.) (M–U)

Livingston, M. C. (Sel.). (1988). *Space Songs.* New York: Holiday House. (M–U)

Livingston, M. C. (Sel.). (1990). *Dog Poems.* New York: Holiday House. (M–U)

Livingston, M. C. (Sel.). (1990). *If the Owl Calls Again: A Collection of Owl Poems.* New York: McElderry Books. (U)

Livingston, M. C. (Sel.). (1992). *If You Ever Meet a Whale.* New York: Holiday House. (P–M)

Livingston, M. C. (Sel.). (1993). *Roll Along: Poems on Wheels.* New York: McElderry. (M–U)

Morrison, L. (1985). *The Break Dance Kids: Poems of Sport, Motion, and Locomotion.* New York: Lothrop, Lee & Shepard. (U)

Morrison. L. (1995). *Slam Dunk: Basketball Poems.* New York: Hyperion. (M–U)

Newman, F. (1980). *Round Slice of Moon and Other Poems for Canadian Kids.* Toronto: Scholastic. (P–M) 🍁

O'Huigan, S. (1983). *Scary Poems for Rotten Kids.* Toronto: Black Moss Press. (P–M) 🍁

O'Huigan, S. (1983). *Well, You Can Imagine.* Windsor: Black Moss Press. (P–M) 🍁

Prelutsky, J. (1984). *It's Snowing! It's Snowing!* New York: Greenwillow. (P–M)

Prelutsky, J. (1988). *Tyrannosaurus Was a Beast: Dinosaur Poems.* New York: Greenwillow. (P–M)

Robb, L. (1995). *Snuffles and Snouts.* New York: Dial. (Poems about pigs) (P–M)

Sullivan, C. (1993). *Cowboys.* New York: Rizzoli. (P–M)

Yolen, J. (1990). *Bird Watch: A Book of Poetry.* New York: Philomel. (M–U)

Yolen, J. (1990). *Dinosaur Dances.* New York: Putnam. (M)

Yolen, J. (1993). *Weather Report: Poems.* Honesdale, PA: Wordsong. (M–U)

Yolen, J. (1995). *Water Music: Poems for Children.* Honesdale, PA: Wordsong. (M–U)

P = primary grades (K–2); M = middle grades (3–5); U = upper grades (6–8).

Figure 6–12 Poetry Books for Thematic Units and Holiday Celebrations

ASSESSING STUDENTS' EXPERIENCES WITH POEMS

Teachers assess students' experiences with poetry by observing as they read poems; by keeping anecdotal notes of students as they read and respond to poems; and by reading students' reading logs and monitoring their projects. Teachers conference with students and ask them about favourite poems and poets to assess their interest in poetry. They notice students' attention to the ways poets use wordplay and poetic devices. Students can also write reflections about their learning and work habits during the poetry activities, providing valuable assessment information.

During poetry units, teachers prepare assessment checklists and keep track of students' reading and response activities. For example, grade 4 students might be assessed on these activities:

- Read twenty poems.
- Keep a list of the twenty poems read.
- Write in a reading log about five favourite poems.
- Participate in choral reading activities.
- Participate in minilessons about choral reading techniques, poet Jack Prelutsky, rhyme, and word pictures.
- Make a page for a class book on a favourite poem.
- Do a project about a poem.

It is difficult to grade students on reading poetry, but students can earn points for these activities, and the points can be added together for a grade.

Writing Stories

As students read and talk about literature, they learn how writers craft stories. Writers draw from stories they have read as they create their own stories, intertwining several story ideas and adapting story elements to meet their own needs (Atwell, 1987; Graves, 1989; Hansen, 1987; Harste, Short, & Burke, 1988; Harwayne, 1992). Cairney (1990) found that elementary students do think about stories they have read as they write, and Blackburn (1985) describes a cycle of intertextuality: students read and talk about books, they weave bits of stories they have read into stories they write, share their compositions, and bits of these compositions make their way into classmates' compositions. Students make intertextual links in different ways, such as

- Using specific story ideas without copying the plot
- Copying the plot from a story, but adding new events, characters, and settings
- Using a specific genre they have studied for a story
- Using a character borrowed from a story read previously
- Writing a retelling of the story
- Incorporating content from an informational book into a story
- Combining several stories into a new story

The first two strategies were the ones most commonly used in Cairney's study of sixth graders. Interestingly, the next-to-the-last strategy was used only by less capable readers, and the last only by more capable readers.

Students incorporate what they have learned about stories when they write stories, and use the writing process to draft and refine their work. They write stories as part of resource-based units, during thematic units, and in writers workshop. Stories are probably the most complex writing form that elementary students use. It is difficult to craft well-formed stories incorporating plot, character development, and other elements of story structure.

Students make intertextual links and write retellings of stories, new stories using patterns from stories they have read, sequels to stories they have read, and original genre stories.

WRITING RETELLINGS OF STORIES

Elementary students often write retellings of stories they have read and enjoyed. As they retell a story, they internalize the structure of the story and play with the language the author used.

Students can work together as a group to write or dictate the retelling, or they can divide the story into sections or chapters and have each student or pair of students write a small part. Then the parts are compiled. A grade 1 class worked together to dictate their retelling of *Where the Wild Things Are* (Sendak, 1963), which was published as a big book:

Page 1:   *Max got in trouble. He scared his dog and got sent to bed.*
Page 2:   *This room turned into a jungle. It grew and grew.*
Page 3:   *A boat came for Max. It was his private boat.*
Page 4:   *He sailed to where the wild things lived.*
Page 5:   *They made him king of all the wild things.*
Page 6:   *The wild things had a wild rumpus. They danced and hung on trees.*
Page 7:   *Max sent them to bed without any supper.*
Page 8:   *Then Max wanted to come back home. He waved goodbye and sailed home on his boat.*
Page 9:   *And his dinner was waiting for him. It was still hot from the microwave.*

As the grade 1 students dictated the retelling, their teacher wrote it on chart paper. Then they read over the story several times, making revisions. Next, the students divided the text into sections, recopied the text onto each page for the big book, drew pictures, and added a cover and title page. Students also wrote their own books, including the major points at the beginning, middle, and end of the story.

Sometimes students change the point of view in their retellings. A grade 4 student wrote this retelling of "Goldilocks and the Three Bears" from Baby Bear's perspective:

One day mom got me up. I had to take a bath. I hate to take baths, but I had to. While I was taking my bath, Mom was making breakfast. When I got out of the tub breakfast was ready. But Dad got mad because his breakfast porridge was too hot to eat. So Mom said, "Let's go for a walk and let it cool." I thought, "Oh boy, we get to go for a walk!" My porridge was just right, but I could eat it later.

When we got back our front door was open. Dad thought it was an animal so he started to growl. I hate it when Dad growls. It really scares me. Anyway, there was no animal anywhere so I rushed to the table. Everybody was sitting down to eat. I said, "Someone ate my porridge." Then Dad noticed someone had tasted his porridge. He got really mad.

Then I went into the living room because I did not want to get yelled at. I noticed my rocking chair was broken. I told Dad and he got even madder.

Then I went into my bedroom. I said, "Someone has been sleeping in my bed and she's still in it." So this little girl with long blond hair raises up and starts to scream. Dad plugged his ears. She jumped up like she was scared of us and ran out of the house. We never saw that little girl again.

Retelling of stories gives teachers the opportunity to explore or develop and review different story elements with students. Students enjoy the opportunity to manipulate various elements such as point of view or characterization in a story in their retelling. These opportunities help reinforce the concept of story in their minds.

Figure 6–13 A Grade 1 Student's Circle Diagram for *If You Give a Mouse a Cookie*

Writing Innovations on Texts. Many stories have a repetitive pattern or refrain, and students can use this structure to write their own stories. As part of a resource-based unit on mice, a grade 1 class read *If You Give a Mouse a Cookie* (Numeroff, 1985) and talked about the circle structure of the story. The story begins with giving a mouse a cookie and ends with the mouse getting a second cookie. Grade 1 students wrote stories about what they would do if they were given a cookie. A student named Michelle drew the circle diagram shown in Figure 6–13 to organize her story, and wrote this story, which has been transcribed into conventional English spelling:

> If you gave Michelle a cookie she would probably want some pop. Then she would want a napkin to clean her face. That would make her tired and she would go to bed to take a nap. Before you know it, she will be awake and she would like to take a swim in a swimming pool. Then she would watch cartoons on TV. And she would be getting hungry again so she would probably want another cookie.

Writing Sequels. Students often write sequels as projects during resource-based units. For example, they might want to continue the escapades of Newton after reading *Newton and the Giant* (McGowan, 2003). Newton is a 10-year-old science geek who tries to avoid his four older brothers intent on making him pay for any number of things he has done to embarrass them. In the process of avoiding them, Newton encounters a massive, hairy, spectacularly unattractive giant named Herbert. Newton and Herbert form an alliance to help each other with their pressing problems. Students will enjoy reading about Newton's struggles and writing his next adventure. Similarly, they will want to write additional adventures about the boa constrictor after reading *The Day Jimmy's Boa Ate the Wash* (Noble, 1980). Many stories lend themselves to sequels, and students enjoy extending a favourite story.

Writing Genre Stories. During some resource-based units, students read books and learn about a particular genre, such as folktales, historical fiction, myths, or fables. Students try their hand at writing stories that incorporate the characteristics of the genre.

ASSESSING THE STORIES STUDENTS WRITE USING RUBRICS

Assessment involves far more than simply judging the quality of the finished stories. Assessment also takes into account students' knowledge of story structure as well as the activities they engage in while writing and refining their stories. A vehicle that can be used to guide a teacher's judgment is the rubric. A scoring rubric consists of a fixed scale and a list of characteristics describing performance for each of the points on the scale (Marzano, Pickering, & McTighe, 1993).

For example, teachers might consider four components in assessing students' stories: students' knowledge of the elements of story structure, their application of the elements in writing, their use of the writing process, and the quality of the finished stories. Determining whether students learned about the element and applied what they learned in their stories is crucial. A rubric might be considered for some of these components as follows:

A.   Students demonstrate knowledge of story structure by
   3.   Applying the element in the story he or she has written
   2.   Explaining how the element was used in a particular story
   1.   Defining or identifying the characteristics of the element

B.   Students demonstrate the stages of the writing process by
   4.   Completing all stages of the process including a rough draft, participating in a writers' group, revising and proofreading the story, and sharing the story with others
   3.   Completing the story with limited revision and proofreading and by sharing work with others
   2.   Completing the story without revision or proofreading
   1.   Writing a rough draft only without the participation with others

C.   Students write high-quality, interesting stories:
   4.   The story is of high quality, interesting, creative, and well organized using elements of story structure to advantage.
   3.   The story is interesting, creative, and well organized.
   2.   The story is interesting and creative.
   1.   The story is poorly organized, without good use of story structure elements.

Journals: Writing Our Personal Stories

All kinds of people—artists, scientists, dancers, politicians, writers, assassins, and children—keep journals (Mallon, 1984). People usually record in their journals the everyday events of their lives and the issues that concern them. These journals, typically written in notebook form, are personal records, not intended for public display. Other journals might be termed "working" journals, in which writers record observations and other information to use for another purpose; for example, farmers might record weather or crop data, or gardeners the blooming cycle of their plants.

Elementary students use journals for a variety of purposes, just as adults do. Types of journals are described in the Teacher's Notebook on pages 252–253. In each type of journal the focus is on the writer, and the writing is personal and private. Students' writing is spontaneous and loosely organized and it often contains mechanical errors because students are focusing on thinking, not on spelling, capitalization, and punctuation. Some of the purposes for journal writing are to

- Record experiences
- Stimulate interest in a topic

- Explore thinking
- Personalize learning
- Develop interpretations
- Wonder, predict, and hypothesize
- Engage the imagination
- Ask questions
- Activate prior knowledge
- Assume the role of another person
- Share experiences with trusted readers

Simulated Journals. Students assume the role of a book character or a historical personality and write journal entries from that person's viewpoint. Students include details from the story or historical period in their entries.

A child writes and draws about her personal experiences in a personal journal.

Teacher's Notebook

Types of Journals

Personal Journals
Students write about events in their own lives and other topics of special interest in personal journals. These journals are the most private type. The teacher responds as an interested reader, often asking questions and offering comments about his or her own life.

Dialogue Journals
Dialogue journals are similar to personal journals except that they are written to be shared with the teacher or a classmate. The person who receives the journal reads the entry and responds to it. These journals are like a written conversation.

Reading Response Logs
Students respond to stories, poems, and informational books they are reading in reading logs. They write and draw entries after reading, record key vocabulary words, make charts and other diagrams, and write memorable quotes.

Double-Entry Journals
Students divide each page of their journals into two columns and write different types of information in each column. Sometimes they write quotes from a story in one column and add reactions to the quotes in the other, or write predictions in one column and what actually happened in the story in the other.

Language Arts Notebooks

Students take notes, write rules and examples, draw diagrams, and write lists of other useful information about language arts in these notebooks. Students use these notebooks during minilessons and refer to the information during resource-based units and readers and writers workshops.

Learning Logs

Students write in learning logs as part of social studies and science thematic units and math units. They write quickwrites, draw diagrams, take notes, and write vocabulary words.

Simulated Journals

Students assume the role of a book character or a historical personality and write journal entries from that person's viewpoint. Students include details from the story or historical period in their entries.

PERSONAL JOURNALS

Students often keep personal journals in which they recount events in their lives and write about topics of their choice. It is normal for students to misspell a few words in their entries; when students write in personal journals, the emphasis is on what they say, not how correctly they write.

It is often helpful to develop a list of possible journal-writing topics on a chart in the classroom or on sheets of paper for students to clip inside their journal notebooks. For personal journals, they choose their own topics. Although they can write about almost anything, some students will complain that they don't know what to write about, so a list of topics gives them a crutch. Figure 6–14 on page 254 shows a list of possible journal-writing topics developed by a class of fourth and fifth graders. Students can add topics to their lists throughout the year, which may include more than a hundred topics by the end of the school year. Referring students to the list or asking them to brainstorm a list of topics encourages them to become more independent writers and discourages them from relying too heavily on teachers for writing topics.

Privacy becomes an important issue as students grow older. Most young children are willing to share what they have written, but by third or fourth grade students grow less willing to read their journal entries aloud to the class (although they are usually willing to share the entries with a trusted teacher). Teachers must be scrupulous about respecting students' privacy and not insist that they share their writing when they are unwilling to do so. It is also important to talk with students about respecting each other's privacy and not reading each other's journals. To protect students' privacy, many teachers keep personal journals on an out-of-the-way shelf when they are not in use.

When students share personal information with teachers through their journals, a second issue arises. Sometimes, teachers learn details about students' problems and family life that they do not know how to deal with. Entries about child abuse, suicide, or drug use may be the child's way of asking for help. Although teachers are not counsellors, they do have a legal obligation to protect their students and report possible problems to appropriate school personnel. Occasionally, a student invents a personal problem in a journal entry as an attention-getting tactic; however, asking the student about the entry or having a school counsellor do so will help to ensure that the student's safety is fully considered.

DIALOGUE JOURNALS

Students converse in writing with the teacher or a classmate through dialogue journals (Bode, 1989; Gambrell, 1985; Staton, 1980, 1987). These journals are interactive and conversational

---

Things to Write About in Personal Journals

my favourite place in town	if I had three wishes
boyfriends/girlfriends	my teacher
things that make me happy or sad	TV shows I watch
music	my favourite holiday
an imaginary planet	if I were stranded on an island
cars	what I want to be when I grow up
magazines I like to read	private thoughts
what if snow were hot	how to be a superhero
dreams I have	dinosaurs
cartoons	my mom/my dad
places I've been	my friends
favourite movies	my next vacation
rock stars	love
if I were a movie/rock star	if I were an animal or something else
poems	books I've read
pets	favourite things to do
football	my hobbies
astronauts	if I were a skydiver
the prime minister	when I get a car
jokes	if I had a lot of money
motorcycles	dolls
things that happen in my school	if I were rich
current events	wrestling and other sports
things I do on weekends	favourite colours
a soap opera with daily episodes	questions answered with "never"

or ANYTHING else I want to write about

Figure 6–14 Grade 4 and 5 Students' List of Possible Journal-Writing Topics

in tone. Most important, dialogue journals are an authentic writing activity and provide the opportunity for real communication between students or between a student and the teacher. Students write informally about something of interest, a concern, a book they are reading, or what they are learning in a thematic unit. Students choose their own topics and usually control the direction the writing takes.

When teachers or classmates respond to students' entries, they answer as they would in an oral conversation. They react to students' comments, ask questions, and offer suggestions. Staton (1987) offers these suggestions for teachers who are responding to students' writing and continuing the dialogue:

1. Acknowledge students' ideas and encourage them to continue to write about their interests.
2. Support students by complimenting them about behaviour and schoolwork.
3. Provide new information about topics, so that students will want to read your responses.
4. Write less than the students do.
5. Avoid unspecific comments like "good idea" or "very interesting."
6. Ask few questions; instead, encourage students to ask you questions.

Teachers' responses do not need to be lengthy; a sentence or two is often enough. Even so, it is time-consuming to respond to twenty-five, thirty, or more journal entries every day. As an alternative, many teachers read and respond to students' journal entries on a rotating basis. They might respond to one group of students one week and another group the next week.

In this grade 5 student's dialogue journal, Daniel shares the events and problems in his life with his teacher, and she responds sympathetically. Daniel writes:

> Over spring break I went down to my grandma's house and played basketball in their back-yard and while we were there we went to see some of my uncles who are all Aboriginal. Out of my whole family down there they are all Aboriginal except Grandpa Russell.

And Daniel's teacher responds:

> What a fun spring break! That is so interesting to have Aboriginal peoples in your family. I think I might have some Aboriginal ancestors too. Do you still plan to go to Vancouver Island for the summer?

The next day Daniel writes:

> My family and I plan to go to Vancouver Island in June and I imagine we will stay there for quite a while. I think the funnest part will probably be swimming or camping or something like that. When we get there my mom says we will probably stay in a nice motel.

Daniel's teacher responds:

> That really sounds like a fun vacation. I think swimming is the most fun, too. Who will go with you?

Daniel continues to talk about his family, now focusing on the problems he and his family are facing:

> Well, my mom and dad are divorced so that is why I am going to court to testify on Tuesday but my mom, me, and my sister and brother are all going and that kind of makes me sad because a couple of years ago when my mom and dad were together we used to go a lot of places like camping and hiking but now after what happened we hardly go anywhere.

His teacher responds:

> I am so sorry your family is having problems. It sounds as if your mom and dad are having problems with each other, but they both love you and want to be with you. Be sure to keep talking to them about how you feel.

Daniel replies:

> I wish my mom and dad did not have problems because I would have a lot more fun and get to go and do a lot more things together, but since my mom and dad are divorced I have to take turns spending time with both of them.

His teacher offers a suggestion:

> I'm sure that is hard. Trevor and Carla have parents who are divorced, too. Maybe you could talk to them. It might help.

This journal is not a series of teacher questions and student answers. Instead, the student and teacher are having a dialogue, or conversation, and the interchange is built on mutual trust and respect.

Dialogue journals can also be effective in dealing with students who have behaviour problems or other types of difficulties in school (Staton, 1980). The teacher and student write back and forth about the problem and identify ways to solve it. In later entries the student reflects on his or her progress toward solving the problem. The teacher responds to the student's message, asks clarifying questions, or offers sympathy and praise.

Atwell suggests that teachers affirm, challenge, or extend a student's responses in their inter-actions with them. "There isn't one set of questions for teachers to ask students in their reading journals. Instead there are all of these individual readers with their own strategies, questions, tastes, needs, opinions, backgrounds and experiences" (Atwell, 1998, p. 283).

Kreeft (1984) believes that the greatest value of dialogue journals is that they bridge the gap between talking and writing—they are written conversations. As the journal excerpts between Daniel and his teacher show, a second value is the strong bond that develops between student and teacher through their writing back and forth.

Dialogue journals are especially effective in promoting the writing development of children who are learning English as a second language. Researchers have found that these students are more successful writers when they choose their own topics for writing and when their teachers contribute to the dialogue with requests for a reply, statements, and other comments (Peyton & Seyoum, 1989; Reyes, 1991). Not surprisingly, researchers found that students wrote more when teachers requested a reply than when teachers made comments that did not require a response. Also, when a student was particularly interested in a topic, it was less important what the teacher did, and when the teacher and the student were both interested in a topic, the topic seemed to take over as they shared and built on each other's writing. Reyes also found that bilingual students were much more successful in writing dialogue journal entries than in writing in response to books they had read.

Students use dialogue journals to write to classmates or the teacher about books they are reading (Barone, 1990; Dekker, 1991; Nash, 1995). In these journal entries, students write about the books they are reading, compare the books to others by the same author or other authors they have read, and offer opinions about the book and whether a classmate or the teacher might enjoy reading it. They also write about their book-selection strategies and their reading behaviour.

This approach is especially effective in readers workshop classrooms when students are reading different books. Students are often paired and write back-and-forth to their reading buddies. This activity provides the socialization that independent reading does not. Depending on whether students are reading relatively short picture books or longer chapter books, they can write dialogue journal entries every other day or once a week, and then classmates write back.

Fourth graders wrote these entries to classmates and their teacher about informational books they were reading during readers workshop:

Dear Adam,
I'm reading the coolest book. It's about snakes and it's called A Snake's Body [Cole, 1981]. Look at the pictures on pages 34, 35, 36, 37, 38, 39, 40, 41, and 42 to see how a python strangles and eats a chick. It's awesome.
Your Friend, Todd

Dear Mrs. Parker,
I just finished reading The Magic School Bus Inside the Human Body [Cole, 1989]. I think you would like it, too, because it's about a teacher named Ms. Frizzle and she's sort of magic. She takes her kids on a field trip and Ms. Frizzle drives the school bus inside a human body. The book takes a long time to read because it has lots of cartoons and extra things to read and look at. I'd say it was one of the best books I've ever read. I think everyone in our class should read it. What do you think?
Love, Ali

Trevor,
The book I'm reading is A Wall of Names [Donnelly, 1991]. It's ok, if you want to know about the Vietnam wall memorial. I picked this book because my Gramps was in that war and last summer we went to Washington, D.C. on vacation and I got to see the wall. It's shiny and black and all the names of the soldiers that died fighting in it are written on the wall. Have you ever heard of it?
From your friend, David

Before the students began writing dialogue journal entries, the teacher taught a minilesson about how to format their entries, about how to capitalize and underline book titles, and about the importance of asking questions in their entries so that respondents could answer them in their replies. In their entries, most students incorporated what they had learned in the minilesson.

READING RESPONSE LOGS

Students write in reading logs about the stories and other books they are reading or listening to the teacher read aloud during resource-based units and readers workshop. Rather than simply summarize their reading, students relate their reading to their own lives or to other literature they have read. Students may also list interesting or unfamiliar words, jot down memorable quotes, and take notes about characters, plot, or other story elements; but the primary purpose of these journals is for students to think about the book, connect literature to their lives, and develop their own interpretations. These journals go by a variety of names, including literature response journals (Hancock, 1992), literature journals (Five, 1986), and reading journals (Wollman-Bonilla, 1989); but no matter what they are called, their purpose remains the same.

Teachers and researchers (Barone, 1990; Dekker, 1991; Hancock, 1992) have examined students' reading log entries and have identified these categories of response:

- Questions related to understanding the text
- Interaction with characters
- Empathy with characters
- Prediction and validation
- Personal experiences
- Personal feelings and opinions
- Simple and elaborate evaluations
- Philosophical reflections
- Retellings and summaries

Grade 7 students' reading log entries about *The Giver* (Lowry, 1993) are shown in Figure 6–15 on page 258. In these entries, students react to the book, make predictions, deepen their understanding of the story, ask questions, assume the role of the main character, and value the story.

When students begin writing entries in reading logs, their first entries are often retellings and plot summaries, but as students gain experience reading and responding to literature, their entries become more interpretive and personal. Teachers can model writing "I think" reactions, share student entries that are interpretive, and respond to students' entries by asking questions.

Teachers and researchers have examined students' responses and noticed patterns in their reading log entries. Hancock (1992, 1993) identified these eight categories:

1. *Monitoring understanding.* Students get to know the characters and explain how the story is making sense to them. These responses usually occur at the beginning of a book.

2. *Making inferences.* Students share their insights into the feelings and motives of a character. They often begin their comments with "I think."

3. *Making, validating, or invalidating predictions.* Students speculate about what will happen later in the story and also confirm or deny predictions they made previously.

4. *Expressing wonder or confusion.* Students reflect on the way the story is developing. They ask "I wonder why" questions and write about confusions.

5. *Character interaction.* Students show that they are personally involved with a character, sometimes writing "If I were _____, I would ... " They express empathy and share related experiences from their own lives. Also, they may give advice to the character.

6. *Character assessment.* Students judge a character's actions and often use evaluative terms such as "nice" or "dumb."

I think the book *The Giver* is very scary because when you do something wrong you get released from the community. I think it would be terrible to be pushed out of your community and leave your family. Your family would be ashamed and embarrassed. It is like you are dead.

I don't think I could handle being a friend of Jonas's. In other words NO I would not like to be a friend of his. There would be too much pain involved and most of the time I wouldn't see Jonas.

The part that hooked me was when the book said Jonas took his pills and did not have feelings about Fiona.

As I'm reading I'm wondering if they get married at twelve because they get jobs at twelve.

Something that surprised me so far in the story was when Lily said she wanted to be a birthmother. Lily's mom became mad and said three years, three births, and then you're a labourer. Being a birthmother is not a good job at least after the three years. I hope that doesn't happen to Lily but I don't know what other job she should have.

So far I think that the story is really sad. The story is sad because everyone has sameness except Jonas and the Giver. Jonas and the Giver are the only ones who can see colour because of the memories. The story is also sad because no one has feelings.

Why didn't Jonas use the fire in his favourite memory to stay warmer on his long journey through the rain, and snow, and the terrible coldness? Also, why didn't the author explain more about the things that are between the lines so the reader could really grasp them?

Well, I can't really make a prediction of what is going to happen because I already read the book. If I hadn't read ahead my prediction would be that Jonas would get drowned in the river because he couldn't handle the pain.

I think Jonas will confront his father. He won't ever forget what he saw his father do and it is wrong. Just wrong, wrong, wrong. If my father ever did that to an innocent little baby I would never forgive him. I would confront him and tell him that I know. I will always know and so will God.

I don't exactly understand what happens at the end. It sounds like they froze to death. I think they died but I wish they found freedom and happiness. It is very sad.

The ending is cool. Jonas and Gabe come back to the community but now it is changed. There are colours and the people have feelings. They believe in God and it is Christmas.

At first I thought it would be good to have a perfect community. There would be no gangs and no crime and no sickness. but there is a lesson in this story. Now I think you can't have a perfect community. Even though we have bad things in our community we have love and other emotions and we can make choices.

Figure 6–15 Entries from Grade 7 Students' Reading Logs about *The Giver*

7. ***Story involvement.*** Students reveal their involvement in the story as they express satisfaction with how the story is developing. They may comment on their desire to continue reading or use terms such as "disgusting," "weird," or "awesome" to react to sensory aspects of the story.

8. ***Literary criticism.*** Students offer "I liked/I didn't like" opinions and praise or condemn an author's style. Sometimes students compare the book with others they have read or compare the author with other authors with whom they are familiar.

The first four categories are personal meaning-making options in which students make inferences about characters, offer predictions, ask questions, or discuss confusions. The next three categories focus on character and plot development. Students are more involved with the story, and they offer reactions to the characters and events of the story. The last category is literary evaluation, in which students evaluate books and reflect on their own literary tastes.

These categories can extend the possibilities of response by introducing teachers and students to a wide variety of response options. Hancock (1992, 1993) recommends that teachers begin by assessing the kinds of responses students are currently making. They can read students' reading logs, categorize the entries, tally the categories, and make an assessment. Often students use only a few types of responses, not the wide range that is available. Teachers can teach minilessons and model types of responses that students aren't using, and they can ask questions when they read journals to prompt students to think in new ways about the story they are reading.

DOUBLE-ENTRY JOURNALS

For double-entry journals, students divide each entry into two parts (Barone, 1990; Berthoff, 1981). Often, students divide their journal pages into two columns; in the left column they write quotes from the story or other book they are reading, and in the right column they relate each quote to their own lives and to literature they have read. Through this type of journal, students become more engaged in what they are reading, note sentences that have personal connections, and become more sensitive to the author's language.

Students in a grade 5 class kept a double-entry journal as they read C. S. Lewis's classic *The Lion, the Witch and the Wardrobe* (1950). After they read each chapter, they reviewed it and selected one, two, or three brief quotes. They wrote these excerpts in the left column of their journals, and they wrote reactions beside each quote in the right column. Excerpts from a grade 5 student's journal are presented in Figure 6–16. This student's responses indicate that she is engaged in the story and is connecting it to her own life as well as to another story she has read.

In the Text	My Response
Chapter 1 I tell you this is the sort of house where no one is going to mind what we do.	I remember the time that I went to Saskatoon to stay with my aunt. My aunt's house was very large. She had a piano and she let us play it. She told us we could do whatever we wanted to.
Chapter 5 "How do you know?" he asked, "that your sister's story is not true?"	It reminds me of when I was little and I had an imaginary place. I would go there in my mind. I made up all kinds of make-believe stories about myself in this imaginary place. One time I told my big brother about my imaginary place. He laughed at me and told me I was silly. But it didn't bother me because nobody can stop me from thinking what I want.
Chapter 15 Still they could see the shape of the great lion lying dead in his bonds. They're nibbling at the cords.	When Aslan died I thought about when my Uncle Carl died. This reminds me of the story where the lion lets the mouse go and the mouse helps the lion.

Figure 6–16 Excerpts from a Grade 5 Student's Double-Entry Journal about *The Lion, the Witch and the Wardrobe*

Double-entry journals can be used in several other ways. Instead of recording quotes from the book, students can write "Reading Notes" in the left column and then add "Reactions" in the right column. In the left column students write about the events they read about in the chapter. Then, in the right column they make personal connections to the events.

As an alternative, students can use the heading "Reading Notes" for one column and "Discussion Notes" for the second column. Students write reading notes as they read or immediately after reading. Later, after discussing the story or chapter of a longer book, students add discussion notes. As with other types of double-entry journals, it is in the second column that students make more interpretive comments.

Younger students can use the double-entry format for a prediction journal (Macon, Bewell, & Vogt, 1991). They label the left column "Predictions" and the right column "What Happened." In the left column they write or draw a picture of what they predict will happen in the story or chapter before reading it. Then, after reading, they draw or write what actually happened in the right column.

SIMULATED JOURNALS

Some children's books, such as *Catherine, Called Birdy* (Cushman, 1994), *Stranded at Plimoth Plantation, 1626* (Bowen, 1994), and *Eleanora's Diary* (Parry, 1994) are written as journals, and the authors assume the role of a character and write from the character's point of view. We call these books *simulated journals*. They are rich with historical details and feature examples of both words and phrasing of the period. At the end of the book, authors often include information about how they researched the period and explanations about the liberties they took with the character, setting, or events that are recorded.

Elementary students, too, can write simulated journals. They can assume the role of another person and write from that person's viewpoint. They can assume the role of a historical figure when they read biographies or as part of social studies thematic units (Tompkins, 1995). As they read stories, students can assume the role of a character in the story. In this way students gain insight into other people's lives and into historical events.

Students can use simulated journals in two ways. They can use them as a tool for learning or as a project. When students use simulated journals as a tool for learning, they write the entries as they are reading a book in order to get to know the character better, or during the thematic unit as they are learning about the historical period. In these entries, students are exploring concepts and making connections between what they are learning and what they already know. These journal entries are less polished than when students write a simulated journal as a project. Students might choose to write a simulated journal as a culminating project for a resource-based unit or a thematic unit. As a project, students plan out their journals carefully, choose important dates, and use the writing process to draft, revise, edit, and publish their journals.

One variation of simulated journals is simulated letters (Roop, 1995). Students assume the role of a book character or historical figure, as they do for simulated journals, but students write a letter—not a journal entry—to another character in the book or to another historical figure. Students can exchange letters with classmates or the teacher and write replies.

YOUNG CHILDREN'S JOURNALS

For more information on invented spelling, see Chapter 9, "Words and the Language Tools to Use Them: Spelling, Grammar, and Handwriting," pages 373–375.

Young children can write in journals by drawing, or they can use a combination of drawing and writing (Hipple, 1985; McGee & Richgels, 1985; Nathan, 1987). Children may write scribbles, random letters and numbers, simple captions, or extended texts using invented spelling. Their invented spellings often seem bizarre by adult standards, but they are reasonable in terms of children's knowledge of phoneme–grapheme correspondences and spelling patterns. Other children want parents and teachers to take their dictation and write the text. After the text has been written, children can usually read it immediately, and they retain recognition of the words for several days.

Young children usually begin writing in personal or dialogue journals and then expand their repertoire of journal forms to include reading logs and learning logs. Four kindergartners'

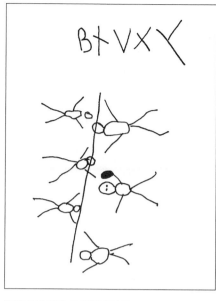

Figure 6–17 Entries from Young Children's Journals

journal entries are presented in Figure 6–17. The top two entries are from personal journals, and the bottom two are from reading logs. In the top left entry, a five-year-old focuses on the illustration, drawing a detailed picture of a football game (note that the player in the middle right position has the ball); he adds five letters for the text so that his entry will have some writing. In the top right entry the kindergartner writes, "I spent the night at my dad's house." The child wrote the entry on the bottom left after listening to his teacher read *The Three Billy Goats Gruff* (Stevens, 1987) and then acting out the story. As he shared his entry with classmates, he read the text this way: "You are a mean bad troll." The kindergartner wrote the entry on the bottom right after listening to the teacher read *The Jolly Postman, or Other People's Letters* (Ahlberg & Ahlberg, 1986). This child drew a picture of the three bears receiving a letter from Goldilocks. She labelled the mom, dad, and baby bear in the picture and wrote, "I [am] sorry I ate your porridge."

For more information on how young children emerge into writing, see Chapter 3, "Emergent Literacy," pages 115–122.

Adapting

Journal Writing to Meet the Needs of Every Student

1. **Draw Journal Entries**
   Students can draw their thoughts and ideas in journal entries instead of writing them, or they can draw pictures before writing. What is important is that students explore their thoughts and feelings or record important information they are learning.

2. **Talk Before Writing**
   Students can talk about topics to generate and narrow ideas before beginning to write. As they talk, students find the words and sentences to express their ideas, and they use these words and expand on them as they write.

3. **Dictate Entries**
   Teachers or cross-age tutors can take students' dictation and write the entries for students. Then students reread their dictation with the teacher's or cross-age tutor's assistance. They can also pick key words and phrases from the dictated text and use the words to label drawings.

4. **Share in Small Groups**
   Sharing is an important part of writing, but some students may not feel comfortable sharing with the whole class. These students may prefer sharing their journal entries with a partner or in small groups, which are less threatening than large groups.

5. **Focus on Ideas**
   Students focus on ideas, not mechanical correctness, as they write journal entries because they use journal writing to develop writing fluency and explore the ideas they are learning. Similarly, when teachers assess students' entries, they should consider whether or not students have developed their ideas and not correct their mechanical errors.

6. **Use Flow Writing**
   Children listen to a story, such as Cynthia Rylant's *The Relatives Came* (1985) or Christine Perry's *If* (1995), and then write for 10 minutes using a prompt from the story such as "I remember . . ." or "If caterpillars were toothpaste . . . "

Through a variety of forms and purposes, journal writing helps elementary students discover the power of writing to record information and explore ideas. Students usually cherish their journals and are amazed by the amount of writing they contain. The box above outlines some strategies for adapting journal writing to meet the needs of every student.

Writing Poetry

Elementary students can have successful experiences writing poetry if they write formula poems by beginning each line with particular words, as is the case with colour poems; by counting syllables, as for haiku; or by creating word pictures, as in concrete poems. These formulas serve as scaffolds, or temporary writing frameworks, so that students focus on ideas rather than on the mechanics of writing poems (Cecil, 1994). Poetry also allows students more freedom in punctuation, capitalization, and page arrangement.

An excellent place to begin is with children's literature that evokes patterned responses. After reading Cynthia Rylant's *All I See* (1988), children can then write their own responses using the stem, "All I see is ____," for example. Another favourite book is Barbara Reid's *The Party* (1997). Grade 2 students listened to the story, talked about different times in their lives when relatives came to visit or other special gatherings, and then wrote using the sentence frame, "I remember . . ."

Another excellent resource is the picture book *If* by Sarah Perry (1995). Each page depicts strange and unique wonderings about our world, such as "if caterpillars were toothpaste" or "if worms had wheels." The last page invites children to create more wonderings if they are so inclined. They enjoy responding to the challenge.

Five types of poetic forms are formula poems, free-form poems, syllable- and word-count poems, rhymed verse poems, and model poems. Elementary students' poems illustrate each poetic form. Kindergartners' and first-graders' poems may seem little more than lists of sentences compared with the more sophisticated poems of older students. The range of poems produced by elementary and middle-grade students shows how they grow in their ability to write poetry through these writing activities.

FORMULA POEMS

The poetic forms are not intended to be followed rigidly. Rather, they provide a scaffold, organization, or skeleton. After collecting words, images, and comparisons through brainstorming, clustering, quickwriting, or another prewriting strategy, students craft their poems, choosing words and arranging them to create a message. Meaning is always most important, and form follows the search for meaning. Children "dig for poems" (Valentine, 1986) through words, ideas, poetic forms, rhyme, rhythm, and conventions. Poet Kenneth Koch (1980) developed some simple formulas that make it easy for nearly every child to become a successful poet. These formulas call for students to begin every line the same way or to insert a particular kind of word in every line. The formulas use repetition, a stylistic device that is more effective for young poets than rhyme. Some forms may seem more like sentences than poems, but the dividing line between poetry and prose is a blurry one, and these poetry experiences help children move toward poetic expression.

"I Wish . . ." Poems. Children begin each line of their poems with the words "I wish" and complete the line with a wish (Koch, 1980).

Colour Poems. Students begin each line with a colour. They can repeat the same colour in each line or choose a different colour (Koch, 1980).

Writing colour poems can be coordinated with teaching young children to read and write colour words. Instead of having students in kindergarten and grade 1 read worksheets and colour pictures in the designated colours, students can create colour poems in booklets. They write and illustrate one line of the poem on each page.

Five-Senses Poems. Students write about a topic using each of the five senses. Sense poems are usually five lines long, with one line for each sense, as this poem written by a student in grade 6 demonstrates:

> **Being Heartbroken**
>
> Sounds like thunder and lightning
> Looks like a carrot going through a blender
> Tastes like sour milk
> Feels like a splinter in your finger
> Smells like a dead fish
> It must be horrible!

It is helpful to have students develop a five-senses cluster diagram and collect ideas for each sense. Students select from the cluster the strongest or most vivid idea for each sense.

"If I Were ... " Poems. Children write about how they would feel and what they would do if they were something else—a tyrannosaurus rex, a hamburger, or sunshine (Koch, 1980). They begin each poem with "If I were" and tell what it would be like to be that thing.

Definition Poems. In definition poems, students describe what something is or what something or someone means to them. To begin, the teacher or students identify a topic to fill in the blank, such as anger, a friend, liberty, or fear; then students start each line with " . . . is" and describe or define that thing. A group of grade 2 students wrote the following poem as a part of their weather unit:

Thunder Is . . .

Thunder is someone bowling.
Thunder is a hot cloud bumping against a cold cloud.
Thunder is someone playing basketball.
Thunder is dynamite blasting.
Thunder is a brontosaurus sneezing.
Thunder is people moving their furniture.
Thunder is a giant laughing.
Thunder is elephants playing.
Thunder is an army tank.
Thunder is Bugs Bunny chewing his carrots.

Students often write powerful poems using this formula once they move beyond the cute "Happiness is . . . " and "Love is . . . " patterns.

Acrostic Poems. Students write acrostic poems by choosing a keyword and writing it vertically on a sheet of paper. Then they create lines of poetry, each beginning with a letter of the word. Students can use their names during a unit on autobiography or names of characters during a resource-based unit. For example, after reading *Officer Buckle and Gloria* (Rathmann, 1995), grade 1 students wrote this acrostic using the dog's name, Gloria, for the keyword.

Gloria
Loves to do tricks.
Officer Buckle tells safety
Rules at schools.
I wish I had
A dog like Gloria.

Students also write acrostics using keywords from social studies and science thematic and inquiry-based units. A grade 6 student wrote,

Every
Golden treasure lies still
Young in beauty and
Precious in value beneath the earth
The Egyptians adorned themselves in never-ending splendour.

FREE-FORM POEMS

In free-form poems, children choose words to describe something, express a thought, or tell a story, without concern for rhyme or other arrangements. The number of words per line and the use of punctuation vary. In the following poem, a grade 8 student uses only 15 well-chosen words:

Loneliness

A lifetime
Of broken dreams
And promises
Lost love

Hurt
My heart
Cries
In silence

Students can use several methods for writing free-form poems. They can select words and phrases from brainstormed lists and cluster diagrams, or they can write a paragraph and then "unwrite" it by deleting unnecessary words. They arrange the remaining words to look like a poem.

Concrete Poems. Students create concrete poems through art and the careful arrangement of words on a page. Words, phrases, and sentences can be written in the shape of an object, or word pictures can be inserted within poems written left to right and top to bottom. Two concrete poems are shown in Figure 6–18. In "Ants," the words ants, cake, and frosting create the image of a familiar picnic scene, and in "Cemetery," repetition and form create a reflection of peace. Three books of concrete poems are *Splish Splash: Poems* (Graham, 1994), *Seeing Things* (Froman, 1974), and *Walking Talking Words* (Sherman, 1980).

Found Poems. Students create poems by culling words from other sources, such as stories, songs, and newspaper articles. A grade 3 class created a lengthy found poem, with a section for each chapter as they read *Sarah, Plain and Tall* (MacLachlan, 1985). This section is from Chapter 3, "The Arrival":

Papa drove off,
New wife,
New mother.
Maybe? Maybe?

Rocking on the porch,
Rolling the blue marble,
Back and forth,
Back and forth.
Caleb saw it too,
Not smiling.
We do not have the sea here.
Perfect? Perfect?

Figure 6–18 Students' Concrete Poems

During a thematic unit on Aboriginal Canadians, students write found poems using words and phrases from books they have read.

SYLLABLE- AND WORD-COUNT POEMS

Haiku and other syllable- and word-count poems provide a structure that helps students succeed in writing; however, the need to adhere to these poems' formulas may restrict freedom of expression. The exact syllable counts force students to search for just the right words and provide an opportunity for students to use thesauri and dictionaries.

Haiku. Haiku (high-KOO) is a Japanese poetic form consisting of 17 syllables arranged in three lines of 5, 7, and 5 syllables. Haiku poems present a single clear image. A grade 4 student wrote this haiku poem:

> Spider web shining
> Tangled on the grass with dew
> Waiting quietly.

Books of haiku to share with students include *Haiku—One Breath Poetry* (Wakan, 1993), *Black Swan/White Crow* (Lewis, 1995), *Spring: A Haiku Story* (Shannon, 1996), *Shadow Play: Night Haiku* (Harter, 1994), *In a Spring Garden* (Lewis, 1965), *Cricket Songs* (Behn, 1964), and *More Cricket Songs* (Behn, 1971). The photographs and artwork in these books may give students ideas for illustrating their haiku poems.

Tanka. Tanka (TANK-ah) is a Japanese verse form containing 31 syllables arranged in five lines, 5-7-5-7-7. A grade 8 student wrote this tanka poem:

> The summer dancers
> Dancing in the midnight sky,
> Waltzing and dreaming
> Stars glistening in the night sky.
> Wish upon a shooting star.

Cinquain. A cinquain (SIN-cane) is a five-line poem containing 22 syllables in a 2-4-6-8-2 syllable pattern. Students ask themselves what their subject looks like, smells like, sounds like, and tastes like, and record their ideas using a five-senses cluster as follows:

Line 1:   A one-word subject with two syllables
Line 2:   Four syllables describing the subject
Line 3:   Six syllables showing action
Line 4:   Eight syllables expressing a feeling or an observation about the subject
Line 5:   Two syllables describing or renaming the subject

Here is a cinquain poem written by an upper-grade student:

> Wrestling
> skinny, fat
> coaching, arguing, pinning
> trying hard to win
> tournament

Some lines in this poem are short a syllable or two. The student bent some of the guidelines to create a powerful image of wrestling; however, the message of the poem is more important than adhering to the formula.

Diamante. Tiedt (1970) invented the diamante (dee-ah-MAHN-tay), a seven-line contrast poem written in the shape of a diamond. This poetic form helps students apply their knowledge of opposites and parts of speech. The formula is as follows:

Line 1:   One noun as the subject
Line 2:   Two adjectives describing the subject
Line 3:   Three participles (ending in -*ing*) telling about the subject
Line 4:   Four nouns (the first two related to the subject and the second two related to the opposite)
Line 5:   Three participles telling about the opposite
Line 6:   Two adjectives describing the opposite
Line 7:   One noun that is the opposite of the subject

A grade 3 class wrote this diamante poem:

> Baby
> wrinkled tiny
> crying wetting sleeping
> rattles diapers money house
> caring working loving
> smart helpful
> Adult

Notice that the students created a contrast between *baby*, the subject in the first line, and *adult*, the opposite in the last line. This contrast gives students the opportunity to play with words and apply their understanding of opposites. The third word in the fourth line, *money*, begins the transition from *baby* to its opposite, *adult*.

RHYMED VERSE FORMS

Rhymed verse forms such as limericks can be used effectively with middle- and upper-grade students. It is important that teachers try to prevent the forms and rhyme schemes from restricting students' creative and imaginative expression.

Limericks. The limerick is a form of light verse that uses both rhyme and rhythm. The poem consists of five lines; the first, second, and fifth lines rhyme, while the third and fourth lines rhyme with each other and are shorter than the other three. The rhyme scheme is a-a-b-b-a, and a limerick is arranged this way:

Line	Rhyme
1 _____	a
2 _____	a
3 _____	b
4 _____	b
5 _____	a

The last line often contains a funny or surprise ending, as in this limerick written by a grade 8 student:

> There once was a frog named Pete
> Who did nothing but sit and eat.
> He examined each fly
> With so careful an eye
> And then said, "You're dead meat."

Writing limericks can be a challenging assignment for many upper-grade students, but middle-grade students can also be successful with this poetic form, especially if they write a class collaboration.

Limericks were first popularized over a century ago by Edward Lear (1812–1888). Poet X. J. Kennedy (Kennedy & Kennedy, 1982) described limericks as the most popular type of poem in the English language today. Teachers can introduce students to limericks by reading aloud some of Lear's verses so that students appreciate the rhythm of the verse. Two collections of Lear's limericks are *Daffy Down Dillies: Silly Limericks by Edward Lear* (Lear, 1995) and *Lots of Limericks* (Livingston, 1991). Arnold Lobel has also written a book of unique pig limericks, *The Book of Pigericks* (1983). After reading Lobel's pigericks, students will want to write "birdericks" or "fishericks."

MODEL POEMS

Students can model their poems on poems composed by adult poets. Koch suggested this approach in *Rose, Where Did You Get That Red?* (1990); students read a poem and write their own, using the theme expressed in the model poem. Paul Janeczko's *Poetry from A to Z: A Guide for Young Writers* (1994) and Nancy Cecil's *For the Love of Language* (1994) offer other examples of model poems.

TEACHING STUDENTS TO WRITE POEMS

As they write poems, students use what they have learned about poetry through reading poems and the information presented in minilessons on the poetic forms. They often have misconceptions that interfere with their ability to write poems. Many students think poems must rhyme, and in their search for rhymes they create inane verse. It is important that teachers help students develop a concept of poetry and what poems look like on a page as students begin writing poems. An excellent resource is Diane Dawber's *My Underwear's Inside Out: The Care and Feeding of Younger Poets* (1991).

The collection of poetry is interspersed with instructions at the end of each section to help young poets write. Children will experience both the world of poetry and the excitement of poetic writing as they read and respond to the book.

Minilessons on Poetry. Teachers use minilessons to teach students about the procedures, concepts, and strategies and skills for reading and writing poetry. As part of poetry writing activities, teachers teach minilessons to introduce students to particular poetic forms or to review the forms. Steps in teaching a minilesson on a poetic formula are shown in the following Step by Step box:

Step by Step

A Minilesson on a Poetic Formula

1. *Explain the poetic form.*   The teacher describes the poetic form to students and explains what is included in each line or stanza. Then the teacher displays a chart that describes the form, or has students write a brief description of the poetic form in their poetry notebooks.

2. *Share sample poems.*   The teacher reads aloud poems that are written by children and adults and that adhere to the form. The teacher can share sample poems from this chapter and poems written by students in previous years, or share poems from poetry collections written for children by adults. After reading and responding to each poem, students point out how the writer used the form.

3. *Write class collaboration poems.*   Students write a class collaboration poem, or poems, in small groups before writing individual poems. Each student contributes a line for a class collaboration "I wish . . . " poem or a couplet for a contrast poem. To write other types of poems, such as concrete poems, students can work together by suggesting ideas and words. They dictate the poem to the teacher, who records it on the chalkboard or on chart paper. Older students work in small groups to create poems. Through collaborative poems, students review the form and gather ideas to use later in writing their own poems. The teacher should compliment students when they play with words or use poetic devices. Students also need information about how to arrange the poem on the page, how to decide about capital letters and punctuation marks, and why it may be necessary to "unwrite" and delete some words.

Teachers often simply explain several poetic forms, and then allow students to choose a form and write a poem. This approach ignores the teaching component; it's back to the "assign and do" syndrome. Instead, students need to experiment with each poetic form. After these preliminary experiences, they can apply what they have learned and write poems that adhere to any of the forms they have learned during writers workshop or as part of resource-based units, thematic units, and inquiry-based units. Class collaborations are crucial because they are a practice run for children who are not sure what to do. The five minutes it takes to write a class collaboration poem can be the difference between success and failure for would-be poets.

Teachers teach many other poetry minilessons on wordplay, arranging lines of poetry for the greatest impact, punctuating poems, and how to read poems, for example. A list of topics for mini-lessons related to reading and writing poetry is presented on pages 271–272.

Georgia Heard (1989) emphasizes the importance of teaching students about line breaks and white space on the page. Young children often write poems with the same page arrangement as stories, but as they gain more experience reading poems and experimenting with line breaks, they shape their poems to emphasize rhythm and rhyme, images, and poetic devices. Students learn that there are no right or wrong ways to arrange a poem on a page, but that the way the lines are broken affects both how the poem looks and how it sounds when read aloud.

The Teacher's Notebook on page 270 summarizes some guidelines for teaching children to write poetry.

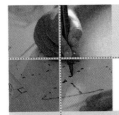

Teacher's Notebook

Guidelines for Writing Poems

1. **Explain the Concept of Poetry**
   The teacher explains what poetry is and what makes a good poem. Too often students assume that all poems must rhyme, are written on topics such as love and flowers, must be punctuated in a particular way, or have other restrictions.

2. **Include Poetry Books in the Classroom**
   Poetry books are set out in a special section of the classroom library. Students learn about poetry through reading, and some poems can serve as models for the poems students write.

3. **Teach Formulas**
   Students learn five to ten formulas to use when they write poems so that they have a range of formulas from which to choose. At the same time, it is important that students know that they can break the formulas in order to express themselves more effectively.

4. **Teach Minilessons on Poetic Devices**
   The teacher presents minilessons on comparison, alliteration, onomatopoeia, and repetition, and encourages students to use poetic devices other than rhyme.

5. **Encourage Wordplay**
   The teacher encourages students to play with words, invent new words, and create word pictures as they write poems.

6. **Write Poetry**
   Students write poetry as part of resource-based units, thematic, and inquiry-based units. Students can write found poems using excerpts from books, write poems about characters in stories, and write poems about topics related to themes.

7. **Create a Class Anthology**
   The teacher and students create a class anthology of students' poems, and duplicate copies of the anthology for each student.

For more information on readers and writers workshops, see Chapter 2, "Teaching the Language Arts," pp. 61–63, and Chapter 11, "Putting It All Together," pp. 461–471.

In Writers Workshop. After students learn about various poetic forms, they often choose to write poems during writers workshop. They write poems about favourite topics or to express their feelings. They also experiment with forms introduced during recent minilessons. Students who especially like to write poems can publish collections of their poems during writers workshop and share them with their classmates. This sharing often stimulates other students to write poetry.

Teachers also plan poetry workshops that incorporate components of both readers and writers workshops. Students read and respond to poems during the readers workshop component, and then they write poems during the writers workshop component. One possible schedule for a two-hour poetry workshop is as follows:

15 minutes	The teacher leads a whole-class meeting to • Give a book talk on a new poetry book • Talk about a poet • Read several favourite poems using choral reading • Talk about a "difficult" or "confusing" poem
30 minutes	Students read poems independently.
15 minutes	Students share poems with classmates.
15 minutes	The teacher teaches a poetry minilesson.
30 minutes	Students write poems using the writing process.
15 minutes	Students share poems they have written.

Duthie and Zimet (1992) describes a similar poetry workshop for first graders that combines reading and writing. Students read poetry, and the teacher reads poetry aloud to students. Writers workshop follows readers workshop, and students also write poems. They draft poems and share them with classmates from the author's chair. Teachers also teach minilessons comparing rhyming versus nonrhyming poetry, creating invented words, introducing comprehensive anthologies and other poetry books, arranging lines of poetry, experimenting with sound words and alliteration, inventing titles for poems, and crafting shape poems. As a culminating project, students compile an anthology of original poems.

For more information on the author's chair, see Chapter 3, "Emergent Literacy," pages 120–122.

Minilessons

Reading and Writing Poetry

	Procedures	Concepts	Strategies and Skills
Wordplay	Craft riddles Create word pictures Invent words Craft tongue twisters	Wordplay Word picture Metaphors Similes Alliteration Onomatopoeia Repetition Rhyme	Rhyme Compare Use alliteration Use onomatopoeia Use repetition
Reading Poetry	Read a poem interpretively Do choral reading Share poems Respond to poems in quickwrites Discuss poems Do a project Compile an anthology	Poetry Rhymed verse Narrative poems Free verse Concrete poems Information about poets Arrangements for choral reading	Vary tempo Emphasize rhythm Vary pitch Stress juncture

(continued)

(continued)	Procedures	Concepts	Strategies and Skills
Writing Poetry	Write formula poems	Poetic form	Use poetic forms
	Write "I wish . . ." poems		Create sensory images
	Write colour poems		Paint word pictures
	Write five-senses poems		Unwrite
	Write "If I were . . ." poems		Use model poems
	Write contrast poems		Write rhymes
	Write definition poems		Punctuate poems
	Write preposition poems		Capitalize poems
	Craft found poems		Arrange poems on the page
	Write free-form poems		
	Design concrete poems		
	Write haiku poems		
	Write cinquain poems		
	Write diamante poems		
	Write limericks		
	Write model poems		

In Resource-Based Units. Students often write poems as part of resource-based units. They write poems together as a class during the exploring stage, or individually or in small groups as projects during the extending stage. To explore the language of a book, students might write found poetry using a paragraph from a favourite book. Or students might write acrostic poems about a book title or a character's name. This acrostic poem about *Jumanji* (Van Allsburg, 1981) was written by a grade 4 student:

> **J**ungle adventure game and
> f**U**n for a while.
> **M**onkeys ransacking kitchens
> **A**nd boa constrictors slithering past.
> **N**o way out until the game is done—
> **J**ust reach the city of Jumanji,
> **I** don't want to play!

Sometimes poetry writing activities are planned, and at other times they happen spontaneously. During a unit on Patricia MacLachlan's *Sarah, Plain and Tall* (1985), a grade 3 class was discussing the two kinds of dunes in the story, and wrote this free-form poem:

> **Dunes**
>
> Dunes of sand
> on the beach.
> Sarah walks on them
> and watches the ocean.
> Dunes of hay
> beside the barn.
> Papa makes them for Sarah
> because she misses Maine.

In Thematic Units. Students also write poems as projects during thematic units. A small group of grade 3 students composed the following found poem after reading *Sarah Morton's Day: A Day in the Life of a Pilgrim Girl* (Waters, 1989):

This Is My Day

Good day.
I must get up and be about my chores.
The fire is mine to tend.
I lay the table.
I muck the garden.
I pound the spices.
I draw vinegar to polish the brass.
I practise my lessons.
I feed the fire again.
I milk the goats.
I eat dinner.
I say the verses I am learning.
My father is pleased with my learning.
I fetch the water for tomorrow.
I bid my parents good night.
I say my prayers.
Fare thee well.
God be with thee.

To compose the found poem, the students collected their favourite words and sentences from the book and organized them sequentially to describe the pilgrim girl's day.

ADAPTING TO MEET THE NEEDS OF EVERY STUDENT

Poetry should be an important part of reading and writing, and teachers must find ways to involve all students in poetry activities. Poetry written for children is available today that will evoke strong feelings and powerful images in students. Writing poetry is a valuable way for students to play with language and express themselves. As teachers plan poetry workshops and connect reading and writing poetry activities to resource-based and thematic units, they must find ways to adapt the activities to meet the needs of every student. An extensive list of poetry resources can be found in Figure 6–19 on pages 274–275.

ASSESSING POEMS THAT STUDENTS WRITE

As teachers read, respond to, and assess the poems that students write, they need to recognize the nuggets of promise in the poems and support and build on them, instead of noticing children's lack of adult conventions (Tway, 1980). Donald Graves (1992) recommends that teachers focus on the passion and wonder in students' writing and on students' ability to make the common seem uncommon. Teachers can also notice the specific details, strong images, wordplay, comparisons, onomatopoeia, alliteration, and repetitions of words and lines that students incorporate in their poems.

The poetic formulas discussed in this chapter provide options for students as they experiment with ways to express their thoughts. Although children experiment with a variety of forms during the elementary grades, it is not necessary to test their knowledge of particular forms. Knowing that haiku is a Japanese poetic form composed of seventeen syllables arranged in three lines will not make a child a poet. Descriptions of the forms should instead be posted in the classroom or added to language arts notebooks for students to refer to as they write.

Assessing the quality of students' poems is especially difficult, because poems are creative combinations of wordplay, poetic forms, and poetic devices. Instead of trying to give a grade for quality, teachers can assess students on other criteria:

- Has the student experimented with the poetic form presented in a minilesson?
- Has the student used the process approach in writing, revising, and editing the poem?
- Has the student used wordplay or another poetic device in the poem?

Booth, D. (1993). *Doctor Knickerbocker*. Toronto: Kids Can Press.
RL 3   IL 3–8 🍁

Booth, D. (Ed.) (1989). *Til All the Stars Have Fallen: Canadian Poems for Children*. Toronto: Kids Can Press.
RL 3   IL 2–6 🍁

Booth, D. (Ed.) (1990). *Voices on the Wind: Poems For All Seasons*. Toronto: Kids Can Press.
RL 3   IL 3–7 🍁

Bouchard, D. (1990). *The Elders Are Watching*. Tofino: Eagle Dancer Enterprises.
RL 4   IL 4 and up 🍁

Bouchard, D. (1997). *Prairie Born*. Victoria: Orca Books.
RL all ages   IL all ages 🍁

Bouchard, D. (1999). *A Barnyard Bestiary*. Victoria: Orca Books.
RL 3   IL 6 and up 🍁

Chase, E. and Reid, B. (1984). *The New Baby Calf*. Toronto: Scholastic.
RL 2   IL 1–4 🍁

Cohen, L. (1995). *Dance Me to the End of Love*. New York: Welcome Enterprises.
RL 6   IL 6 and up 🍁

Dawber, D. (1991). *My Underwear's Inside Out: The Care and Feeding of Younger Poets*. Kingston: Quarry Press.
RL 4   IL 3–6 🍁

Dawber, D. (1997). *How Do You Wrestle a Goldfish?* Nepean: Borealis Press.
RL 6   IL 12 and up 🍁

Day, D. (1991). *Aska's Animals*. Toronto: Doubleday.
RL 3   IL 3–6 🍁

Day, D. (1992). *Aska's Birds*. Toronto: Doubleday.
RL 3   IL 3–6 🍁

Day, D. (1994). *Aska's Sea Creatures*. Toronto: Doubleday.
RL 3   IL 3–6 🍁

Denton, K.M. (Ed.) (1998). *A Child's Treasury of Nursery Rhymes*. Toronto: Kids Can Press.
RL 3   IL preschool and up 🍁

Downie, A., and Robertson, B. (Compilers) (1984). *The New Wind Has Wings: Poems from Canada*. Toronto: Oxford University Press.
RL 5   IL 4 and up 🍁

Dunn, S. (1994). *Gimme a break, Rattlesnake*. Toronto: Stoddart.
RL 3   IL 1–5 🍁

Esbenson, B. (1992). *Who Shrank My Grandmother's House?* Vancouver: Douglas & McIntyre.
RL 3   IL 2–5 🍁

Fitch, S. (1991). *Merry-Go-Day*. Toronto: Doubleday.
RL 2   IL K–3 🍁

Fitch, S. (1992). *There Were Monkeys in My Kitchen*. Toronto: Doubleday.
RL 2   IL K–3 🍁

Fitch, S. (1995). *I Am Small*. Toronto: Doubleday.
RL 2   IL preschool–2

Fitch, S. (1995). *Mabel Murple*. Toronto: Doubleday.
RL 1   IL K–4 🍁

Fitch, S. (1997). *There's a Mouse in My House*. Toronto: Doubleday Canada.
RL 3   IL 8 and up 🍁

Fleischman, P. (1988). *Joyful Noise*. New York: Harper & Row.
RL 5   IL 5–10 🍁

Harrison, T. (2002). *O Canada*. Toronto: Kids Can Press.
RL 2   IL K–5 🍁

Heidbreder, R. (1999) *Python Play and Other Recipes for Fun*. Toronto: Stoddart.
RL K2 IL 4–7 🍁

Kouhi, E. (1993). *North Country Spring*. Waterloo, ON: Penumbra Press.
RL 3   IL all ages 🍁

Kovalski, M. (1992). *Take Me Out to the Ballgame*. Toronto: North Winds Press.
RL 2   IL preschool–3 🍁

Lear, E. (illustrated by Lemieux, M.) (1995). *There Was an Old Man ... A Collection of Limericks*. Toronto: Kids Can Press.
RL 3   IL all ages 🍁

Lee, D. (1974). *Alligator Pie*. Toronto: Macmillan.
RL 4   IL 2–7 🍁

Lee, D. (1991). *The Ice Cream Store*. Toronto: HarperCollins.
RL 4   IL 2–7 🍁

Lee, D. (1993). *Ping and Pong*. Toronto: HarperCollins.
RL 1   IL preschool–1 🍁

Lesynski, L. (1999). *Dirty Dog Boogie*. Toronto: Annick Press.
RL 2   IL preschool–3 🍁

Lotteridge, C. (Ed.) (1994). *Mother Goose: A Canadian Sampler*. Toronto: Groundwood.
RL 1   IL all ages 🍁

Loughead, D. (1998). *All I Need and Other Poems for Kids*. Etobicoke: Moonstruck Press.
RL 4–6 IL 8 and up 🍁

McArthur, W., and Ursell, G. (Eds.) (1989). *Jumbo Gumbo: Songs, Poems and Stories for Children*. Regina: Coteau Books.
RL 4   IL 2–5 🍁

(continued)

Figure 6–19 Other Poetry Resources

McNeil, F. (Ed.) (1990). *Do Whales Jump at Night?: Poems for Kids*. Toronto: Douglas & McIntyre.
RL 6   IL 5–9 🍁

Middleton, J. E. (1990). *The Huron Carol*. Toronto: Lester & Orpen Dennys.
RL 3   IL preschool–12 🍁

Moore, C. (illustrated by K. Fernandes) (1998). *A Visit from St. Nicholas*. Toronto: Doubleday.
RL 2   IL preschool–3 🍁

Muller, R. (1992). *Hickory, Dickory, Dock*. Richmond Hill, ON: North Winds Press.
RL 2   IL preschool–4 🍁

Neaman, E. (1992). *Folk Rhymes from Around the World*. Vancouver: Pacific Educational Press.
RL 3   IL K–5 🍁

Nichol, B. (1997). *Biscuits in the Cupboard*. Toronto: Stoddart Kids.
RL 3   IL K–5 🍁

Nickel, B. (1999). *From the Top of a Grain Elevator*. Vancouver: Beach Holme.
RL 3–7 IL 9 and up 🍁

Noyes, A. (illustrated by C. Keeping) (1981). *The Highwayman*. Oxford: Oxford University Press.

Obed, E. B. (1988). *Borrowed Black*. St. John's: Breakwater Books.
RL 4   IL 2–6 🍁

Obed, E. B. (1990). *Wind in My Pocket*. St. John's: Breakwater Books.
RL 3   IL 3–6 🍁

Parry, C. (Ed.) (1991). *Zoomerang a Boomerang*. Toronto: Kids Can Press.
RL 2   IL K–3 🍁

Perry, S. (1995) *If*. Malibu, CA: J. P. Getty Museum and Children's Library Press.
RL 2   IL 2 and up 🍁

Pilling, A. (1990). *Before I Go to Sleep*. Toronto: Kids Can Press.
RL 4   IL 3–6 🍁

Priest, R. (1994). *The Ballad of the Blue Bonnet*. Toronto: Groundwood Books.
RL 1   IL preschool–1 🍁

Raffi (1988). *Wheels on the Bus*. New York: Crown Publishers.
RL 1   IL preschool–3 🍁

Reid, B. (illustrator) (1987). *Sing a Song of Mother Goose*. Richmond Hill, ON: North Winds Press.
RL 1   IL preschool–3 🍁

Robertson, J. (1991). *Sea Witches*. Toronto: Oxford University Press.
RL 2   IL 2–3 🍁

Rylant, C. (1985). *The Relatives Came*. New York: Bradbury.
RL 2   IL 3–6

Rylant, C. (1988). *All I See*. New York: Orchard.
RL 3   IL 3–6 🍁

Service, R. (illustrated by T. Harrison) (1986). *The Cremation of Sam McGee*. Toronto: Kids Can Press.
RL 4   IL 4 and up 🍁

Service, R. (illustrated by T. Harrison) (1988). *The Shooting of Dan McGrew*. Toronto: Kids Can Press.
RL 5   IL 5 and up 🍁

Stevenson, R. L. (illustrated by V. Gad) (1985). *Happy Thought: Poems For Children*. Toronto: Midway Publications.
RL 2   IL 1–4 🍁

Swede, G. (1991). *I Want to Lasso Time*. Toronto: Simon & Pierre.
RL 4   IL 4–8 🍁

Thomas, D. (illustrated by M. Kimber) (1997). *Fern Hill*. Red Deer: Red Deer College Press.
RL 6   IL 4 and up 🍁

Tynes, M. (1991). *Save the World for Me*. East Lawrencetown: Pottersfield Press.
RL 3   IL 2–5 🍁

Wakan, N. (1993). *Haiku—One Breath Poetry*. Vancouver: Pacific Rim Publishers.
RL 7   IL 7 and up 🍁

Ward, K. (1989). *Twelve Kids One Cow*. Toronto: Kids Can Press.
RL 2   IL preschool–2 🍁

Wilkins, C. (1989). *Old Mrs. Schmatterbung and Other Friends*. Toronto: McClelland & Stewart.
RL 3   IL 1–5 🍁

Yolen, J. (1996). *Sacred Places*. New York: Harcourt Brace.
RL 6   IL 4 and up 🍁

(RL – Reading Level; IL – Interest Level)

Figure 6–19 Other Poetry Resources *(continued)*

Teachers also ask students to assess their own progress in writing poetry. Students choose their best efforts and poems that show promise. They can explain which writing strategies they used in particular poems and which poetic forms they used.

Students keep copies of their poems in their writing folders or poetry booklets so that they can review and assess their own work. They may also place copies of some poems in their language arts portfolios. If a grade for quality is absolutely necessary, students should choose several of the poems in their writing folders for the teacher to evaluate.

■ Review

During the elementary grades students learn about five elements of story structure: plot, characters, setting, point of view, and theme. Students apply this knowledge as they read and write stories. They read stories aesthetically and develop interpretations as they read and respond to stories. Students read stories as part of resource-based units, readers workshop, and thematic units. Students use the writing process to write retellings of familiar stories, new versions of stories, sequels, and original stories during resource-based units, in thematic units, and in writers workshop. They also use journal writing to share events in their lives and record what they are learning in resource-based units and thematic units.

Poetry is also an important part of the language arts curriculum. Elementary students participate in wordplay activities and read and write poetry as part of resource-based units, readers and writers workshops, and thematic units.

The following key concepts are presented in this chapter:

1. Students acquire a concept of story by reading and writing stories and by learning about the elements of story structure.

2. Stories have unique structural elements that distinguish them from other forms of writing: plot, characters, setting, point of view, and theme.

3. The goal of aesthetic reading is comprehension, the negotiation of meaning between the reader and the text.

4. Students use the following strategies to respond to stories: visualizing, predicting, engaging, empathizing, identifying, elaborating, noticing opposites, monitoring, and connecting to personal experiences.

5. Storyboards, story boxes, open-mind portraits, setting maps, sketch-to-stretch, and story quilts are six ways to explore stories.

6. Students use intertextuality as they incorporate ideas from the stories they have read into the stories they write.

7. Students write in seven kinds of journals: personal journals, dialogue journals, reading response logs, double-entry journals, language arts notebooks, learning logs, and simulated journals.

8. Dialogue journals are especially useful for students learning English as a second language.

9. Reading response logs, double-entry journals, language arts notebooks, and simulated journals are often used during resource-based units.

10. Even young children can draw and write in personal journals and reading logs.

11. The focus in journal writing is on developing writing fluency and using writing as a tool for learning.

12. Wordplay activities with riddles, comparisons, rhyme, and other poetic devices provide the background of experiences students need for reading and writing poetry.

13. The focus in teaching students to read and respond to poems is enjoyment.

14. Tempo, rhythm, pitch, and juncture are four elements to consider when reading poetry aloud.

15. Choral reading is an effective way for students to read poetry.

16. Students can write poems successfully using poetic formulas in which they begin each line with particular words, count syllables, or create word pictures.

17. Because rhyme is a sticking point for many students, they should be encouraged to experiment with other poetic devices in their writing.

Extensions

1. Compile a list of books to use in teaching about story elements at the grade level you teach or plan to teach. Write a brief summary for each book, commenting specifically on the element of story structure or genre that the book exemplifies.

2. Interview several students about their concept of story and what they think about as they read and write stories. Ask questions such as these:

   - Tell me about a story you have read that is really a good one.
   - What things do authors include in stories to make them good?
   - Do you like to read stories? Write stories?
   - Tell me about some of the stories you have written.
   - Tell me some of the things you think about while you are writing a story.
   - What do you include in stories you write to make them good?
   - What have your teachers taught you about reading and writing stories?

3. Teach a series of minilessons about reading strategies or one of the elements of story structure to a small group of students. Use the teaching strategy presented in this chapter.

4. Plan a resource-based unit on a picture book or a chapter book.

5. Collect samples of children's stories and examine them to see how students use the elements of story structure.

6. Plan an author study unit. Collect information about the author and copies of the stories the author has written.

7. Using dialogue journals, write back and forth with three students who are having difficulty in your classroom. Continue for several weeks. Use this opportunity to get to know these students better and make the activity a positive experience for students. What changes do you see in students' entries and your own over the period?

8. Keep a personal journal in which you record experiences and feelings, or keep a double-entry journal in which you reflect on the material in this book as well as your teaching experiences for the remainder of the school term.

9. Plan and teach a minilesson on a language arts topic to a small group of students, and have the students make notes in their language arts notebooks.

10. Plan and teach a two-week poetry workshop. During the workshop, involve students with activities in reading and writing poetry, and teach minilessons on topics from the list on pages 271–272.

11. Collect a group of poems for choral reading and teach a group of students to do choral reading using the four arrangements listed on page 244.

12. Teach a small group of students to write several types of poems, and have students compile their poems in a class anthology or in hardbound books.

chapter seven

Reading and Writing Expository Text

PROFILE

Changing
Information
into
Knowledge

Procedure

In a five-week unit called Exploring Ancient Egypt, my goal was to motivate students to research areas of Ancient Egypt that interested them and to give them the skills to sift through masses of resources and synthesize information into a concise, useable, and memorable project. It was all about changing information into knowledge. What fun we had! We chose ancient Egypt because all of the students were very interested in that topic. The grade 7 social studies curriculum included culture and because the ancient Egyptian culture was so different from our Canadian one, it made for great comparisons when I later taught the regular social studies topic.

> "This unit was so much fun to teach because . . . I was able to choose skills from both the language arts and social studies curricula to integrate into the learning."

Dawn King-Hunter
G. S. Lakie Middle School
Lethbridge, Alberta

We started out by taking a 17" × 11" piece of paper and folding it in half three times. This gave us a tracking sheet with 8 equal squares on each side. As a class, we brainstormed topics that people wanted to explore. Students wrote a topic at the top of each square, coming up with many different ones, including ancient Egyptian food, religion, clothing, farming, lifestyles, language, writing, pharaohs, the Nile, holidays, festivals, art, class system, housing, architecture, transportation, education, mummification and burial ceremonies. One of the squares was entitled "Bibliography" and students recorded each informational resource they used.

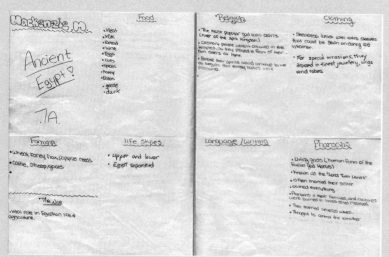

The handwritten tracking sheet shows:

Mackenzie M.

Ancient Egypt♥

7A.

Food
- Meat
- Milk
- Bread
- Wine
- Eggs
- Nuts
- Spices
- Honey
- Dates
- goose
- duck

Religion
- The most popular god was Osiris (ruler of the afterlife/kingdom.)
- Ordinary people weren't allowed in the temples; so they prayed in front of their own alters at home.
- Before their spirits could continue to live on to reach their eternal bodies were preserved.

Clothing
- Sleeveless tunics with extra sleeves that could be sewn on during cold weather.
- For special occasions, they dressed in finest jewellery, wigs and robes.

Farming
- Wheat, barley, flax, papyrus reeds
- cattle, sheep, goats

Life Styles
- Upper and lower
- Egypt separated

Language/Writing

Pharaohs
- Living gods (human form of the falcon god Horus)
- Known as the "Lord Two Lands"
- often married their sister
- owned everything
- Pharaohs & their families, and captives were buried in tombs called mastaba.
- They married several wives.
- Thought to control the weather

The Nile
- Vital role in Egyptian and agriculture.

Students track their research and eventually use the information to creatively present the topic to others.

As a facilitator, I then tried to inundate them with all sorts of different information material. We examined library books, flipped through *National Geographic* magazines, and surfed the Internet. On day one, I read information from a few different books and as a class we practised how to pinpoint the main idea and copy a point-form phrase on our tracking sheet. I modelled this on the board. Day two gave the students an opportunity to share the materials we had in the classroom and take more notes. Students were allowed to work with a partner reading the information, but both students needed to record important points. On day three, we accessed a class set of laptop computers and students used a variety of search engines to find more information. Throughout our research, students recorded information in point form in the appropriate square on their own tracking sheets. We continued researching this way for about a week. At one point, we invited one of our ESL students to teach us basic Egyptian Arabic.

From the beginning of the unit, all students were extremely interested in the mummification process so we researched how this was done and everyone participated in a hands-on chicken mummification experience. After completing a mummification game on the Internet at www.bbc.co.uk/history/ancient/egyptians/launch_gms_mummy_maker.shtml, students divided into groups and each group was given a chicken to mummify. After five weeks of processing the chickens, each group wrapped the mummy in gauze bandages and adorned the bodies with precious gems. By this time, each mummy had been named (for instance, King Cluck, Princess Cluckopatra) and students had turned a shoebox into a beautifully designed sarcophagus. We had a classroom burial ceremony and the mummies were placed in the G. S. Lakie School resident tomb (the classroom back closet).

Assessment

Students were required to create a project to present the information they gleaned during the unit to the rest of the class. Each specific project was left open-ended so students could choose a project and method of presentation that appealed to their strongest intelligence. For example, a student with a strong visual intelligence chose to present information in poster format and another built an intricate 3-D model of the pyramids. Three students worked together on a video mockumentary showing a new discovery of an ancient tomb. One student with a strong proficiency in writing composed a fictional story of a slave girl's life of catering to a famous pharaoh. The entire unit was based on a pass/fail grade, so if students participated in the research and had a final project, they passed.

Reflections

This unit was so much fun to teach because, first of all, the students were really interested in ancient Egypt. Secondly, it was a topic that lent itself well to the integration of many different subjects. I was able to choose skills from both the language arts and social studies curricula to integrate into the learning. As a group, we learned together and I adjusted my lessons according to the information we were unearthing on a daily basis. The tracking sheet is an extremely useful tool because it teaches students to organize research material all in one place. By insisting that students write the main idea in point form rather than copying reams of sentences directly from the resources, it also teaches them how to make the knowledge their own, without plagiarizing. Finally, the real learning comes through having participated in individual research, creating a final project, and then observing and experiencing everyone else's presentation.

As part of a theme unit on quilt-making and shapes, Joanne Takasaki and her grade 4 class created this quilt. Students read *Selina and the Bear Paw Quilt* (1995) by Barbara Smucker. They also studied symmetrical and asymmetrical two-dimensional shapes. By bringing together literature and mathematics, these students created one large quilt requiring them to estimate, measure, rearrange patterns, read, and write. Later, the class chose to donate the quilt to Harbour House, a local shelter for women and children.

In a thematic unit on whales, a teacher might say, "I have an exciting story to read to you today about how whales migrate" and "What a wonderful story you've written, and I learned a lot about baleen whales!" These books about whales may be stories, but it is more likely that they are informational or nonfiction books because their primary purpose is to provide information. Teachers sometimes use the word *story* as a generic term for all books students read, thinking that *story* is an easier term for them to understand. But it is somewhat unfair to students to do this. Stories and informational books are different genres, although they overlap. Chapman and Sopko (2003) refer to the books in which information and story overlap as *combined-texts*. Combined-texts, such as *The Magic School Bus Inside a Hurricane* (Cole, 1995), use a story-like format, but the emphasis is on providing information (Freeman & Person, 1992).

Teachers have assumed that constructing stories in the mind is a fundamental way of learning (Wells, 1986). Recent research, however, suggests that stories are not easier for children to understand, and that children are able to understand informational texts as well as they do stories (Pappas, 1991, 1993). Classroom reading instruction should involve instruction that goes beyond what can be taught through stories. Instruction should involve students in recognizing different genres; using different informational text formats (e.g., graphs, glossaries, and indexes); assessing the content in informational text; and using multiple sources (Kamil & Lane, 1997). Children are interested in learning about their world—about baleen whales, how a road is built, threats to the environment of Antarctica, or Helen Keller's courage—and informational books provide this knowledge.

Students often assume the efferent stance as they read informational books to locate facts, but this is not always the case (Rosenblatt, 1978, 1991). Many times they pick up an informational book to check a fact, and then they continue reading—aesthetically, now—because they are fascinated by what they are reading. Similarly,

To Guide Your Reading

As you read this chapter, prepare to

Describe the nature and features of informational text

•

Explain how informational text differs from stories

•

Describe the five most common expository text structures

•

Explain how teachers can teach students to read and learn from expository text

•

Explain how teachers facilitate students' writing of various types of informational prose, including reports and letters

they read information from websites and CD-ROMs well beyond the particular fact they sought. At other times students read books about topics they are interested in, and they read aesthetically, engaging in the experience of reading and connecting what they are reading to their own lives and prior reading experiences.

For more information on aesthetic and efferent reading, see Chapter 4, "The Reading and Writing Processes," pages 128–129

Janet Lunn, co-author of *The Story of Canada*, the first illustrated history of Canada for young people, talks about how children become engaged in reading informational books. She suggests that adults and children together share this type of literature. Lunn says, "I can't see too many kids sitting down and reading it from beginning to end, but they will dip into it, and read this and that story" (Reed, 1992, p. 295). In addition, she notes the important role that illustrations play in an informational book, indicating that these "in large part are responsible for the book's appeal" (1992, p. 295). In a similar way, Mel Hurtig talks about the comprehensive resource, *The Junior Encyclopedia of Canada*, a reference work on Canada for young Canadians. According to Hurtig, the visual presentation of informational books geared for children, young and old, must be both interesting and inviting. He advocates the use of charts, chronological tables, illustrations, and examples. As he says, "children have to be drawn into the Junior. They must want to use it" (Zatlokal, 1990, p. 54). It is important that teachers in the higher grades critically evaluate non-fiction texts to ensure these are engaging for students.

As students read informational books and listen to them read aloud, they learn about the world around them and many other things as well. They learn how to vary their reading, depending on their purpose. Sometimes they read informational books from beginning to end like stories, or they may use the index to locate a specific topic and then read just that section. They learn how to use an index and a table of contents, and how to read charts, graphs, maps, and diagrams. They also notice the different ways expository texts are organized and how authors develop interrelationships among the pieces of information being presented.

Students also write informational books about concepts and information they are learning during thematic units and in lessons in other areas of the curriculum. The informational trade books they have read serve as models for their writing, and they organize the information that they present using the same types of patterns or structures used in informational books (Freeman, 1991; Tompkins, Smith, & Hitchcock, 1987). Students also learn to read expository text from other sources, including the Internet and CD-ROMs. As discussed in Chapter 8, "Viewing and Visually Representing," they learn to visually represent information in the ways they experience them in these sources.

Types of Informational Books

A new wave of engaging and artistic informational books is now available, and these books show increased respect for children. Peter Roop (1992) explains that for years informational books were the "ugly duckling" of children's literature, but now they have grown into a beautiful swan.

Four qualities of informational books are accuracy, organization, design, and style (Vardell, 1991). First and foremost, the facts must be current and complete. These books must be well researched, and, when appropriate, varying points of view should be presented. Stereotypes are to be avoided, and the details in both the text and the illustrations must be authentic. Second, information should be presented clearly and logically, using organizational patterns to increase the book's readability. Third, the design of the book should be eye-catching and should enhance its usability. Illustrations should complement the text, and explanations should accompany each illustration. Last, the book should be written in a lively and stimulating style so as to engage the reader's curiosity and wonder. The same four characteristics are true of expository texts presented in other contexts, such as the Internet and CD-ROMs.

A wide variety of informational books are available today. Topics include the biological sciences, the physical sciences, the social sciences, the arts, and biographies. *Exploring the Sky by Day* (Dickinson, 1988) is a fine informational book about weather and the atmosphere. It provides readable descriptions of the atmosphere and captivating illustrations using photographs and drawings. Another book—*Chew On This: Everything You Don't Want to Know About Fast Food* (Schlosser & Wilson, 2006)—documents the far-reaching negative effects of the fast food industry. Books like *Move!* (Jenkins & Page, 2006) show how a variety of animals move with bright colourful illustrations and simple yet engaging text.

Other books present historical and geographic concepts. *A Pioneer Story: The Daily Life of a Pioneer Family in 1840* (Greenwood, 1995) helps readers experience nineteenth-century Ontario by spending a year with the Robertson family on their remote and isolated backwoods farm. The book contains fact, fiction, illustrations, and hands-on activities. Another fine book, *Buried in Ice* (Beattie, Geiger, & Tanaka, 1992), recreates the ill-fated Arctic expedition led by Sir John Franklin. It combines fictionalized accounts with present-day speculations about the disappearance of the explorers. These books are exciting to read, and they provide an engaging and enriching reading experience for elementary students. *Invisible Allies: Microbes that Shape Our Lives* (Farrell, 2005) is a readable book of science that talks about the beneficial role played by microbes on Earth.

Life stories are another type of informational book; one type of life story is biography, and another is autobiography. Life stories being written today are more realistic than in the past, and they present well-known personalities, warts and all. Linda Granfield's portrait of John McCrae in *In Flanders Fields: The Story of the Poem by John McCrae* (1995) is among the best known, and *John Lennon: All I Want is the Truth* (Partridge, 2005) is an award-winning biography of Lennon's life and death. Another excellent resource is Wendy Long's *Celebrating Excellence: Canadian Women Athletes* (1995) which shows how other subject areas can be enhanced through books and reading. Authors often include notes in the back of books to explain how the details were researched and to provide additional information.

Although few autobiographies are available to elementary students today, more are being published each year. Autobiographies about authors and illustrators, such as Jean Little's *Little by Little* (1987) and *Stars Come Out Within* (1990), provide insight into one person's courage, perseverance, and talent, and are popular with students. Two recent publications make a significant contribution to information available to young readers regarding Canadian art and artists. They are *Capturing Joy: The Story of Maud Lewis* (Bogart, 2002) and *Breaking Free: The Story of William Kurelek* (Ebbit-Cutler, 2002).

Kindergarten students learn about sequence as they arrange information boards made from two copies of an informational book about the life cycle of a chicken.

In addition to these main types of informational books, there are other, more specialized, types. Four types that elementary students read are

1. ***Alphabet and counting books.*** While many alphabet and counting books with pictures of familiar objects are designed for young children, others provide a wealth of information on various topics. In *Eh? To Zed: A Canadian AbeCedarium*, Kevin Major (2000) focuses on uniquely Canadian objects and artifacts to produce his alphabet book; in *A Northern Alphabet* (1982), Ted Harrison uses many elements from the Cree culture to inform his work; and in *Wildlife ABC: A Nature Alphabet* (1988), Jan Thornhill describes many Canadian animals and examines the ecology supporting them. Jo Bannatyne-Cugnet presents information about the Prairies in *A Prairie Alphabet* (1992), and Denise Fleming uses handmade paper artwork to create an alphabet book highlighting construction activities in *Alphabet Under Construction* (2002). In some of these books, new terms are introduced and illustrated, and in others new terms are explained in a sentence or a paragraph.

2. ***Books that present information through a song or poem.*** In these powerful books, songs and poems are illustrated with a word, line, or stanza on each page. Together the text and illustrations provide information. In *Mummer's Song* (Davidge, 1990), Bud Davidge's song—well known in Newfoundland and Labrador—is accompanied by Ian Wallace's captivating pictures of that province's mummering tradition. Old-fashioned dress-ups and Christmas traditions are described and celebrated through pictures and song. Joyce Sidman's poetry and Beckie Prange's illustrations combine to describe the life of ponds through melodic verse and woodcut art in *Song of the Water Boatman and Other Pond Poems* (2005). *Ann and Seamus* (2003), the story of an Irish shipwreck off the coast of Newfoundland and Labrador, is told by award-winning author Kevin Major and exquisitely illustrated by East Coast artist David Blackwood.

3. ***Books that present information within a story.*** Authors are devising innovative strategies for combining information with a story in combined-texts. Michele Martin Bossley's *The Perfect Gymnast* (1996) provides detailed and powerful information about gymnastics, bulimia, and interpersonal relationships. In a historical vein, several good books are available. In *Selina and the Bear Paw Quilt* (1995), Barbara Smucker documents a Mennonite family's move to Upper Canada to avoid the US Civil War, and *Arizona Charlie and the Klondike Kid* (2003) by Julie Lawson is set during the Yukon Gold Rush era. These books present factual material through interesting and thought-provoking stories. Flashback is another useful technique for presenting information. In *Just Like New* (Manson, 1995), flashback is used to contrast Canada with war-torn England in the 1940s. Karen Reczuch cleverly uses black and white and colour illustrations to contrast the settings in these two countries.

   Some combination informational/story books are imaginative fantasies. *The Magic School Bus* series, written by Joanna Cole and illustrated by Bruce Degen, is perhaps the best known. In *The Magic School Bus Inside a Hurricane* (1995), for example, Ms. Frizzle and her class study weather up close as their bus survives both a hurricane and a tornado on its way to a weather station. Charts and reports with factual information and suggestions for projects are presented throughout the book. Another fantasy story with factual information is Faith Ringgold's *Aunt Harriet's Underground Railroad in the Sky* (1992). Information and a map about the Underground Railroad and a biographical sketch of Harriet Tubman are included in the back of the book.

   Other authors use the story format to tell about experiences in their own lives. *My School Is Alive!* (Barnes, 2005) tells the story of one school garden that grew into a place of refuge and study for plants, animals, and the school community. It is written by elementary schoolteacher David Barnes and told through the voice of a grade 2 student. *A Child in Prison Camp* (Takashima, 1971) is the story of a child living in a Japanese internment camp during the Second World War. In both of these books, factual information about the topics is woven into the text. Still other authors use combined texts to write autobiographically. For example,

Martin (1998) tells the life story of Wilson Bentley in narrative while also detailing the development of specialized photography technique through marginal notes in *Snowflake Bentley*, a Caldecott Medal winner.

4. ***Journals and letters.*** Journals and letters are types of informational books, and these artifacts provide a glimpse into historical periods and the lives of historical personalities. One all-encompassing example is the previously mentioned *The Story of Canada* (Lunn & Moore, 1992). This encyclopedic volume follows the buffalo hunt, the Klondike gold rush, and features information about the lives of such notable Canadians as Terry Fox and Roberta Bondar. The book is well researched and contains paintings, historical photographs, maps, and posters, making it visually appealing to children and adults alike.

Some journals and collections of letters are authentic accounts, but others are fictionalized. Shelley Tanaka's *I Was There: On Board the Titanic* (1996) is an award-winning informational book that focuses on the lives of two young men who actually survived the sinking of the Titanic. The author weaves together memories and factual information to produce an outstanding account of the voyage and its tragic demise. Even the fictionalized accounts can be used in conjunction with informational books, but teachers and students should be aware of the differences between the two types.

EXPOSITORY TEXT STRUCTURES

Just as stories are structured using plot, characters, and the other elements of story structure, informational books are organized or patterned in particular ways called *expository text structures*. These structures are commonly found in textbooks, in informational trade books, on the Internet, in CD-ROMs, in magazines, and in newspapers. Five of the most common organizational patterns are description, sequence, comparison, cause and effect, and problem and solution (Meyer & Freedle, 1984; Niles, 1974). Figure 7–1 on pages 286–287 describes these patterns and presents sample passages and cue words that signal use of each pattern. In stories, the elements of story structure interact together to create the story framework; however, in informational text, expository text structures may be used separately.

Description. In this pattern, the author describes a topic by listing characteristics, features, and examples. Phrases such as *for example, characteristics are,* and *consists of* cue this structure. Examples of books using description include *Touching All the Bases: Baseball for Kids of all Ages* (Mackay, 1994) and *Birdwise* (Hickman, 1988). In these books the authors describe many facets of their topic. When students delineate any topic, such as the Mackenzie River, wolves, or the Rocky Mountains, they use description.

Sequence. In this pattern, the author lists items or events in numerical or chronological order. Cue words include *first, second, third, next, then,* and *finally.* Caroline Arnold describes the steps in creating a museum display in *Dinosaurs All Around: An Artist's View of the Prehistoric World* (1993), and David Macaulay describes how a castle was constructed in *Castle* (1977). Students use the sequence pattern to write directions for completing a math problem, the stages in an animal's life cycle, or events in a biography.

Comparison. In this pattern, the author explains how two or more things are alike and/or different. *Different, in contrast, alike, same as,* and *on the other hand* are cue words and phrases that signal this structure. In *Horns, Antlers, Fangs, and Tusks* (Rauzon, 1993), for example, the author compares animals with these distinctive types of headgear. When students compare and contrast book and video versions of a story, reptiles and amphibians, or life in ancient Greece with life in ancient Egypt, they use this organizational pattern.

Cause and Effect. In this pattern, the author describes one or more causes and the resulting effect or effects. *Reasons why, if . . . then, as a result, therefore,* and *because* are words and phrases that cue this structure. Explanations of why dinosaurs became extinct or the effects of pollution on the environment use the cause-and-effect pattern. Celia Godkin's *Ladybug Garden* (1995) and Nicole Mortillaro's *Sun and Storms: Canadian Summer Weather* (2005), from the Canada Close Up Series, are two informational books that exemplify the cause-and-effect structure.

Problem and Solution. In this pattern, the author states a problem and offers one or more solutions. In *Real Live Science: Top Scientists Present Amazing Activities Any Kid Can Do* (1992), Jay Ingram suggests experiments to test real-life problems. A variation is the question-and-answer (or Q&A) format, in which the author poses a question and then answers it; one Q&A book is *The New Kids' Question and Answer Book: Questions Kids Ask about Nature, Science and the Environment* (Farris, 1993). Cue words and phrases include *problem is, dilemma is, puzzle is, solve,* and *question . . . answer.* Students use this structure when they write about why money was invented, saving endangered animals, and building dams to stop flooding. They often use the problem–solution pattern in writing advertisements and in other persuasive writing.

These organizational patterns correspond to the traditional organization of main ideas and details within paragraphs. The main idea is embodied in the organizational pattern, and the details are the elaboration; for example, in the sample passage of the comparison pattern in Figure 7–1, the main idea is that the modern Olympic games are very different from the ancient Olympics. The details are the specific comparisons and contrasts.

Graphic organizers can help students organize and visually represent ideas for the five organizational patterns (Piccolo, 1987; Smith & Tompkins, 1988). Students might use a cluster for description, a Venn diagram or T-chart for comparison, or a series of boxes and arrows for cause and effect (Bromley, 1991; Yopp & Yopp, 1996). Diagrams of a variety of graphic organizers also appear in Figure 7–1. Most of the research on expository text structures has focused on older students' use of these patterns in reading; however, elementary students also use the patterns and cue words in their writing (Langer, 1986; Raphael, Englert, & Kirschner, 1989; Tompkins, 1994).

Even though the expository text structures are used with informational texts, some books that are classified as stories also involve sequence, cause and effect, or one of the other expository text structures. Teachers can point out these structures or use graphic organizers to help students look more closely at the story. The popular *The Very Hungry Caterpillar* (Carle, 1969), for example, involves two sequences. Eric Carle uses sequence to show the development of the caterpillar from egg to butterfly and to list what the caterpillar ate each day. Problem and solution is illustrated in *A New Coat for Anna* (Ziefert, 1986), a story set in war-torn Europe, as Anna's mother makes a series of trades to get a new coat for her daughter.

TEACHING STUDENTS TO READ AND LEARN FROM EXPOSITORY TEXT

Reading expository text, just like reading narrative text, requires students to monitor their reading to make sure that what they read makes sense. Ruddell (2001) suggest students need to do six things to read and learn from expository text. Figure 7–2 on page 288 explains those six things.

Students also need to learn about the five expository text structures and how to use them to improve their reading comprehension as well as to organize their writing (Flood, Lapp, & Farnan, 1986; McGee & Richgels, 1985; Piccolo, 1987). Teachers teach students about expository text structure by presenting minilessons. The minilesson procedure explained in Chapter 1, "Learning and the Language Arts," can be adapted to teach expository text structure and how to learn from expository text. The informational books listed in Figure 7–5 on pages 296–297 exemplify each of the expository text structures. They can be used as examples when teachers present minilessons. The steps in teaching minilessons on expository text structure are presented in the Step by Step box on page 288.

Figure 7–1 The Five Expository Text Structures

Pattern	Description	Cue Words	Graphic Organizer	Sample Passage
Description	The author describes a topic by listing characteristics, features, and examples.	for example characteristics are consists of		The Olympic symbol consists of five interlocking rings. The rings represent the five continents—Africa, Asia, Europe, North America, and South America—from which athletes compete in the games. The rings are coloured black, blue, green, red, and yellow. At least one of these colours is found in the flag of every country sending athletes to compete in the Olympic games.
Sequence	The author lists items or events in numerical or chronological order.	first, second, third next then finally	1. 2. 3. 4. 5.	The Olympic games began as athletic festivals to honour the Greek gods. The most important festival was held in the valley of Olympia to honour Zeus, the king of the gods. It was this festival that became the Olympic games in 776 BC. These games were ended in AD 394 by the Roman Emperor who ruled Greece. No Olympic games were held for more than 1500 years. Then the modern Olympics began in 1896. Almost 300 male athletes competed in the first modern Olympics. In the games held in 1900, female athletes were allowed to compete. The games have continued every four years since 1896 except during World War II, and they will most likely continue for many years to come.
Comparison	The author explains how two or more things are alike and/or how they are different.	different in contrast alike same as on the other hand		The modern Olympics is very unlike the ancient Olympic games. Individual events are different. While there were no swimming races in the ancient games, for example, there were chariot races. There were no female contestants and all athletes competed in nude. Of course, the ancient and modern Olympics are also alike in many ways. Some events, such as the javelin and discus throws, are the same. Some people say that cheating, professionalism, and nationalism in the modern games are a disgrace to the Olympic tradition. But according to the ancient Greek writers, there were many cases of cheating, nationalism, and professionalism in their Olympics, too.

Cause and Effect	The author lists one or more causes and the resulting effect or effects.	*reasons why* *if … then* *as a result* *therefore* *because*	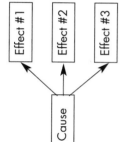 There are several reasons why so many people attend the Olympic games or watch them on television. One reason is tradition. The name *Olympics* and the torch and flame remind people of the ancient games. People can escape the ordinariness of daily life by attending or watching the Olympics. They like to identify with some-one else's individual sacrifice and accomplishment. National pride is another reason, and an athlete's or a team's hard earned victory becomes a nation's victory. There are national medal counts and people keep track of how many medals their country's athletes have won.
Problem and Solution	The author states a problem and lists one or more solutions for the problem. A variation of this pattern is the question-and-answer format in which the author poses a question and then answers it.	*problem is* *dilemma is* *puzzle is* *solved* *question …* *answer*	One proble with the modern Olympics is that it has become very big and expensive to operate. The city or country that hosts the games often loses a lot of money. A stadium, pools, and playing fields must be built for the athletic events, and housing is needed for the athletes who come from around the world. And all of these facilities are used for only 2 weeks! In 1984, Los Angeles solved these problems by charging a fee for companies who wanted to be official sponsors of the games. Companies like McDonald's paid a lot of money to be part of the Olympics. Many buildings that were already built in the Los Angeles area were also used. The Coliseum where the 1932 games were held was used again, and many colleges and universities in the area became playing and living sites.

Cause → Effect #1, Effect #2, Effect #3

Problem → Solution

Step by Step

Teaching Minilessons on Expository Text Structure

1. *Introduce an organizational pattern.*   The teacher explains the pattern and when writers use it, noting cue words that signal the pattern. Then the teacher shares an example of the pattern and describes the graphic organizer for that pattern.

2. *Analyze examples of the pattern in informational books, not in stories.*   Figure 7–5 lists books that illustrate each of the five expository text structures. Sometimes the pattern is signalled clearly by means of titles, topic sentences, and cue words, and sometimes it is not. Students learn to identify cue words, and they talk about why writers may or may not explicitly signal the structure. They also diagram the structure using a graphic organizer.

3. *Write paragraphs using the pattern.*   The first writing activity may be a whole-class activity; later, students can write paragraphs in small groups and individually. Students choose a topic, gather information, and organize it using a graphic organizer. Next they write a rough draft of the paragraph, inserting cue words to signal the structure. They revise, edit, and write a final copy of the paragraph. Then they share the paragraphs they have written and explain how they have used the particular organizational pattern in their writing.

4. *Repeat steps 1 to 3 for each pattern.*   The teacher repeats the first three steps in the teaching strategy to teach each of the five expository text structures.

5. *Choose the most appropriate pattern.*   After students have learned to use the five patterns, they need to learn to choose the most appropriate pattern to communicate effectively. Students can experiment to discover the appropriateness of various patterns by writing paragraphs about one set of information using different organizational patterns. For example, information about igloos might be written as a description, as a comparison to modern housing, or as an example of the use of local resources within a unique environment.

To read and learn from expository text, students need to

1. **Organize information before reading.** Students think about what they know, raise questions, and predict.
2. **Organize information while reading.** Students confirm or adjust predictions, relate new information to that known, and visualize concepts presented.
3. **Organize information after reading.** Students respond to text in an important way (e.g., mapping, writing) and perceive relationships with prior knowledge.
4. **Synthesize and articulate new learning.** Students arrive at new understandings and integrate new information with known, prepare for further learning.
5. **Learn vocabulary that labels important concepts, elements, and relationships.** Students identify new words and concepts and use them in meaningful ways.
6. **Produce or create something new and apply new information.** Students work through new ideas in writing; build or create something new; perform.

Figure 7–2 What Students Need to Do to Read and Learn from Expository Text
Source: Adapted from Ruddell (2001).

Teachers also teach students specific strategies to help them read expository text comprehensively, a skill especially important to upper-elementary and middle-school students who are expected to read and study independently with textbooks and other sources of informational text. Three strategies they teach are mapping, SQ4R (Survey, Question, Read, Recite, Review, Reflect), and ReQuest (Manzo, 1969). These strategies work well when students apply them to build their understandings of expository texts from content area or subject textbooks, or magazines for young readers such as *Pop*, or from informational websites such as *National Geographic* for Kids (**www.nationalgeographic.com/kids/index.html**) or CBC.ca/kids (**www.cbc.ca/kids**).

Mapping. Visual structures are powerful tools for comprehension instruction because they offer concrete, memorable representations of abstract thinking processes (Alvermann & Boothby, 1986; Calfee & Patrick, 1995; and Norton, 1992). Visual structures, sometimes referred to as *clusters*, *maps*, or *graphic organizers*, help students organize large amounts of textual information in ways that show relationships and connections among the ideas and concepts contained in the text. Each expository text structure lends itself to meaningful visual mapping as shown in Figure 7–1.

Students learn to construct maps through viewing examples, teacher modelling, and experimenting with creating maps. After presenting minilessons focused on students learning each text structure, teachers show students how to graphically represent text. As we'll see in Chapter 8, "Viewing and Visually Representing," software such as Inspiration can be used to create complex and sophisticated visual representations of information.

Concept maps are one of the most basic visual structures teachers show students how to construct. Concept maps are often used to help students understand concepts and ideas that are foundational to understanding extended selections of expository text or informational books.

SQ4R: Survey, Question, Read, Recite, Review, Reflect. Traditionally, teachers taught students SQ3R (Robinson, 1946), perhaps the oldest study strategy ever presented—Survey, Question, Read, Recite, Review. Currently, several derivatives of the strategy are popular in elementary and middle school classrooms. With increasing attention to reflection as a valid form of learning, it is popular to add the fourth *R—Reflect—*to the processing of text. We have also explored having *"Represent"* as the fourth *R*, but have no experimental data at this point to demonstrate its effect. Slavin (1997) changed the first step from *Survey* to *Preview* (PQ3R), but regardless of labels, all engage students in essentially the same systematic and thorough processing of text. Teaching students to use SQ4R, like teaching most strategies, requires time, modelling, and guided practice before students can be expected to use it independently. The SQ4R study strategy consists of the following steps:

1. *Survey.* The reader skims the text, seeking a general overview of content and message; reading headings and subheadings; and noting illustrations, charts, graphs, and other text features.
2. *Question.* The reader poses questions by converting headings and subheadings into questions.
3. *Read.* The reader reads the entire text to answer the questions posed.
4. *Recite.* The reader states answers to the questions either to self or a reading partner.
5. *Review.* The reader goes back over what has been learned, reading chapter summaries and rereading as necessary.
6. *Reflect.* The reader thinks about the reading, writes journal entries, or makes notes to clarify learning.

Students need step-by-step guidance to learn to effectively apply the strategy to their reading. Teachers provide this instruction through minilessons concerning each step, then follow the lessons with opportunities for practice. Only after practice can students be expected to use the strategy independently.

ReQuest. ReQuest (Manzo, 1969) is a strategy intended to increase students' understanding of text through shared or reciprocal questioning between student and teacher. Reciprocal questioning is based on the idea that learning to answer good questions benefits reading comprehension, and that if students repeatedly hear teachers asking good questions, they in turn will follow the modelling and ask good questions about text. ReQuest is used in one-to-one situations and in working with groups, both large and small. The ReQuest strategy consists of the steps shown in the following Step by Step box:

Step by Step

ReQuest Strategy

1. *Read and ask questions.* The teacher and students silently read a selection of text. After reading, the teacher closes the book and the students are invited to ask as many questions as they wish. The teacher answers all questions as completely as possible.

2. *Ask follow-up questions* The students close books and the teacher asks questions that follow up on questions asked by the students, raising new issues, and/or calling attention to important information in the text.

3. *Read further and ask more questions.* A new selection of text is read silently and the questioning by students and teacher continues. The teacher's questions require the students to integrate information from one selection of text to another and to see relationships among the points of information in each selection. For example, when the text concerns the loss of natural resources, the teacher might ask, "In the last paragraph, we read that cod stocks are diminishing because of over fishing. What effects do you think this might have on the employment in the coastal provinces?"

4. *Predict and set the purpose for more reading.* The reciprocal questioning continues until a point in the text where students can reasonably predict the rest of the information or can see how they can continue independently reading the rest of the text and complete any assigned follow-through activities. In other words, the questioning continues until students can set a clear purpose for finishing the reading. The teacher helps students frame that purpose by asking them to form a question they can only answer by reading the rest of the text. Purpose-setting questions often begin with, "On the basis of what we have read so far . . ."

5. *Have students write and finish reading.* Students write the purpose-setting question and finish the reading.

6. *Respond and discuss.* Teacher–student questioning and discussion continues after the teacher asks the purpose-setting question. If the purpose-setting question cannot be answered from the text, then it is considered to be an imperfect question. That is, the students' prediction about the rest of the text was flawed. The teacher then guides the students to compose another question that the text does answer. This leads to further discussion about the content of the text.

    Teachers ask questions at three levels of comprehension—literal, interpretive, and applied. They ask questions to which the answer is easily found in the text, questions that require making connections across the text, questions that require connections to the students' prior knowledge, questions to which there is no one right answer but that are worth thinking about, and questions that ask students to interpret information.

ReQuest is a powerful strategy, one that students can learn relatively easily, but it does require practice over time to ensure that the questions asked by both teacher and students lead to clear, in-depth understandings and perceptions. And, as noted in earlier discussion of sustaining talk in classrooms, reciprocal questioning requires both teacher and students to listen attentively.

READING CONTENT-AREA TEXTBOOKS

Content-area textbooks are often used as the primary print resource in social studies or science. Although the quality of textbooks available for use in Canadian classrooms is generally high, typically they survey topics; other instructional materials are needed to provide depth and understanding. Students need to read, write, and discuss topics. It is most effective to use the reading process and then extend students' learning with projects. Developing thematic units or inquiry-based units and using content-area textbooks as one resource is recommended. There are a variety of excellent nonfiction books available to support the teaching of curriculum topics. Examples include *If the World Were a Village* (Smith & Armstrong, 2002), which provides a picture of the world as if it were a global village of one hundred people, and *Marconi's Secret* (Browne & D'Souza, 2001), which tells the story of Guglielmo Marconi's reception of the first transatlantic radio signal at Signal Hill in St. John's, Newfoundland and Labrador.

USING CONTENT-AREA TEXTBOOKS

Content-area textbooks are often difficult for students to read—more difficult, in fact, than many informational books. One reason textbooks are difficult is that they briefly mention many topics without developing any of them. A second reason is that content-area textbooks, like all expository text, are read differently from stories. Teachers need to show students how to approach content-area textbooks and teach students how to use specific expository text reading strategies and procedures to make comprehension easier. The Teacher's Notebook on page 292 presents guidelines for using content-area textbooks.

Teachers can make content-area textbooks more readable and show students ways to remember what they have read. Some activities are used before reading and others after reading. The before-reading activities are used to help students activate prior knowledge, set purposes for reading, or build background knowledge. The after-reading activities help students identify and remember main ideas and details. Other activities are used when students want to locate specific information. Seven activities to make content-area textbooks more readable are

1. *Previewing.* Teachers introduce the reading assignment by asking students to note main headings in the chapter and then skim or rapidly read the chapter to get a general idea about the topics covered in the reading assignment.

2. *Prereading plan (PReP).* Teachers introduce a key concept discussed in the reading assignment and ask students to brainstorm words and ideas related to the concept before reading (Langer, 1981).

3. *Anticipation guides.* Teachers present a set of statements on the topic to be read. Students agree or disagree with each statement and then read the assignment to see if they were right (Head & Readence, 1986).

4. *Exclusion brainstorming.* Teachers distribute a list of words, most of which are related to the key concepts to be presented in the reading assignment. Teachers ask students to circle the words that are related to a key concept and then read the assignment to see if they circled the right words (Johns, Van Leirsburg, & Davis, 1994).

5. *Clusters.* Teachers distribute a cluster, map, or other graphic organizer with main ideas marked. Students complete the graphic organizer by adding details after reading each section.

6. *Note-taking.* Students develop an outline by writing the headers and then take notes after reading each section.

7. *Scanning.* Students reread quickly to locate specific information.

No longer are content-area texts viewed as the only source for learning, but they continue to be useful tools for learning across the curriculum and are available in most classrooms. Tierney and Pearson (1992) recommend that teachers shift from teaching *from* textbooks to teaching *with* textbooks and include other types of reading materials and other types of activities in their instructional programs.

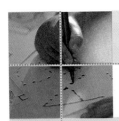

Teacher's Notebook

Guidelines for Using Content-Area Textbooks

1. Use Comprehension Aids
The teacher teaches students how to use the comprehension aids in content-area textbooks, including chapter overviews; headings that outline the chapter; helpful graphics such as maps, charts, tables, graphs, diagrams, photos, and drawings; technical words defined in the text; end-of-chapter summaries; and review questions.

2. Have Students Revise Section Headings to Questions
The teacher divides the reading of a chapter into sections. Before reading each section, students turn the section heading into a question and read to find the answer to the question. As they read, students take notes about the section and then answer the question they created using the section heading after reading.

3. Teach Expository Text Structures
The teacher teaches students about expository text structures and assists students in identifying the patterns used in the reading assignment, especially cause and effect or problem and solution, before reading.

4. Introduce Vocabulary
The teacher introduces only the key terms as part of an introductory presentation or discussion before students read the textbook assignment. The teacher presents other vocabulary during reading, if needed, and after reading, develops a word wall with important words.

5. Focus on Key Concepts
The teacher has students focus on key concepts or the big ideas instead of having students try to remember all the facts or details.

6. Use Content-Area Reading Techniques
The teacher uses content-area reading techniques, such as PReP, exclusion brainstorming, or anticipation guides, to help students identify and remember main ideas and details after reading.

7. Encourage Students to Use Headings
The teacher encourages students to use headings and subheadings to select and organize relevant information. Headings can be used to create a semantic map, and students add details as they read.

8. Apply the Listen–Read–Discuss Format
First, the teacher presents the key concepts orally, and then students read and discuss the chapter. Or, the teacher has students read the chapter as a review activity rather than as the introductory activity.

READING AND WRITING HYPERTEXT—A SPECIAL FORM OF EXPOSITORY TEXT

Students read from many sources, not just books. Their reading from such sources as CD-ROMs and the Internet requires that they be able to process text that is not linear. In other words, linear text is essentially structured with a definitive beginning and ending with identifiable structure and order of information (see Figure 7–1) between the beginning and ending. Hypertext, on the other hand, is not linear and not sequential. *Hypertext* comprises any nonlinear text that provides readers with options to explore links among individual segments of text (Reinking, 1997). *Hypermedia* is a broader term used to describe hypertext that includes visual and audio components. Readers of hypertext and hypermedia must make decisions regarding the order in which they read and the connections they form among pieces of information presented. Reinking describes the reading of hypertext as being a process of many digressions. He suggests that reading hypertext, whether on CD-ROM or the Internet, is like looking up one topic in an encyclopedia and, while looking, digressing to read other related and sometimes marginally related topics. It could be said that readers become authors in that they decide which links to follow and thus they shape or create the text that they read.

Imagine two grade 6 students beginning to research the rain forest from a well-constructed website. Together they read the introduction and then must make a choice. They can "click here" to learn about the animals of the rain forest or "click here" to learn more about the overarching canopy and lower structures of trees and plants. They choose to read about the animals and click to take them to that webpage. They are anxious to solve their curiosity concerning the preying nature of the jaguar. Within minutes they are attempting to print the picture of the sleek beast, thinking that it will make an attractive cover for their report.

Scenarios such as this are common. The plethora of information available in highly attractive formats—print and digital—can be highly motivational and engaging for students, but can also be confusing and somewhat overwhelming if they are not able to systematically process the text. Teachers need to guide students' reading and help them develop the strategies required to follow a variety of texts.

For more information on new literacies, see Chapter 1, "Learning and the Language Arts," pages 14–25.

Given the great diversity of written material available, reading comprehension is by nature so sophisticated that no single teaching strategy is sufficient for all readers with all texts in all learning situations (Snow, Burns, & Griffin, 1998). The teaching strategies previously described in this chapter and elsewhere in this text are not only applicable to traditional print, but also to hypertext and hypermedia. However, teaching students how to read hypertext and hypermedia requires that the nature of electronic text be considered. Karchmer (2001) points out four characteristics of electronic text:

1. **It is interactive and malleable.** Reading material on the computer can be manipulated and modified through such things as adding pronunciations, graphing, and video.

2. **It seamlessly incorporates audiovisual features.** Graphics are integral within an electronic environment, whereas they are considered supplementary in traditional printed text.

3. **It makes it possible to access multiple related resources.** Through electronic links, authors can make relevant supplementary information easily available to readers.

4. **It is not linear.** Readers have a more active role in the navigation of electronic text than in traditional text.

Two strategies considerate of electronic text we have seen students use effectively are graphic organizers and study guides. Graphic organizers may follow the expository text structures shown in Figure 7–1 or may take the form of data charts as illustrated in Figure 7–3. Data charts help students organize information from various sections of one website or from multiple sources.

Study guides are a way for teachers to guide students through the reading of a particular text—traditional print or electronic. They help students identify important information (key concepts and

Name	Appearance	Size	Where It Grows	Flower Family
Buttercup	• Five yellow waxy petals • Long thin green stems	30–40 cm tall	Fields and roadside ditches	Buttercup
Dog-toothed Violet (or Glacier Lily)	• Yellow flowers on green stems • Each flower has six petals and six stamens • Two long green leaves	15–30 cm tall	Alpine meadows	Lily
Mountain spirea	• Dense, flat-topped deep pink flower clusters • Leaves are oval; stems are light brown	50–90 cm tall	Wet meadows and boggy ground	Rose
Indian Paintbrush	• Narrow, tubular flowers with many little petals like a brush—pink, red, orange; rarely yellow or white	10–60 cm tall	Well-drained areas and rocky slopes	Figwort

Figure 7–3 Data Chart on Canadian Wildflowers

supporting details) and focus on the content that the teacher considers essential to their learning and meeting curricular objectives. See Figure 7–4 for a sample study guide for a reading from the Internet. The steps in preparing and using study guides are presented in the following Step by Step box:

Step by Step

Preparing and Using Study Guides

1. *Select the text to be read.*   If text is on the Internet, the teacher bookmarks it for easy access by students.

2. *Identify the purpose or purposes for the reading.*   The teacher states, in simple terms, the objectives of the students' reading.

3. *Identify the most crucial information to student understanding.*   The teacher points out to students the key concepts about which they will be reading.

4. *Develop questions to guide students through the text.*   The teacher identifies the segments of text where students can find answers to the questions. If necessary, the teacher indicates which links to follow. Question format can be extended to include having students make note of particular information. For example, students might be asked to list information or draw and label a diagram to show information read.

5. *Have students complete the study guide as they read.*   The teacher provides space in the study guide for students to include questions that arise as they seek answers to the questions provided.

6. *Discuss students' answers in large or small groups.*   If disputes over students' interpretation of the text arise, the teacher clarifies the information so that students are left with accurate notes for future reference.

Structure of the Government of Canada
http://Canada.gc.ca/howgoc/glance_e.html

Purpose for Reading
The purpose for your reading is to learn about the Government of Canada and its structure. Also, read any aspect of the site you think appropriate to answer the challenge questions. By answering them, you will learn about other important and interesting facts releated to the Government of Canada.

Go to **http://Canada.gc.ca/howgoc/glance_e.html**
Scroll down to About Government and click
Click on Structure of the Government of Canada
Click on Governors General Since Confederation

1. During what years was the first Governor General appointed?
2. What was his name?
3. Describe an interesting fact about the Right Honourable Jeanne Mathilde Sauvé.

Go back to the first page. (Use the Back button to go back one page.)
Scroll down to The Prime Minister and click.

1. Find six (6) interesting facts about the Prime Minister of Canada.

Go back to the main page. (Use the Back button to go back two pages.)
Click on About Government
Click on Provincial and Territorial Governments.

1. Find your province or territory.
2. Draw and colour its flag.

Fill in the chart:

Flag	Name the capital city.

Challenge Questions

1. If our class went to Rideau Hall, whose home would we be visiting?
2. What would we see in the home?

Figure 7–4 A Study Guide for a Reading from the Internet

Students also write hypertext and hypermedia texts. Increasingly, classrooms are equipped to support students' creation of the kinds of texts they experience on CD-ROMs and the Internet. Teachers facilitate their hypertext writing in at least two ways. They provide them with models and the opportunity to discover the characteristics of the models through such activities as discussion of the decisions authors make about how to present their texts—print, visual, and audio—singularly or in combination. Teachers also make time and equipment available during each stage of the writing process for students to compose electronic texts. Students we recently observed were deeply involved in producing an animated, interactive retelling of Clement Moore's "The Night Before Christmas." Their work was complete with their drawings and digital photos to let readers know "to their wondering eyes did appear . . . a shiny SUV loaded with hockey gear"! The interactive and nonlinear characteristics of hypertext and hypermedia extend the ways in which meaning can be made and thought represented (Hammerberg, 2001). Whether students are writing independently or collaboratively, they benefit from the opportunities teachers provide them to take writing beyond the limitations of traditional print.

ASSESSING STUDENTS' USE OF EXPOSITORY TEXT STRUCTURES

Teachers can assess how students use expository text structures to comprehend as they read and listen to informational books read aloud. Students should learn to recognize the structural patterns and use graphic organizers to classify information, take notes, and generalize main ideas. Teachers can monitor students as they participate in discussions about informational books and review students' learning log entries during thematic units to assess their understanding of key concepts and their use of graphic organizers.

Teachers can also assess how well students organize information when they write paragraphs, reports, and other across-the-curriculum pieces. When students write to present information, they

- Choose the most appropriate structure
- Develop a graphic organizer before writing
- Write a topic sentence that identifies the structure
- Use cue words to signal the structure

These four components can be used to develop a checklist or rubric to assess students' use of expository text structures.

Description

Beattie, O., Geiger, J., & Tanaka, S. (1992). *Buried in Ice*. Toronto: Madison Press Books. (M–U) 🍁

Dixon, N. (1995). *Kites*. Toronto: Kids Can Press. (P–M) 🍁

Hoyt, E. (1991). *Meeting the Whales*. Camden East: Camden House. (M–U)

Jenkins, S. (2005). *Prehistoric Actual Size*. New York: Houghton Mifflin. (P) 🍁

Kaner, E. (1995). *Towers and Tunnels*. Toronto: Kids Can Press. (M–U) 🍁

Lawrence, R. D. (1990). *Wolves*. Toronto: Key Porter. (U) 🍁

Scowen, K. (2006). *My Kind of Sad: What It's Like to Be Young and Depressed*. Toronto: Annick Press. (U) 🍁

Szpirglas, J. (2005). *They Did What?! Your Guide to Weird & Wacky Things People Do*. Vancouver: Maple Tree Press. (M–U) 🍁

Tanaka, S. (1996). *I Was There: On Board the Titanic*. Ill. K. Marshall. Toronto: Scholastic. (M–U) 🍁

Sequence

The Making-a-Book Activity Book. Based on the 1988 Vancouver Art Gallery exhibition, "Once upon a time" sponsored by Placer Dome Inc., Vancouver: Douglas & McIntyre Ltd. (M–U) 🍁

Bateman, R. (2005). *Backyard Birds: An Introduction*. Toronto: Scholastic Canada/Madison Press. (P–M) 🍁

Reid, B. (1991). *Zoe's Rainy Day*. Toronto: HarperCollins Publishers. (P) 🍁

Reid, B. (1991). *Zoe's Snowy Day*. Toronto: HarperCollins Publishers. (P) 🍁

Reid, B. (1991). *Zoe's Sunny Day*. Toronto: HarperCollins Publishers. (P) 🍁

Reid, B. (1991). *Zoe's Windy Day*. Toronto: HarperCollins Publishers. (P) 🍁

Steltzer, U. (1995). *Building an Igloo*. New York: Holt. (P–M)

Zimmermann, H. (1990). *Alphonse Knows—The Colour of Spring*. Toronto: Oxford University Press. (P) 🍁

(continued)

Figure 7–5 Informational Books Representing the Expository Text Structures

Comparison

Barretta, G. (2006). *Now & Ben: The Modern Inventions of Benjamin Franklin*. New York: Holt. (P)

Chaconas, D. (2006). *Cord & Fuzz: Short and Tall*. New York: Viking. (P)

Markle, S. (1993). *Outside and Inside Trees*. New York: Bradbury Press. (M)

Rauzon, M. J. (1993). *Horns, Antlers, Fangs, and Tusks*. New York: Lothrop, Lee & Shepard. (P–M)

Sewall, M. (1995). *Thunder from the Clear Sky*. New York: Atheneum. (M–U)

Singer, M. (1995). *A Wasp Is Not a Bee*. New York: Holt. (P)

Cause and Effect

Andrews, W. (1994). *Protecting the Ozone Layer*. Toronto: Health Canada Ltd. (M–U)

Andrews, W. (1995). *Understanding Global Warming*. Toronto: Health Canada Ltd. (M–U)

Bourgeois, P. (1987). *The Amazing Apple Book*. Toronto: Kids Can Press. (P–M)

Casey, D. (1995). *Weather Everywhere*. New York: Macmillan. (P)

Dixon, N. (1995). *Kites*. Toronto: Kids Can Press. (M)

Farris, K. (Ed.). (1993). *The New Kids' Question and Answer Book*. Toronto: Greey de Pencier. (M)

Golick, M. (1995). *Wacky Word Games*. Markham: Pembroke Publishers. (M–U)

Gryski, C. (1993). *Boondoggle: Making Bracelets with Plastic Lace*. Toronto: Kids Can Press. (M)

Gryski, C. (1995). *Favourite String Games*. Toronto: Kids Can Press. (M)

Lauber, P. (1995). *Who Eats What? Food Chains and Food Webs*. New York: HarperCollins. (M)

Souza, D. M. (1994). *Northern Lights*. Minneapolis: Carolrhoda.

Suzuki, D. (1988). *Looking at Weather*. Toronto: Stoddart. (M–U)

Zoehfeld, K. W. (1995). *How Mountains Are Made*. New York: HarperCollins. (M)

Problem and Solution

Arnosky, J. (1995). *I See Animals Hiding*. New York: Scholastic. (P)

Bourgeois, P. (1990). *The Amazing Dirt Book*. Toronto: Kids Can Press. (P)

Geisert, B. (1995). *Haystack*. Boston: Houghton Mifflin. (P)

Hickman, P. (1985). *Bugwise*. Toronto: Kids Can Press. (P–M)

Johnson, S. A. (1995). *Raptor Rescue! An Eagle Flies Free*. New York: Dutton. (M)

Lauber, P. (1990). *How We Learned the Earth Is Round*. New York: Crowell. (P–M)

Mackay, C. (1987). *Pay Cheques and Picket Lines: All about Unions in Canada*. Illus. by Eric Parker. Toronto: Kids Can Press. (U)

Savan, B. (1991). *Earthcycles and Ecosystems*. Toronto: Kids Can Press. (M–U)

Things to Do

Badone, D. (1992). *Time Detectives: Clues from Our Past*. Willowdale: Annick Press. (M–U)

Coombs, E., & Tanaka, S. (1991). *Mr. Dressup's Things to Make and Do*. Toronto: Stoddart. (P–M)

Irvine, J. (1992). *How to Make Super Pop-ups*. Ill. by Linda Hendry. Toronto: Kids Can Press. (M)

Jenkins, P. (1991). *Flip Book Animation: And Other Ways to Make Cartoons Move*. Toronto: Kids Can Press. (M–U)

Kaner, E. (1995). *Towers and Tunnels*. Toronto: Kids Can Press. (M)

Schendlinger, M. (2005). *Prepare to be Amazed: The Geniuses of Modern Magic*. Toronto: Annick Press. (M–U)

Thurman, M. (1992). *Fun-tastic Collages*. Markham: Pembroke Publishers. (M)

Figure 7–5 Informational Books Representing the Expository Text Structures (*continued*)

Reports

Students in the elementary grades—even in the primary grades—write both class collaborative and individual reports (Duthie, 1994; Krogness, 1987; Queenan, 1986). Early, successful experiences with informative writing teach students about content-area topics as well as how to interview, collect data, and write reports. Not only do primary and elementary students write traditional text-based reports, but also they transform their reports into multimedia presentations, demonstrating clearly that there is no need to delay the writing of expository text until upper grades.

YOUNG CHILDREN'S REPORTS

Contrary to the popular assumption that young children's first writing is narrative, educators have found that kindergartners and first graders write many non-narrative compositions in which they provide information about familiar topics, including "Signs of Fall," or directions for familiar activities, such as "How to Feed Your Pet" (Bonin, 1988; Sowers, 1985). Many of these writings might be termed "All about . . ." books, and others are informational pieces that children dictate for the teacher to record. These two types introduce young children to informational writing.

In young children's "All about . . ." books, they write an entire booklet on a single topic. Usually one piece of information and an illustration appear on each page. A second grader wrote an "All about . . ." book called *Snowy Thoughts*, shown in Figure 7–6. It was written as part of a theme on the four seasons. Even though the student omitted some capital letters and punctuation marks and used invented spelling for a few words in his book, the information can be easily deciphered.

Figure 7–6 A Grade 2 Student's "All about . . ." Book

Young children can dictate reports to their teacher, who serves as scribe to record them. After listening to a guest speaker, viewing a film, or reading several books about a particular topic, kindergartners and first graders can dictate brief reports. A class of kindergartners compiled this book-length report on police officers:

Page 1: *Police officers help people who are in trouble. They are nice to kids. They are only mean to robbers and bad people. Police officers make people obey the laws. They give tickets to people who drive cars too fast.*

Page 2: *Men and women can be police officers. They wear blue uniforms like Officer Jerry's. But sometimes police officers wear regular clothes when they work undercover. They wear badges on their uniforms and on their hats. Officer Jerry's badge number is 3407. Police officers have guns, handcuffs, whistles, sticks, and two-way radios. They have to carry all these things.*

Page 3: *Police officers drive police cars with flashing lights and loud sirens. The cars have radios so the officers can talk to other police officers at the police station. Sometimes they ride on police motorcycles or on police horses or in police helicopters or in police boats.*

Page 4: *Police officers work at police stations. The jail for the bad people that they catch is right next door. One police officer sits at the radio to talk to the police officers who are driving their cars. The police chief works at the police station, too.*

Page 5: *Police officers are your friends. They want to help you so you shouldn't be afraid of them. You can ask them if you need some help.*

Page 6: *How We Learned about Police Officers for Our Report 1. We read this book: Bourgeois, Paulette (1992). Canadian Police Officers. Illustrated by Kim LaFave. Toronto: Kids Can Press. 2. We interviewed Officer Jerry. 3. We visited the police station.*

The teacher read two books aloud to the students, and Officer Jerry visited the classroom and talked to the students about his job. The students also took a field trip to the police station. The teacher took photos of Officer Jerry, his police car, and the police station to illustrate the report. With this background, the students and the teacher together developed a cluster with these five main ideas: what police officers do, what equipment police officers have, how police officers travel, where police officers work, and police officers are your friends. The students added details to the five main ideas until each one developed into one page of the report. The background of experiences and the clustering activity prepared students to compose their report. After students completed the report, included a bibliography called "How We Learned about Police Officers for Our Report," and inserted the photographs, it was ceremoniously presented to the school library to be enjoyed by all students.

COLLABORATIVE REPORTS

A successful first report-writing experience for middle- and upper-grade students is a class collaboration research report. Small groups of students work together to write sections of the report, which are then compiled. Students benefit from writing a group report in two ways: first, they learn the steps in writing a research report—with the group as a scaffold or support system—before tackling individual reports; and second, working in groups lets them share the laborious parts of the work.

A quartet of grade 4 students wrote a collaborative report on hermit crabs. The students sat together at one table and watched hermit crabs in a terrarium. They cared for the crustaceans for two weeks and made notes of their observations in learning logs. After this period, the students were bursting with questions about the hermit crabs and eager for answers. They wanted to know about the crabs' natural habitat, what the best habitat was for them in the classroom, how they breathed air, why they lived in "borrowed" shells, why one pincer was bigger than the other, and so on. Their teacher provided some answers and directed them to books that would provide additional information. As they collected information, they created a cluster that they taped to the table next to the terrarium. The cluster became inadequate for reporting information, so they decided to share their knowledge by writing a book entitled

The Encyclopedia about Hermit Crabs. Chapters from this book and the cluster used in gathering the information appear in Figure 7–7. The students decided to share the work of writing the book, and they chose four main ideas, one for each participant to write: what hermit crabs look

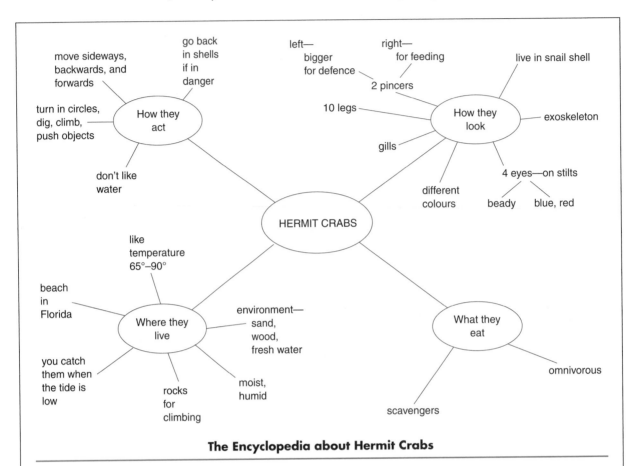

The Encyclopedia about Hermit Crabs

How They Look
Hermit crabs are very much like regular crabs but hermit crabs transfer shells. They have gills. Why? Because they are born in water and when they mature they come to land and kill snails so they can have a shell. They have two beady eyes that look like they are on stilts. Their body is a sight! Their shell looks like a rock. Really it is an exoskeleton which means the skeleton is on the outside. They have two pincers. The left one is bigger so it is used for defence. The right one is for feeding. They also have ten legs.

Where They Live
Hermit crabs live mostly on beaches in Florida where the weather is 65°–90°. They live in fresh water. They like humid weather and places that have sand, wood, and rocks (for climbing on). The best time to catch hermit crabs is a low tide.

What They Eat
Hermit crabs are omnivorous scavengers which means they eat just about anything. They even eat leftovers.

How They Act
Hermit crabs are very unusual. They go back into their shell if they think there is danger. They are funny because they walk sideways, forwards, and backwards. They can go in circles. They can also get up when they get upside down. And that's how they act.

Figure 7–7 Grade 4 Students' Cluster and Collaborative Report on Hermit Crabs

like, how they act, where they really live, and what they eat. A different student wrote each section and they then returned to the group to share their respective rough drafts. The students gave each other suggestions and made revisions based on the discussion. Next, they edited their report with the teacher and added an introduction, a conclusion, and a bibliography. Finally, they recopied their report and added illustrations in a cloth-bound book, which they read to each class in the school before adding it to the school library.

Students can organize reports in a variety of formats—formats they see used in informational books. One possibility is a Q&A format; another possibility is an alphabet book. A group of fourth-grade students wrote an alphabet book about filmmaking with one page for each letter of the alphabet. The "A" page appears in Figure 7–8.

INDIVIDUAL REPORTS

Toby Fulwiler (1985) recommends that students do "authentic" research in which they explore topics that interest them or hunt for answers to questions that puzzle them. When students become immersed in content-area study, questions arise that they want to explore. A grade 4 class

Figure 7–8 Grade 4 Students' "A" Page from an Alphabet Book on Filmmaking

How to Recognize an Egret!

An egret is a bird with white feathers. Some egrets have black and red feathers but the egrets around Marysville are white. They have very long necks and long beaks because they stick their heads under water to catch fish. An egret can be from 20 to 41 inches tall. When they are just standing, they look like in the picture but when they are flying their wing span can stretch to one-and-a-half feet.

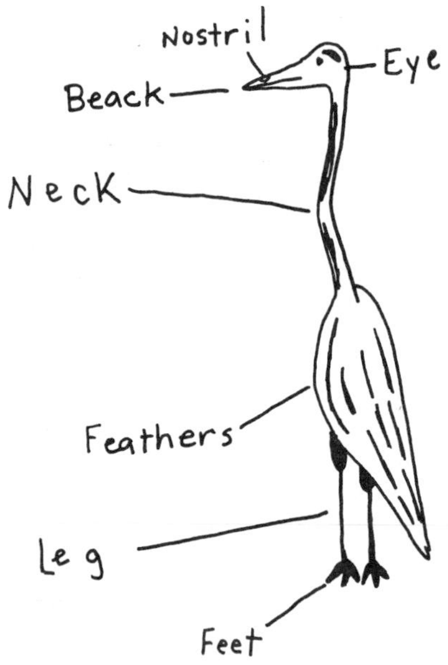

Nostril
Beack
Eye
Neck
Feathers
Leg
Feet

Figure 7–9 An Excerpt from a Grade 4 Student's Report on Egrets

began a unit on birds by brainstorming questions they wanted to answer. The teacher encouraged them to search for answers in the books they had checked out of the school and community libraries, and during an interview with an ornithologist from the local zoo. Once they learned the answers to their questions, the students were eager to share their new knowledge and decided to write reports and publish them as books.

Each student's book had a table of contents, four or five chapters, a glossary, a bibliography, and an index. An excerpt from one fourth-grader's book on egrets is presented in Figure 7–9. The text was word-processed, and then the student added the illustrations.

TEACHING STUDENTS TO WRITE REPORTS

Students learn how to write reports through experience. As they write "All about . . ." books and collaborative reports, they learn how to search for answers to questions about a topic and then compose a report to share what they have learned. Designing questions and gathering information comprise the prewriting stage; then students draft, polish, and make final copies of their reports. Teachers also present minilessons on procedures, concepts, and strategies and skills related to report writing.

Writing Class Collaboration Reports. To apply the process approach in writing class collaboration reports, students follow six steps, as laid out in the accompanying Step by Step box.

Writing Individual Reports. Writing an individual report is similar to writing a class collaborative report. Students continue to devise research questions, gather information to answer the questions, and compile what they have learned in a report. However, writing individually

Step by Step

Writing Class Collaborative Reports

1. *Choose a topic.* The first step is to choose a topic, which should be something students are studying or want to study. Almost any social studies, science, or current events topic that can be subdivided into four to ten parts works well for class collaboration reports. Usually, general topics, such as the human body, the solar system, or the Middle Ages, come from the program of studies or curriculum. From the general topic, students choose specific topics for small groups or pairs of students to research. For some topics, students may not be able to identify the specific topic they will research until they have learned more and designed research questions. This is especially true of upper-elementary and middle-grade students when relatively sophisticated study of topics is required.

2. *Design research questions.* Research questions emerge as students study a topic. Students brainstorm a list of questions on a chart posted in the classroom, and they add to the list as other questions arise. If they are planning a report on the human body, for example, the small groups that are studying each organ may decide to research the same three, four, or five questions: What does the organ look like? What job does the organ do? Where is the organ located in the human body? Students studying a theme such as the Middle Ages might brainstorm the following questions about life in that era: What did the people wear? What did they eat? What were their communities like? What kind of entertainment did people enjoy? What were their occupations? How did people protect themselves? What kinds of transportation did they use? Each small group selects one of the questions as the specific topic for its report and chooses questions related to the specific topic.

To provide a rehearsal before students research and write their section of the report, the teacher and students may work through the procedure using a research question that no one chose. Together as a class, students gather information, organize it, and write the section of the report using the drafting, revising, and editing stages of the writing process.

3. *Gather and organize information.* Students work in small groups or in pairs to search for answers to their research questions. The questions provide the structure for data collection, because students are seeking answers to specific questions, not just randomly writing down information. Students can use clusters or data charts to record the information they gather. The research questions are the same for each data-collection instrument. On a cluster, students add information as details to each main-idea ray; if they are working with data charts, they record information from the first source in the first row under the appropriate question, from the second source in the second row, and so on. These two instruments are effective because they organize the data collection question by question and limit the amount of information that can be gathered from any one source. Students list their sources of information for clusters and data charts on the back of the paper.

Students gather information from a variety of reference materials, including trade books, textbooks, encyclopedias, magazines, films, videos, filmstrips, CD-ROMs, the Internet, field trips, interviews, demonstrations, and observations. Teachers often require that students consult two or three different sources and that no more than one source be an encyclopedia.

Traditionally, report writing was equated with copying facts out of an encyclopedia, but with the multiplicity of information sources available in most schools, source options have been greatly expanded. Students, even young ones, need to learn respect for sources and to understand what plagiarism is and why it is wrong. Primary-grade students realize they should not "borrow" items belonging to classmates and pretend the items are theirs. Similarly, students should not "borrow" someone else's words, especially without giving credit in the composition. The format of clusters and data charts makes it easier for students to take notes without plagiarizing.

After students gather information, they read it over to check that they have answered their research questions fully and to delete unnecessary or redundant information. Next, they consider how they will sequence the information in their rough drafts. Some students tentatively number the research questions in the order they plan to list them in their composition. They also identify a piece of information that is especially interesting to use as the lead-in to the section.

4. *Draft the sections of the report.*   Students write their report sections using the process approach to writing. They write the rough draft, skipping every other line to allow space for revising and editing. Because students are working in pairs or in small groups, one student can be the scribe to write the draft while the other student or students in the group dictate the sentences, using information from a cluster or a data chart. Next, they share their draft with students from other small groups and revise it on the basis of feedback they receive. Last, students proofread and correct mechanical errors.

5. *Compile the sections.*   Students compile their completed sections of the research report and, as a class, write the introduction, conclusion, and bibliography to add to the report. A list at the end of the report should identify the authors of each section. After all the parts are compiled, students read the entire report aloud to catch inconsistencies or redundant passages.

6. *Publish the report.*   The last step in writing a class collaboration research report is to publish it. A final copy is made with all the parts of the report in the correct sequence. If the report has been written on a computer, it is easy to print out the final copy; otherwise, the report can be typed or recopied by hand. Copies are made for each student, and special bound copies can be constructed for the class or school library.

demands two significant changes: first, students narrow their topics, and second, they assume the entire responsibility for writing the report. The steps in writing individual reports are described in the following Step by Step box:

Step by Step

Writing Individual Reports

1. *Choose and narrow a topic.*   Students choose topics for research reports from a content area, hobbies, or other interests. After choosing a general topic, such as cats or the human body, they need to narrow the topic so that it is manageable. The broad topic of cats might be narrowed to pet cats or tigers, and the human body to one organ or system.

2. *Design research questions.*   Students design research questions by brainstorming a list of questions in a learning log. They review the list, combine some questions, delete others, and finally arrive at four to six questions that are worthy of answering. When they begin their research, they may add new questions and delete others if they reach a dead end.

3. **Gather and organize information.** As in collaborative reports, students use clusters or data charts to gather and organize information. Data charts, with their rectangular spaces for writing information, serve as a transition for upper-grade students between clusters and note cards.

4. **Draft the report.** Students write a rough draft from the information they have gathered. Each research question can become a paragraph, section, or chapter in the report.

5. **Revise and edit the report.** Students meet in writers groups to share their rough drafts, and then they make revisions based on the feedback they receive from their classmates. After they revise, students use an editing checklist to proofread their reports and identify and correct mechanical errors.

6. **Publish the report.** Students recopy their reports in books and add bibliographic information. Research reports can also be published in several other ways—for example, as a filmstrip or video presentation, as a series of illustrated charts or dioramas, as a PowerPoint presentation, or as a dramatization.

ASSESSING STUDENTS' REPORTS

Students need to know the requirements for the research project and how they will be assessed or graded. Many teachers distribute a checklist of requirements for the project before students begin working so that the students know what is expected of them and can assume responsibility for completing each step of the assignment. The checklist for an individual report might include these observation behaviours and products:

- Choose a narrow topic.
- Identify four or five research questions.
- Use a cluster to gather information to answer the questions.
- Write a rough draft with a section or a chapter to answer each question.
- Meet in writers groups to share your report.
- Make at least three changes in your rough draft.
- Complete an editing checklist with a partner.
- Add a bibliography.
- Write the final copy of the report.
- Share the report with someone.

The checklist can be simpler or more complex depending on a student's age and experiences. Students staple the checklist to the inside cover of the folder in which they keep all the work for the project, and they check off each requirement as they complete it. A checklist enables students to monitor their own work and learn that writing is an involved process, not just a final product. It also helps teachers assess students' progress as the work continues.

After completing the project, students submit their folders to the teacher for assessment. The teacher considers all the requirements on the checklist in determining a student's grade. If the checklist has 10 requirements, each requirement might be worth 10 points, and the grading can be done objectively on a 100-point scale. Thus, if the student's project is complete and meets all criteria, the student scores 100, or a grade of A.

Letters

Letters are a way of talking to people who live too far away to visit. While much communication, both personal and business, is now conducted electronically, elementary and middle-school students benefit from knowing letter conventions. Audience and purpose are important considerations, but form is also important in letter writing. Although letters may be personal, they involve a genuine audience of one or more persons. Students have the opportunity not only to sharpen their writing skills through letter writing but also to increase their awareness of audience. Because letters are written to communicate with a specific and important audience, students take more care to think through what they want to say, to write legibly, and to use spelling, capitalization, and punctuation correctly.

Letters are typically classified as friendly or business letters. Formats for friendly and business letters are shown in the accompanying Teacher's Notebook. The choice of format depends on the purpose of the letter. Friendly letters might be informal, chatty letters to pen pals or thank-you notes to a parent volunteer who has assisted in the classroom. When students write to Parks Canada requesting information about the Waterton Lakes National Park or another park or send letters to the prime minister expressing an opinion about current events, they use the more formal, business letter–style. Before students write both types of letters, they need to learn how to format them.

Friendly and business letter formats are accepted writing conventions, and most teachers simply explain the formats to students and prepare a set of charts to illustrate them. Attention to format should not suggest, however, that form is more important than content; rather, it should highlight formatting considerations of letter writing that elementary students are typically unfamiliar with.

FRIENDLY LETTERS

After teachers have introduced the format for friendly letters, students need to choose a "real" someone to write to. Writing authentic letters that will be delivered is much more valuable than writing practice letters to be graded by the teacher. One way of facilitating friendly letter writing is through pen pals. Remember that receiving letters is the reward for writing!

Pen Pal Letters. Teachers can arrange for their students to exchange letters with students in another class by contacting a teacher in a nearby school or local educational associations, by answering advertisements in educational magazines, or by making connections on the Internet.

Another possible arrangement is to have an elementary class become pen pals with university students in a language arts methods class. Over a semester the elementary students and preservice teachers can write back and forth to each other four, five, or six times, and perhaps can even meet each other at the end of the semester. The children have the opportunity to be pen pals with university students, and the university students have the opportunity to get to know an elementary student and examine the student's writing.

In a study by Greenlee, Hiebert, Bridge, and Winograd (1986), a class of grade 2 students became pen pals with a class of university students who were majoring in elementary education. The researchers investigated whether having a genuine audience would influence the quality of the letters the students wrote. They compared the second-graders' letters to ones written by a control group who wrote letters to imaginary audiences and received traditional teacher comments on their work. The researchers found that the students who wrote to pen pals composed longer and more complex letters once they received responses to their letters. The results of this study emphasize the importance of providing real audiences for student writing.

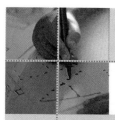

Teacher's Notebook

Forms for Friendly and Business Letters

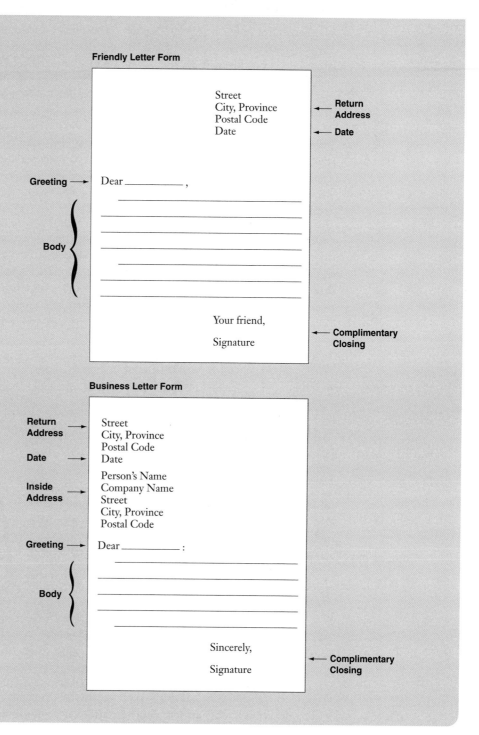

Friendly Letter Form

Street
City, Province
Postal Code
Date

← **Return Address**
← **Date**

Greeting → Dear _____ ,

Body {

Your friend,

Signature

← **Complimentary Closing**

Business Letter Form

Return Address →
Date →

Street
City, Province
Postal Code
Date

Inside Address →

Person's Name
Company Name
Street
City, Province
Postal Code

Greeting → Dear _____ :

Body {

Sincerely,

Signature

← **Complimentary Closing**

When writing pen pal letters as a class, students use the writing process. In the prewriting stage they decide what to include in their letters. Brainstorming and clustering are effective strategies to help students choose information to include and questions to ask. Figure 7–10 shows a cluster with four rays developed by a third-grade class for pen pal letters. As a class, the students brainstormed a list of possible topics and finally decided on the four main-idea rays (me and my family, my school, my hobbies, and questions for my pen pal). Then students completed the clusters by adding details to each main idea.

Students' rough drafts incorporated the information from one ray into the first paragraph, information from a second ray into the second paragraph, and so on, for the body of the letters. After writing their rough drafts, students met in writers groups to revise content and edit to correct mechanical errors, first with a classmate and later with the teacher. Next, they recopied their final drafts, addressed envelopes, and mailed them. A sample letter is also presented in Figure 7–10. Comparing each paragraph of the letter with the cluster reveals that using the cluster helped the student write a well-organized and interesting letter that was packed with information.

Courtesy Letters. Invitations and thank-you notes are two other types of friendly letters that elementary students write. They may write to parents to invite them to an after-school program, to the class across the hall to invite them to visit a classroom exhibit, or to a community person to invite him or her to be interviewed as part of a content-area unit. Similarly, children write letters to thank people who have been helpful.

Letters to Authors and Illustrators. Students write letters to favourite authors and illustrators to share their ideas and feelings about the books they have read. They ask questions about how a particular character was developed or why the illustrator used a certain art medium. Students also describe the books they have written. Here are questions from teacher Deanna Andres's grade 2 students to Robert Munsch. These questions were sent in a letter at the end of an author study:

How many books have you written?

Do you like to read?

Where do your ideas come from for your books?

Who is the character, Jule Ann, in the book *The Boy in the Drawer* based on?

Most authors and illustrators reply to student's letters when possible, and Robert Munsch answered these grade 2 students' questions. However, authors and illustrators receive thousands of letters from children every year and cannot be pen pals with students. Beverly Cleary's award-winning book *Dear Mr. Henshaw* (1983) offers a worthwhile lesson about what students (and their teachers) can realistically expect. We suggest the following guidelines for students writing to authors and illustrators:

- Follow the correct business letter format with return address, greeting, body, closing, and signature.
- Use the process approach to write, revise, and edit the letter. Be sure to proofread and correct errors.
- Avoid asking personal questions such as how much money he or she earns.
- Do not ask for free copies of books.
- Recopy the letter so that it will be neat and easy to read.
- Write the return address on both envelope and letter.
- Include a stamped, self-addressed envelope for a reply.
- Be polite in the letter; use the words *please* and *thank you*.

Students should write genuine letters to share their thoughts and feelings about the author's writing or the illustrator's artwork. Students send their letters to the author/illustrator in care of

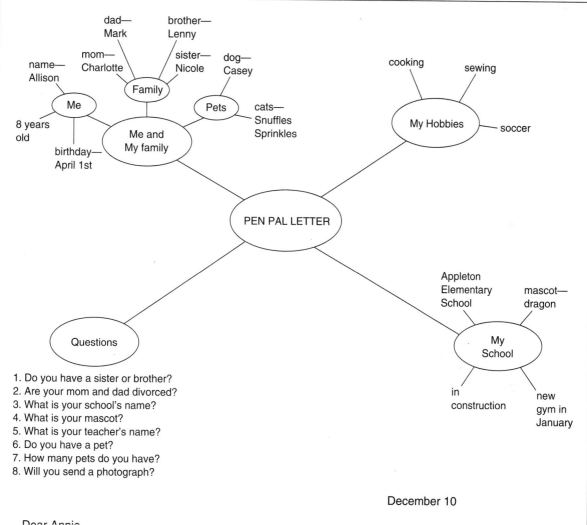

1. Do you have a sister or brother?
2. Are your mom and dad divorced?
3. What is your school's name?
4. What is your mascot?
5. What is your teacher's name?
6. Do you have a pet?
7. How many pets do you have?
8. Will you send a photograph?

December 10

Dear Annie,

I'm your pen pal now. My name is Allison and I'm 8 years old. My birthday is on April 1st.

I go to Appleton Elementary School. Our mascot is a dragon. We are in construction because we're going to have a new gym in January.

My hobbies are soccer, sewing, and cooking. I play soccer, sewing I do in free time, and I cook dinner sometimes.

My pets are two cats and a dog. The dog's name is Casey and he's a boy. He is two years old. The cat is a girl and her name is Snuffles. She is four years old. The kitten is a girl and her name is Sprinkles. She is two months old.

My dad's name is Mark and my mom's name is Charlotte. Her birthday is the day after Mother's Day. My brother's name is Lenny. He is 13 years old. My sister's name is Nicole. She is 3 years old.

I have some questions for you. Do you have a sister or a brother? Are your mom and dad divorced? Mine aren't. What is your school's name? What is your mascot? What is your teacher's name? Do you have a pet? How many pets do you have? Will you send me a photograph of yourself?

Your friend,
Allison

Figure 7–10 A Grade 3 Student's Cluster and Pen Pal Letter

the publisher (the publisher's name normally appears on both the book's spine and title page, and the address usually appears on the copyright page—the page following the title page). If students cannot find the complete mailing address, they can check the most recent *Canadian Publishers Directory*, a reference book that is available in most public libraries.

BUSINESS LETTERS

Students write business letters to seek information, to complain and compliment, and to transact business. They use this more formal letter style and format (as shown in the Teacher's Notebook on page 307) to communicate with businesses, local newspapers, and governmental agencies. Students can also write to local, provincial, and federal government officials to express concerns, make suggestions, or seek information. Addresses of local elected officials are listed in the telephone directory, and addresses of provincial and federal officials are available in the reference section of the public library. *The Canadian Global Almanac 2004* provides Internet sites for the Canadian federal government, Canadian cabinet members, members of Canada's Senate, and members of Parliament. Here are the addresses of the prime minister, the House of Commons, and the Senate of Canada:

Office of the Prime Minister
Langevin Block
Ottawa, ON
K1A 0A2

The Senate of Canada
Ottawa, ON
K1A 0A4

The House of Commons
Centre Block, Parliament Bldg.
Ottawa, ON K1A
0A6

Students may also write other types of business letters to request information and free materials. One source of free materials is *Free Stuff for Kids* (Free Stuff Editor, & Meadowbrook, 2002). This book is updated regularly and lists hundreds of free or inexpensive materials that elementary students can write for. They can also find free materials at **www.canadianfreestuff.com/kids.html** and at **www.webfreebees.net/kids.html**.

SIMULATED LETTERS

Students can also write simulated letters, in which they assume the identity of a historical or literary figure. Simulated letters are similar to simulated journals except that they are written as letters using the friendly letter form. Students can write to a fairy tale character, as one student did in Figure 7–11, or from one book character to another; for example, after reading *Sarah, Plain and Tall* (MacLachlan, 1985), students can assume the persona of Sarah and write a letter to her brother William, as a third grader did in this letter:

Dear William,

I'm having fun here. There was a very big storm here. It was so big it looked like the sea. Sometimes I am very lonesome for home but sometimes it is very fun here in Ohio. We swam in the cow pond and I taught Caleb how to swim. They were afraid I would leave. Maggie and Matthew brought some chickens.

Love, Sarah

Even though these letters are never mailed, they are written to a specific audience. Classmates can assume the role of the addressee and respond to the letter. Also, these letters show clearly how well students comprehend the story, and teachers can use them to monitor students' learning.

Figure 7–11 A Grade 1 Student's Letter to Goldilocks

TEACHING STUDENTS TO WRITE LETTERS

Teachers teach a variety of minilessons so that students will know how to write letters and how the format and style of letters differs from the format and style of stories, informational books, and journals. Topics for minilessons include using the letter-writing forms, focusing on your audience, organizing information in the letter, and asking questions. Teachers also teach minilessons on capitalizing proper nouns, addressing an envelope, using paragraphs, and being courteous.

Students use the process approach to writing letters so that they can make their letters interesting, complete, and readable. The steps in writing letters are presented in the following Step by Step box:

Step by Step

Writing Letters

1. Gather and organize information for the letter. Students participate in prewriting activities, such as brainstorming or clustering, to decide what information to include in their letters. If they are writing friendly letters, particularly to pen pals, they also identify several questions to include.

2. *Review the friendly or business letter form.*   Before writing the rough drafts of their letters, students review the friendly or business letter form.

3. *Draft the letter.*   Students write a rough draft, incorporating the information developed during prewriting and following either the friendly or the business letter style.

4. *Revise the letter.*   Next, students meet in a writers group to share their rough drafts, receive compliments, and get feedback. They make changes based on the feedback in order to communicate more effectively.

5. *Edit the letter.*   Students edit their letters with a partner, proofreading to identify errors and correcting as many as possible. They also make sure they have used the appropriate letter format.

6. *Make the final copy of the letter.*   After making all the mechanical corrections, students recopy or edit and format if word-processing their letters and address envelopes. The teacher often reviews how to address an envelope during this step, too.

7. *Mail the letter.*   The crucial last step is to mail the letters and wait for a reply.

A variety of books that include letters have been published for children. Some of these are stories with letters that children can take out of envelopes and read. *The Jolly Postman, or Other People's Letters* (Ahlberg & Ahlberg, 1986) and *Dear Peter Rabbit* (Potter, 1995) are collections of letters that have been published for children. Figure 7–12 presents a list of books that includes letters that teachers can share with students as part of letter-writing activities.

ASSESSING STUDENTS' LETTERS

Traditionally, students wrote letters and turned them in for the teacher to grade. The letters were returned to the students after they were graded, but they were never mailed. Educators now recognize the importance of having an audience for student writing, and research suggests that students write better when they know that someone other than the teacher will read their writing. Whereas it is often necessary to assess student writing, it would be inappropriate for the teacher to put a grade on the letter if it is going to be mailed to someone. Teachers can instead develop a checklist or rubric for evaluating students' letters without marking on them.

A grade 3 teacher developed the checklist for assessing students' pen pal letters in Figure 7–13; it identifies specific behaviours and measurable products. The teacher shares the checklist with students before they begin to write so that they know what is expected of them and how they will be graded. At an evaluation conference before the letters are mailed, the teacher reviews the checklist with each student. The letters are mailed without evaluative comments or grades written on them, but the completed checklist goes into students' writing folders. A grading scale can be developed from the checklist; for example, points can be awarded for each check mark in the "Yes" column, or five check marks can be determined to equal a grade of A, four check marks a B, and so on.

ADAPTING TO MEET THE NEEDS OF EVERY STUDENT

Teachers can make adaptations as students read and write informational books so that every student can be successful. A list of recommendations is presented in the Adapting box on page 314. It is important to teach students about the genre of informational books and the

Books That Include Letters

Ahlberg, J., & Ahlberg, A. (1986). *The Jolly Postman, or Other People's Letters.* Boston: Little, Brown. (P)

Avi. (1991). *Nothing But the Truth.* New York: Orchard. (U)

Cartlidge, M. (1993). *Mouse's Letters.* New York: Dutton. (P)

Cartlidge, M. (1995). *Mouse's Scrapbook.* New York: Dutton. (P)

George, J. C. (1993). *Dear Rebecca, Winter Is Here.* New York: HarperCollins. (M)

Harrison, J. (1994). Dear Bear. Minneapolis: Carolrhoda. (P)

Heisel, S. E. (1993). *Wrapped in a Riddle.* Boston: Houghton Mifflin. (M–U)

Hesse, K. (1992). *Letters from Rifka.* New York: Holt. (U)

James, E., & Barkin, C. (1993). *Sincerely Yours: How to Write Great Letters.* New York: Clarion. (M–U)

Johnston, T. (1994). *Amber on the Mountain.* New York: Dial. (P–M)

Keith, Agnes Newton (1982). *Three Came Home.* Toronto: McClelland and Stewart Ltd. (U) 🍁

Kitagawa, M. (1986). *This Is My Own: Letter to Wes and Other Writings on Japanese Canadians, 1941–1948.* Vancouver: Talonbooks. (M–U) 🍁

Langen, A., & Droop, C. (1994). *Letters from Felix: A Little Rabbit on a World Tour.* New York: Abbeville Press. (M)

Neering, R. (1990). *Pioneers: Canadian Lives Series.* Markham, Ontario: Fitzhenry and Whiteside. (M–U) 🍁

Nichol, B. (1993). *Beethoven Lives Upstairs.* New York: Orchard. (M–U)

Parry, C. (1994). *Eleanora's Diary.* Richmond Hill: Scholastic Canada. (U) 🍁

Pinkney, A. D. (1994). *Dear Benjamin Banneker.* San Diego: Gulliver/Harcourt Brace. (M)

Potter, B. (1995). *Dear Peter Rabbit.* New York: Warne. (P–M)

Rabbi, N. S. (1994). *Casey Over There.* San Diego: Harcourt Brace. (P–M)

Takashima, S. (1971). *A Child in Prison Camp.* New York: William Morrow and Company. (U)

Tryon, L. (1994). *Albert's Thanksgiving.* New York: Atheneum. (P)

P = primary grades (K–2); M = middle grades (3–5); U = upper grades (6–8).

Figure 7–12 Books That Include Letters

Pen Pal Letter Checklist

Name _____

	Yes	No
1. Did you complete the cluster?	❏	❏
2. Did you include questions in your letter?	❏	❏
3. Did you put your letter in the friendly letter form?	❏	❏

_____ return address

_____ greeting

_____ 3 or more paragraphs

_____ closing

_____ salutation and name

	Yes	No
4. Did you write a rough draft of your letter?	❏	❏
5. Did you revise your letter with suggestions from people in your writers group?	❏	❏
6. Did you proofread your letter and correct as many errors as possible?	❏	❏

Figure 7–13 A Checklist for Assessing Students' Pen Pal Letters

Adapting

Reading and Writing Information to Meet the Needs of Every Student

1. **Examine Informational Books**
   Informational books are organized differently than stories, and they often have unique conventions. Teachers can help students examine this genre and compare these books with stories so that they can recognize the differences.

2. **Compare Aesthetic and Efferent Reading**
   Students read informational books efferently to locate specific information, and aesthetically for the lived-through experience of reading. Too often, less fluent readers read efferently and assume that they must read the entire book and remember everything, even when they are reading to locate a specific piece of information. These students need to learn how to assume an efferent stance to locate specific information and an aesthetic stance at other times.

3. **Teach Students How to Read Hypertext**
   Less capable readers can be paired with more able readers to read selections from the Internet or CD-ROMs. Following the nonlinear nature of hypertext can be confusing and some students may need guidance to maintain their focus on main ideas. Written study guides or outlines may be provided to help readers follow a logical path and/or to make clearly organized notes.

4. **Have Students Write "All about . . ." Books**
   Less experienced writers can write "All about . . ." books. In these books students write information they are learning during thematic units or information about hobbies. Because students draw a picture and write only a sentence or two on each page, they are able to complete the project before they lose interest or become frustrated.

5. **Arrange for Students to Write Authentic Letters**
   Teachers can arrange for students to write friendly and business letters so that students can have the experience of writing to a real audience. Receiving a reply is one of the best ways to stimulate students' interest in writing!

characteristics of expository text from multiple sources, and the unique conventions they have to help readers—including diagrams, glossaries, and indexes. Students also need to learn about the five expository text structures because research has shown that less fluent readers are not as conscious of them as better readers are. Informational books are available on a wide variety of topics and at a range of reading levels, so selecting reading materials to meet the needs of every student should not be too difficult.

Students can write a variety of reports, ranging from posters and "All about . . ." books to more formal individual reports. Teachers should guide students to choose a format that is appropriate for their information and message. For letter writing, too, students can make choices regarding form and content. What is most important is that students write authentic letters that are mailed. Receiving a reply makes the work that goes into writing a letter worthwhile. Teachers can coordinate letter-writing activities with thematic units, resource-based units, or pen pals.

Too often, less capable readers don't have opportunities to read life-stories, but there are many interesting picture book biographies. All students should have opportunities to read these books as they are a rich source of informational text. Students also benefit from opportunities to write their own autobiographies. Young children and those who find extensive writing difficult can create "Me Boxes" in which they collect small items such as pictures and favourite toys that represent their life-stories. They can then tell their stories using the items as props. Older children can write and illustrate their life-stories after reading biographies of others.

Review

Research suggests that reading and writing information may be as primary as reading and writing stories. Three types of informational texts that elementary and middle school students read and write are reports and other informational books, life stories, and letters.

The following key concepts are presented in this chapter:

1. Students read expository texts to learn information (from books, the Internet, CD-ROMs, newspapers, and magazines), and they write expository text (in reports, informational books, posters, etc.) to share information with others.

2. Students may use either efferent or aesthetic reading when reading informational books, depending on their purpose for reading.

3. Informational writing is organized into five expository text structures: description, sequence, comparison, cause and effect, and problem and solution.

4. Students use their knowledge of expository text structures when reading and writing informational texts.

5. Reading and writing hypertext requires students to use many of the same strategies as traditional print, but also requires them to make decisions regarding structure and links across text.

6. Students write both collaborative and individual reports using the stages of the writing process.

7. Students can organize reports in a variety of formats, including posters, alphabet books, and question-and-answer (Q&A) books.

8. The friendly and business letters that students write should be mailed to authentic audiences.

9. Students write simulated letters in connection with resource-based units and social studies and science thematic units.

Extensions

1. Follow the guidelines in this chapter to write a class collaborative report with a group of elementary students on a social studies topic, such as modes of transportation, or on a science topic, such as the solar system.

2. Choose a topic related to teaching language arts, such as writing in journals or the uses of drama. Research the topic and write an "All about . . ." book to share with colleagues.

3. With students in a local elementary school, write biographies of Canadian heroes, using graphic organizers to collect the information.

4. Assist a group of students write friendly letters to pen pals in another school.

chapter eight

Viewing and Visually Representing

Giving New Meaning to "Sounding Out" Words

Procedure

The French Language Arts program in my grade 4 immersion class is literature-based. Once a month, an author is spotlighted as author of the month. The featured books are a springboard for our reading, writing, and drama activities. Recently, I have been using a variety of drama activities that focus on image, gesture, and sound to enhance student meaning of the material.

As a post-reading learning experience, drama helps shoulder the more privileged reading and writing activities. One very successful drama activity that I use is "Soundtracking" (Neelands, 1990), or soundscapes, that could be considered the background musical score of a movie. I invite students to represent a novel by using sounds to convey their found meanings of parts of the text.

After reading through the selected novel as a class, students are put into groups of four. They are assigned a chapter of the book to represent. At their initial meeting, they reread the text, and make plans as to what they will represent and how. To produce their sounds, students are permitted to use anything at their disposal: voice, buckets of water, hockey sticks, music instruments, etc. Students are responsible for collecting all materials they need.

> "The 'novel soundtrack' enhances students' attitude toward reading, understanding of written text, and understanding of self."

Paul Comeau
Grade 4 Teacher
St. Peter's Elementary School,
Mount Pearl, Newfoundland

Students are given approximately 20 minutes at the next group session to produce a soundscape of their designated chapter. They then present their draft representation to their classmates who in turn have the opportunity to question the group and suggest additional sounds. The foursomes regroup to refine and edit the

Adaptations

Novels can also be represented by a dramatic collage of images. Students thumb through old magazines to find pictures and images that could possibly represent characters, setting, plot, words, feelings, or actions of a novel. Working through the process of collage making, students inevitably discuss the novel at length. They also learn to respect and appreciate the various interpretations individuals may have of the same story.

Reflections

The novel soundtrack enhances students' attitude toward reading, understanding of written text, and understanding of self. By its design, it provides concreteness to the abstractness of the text. It also imitates a simple writing process concretely. Students engage in drafting, revising, editing, and publishing sounds by negotiating and collaborating efforts. This enriched learning experience gives new meaning to "sounding out" what one reads.

soundscapes. The final step is to record the edited sounds, as they would appear in the novel, to publish the "novel soundtrack." The audio tape is forwarded to the author in anticipation of a favourable response.

Assessment

The student response-journal is an invaluable tool to assess students' language and personal growth. Students reflect on questions such as "How did you feel by working through this activity? What did you learn? What contribution did you make to this group activity?" The student reflection is reinforced with a class discussion to share feelings and acquisitions. This self-evaluation is complemented by teacher anecdotal observations to form the basis of an effective formative assessment. The information gathered can be used to organize instruction, to guide students' development, and to communicate student progress to parents.

November 17

I think that this project was very interesting and fun. It was work but a special kind of work. It was work in disguise. I think that everybody learned that you can't do a project right off the bat. You've got to work at it. I did not realize that there were so many sounds in the book we used. I helped the group by making sounds to represent seals, a horse, and a hockey game. For the game we hit hockey sticks together. Almost everyone involved in the project thought that if they could do it a second time they could improve something they did.

Journal entry by grade four student Gregory Bruslett.

In her grade 2 and 3 class, Karen Hipkin bases assessment and evaluation of student learning on portfolios. The students' portfolios contain samples of writing, recordings of readings, and work from other areas of the curriculum. The children choose some samples and Karen highly recommends others to be included. In each reporting period, children meet with parents and teacher to show their portfolios, explaining the goals they have reached and those they have set for the next period. Parents are asked to give the children "three stars and a wish" in response to the portfolios. Parents and children are thrilled with the learning stories the portfolios tell.

To Guide Your Reading

As you read this chapter, prepare to

Define visual literacy

•

Describe the viewing and visually representing processes

•

Explain how viewing and visually representing support and enhance listening, speaking, reading, and writing

•

Explain how the concepts of aesthetic, efferent, and critical information processing described in Chapter 5 apply to viewing and visually representing

•

Describe how viewing and visually representing can be taught as part of language arts units

For decades, listening, speaking, reading, and writing were considered the language arts. With the introduction and increased availability in the early 1980s of microcomputers and other video equipment, educators acknowledged the need to recognize viewing as an essential communication art. Hence, viewing became the fifth language art. As technological advances made possible the easy production of print and nonprint media, educators recognized the role of representation of knowledge in meaning construction and communication, and visually representing became the sixth language art.

This chapter will focus on how teachers teach the two newest language arts—viewing and visually representing—and how they contribute to students' learning.

Viewing is a way students acquire, appreciate, and critique information thoughts, ideas, and feelings that are visually conveyed. Students encounter many opportunities to view a variety of formats, including visuals (such as photographs, illustrations, and charts), drama (such as puppets, tableaux, and skits), and multimedia (such as videos, CD-ROMs, DVDs, and television). Viewing enhances listening when students attend to nonverbal communication or visual elements of presentations.

Visually representing is a way for students to convey information learned, thoughts, and ideas through creation of visual texts and art forms. Students create meaning through multiple sign systems such as drawings, videos, digital images, drama, sculptures, models, and posters. Often, visual representation projects lead students to deeper understanding of texts they have read or heard. Visually representing also enhances speaking when students support their oral presentations with visuals.

Viewing and visually representing broaden the ways in which students can understand and communicate their learning. Traditionally, the emphasis in language arts has been on representing thoughts, ideas, and feelings in written and spoken forms, but currently in Canadian classrooms students also use visual, dramatic, and multimedia formats, both independently and as support to their written and spoken messages.

Technology and access to the Internet have changed what it means for students to be literate and what language arts strategies and skills teachers need to help them develop. Whereas the term *literacy* traditionally refers to ability to read and write, it is now readily accepted that literacy includes construction of meaning from multiple information sources, not just print. Hence, the concept of visual literacy has evolved to refer to the ability to create, read, and respond to visual images.

Visual Literacy

Visual literacy is an area of literacy that deals with what can be seen and how what is seen is interpreted. *Visual literacy* can be defined as the ability to understand communications composed of visual images as well as being able to use visual imagery to communicate with others. In other words, visual literacy is the ability to see, understand, think, create, and communicate graphically. There is a proliferation of images in our students' worlds—in books, on television, in newspapers, magazines, video games, and movies, in advertising, and on the Web. As students are exposed to more and more information and entertainment through nonprint media, their ability to think critically and visually about the images they see becomes a vital life-skill. Teachers must help students develop the skills to read and create visually in thoughtful and critical ways.

Visual literacy is learned, just as reading and writing are learned. Students learn to process visual images efficiently and understand the impact they have on viewers. The visually literate student looks at images carefully and critically to discover the intention of the image creator, just as a skilled reader discovers the intention of the author. Visual literacy allows students to gather information and ideas contained in images, put them in context, and determine their meaning in relation to that context and beyond. Visually literate students can apply their skills to reading a variety of images including (but not limited to) photographs, charts and graphs, drawings, paintings, films, sculptures, maps, and book illustrations.

Like reading words, visual literacy involves more than one level of skill. Just as the first level of reading printed text is decoding of words and sentences, the first level of visual literacy is identification of the subject or elements in the image. But just as reading comprehension is the goal of reading printed text, understanding what is seen and comprehending the visual information and relationships is the goal of visual literacy. Higher-level visual literacy skills require critical thinking, and they are essential to students' reading, especially in subject areas where information is conveyed through visual texts such as graphs, diagrams, and maps.

Visual texts make meaning with images or with a combination of images and words. Think of a map, for instance. The words are needed to name the places, while the images are needed to show where those places are and the relationship of one place to another. Some kinds of information are best expressed in words, others in images, while still others are best expressed in a combination of words and images. As students learn to view and represent, they must learn to distinguish types of information and how they are most clearly communicated.

Teachers work with students in many ways to help them see, read, and create visual images. Just as verbally literate students must be able to manipulate the basic components of written language—the letters, words, spelling, grammar, and syntax—visually literate students must be able to recognize the use of and employ the basic visual elements. Bartel (2005) explains that just as the organization, sentence structure, style and so on can make or break a good story, the way the elements are arranged can make or break a good picture idea. Being familiar with the basic elements of visual communication makes it possible for students to read and use many visual forms and media. Although there is variation among visual artists in regard to which elements are considered basic, we know that knowledge of the elements and how they function helps students understand and compose meaningful visual messages. Figure 8–1 provides a guide to the visual elements and their functions that students in elementary schools use to interpret and construct visual messages.

Responses to visual texts are a form of personal expression, just as written responses to literature are unique to the reader. Teachers help students respond to visual texts by creating a climate of trust and respect for the opinions of all students. Having many students share their perspectives

Dot is the most basic of visual elements. It is a pointer or a marker of space. A dot standing alone can direct attention to a specific point. A group of dots can suggest motion or direction. Contemporary visual media such as television, video, computer screen print, and animation are patterns of dots.

Line is a simple, but powerful, visual tool. Line comprises a series of very closely spaced dots that can show motion and direction. Horizontal lines create a sense of equilibrium; diagonal lines create visual stress and imply movement.

Hue refers to colour. All the colours of the rainbow are actually different hues in the visible spectrum of light. Hues are warm (red, orange, and yellow) and cool (blue and closely related colours) Warm hues imply warmth, comfort, and ease, while cool hues imply distance, anxiety, and tension.

Lighting refers to the use of varying levels of light and colour to create mood and feelings or show change in mood or time.

Sound is the presence or absence of music or special sounds to create a mood, convey action, or signal change.

Composition is the arrangement of masses and spaces including the arrangement of objects, people, and places within a scene or screen.

Shapes may be the outlines of objects or may be the negative shapes (spaces) between objects. Circle and curvy shapes suggest warmth, comfort, and calm. Squares can be read as dull, stable, or lacking imagination. Triangles are interpreted as action, tension, or conflict.

Form is three-dimensional quality as in height, width, and depth. Dimension is created through use of linear perspective, often enhanced by colour manipulation. Two-dimensional visual objects such as photographs, drawings, and paintings are created such that they imply that three dimensional, real objects are being seen.

Perspective is the illusion of distance and point of view created by techniques such as size, overlapping, atmosphere, sharpness or blurriness, and angles.

Texture is the feel of an object's surface, both to the touch of fingers and the way the viewer's eyes *feel* a visual image. Visual texture is interpreted through minute variations in dimension. Viewers perceive visual texture because their sense of touch cooperates with their eyes to help them better understand their surroundings.

Figure 8–1 Elements of Visual Art and Concept Design

Source: Adapted from Cornett & Smithrim (2001) and the On-line Visual Literacy Project, Pomona College. Retrieved March 7, 2004, from www.pomona.edu/Academics/courserelated/classprojects/Visual-lit/intro/intro.html.

enhances all students' understanding and helps students appreciate the importance of nonverbal communication. To make viewing images a meaningful experience, teachers guide students to consider the ways the elements of design are used and the effect the image has upon viewers. Similarly, teachers guide students to create visual messages attending to the same elements. Students can be asked, for example, to apply these principles when they create their own interpretation of a poem or story through a visual art activity such as drawing a picture, making a collage, or creating their own multimedia productions.

The Viewing Process

More than a decade ago, Neil Postman (1992) claimed that children needed no instruction to watch television; there are no skills involved and "that is why there is no such thing as remedial television-watching" (p. 152). While he was correct about there being no remedial television watching, we disagree regarding the skills needed for viewing. In their worlds today, children are bombarded with visual images not only on television, but also on videos, CD-ROMs, DVDs, and websites, as well as images in books and other print and nonprint sources. Viewing is more than just seeing. Students must be taught how to view. They need to learn that visual images, like words, convey ideas, beliefs, and values. Hence, the important place of viewing across Canadian provincial language arts curricula, often closely associated with curriculum concerning technology.

Viewing, like reading and writing, is an active process of constructing meaning. By attending to and comprehending visual information, students broaden the ways in which they interpret and understand their worlds.

STEPS IN THE VIEWING PROCESS

Like the listening process, viewing involves three steps: receiving, attending, and assigning meaning. In the first step, the viewer receives the visual stimuli. In the second step, the viewer attends to the attributes of the stimuli, such as colour and shape. Stimuli are always present in a context, and viewers must be aware of the influence of the context as they develop meaning. Attributes and context contribute to the viewer's interpretation. In the third step, the viewer, like a reader, assigns meaning to a text based on previous experience and prior knowledge. Teachers provide experiences for students to view a variety of materials, both print and nonprint, for a variety of purposes. Like listeners, students view in different ways for different purposes. Many parallels can be drawn between the viewing process and efferent and aesthetic listening.

PURPOSES FOR VIEWING

Little teaching and learning in any discipline is bereft of the use of visual images. Visual images enhance students' understanding and motivation for learning. Because visual images are complex and multi-layered, they require skill in their interpretation. Students need to learn to analyze visual images and to understand the creator's technique and intent to be able to respond to them. In language arts units, students view for at least three primary purposes. They often view to deepen their understanding of text composed by others. For example, when students examine picture book illustrations, seeing the illustrator's interpretation of the text deepens their understanding. Students also view and consider the effects of visual images to create visual texts that enrich the messages they wish to convey. For example, when they create posters or scrapbooks to tell their family stories, they plan ways to catch viewers' attention. Finally, students view print and nonprint media to gain more information or a fuller understanding of topics. For example, they may seek more information to be included in their writing projects or their studies in content areas of the curriculum.

TEACHING VIEWING STRATEGIES

Although students must be taught how to view and teachers must pay specific attention to the viewing process, opportunities for viewing alone are rare in classrooms. Students are usually involved in both processes simultaneously when they listen to teachers read aloud from picture books and see the illustrations, watch videos, watch television, engage with interactive CD-ROMs, DVDs, and websites, and attend to dramatic productions. A few exceptions for viewing alone would include watching mime, viewing art objects or models, and reading wordless picture books. During these activities students must rely only on the visual information to construct meaning.

Students often view videos or DVDs of children's literature as part of language arts units, and it is important that teachers take advantage of the unique capabilities of this technology (Green, 1989).

Some precautions, however, are necessary to make the most of both the students' reading, or being read to by the teacher, and the viewing of the literature selection. In many classrooms we visit, it is usual for the book to be read first and the video watched when the reading is complete. While this may sometimes be appropriate, we stress that other options should be considered. Teachers decide upon the purpose for viewing and they decide whether students view the video before or after reading, or whether the viewing is interspersed with the reading. They also decide how much of the video students watch in the classroom. Purpose and students' needs and interests guide all of these decisions.

Students with limited background knowledge often benefit from viewing before reading or listening to the book read aloud, but for other students, watching a video before reading would curtail their interest in reading the book. Showing a short clip of the video to introduce the book can be instructive concerning some aspects such as unfamiliar settings and can heighten student interest in reading. Similarly, showing clips as reading progresses can clarify aspects of plot or character development and can facilitate discussion and deepening of meaning. Showing the complete video upon completion of reading can also deepen meaning and raise many points for discussion. As Golden (2001) reminds us, students tend to be visually oriented, able to see significant aspects of visual media, and the skills they use to decode visual images are the same skills they use for written text. Presenting both visual and written text maximizes possible transfer of decoding and analytical skills.

In language arts units, teachers often ask students to make comparisons between the book and video versions of a story and choose the one they like better. Interestingly, less capable students who don't visualize the story in their minds often prefer the video version, while more capable readers often prefer the book version because the video doesn't meet their expectations. They can also examine some of the conventions used in video productions, such as narration, music, and sound effects, the visual representation of characters and the setting, the camera's perspective, and any changes from the book version. Making comparisons between video and writing techniques deepens understanding of both meaning of the story and effect of techniques. General guidelines for using visual media in the classroom are listed in the accompanying Teacher's Notebook.

Besides making comparisons of book and digital versions (video, CD-ROM, or DVD) of a story, students can also compare two digital versions or plan and create their own digital version. Many digital storybooks include the same illustrations and printed text with the added feature of being able to animate the illustrations in some way, often with a click of the mouse. When reading comprehension is compared after reading print books and reading CD-ROM books, results suggest that readers' comprehension can be improved by the electronic texts (Matthew, 1996, 1997).

Viewing strategies can be learned through many activities. Projects that help students learn to comprehend visual information can be closely linked to reading and responding to literature, and to learning across the curriculum. Figure 8–2 on page 324 lists projects that allow students to learn viewing and visually representing strategies while engaged in meaningful integrated language arts tasks.

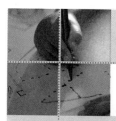

Teacher's Notebook

Guidelines for Using Visual Media in the Classroom

1. **Preview**
Before showing a video, CD-ROM, or DVD, make sure it is suitable for students and contributes significantly to making information available to them. It may be necessary to skip some portions due to excessive length or unsuitable content when showing visual media to students.

2. **Plan How to Use**
Plan how the media will be used. Plan an introduction, interaction during the viewing, and a follow-up. Plan how it will be shown—all at once or in short segments. Students who have little background knowledge on the topic or students for whom the sentence structure or vocabulary is difficult may benefit from previewing, with or without sound, with teacher guidance before viewing and listening independently.

3. **Set the Purpose and Give Students Viewing Guidelines**
Explain the purpose for viewing and explain whether students should use primarily aesthetic, efferent, or critical listening. Indicate to students what will be expected of them during and after viewing.

4. **Use the Pause Function**
Stop the presentation periodically in order for students to make predictions, reflect on their use of a listening strategy, talk about the story or information, or compare the book and electronic versions. If students are listening and viewing an informational presentation, they may need to stop periodically to take notes.

5. **Re-view**
Consider showing the video or CD-ROM more than once because re-viewing is as beneficial as rereading. Teachers can show particular scenes twice while students are viewing, or teachers can show the video without interruption the first time and then play it a second time.

6. **Vary the Procedure Used**
Teachers sometimes show the beginning of a story on the video, CD-ROM, or DVD and then read aloud the entire book. Afterwards, students view the entire video CD-ROM, or DVD. Or, teachers can alternate reading and viewing sections of text.

7. **Consider the Visual and Sound Elements and Effects**
Depending upon the content of the video CD-ROM, or DVD (story or expository information), students can examine the impact of the narration, music, sound effects, camera angles, and the visual representation of the characters and setting as appropriate.

8. **Provide Opportunities for Response**
Provide opportunities for students to respond to visual media presentations. Students can respond in many ways including participating in grand conversations and writing in reading logs.

The Viewing Process

Viewing Projects

1. View footage from television, film, CD-ROM, or video and analyze use of some of the visual elements and their use in portraying meaning.
2. Compare the illustrations in several versions of the same story. Multiple versions of folktales and other traditional stories are available and appropriate for comparison.
3. Analyze the illustrator's craft and medium to discover the questions illustrators must ask and answer as they work.
4. Ask students to choose a piece of art (e.g., painting or sculpture) that relates to a book or other text (poem) and share their interpretation of the art with the class.
5. View a CD-ROM version or online version of a book. Note how the text is made interactive and discuss the effects of the interactive components on meaning construction.
6. View artifacts or pictures related to a book and use them to predict story plot and events.
7. View the work of one illustrator in several books. Look for commonalities. The websites of many illustrators provide insight into their work.
8. Ask students to solve visual puzzles such as identifying differences between two similar pictures.
9. View a series of portraits or illustrations of characters in books and discuss the contribution of the visuals to character development.
10. View the same picture in black and white and in colour. Discuss differences and effects upon meaning.

Visually Representing Projects

1. Experiment with the illustration techniques (e.g., collage, watercolour, line drawing) used in favourite books. Examine other books illustrated with the same technique.
2. Make a diagram or model using information from a book.
3. Create a collage to represent the theme of a book or mood of a poem.
4. Design a book jacket, laminate it, and place it on the book.
5. Make a diorama or other miniature scene of an episode from a favourite book. Use toys, clay figures, or other objects to represent characters and objects in the story. Include a display sign to describe the scene.
6. Make a set of storyboards with one card for each episode, chapter, or scene of a text.
7. Make a map or relief map of a book's setting or something related to the book.
8. Construct a mobile illustrating a book.
9. Make a comic strip to illustrate the sequence of events in a book.
10. Prepare bookmarks for a book and distribute them to classmates.
11. Prepare flannel board pictures or puppets to use in retelling the story.
12. Create a Power Point presentation using pictures from the Internet and written text to retell the story.
13. Experiment with colour, font, and other design techniques when publishing students' written work. Note effects on impression, mood, and meaning of the text.
14. Create a Venn diagram to compare the book and film versions of a story.
15. Make a chart to analyze several versions of the same story or a text set of books by one author.
16. Make a character cluster or sociogram showing relationships among characters.
17. Create tableaux to represent scenes from a story or novel. Include costumes and props.
18. Use drawing software to make a plot profile or story timeline.
19. Create a PowerPoint presentation to report information. Include digital pictures and text.
20. Create models (life size or smaller) of characters or significant story objects from clay, Plasticine, papier mâché, cardboard, or other collected materials.

Figure 8–2 Viewing and Visually Representing Projects

Critical Viewing and Listening

For more information on critical listening, see Chapter 5, "Listening and Speaking in the Classroom," page 175.

Students—even those in the primary grades—need to develop critical viewing and listening skills because they are exposed to many types of persuasion and propaganda. Interpreting and constructing meaning from books and media requires critical thinking, listening, and viewing. As will be pointed out later in this chapter, students' must also be able to apply their critical thinking, listening, and viewing skills to their representation activities. Critical thinking, viewing, and listening are not limited to language arts. Social studies and science lessons on topics such as pollution, political candidates, and drugs demand that students think critically.

Television, magazines, and Internet commercials are prominent forms of persuasion and source of propaganda in students' lives. Because many commercials are directed at children, it is essential that they be able to listen and view critically and learn to judge advertising claims. Teachers often choose to teach critical listening and viewing through projects focused on advertisements. Teachers extend such language arts units to include persuasive writing and identification of writers' techniques in printed text.

PERSUASION AND PROPAGANDA

Advertisers use many devices, gimmicks, and strategies to attract attention and persuade viewers and listeners. There are, however, three basic ways to persuade people. The first is by reason. People seek logical conclusions, whether from facts or from strong possibilities; for example, people can be persuaded to practise more healthful living as the result of medical research. It is necessary, of course, to distinguish between reasonable arguments and unreasonable appeals. For instance, to suggest that diet pills will bring about extraordinary weight loss is an unreasonable appeal.

The second way to persuade people is by an appeal to character. We can be persuaded by what another person recommends if we trust that person. Trust comes from personal knowledge or the reputation of the person who is trying to persuade. We must always question whether we can believe the persuader. We can believe what scientists say about the dangers of nuclear waste, but can we believe what a sports personality says about the effectiveness of a particular sports shoe?

The third way to persuade people is by appealing to their emotions. Emotional appeals can be as strong as intellectual appeals. We have strong feelings and concern for ourselves, other people, and animals. Fear, a need for peer acceptance, and a desire for freedom of expression are all strong feelings that influence our opinions and beliefs.

Any of the three types of appeals can be used to try to persuade someone. Students need to learn to recognize and appropriately use all three types. To persuade classmates to read a particular book in a book report "commercial," a student might argue that it is short and interesting (reason); or it is the most popular book in grade 5 and everyone else is reading it (character); or it is hilarious and they'll laugh (emotion).

Children need to learn to become critical consumers of advertisements (Lutz, 1989; Rudasill, 1986; Tutolo, 1981) and, more specifically, to understand the symbiotic relationship between words and images (Burmark, 2002). Increasingly, kids are bombarded with clever advertising on television and the Internet. Integrating the techniques of "adbusting" into our curricula will equip students with the critical awareness they need to be discriminating consumers (Curry-Tash, 1998).

In addition to techniques of persuasion used by advertisers, students also need to learn about propaganda. Advertisers use appeals to reason, character, and emotion to promote products, ideas, and services; however, advertisers may also use propaganda to influence our beliefs and actions. Propaganda suggests something shady or underhanded. Like persuasion, propaganda is designed to influence people's beliefs and actions, but propagandists may distort, conceal, and exaggerate. Two propaganda techniques are *deceptive language* and *propaganda devices*.

Loaded Words	Doublespeak
best buy	bathroom tissue (toilet paper)
better than	civil disorder (riot)
carefree	correctional facility (jail, prison)
discount	dentures (false teeth)
easier	disadvantaged (poor)
extra strong	encore telecast (rerun)
fortified	funeral director (undertaker)
fresh	genuine imitation leather (vinyl)
guaranteed	inner city (slum, ghetto)
improved	memorial park (cemetery)
longer lasting	mobile home (house trailer)
lowest	nervous wetness (sweat)
maximum	occasional irregularity (constipation)
more natural	passed away (died)
more powerful	people expressways (sidewalks)
new/newer	personal preservation flotation device (life preserver)
plus	pre-owned or experienced (used)
stronger	pupil station (student's desk)
ultra	senior citizen (old person)
virtually	terminal living (dying)

Figure 8–3 Examples of Deceptive Language
Source: Lutz, 1989.

People seeking to influence us often use words that evoke a variety of responses. They claim that something is "improved," "more natural," or "50 percent better"—loaded words and phrases that are deceptive because they are suggestive. When a product is advertised as 50 percent better, for example, consumers need to ask, "50 percent better than what?" Advertisements rarely answer that question.

Doublespeak is another type of deceptive language characterized as evasive, euphemistic, confusing, and self-contradictory. It is language that "pretends to communicate but really does not" (Lutz, 1991, p. 17). Lutz cites a number of kinds of doublespeak, and elementary students can easily understand two kinds: euphemisms and inflated language. *Euphemisms* are words or phrases (e.g., "passed away") that are used to avoid a harsh or distasteful reality, often out of concern for someone's feelings rather than to deceive. *Inflated language* includes words intended to make the ordinary seem extraordinary. Thus, garbage collectors become "sanitation engineers," and used cars become "pre-owned" vehicles. Examples of deceptive language are listed in Figure 8–3. Students need to learn that people sometimes use words that only pretend to communicate; sometimes they use words to intentionally misrepresent, as when someone advertises a vinyl wallet as "genuine imitation leather" or a ring with a glass stone as a "faux diamond." Students need to be able to interpret deceptive language and to avoid using it themselves.

To sell products, advertisers use propaganda devices such as testimonials, the bandwagon effect, and rewards. Ten propaganda devices that elementary students can learn to identify are listed in Figure 8–4. Students can listen to commercials to find examples of each propaganda device and discuss the effect the device has on them. They can also investigate to see how the same devices vary in commercials directed toward different audiences. For example, a snack food commercial with a sticker or toy in the package will appeal to young children while and a cell phone advertisement offering a factory rebate will appeal to teenagers and adults. The propaganda device for both

1. **Glittering Generality**
Generalities such as "motherhood," "healthy lifestyle," and "All Canadian" are used to enhance the quality of a product or the character of a political figure. Propagandists select a generality (such as motherhood or healthy lifestyle) so attractive that viewers and listeners do not challenge the real point.

2. **Testimonial**
To convince people to purchase a product, an advertiser associates it with a popular personality such as an athlete or film star. Viewers and listeners assume that the person offering the testimonial has the expertise to judge the quality of the product.

3. **Transfer**
Persuaders try to transfer the prestige, good looks, or ideas of a person or object to another person or object that will then be accepted. A film star, for example, is shown using Super Soap, and viewers are to believe that they can have youthful skin if they use this soap. Likewise, politicians appear with famous athletes or entertainers so that the lustre of the stars will rub off on them.

4. **Name-Calling**
Advertisers try to pin a bad label or negative image on something they want viewers and listeners to dislike. The purpose is to cause unpleasant associations to rub off on the competition whether a product, person, political party, or company.

5. **Card Stacking in Comparisons**
Persuaders choose only items that favour one side of an issue. Unfavourable facts are ignored. Viewers and listeners are led to believe one product or person or political party is better than another on basis of limited information included.

6. **Bandwagon**
This technique appeals to people's need to be a part of a group. Advertisers claim that everyone is using this product or is part of this group and you should be, too. Viewers and listeners must ask if this is the case and if so, why.

7. **Snob Appeal**
Persuaders use snob appeal to attract the attention of people who want to be part of an exclusive group. Advertisements for expensive clothes, cosmetics, and gourmet foods often use this technique. Viewers and listeners must consider whether the product is of high quality or merely has an expensive nametag.

8. **Rewards**
Advertisers often offer rewards or rebates for buying their products. Viewers and listeners must consider the value of rewards and how they increase the product's cost.

9. **Faulty Cause and Effect**
Advertisers portray that use of a product or technique results in a positive effect when no real evidence of causality is shown. Viewers and listeners are intended to take the message at face value.

10. **Repetition**
Advertisers repeat the name or keywords or phrases several times to invoke a lasting image and associate the particular brand name or quality with the product.

Figure 8–4 Propaganda Devices
Source: Devices adapted from Devine, 1982, pp. 39–40 and www.think.com.

ads is the same: a reward! Propaganda devices can be used to sell ideas as well as products. Public service announcements about smoking or wearing seatbelts, as well as political advertisements, endorsements, and speeches, use these devices.

When students locate advertisements and commercials they believe are misleading or deceptive, they can write letters of complaint to the following watchdog agencies:

- Canadian Radio-television and Telecommunications Commission (CRTC), Les Terrasses de la Chaudière, Central Building, 1 Promenade du Portage, Gatineau, Quebec J8X 4B1
- Canadian Direct Marketing Association, 1 Concorde Gate, Suite 607, Don Mills, Ontario M3C 3N6
- The Canadian Association of Broadcasters, 350 Sparks Street, Suite 306, Ottawa, Ontario K1R 7S8
- Children's Advertising Review Unit, Council of Better Business Bureau, 70 West 36th Street, 13th Floor, New York, NY 10018

In their letters, students should carefully describe the advertisement and explain what bothers them about it. They should also tell where and when they saw or heard the advertisement.

STRATEGIES FOR CRITICAL VIEWING AND LISTENING

Viewing and listening critically means evaluating the message. Students learn to use evaluating strategies to determine and judge the author's message. To evaluate visual images, especially those in print media, students consider a variety of points simultaneously. Key questions they ask are

- Does this appeal to my sense of reason, and if so, how?
- Is there an appeal to my sense of good character?
- Is there an emotional appeal?
- Are propaganda devices being used?
- Are deceptive words or inflated language used?

Students also learn to critically view nonprint media. Among the nonprint media students evaluate are television, videos, DVDs, websites, and films. In evaluating these, students learn to be mindful that such products contain points of view about the world. They also learn that those produced for commercial (and not educational) purposes are never neutral or value-free; they are designed to attract and appeal to certain audiences.

As students listen to books read aloud, hear and view commercials and advertisements, listen to speakers, and view videos, documentaries, and films, they need to ask themselves questions such as those above in order to critically evaluate the message. Students might also ask

- Who created the media work and how are the creators' values and viewpoint reflected?
- Who is the intended audience?
- What content has been left out or whose viewpoint is not expressed?
- How might this work be different in a different medium?

Students also use efferent listening strategies while evaluating because critical listening is an extension of efferent listening. They organize ideas, generalize main ideas, and monitor their understanding of a presentation. Figure 8–5 lists books that encourage critical listening. Few messages are presented in one medium; therefore teachers help students use multiple questions and criteria to become critical viewers and listeners.

An elementary school teacher shares a picture book with his culturally diverse students.

Avi. (1991). *Nothing but the Truth.* New York: Orchard. (U)

Bedard, M. (1990). *Redwork.* Toronto: Lester & Orpen Dennys. (M) 🍁

Bondar, B., & Bondar, R. (1993). *On the Shuttle: Eight Days in Space.* Toronto: Greey de Pencier Books. (P–M–U) 🍁

Brennan-Nelson, D. (2004). *My Teacher Likes to Say.* Chelsea, MI: Sleeping Bear Press.

Creech, S. (2001). *Love That Dog.* New York: HarperCollins. (M)

Creech, S. (2000). *The Wanderer.* New York: HarperCollins. (U)

Edwards, W. (2004). *Monkey Business.* Toronto: Kids Can Press. (P–M) 🍁

Fitch, S. (1999). *There's a Mouse in the House.* Buffalo, NY: Firefly Books. (P–M)

Kogawa, J. (1986). *Naomi's Road.* Toronto: Oxford University Press. (M) 🍁

Lowry, L. (1993). *The Giver.* Boston: Houghton Mifflin. (U)

Mollel, T. (1990). *The Orphan Boy.* Toronto: Oxford University Press. (P–M) 🍁

Pearson, K. (1991). *Looking at the Moon.* Toronto: Viking. (M) 🍁

Porter, P. (2005). *Crazy Man.* Toronto: Groundwood Books. (U) 🍁

Sis, P. (1998). *Tibet Through the Red Box.* Toronto: Douglas & McIntyre. (U) 🍁

Sachar, L. (1998). *Holes.* New York: Random House Children's Books. (U)

Smucker, B. (1977). *Underground to Canada.* New York: Irwin and Co. Ltd. (M) 🍁

Taylor, C. (1997). *Vanishing Act.* Red Deer, AB: Red Deer College Press. (M) 🍁

Wynne-Jones, T. (2003). *Ned Mouse Breaks Away.* Toronto: Groundwood Books. (P) 🍁

Yee, P. (1996). *Ghost Train.* Toronto: Groundwood Books. (P) 🍁

P = primary grades (K–2); M = middle grades (3–5); U = upper grades (6–8).

Figure 8–5 Books That Encourage Critical Listening

The Visually Representing Process

Visual art has long been associated with literacy, but only recently has visually representing been recognized in curriculum documents as the sixth language art. *Visually representing*, or representing, is creating, constructing, and communicating meaning through a variety of media and forms including drawing, sounds, pictures, illustrations, charts, graphs, posters, murals, photographs, dioramas, puppets, mime, sculptures, models, dramas, videos, and digital text with graphics. Visually representing is a way for students to construct both original meaning and their interpretations of text or other nonprint media. It enables students to communicate information and their ideas and understandings through alternative ways, often enhancing what they might communicate through oral or written text alone. Visually representing is not easily separated from the other language arts. Together with one or more other processes, it is a powerful means of communicating and learning. It allows students to both understand and employ the many ways in which images and language can be used to convey ideas, values, and beliefs.

Traditionally, the emphasis in language arts has been on representing thoughts, ideas, and feelings in written or spoken forms. Today, a broader concept of literacy and the availability of communication technology and multimedia have placed more emphasis on expression through multiple forms of communication. Language arts units give students opportunities to use visual, dramatic, and multimedia formats as both support their written and spoken messages and as stand alone forms of communication.

PURPOSES FOR VISUALLY REPRESENTING

Students in language arts classrooms use a wide variety of representation for many purposes, mostly to help conceptualize and organize ideas, thoughts, or beliefs. They use concept maps, sets of pictures, sketches, and diagrams to help organize, often before writing. They enhance the meaning they construct of text or other media through constructing models, creating collages, creating illustrations, and producing dramatic presentations. They demonstrate their interpretation of text through drama, visual arts, and multimedia presentations. Arnheim (1989) points out that "images produced for practical purposes have more sophistication than that of supplying faithful duplicates . . . what an illustration needs to show is not an object as such, but some of its significant properties" (p. 30). Taking this advice and remembering that students' representations take many forms, not just visual arts, teachers encourage students to construct meaning of whole pieces of text, develop their conceptual understandings, and show their interpretation of theme or characters using visual media. Increasingly, students use multiple forms of media such as digital pictures and sound recordings to illustrate their understanding or interpretation of a text and to create their own original text.

TEACHING REPRESENTATION STRATEGIES

Learning to represent is not limited to language arts lessons. The strategies and techniques involved are often considered a part of art, technology, and drama curricula, but they are integrated into language arts units. During a thematic unit on penguins, a grade 1 class made an information quilt. One quilt square is shown in Figure 8–6. Before making the quilt, the teacher read aloud to the children from several informational books about penguins. They recorded what they learned on a class chart and referred to the chart as they created their quilt squares.

When teachers teach how to understand and use visual symbols, they involve students in thinking about and expressing what is often beyond their linguistic capabilities. That is,

Figure 8–6 A Square for a Grade 1 Information Quilt on Penguins

imagery and metaphor are keys to thinking and learning that are used from early childhood—initially unconsciously and later consciously. Students involved in using multiple sign systems declare that having a range of systems available gives them opportunity to think more broadly, to consider other ideas, to connect to memories, and to think through feelings (Short, Kauffman, & Kahn, 2003). Through representation, they often create sophisticated meaning and stretch their understanding past what they might do in writing or oral presentations. The representations are a way of knowing what students think, understanding their thoughts, and assessing their thinking. In doing so, respect for diversity and creativity are developed.

Teachers do not need to be artists or dramatists to facilitate students' visual representations. As well, students need only basic skills to create their representations. For example, after students are taught the essential elements of visual art and design through experience and example, they can apply these elements to create and critique their own and their classmates' products. The elements and concepts shown in Figure 8–1 apply to both visual art products (such as watercolour paintings) and multimedia products (such as PowerPoint presentations and websites). Even young children can become aware of the impact on their communication of each of the elements. Individuals, small groups, or whole classes may do visually representing projects. One grade 5 class that read Gary Paulsen's *Hatchet* (1987) created dioramas to depict each week of the harrowing experience of survival. The class became acutely aware of the passage of time in the plot as the students attempted to distinguish one time frame from the next. Project suggestions in Figure 8–2 describe the kinds of representation students undertake.

Teachers can teach students about visual representation by making connections to the literature they are reading. Picture books provide excellent examples of one or more forms of representation and various art media. Figure 8–7 on pages 332–333 lists picture books according to medium.

Cartoons and Caricature

Harrison, T. (1997). *Don't Dig So Deep, Nicholas!* Toronto: Owl Books. 🍁

Henkes, K. (1993). *Owen.* New York: Greenwillow Books.

Rae, J. (1998). *Dog Tales.* Vancouver: Whitecap Books. 🍁

Collage

Carle, E. (1998). *Hello, Red Fox.* New York: Simon & Schuster.

Cleaver, E. (1969) *How Summer Came to Canada.* Toronto: Oxford University Press. 🍁

Jocelyn, M. (2000). *Hannah's Collections.* New York: Dutton Children's Books.

Oppenheim, J. (1996). *Have You Seen Bugs?* Richmond Hill, ON: Scholastic Canada. 🍁

Yerxa, L. (1993). *Last Leaf First Snowflake to Fall.* Vancouver: Douglas & McIntyre. 🍁

Crayons and Coloured Pencils

Coffey, M. (1998). *A Cat in a Kayak.* Toronto: Annick Press. 🍁

Gregory, N. (1995). *How Smudge Came.* Red Deer, AB: Red Deer College Press. 🍁

MacFarlane, S.(1993) *Waiting for the Whales.* Victoria, BC: Orca Book Publishers. 🍁

Zeeman, L. (1999). *Sinbad: From the Tales of the Thousand and One Nights.* Montreal: Tundra Books. 🍁

Drawing

Greenwood, B. (1999). *Pioneer Thanksgiving.* Toronto: Kids Can Press. 🍁

Johnson, C. (1965). *Harold and the Purple Crayon.* New York: Harper & Row.

Macaulay, D. (1977). *Castle.* Boston: Houghton Mifflin.

Munsch, R. (1992). *Purple, Green, and Yellow.* Toronto: Annick Press. 🍁

Wynne-Jones, T. (1992). *Zoom Upstream.* Toronto: Groundwood Books. 🍁

Mixed Media

Goble, P. (2003). *Mystic Horse.* New York: HarperCollins.

Lunn, J. (1992). *Story of Canada.* Toronto: Key Porter Books. 🍁

Lunn, J. (1992). *Story of Canada.* Toronto; Key Porter Books. 🍁

Major, K. (2000). *Eh? To Zed: A Canadian ABcDarium.* Calgary: Red Deer Press. 🍁

Tolowa, M. (1995). *The Orphan Boy.* Don Mills, ON: Stoddart. 🍁

Painting

Butler, G. (1995). *The Killick: A Newfoundland Story.* Montreal: Tundra Books. 🍁

Carney, M. (1997). *At Grandpa's Sugar Bush.* Toronto: Kids Can Press. 🍁

Graham, G. (1998). *The Strongest Man This Side of Cremona.* Red Deer, AB: Northern Lights/Red Deer College Press. 🍁

Harrison, T. (2002). *O Canada.* Toronto: Kids Can Press. 🍁

McGugan, J. (1994). *Josepha: A Prairie Boy's Story.* Red Deer, AB: Red Deer College Press. 🍁

Taylor, C. (1992). *Little Water and the Gift of the Animals: A Seneca Legend.* Montreal: Tundra Books. 🍁

Pastels (Chalk)

Coerr, F. (1993) *Sadako.* New York: Putnam.

Dewey, A. (1995). *The Sky.* Seattle, WA: Green Tiger Press.

Sisulu, E. (1996). *The Day Gogo Went to Vote.* Boston: Little Brown.

Van Allsburg, C. (1985). *The Polar Express.* Boston: Houghton Mifflin.

Pen and Pencil/Ink

Anfousse, G. (1978). *Chicken Pox.* Toronto: New Canada Publications. 🍁

Downie, M. & Rawlyk, G. (1980). *A Proper Acadian.* Toronto: Kids Can Press. 🍁

Lionni, L. (1961). *On My Beach There Are Many Pebbles.* London: Mulberry Books.

Sis, P. (1998). *Tibet Through the Red Box.* Toronto: Douglas & McIntyre. 🍁

Stinson, K. (1982). *Red Is Best.* Toronto: Annick Press. 🍁

Photography

Hoban, T. (2000). *Cubes, Cones, Cylinders and Spheres.* New York: Greenwillow.

Johnston, S. (1995). *Alphabet City.* Toronto: Penguin Books Canada. 🍁

Kissinger, K. (1994). *All the Colours We Are.* St. Paul, MN: Redleaf Press.

McGraw, S. (1990). *Papier-mâché Today.* Toronto: Firefly Books. 🍁

(continued)

Figure 8–7 Picture Book Examples of a Variety of Art Media

Onyefulu, I. (1993). *A Is for Africa*. Toronto: Penguin Canada. ✤

Plasticine

Bogart, J. (1994). *Gifts*. Richmond Hill, ON: North Winds Press. ✤

Burton, K. (1995). *One Grey Mouse*. Toronto: Kids Can Press. ✤

Reid, B. (1997). *The Party*. Toronto: Scholastic Canada. ✤

Reid, B. (2003). *The Subway Mouse*. Toronto: Scholastic Canada. ✤

Printmaking

Ballantyne, A. (1991). *Wisakyjak and the New World*. Waterloo, ON: Penumbra Press. ✤

Bouchard, D. (1990). *The Elders Are Watching*. Tofino, BC: Eagle Dance Enterprises. ✤

Martin, J. (1998). *Snowflake Bentley*. Boston: Houghton Mifflin.

Sculpture

Feelings, M. (1974). *Jambo Means Hello: Swahili Alphabet*. New York: Dial Books for Young Readers.

Flemming, D. (1994). *Barnyard Banter*. New York: Henry Holt.

Hoyt-Goldsmith, D. (1990). *Totem Pole*. New York: Holiday House.

Watercolour

Bouchard, D. (1996). *The Dust Bowl*. Toronto: Kids Can Press. ✤

Chase, E. (1996). *Secret Dawn*. Richmond Hill, ON: North Winds Press. ✤

Gay, M-L. (2000). *Stella Queen of the Snow*. Toronto: Douglas & McIntyre. ✤

Lawson, J. (1992). *A Morning to Polish and Keep*. Red Deer, AB: Red Deer College Press. ✤

LeFord, B. (1995). *A Blue Butterfly: A Story About Claude Monet*. New York: Doubleday.

Waterton, B. (1978). *A Salmon for Simon*. Vancouver: Douglas & McIntyre. ✤

Figure 8–7 Picture Book Examples of a Variety of Art Media *(continued)*

Teaching Critical Listening, Viewing, and Visually Representing

The steps in teaching students to be critical listeners, viewers, and visual represented are similar to the steps in teaching aesthetic and efferent listening strategies. In the following teaching strategy, students view television commercials to examine propaganda devices and persuasive language. Later they can create their own commercials and advertisements using available print and digital technology. The steps in a listening, viewing, and visually representing strategy are presented in the following Step by Step box:

Step by Step

Listening, Viewing, and Visually Representing Strategy

1. *Introduce commercials.* The teacher talks about commercials and asks students about familiar commercials. The teacher collects some commercials on video and views them with students. The teacher leads discussion about the purpose of each commercial, and uses these questions about commercials to probe students' thinking about persuasion and propaganda:

   ● What is the purpose of the commercial?
   ● Is there evidence of bias?

- Does the commercial make sweeping generalizations or unsupported inferences?
- Do opinions predominate the talk?
- Does the commercial make use of any propaganda devices?
- Do you accept the message? (adapted from Devine, 1982, pp. 41–42)

2. *Explain persuasion and propaganda.*   The teacher presents the terms *persuasion* and *propaganda*. The teacher introduces the persuasion and propaganda devices and shows the commercials again to look for examples of each device. Then, the teacher introduces the terms *loaded words* and *doublespeak*, and shows the commercials a third time to look for examples of deceptive language.

3. *Analyze deceptive language.*   The teacher has students work in small groups to critique a commercial (print or nonprint) as to the types of persuasion, propaganda devices, and deceptive language used. Students might also want to test the claims made in the commercial.

4. *Review concepts.*   The teacher reviews the concepts about persuasion, propaganda devices, and deceptive language introduced in the first three steps. It may be helpful for students to make charts about these concepts.

5. *Provide practice.*   The teacher presents a new set of commercials for students to critique. The teacher asks students to identify persuasion, propaganda devices, and deceptive language in the commercials.

6. *Have students create commercials.*   The teacher has students apply what they have learned about persuasion, propaganda devices, and deceptive language by creating their own products and writing and producing their own commercials to advertise them. Possible products include breakfast cereals, toys, beauty and diet products, and sports equipment. Students might also create homework and pet-sitting services to advertise, or choose community or environmental issues to campaign for or against. An excerpt from a storyboard for a commercial created by a group of grade 5 students appears in Figure 8–8. As the students present the commercials, classmates act as critical listeners and viewers to detect persuasion, propaganda devices, loaded words, and doublespeak.

Using Advertisements. Students can use the same step-by-step procedures and activities with advertisements collected from magazines and product packages. Children collect advertisements and display them on a bulletin board. Written advertisements also use deceptive language and propaganda devices. Students examine advertisements and then decide how the writer is trying to persuade them to purchase the product. They can also compare the proportion of text and pictures in the advertisements. Toy advertisements often feature large, colourful pictures; cosmetic advertisements feature large pictures of beautiful women; but advertisements for medicines devote more space to text. Students point out sports stars and entertainment personalities in many advertisements. Even primary-grade students recognize intellectual, character, and emotional appeals in these advertisements.

Students often apply what they have learned about persuasion in advertisements when they create their own. Figure 8–9 shows the "Wanted" poster that a grade 2 student made after reading *Sylvester and the Magic Pebble* (Steig, 1969), the story of a donkey who is lost after he is magically turned into a stone. Before students made these posters, the teacher taught a minilesson about persuasion and shared examples of advertisements with the students. With this introduction, students decided to feature large pictures of the donkey, emotional appeals, reward offers, and their telephone numbers. Students can also make advertisements about favourite books as part of their response to the literature, both fiction and nonfiction.

Figure 8–8 An Excerpt from Grade 5 Students' Storyboard for Their "Dream Date" Commercial

Figure 8–9 A Grade 2 Student's "Wanted" Poster

Minilessons on Critical Listening, Viewing, and Visually Representing. Teachers teach mini-lessons to introduce, practise, and review procedures, concepts, and strategies and skills related to critical listening and viewing. Chapter 5, "Listening and Speaking in the Classroom," presents a list on page 185 of topics for minilessons on critical listening. These topics can be taught when students are studying commercials or writing advertisements as part of language arts units, or social studies or science lessons.

Using Picture Books to Teach Critical Viewing. In picture books the message depends upon the pictures as much as or more than the text. The pictures must be accurate and synchronized with the text, but they extend the text. When students view picture books, they first see each picture as a whole then notice the individual details that make up the whole. When teachers present books to children, they provide time and guidance for careful viewing, pointing out the illustrator's use of such techniques as line, colour, space, and shape for particular effects. For example, a teacher might draw attention to how cross-hatch lines are used to give texture in *Where the Wild Things Are* (Sendak, 1963); how colours replicate the African landscape in *We All Went on Safari* (Krebs & Cairns, 2003) and *The Orphan Boy* (Mollel, 1990); and how shape and space are used together to show form in *Inside Freight Train* (Crews, 2001) Young children's attention is also drawn to special effects such as the foil scales of Marcus Pfister's *The Rainbow Fish* and the soft-to-touch feel of Arctic bear in *Snow Bear* (Harper, 2002).

The techniques and materials used in picture book illustrations are often difficult for classroom teachers to determine. Some information can be found in a Foreword or Afterward, or on the jacket flap, cover, or last page of the book. Teachers also learn about illustrations by consulting the author's and illustrator's websites. Figure 8–10 lists award-winning picture books that teachers use to teach illustration media and critical viewing.

ADAPTING TO MEET THE NEEDS OF EVERY STUDENT

Because students of all ages and all reading abilities are bombarded with visual images, it is especially important that all students be thoughtful and critical viewers. Students need to learn not only the specific critical viewing skills related to persuasion and propaganda, but the more general skill of varying the way they view images in accordance with the purposes for which they are viewing.

The Amelia Frances Howard-Gibbon Illustrator's Award honours excellence in children's illustration in a book published in Canada.

1995	Barbara Reid. *Gifts* by Jo Ellen Bogart. Richmond Hill: North Winds Press, 1994.
1996	Karen Reczuch. *Just Like New* by Ainslie Manson. Toronto: Groundwood Books, 1995.
1997	Harvey Chan. *Ghost Train* by Paul Yee. Toronto: Groundwood Books, 1996.
1998	Barbara Reid. *The Party* by Barbara Reid. Richmond Hill: Northwinds Press, 1997.
1999	Kady MacDonald Denton. *A Child's Treasury of Nursery Rhymes*. Toronto: Kids Can Press, 1998.
2000	Zhong-Yang Huang. *The Dragon New Year* by David Bouchard. Vancouver: Raincoast Books, 1999.
2001	Laura Fernandez and Rick Jacobson. *The Magnificent Piano Recital* by Marilynn Reynolds. Victoria: Orca Book Publishers, 2000.

(continued)

Figure 8–10 Recently Published Award-Winning Picture Books Teachers Use to Teach Illustration Media and Critical Viewing

2002   Frances Wolfe. *Where I Live.* Toronto: Tundra Books, 2001. ❦

2003   Susan Vande Griek and Pascal Milelli. *The Art Room.* Toronto: Groundwood Books, 2002. ❦

2004   Bill Slavin. *Stanley's Party* by Linda Bailey. Toronto: Kids Can Press, 2003. ❦

2005   Wallace Edwards. *Monkey Business.* Toronto: Kids Can Press, 2004 ❦

The Elizabeth Mrazik-Cleaver Canadian Picture Book Award is presented annually to a Canadian children's book illustrator whose work on a new book is deemed both original and worthy.

1995   Murray Kimber. *Josepha: A Prairie Boy's Story* by Jim McGugan. Red Deer: Red Deer College Press, 1994. ❦

1996   Janet Wilson. *Selina and the Bear Paw Quilt* by Barbara Smucker. Toronto: Lester Publishing, 1995. ❦

1997   Harvey Chan. *Ghost Train* by Paul Yee. Toronto: Groundwood Books, 1996. ❦

1998   Pascal Milelli. *Rainbow Bay* by Stephen Eaton Hume. Vancouver: Raincoast Books, 1997. ❦

1999   Kady MacDonald Denton. *A Child's Treasury of Nursery Rhymes.* Toronto: Kids Can Press, 1998. ❦

2000   Michele Lemieux. *Stormy Night.* Toronto: Kids Can Press, 1999. ❦

2001   Marie Louise Gay. *Stella, Queen of the Snow.* Toronto: Groundwood Books, 2000. ❦

2002   Janie Jaehyun Park. *The Tiger and the Dried Persimmon.* Groundwood Books, 2002. ❦

2003   Pierre Pratt. *Where's Pup?* by Dayle Ann Dodds. Toronto: Tundra Books, 2003. ❦

2004   Stephan Poulin. *Un chant de Noel* by Lucie Papineau. Saint-Lambert, QC: Dominique et compagnie, 2004. ❦

For a complete list of each award since its inception, see the Canadian Children's Book Centre website at www.bookcentre.ca.

Figure 8–10 Recently Published Award-Winning Picture Books Teachers Use to Teach Illustration Media and Critical Viewing *(continued)*

To do this, they must learn to recognize the elements that affect their viewing, and the ways those elements affect the meanings they construct from the visual texts. See page 338 for a list of ways to adapt viewing and visually representing instruction to meet the needs of every student.

ASSESSING STUDENTS' CRITICAL VIEWING AND VISUALLY REPRESENTING

Teachers can assess students' knowledge of critical listening, viewing, and visually representing by having them first view and listen to commercials, advertisements, or other oral and visual presentations, then critique them indicating their recognition of techniques used and their effects. Teachers can also evaluate their students' recognition and use of critical techniques in their own productions of commercials, advertisements, or other visual presentations. A third way to assess students' understanding of critical viewing is to have them critique picture book illustrations or the visuals presented in nonprint media such as DVDs. Critical listening and viewing are interrelated in such tasks and teachers should consider both when assessing students' knowledge and skills. Further, the

Adapting

Viewing and Visually Representing Instruction to Meet the Needs of Every Student

1. **Identify a Purpose for Viewing**
   When students view images, they need to have a specific purpose for viewing and to know what they will be expected to do after viewing. Ask students to state their purpose and how they will use the information gathered. Because viewing can be a passive activity if not structured, teachers need to help students clarify the reason for viewing and how the information will be used.

2. **Provide Frequent Opportunities to View**
   Learning to view, like learn to read, requires time on task. Provide students with frequent opportunities to view for multiple purposes followed by an opportunity to discuss what was viewed. Teachers can include words that describe visual elements and techniques in the classroom word wall to assist students in using appropriate vocabulary in discussions.

3. **Make the Viewing Process Visible**
   Viewing is an invisible process. Teachers can help students make it visible by asking them to speak and write about what they do when they view. Teachers encourage students to think about how the author of the visual image perceived the information, and what techniques the author chose and why to convey information.

4. **Explore Many Examples of Visual Images**
   Teachers guide students to explore and read the many visual images they encounter, including, but not limited to the visual images in their textbooks (graphs, illustrations, charts, etc.) and those contained in other texts they read in school, such as websites. Teachers provide practice in interpreting the information and opportunity to share their interpretations.

5. **Provide Frequent Opportunities to Represent**
   Students need many opportunities to communicate their ideas and demonstrate their learning in a variety of forms. They need to explore use of various media and forms to discover the characteristics, purposes, and effects of using each one. For some students, visual communication may be a means of significantly clarifying or enhancing the message they are able to convey.

6. **Give Students Guidance and Explicit Instruction**
   Although much is learned by observing and exploring, students also need explicit instruction in how to use specific visually representing strategies. Specific and well-paced instruction in strategies such as story mapping, storyboarding, graphing, charting, role-playing, and creating models or pictorial displays helps students develop effective visually representing skills. Similarly, students also need explicit and well-paced instruction to enable them to use technology to visually represent and communicate their thoughts and ideas.

production of illustrations for a variety of purposes and the creation of webpages requires application of critical analysis and can provide assessment information regarding student learning.

Review

Viewing and visually representing are the most recent additions to the language arts. A broader concept of literacy and the ready availability of communication technology and multimedia in students' lives have made them essential parts of the curriculum. Through viewing and visually representing activities, students learn to vary the way they view for different purposes, and they learn the various ways authors use visual images to convey information and ideas. In turn, they learn to create their own visual images, to visually represent, using different procedures, strategies, and skills to communicate their knowledge, understandings, and beliefs.

The following key concepts are presented in this chapter:

1. Viewing and visually representing are essential language arts.
2. Visual literacy is the ability to see and understand, and to think, create, and communicate graphically.
3. Students need to learn viewing strategies to make the most of their learning from visual images.
4. Students need to learn to use visually representing strategies to enhance their communication abilities.
5. Viewing, like listening, is a three-step process: receiving, attending, and assigning meaning.
6. Critical viewing, like critical listening, involves students in evaluation of messages from others.
7. Picture books, commercials, and advertisements are excellent resources for teaching visual literacy.
8. Students need to learn elements of visual art and design and techniques of propaganda and persuasion to view critically and create meaning through representation.
9. Students need to learn to view critically because they are exposed to many types of persuasion and propaganda.
10. Students need multiple opportunities to visually represent their learning using a variety of strategies because representation enhances learning not only of the language arts, but in other areas of curriculum.

Extensions

1. Visit a classroom and observe how viewing and visually representing are taught and how students use their viewing and representing skills.
2. Interview primary students about how they read picture books. Ask questions such as these:
   - When you read a picture book, do you look at the pictures first?
   - What do you think the illustrator was thinking when he/she created these pictures? (Show the students a particular picture from a familiar book.)
   - Do you use the pictures to help with words you do not recognize?
3. Read a wordless picture book with primary students. Take note of how they read the illustrations to compose a story. What elements of the illustrations do they attend to, in order to help compose their stories?
4. Work with middle- and upper-grade students to create illustrated stories using pictures and symbols available online.
5. Work with students to enhance written informational text with visual images. As they work, talk with students about their choices of strategies such as graphs, diagrams, and charts.
6. Study the illustrations of one or more picture books. Read the illustrators' websites to gain insights into the techniques.
7. Experiment with software designed to help create visual images of concepts, such as Inspiration, to create images of your understandings of a topic related to learning and teaching the language arts.
8. Using the information presented on critical listening, viewing, and visually representing, teach a lesson in which students critique and create commercials or advertisements. Reflect on their understanding of propaganda techniques.

chapter nine

Words and the Language Tools to Use Them: Spelling, Grammar, and Handwriting

Procedure

Structures is a process of math (and science) investigation initiated by Dr. Otto Weininger of the Ontario Institute of Studies in Education (OISE).

Simply put, my kindergarten children choose from 30+ bins of building materials, ranging from trade materials, such as base-ten blocks, Construx, Duplo, Tinkertoys, and Polydrons, to "found" materials such as yogourt containers, wood scraps, paper rolls, film canisters, Styrofoam pieces, and plastic shapes. They go to their own space, taking a Structures mat (laminated 46 cm x 60 cm construction paper), and they build! Through the medium of play—directed by previous instruction and extensive modelling, but with free rein when they work—the children explore and internalize math concepts through manipulation of materials provided. A significant component of this process is language development—a wonderful example of language arts integrated across the curriculum.

Work periods vary from 10 to 30 minutes. Normally the children work in silence, allowing them a rare opportunity to be quiet and to rely on their own ideas and initiative.

Work periods can be unstructured or the children can be given direction ("See how you can use your materials to build the tallest structure possible," "Can you cover all of your mat before you begin to build up?" or "Think about ways you can change your original idea").

> "I have used Structures as a language arts and math tool for more than eight years with children ranging in age from four to twelve . . . For me, Structures is often 'as good as it gets' in teaching."
>
> Karen Dicks
> Kindergarten Teacher
> J. H. Sissons School,
> Yellowknife, NWT

Before introducing the materials, and before each session, we talk about possibilities. Children verbalize scenarios, listen to others' ideas, comment, and make

This is a squishy moshen wik clay and stiks.

suggestions. The teacher models: "I have a bin of cylindrical solids. They are different heights; they are different thicknesses; they are different colours. How many ways can I use them?" We work on vocabulary generated by discussion, orally, and in written form. I introduce and reinforce vocabulary I anticipate they will need. Some language arts learning activities:

- Shape books related to what we have discussed
- Vocabulary lists sorted and grouped on chart paper
- Flash cards—actions (stack, balance, sort, compare, substitute), outcomes (tower, symmetry, pattern, balance), names of shapes, names of 3-D solids, colour words, number words—used throughout the kindergarten day in various settings
- Stories/accounts recorded on chart paper for reading and rereading
- Journals—in kindergarten, we keep a class journal, and children also write in their personal journals after Structures sessions
- A master list, in large print, of available materials. Children read down the list and consider what they might work with next. The names of materials are alphabetized
- Post-activity tours, when children circulate, comment, question, and bring observations back to the group
- A home journal, a photographic account of what we do during sessions, with some dialogue provided by the children. It travels home with the children and also acts as an introduction for children and parents new to our classroom.

Assessment

I draw a grid, one name per box, recording observations, noting what materials each child uses. In a 30-minute period, I make detailed notes of observations on a third of the children; the next two times, I observe the rest of the children. I always have an extra sheet handy to record "Eureka!" occurrences and quotes from the children.

I tape conversations we have, both pre- and post-activity period.

I regularly take photos and have the children dictate accompanying dialogue. This is a favourite book during reading periods.

I have colleagues come in during sessions to provide feedback. Sometimes I ask them to watch a particular child; at other times I let them choose.

Adaptations

We have days when two children can work together with either one bin or two in combination. Big Buddies also come to work with us. Parents are invited to come in and join us . . . guess who gets the most carried away! Older kids can keep their own math journals—illustrating what they've done and adding text to describe processes.

Reflections

I have used Structures as a language arts and math tool for more than eight years with children ranging in age from four to twelve (I know colleagues who use it through the end of high school). For me, Structures is often "as good as it gets" in teaching. While few of the children master the technical vocabulary, they become familiar with and curious about the whole process of language and have a base from which to extend as they grow.

This aspiring author in Enchant School is learning to use both invented and conventional spelling to express her ideas. She and her teacher talked together to organize her writing, then her teacher wrote a model for her first sentence. She will add to her story using her growing knowledge of how print works.

Words are the meaning-bearing units of language. Of the three-quarters of a million words in English, most people use only about 20 000, and most of the words we commonly use come from a body of approximately 5000 to 7000 words (Klein, 1988). To construct meaning, readers and writers need to know many words, how to choose the right words, and how to connect words together in ways that are understood by others; that is, they need to have and use rich vocabularies and know and use Standard English grammar. If they are to communicate with others, they also need to know how to use the tools of language—spelling and handwriting. Traditionally, use of Standard English grammar, conventional spelling, and neat handwriting have been considered the hallmarks of an educated person. Today, more and more people see grammar, spelling, and handwriting as tools for communicating *through* language—as means to an end, rather than the goal of education. Although how they are perceived may be changing in response to influences such as communication technology, these tools have been and continue to be important parts of language arts instruction. In this chapter we will first look at some types of words and students' vocabulary development. Then we will discuss the language tools of spelling, grammar, and handwriting, and how to teach students to use them.

Words and Their Meanings

Learning about words and how to choose the right one to express the meaning you intend is what vocabulary is all about. Vocabulary is not decoding or word identification; rather, the focus is on meaning. Choosing the best word to express meaning is important to all language users. When we listen and read, we must understand the meaning that someone else intends, and when we speak and write, we must choose exactly the right word so that our audience will understand our message.

Students begin kindergarten with approximately 5000 words in their vocabularies, and their vocabularies grow at a rate of about 3000 words a year (Nagy &

To Guide Your Reading

As you read this chapter, prepare to

Identify what teachers teach young students about the meanings of words.

•

Explain how teachers focus on words during resource-based units, thematic units, and inquiry-based units

•

Explain how teachers teach spelling, grammar, and handwriting in the elementary grades

•

Explain how teachers teach the language tools integrated with meaningful, functional, and genuine language arts activities

Herman, 1985; Blachowicz & Fisher, 2000). Through reading and other experiences with language, students not only learn more, but also become sophisticated about words and their literal and figurative meanings. During the elementary grades, students learn about words and word parts, words that mean the same as and the opposite of other words, words that sound alike, words with multiple meanings, the figurative language of idioms, and how words have been borrowed from languages around the world. They also learn about how words are created and they have fun playing with words (Tompkins, 1994). What follows is a teachers' guide to those aspects of words most often explored in elementary classrooms.

ROOT WORDS AND AFFIXES

A *root word* is a morpheme, the basic and meaning-bearing part of a word to which affixes are added. Some root words are whole words, and others are parts of words. Many words are developed from a single root word; for example, the Latin word *portare* ("to carry") is the source of at least nine Modern English words: *deport, export, import, port, portable, porter, report, support,* and *transportation.* Latin is one source of English root words, and Greek and Old English are two other sources. A list of root words appears in the Teacher's Notebook on page 344. Students can compile lists of words developed from these root words, and they can draw root word clusters to illustrate the relationship of the root word to the words developed from it. Figure 9–1 shows a root word cluster for the Greek root *graph*, which means "to write." Recognizing basic elements from word to word helps students cut down on the amount of memorizing necessary to learn meanings and spellings.

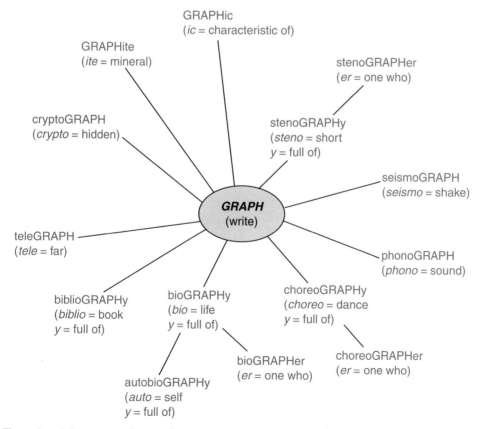

Figure 9–1 A Cluster for the Root Word *Graph*

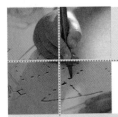

Teacher's Notebook

Root Words

ann/enn (year): anniversary, annual, biennial, centennial, perennial

ast (star): aster, asterisk, astrology, astronaut, astronomy

auto (self): autobiography, automatic, automobile

bio (life): autobiography, biodegradable, biography, biology

cent (hundred): cent, centennial, centigrade, centipede, century

circ (around): circle, circular, circus, circumspect

corp (body): corporal, corporation, corps

cycl (wheel): bicycle, cycle, cyclist, cyclone, tricycle

dict (speak): contradict, dictate, dictator, predict, verdict

geo (earth): geography, geology, geometry

gram (letter): diagram, grammar, monogram, telegram

graph (write): biography, graphic, paragraph, phonograph, stenographer

grat (pleasing, thankful): congratulate, grateful, gratitude

jus/jud/jur (law, right): injury, judge, justice

man (hand): manacle, manual, manufacture, manuscript

mand (order): command, demand, mandate, remand

mar (sea): aquamarine, marine, maritime, submarine

meter/metre (measure): barometer, centimetre, diameter, speedometer, thermometer

min (small): miniature, minimize, minor, minute

mort (death): immortal, mortal, mortality, mortician, post-mortem

ped/pod (foot): pedal, pedestrian, podiatry, tripod

phon (sound): earphone, microphone, phonics, phonograph, saxophone, symphony

photo (light): photograph, photographer, photosensitive, photosynthesis

quer/ques/quis (seek): query, question, inquisitive

rupt (break): abrupt, bankrupt, interrupt, rupture

scope (see): horoscope, kaleidoscope, microscope, periscope, telescope

struct (build): construction, indestructible, instruct

tele (far): telecast, telegram, telegraph, telephone, telescope, telethon, television

terr (land): terrace, terrain, terrarium, territory

tract (pull, drag): attraction, subtract, tractor

vict/vinc (conquer): convict, convince, evict, victor, victory

vis (see): television, visa, vision, visual

viv/vit (live): survive, vitamin, vivid

volv (roll): involve, revolutionary, revolver

Affixes are bound morphemes that are added to words and root words. Affixes can be prefixes or suffixes. Prefixes are added to the beginning of words, such as *re-* in *reread*, and suffixes are added to the ends of words, such as *-ing* in *singing* and *-er* in *player*. Like root words, affixes come from Old English, Latin, and Greek. They often change a word's meaning, such as adding *un-* to *happy* to form *unhappy*. Sometimes they change the part of speech, too. For example, when *-ion* is added to *attract* to form *attraction*, the verb *attract* becomes a noun.

When an affix is "peeled off" or removed from a word, the remaining word is usually a real word. For example, when the prefix *pre-* is removed from *preview*, the word *view* can stand

Grade 4 students play word card games to learn homonyms.

alone; and when the suffix -ful is removed from careful, the word care can stand alone. One caution should be pointed out to students. Some words include letter sequences that look like affixes, but because the remaining word cannot stand alone, they are not affixes. For example, the in- at the beginning of include is not a prefix because clude is not a word. Such "phantom" affixes can be confusing to students when they are using the affixes to unlock the meaning of unfamiliar words.

A list of prefixes and suffixes is presented in the Teacher's Notebook on page 346. White, Sowell, and Yanagihara (1989) researched affixes and identified those that are most commonly used in English words; these are marked with an asterisk in the Teacher's Notebook. White and his colleagues recommend that the commonly used affixes be taught to middle- and upper-grade students because affixes help determine spelling and word meaning.

SYNONYMS AND ANTONYMS

Synonyms are words that have the same or nearly the same meanings as other words. Synonyms are useful because they provide options, allowing us to express ourselves with more exactness. Students can check a dictionary or thesaurus to locate synonyms for words to assist them to clearly and expressively present their ideas in their writing.

Antonyms are words that express opposite meanings. For example, antonyms for loud include soft, subdued, quiet, silent, inaudible, sedate, sombre, and dull. These words express shades of meaning just as synonyms do, and some opposites are more appropriate for one meaning of loud than for another.

Two important references for examining the meanings of words are dictionaries and thesauri, both hard texts and online editions. Beginning with pictionaries, students can learn to use these resources as soon as they begin to read and write. Among our favourites are The Canadian Oxford Picture Dictionary (1996), the Gage Canadian Dictionary (2000), and Scholastic Children's Thesaurus (1998). These and other reference books are annotated in Figure 9–2 on pages 347–348.

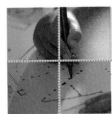

Teacher's Notebook

Affixes

Prefixes	Suffixes

Prefixes

a/an- (not): atheist, anaerobic
amphi- (both): amphibian
anti- (against): antiseptic
bi- (two, twice): bifocal, biannual
contra- (against): contradict
de- (away): detract
di- (two): dioxide
***dis-** (not): disapprove
***dis-** (reversal): disinfect
ex- (out): export
hemi- (half): hemisphere
***il-/im-/in-/ir-** (not): illegible, impolite,
    inexpensive, irrational
***in-** (in, into): indoor
inter- (between): intermission
kilo/milli- (one thousand): kilometre, milligram
micro- (small): microfilm
***mis-** (wrong): mistake
mono- (one): monarch
multi- (many): multimillionaire
omni- (all): omnivorous
***over-** (too much): overflow
poly- (many): polygon
post- (after): postwar
pre-/pro- (before): precede, prologue
quad-/quart- (four): quadruple, quarter
re- (again): repay
***re-/retro-** (back): replace, retroactive
***sub-** (under): submarine
super- (above): supermarket
trans- (across): transport
tri- (three): triangle
***un-** (not): unhappy
***un-** (reversal): untie

Suffixes

-able/-ible (worthy of, can be): lovable, audible
***-al/-ial** (action, process): arrival, denial
-ance/-ence (state or quality): annoyance,
    absence
-ant (one who): servant
-ard (one who is): coward
-ary/-ory (person, place): secretary, laboratory
-dom (state or quality): freedom
-ed (past tense): played
-ee (one who is): trustee
***-er/-or/-ar** (one who): teacher, actor, liar
-er/-or (action): robber
-ern (direction): northern
-et/-ette (small): booklet, dinette
-ful (full of): hopeful
-hood (state or quality): childhood
-ic (characterized by): angelic
-icle/-cule (small): particle, molecule
-ify (to make): simplify
-ing (participle): eating, building
-ish (like): reddish
-ism (doctrine of): communism
-less (without): hopeless
-ling (young): duckling
-logy (the study of): zoology
***-ly** (in the manner of): slowly
-ment (state or quality): enjoyment
***-ness** (state or quality): kindness
-s/-es (plural): cats, boxes
-ship (state, or art or skill): friendship, seamanship
***-sion/-tion** (state or quality): tension, attraction
-ster (one who): gangster
-ure (state or quality): failure
-ward (direction): homeward
***-y** (full of): sleepy

* = most commonly used affixes

Source: White, Sowell, & Yanagihara, 1989.

Dictionaries

Canadian Children's Dictionary. (1991). Toronto: Houghton Mifflin Canada Ltd. (M) ⚜

* This dictionary is intended for use in schools in grades 3 through 6. It contains more than 1500 illustrations in addition to word histories and a pronunciation key. A beginning section helps readers become acquainted with the dictionary.

Canadian Junior Dictionary. (2000). Toronto: Gage Educational Publishing Ltd. (M) ⚜

* This dictionary lists and defines approximately 30 000 words. It includes a pronunciation key, fistnotes, and student activities.

Canadian Primary Dictionary. (1991). Toronto: Houghton Mifflin Canada Ltd. (P) ⚜

* This dictionary contains 1700 words and 600 full-colour illustrations to represent a broad selection of words children see and use every day. Every word is defined and illustrations are used to enhance definitions.

Gage Canadian Dictionary Intermediate. (1997). Toronto: Gage Educational Publishing Ltd. (U) ⚜

* This dictionary builds on the smaller *Junior* volume. Recently revised and updated, it is ideal for grades 6 to 10 and ESL students. It offers fistnotes, pronunciation, homonyms, usage information, synonyms, and etymologies.

Harcourt Brace Canadian Dictionary for Students. (1998). Toronto: Harcourt Canada. (M–U) ⚜

* This dictionary is intended for grades 4 through 8.

Kenny, C. (Ed.) (1999). *The Kids Can Press French & English Phrase Book.* Ill. by L. Hendry. Toronto: Kids Can Press. (M–U) ⚜

* This reference book has more than 200 useful phrases clearly illustrated in French and English.

McIlwain, J. (1994). *The DK Children's Illustrated Dictionary.* London: Dorling Kindersley. (P)

* This dictionary has 5000 main entries and 7000 related words accompanied by 2500 colour photographs and illustrations. In each entry, the part of speech is identified, multiple meanings are listed, and sample sentences are provided. A pronunciation guide and antonyms are provided as needed. The entries are arranged in four columns on each page.

My First Canadian Oxford Dictionary. (2003). Don Mills, ON: Oxford University Press Canada. (P) ⚜

* This dictionary is intended for children ages 5 and up. It contains lively, colourful illustrations of over 550 words.

Nelson Canadian Dictionary of the English Language. (1998). Toronto: ITP Nelson. (T) ⚜

Parnwell, E., & Grennan, M. (1996). *The Canadian Oxford Picture Dictionary: Monolingual Edition.* Toronto: Oxford University Press. (P–M) ⚜

* This useful dictionary is designed to be a basic tool to aid acquisition of Canadian English vocabulary. It contains over 2400 words and full-colour illustrations portraying Canadian culture.

Scholastic Children's Dictionary. (1996). New York: Scholastic. (M)

* Approximately 13 000 words are included in this dictionary with colour illustrations and colourful page decorations. Guide words, pronunciation guides, and attractively designed boxes with information about synonyms, affixes, and word histories are included.

Thesauri

Beal, G. (1996). *The Kingfisher Illustrated Pocket Thesaurus.* New York: Kingfisher. (U)

* In this pocket-size paperback book, over 5000 entries with sample sentences are presented. Antonyms are marked with a star, which is somewhat confusing.

Bellamy, J. (1996). *The Webster's Children's Thesaurus.* New York: Barnes and Noble. (M–U)

* More than 6000 entries are included in this thesaurus. For each entry, synonyms and antonyms are listed, and there are a few two-colour illustrations.

Bollard, J. (1998). *Scholastic Children's Thesaurus.* Richmond Hill, ON: Scholastic (M–U) ⚜

* This comprehensive thesaurus provides a sample sentence for each synonym listed. It also includes an extensive index.

The Harcourt Brace Student Thesaurus. (1991). San Diego: Harcourt Brace. (M–U)

* Over 800 entries with more than 3500 synonyms are listed in this thesaurus. There are 150 colour illustrations. For each entry, the part of speech is listed, definitions and synonyms are provided, and sample sentences are presented. Antonyms are listed for appropriate entries.

My First Canadian Oxford Thesaurus (2003). Don Mills, ON: Oxford University Press Canada. (P–M) ⚜

* This thesaurus includes 100 headwords and more than 1000 alternative words, including opposites. It is intended for children 5 years and up.

(continued)

Figure 9–2 Reference Books for Elementary Students

Roget's Student Thesaurus (Rev. ed.). (1994). New York: HarperCollins. (M–U)
- Over 4000 synonyms with sample sentences are listed in this thesaurus. The pronunciation guide is listed in the index.

Young Canada Thesaurus (1996). Scarborough, ON: Nelson Canada. (U) 🍁
- Over 5000 entries with keywords are included in this thesaurus. An appendix includes lists of words about Canadian and world geography, computers, weather, and other topics.

P = primary grades (K–2); M = middle grades (3–5); U = upper grades (6–8); T = teacher.

Figure 9–2 Reference Books for Elementary Students (*continued*)

HOMONYMS

Homonyms, words that have sound and spelling similarities, are divided into three categories: homophones, homographs, and homographic homophones. *Homophones* are words that sound alike but are spelled differently. Most homophones developed from entirely different root words, and it is only by accident that they have come to sound alike; for example, *right* and *write*.

Homographs are words that are spelled the same but pronounced differently. Their meaning is dependent on the pronunciation. Examples of homographs are *bow, close, lead, minute, record, read,* and *wind*.

Homographic homophones are words that are both spelled and pronounced alike, such as *bark, bat, bill, box, fair, fly, hide, jet, mine, pen, ring, row, spell, toast,* and *yard*. Some are related words; others are linguistic accidents. There are many books of homonyms for children, including Gwynne's *The King Who Rained* (1970), *A Chocolate Moose for Dinner* (1976), *The Sixteen Hand Horse* (1980), and *A Little Pigeon Toad* (1988); Maestro's *What's a Frank Frank?* (1984); and Terban's *Hey, Hay! A Wagonful of Funny Homonym Riddles* (1991). Elementary students enjoy reading these books and making their own word books. Figure 9–3 shows a page from a grade 2 student's homophone book.

MULTIPLE MEANINGS

Many words have more than one meaning. Such words are referred to as *polysemous* words. The word *bank*, for example, has as many as twelve meanings. Why does this happen? One possibility is word origin, such as when words of similar pronunciation but different meanings were borrowed from different languages. Another possibility is the evolution of meanings as society became more complex and needed finer shades of meaning. Other polysemous words may be linguistic accidents. Students can create posters with word clusters to show multiple meanings of words (Bromley, 1996). Figure 9–4 shows a cluster with ten meanings of the word *hot* sketched from a poster made

Figure 9–3 A Page from a Grade 2 Student's Homophone Book

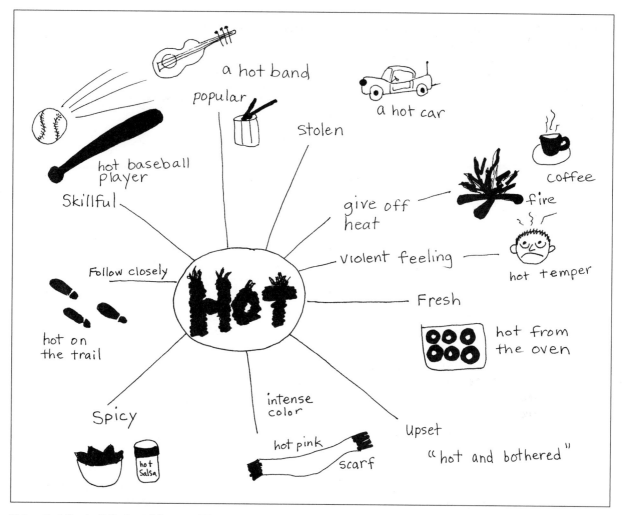

Figure 9–4 Grade 7 Students' Poster of Ten Meanings for *Hot*

by three grade 7 students. Students can also compile lists of words containing the same root word or make booklets illustrating polysemous words.

IDIOMS AND METAPHORS

Many words have both literal and figurative meanings. Literal meanings are the explicit, dictionary meanings, and figurative meanings are metaphorical or use figures of speech. For example, to describe winter as the coldest season of the year in Canada is literal, but to say that winter has icy breath is figurative. Two types of figurative language are idioms and metaphors.

Idioms are groups of words, such as "let the cat out of the bag," that have a special meaning. There are hundreds of idioms in English, and we use them every day to create word pictures that make language more colourful. Some examples are "out in left field," "a skeleton in the closet," and "stick your neck out." Some of these idioms are new, and others are hundreds or thousands of years old.

Idioms can be confusing to students because they must be interpreted figuratively rather than literally. They can be particularly troublesome to students learning English as a second language. It is important that children move beyond the literal meanings to learn flexibility in using language. One

Figure 9–5 A Grade 4 Student's Idiom Poster

way for students to learn flexibility is to create idiom posters, as illustrated in Figure 9–5. Another way is to use literature to introduce figurative language. Young students enjoy the clever use of homonyms and idioms made by the author Peggy Parish in her series of books about Amelia Bedelia. Four other excellent books of idioms for students are *Put Your Foot in Your Mouth and Other Silly Sayings* (Cox, 1980), *Punching the Clock: Funny Action Idioms* (Terban, 1990), and *In a Pickle and Other Funny Idioms* (Terban, 1983). Another good reference book is *Canadian English Idioms: Sayings and Expressions* (Magnuson, 1989). This book provides meanings and examples of idioms that are used every day in Canada.

Metaphors and similes compare something to something else. A *simile* is a comparison signalled by the use of *like* or *as:* "The crowd was as rowdy as a bunch of marauding monkeys" and "In the moonlight the dead tree looked like a skeleton" are two examples. In contrast, a *metaphor* compares two things by implying that one is something else, without using *like* or *as*. "The children were frisky puppies playing in the yard" is an example. Metaphors are a stronger comparison, as these examples show:

The two old men crossed the street as slowly as snails.
The two old men were snails crossing the street.
In the moonlight, the dead tree looked like a skeleton.
In the moonlight, the dead tree was a skeleton.

Differentiating between the terms *simile* and *metaphor* is less important than understanding the meaning of comparisons in books students are reading and having students use comparisons to make their writing more vivid.

SOURCES OF NEW WORDS

Knowing the history of English and how words entered the language contributes greatly to understanding the language and its words—their meanings and spelling patterns. When teachers know about the language and its history, they can help students understand some of the complexities of English.

The fact that English is a historic language accounts for word meanings and some spelling inconsistencies. English has a variety of words for a single concept, and the history of English in general, and the etymology of the words in particular, explain apparent duplications. Consider these words related to water: *aquatic, hydrant, aquamarine, waterfall, hydroelectric, watercress, watery, aquarium, waterproof, hydraulic, aqualung,* and *hydrogen,* to name a few. These words have one of three root words that each mean "water": *water* is English, of course, while *aqua* is Latin, and *hydro* is Greek. The root word that is used depends on the people who created the word, the purpose of the word, and when the word entered English. Helping children understand and appreciate the origins of words is an excellent way to help build meaning vocabulary. Where and how did a word like *snob* enter our language?

Dating back to Old English times, the most common way of expanding English is to borrow words from other languages. Perhaps as many as 75 percent of our words have been borrowed from other languages and incorporated into English. Among the most interesting borrowed words are those from Aboriginal North Americans. The early North American colonists encountered many unfamiliar animals, plants, foods, and aspects of Aboriginal life in America. They borrowed the Aboriginal North American terms for these objects or events and tried to spell them phonetically. Aboriginal North American loan words include *chipmunk, hickory, moccasin, moose, muskrat, opossum, papoose, powwow, raccoon, skunk, toboggan, tomahawk,* and *tepee.*

New words continually appear in English. Not all are borrowed. Many of them are created to describe new phenomena, inventions, and scientific projects. They are created in a variety of ways, including coining, compounding, and clipping.

Creative people have always coined new words. Lewis Carroll, author of *Alice in Wonderland* and *Through the Looking Glass,* is perhaps the best-known inventor of words. He called his inventions *portmanteau words* (borrowing from the British word for a suitcase that opens into two halves) because they blended two words into one. His most famous example, *chortle,* a blend of *snort* and *chuckle,* is from the poem "Jabberwocky." Other examples of blended words include *brunch* (*breakfast* + *lunch*), *electrocute* (*electric* + *execute*), *guesstimate* (*guess* + *estimate*), and *smog* (*smoke* + *fog*).

In addition to blending, some new words are created through compounding or combining two existing words to create a new word. *Friendship* and *childhood* are two words the Anglo-Saxons compounded, while recent compoundings include *latchkey kids, skateboard,* and *software.* Canadian author Jane Barclay (1998) shows the playfulness of combining words in *How Cold Was It?* when she writes of a "freezing, sneezing, goose-bumpy, teeth-chattering, can't-get-out-of-bed, blanket-over-my-head kind of cold."

Clipping, the process of shortening existing words, is another way of creating new words. For example, *bomb* is the shortened form of *bombard,* and *zoo* comes from *zoological park.* Most clipped words are only one syllable and are used in informal conversation.

Two other types of coined words are trademarks and acronyms. Examples of well-known trademarks and brand names that are used generically as words include *Kleenex* (to mean tissue) and *Xerox* (to mean photocopy). Acronyms, words formed by combining the initial letters of several words, include *radar, laser,* and *scuba. Scuba,* for example, was formed by combining the initial letters of *self-contained* underwater breathing apparatus.

Authors also create new words in their stories, and students should be alert to the possibility of finding a created word when they read or listen to stories. The Howes (1979) created *Bunnicula* to name their spooky young rabbit (*bunny* + *dracula*), and Chris Van Allsburg (1981) invented the word *Jumanji* to name his adventure game. J.K. Rowling (1998) introduced readers to Harry Potter's associates *Wormtail, Dumbledore,* and *Lord* Voldemort, whose wizardry was aided by a *portkey.* Although it is unlikely that your students will create new words that will eventually appear in the dictionary, they do create words to add pizzazz to their speech and their writing, and some invented words become part of the everyday jargon in families and classrooms. For instance, a young wordsmith in kindergarten in rainy Halifax told her teacher that for her birthday she wanted a *rainbrella.*

TEACHING STUDENTS ABOUT WORDS

Students' vocabularies grow at an astonishing rate—about 3000 words a year, or roughly seven to ten new words every day (Nagy & Herman, 1985). By the time students finish high school, their vocabularies reach 40 000 words. Teachers often assume that students learn words primarily through the lessons they teach, but students actually learn the meanings of many more words through independent reading and writing projects than through instruction. Media, too, have a significant impact on children's vocabularies. It remains true, however, that encouraging students to read is probably the most important way teachers promote vocabulary growth (Nagy, 1988). Repeated exposure to words is crucial because students need to see and use a new word many times before it becomes a part of their ownership dictionaries—words they understand and use competently.

Once words have been introduced, effective vocabulary instruction calls for frequent, rich and extended instruction (Beck, McKeown, & Kucan, 2002). Multiple encounters with new words are required if students are to retain meanings for the words. Words need to be encountered eight to ten times in a rich instructional environment, one that gets children using and thinking about word meanings and creating associations among the words, so that new words learned become an active part of a student's vocabulary. The measure of success is the frequency with which new vocabulary is incorporated into the writing of new ideas and stories.

Not all the words students learn are equally hard or easy to learn; the degree of difficulty depends on what the student already knows about the word. M. Graves (1985) identifies four possible situations for unfamiliar words:

1. *Sight word.* Students recognize the word, know what it means when they hear someone say it, and can use it orally, but don't recognize its written form. New sight words are probably the easiest words for students to learn because they already use the word orally.
2. *New word.* Students have a concept related to the word, but are not familiar with the word, either orally or in written form.
3. *New concept.* Students have little or no background knowledge about the concept underlying the word, and don't recognize the word itself. New concept words are the most difficult words for students to learn because they must both learn the concept and attach the word label.
4. *New meaning.* Students know the word, but are unfamiliar with the way the word is used and its meaning in this situation.

Vocabulary instruction may take many forms in classroom instruction and may be included in many curriculum areas, not just the language arts. For example, students need to learn the vocabulary of the science and mathematical concepts they are studying. Instruction may be presented in minilessons and other word-study activities. The most successful activities are meaningful to students and involve students in manipulating words from books they are reading or words related to science and social studies themes they are studying. Some lessons may focus on the meaning of selected words, but teachers also need to teach students how to independently figure out the meaning of unfamiliar words (Blachowicz & Lee, 1991). Traditionally, the most common vocabulary activities involve listing new words and directing students to write the words and copy the definitions from a dictionary or use the words in sentences. These activities are not effective and are no longer recommended as they often fail to produce in-depth understanding (Nagy, 1988).

WORD WALLS

One important way to focus students' attention on words is to write keywords on word wall charts and post them in the classroom. Teachers hang blank word walls, made from large sheets of butcher paper, in the classroom at the beginning of a unit. As they plan a unit, teachers identify key vocabulary to understanding the unit concepts and literature. As the unit begins, students and the teacher use the word wall to record interesting, confusing, and important words related to the topic and from the

This student lists important words from books the class is reading on the word wall.

books they are reading or from other media texts they are using. Words are added to the word wall as they come up during unit activities.

Teachers choose the most important words for explicit instruction. Important words include words that are essential to understanding the texts, words that may confuse students, and words that students will use as they read and write throughout the unit. For example, during a unit on the Canadian Pacific Railway, grade 7 students listed these words on their word wall:

ambitious	North-West Rebellion	surveyors
Métis	Chinese workers	Louis Riel
dangerous	Batoche	William Van Horne
Mounted Police	prairies	Canadian troops
mountains	Iron Horse	construction
iron	rock falls	investors
dynamite	wood burning locomotives	explosions
winter cold	Grand Trunk Railway	6000 workers
1885	24 kilometres per hour	bankrupt
engines	John A. Macdonald	hazards
last spike	east to west	bone-rattling
Craigellachie, BC	train robbery	Pacific
train	Westward Ho!	CPR
coast to coast	locomotive	

Even though all of these words and perhaps more will be included on the word wall, remember that not all will be directly taught to students. As they plan, teachers try to identify which words will be sight words for students and which words represent new concepts, new words, and new meanings for students. From this list, teachers choose the keywords—the ones that are critical to understanding the book or the theme—and these are the words that teachers plan to highlight or include in minilessons. They also choose any words that must be introduced before reading.

According to Lev Vygotsky's notion of a "zone of proximal development," teachers need to be alert to individual students and what words they are learning to provide instruction when students are most interested in learning more about a word.

Identifying some words on the word wall as keywords doesn't mean that the other words are unimportant. Students have many opportunities to use all the word wall words as they write and talk about what they are reading and studying. For example, students often use the word wall to locate a specific word they want to use to make a point during a discussion or to check the spelling of a word they are writing in a reading log or in a report. Teachers choose from the words listed on the word wall for word-study activities, including spelling of keywords when appropriate.

WORD-STUDY ACTIVITIES

Word-study activities provide students with opportunities to explore the meaning of words listed on word walls, other words related to books they are reading, and words they are learning during social studies, science, or other curriculum areas. Although the primary goal of word-study activities is to help students expand their vocabulary and knowledge of words, many teachers combine word study and spelling instruction. They engage students in activities that involve both oral and written use of the words to maximize their learning. Here are six types of word-study activities:

1. *Word posters.* Students choose a word from the word wall and write it on a small poster. They then illustrate the word and may also add a sentence or two to their poster, using the keyword. Pictures may be hand-drawn and coloured or created with drawing and paint software.

2. *Word clusters.* Students choose a word to write in the centre circle of a cluster. Then they draw rays, write information about the word, and make connections between the word and the literature they are reading. Word clusters can be hand-drawn or created with software such as Inspiration. Figure 9–6 shows three types of word clusters. Grade 1 students made the first cluster after reading *The Adventures of Taxi Dog* (Barracca & Barracca, 1990). The second is a cluster that grade 3 students made after reading *Sugaring Time* by Kathryn Lasky (1983). For the third cluster, grade 7 students considered the definition of *reminiscent*, its history or etymology, its part of speech, other related forms, its word parts, and its synonyms.

3. *Dramatizing words.* Students choose a word from the word wall and dramatize it for classmates to guess. Teachers might also want to choose a word from the word wall for a "word of the day."

4. *Word sorts.* Students sort a collection of words taken from the word wall into two or more categories (Bear, Templeton, Invernizzi, & Johnston, 1996). Usually students choose which categories they will use for the sort, but sometimes the teacher chooses. For example, words from a story might be sorted by character, or words from a theme on machines might be sorted according to type of machine. The words can be written on cards, and then students sort a pack of word cards into piles. Or, students can cut apart a list of words, sort the words into categories, and then paste each group on a sheet of paper. Figure 9–7 on page 356 shows a word sort done by a small group of grade 5 students during a theme on the history of Canada. Students chose the three categories—The First Nations, The First Europeans, and Forming a New Nation—and sorted word cards for each category. Then they glued the word cards onto a large sheet of paper.

5. *Books about words.* There are a variety of books for children that are collections of words or explain words related to particular concepts. Teachers often include sharing books about words in their unit activities and as the focus of minilessons. For example, a minilesson on comparative and superlative forms might include *Super, Super, Superwords* (McMillan, 1989), or a minilesson on collective nouns might include *A Cache of Jewels and Other Collective Nouns* (Heller, 1987). Jesse Sheidlower answers questions about the origin of words and explains strange expressions like "kit and caboodle" and "by the skin of one's teeth" in *Jesse's Word of the Day* (Sheidlower, 1998). These and other books about words are listed in Figure 9–8 on page 356.

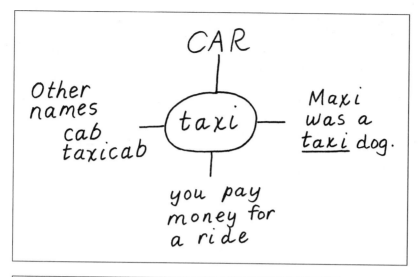

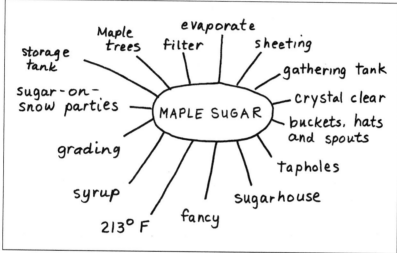

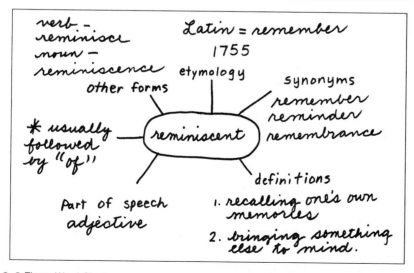

Figure 9–6 Three Word Clusters

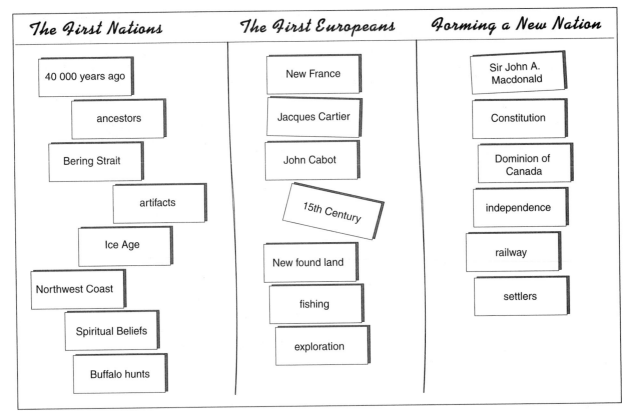

Figure 9–7 Grade 5 Students' Word Sort on the History of Canada

Agard, J. (1989). *The Calypso Alphabet*. Illus. by J. Bent. Toronto: Fitzhenry & Whiteside. (P)

Bannatyne-Cugnet, J. (1992). *A Prairie Alphabet*. Illus. by Y. Moore. Montreal: Tundra Books. (M) 🍁

Barnette, M. (2003). *Dog Days and Dandelions*. New York: St. Martin's Press. (M–U)

Base, G. (1988). *Animalia*. Toronto: Stoddart. (M) 🍁

Blades, A. (1985). *By the Sea: An Alphabet Book*. Toronto: Kids Can Press. (P) 🍁

Browne, P. (1996). *A Gaggle of Geese: The Collective Names of the Animal Kingdom*. New York: Atheneum. (M)

Dewar, T. (1992). *Inside the Whale and Other Animals*. London: Dorling Kindersley. (M–U)

Dewey, A. (1995). *Naming Colours*. New York: HarperCollins. (M)

Ehlert, L. (1990). *Feathers for Lunch*. Orlando, FL: Harcourt Brace. (P–M)

Feder, J. (1995). *Table, Chair, Bear: A Book in Many Languages*. New York: Ticknor. (P–M)

Garg, A. (2002). *A Word a Day*. London: Wiley. (M–U)

Gibbons, G. (1990). *Weather Words and What They Mean*. New York: Holiday House. (P–M)

Graham-Barber, L. (1995). *A Chartreuse Leotard in a Magenta Limousine: And Other Words Named After People and Places*. New York: Hyperion. (M–U)

Heller, R. (1983). *The Reason for a Flower*. New York: Sandcastle. (See other books in the series by this author.) (M)

Heller, R. (1987). *A Cache of Jewels and Other Collective Nouns*. New York: Grosset & Dunlap. (M–U)

Hepworth, C. (1992). *Antics! An Alphabetical Anthology*. New York: Putnam. (M–U) Hunt, J. (1989). *Illuminations*. New York: Bradbury. (M–U)

Lobel, A. (1990). *Alison's Zinnia*. New York: Greenwillow. (M)

Maestro, B., & Maestro, G. (1989). *Taxi: A Book of City Words*. New York: Clarion. (P–M)

McMillan, B. (1989). *Super, Super, Superwords*. New York: Lothrop, Lee & Shepard. (P)

Moss, L. (1995). *Zin! Zin! Zin! A Violin*. New York: Simon & Schuster. (P–M)

Most, B. (1991). *A Dinosaur Named After Me*. Orlando, FL: Harcourt Brace. (P–M)

Onyefulu, I. (1993). *A Is for Africa*. New York: Cobblehill Books. (M)

(continued)

P = primary grades (K–2); M = middle grades (3–5); U = upper grades (6–8); T = teacher.

Figure 9–8 Books about Words

Pallotta, J. (1994). *The Desert Alphabet Book.* Watertown, MA: Charlesbridge. (See other alphabet books by the same author.) (M–U)

Palmer, S. (2000). *A Little Alphabet Book.* London: Oxford University Press. (P–M)

Parker, N. W., & Wright, J. R. (1990). *Frogs, Toads, Lizards, and Salamanders.* New York: Greenwillow. (M)

Rotner, S. (1996). *Action Alphabet.* New York: Atheneum. (P–M)

Sheidlower, J. (1998). *Jesse's Word of the Day.* New York: Random House. (M–U)

Terban, M. (1988). *Guppies in Tuxedos: Funny Eponyms.* New York: Clarion. (M–U)

Terban, M. (1989). *Superdupers! Really Funny Real Words.* New York: Clarion. (M–U)

Terban, M. (1993). *It Figures! Fun Figures of Speech.* New York: Clarion. (M)

Thomas, L. (1988). *What's It?: Gadgets, Objects, Machines and More.* Toronto: Greey de Pencier. (M–U) 🍁

P = primary grades (K–2); M = middle grades (3–5); U = upper grades (6–8); T = teacher.

Figure 9–8 Books about Words (*continued*)

6. **Word chains.** Students choose a word from the word wall and then identify three or four words to sequence before or after the word to make a chain. For example, the word *tadpole* can be chained this way: *egg, tadpole, frog*; and the word *aggravate* can be chained like this: *irritate, bother, aggravate, annoy.* Students can draw and write their chains on a sheet of paper, or write words on cards and place them in order in a pocket chart, or they can make a construction paper chain and write the words on each link.

MINILESSONS ON WORD MEANINGS

The goal of vocabulary instruction is for students to learn new words. Carr and Wixon (1986) provide four guidelines for effective instruction:

- Students relate new words to their background knowledge.
- Students acquire ownership-level word knowledge.
- Students are actively involved in learning new words.
- Students develop strategies for learning new words independently.

For more information on teaching strategy, see Chapter 1, "Learning and the Language Arts," pages 37–40.

The teaching strategy presented in Chapter 1, "Learning and the Language Arts," embodies these guidelines of effective vocabulary instruction, and it can be used to teach minilessons on strategies for unlocking word meanings, on specific keywords and groups of related words, or on a lexical concept such as idioms, prefixes, or homonyms. The steps in teaching a minilesson on vocabulary are presented in the following Step by Step box:

Step by Step

A Minilesson on Vocabulary

1. **Introduce the topic.**   The teacher introduces a word-identification strategy, a keyword or group of related words, or a lexical concept. During the brief introduction, the teacher connects the topic to students' background knowledge and shares examples from books students are reading or from a thematic unit.

2. **_Presents information related to the topic._**   The teacher demonstrates how to use the strategy, presents information related to the keyword or group of words, or shares examples of the lexical concept. The teacher begins with examples from students' own writing or books they are reading. The teacher also invites students to suggest other information or examples.

3. **_Apply word knowledge._**   The teacher involves students in an activity to bring together all the information—semantic, morphological, and contextual—presented earlier. Students might sort words, make word clusters or word chains, or locate additional examples of the word or lexical concept in books they are reading or in their writing.

4. **_Review the topic._**   Students and the teacher review the strategy, the keyword or words, or the lexical concept. Students can add the words to vocabulary notebooks or make a poster to review the strategy or lexical concept they have learned.

5. **_Provide meaningful opportunities to use the topic._**   Students use the strategy, keywords, or lexical concept in meaningful ways in projects and through writing, speaking, and reading.

Minilessons

Words

Procedures	Concepts	Strategies and Skills
Choose words for word walls	History of English	Use phonics to pronounce a word
Extrapolate the etymology	Root words	Use structural analysis to identify a word
"Peel off" affixes	Affixes	Use context clues to identify a word
Make a word poster	Prefixes	Consider shades of meaning in selecting a word
Make a word cluster	Suffixes	Use a thesaurus to choose a better word
Do a word sort	Synonyms	Use a dictionary to identify a word
Make a word chain	Antonyms	Avoid trite language
Locate a word in a dictionary	Homophones	Consider multiple meanings of words
Locate a word in a thesaurus	Homographs	
Assess use of words in a resource-based unit	Homographic homophones	
Assess use of words in a thematic unit or an inquiry-based unit	Multiple meanings of words	
	Idioms	
	Literal meanings	
	Figurative meanings	
	Borrowed words	
	Compound words	
	Coined words	
	Clipped words	
	Invented words	

Students need to know about the English language, words and their meanings, and strategies to figure out the meanings of words independently. Students in the elementary grades learn about multiple meanings as well as about root words and affixes; homonyms, synonyms, and antonyms; and figurative meanings of words, such as idioms. The accompanying box presents a list of topics for minilessons on words.

ADAPTING TO MEET THE NEEDS OF EVERY STUDENT

Because learning about words is an important part of language arts, it is crucial that teachers find ways to help all students use the words they are learning. Having a word wall to accompany every unit is one of the simplest and best ways to focus students' attention on words. Teachers also need to provide a variety of word-study activities to meet the needs of every student. A list of suggestions for adapting vocabulary instruction is presented below. These suggestions focus on using vocabulary in meaningful, functional, and genuine ways.

For more information on planning thematic units, see Chapter 11, "Putting It All Together," pages 454–457.

ASSESSING STUDENTS' USE OF WORDS

Teachers assess students' use of words in a variety of ways. They listen while students participate in discussions, examine students' writing and projects, and ask students to speak or write about the literature and themes and what they have learned. Here are some specific strategies to determine whether students have learned and are applying new words:

- Check reading logs, learning logs, or simulated journals for words related to the unit.
- Use unit-related words in a conference and note the student's response.
- Listen for vocabulary when students give oral reports.
- Ask students to make a cluster or do a quickwrite about some aspect of the unit or about specific words.
- Ask students to brainstorm a list of words and phrases about the unit.
- Check students' reports, biographies, poems, stories, or other writings for unit-related words.
- Ask students to write a letter to you, telling what they have learned in the unit.

Adapting

Vocabulary Instruction to Meet the Needs of Every Student

1. **Highlight Keywords on Word Walls**
   Teachers might highlight words on word walls by writing them with coloured pens. Also, they can add pictures to illustrate the words.

2. **Use Word Sorts**
   The word-sorting activity is very useful for students who need additional opportunities to categorize words or learn relationships among words. After reading a story, students can sort words according to characters, or during a thematic unit they can sort words according to key concepts. Simplify sorts by using a limited number of words.

3. **Teach Idioms**
   Students who are learning English as a second language may need to learn about idioms and separate their literal and figurative meanings. Teachers explain that some phrases in English have two

meanings. These phrases are called idioms. Examples of idioms are "get up on the wrong side of the bed" (wake up in a bad mood) and "rain cats and dogs" (rain hard). Students can dramatize or draw pictures of the two meanings of idioms.

4. **Teach Multiple Meanings of Words**
Students can draw diagrams to show multiple meanings of words. For example, students can draw a diagram to chart two meanings of watch:

$$\text{watch} \diagup\diagdown \begin{matrix} \text{to look at something} \\ \text{a small clock on your wrist} \end{matrix}$$

Students can add drawings to the diagram or use the word in sentences.

5. **Introduce New Concepts**
Some students may need assistance in developing a concept before learning related words. Teachers need to anticipate how difficult a word might be for students and provide opportunities involving hands-on experiences, dramatic activities, or pictures. Introduce one concept at a time and allow for guided and independent practice using the new vocabulary.

Teachers can also give tests on the vocabulary words, but this is probably the least effective approach, because a correct answer on a test does not indicate whether students have ownership of a word or whether they are applying it in meaningful and genuine ways.

Grammar

Children learn the structure of the English language—its grammar—intuitively as they learn to talk; the process is an unconscious one. They have almost completed it by the time they enter kindergarten. The primary purpose of grammar instruction, then, is to make this intuitive knowledge about

This teacher presents a minilesson on how to unlock word meanings using words from books students are reading in class.

the English language explicit and to provide labels for words within sentences, parts of sentences, and types of sentences.

Grammar is probably the most controversial area of language arts. Teachers, parents, and the community disagree about the content of grammar instruction, how to teach it, and when to begin teaching it. Some people believe that formal instruction in grammar is unnecessary. Others believe that grammar instruction should be a key component of language arts instruction. They argue that knowing how to use Standard English is essential to success in oral and written communication. In keeping with conventional wisdom, they think knowledge about grammar and usage improves students' oral language and writing. Research since the beginning of the century, however, has not confirmed this assumption.

Before going further, let's clarify the terms *grammar* and *usage*. Grammar is the description of the syntax or structure of a language and prescriptions for its use (Weaver, 1996). It involves principles of word and sentence formation. In contrast, usage is correctness, or using the appropriate word or phrase in a sentence. It is the socially preferred way of using language within a dialect. Fraser and Hodson explain the distinction between grammar and usage this way: "Grammar is the rationale of a language; usage is its etiquette" (1978, p. 52).

WHY TEACH GRAMMAR?

Teachers, parents, and the community at large cite many reasons for teaching grammar. Many teachers feel that teaching grammar will help students understand sentence structure and form sentences to express their thoughts. Another reason is that parents expect that grammar will be taught, and teachers must meet these expectations. Other teachers explain that they teach grammar to prepare students for the next grade or for instruction in a foreign language. Others pragmatically rationalize grammar instruction because it is a part of norm-referenced achievement tests.

Despite the controversy about teaching grammar and its value for elementary students, grammar is a part of the elementary language arts curriculum and will undoubtedly remain so for some time. Given this fact, it is only reasonable that grammar should be taught in the most beneficial manner possible. Researchers suggest that integrating grammar study with reading and writing produces the best results (Noguchi, 1991; Noyce & Christie, 1983). L. M. Calkins has argued for more than two decades that "basic skills belong in context" (1980, p. 567). Researchers view grammar as a tool for writers and recommend integrating grammar instruction with the revising and editing stages of the writing process.

GRAMMATICAL CONCEPTS

The four most common types of information about grammar taught during the elementary grades are parts of speech, parts of sentences, types of sentences, and usage.

Parts of Speech. Grammarians have sorted English words into eight groups, called parts of speech: nouns, pronouns, verbs, adjectives, adverbs, prepositions, conjunctions, and interjections. Words in each group are used in essentially the same way in all sentences. Nouns and verbs are the basic building blocks of sentences, and pronouns substitute for nouns. Adjectives, adverbs, and prepositions build on and modify the nouns and verbs. Conjunctions connect individual words or groups of words, and interjections express strong emotion or surprise.

Parts of Sentences. A *sentence* is made up of one or more words to express a complete thought and, to express the thought, must have a subject and a predicate. The *subject* names who or what the sentence is about, and the *predicate* includes the verb and anything that completes or modifies it. In a simple sentence with one subject and one predicate, everything that is not part of the subject is part of the predicate.

Types of Sentences. Sentences are classified in two ways. First, they are classified according to structure, or how they are put together. The structure of a sentence may be simple, compound, complex, or compound-complex according to the number and type of clauses. A *clause* consists of a subject and predicate, and there are two types of clauses. If the clause presents a complete thought and can stand alone as a sentence, it is an *independent clause*. If the clause is not a complete thought and cannot stand alone as a sentence, it is a *dependent clause* because it depends on the meaning expressed in the independent clause. A *simple sentence* contains only one independent clause, and a *compound sentence* is made up of two or more independent clauses. A *complex sentence* contains one independent clause and at least one dependent clause. A *compound-complex sentence* contains more than one independent clause and at least one dependent clause.

Second, sentences are classified according to the type of message they contain. Sentences that make statements are *declarative*, those that ask questions are *interrogative*, those that make commands are *imperative*, and those that communicate strong emotion or surprise are *exclamatory*.

Usage. Usage is the customary or "correct" way in which a language is spoken or written. Using a single negative, not a double negative, in the sentence "I don't have any money" (rather than "I ain't got no money"), or subjective pronouns, not objective pronouns, for the subject in the sentence "He and I have dirt bikes" (rather than "Him and me have dirt bikes") are examples of Standard English usage. Ten types of usage errors that students can learn to correct are

1. ***Irregular verb forms.*** Students form the past tense of irregular verb forms as they would a regular verb; for example, *catch* + *ed* to make *catched* instead of *caught*.

2. ***Past-tense forms.*** Students use present-tense or past-participle forms in place of past-tense forms, such as *she run* for *she ran*, or *he seen* for *he saw*.

3. ***Nonstandard verb forms.*** Students use *brung* for *brought* or *had went* for *had gone*.

4. ***Double subjects.*** Students include both a noun and a pronoun in the subject, such as "My mom *she* . . ."

5. ***Nonstandard pronoun forms.*** Students use nonstandard pronoun forms, such as *hisself* for *himself*, or *them books* for *those books*.

6. ***Objective pronouns for the subject.*** Students use objective pronouns instead of subjective pronouns in the subject, such as "*Me* and my friend went to the store" or in response to "How are you?" "I am fine, thank you. How about *yourself*?"

7. ***Lack of subject–verb agreement.*** Students use *we was* for *we were* and *he don't* for *he doesn't*.

8. ***Double negatives.*** Students use two negatives when only one is needed; for example, "I *don't* got *none*" and "Joe *don't* have *none*."

9. ***Confusing pairs of words.*** Some students confuse word pairs such as *learn–teach*, *lay–lie*, and *leave–let*. They might say, "I'll *learn* you to read" instead of "I'll *teach* you to read"; "Go *lay* down" instead of "Go *lie* down"; and "*Leave* me do it" instead of "*Let* me do it." Other confusing pairs and combinations include *bring–take*, *among–between*, *fewer–less*, *good–well*, *passed–past*, *real–really*, *set–sit*, *than–then*, *who–which–that*, *who–whom*, *it's–its*, and *your–you're*.

10. ***"I" as an objective pronoun.*** Students incorrectly use *I* instead of *me* as an objective pronoun. Students say or write "It's for Bill and *I*" instead of "It's for Bill and *me*" (Pooley, 1974; Weaver, 1996).

Students who speak nonstandard dialects learn Standard English forms as alternatives to the forms they already know. Rather than trying to substitute their standard forms for students' nonstandard forms, teachers can explain that Standard English is the language of school. It is the language used in books, and students can easily locate Standard English examples in books they are reading. Calling Standard English "book language" also helps to explain the importance of proofreading to identify and correct usage errors in students' writing.

TEACHING GRAMMAR IN THE ELEMENTARY GRADES

An effective approach to teaching grammar to elementary students is to connect grammar with reading and writing activities and to teach minilessons about the function of words in sentences and ways of arranging words into sentences (Cullinan, Jaggar, & Strickland, 1974; Tompkins & McGee, 1983). Guidelines for teaching grammar are listed in the Teacher's Notebook on page 364.

Connecting Grammar and Reading. Students learn many things about the structure of the English language through reading. Some learn simply through the experience of reading and others need teachers' guidance to learn from the examples contained in the language of the books they are reading. Teachers bring the features of the text to students' attention through reading aloud examples or drawing attention through discussion. Students learn more sophisticated language, a more formal register than they speak, and sophisticated ways of phrasing ideas and arranging words into sentences when they read literature. Students reading Lois Burdett's Shakespeare for Kids series, for example, gain experience with language rich in vocabulary and variations of word order. Many opportunities for conversation about grammar and language arise when students read passages of Shakespearean dialogue, such as when Oberon approaches the sleeping Titania in *A Midsummer Night's Dream*:

> What thou see'st when thou dost wake Do it for they true-love take; Be it lynx or cat or bear, Leopard, or boar with bristled hair, When thou wak'st, it is they dear. Wake when some vile thing is near. (1997, p. 38)

Students often read sentences that are longer than the ones they speak and learn new ways to string words into sentences. In *Chrysanthemum* (Henkes, 1991), the story of a mouse named Chrysanthemum who loves her name until she starts school and is teased by her classmates, the author uses a combination of long and short sentences very effectively: "Chrysanthemum could scarcely believe her ears. She blushed. She beamed. She bloomed" (n.p.).

Students read sentences exemplifying all four sentence message types in many books. One example is the Caldecott Medal-winning *Officer Buckle and Gloria* (Rathmann, 1995), the story of a police officer and his dog, Gloria. "Officer Buckle loved having a buddy" and "that night Officer Buckle watched himself on the 10 o'clock news" (n.p.) are statements, or declarative sentences. "How about Gloria?" and "could she come?" (n.p.) are questions, or interrogative sentences. Officer Buckle's safety tips, such as "keep your shoelaces tied" and "do not go swimming during electrical storms!" (n.p.), are imperative sentences. The children loved Gloria and her tricks, and they cheered "bravo!" (n.p.)—an example of an exclamation, or exclamatory sentence.

Students also read all sentence structure types—simple, compound, complex, and compound-complex sentences. Kevin Henkes includes all of these types of sentences in his wonderful book, *Lilly's Purple Plastic Purse* (1996):

Simple Sentence: "Lilly loved school."
Compound Sentence: "She loved the fish sticks and chocolate milk every Friday in the lunchroom."
Complex Sentence: "Whenever the students had free time, they were permitted to go to the Lightbulb Lab in the back of the classroom."
Compound-Complex Sentence: "When all the students were buttoned and zipped and snapped and tied and ready to go home, Mr. Slinger strolled over to Lilly and gave her purple plastic purse back." (n.p.)

Some authors write dialogue and other text in nonstandard English that is appropriate to the characters and setting they are creating. In *Shiloh* (Naylor, 1991), for example, the story of a boy named Marty who will do anything to save a beagle puppy, Marty says, "thinking don't cost nothing" (p. 31), and this language is appropriate for the rural setting of the book. Understanding that authors (and all language users) make choices about Standard and nonstandard English according to the situation in which it is used is important in helping students who speak nonstandard English become aware of Standard English options.

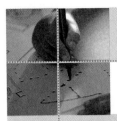

Teacher's Notebook

Guidelines for Teaching Grammar

1. Teach Minilessons on Grammar and Usage
The teacher teaches minilessons on grammar and usage concepts and has students locate examples of grammar and usage concepts they are learning from books they are reading and books they are writing.

2. Share Concept Books
The teacher shares concept books when students are studying parts of speech, and students also create their own concept books.

3. Manipulate Sentences
Students use sentences from books they are reading for grammar activities, such as sentence slotting, sentence expansion, sentence manipulation, and combining sentences.

4. Collect Sentences
Students collect favourite sentences from books they are reading and use the sentences for grammar and usage activities.

5. Use Sentence Frames
Students write innovations, or new versions of books, using sentence frames or patterns in books they have read.

6. Make Grammar Posters
Students can make grammar posters to visually represent parts of speech, sentence types, or usage rules they are learning.

7. Teach Students to Proofread
Students need to learn how to proofread so that they can locate and correct grammar and usage errors in their own writing.

8. Acknowledge Alternatives to Standard English
The teacher explains that Standard English is the language of school and is one way of speaking and writing. It is important that students understand that the purpose of grammar instruction is to expand their repertoire of language options, not to replace their home language.

One way to help students focus on sentences in stories is sentence collecting (Speaker & Speaker, 1991). Students collect favourite sentences and share them with classmates. They copy their sentences on chart paper or on long strips of tagboard and post them in the classroom. Students and the teacher talk about the merits of each sentence, focus on word choice, and analyze the sentence types. Through this discussion, students gradually learn to comprehend more syntactically complex sentences. Students can cut the words in the sentences apart and rebuild them, either in the author's original order or in an order that appeals to them. These sentences can also be used in the minilessons described later in this section.

Connecting Grammar and Writing. Not only do students notice the way sentences are phrased in the books they read or listen to read aloud, but they also use the structures in their writing. Kathy Egawa (1990) reports that a grade 1 student used the structure and rhythm of Jane Yolen's

Owl Moon (1987) in writing a book called *Salamander Sun*. *Owl Moon* begins this way: "It was late one winter night, long past my bedtime when Pa and I went owling." The child's book, written in invented spelling, begins this way: "it was lat one spring afternoon a long time after lunch when ma tact me sawlumendering" (p. 586). This grade 1 student was not plagiarizing Yolen's book, but adapting and incorporating the structure in his own writing.

Because children's knowledge of grammar and usage is dependent on the language spoken in their homes and neighbourhoods, some primary- and middle-grade students do not recognize a difference between "me and him" and "he and I." When the error is brought to their attention, they do not understand, because semantically—at a meaning level—the two versions are identical. Moreover, "me and him" sounds right to these students. When other corrections are pointed out to middle- and upper-grade students, they repeat the correct form, shake their heads, and say that it doesn't sound right. "Real" sounds better to some than "really" because it is more familiar. An explanation that adverbs rather than adjectives modify adjectives is not useful either, even if students are familiar with the parts of speech. Correction of nonstandard English errors can be perceived as a repudiation of the language spoken in children's homes and must be done with sensitivity. Rather than any suggestion of right and wrong, teachers can explain that written language requires a more formal language register or dialect than general conversation.

Using a problem-solving approach during the editing stage of the writing process can be effective. Locating and correcting errors in students' writing is not as threatening to students as correcting their talk, because it is not as personal. Also, students can more easily accept that "book language" is a different kind of English. During editing, students are hunting for errors, trying to make their papers "optimally readable" (Smith, 1982). They recognize that it is a courtesy to readers to make their papers as correct as possible. Some errors, however, should be ignored, especially those made by young children and students learning English as a second language; correcting too many errors teaches students only that their language is inferior or inadequate. The goal in dealing with nonstandard English speakers is not to replace their dialects but to add Standard English to their language options.

Middle-school students use resources to help them create a crossword puzzle based on synonyms.

For more information on students learning English as a second language, see Chapter 1, "Learning and the Language Arts," pages 18–20.

For the steps in teaching a minilesson, see Chapter 2, "Teaching the Language Arts," page 59.

Minilessons and Other Grammar Lessons. Teachers identify topics for grammar minilessons in two ways. The preferred way is to identify concepts by assessing students' writing and noting what types of grammar and usage errors they are making. At other times, teachers choose topics from lists of skills they are expected to teach at their grade level. The topics can be taught to the whole class or to small groups of students, but only to students who don't already know them. Atwell (1987) suggests using minilessons because of their immediate connections to reading and writing.

Teachers use the steps in teaching minilessons outlined in Chapter 2, "Teaching the Language Arts." Worksheets are not recommended; instead, excerpts from books students are reading or from students' own writing are used. Students can write words on cards and manipulate them into sentences, or write sentences on overhead transparencies to share with classmates. Teachers introduce a concept and its related terminology; then they provide opportunities for students to experiment with sentence construction. A variety of approaches to teaching minilessons on grammar are presented in the following paragraphs, and topics for minilessons on grammar appear on page 386.

1. ***Parts of speech.*** Students work in small groups to identify words representing one part of speech or all eight parts of speech from books they are reading or from their own writing. A group of grade 5 students identified the following words representing each part of speech from Van Allsburg's *The Polar Express* (1985):

   - *Nouns:* train, children, Santa Claus, elves, pajamas, roller coaster, conductor, sleigh, hug, clock, Sarah
   - *Pronouns:* we, they, he, it, us, you, his, I, me
   - *Verbs:* filled, ate, flickered, raced, were, cheered, marched, asked, pranced, stood, shouted
   - *Adjectives:* melted, white-tailed, quiet, no, first, magical, cold, dark, polar, Santa's
   - *Adverbs:* soon, faster, wildly, apart, closer, alone
   - *Prepositions:* in, through, over, with, of, in front of, behind, at, for, across, into
   - *Conjunctions:* and, but
   - *Interjections:* oh, well, now

   Similarly, students can hunt for parts of sentences or sentence types in books of children's literature.

   After collecting words representing one part of speech from books they are reading or from books they have written, students can create a book using some of the words they collected. Figure 9–9 shows the cover and a page from an alphabet book focusing on adjectives that one grade 2 class developed.

2. ***Grammar concept books.*** Students examine concept books that focus on one part of speech or another grammatical concept. For example, Barrett describes the essential characteristics of a variety of animals in *A Snake Is Totally Tail* (1983), and most of the descriptions include an adverb. After students read the book and identify the adverbs, they can write their own sentences, following the same pattern, and illustrate the sentences using posters, mobiles, a mural, or a class book. Books that illustrate grammar concepts are listed in Figure 9–10 on page 368.

   Students in a grade 8 class divided into small groups to read Ruth Heller's books about parts of speech, including *Up, Up and Away: A Book About Adverbs* (1998), *Behind the Mask: A Book of Prepositions* (1995), and *Merry-Go-Round: A Book About Nouns* (1990). After reading one of her books, students made a poster with information about a part of speech, which they presented to the class. The students' poster for adverbs is shown in Figure 9–11 on page 369. Later, students divided into small groups to do a word sort. In this activity,

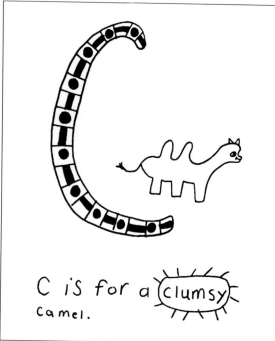

Figure 9–9 An Excerpt from a Grade 2 Class Book on Adjectives

students cut apart a list of words and sorted them into groups according to the part of speech. All of the words had been taken from posters that students created, and students could refer to the posters if needed.

3. **Sentence slotting.** Students experiment with words and phrases to see how they function in sentences by filling in sentences that have slots, or blanks. Sentence slotting teaches students about several different grammatical concepts. They can experiment with parts of speech using a sentence like this:

The snake slithered _____ the rock.

> over
>
> around
>
> under
>
> to

Students brainstorm a number of words to fill in the slot, all of which will be prepositions; adjectives, nouns, verbs, and adverbs will not make sense. This activity can be repeated to introduce or review any part of speech.

Sentence slotting also demonstrates to students that parts of speech can substitute for each other. In the following sentence, common and proper nouns as well as pronouns can be used in the slot:

_____ knew more safety tips than anyone else in Napville.

The man
Officer Buckle
He
The police officer

Nouns

Heller, R. (1987). *A Cache of Jewels and Other Collective Nouns.* New York: Grosset & Dunlap. (M–U)

Heller, R. (1990). *Merry-go-round: A Book About Nouns.* New York: Grosset & Dunlap. (M–U)

Heller, R. (1995). *Behind the Mask: A Book About Prepositions.* New York: Grosset & Dunlap. (M–U)

Hoban, T. (1981). *More Than One.* New York: Greenwillow. (P)

MacCarthy, P. (1991). *Herds of Words.* New York: Dial. (M)

Terban, M. (1986). *Your Foot's on My Feet! and Other Tricky Nouns.* New York: Clarion. (M)

Wildsmith, B. (1968). *Fishes.* New York: Franklin Watts. (M)

Verbs

Beller, J. (1984). *A-B-Cing: An Action Alphabet.* New York: Crown. (P–M)

Burningham, J. (1986). *Cluck Baa, Jangle Twang, Slam Bang, Skip Trip, Sniff Shout, Wobble Pop.* New York: Viking. (P–M)

Crystal, D. (2001). *Language and the Internet.* Cambridge: Camrbridge University Press.

Heller, R. (1988). *Kites Sail High: A Book About Verbs.* New York: Grosset & Dunlap. (M–U)

Hoban, T. (1975). *Dig, Drill, Dump, Fill.* New York: Greenwillow. (P)

Maestro, B., & Maestro, G. (1985). *Camping Out.* New York: Crown. (P–M)

Neumeier, M., & Glasser, B. (1985). *Action Alphabet.* New York: Greenwillow. (M)

Parrish, T. (2002). *The Grouchy Grammarian.* London: Wiley. (M)

Rotner, S. (1996). *Action Alphabet.* New York: Atheneum. (P–M)

Schneider, R. M. (1995). *Add it, Dip It, Fix It: A Book of Verbs.* Boston: Houghton Mifflin. (M)

Shiefman, V. (1981). *M Is for Move.* New York: Dutton. (P–M)

Terban, M. (1984). *I Think I Thought and Other Tricky Verbs.* New York: Clarion. (M)

Adjectives

Boynton, S. (1983). *A Is For Angry: An Animal and Adjective Alphabet.* New York: Workman. (M–U)

Duke, K. (1983). *Guinea Pig ABC.* New York: Dutton. (P)

Heller, R. (1989). *Many Luscious Lollipops: A Book About Adjectives.* New York: Grosset & Dunlap. (M–U)

Hoban, T. (1981). *A Children's Zoo.* New York: Greenwillow. (P)

Hubbard, W. (1990). *C Is for Curious: An ABC Book of Feelings.* San Francisco: Chronicle Books. (M)

Maestro, B., & Maestro, G. (1979). *On the Go: A Book of Adjectives.* New York: Crown. (P–M)

McMillan, B. (1989). *Super, Super, Superwords.* New York: Lothrop, Lee & Shepard. (P)

Adverbs

Barrett, J. (1983). *A Snake Is Totally Tail.* New York: Atheneum. (M–U)

Heller, R. (1991). *Up, Up and Away: A Book About Adverbs.* New York: Grosset & Dunlap. (M–U)

Prepositions

Bancheck, L. (1978). *Snake in, Snake Out.* New York: Crowell. (P–M)

Berenstain, S., & Berenstain, J. (1968). *Inside, Outside, Upside, Down.* New York: Random House. (M)

Berenstain, S., & Berenstain, J. (1971). *Bears in the Night.* New York: Random House. (P–M)

Hoban, T. (1973). *Over, Under, and Through and Other Spatial Concepts.* New York: Macmillan. (P)

Hoban, T. (1991). *All About Where.* New York: Greenwillow. (P)

Lillie, P. (1993). *Everything Has a Place.* New York: Greenwillow. (P)

P = primary grades (K–2); M = middle grades (3–5); U = upper grades (6–8).

Figure 9–10 Books That Illustrate Grammar Concepts

A similar sentence-slotting example demonstrates how phrases can function as an adverb:

The dog growled _____.

ferociously

with his teeth bared

daring us to reach for his bone

In this example, the adverb *ferociously* can be used in the slot, as well as prepositional and participial phrases.

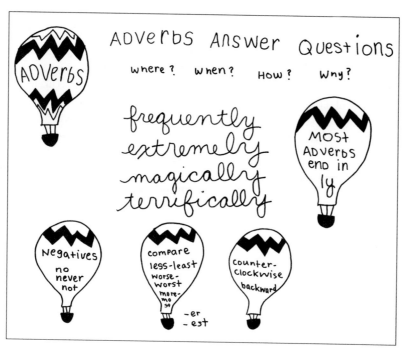

Figure 9–11 A Grade 8 Poster on Adverbs

Sentences with an adjective slot can be used to demonstrate that phrases function as adjectives. The goal of this activity is to demonstrate the function of words in sentences. Many sentence-slotting activities, such as the last example, also illustrate that sentences become more specific with the addition of a word or phrase. The purpose of these activities is to experiment with language; they should be done with small groups of students or the whole class, not as worksheets.

4. **Sentence expansion.** Students expand simple sentences, such as "a frog leaps" or "the car raced," by adding modifiers. The words and phrases with which they expand the sentence can add qualities and attributes, details, and comparisons. Using the "5 *W*s plus one" (*who, what, when, where, why,* and *how*) helps students focus on expanding particular aspects of the sentence; for example:

Sentence	A frog leaps.
Who?	A frog
What kind?	green, speckled
When?	noon
How?	high into the air
Where?	from a half-submerged log and lands in the water with a splash
Why?	to retreat from the hot noon sun
Expanded Sentence	To retreat from the hot noon sun, a green, speckled *frog leaps* high into the air from a half-submerged log and lands in the water with a splash.

Depending on what questions are asked and students' answers, many other expanded sentences are possible from the same basic sentence. Students enjoy working in small groups to expand a basic sentence so that they can compare their expanded version with those of the other groups. Instead of using the "5 *W*s plus one" questions to expand sentences, teachers can ask older students to supply a specific part of speech or modifier at each step of expansion.

Students or the teacher can create basic sentences for expansion or take them from children's literature. Very few basic sentences appear in stories, but a basic sentence within an expanded sentence can be identified. Students enjoy comparing their expanded versions of the basic sentence with the author's. When students are familiar with the story the sentence was taken from, they can try to approximate the author's meaning. Even so, it is likely that they will go in a variety of directions, and because students' expanded sentences may vary greatly from the author's, they come to realize the power of modifiers to transform a sentence.

5. **Sentence manipulation.** Hudson (1980) suggests "moving language around" to help students learn about the structure of English and how to manipulate sentences. Students begin with a sentence and then apply four operations to it: They add, delete, substitute, and rearrange. With the sentence "children play games," these manipulations are possible:

Add	Children play games at home.
	Children like to play games.
Delete	Children play.
Substitute	Adults play games.
	Children like games.
	Children play Nintendo.
Rearrange	Games are played by children.

Practice with sentence manipulation may be closely linked to revising students' writing. Through sentence manipulation, teachers show students how their writing can be strengthened and enriched. Examples for collaborative manipulation may be taken from the students' writing and become the focus for a minilesson. Without naming the author, teachers display sentences on a whiteboard or on word cards in a pocket chart and asks students to make suggestions for revisions. Students then discuss the effect of each suggestion on the meaning and impact of the sentence.

6. **Combining sentences.** In sentence combining, students combine and rearrange words in sentences to make the sentences longer and more conceptually dense (Strong, 1996). The goal of sentence combining is for students to experiment with different combinations. Sentences can be joined or embedded in a variety of ways. In the following example, two sentences (S) about *Sylvester and the Magic Pebble* (Steig, 1969) are transformed or combined to create two combined sentences (C1) and (C2):

(S)	Sylvester found a red pebble.
(S)	The pebble was magic.
(C1)	Sylvester found a red pebble that was magic.
(C2)	Sylvester found a magic red pebble.

The two combined sentences illustrate embedding the adjective *magic*. The first combined sentence uses a relative clause transformation; the second uses an adjective transformation. Neither combined sentence is right or wrong; rather, they provide two options. Teachers and students can create many other sentences to combine. They can take examples from books they are reading or from their own writing, or they can create the sentences themselves on a variety of topics.

Sentence-combining activities give students opportunities to manipulate sentence structures; however, they are rather artificial. They are most effective when combined with other writing assignments. Weaver cautions that "sentence combining activities are only an adjunct to the writing program and the writing process and should never be used as substitutes for actual writing" (1979, pp. 83–84).

7. *Sentence frames.* Students in the primary grades often create new books or "innovations" using the structure in repetitive books. Young children write their own versions of *Brown Bear, Brown Bear, What Do You See?* (Martin, 1983) and *The Very Hungry Caterpillar* (Carle, 1969). Teachers often write these collaboratively with groups of children. Similarly, middle-grade students write new verses following the rhyming pattern in Laura Numeroff's *Dogs Don't Wear Sneakers* (1993) and the sequel, *Chimps Don't Wear Glasses* (1995).

A grade 3 class used Numeroff's frame to write verses, and one small group composed this verse, rhyming *TV* and *bumblebee:*

> Ducks don't have tea parties,
> Lions don't watch TV,
> And you won't see a salamander
> being friends with a bumblebee.

Middle- and upper-grade students can take a favourite sentence and imitate its structure by plugging in new words. Dunning and Stafford (1992) call this procedure "copy changes." For example, grade 8 students chose sentences from *The Giver* (Lowry, 1993) for copy changes. The original sentence was "Dimly, from a nearly forgotten perception as blurred as the substance itself, Jonas recalled what the whiteness was" (p. 175). A student created this sentence using the sentence frame: "Softly, from a corner of the barn as cozy and warm as the kitchen, the baby kitten mewed to its mother."

ADAPTING TO MEET THE NEEDS OF EVERY STUDENT

The goal of grammar instruction is to increase students' ability to structure and manipulate sentences and to expand their repertoire of sentence patterns. Teaching grammar is a controversial issue, and it is especially so for students whose native language is not English or for students who speak a nonstandard form of English. The best way to encourage students' language development and the acquisition of Standard English is to encourage students to talk without fear of being corrected in a way that will cause embarrassment. Teachers and classmates model Standard English through their talk, and students also learn Standard English syntactic patterns in the books they read. Teachers can deal with nonstandard English in older students' compositions during the editing stage of the writing process.

Students with limited language fluency especially benefit from creating innovations on repetitive books so that they can expand their repertoire of sentence forms and lengthen the sentences they speak and write. Building and manipulating sentences are other useful activities to help these students increase their ability to use a variety of sentence types. A list of recommendations for adapting grammar instruction to meet the needs of every student is presented on page 372.

ASSESSING STUDENTS' KNOWLEDGE ABOUT GRAMMAR

The best gauge of students' knowledge of grammar is how they arrange words into sentences as part of genuine communication projects. Teachers can develop checklists of grammar and usage skills to teach at a particular grade level, or they can list errors they observe in students' writing. Then teachers observe students as they write and examine their compositions to note errors, plan and teach minilessons based on students' needs, note further errors, plan and teach other minilessons, and so on. As teachers identify grammar and usage problems, they should plan minilessons to call students' attention to the problems that make a bigger difference in writing (Pooley, 1974).

Spelling

Spelling is a tool for writers that allows them to communicate conventionally with readers. As D. H. Graves explains, "Spelling is for writing. Children may achieve high scores on phonic inventories, or weekly spelling tests. But the ultimate test is what the child does under 'game conditions,' within the process of moving toward meaning" (1983, pp. 193–194). Students need to learn to spell words conventionally so that they can communicate effectively through writing. English spelling is complex, and attempts to teach spelling through weekly lists have not been consistently successful. Rather, ability to use skills such as spelling conventionally is best fostered by teaching the skills in the context of their use (Routman, 1996). In fact, we recommend that all language tools—grammar, spelling, and handwriting—be taught as part of integrated reading and writing instruction.

CHILDREN'S SPELLING DEVELOPMENT

The alphabetic principle suggests a one-to-one correspondence between phonemes and graphemes, but English spelling is phonetic only about half the time.

Adapting

Grammar Instruction to Meet the Needs of Every Student

1. **Encourage Reading and Writing**
   As students become more fluent readers and writers, they will acquire more Standard English syntactic forms. Teachers should provide daily reading and writing opportunities for all students, but these opportunities are especially important for students who speak nonstandard English. As well as reading independently, students who struggle benefit from being read to, especially materials they could not read independently. They should be encouraged to read and be read to from a wide variety of genres to give them broad experience with language.

2. **Identify Grammar and Usage Concepts to Teach by Examining Students' Writing**
   Teachers analyze students' writing to identify topics for grammar minilessons. As they teach minilessons, teachers explain that Standard English is the language of books, an alternative language form, and they ask students to apply what they are learning in their writing.

3. **Teach Students How to Proofread**
   Students learn to proofread so that they can correct many of the grammar and usage errors they make in their writing. Proofreading activities help students focus on the words and sentences in their own writing. Children who struggle with writing may benefit from working with classmates as editing partners.

4. **Have Students Write Innovations on Texts**
   Encourage students to write innovations, or new versions, of familiar patterned texts. As they use the author's sentence forms to create new versions, students practise using more complex syntactic structures than they might normally use themselves.

5. **Correct Grammatical Errors in Students' Writing, Not in Their Speech**
   Students make grammatical errors both when they speak and when they write, but because their speech is so personal, teachers are likely to damage students' self-confidence when they correct their speech. A better way to develop students' abilities in Standard English is to focus on errors in their writing.

Elementary students learn to spell the phonetic elements of English as they learn about phoneme–grapheme correspondences, and they continue to refine their spelling knowledge through reading and writing. Children's spelling that reflects their growing awareness of English orthography is known as *invented spelling*. During their development children move from using scribbles and single letters to represent words through a series of stages until they adopt conventional spellings.

For more information on young children's writing, see Chapter 3, "Emergent Literacy," pp.115–119.

Invented Spelling. As young children begin to write, they create unique spellings, called invented spellings, based on their knowledge of English orthography. Other names for invented spelling include *temporary spelling* and *kid spelling*. Charles Read (1975, 1986), one of the first researchers to study preschoolers' efforts to spell words, discovered that they used their knowledge of phonology to invent spellings. These children used letter names to spell words such as U (*you*) and R (*are*), and they used consonant sounds rather consistently: GRL (*girl*), TIGR (*tiger*), and NIT (*night*). The preschoolers used several unusual but phonetically based spelling patterns to represent affricates. They spelled *tr* with *chr* (e.g., CHRIBLES for *troubles*) and *dr* with *jr* (e.g., JRAGIN for *dragon*), and they substituted *d* for *t* (e.g., PREDE for *pretty*). Words with long vowels were spelled using letter names: MI (*my*), LADE (*lady*), and FEL (*feel*). The children used several ingenious strategies to spell words with short vowels. The three-, four-, and five-year-olds rather consistently selected letters to represent short vowels on the basis of place of articulation in the mouth. Short *i* was represented with *e* as in FES (*fish*), short *e* with *a* as in LAFFT (*left*), and short *o* with *i* as in CLIK (*clock*). The children often omitted nasals within words (e.g., ED for *end*) and substituted -*eg* or -*ig* for -*ing* (e.g., CUMIG for *coming* and GOWEG for *going*). Also, they often ignored the vowel in unaccented syllables, as in AFTR (*after*) and MUTHR (*mother*). These spellings may seem odd to adults, but they are based on phonetic relationships and reflect children's growing awareness of how English is written conventionally.

In summary, Read found that children developed strategies for their spellings based on their knowledge of the phonological system and of letter names, their judgments of phonetic similarities and differences, and their ability to abstract phonetic information from letter names. Based on Read's seminal work, other researchers began to systematically study the development of children's spelling abilities. Henderson and other researchers (Beers & Henderson, 1977; Gentry, 1981; Templeton, 1979; Zutell, 1979) have studied the manner in which children proceed developmentally from invented spelling to conventional spelling. It is generally agreed that learning to spell entails understanding increasingly abstract relationships that begin at the level of individual letters and sounds, and progressively advance through patterns and meaning. (Ehri, 1993; Henderson, 1990).

Based on observations of children's spellings, researchers have identified five stages that children move through on their way to becoming conventional spellers, and at each stage they use different types of strategies. The stages are precommunicative spelling, semiphonetic spelling, phonetic spelling, transitional spelling, and conventional spelling (Gentry, 1981, 1982, 1987; Gentry & Gillet, 1993). The characteristics of each of the five stages of invented spelling are summarized in Figure 9–12 on page 374.

1. *Precommunicative spelling.* Children string scribbles, letters, and letter-like forms together, but they do not associate the marks they make with any specific phonemes. Precommunicative spelling represents a natural, early expression of the alphabet and other concepts about writing. Children may write from left to right, right to left, top to bottom, or randomly across the page. Some precommunicative spellers have a large repertoire of letter forms to use in writing, while others repeat a small number of letters over and over. Children use both upper- and lowercase letters, but they show a distinct preference for uppercase letters. At this stage, children have not discovered how spelling works or that letters represent sounds in words. This stage is typical of preschoolers, ages three to five.

Stage 1: Precommunicative Spelling

Child uses scribbles, letter-like forms, letters, and sometimes numbers to represent a message.

Child may write from left to right, right to left, top to bottom, or randomly on the page.

Child shows no understanding of phoneme–grapheme correspondences.

Child may repeat a few letters again and again or use most of the letters of the alphabet.

Child frequently mixes upper- and lowercase letters but shows a preference for upper-case letters.

Stage 2: Semiphonetic Spelling

Child becomes aware of the alphabetic principle that letters are used to represent sounds.

Child uses abbreviated one-, two-, or three-letter spelling to represent an entire word.

Child uses letter-name strategy to spell words.

Stage 3: Phonetic Spelling

Child represents all essential sound features of a word in spelling.

Child develops particular spellings for long and short vowels and plural and past-tense markers.

Child chooses letters on the basis of sound without regard for English letter sequences or other conventions.

Stage 4: Transitional Spelling

Child adheres to basic conventions of English orthography.

Child begins to use morphological and visual information in addition to phonetic information.

Child may include all appropriate letters in a word but reverse some of them.

Child uses alternative spellings for the same sound in different words, but only partially understands the conditions governing their use.

Child uses a high percentage of correctly spelled words.

Stage 5: Conventional Spelling

Child applies the basic rules of the English orthographic system.

Child extends knowledge of word structure, including the spelling of affixes, contractions, compound words, and homonyms.

Child demonstrates growing accuracy in using silent consonants and doubling consonants before adding suffixes.

Child recognizes when a word doesn't "look right" and can consider alternative spellings for the same sound.

Child learns irregular spelling patterns.

Child learns consonant and vowel alternations and other morphological structures.

Child knows how to spell a large number of words conventionally.

Figure 9–12 Characteristics of the Five Stages of Invented Spelling

Sources: Adapted from Gentry, 1982; Gentry & Gillet, 1993.

2. ***Semiphonetic spelling.*** Children begin to represent phonemes in words with letters, indicating that they have a rudimentary understanding of the alphabetic principle—that a link exists between letters and sounds. Spellings are quite abbreviated, and children use only one, two, or three letters to represent an entire word. Examples of stage 2 spelling are DA (*day*), KLZ (*closed*), and SM (*swimming*). As these examples illustrate, semiphonetic spellers use a letter-name strategy to determine which letters to use to spell a word, and their spellings represent some sound features of words while ignoring other, equally important, features. Typically, five- and six-year-olds spell semiphonetically.

3. **Phonetic spelling.** Children's understanding of the alphabetic principle is further refined in this stage. They continue to use letter names to represent sounds, but they also use consonant and vowel sounds at this stage. Examples of stage 3 spelling are LIV (*live*), DRAS (*dress*), and PEKT (*peeked*). As these examples show, children choose letters on the basis of sound alone, without considering acceptable English letter sequences (e.g., using -*t* rather than -*ed* as a past-tense marker in *peeked*). These spellings do not resemble English words, but they can be deciphered. The major achievement of this stage is that for the first time children represent all essential sound features in the words. Henderson (1980) explains that words are "bewilderingly homographic" at this stage because children spell on the basis of sound alone; for example, *bat, bet,* and *bait* might all be spelled BAT. Typically, phonetic spellers are about six years old.

4. **Transitional spelling.** Transitional spellers come close to the conventional spellings of English words. They spell many words correctly but continue to misspell words with irregular spellings. Examples of stage 4 spelling are HUOSE (*house*), TRUBAL (*trouble*), EAGUL (*eagle*), and AFTERNEWN (*afternoon*). This stage is characterized by children's growing ability to represent the features of English orthography. They include a vowel in every syllable and demonstrate knowledge of vowel patterns even though they might make a faulty decision about which marker to use. For example, *toad* is often spelled TODE when children choose the wrong vowel marker, or TAOD when the two vowels are reversed. Also, transitional spellers use common letter patterns in their spelling, such as YOUNIGHTED for *united* and HIGHCKED for *hiked*. In this stage, children use conventional alternatives for representing sounds, and although they continue to misspell words, transitional spelling resembles English orthography and can easily be read. As the examples show, children stop relying entirely on phonological information and begin to use visual clues and morphological information. Transitional spellers are generally seven, eight, and nine years old.

5. **Conventional spelling.** As the name implies, children spell most words (90 percent or more) conventionally (as they are spelled in the dictionary) at this stage. They have mastered the basic principles of English orthography. Children typically reach stage 5 by the age of eight or nine. During the next four or five years, children learn to control homonyms (e.g., *road–rode*), contractions, affixes (e.g., *running*), and vowel and consonant alternations. They also learn to spell common irregularly spelled words (e.g., *school* and *they*). If the curriculum expects students to study lists of spelling words and take weekly spelling tests, they should not begin these tests until they reach the conventional stage (Gentry, 1981, 1982; Gentry & Gillet, 1993).

Teachers can do many things to scaffold children's spelling development as they move through the development stages. Figure 9–13 on page 376 presents a list of ways to support young children's spelling development.

Older Students' Spelling Development. Researchers are continuing to study children's spelling development beyond age eight. Hitchcock (1989) studied children's spellings in grades 2 through 6 and classified the errors that these older, conventional- stage spellers continue to make as semiphonetic, phonetic, and transitional-stage spellings. More than half of their errors were classified as phonetic spellings, in which students spell words according to the way they sound or as they pronounce them (e.g., *wat* for *want*, *to* for *two*, *babes* for *babies*). That students continue to misspell words by spelling them phonetically is not surprising, because teachers and parents often encourage students to sound out the spelling when children ask how to spell an unknown word.

Other research has focused on the relationship between reading and spelling (Anderson, 1985). Researchers have examined the spelling strategies of poor readers in fourth through sixth grade and found that these students were likely to use a sounding-out strategy. Good readers, on the other hand, used a variety of spelling strategies, including visual information, knowledge about root words and affixes, and analogy to known words.

Stage 1: Precommunicative Spelling

Allow the child to experiment with making and placing marks on the paper.
Suggest that the child write with a pencil and draw with a crayon.
Model how adults write.
Point out the direction of print in books, from top to bottom and left to right across a page.
Encourage the child to notice letters in names and environmental print.
Ask the child to talk about what he or she has written.

Stage 2: Semiphonetic Spelling

Demonstrate how to say a word slowly, stretch it out, and isolate one, two, or three
    sounds in the word to write. (Emphasize only consonant sounds and long-vowel
    sounds at this stage.)
Show the child how to form letters in names and other common words.
Sing the alphabet song and name letters of the alphabet with the child.
Have the child pick out common objects beginning with particular letters and consonant
    sounds.
Encourage the child to read the names of classmates and look for names that begin with
    the same letter.
Ask the child to read what he or she has written.

Stage 3: Phonetic Spelling

Model how to write phonetically, segmenting words into beginning, middle, and ending
    sounds.
Use Elkonin boxes to help the child segment words into beginning, middle, and ending
    sounds.
Teach short and long vowels.
Have the child write rhyming words.
Teach the child how to use plural, past tense, and other word markers (e.g., -s, -ed, -ing).
Use "sharing the pen" interactive writing when creating class charts.

Stage 4: Transitional Spelling

Teach consonant and vowel digraphs, vowel diphthongs (e.g., oo in moon, oy in boy),
    and other spelling patterns.
Focus on silent letters in words (e.g., the final e in CVCe words, gh in light, and k in
    know).
Encourage the child to develop visualization skills in order to recognize whether or not
    a word "looks" right.
Help the child identify common sight words that cannot be spelled using phonics (e.g.,
    what, here).
Introduce proofreading so the child can identify and correct misspelled words in
    compositions.

Stage 5: Conventional Spelling

Teach the child to break longer words into syllables for spelling. Introduce root words
    and affixes and how to build longer words using affixes.
Create class charts of spelling options (e.g., ways to spell long o, words that end with
    -able and -ible [adaptable and edible]).
Provide information about other spelling concepts (e.g., possessives, schwa, double letters).
Teach proofreading skills and encourage the child to proofread all writings.
Have the child make a personal dictionary or chart of frequently misspelled words.

Figure 9–13 Ways to Support Young Children's Spelling Development

From time to time the press and concerned parents raise concerns about the perceived lack of spelling ability among students and lack of instruction in classrooms. They often cite examples of inappropriate continued use of invented spelling among students in the middle and upper-elementary grades. In fact, researchers who are examining the types of errors students make have noted that the *number* of misspellings increases in grades 1 through 4, but that the *percentage* of errors decreases as students write longer compositions. The percentage continues to decline in the upper grades, although some students continue to make errors (Taylor & Kidder, 1988). Further, in many classrooms, older students make extensive use of word processing with spell checkers to produce their compositions. Research reports that writing quality, including spelling, improves with word processing (Black, 1989; Outhred, 1987; Owston & Wideman, 1997).

ANALYZING CHILDREN'S SPELLING DEVELOPMENT

Teachers can analyze spelling errors in children's compositions by classifying the errors according to the five stages of spelling development. This analysis will provide information about the child's current level of spelling development and the kinds of errors the child makes, giving the teacher the information needed to provide the appropriate type of instruction. Children who are not yet at the conventional spelling stage—that is, who do not spell at least 90 percent of words correctly and whose errors are not mostly at the transitional level—do not benefit from formal spelling instruction. Instead, early instruction should support students' spelling development. Minilessons that are appropriate to a student's stage of development, such as learning visual and morphological strategies for a transitional speller, are much more beneficial.

A composition written by Marc, a grade 1 student, is presented in the accompanying Figure 9–14. Often, he reverses *b* and *s*, and these two reversals make his writing more difficult to decipher. Here is a translation of Marc's composition:

> Today a person at home called us and said that a bomb was in our school and made us go outside and made us wait a half of an hour and it made us waste our time on learning. The end.

Marc was writing about a traumatic event, and it was appropriate for him to use invented spelling in his composition. Primary-grade students should be encouraged to write using invented spelling. Correct spelling is appropriate when the composition will "go public." That is, it is more important to overall development of primary children's writing skills to support composition than to insist on correct spelling. Teachers can assist with the changing of invented spelling to conventional spelling when children's writing is posted for public reading and their message must be made clear.

Also shown in Figure 9–14 is one way to gauge young students' spelling development. Teachers write the stages of spelling development across the top of the chart and list each word in the student's composition under one of the categories, ignoring proper nouns, capitalization errors, and poorly formed or reversed letters.

Perhaps the most interesting thing about Marc's writing is that he spelled 57 percent of the words correctly. Only one word, *kod* (*called*), is categorized as semiphonetic, and it is classified this way because the spelling is extremely abbreviated, with only the first two and last sounds represented. The eleven words categorized as phonetic are words in which it appears that his spelling represents only the sounds heard; unpronounced letters, such as the final *e* in *made* and the *i* in *wait*, are not represented. Marc pronounces *our* as though it were a homophone for *or*, so *or* is a reasonable phonetic spelling. Homophone errors are phonological because the child focuses on sound, not on meaning.

The words categorized as transitional exemplify a spelling strategy other than sound. In *bome* (*bomb*), for example, Marc applied the final *e* rule he recently learned, even though it isn't appropriate in this word. In time he will learn to spell the word with an unpronounced *b* and will learn that this *b* is needed because *bomb* is a newer, shortened form of *bombard*, in which the *b* in the middle of the word is pronounced. The *b* remains in *bomb* because of the etymology of the word. The word *makde* is especially interesting. Marc pronounced the word "maked," and the *de* is a reversal of letters, a common characteristic of transitional spelling. *Loreneeing* (*learning*) is categorized as transitional because Marc added long-vowel markers (an *e* after *lor* and *ee* after *n*). Because the spelling is based on his pronunciation of *learning*, the long-vowel markers and the conventional spelling of the suffix *-ing* signal a transitional spelling. From the spelling in Marc's composition, he might be classified as a phonetic speller who is moving toward the transitional stage. Marc's paper in Figure 9–14

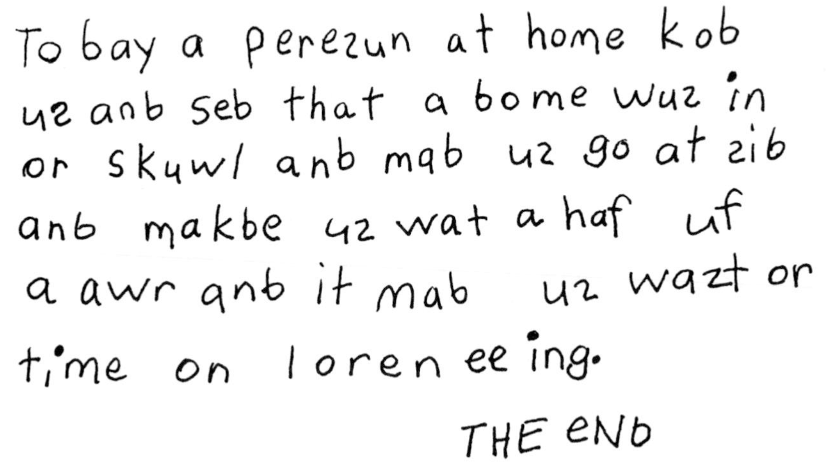

To bay a perezun at home kob uz anb seb that a bome wuz in or skuwl anb mab uz go at zib anb makbe uz wat a haf uf a awr anb it mab uz wazt or time on loren ee ing.

THE eNb

Precommunicative	Semiphonetic	Phonetic	Transitional	Conventional
	kod	sed	peresun	today
		wus	bome	a
		or	skuwl	at
		mad	makde	home
		at sid	uf	us
		wat	loreneeing	and
		haf		that
		awr		a
		mad		in
		wast		and
		or		us
				go
				at
				and
				us
				a
				a
				and
				it
				us
				time
				on
				the
				end

	Precommunicative	Semiphonetic	Phonetic	Transitional	Conventional
Total	0	1	11	6	24
Percent	0	2	26	14	57

Figure 9–14 An Analysis of an Emergent Writer's Invented Spelling

was written in January of grade 1 year, and he is making expected progress in spelling. Categorizing spelling errors in a child's composition and computing the percentage of errors in each category is a useful tool for diagnosing the level of spelling development and deciding whether or not to begin weekly spelling tests.

TEACHING SPELLING IN THE ELEMENTARY GRADES

Spelling instruction is more than learning to spell a given list of words and writing weekly tests. Too often parents and teachers equate spelling instruction with word lists and spelling tests, but a comprehensive spelling program includes much more. Most important, it includes teaching students about English orthography, applying phonics concepts to spelling, and providing students with opportunities to read and write for meaningful, functional, and genuine purposes.

Components of the Spelling Program. A comprehensive spelling program has ten components, including reading and writing opportunities and minilessons about English orthography and spelling procedures.

1. ***Provide daily writing opportunities.*** Providing opportunities for students to write every day is a prerequisite for any spelling program. Spelling is a writer's tool, and it is best learned through the experience of writing. Students who write daily and invent spellings for unfamiliar words move naturally toward conventional spelling. When they write, students use their developing knowledge of sound–symbol correspondences and spelling patterns. Learning to spell is a lot like learning to play the piano. Daily writing opportunities are the practice sessions that lead to achievement.

   When students use the writing process to develop and polish their writings, emphasis on conventional spelling belongs in the editing stage. Through the process approach, children learn to recognize spelling for what it is—a courtesy to readers. As they write, revise, edit, and share their writing with genuine audiences, students understand that they need to spell conventionally so that their audience can read their compositions.

2. ***Provide daily reading opportunities.*** Reading plays an enormous role in students' learning to spell. As they read, students store the visual shapes of words. The ability to recall how words look helps students decide when a spelling they are writing is correct. When students decide that a word doesn't look right, they can rewrite the word several different ways until it does look right, ask the teacher or a classmate who knows the spelling, or check the spelling in a dictionary.

3. ***Post words on word walls.*** One way to direct students' attention to words in books they are reading is through the use of word walls. Students and the teacher choose words to write on word walls, large sheets of paper hanging in the classroom. Then students refer to these word walls for word-study activities and when they are writing. Seeing the words posted on word walls, clusters, and other charts in the classroom and using them in their writing help students to learn to spell the words.

   Teachers also hang word walls with high-frequency words (Cunningham, 1995; Marinelli, 1996). Researchers have identified the most commonly used words and recommend that elementary students learn to spell these words because of their usefulness. The 100 most frequently used words represent more than 50 percent of all the words children and adults write (Horn, 1926)! The Teacher's Notebook on page 385 lists the 100 most frequently used words and suggests ways teachers can teach these words.

4. ***Provide opportunities for students to build words.*** Students arrange and rearrange a group of letter cards to build words (Cunningham & Cunningham, 1992). Primary-grade children can be given a limited number of selected letters to simplify their task. They begin by building two-letter words, then progressively longer words. They can work in small groups and record the words they build on a chart, in columns according to the length of the word. Teachers

Middle-grade students participate in a minilesson on how to form plurals.

often introduce these activities as a whole-class lesson and then set the cards and the word list in a centre for students to use again independently or in small groups. Teachers can use almost any words for word-building activities, but words related to literature students are reading or topics being studied work well.

Given the letters *a, e, b, d, t, s,* and *g,* one group of grade 2 students made the following list:

2-Letter Words	3-Letter Words	4-Letter Words
at	bat	date
be	tea	dead
sea	seat	
ate	babe	
bad		

Students in intermediate grades can increase their knowledge of English orthography and the meanings of affixes and root words by creating new words and their definitions. In one grade 5 classroom, the students called this "Riddlethaurus." The word-building activity requires three packs of word cards, one each of prefixes, root words, and suffixes. Students take one card from each of three piles to form a new word and then they create a definition and sometimes an illustration. One of their favourite inventions is *biphonster*—a person who talks on two telephones at once.

5. ***Teach students to proofread.*** Proofreading is a special kind of reading that students use to locate misspelled words and other mechanical errors in their drafts.

Proofreading should be introduced in the primary grades. Young children and their teachers proofread class collaborative and dictated stories together, and students can be encouraged to reread their own compositions and make necessary corrections soon after they begin writing. This way students accept proofreading as a natural part of both spelling and writing. Proofreading activities are more valuable for teaching spelling than dictation activities, in which teachers dictate sentences for students to write and correctly spell and punctuate.

6. **Teach students to use the dictionary.** Students need to learn how to locate the spelling of unknown words in the dictionary. While it is relatively easy to find a "known" word in the dictionary, it is hard to locate an unfamiliar word, and students need to learn what to do when they don't know how to spell a word. One approach is to predict possible spellings for unknown words, then check the most probable spellings in a dictionary. This procedure involves six steps:

a.   Identify root words and affixes.

b.   Consider related words (e.g., medicine–medical).

c.   Determine the sounds in the word.

d.   Generate a list of possible spellings.

e.   Select the most probable alternatives.

f.   Consult a dictionary to check the correct spelling.

An alternative to using a conventional dictionary is for students to use an online dictionary. To locate unfamiliar words they can use the same strategies as they use with a conventional dictionary.

7. **Teach students to use a spell checker.** When using a word processor to compose, students need to know how to use the spell checker. Most spell checkers offer the writer a variety of choices depending on the type of error made in the original text. Spell checkers frequently fail to produce the intended word as the first option (Montgomery, Karlan, & Coutinho, 2001) and often offer options unrelated in meaning to the intended word. Other options offered include homophones. Teachers must teach students how to choose the correct alternative spelling.

Teachers teach students how to use the spell checker by showing examples. Teachers and students look carefully at the options offered on the computer screen and discuss why each one is correct or incorrect. By showing examples of the types of errors students frequently make, teachers lead students to make correct choices. Teachers must also teach students what to do when the intended word does not appear and when the word in text is correct, but not recognized by the spell checker. Spell checkers and grammar checkers help students reduce mechanical errors, especially non-word errors, but do not replace the need to develop spelling strategies. Spell checkers treat the symptom, not the problem; they help correct, not teach spelling.

8. **Teach spelling options.** In English there are alternative spellings for many sounds because many words that have been borrowed from other languages retain their native spellings. There are many more options for vowel sounds than for consonants. Spelling options sometimes vary according to position in the word. For example, *ff* and *gh* are never used to represent /f/ at the beginning of a word. Common spelling options for phonemes are listed in Figure 9–15 on page 382.

Teachers point out spelling options as they write words on word walls and when students ask about the spelling of a word. They can also use a series of minilessons to teach upper-grade students about these options. During each minilesson, students can focus on one phoneme, such as /f/ or /ar/, and as a class or small group develop a list of the various ways the sound is spelled in English, giving examples of each spelling. A grade 6 class chart for spelling options on long *o* is presented in Figure 9–16 on page 383. In Canadian classrooms, teachers also teach students spelling options related to the national heritage of the orthography. For example, students learn that *cancelled* can be spelled *cancelled* or *canceled* and *honour* as *honour* or *honor*. Generally, the double consonant and *-our* (versus *-or*) patterns are considered Canadian, coming from British heritage, and the single consonant and *-or* patterns are identified with the United States. With increasing globalization and instantaneous communication systems, however, decreasing attention is paid to such spelling attributes.

Sound	Spellings	Examples	Sound	Spellings	Examples
long a	a-e	date	short oo	oo	book
	a	angel		u	put
	ai	aid		ou	could
	ay	day		o	woman
ch	ch	church	ou	ou	out
	t(u)	picture		ow	cow
	tch	watch	s	s	sick
	ti	question		ce	office
long e	ea	each		c	city
	ee	feel		ss	class
	e	evil		se	else
	e-e	these		x(ks)	box
	ea-e	breathe	sh	ti	attention
short e	e	end		sh	she
	ea	head		ci	ancient
f	f	feel		ssi	admission
	ff	sheriff	t	t	teacher
	ph	photograph		te	definite
j	ge	strange		ed	furnished
	g	general		tt	attend
	j	job	long u	u	union
	dge	bridge		u-e	use
k	c	call		ue	value
	k	keep		ew	few
	x	expect, luxury	short u	u	ugly
	ck	black		o	company
	qu	quite, bouquet		ou	country
l	l	last	y	u	union
	ll	allow		u-e	use
	le	automobile		y	yes
m	m	man		i	onion
	me	come		ue	value
	mm	comment		ew	few
n	n	no	z	s	present
	ne	done		se	applause
long o	o	go		ze	gauze
	o-e	note	syllabic *l*	le	able
	ow	own		al	animal
	oa	load		el	cancel
short o	o	office		il	civil
	a	all	syllabic *n*	en	written
	au	author		on	lesson
	aw	saw		an	important
oi	oi	oil		in	cousin
	oy	boy		contractions	didn't
long oo	u	cruel		ain	certain
	oo	noon	*r*-controlled	er	her
	u-e	rule		ur	church
	o-e	lose		ir	first
	ue	blue		or	world
	o	to		ear	heard
	ou	group		our	courage

Figure 9–15 Common Spelling Options for Phonemes

Spelling	Word	Location		
		Initial	Medial	Final
o	oh, obedient	x		
	go, no, so			x
o-e	home, pole		x	
ow	own	x		
	known		x	
	blow, elbow, yellow			x
oa	oaf, oak, oat	x		
	boat, groan		x	
ew	sew			x
ol	yolk, folk		x	
oe	toe			x
ough	though			x
eau	beau			x
ou	bouquet		x	

Figure 9–16 A Grade 6 Class Chart for Spelling Options on Long *o*

9. ***Teach spelling strategies through minilessons.*** Students need to develop a repertoire of strategies in order to spell unfamiliar words (Laminack & Wood, 1996; Wilde, 1993). Some of these spelling strategies are

- Invent spellings for words based on phonological, semantic, and historical knowledge of words.
- Proofread to locate and correct spelling errors.
- Locate words on word walls and other charts.
- Predict the spelling of a word by generating possible spellings and choosing the best alternative.
- Apply affixes to root words.
- Spell unknown words by analogy to known words.
- Locate the spelling of unfamiliar words in a dictionary or other reliable resource.
- Write a string of letters as a placeholder to stand for an unfamiliar word in a rough draft.
- Ask the teacher or a classmate how to spell a word.
- Use a spell checker effectively.

Instead of giving the traditional "sound it out" advice when students ask how to spell an unfamiliar word, teachers should help them use a strategic approach. We suggest that teachers encourage students to "think it out" and to apply one or more of the above strategies.

Teachers teach students about spelling procedures, concepts, and strategies and skills during minilessons. A list of topics for minilessons on spelling is presented on page 386. Some of the topics are appropriate for primary-grade students, and others for older students.

10. ***Develop students' spelling conscience.*** The goal of spelling instruction is to help students develop what Hillerich (1977) calls a "spelling conscience"—a positive attitude toward spelling and a concern for using standard spelling. Two dimensions of a spelling conscience are understanding that standard spelling is a courtesy to readers and developing the ability to proofread to spot and correct misspellings.

Students in the middle and upper grades need to learn that it is unrealistic to expect readers to try to decipher numerous misspelled words. Teachers help students develop a spelling

For more information on proofreading and editing, see Chapter 4, "The Reading and Writing Processes," pages 154–157.

conscience by providing meaningful writing and by teaching them to be strategic in their approach to spelling and proofreading.

Weekly Spelling Tests. Many teachers question the use of spelling tests to teach spelling, since research on invented spelling suggests that spelling is best learned through reading and writing (Gentry & Gillet, 1993; Wilde, 1993). In addition, teachers complain that lists of spelling words in published programs are unrelated to the words students are reading and writing. We recommend that weekly spelling tests, when they are used, be customized so that children learn to spell the words they need for their writing.

In a customized approach to spelling instruction, students and teachers choose the words to be studied. The master list composed by the teacher and students may include words from one or more of the following sources: published spelling programs, topics of study in other areas of curriculum, writing projects specific to language arts, or published lists of frequently misspelled words. In addition to the master list, students can individualize their lists by adding words that they need for their writing projects or that they have misspelled in their writing. In many classrooms, instruction is organized on a weekly basis. Teachers and students compose lists on Monday, study the words during the week, and end their study with a test on Friday.

On Monday the teacher administers a pretest by dictating the master list to the whole class. Students then form pairs and dictate to each other the words they have added to the master list to individualize their lists. Students correct their own pretests and determine the words they must learn throughout the week. One way to organize the lists for the pretest and self-correction is by using test sheets divided into three columns as shown in Figure 9–17. In the first column, the teacher writes the master list and leaves enough space for students to add their individual words. In the second column, students write the pretest. In the third column, students write any words misspelled on the pretest. The first column is folded under so it is not visible while the pretest is being given. It is then unfolded to guide the students when they are self-correcting their tests. Students circle the part of the word they misspelled before writing the word correctly in the third column. These lists are used for study at school and at home during the week.

Master List	Pretest	Correction
volcano	*volcano*	
earthquake	*earthquake*	
lava	*lava*	
spew	*spew*	
ashes	*ash(is)*	*ashes*
spaghetti	*spagh(ti)*	*spaghetti*
veterinarian	*vet(er)narian*	*veterinarian*

Figure 9–17 Test Sheet for Pretest of Spelling List

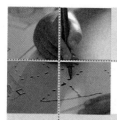

Teacher's Notebook

The 100 Most Frequently Used Words

a	did	in	out	time
about	didn't	into	over	to
after	do	is	people	too
all	don't	it	put	two
am	down	just	said	up
an	for	know	saw	us
and	from	like	school	very
are	get	little	see	was
around	got	man	she	we
as	had	me	so	well
at	have	mother	some	went
back	he	my	that	were
be	her	no	the	what
because	him	not	them	when
but	his	now	then	who
by	home	of	there	will
came	house	on	they	with
can	how	one	things	would
could	I	or	think	you
day	if	our	this	your

Ways to Use This List of Words

1. List these words on bookmarks or tagboard cards that students keep at their desks and refer to when writing.

2. Explain to students the importance of knowing how to spell these words: these 100 words are used again and again, and when students know how to spell them, they will be able to spell half of all the words they write.

3. Make a wall chart with these words and have students add other frequently used words during the school year.

4. For younger students or less capable writers, pick out the 10 or 20 words that your students use most often and make cards with these words for students to keep at their desks.

5. Use words from this list to use in minilessons to contrast "sight words" with words that can be sounded out.

6. Choose words from this list for spelling words since these words are the most frequently used, and high-frequency words should be taught before low-frequency words.

7. These words are also high-frequency reading "sight words." Use this list to develop reading fluency, too.

Minilessons

Language Tools

	Procedures	Concepts	Strategies and Skills
Spelling	Invent spellings	Alphabetic principle	Use placeholders
	Locate words on a word wall	Invented spelling	Sound it out
	Locate words in a dictionary	Homophones	Think it out
	Proofread	Root words and affixes	Visualize words
	Form contractions	Spelling options	Use analogy
	Form plurals	High-frequency words	Apply affixes
	Use other inflectional endings	Dictionary	Generate possible spellings
	Use a thesaurus	Thesaurus	Choose probable alternatives
	Study a spelling word	Spelling conscience	Proofread
	Assess use of spelling strategies	Phoneme–grapheme correspondences	Apply capitalization rules
	Analyze spelling errors	Contractions	Use a spell checker
		Compound words	
		Possessives	
Handwriting	Grip a pencil	Legible	Determine purpose of handwriting
	Form letters	Fluent	Choose manuscript or cursive
	Space between letters	Manuscript handwriting	Apply elements of legibility
	Size letters	Cursive handwriting	Personalize handwriting
	Make letters parallel	D'Nealian handwriting	
	Write manuscript letters	Uppercase letters	
	Write cursive letters	Lowercase letters	
	Make letters touch the baseline	Public and private handwriting	
	Keep letters same size	Elements of legibility	
	Make lines steady and of even thickness		
	Assess handwriting problems		
Grammar	Identify parts of speech	Grammar	Use complete sentences
	Classify sentence types	Usage	Expand sentences
	Slot sentences	Standard English	Rearrange sentences
	Manipulate sentences	Parts of speech	Combine sentences
	Combine sentences	Subject and predicate	Vary sentence length
	Make concept books	Simple sentences	Consider register
	Assess appropriateness of usage	Compound sentences	Proofread to locate usage errors
	Assess use of strategies	Complex sentences	
		Compound-complex sentences	
		Declarative sentences	
		Interrogative sentences	
		Imperative sentences	
		Exclamatory sentences	

Researchers have found that the pretest is a critical component in learning to spell. The pretest eliminates words that students already know how to spell so that they can direct their study toward words that they don't know yet. As long ago as 1957, Ernest Horn recommended that the best way to improve students' spelling is for them to get immediate feedback by correcting their own pretests. His advice is still sound today.

Students spend approximately 5 to 10 minutes studying the words on their study lists each day during the week. Instead of "busy-work" activities, such as using their spelling words in sentences or gluing yarn in the shape of the words, research shows that it is more effective for students to use the following strategy to practise spelling words:

1. Look at the word and say it to yourself.
2. Say each letter in the word to yourself.
3. Close your eyes and spell the word to yourself.
4. Write the word, and check that you spelled it correctly.
5. Write the word again, and check that you spelled it correctly.

This strategy focuses on the whole word rather than breaking it apart into sounds or syllables. During a minilesson at the beginning of the school year, teachers explain how to use the strategy, and then post a copy of the strategy in the classroom. In addition to this word-study strategy, sometimes students trade word lists on Wednesday or Thursday and give each other a practice test.

A final test is administered on Friday. The teacher dictates the master list, and students dictate the individual list to each other. Any words that students misspell should be included on their lists the following week.

This individualized approach is recommended instead of a textbook approach. Typically, in Canadian classrooms, spelling instruction is embedded in the writing program and published spelling programs are used as only one teaching and learning resource.

The words in such programs are often grouped according to spelling patterns or phonetic generalizations, even though researchers question this approach; Johnson, Langford, and Quorm found that "the effectiveness of teaching spelling via phonic generalizations is highly questionable" (1981, p. 586). We, therefore, do not recommend their use alone.

ADAPTING TO MEET THE NEEDS OF EVERY STUDENT

Spelling and the other language tools can be adapted to meet the needs of all students, and the single most important adaptation teachers can make is to understand the relative importance of language tools in the language arts program. Communicative competence is the goal of language arts instruction, and language tools support communication, but they do not equal it. For spelling instruction, that means encouraging students to use invented spelling so that they can communicate with others before they reach the stage of conventional spelling. Students who are learning English as a second language may take longer to move through the five stages of spelling development, and their invented spelling will reflect their pronunciation of words and use of inflectional endings. Students with special needs may experience pervasive and persistent spelling difficulties and should be taught compensatory strategies, including efficient use of dictionaries and spell checkers. A list of recommendations for adapting spelling instruction is presented on pages 388–389.

ASSESSING STUDENTS' PROGRESS IN SPELLING

Grades on spelling tests are the traditional measure of progress in spelling, and they provide a convenient way to assess students. This method of assessing student progress is somewhat deceptive, however, because the goal of spelling instruction is not simply to spell words correctly on tests but to use the words, spelled conventionally, in writing. To determine the carry-over from tests to writing, samples of student writing should be collected periodically. If words that were spelled correctly on tests are not correctly spelled in students' writing, alternative instructional and study strategies should be developed.

When students perform poorly on spelling tests or persistently spell poorly in their writing, teachers try to determine possible causes. They consider whether pronunciation is to blame. They ask students to pronounce words they habitually misspell to see if their pronunciation or dialect differences may be contributing to spelling problems. Students need to recognize that pronunciation does not always predict spelling. For example, in some parts of Canada, people sometimes pronounce *better* as though it were spelled *bedder* and *walked* as though it were spelled *walkt*. Teachers also observe as students proofread to determine what strategies they use to recognize and correct errors. If errors are not recognized, teachers provide minilessons and practice. If the writing sample has been word-processed, errors may be the result of inaccurate use of a spell checker. In this case, the teacher and student work together to give the student an opportunity to share their perceptions of what the correct spelling should be.

Adapting

Spelling Instruction to Meet the Needs of Every Student

1. Read and Write Every Day
Students who are poor spellers often don't read or write very much, but they need to read and write every day in order to become better spellers. Poor spellers benefit from frequent, short writing projects with which they can be successful.

2. Encourage Invented Spelling
Too often poor spellers don't want to write because there are so many words they don't know how to spell. Teachers should encourage students to use invented spelling, no matter how old they are, because it allows them to write independently. Their invented spellings provide valuable insights into what students know about English orthography and what kind of instruction they need. Older students can be taught to underline their best guesses as they write to indicate words that need attention when the writing is edited.

3. Teach High-Frequency Words
Poor spellers should learn to spell the 100 most frequently used words because of their usefulness. Knowing the 100 most frequently used words allows students to spell correctly approximately half of all words they write.

4. Teach the Think-It-Out Strategy
Poor spellers typically rely on a sound-it-out strategy to spell words, while better spellers understand that sound is only a rough guide to spelling. Teachers use minilessons to teach students how to think out and predict the spelling of unfamiliar words, using multiple strategies. Play Interactive Word Games Students learn from each other through interactive word games. Games can provide practice for poor spellers and challenge for proficient spellers. Some computer games also provide practice and challenge.

6. Recognize That Errors Are Part of Learning
Errors indicate what students know and what they need to learn. Both teachers and students can learn from them by working together to identify and correct errors on writing projects that will be published. Too much emphasis on what students misspell does not help them to spell; it teaches them that they cannot spell.

7. Teach Students to Use Word-Processor Spell Checkers

The instant feedback where an incorrect spelling is underlined alerts the student to a possible error and encourages students to look closely at words and patterns. Spell checkers are most helpful to students who already spell reasonably well and whose errors are close to the standard spelling. Writers with major spelling problems are less helped by spell checkers and require guidance in their use.

8. Plan for Success

Many poor spellers achieve success a few words at a time. Divide longer lists to be learned into several shorter ones. Provide opportunities for using the words in written communication.

It is essential that teachers keep anecdotal information and samples of children's writing to monitor their overall progress in spelling. Teachers can examine error patterns and spelling strategies in these samples. Checking to see if students have spelled their spelling words correctly in writing samples provides one type of information, and examining writing samples for error patterns and spelling strategies provides additional information. Fewer misspellings do not necessarily indicate progress because to learn to spell, students must experiment with spellings of unfamiliar words, which will result in errors from time to time. Students often misspell a word by misapplying a newly learned spelling pattern. The word *extension* is a good example. Middle-grade students spell the word *extenshun*, and then change their spelling to *extention* after they learn the suffix *-tion*. Although they are still misspelling the word, they have moved from using sound–symbol correspondences to using a spelling pattern—from a less sophisticated spelling strategy to a more sophisticated one.

Students' behaviour as they proofread and edit their compositions also provides evidence of spelling development. Locating errors is the first step in proofreading; correcting the errors is the second step. It is fairly easy for students to correct the spelling of known words, but to correct unknown words, they must consider spelling options and predict possible spellings before they can locate the words in a dictionary. Teachers can document students' growth in locating unfamiliar words in a dictionary by observing their behaviour when they edit their compositions.

For more information on anecdotal notes, see Chapter 2, "Teaching the Language Arts," pages 70–72.

Handwriting

Like grammar and spelling, handwriting is a tool for writers. While it is easily argued that extensive attention to handwriting cannot be justified given the prominence of word processing, including voice-activated processing, handwriting instruction should not be ignored. Students need to develop a legible and fluent style of handwriting so that they will be able to fully participate in all written language activities. Graves explains: "Children win prizes for fine script, parents and teachers nod approval for a crisp, well-crafted page, a good impression is made on a job application blank . . . all important elements, but they pale next to the substance they carry" (1983, p. 171). Even though Graves was writing of a previous generation of students, the point is well taken, the message is more important than the formation of letters, but handwriting is still an essential communication tool. Students who write legibly, produce better compositions. Legible handwriting frees students to focus on words and ideas (Berninger, 1997).

The goal in handwriting instruction is to help students develop legible forms to communicate effectively through writing. The two most important criteria in determining quality in handwriting are legibility (the writing can be easily and quickly read) and fluency (the writing can be easily and quickly written). It is imperative to recognize the functional purpose of handwriting and convey to students the importance of developing legible handwriting.

HANDWRITING FORMS

Two forms of handwriting are currently used in most Canadian elementary schools: manuscript, or printing, and cursive, or connected writing. These are illustrated in Figure 9–18. Typically, students in the primary grades learn and use the manuscript form; they switch to cursive handwriting in grade 2 or 3. In the middle and upper grades, students use both handwriting forms.

Manuscript Handwriting. Until the 1920s, students learned only cursive handwriting. Marjorie Wise is credited with introducing the manuscript form for primary-grade students in 1921 (Hildreth, 1960). Manuscript handwriting is considered better for young children because the letters require only vertical lines, horizontal lines, and circles, the components of their early drawings. Their drawing practice makes manuscript writing easier when they reach school age (Farris, 1997). In addition, manuscript handwriting is similar to the type style in many primary-level books. Only two lowercase letters, *a* and *g*, are different in typed and handwritten forms. The similarity is assumed to facilitate young children's introduction to reading and writing.

Barbe and Milone (1980) suggest several additional reasons that students in the primary grades should learn manuscript before cursive handwriting. First, manuscript handwriting is easier to learn. Studies show that young children can copy letters and words written in the manuscript form more easily than those written in the cursive form. Also, young children can form the vertical and horizontal lines and circles of manuscript handwriting more easily than the cursive strokes. Furthermore, manuscript handwriting is more legible than cursive handwriting. Because it is easier to read, signs and advertisements are printed in letter forms closely approximating manuscript handwriting. Finally, people are often requested to print when completing applications and other forms. For these reasons, manuscript handwriting has become the preferred handwriting form for young children, as well as a necessary handwriting skill for older children and adults.

Students' use of the manuscript form usually diminishes in the middle grades after they have learned cursive handwriting. The need to develop greater writing speed is often given as the reason for the transfer to cursive handwriting, but research does not show that one form is necessarily written more quickly than the other.

Cursive Handwriting. When most people think of handwriting, the cursive or connected and slanted form comes to mind. The letters in cursive handwriting are joined together to form a word with one continuous movement. Children often view cursive handwriting as the "grown-up" type. Primary-grade students often attempt to imitate this form by connecting the manuscript letters in their names and other words before they are taught how to form and join the letters. Awareness of cursive handwriting and interest in imitating it are indicators that students are ready for instruction.

D'Nealian Handwriting. D'Nealian handwriting is an innovative manuscript and cursive handwriting program developed by Donald Neal Thurber, a teacher in Michigan. The D'Nealian handwriting forms are shown in Figure 9–19 on page 392. In the manuscript form, letters are slanted and formed with a continuous stroke; in the cursive form, the letters are simplified, without the flourishes of traditional cursive. Both forms were designed to increase legibility and fluency and to ease the transition from manuscript to cursive handwriting.

The purpose of the D'Nealian program was to mitigate some of the problems associated with the traditional manuscript form (Thurber, 1987). D'Nealian manuscript uses the same basic letter forms that students will need for cursive handwriting, as well as the slant and rhythm required for cursive. Another advantage of the D'Nealian style is that the transition from manuscript to cursive involves adding only connective strokes to most manuscript letters. Only five

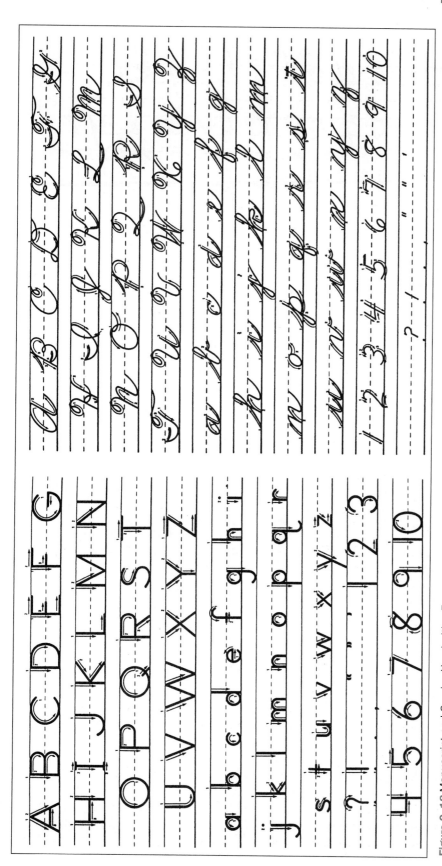

Figure 9–18 Manuscript and Cursive Handwriting Forms

Source: Used with permission of the publisher, Zaner-Blaser, Inc. Columbus, OH, copyright © 1993. From *Handwriting: A Way to Self-Expression*, by Clinton Hackney.

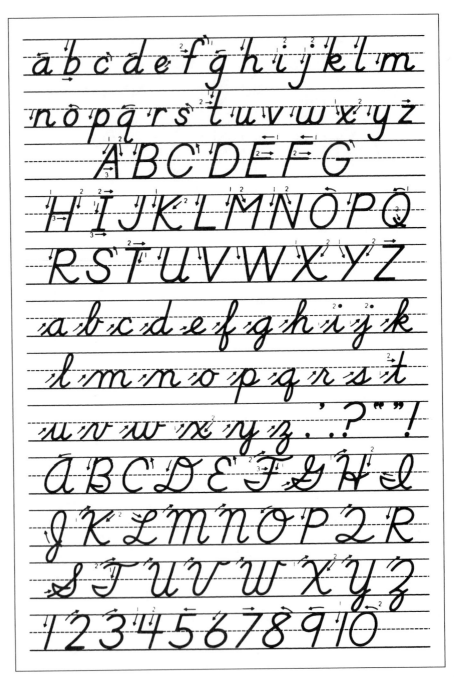

Figure 9–19 D'Nealian Manuscript and Cursive Handwriting Forms

Source: D'Nealian is a registered trademark of Donald Neal Thurber, copyright © 1987 by Scott, Foresman and Company.

letters—*f*, *r*, *s*, *v*, and *z*—are shaped differently in the cursive form. Research (Graham, 1992; Kuhl & Dewitz, 1994) considering its ease of learning and use raises some concerns, but is not conclusive. Some Canadian school districts have adopted the use of D'Nealian handwriting across the grades. Teachers report much satisfaction and appreciate the ease of transition from manuscript to cursive letter forms.

CHILDREN'S HANDWRITING DEVELOPMENT

Children's handwriting grows out of their drawing activities. As they observe words in their environment and see adults writing, they begin to add letter-like forms and scribbles to their drawing. Typically, preschoolers begin to copy words and develop an especially keen interest in copying and writing their names.

During the elementary grades, children grow from using scribbles and letter-like forms in kindergarten to learning the manuscript handwriting form in the primary grades and the cursive form beginning in the middle grades. Students in the middle and upper grades use both forms interchangeably for a variety of handwriting tasks. Examples of children's handwriting from kindergarten through eighth grade are shown in the accompanying Figure 9–20. The excerpts were selected from letters.

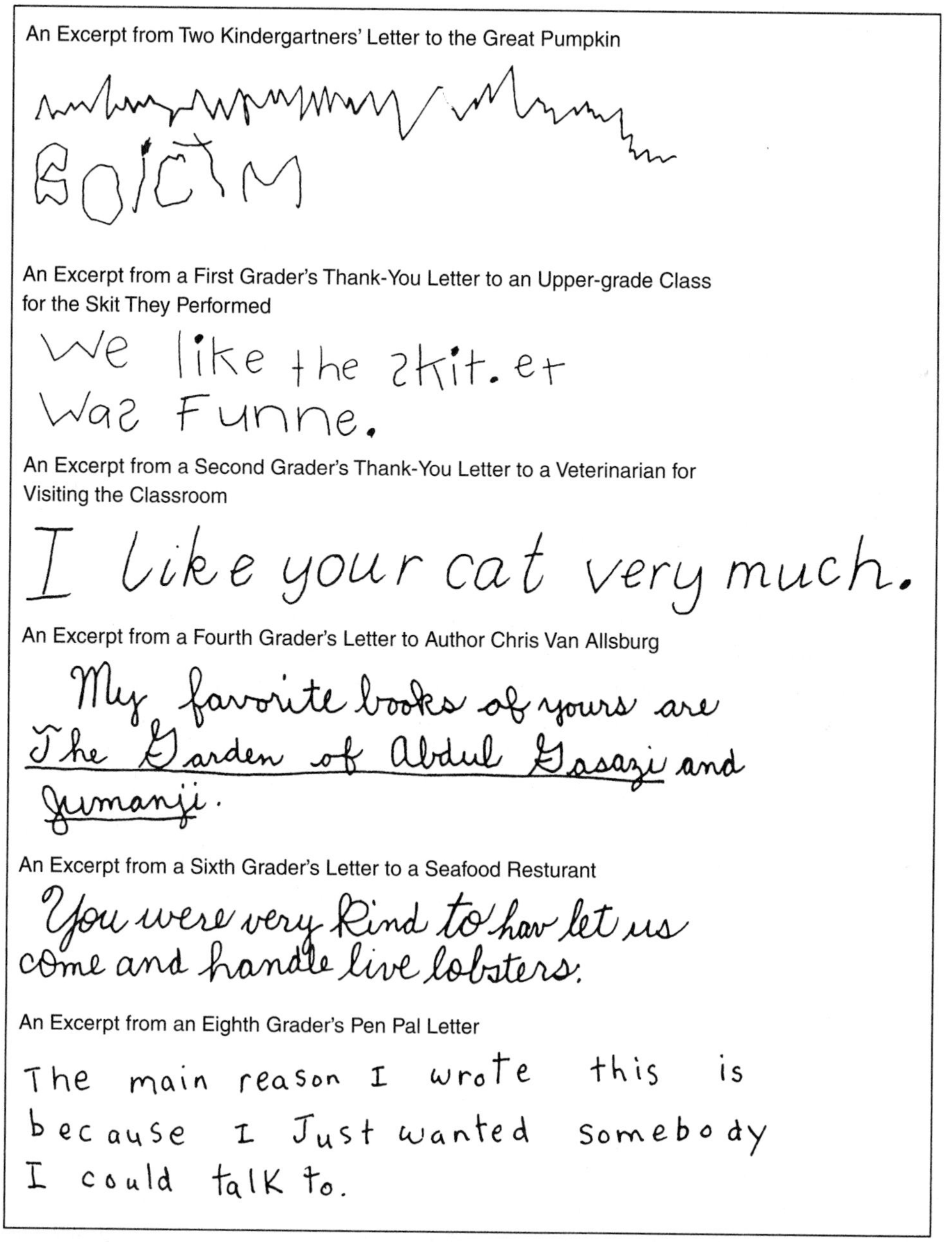

An Excerpt from Two Kindergartners' Letter to the Great Pumpkin

An Excerpt from a First Grader's Thank-You Letter to an Upper-grade Class for the Skit They Performed

We like the zkit. et Waz Funne.

An Excerpt from a Second Grader's Thank-You Letter to a Veterinarian for Visiting the Classroom

I like your cat very much.

An Excerpt from a Fourth Grader's Letter to Author Chris Van Allsburg

My favorite books of yours are The Garden of Abdul Gasazi and Jumanji.

An Excerpt from a Sixth Grader's Letter to a Seafood Resturant

You were very Kind to hav let us come and handle live lobsters.

An Excerpt from an Eighth Grader's Pen Pal Letter

The main reason I wrote this is because I Just wanted somebody I could talk to.

Figure 9–20 Examples of Children's Handwriting

TEACHING HANDWRITING IN KINDERGARTEN AND THE ELEMENTARY GRADES

Teachers must be mindful that young children enter kindergarten with greatly differing backgrounds of drawing and handwriting experience. Some five-year-olds have never held a pencil while others have learned to print their names and other letters. Handwriting instruction in kindergarten typically is somewhat informal and includes four types of activities: stimulating children's interest in writing, developing their ability to hold writing instruments, refining their fine motor control, and letter formation of both upper- and lowercase letters. A hallmark of kindergarten writing is children learning to write their name using one uppercase letter and the rest in lowercase.

In many Canadian schools formal handwriting instruction begins in grade 1. Students learn how to form manuscript letters and space between them, and they develop skills related to the six elements of legibility. In the middle grades, after students have learned both manuscript and cursive handwriting, they need to review both forms periodically. By this time, too, they have firmly established handwriting habits, both good and bad. Instruction at the middle- and upper-grade levels focuses on helping students diagnose and correct their handwriting trouble spots so that they can develop a legible and fluent handwriting style. Older students both simplify their letter forms and also add unique flourishes to their handwriting to develop their own "trademark" styles.

For more information on legibility, see "Elements of Legibility" in this chapter on pages 397–398.

Special pencils and handwriting paper are often provided for handwriting instruction. Kindergartners and first graders have commonly been given "fat" beginner pencils because it has been assumed that these pencils are easier for young children to hold; however, most children prefer to use regular-sized pencils that older students and adults use. Moreover, regular pencils have erasers! Research now indicates that beginner pencils are not better than regular-sized pencils for young children (Graham, 1992). Likewise, there is no clear evidence that specially shaped pencils and small writing aids that slip onto pencils to improve children's grip are effective, but some children appear to be helped, at least temporarily, by them.

Many types of paper, both lined and unlined, are used in elementary classrooms. The few research studies that have examined the value of lined paper in general and paper lined at specific intervals offer conflicting results. One study suggests that younger children's handwriting is more legible when they use unlined paper, and that older children's is better when they use lined paper (Lindsay & McLennan, 1983). In practice, we believe it is best to provide students with experiences with a variety of types of paper as best suited to their writing projects.

Transition to Cursive Handwriting. Students' introduction to cursive handwriting typically occurs in the second semester of grade 2 or the first semester of grade 3. Teachers and students often attach great importance to the transition from manuscript to cursive. Usually, the basic strokes that make up the letters (e.g., slant stroke, undercurve, downcurve) are taught first. Next, the lowercase letters are taught in isolation, and then the connecting strokes are introduced. Uppercase letters are taught later because they are used far less often and are more difficult to form. Which cursive letters are most difficult? The lowercase *r* is the most troublesome letter. The other lowercase letters students frequently form incorrectly are *k*, *p*, and *z*.

The practice of changing to cursive handwriting only a year or two after children learn the manuscript form is sometimes criticized. The argument has been that students need to learn cursive handwriting as early as possible because of their increasing need for handwriting speed. Because of its continuous flow, cursive handwriting was thought to be faster to write than manuscript; however, research suggests that manuscript handwriting can be written as quickly as cursive handwriting (Jackson, 1971). The controversy over the benefits of the two forms of handwriting is likely to continue, but is tempered by concerns for teaching word-processing to facilitate students' writing fluency.

Left-Handed Writers. Approximately 10 percent of our population is left-handed. In the past, left-handed writers were thought to have inferior handwriting skills. In fact, research has shown that there is no significant difference in the quality or speed of left- and right-handed students' writing (Groff, 1963). Teachers and parents should support children's natural tendencies, making any accommodation needed.

Teaching handwriting to left-handed students is not simply the reverse of teaching handwriting to right-handed students (Howell, 1978). Left-handed students have unique handwriting needs, and special adaptations of the procedures for teaching right-handed students are necessary. In fact, many of the difficulties that left-handed students face can be made worse by using the procedures designed for right-handed writers (Harrison, 1981). Special adjustments are necessary to allow left-handed students to write legibly, fluently, and with less fatigue.

The basic difference between right- and left-handed writing is physical orientation. Right-handed students pull their arms toward their bodies as they write, whereas left-handed writers push away. As left-handed students write, they move their left hands across what they have just written, often covering it. Many children adopt a "hook" position to avoid covering and smudging what they have written. Because of their different physical orientation, left-handed writers need to make three major types of adjustments:

1. *Holding pencils.* Left-handed writers should hold pencils or pens an inch or more farther back from the tip than right-handed writers do. This change helps them see what they have just written and avoid smearing their writing. Left-handed writers need to work to avoid "hooking" their wrists. Have them keep their wrists straight and elbows close to their bodies to avoid the awkward hooked position.

2. *Tilting paper.* Left-handed students should tilt their writing papers slightly to the right, in contrast to right-handed students, who tilt their papers to the left. Sometimes it is helpful to place a piece of masking tape on the student's desk to indicate the proper amount of tilt.

3. *Slanting letters.* Whereas right-handed students are encouraged to slant their cursive letters to the right, left-handed writers often write vertically or even slant their letters slightly to the left. Some handwriting programs recommend that left-handed writers slant their cursive letters slightly to the right as right-handed students do, but others advise teachers to permit any slant between vertical and 45 degrees to the left of vertical (Howell, 1978).

Planning Handwriting Instruction. Handwriting is best taught in separate periods of direct instruction and teacher-supervised practice. As soon as skills are taught, they should be applied in real-life writing activities.

Handwriting instruction and practice periods should be brief; 15-minute periods of instruction several times a week are more effective than a single lengthy period weekly or monthly. Regular periods of handwriting instruction are necessary when teaching the manuscript form in kindergarten and grade 1 and the cursive form in grade 2 or 3. Figure 9–21 on pages 396–397 outlines the steps in teaching letter formation. In the middle and upper grades, instruction focuses on specific handwriting problems that students demonstrate and periodic reviews of both handwriting forms.

Minilessons on Handwriting. The teaching strategy presented in Chapter 2 can be adapted to teach minilessons on handwriting. The strategy is multisensory, with visual, auditory, and kinesthetic components, and is based on research in the field of handwriting (Askov & Greff, 1975; Furner, 1969; Graham, 1992; Hirsch & Niedermeyer, 1973). Research has shown the importance of the teacher's active involvement in handwriting instruction and practice. Observing "moving" models—that is, having students watch the teacher write the handwriting sample—is of far greater value than copying models that have already been written (Wright & Wright, 1980). As in the writing process, the teacher's assistance is far more useful while the students are writing than after they have completed writing. The steps in teaching a minilesson on handwriting are shown in the following Step by Step box:

For the steps in teaching a minilesson, see Chapter 2, "Teaching the Language Arts," page 59.

Step by Step

A Minilesson on Handwriting

1. *Introduce the topic.* The teacher demonstrates a specific handwriting procedure, strategy, or skill while students observe. During the demonstration, the teacher describes the steps involved in executing it.

   Example: The teacher demonstrates formation of the letter *p* saying "*p* is made of a stick and a circle. The stick begins at the midline and goes down below the baseline. The circle starts at the midline, goes around to touch the stick, down to sit on the baseline and back up to where it started."

2. *Have students describe the steps.* Students describe the procedure, strategy, or skill and the steps for executing it as the teacher or a classmate demonstrates it again.

3. *Review the topic.* The teacher reviews the specific handwriting procedure, strategy, or skill, summarizing the steps involved.

4. *Circulate as students practise handwriting.* Students practise the procedure, strategy, or skill using pencils, pens, or other writing instruments. As they practise, students softly repeat the steps, and the teacher circulates, providing assistance as needed.

5. *Apply handwriting in writing activities.* Students apply the procedure, strategy, or skill they have learned in their writing.

   Example: At the end of the lesson, students write the sentence, "Some pigs are purple and pink."

   To check that students have learned to handwrite a letter or family of letters, the teacher and students can review writing over a period of several days and mark examples of correct use.

---

1. Introduce the Letter
   Demonstrate the formation of a single letter or family of letters (e.g., the manuscript circle letters—*O, o, C, c, a, e, Q*) on the chalkboard while explaining how the letter is formed.

2. Explain How to Form the Letter
   Have students describe how the letter is formed while you or a student forms the letter on the chalkboard. At first you may need to ask questions to direct students' descriptions. Possible questions include
   • How many strokes are used in making the letter?
   • Which stroke comes first?
   • Where do you begin the stroke?
   • In which direction do you go?
   • What size will the letter be?
   • Where does the stroke stop?
   • Which stroke comes next?

   Students will quickly learn the appropriate terminology, such as *baseline, left-right, slant line, counterclockwise,* and so on, to describe how the letters are formed.

   (continued)

Figure 9–21 Using the Teaching Strategy to Teach Letter Formation

3. Review the Steps

Review the formation of the letter or letter family with students while demonstrating how to form the letter on the chalkboard.

4. Have Students Practise Writing the Letter

Have the students print the letter at the chalkboard, in sand, and with a variety of other materials such as clay, shaving cream, finger paint, pudding, and pipe cleaners. As students form the letter, they should softly describe the formation process to themselves.

Have students practise writing the letter on paper with the accompanying verbal descriptions.

Circulate among students providing assistance and encouragement. Demonstrate and describe the correct formation of the letter as the students observe.

5. Provide Authentic Writing Activities

After the students have practised the letter or family of letters, have them apply what they have learned in authentic writing activities. This is the crucial step!

Figure 9–21 Using the Teaching Strategy to Teach Letter Formation (*continued*)

Elements of Legibility. In order for students to develop legible handwriting, they need to know what qualities or elements determine legibility and then analyze their own handwriting according to these elements (Hackney, 1993). The six elements of legible and fluent handwriting are as follows:

1. *Letter formation.* Letters are formed with specific strokes. Letters in manuscript handwriting are composed of vertical, horizontal, and slanted lines plus circles or parts of circles. The letter *b*, for example, is composed of a vertical line and a circle, and *M* is composed of vertical and slanted lines. Cursive letters are composed of slanted lines, loops, and curved lines. The lowercase cursive letters *m* and *n*, for example, are composed of a slant stroke, a loop, and an undercurve stroke. An additional component in cursive handwriting is the connecting stroke used to join letters.

2. *Size and proportion.* During the elementary grades, students' handwriting becomes smaller, and the proportional size of uppercase to lowercase letters increases. Beginning writers' uppercase manuscript letters are twice the size of lowercase letters. When students first begin cursive handwriting, the proportional size of letters remains 2:1; later, the proportion increases to 3:1 for middle- and upper-grade students.

3. *Spacing.* Students should leave adequate space between letters in words and between words in sentences. Spacing between words in manuscript handwriting should equal one lowercase letter *o*, and spacing between sentences should equal two lowercase *o*'s. The most important aspect of spacing within words in cursive handwriting is consistency. To correctly space between words, the writer should make the beginning stroke of the new word directly below the end stroke of the preceding word. Spacing between sentences should equal one uppercase letter *O*, and the indent for a new paragraph should equal two uppercase letter *O*'s.

4. *Slant.* Letters should be consistently parallel. Letters in manuscript handwriting are vertical, and in the cursive form letters slant slightly to the right. To ensure the correct slant, right-handed students tilt their papers to the left, and left-handed students tilt their papers to the right.

5. *Alignment.* For proper alignment in both manuscript and cursive handwriting, all letters should be uniform in size and consistently touch the baseline.

6. *Line quality.* Students should write at a consistent speed and hold their writing instruments correctly and in a relaxed manner to make steady, unwavering lines of even thickness.

Correct letter formation and spacing receive the major focus in handwriting instruction during the elementary grades. Although the other four elements usually receive less attention, they, too, are important in developing legible and fluent handwriting.

ADAPTING TO MEET THE NEEDS OF EVERY STUDENT

The goal of handwriting instruction is for every student to develop legible and fluent handwriting. Students who experience difficulty producing written work that is easily read may require significant intervention. One possibility is that the D'Nealian handwriting program may be more effective because the letter forms are simplified. Another possibility is that students with severe handwriting problems can be taught to use computers with word-processing programs to produce most of their written work. When teachers make instructional decisions regarding students with severe writing difficulties, they must be mindful of the goals of fluency and legibility. They must remember that handwriting and word processing are tools for communication. The accompanying box presents a list of recommendations for adapting writing instruction.

ASSESSING AND CORRECTING HANDWRITING PROBLEMS

Students and teachers use the six elements of legibility to diagnose handwriting problems. For primary-grade students letter formation and spacing are most important. Older students can examine a piece of handwriting to assess it in respect to all six elements. A checklist for assessing manuscript handwriting is shown in the accompanying Figure 9–22. Checklists can also be developed for cursive handwriting. It is important to involve students in developing the checklists so that they appreciate the need to make their handwriting legible and learn to monitor their progress in writing legibly and fluently. When students experience persistent problems, they require remediation.

TEACHING WORD PROCESSING IN THE ELEMENTARY GRADES

Word processing is a writing tool for students not unlike handwriting. That is, it enables students to express themselves with fluency and legibility. Students often use word processing at all stages of writing: to compose, draft, revise, edit, and publish. Research has shown that students who write using word processors derive motivation for writing from using the computer and they write more (D'Odorico & Zammuner, 1993). Further, students writing on word processors make fewer spelling errors and make more positive changes from first to final drafts. (Black, 1989; Lewis,

---

Handwriting Checklist

Name _____

Writing Project _____

Date _____

_____ 1. Did I form my letters correctly?
                   Did I start my line letters at the top?
                   Did I start my circle letters at 1:00?
                   Did I join the round parts of the letters neatly?
                   Did I join the slanted strokes in sharp points?
_____ 2. Did my lines touch the midline or top line neatly?
_____ 3. Did I make all my letters sit on the baseline?
_____ 4. Did I make my letters straight up and down?
_____ 5. Did I space evenly between letters?
_____ 6. Did I leave enough space between words?

Figure 9–22 A Checklist for Assessing Manuscript Handwriting

Adapting

Writing Instruction to Meet the Needs of Every Student

1. Accommodate the need for repetition to learn letter forms by making additional time available for practice. Make models available to reinforce correct forms during practice.

2. Adjust time available to complete written work so students perceive they have time to write legibly.

3. Modify the quantity of written work. Supplement student writing with peer writing, dictation to teacher's aides, or providing frameworks (fill in the blanks) to compose notes to facilitate focusing on ideas.

4. Provide tutorial assistance in learning to keyboard fluently to help students develop life-long communication skills.

5. Modify writing tools and materials to meet student needs. For example, left-handed writers may find loose-leaf paper easier to use than spiral-bound notebooks. Provide a variety of pens, pencils, crayons, and markers to suit student needs.

6. Seek assistance from an occupational therapist for students with severe difficulties.

Ashton, Haapa, Kieley, & Fielden, 1999). Word processors equipped with voice synthesizers have been shown to facilitate students' writing to a greater extent than those without, especially less-skilled students' writing (Borgh & Dickson, 1986).

For young students to use word processing efficiently, they must learn keyboarding. Learning the placement of keys on the computer keyboard is fundamental for writing fluency. The hunt-and-peck technique places students in a similar handicapped position in respect to fluency as

Karen's class is doing a handwriting lesson.

when they were first learning to print. Some educators recommend that students begin to acquire keyboarding skills as soon as they begin using word processors, but many teachers delay teaching this skill. Curriculum requirements in many provinces support teaching keyboarding in grades 2 and 3. Stoecker (quoted in Langhorne, Dunham, Gross, & Rehmke, 1989) states that a typical unpractised student types at a rate of 6.5 words per minute. With touch-typing instruction for 25 half-hour periods, typing speed increased to 28 to 30 words per minute. Students in grade 3 who learned to type an average of 26 words per minute were able to record thoughts faster than they could by hand (Hiebert, 1989).

Teachers and schools must make a commitment to teaching students word processing, including keyboarding. Students learn most about computers by using them. Even very young students can learn keyboarding and the simple processes of add, delete, and strikeout.

Learning to keyboard can be compared with learning to play the piano or other instruments where brain and fingers must work together. For people who memorize quickly and have good finger dexterity, keyboard can be easy to learn. Speed can usually be increased through practice (Hallows, 2002). Teachers can use the typing tutorials in software packages or more traditional methods of typing instruction to teach children. The letter combination drills help memorization of key locations. Typing tutorials are effective and many provide games and activities that are highly appealing to children while they learn and practise the fundamental skills.

In all keyboard teaching, teachers need to remember that three factors help students succeed in keyboarding: position (sitting up, hands over home row at natural angle), memorization (key locations on keyboard), and motivation (reasons to write fluently). It is difficult to make recommendations regarding particular software programs because upgrades and new programs appear frequently. One program we like because it integrates keyboarding with reading and writing is *Typing to Learn* (Sunburst Communications). Many others are available and teachers need to become familiar with them and devote instructional time to keyboarding and other fundamental aspects of word processing to facilitate students' writing fluency.

◼ Review

Learning about words is an important part of the language arts. Few words have only one meaning, and students in the elementary grades learn about multiple meanings as well as about root words and affixes; homonyms, synonyms, and antonyms; and figurative meanings of words, such as idioms and metaphors. The best measure of students' learning of words is their ability to use the words in meaningful, functional, and genuine activities. In order to engage in meaningful activities, students must develop their abilities to use the tools of language—grammar, spelling, and handwriting. During the elementary grades, students learn the fundamental structures of English, such as types of sentences and parts of speech. They learn to spell conventionally and to proofread their writing. They develop legible and fluent handwriting to facilitate communication and also learn fundamentals of word processing, including use of simple spell checkers and grammar checkers.

The following key concepts are presented in this chapter:

1. English is a historic language, and its diverse origins account for word meanings and some spelling inconsistencies.

2. The fact that students' vocabularies grow at a rate of about 3000 words a year suggests that students learn many words incidentally, especially through reading and writing.

3. Students learn about words, parts of speech, and figures of speech. Idioms and metaphors can be confusing to students because they must be interpreted figuratively rather than literally.

4. All words are not equally difficult or easy to learn; the degree of difficulty depends on what the student already knows about the word.

5. Students use reference books, including dictionaries and thesauri and a variety of word-study activities (word walls, word posters, word clusters, word sorts, and word chains) to learn about words.

6. Grammar is the structure of language, while usage is the socially accepted way of using words in sentences. Study of grammar for elementary students includes learning parts of speech, parts of sentences, types of sentences, and figures of speech.

7. Students move from using scribbles and single letters to represent words through a series of stages that lead to conventional spelling.

8. The five stages of invented spelling are precommunicative, semiphonetic, phonetic, transitional, and conventional.

9. Spelling instruction includes opportunities to read and write and minilessons about spelling procedures, concepts, and strategies and skills.

10. The two traditional handwriting forms are manuscript and cursive, and a newer, form is D'Nealian.

11. The primary purpose of handwriting instruction is to help students develop legible and fluent handwriting.

12. The six elements of legible and fluent handwriting are letter formation, size and proportion, spacing, slant, alignment, and line quality.

13. Students should be taught keyboarding to facilitate fluency in writing.

14. Word processing enhances students writing. Word processing aids students' expression of ideas, spelling, use of Standard English, and production of attractive documents.

■ Extensions

1. Choose a piece of literature (narrative, poem, or nonfiction) for a particular grade level and identify a list of possible words for the word wall. Which words do you think will be sight words, new words, new concepts, or new meanings for students?

2. Observe in an elementary classroom and note how vocabulary is taught both formally and informally. Or, interview an elementary teacher and ask how he or she teaches vocabulary. Compare the teacher's answers with the information presented in this chapter.

3. Plan and teach a grammar lesson using one of the minilesson topics described in this chapter. Choose sentences for the activity from a book that students are reading.

4. Read and analyze a set of stories, reports, or journals written by a class of middle- or upper-grade students. From them identify five possible grammar and usage topics for minilessons. Choose one of the topics and create a lesson plan for teaching a series of minilessons.

5. Observe how spelling is taught in an elementary classroom. How is the spelling program organized? Which components described in this chapter are used in this classroom?

6. Collect samples of a primary-grade student's writing and analyze the spelling errors as shown in Figure 9–12 on page 374 to determine the student's stage of spelling development.

7. Practise forming the manuscript and cursive letters shown in Figures 9–18 and 9–19 on pages 391 and 392 until your handwriting approximates the models. Practising these handwriting forms will prepare you for working with elementary students. Be sure to take note of the handwriting charts displayed in the classroom before beginning to work with students, because several different handwriting programs are used in Canadian classrooms.

8. If possible, observe in a primary-grade classroom where the D'Nealian handwriting program is used. Talk with teachers and students about this innovative form. How do the students like it? What benefits, if any, do teachers notice?

9. Observe students learning to keyboard and to use word-processing programs, including spell checkers and grammar checkers. Note the types of errors they make. How are they helped by the program activities and checkers?

chapter ten

The Language Arts and the Fine Arts

PROFILE

Integrated Learning: Creating Meaningful Connections between Visual Art and Literature in Grade 4

Procedure

I observed early in my teaching career the gasps of wonder and trembles of delight as my grade 4 students entered the classroom and caught sight of the paintbrushes and water cans set out for our weekly art lesson. I continue to take great delight in such obvious joy and enthusiasm. It is my goal as an elementary teacher, and also as an artist, to help students carry this excitement across the curriculum, especially to make linkages between literature and visual art.

Few of the art lessons I use are my original inventions. I attend workshops, exchange units with other teachers, and scan school bulletin boards, teacher resource publications, and various websites for relevant, skill-based art ideas, but I strive to create a meaningful context, the right teaching moment, to introduce the art so that other realms of learning can be applied and reinforced while students are engaged in artistic endeavours that exercise distinct domains of thinking and intelligence. One of my favourite lessons integrates curriculum expectations from the language arts, visual art, and social studies. It involves the students in oral reading, art-making, and procedural writing.

> "I find the writing they produce is confident, well organized, and descriptive. It is also a great way for me to learn about the connections they have made, the concepts they have internalized, and their thoughts and opinions about what we are doing."

Heidi Jardine–Stoddart
Grade 4 Teacher
Elizabeth Ziegler Public School
Waterloo, Ontario

I usually plan this lesson for late fall, after students have spent time in social studies developing mapping skills and familiarity with distinguishing physical features of the provinces and territories of Canada. At this time, in

the language arts my students and I are in the midst of a week-long focus on great Canadian picture books. Using maps mounted around the classroom we indicate the home of each author we read. Students are also near the end of a visual art unit on colour, having reviewed technical components of the colour wheel, experimented with colour mixing, and explored the emotional quality of line and colour in works of art.

At this point, the moment is right to introduce the writing of Robert Service and the art of Ted Harrison. I gather the students around, some on the floor, others on little stools, and more still sharing a wooden bench. I read to them *The Cremation of Sam McGee* (Service, 1986) and they are captivated by the haunting words and mesmerizing pictures. Toward the end of the poem, some are whispering along with me . . . "There are strange things done in the midnight sun by the men who moil for gold. . . ." This leads to energetic discussion about the setting (Yukon Territory), plot, main characters, form, and what it was about this book that caught their attention. Identification of rich examples of word choice and phrases, favourite illustrations, and unusual techniques used by the artist follows our reading. Connections are then made between the work of the author and of the artist, and we talk about how they have created a feeling or mood through their choice of vocabulary or colour. We then brainstorm a list of questions we have about this author, and students break into small groups, each armed with a question to research. Shortly thereafter, we regroup and record the groups' answers and responses on a chart profile of the author. We display our collection of profiles to remind us of all the authors we read.

The next day, I read *O Canada*, another text illustrated by Ted Harrison (2002). The focus this time is on the illustrations that depict each province and territory. We discuss per-

tinent vocabulary, such as "landscape," and I guide students to pay particular attention to the artist's unusual colour choices, application of colour, and how he creates a feeling of space or depth in his artwork.

Students respond eagerly to the concept of unusual or unrealistic use of colour. It seems to open a whole realm of freedom and potential with regard to expression—where you don't have to follow implicit rules of the way things are supposed to be represented or organized. This notion serves us well when we move on to our poetry unit and, most significantly, free verse, which does not have to conform to the usual rules of organization. It becomes evident that choices in visual presentation, in both the written word and pictorial images, can carry great impact when expressing oneself. As one young student in my class later explained at home, "Mom, did you know that trees can be pink and the sky can be green? It all depends on how you look at it and how you feel."

Armed with these insights, I have students target a specific location or region that they want to depict and we set to work on a very prescriptive, step-by-step lesson designed for the successful creation of Ted Harrison–like landscapes. Straight, wavy, and jagged lines are drawn in pencil to create hills, mountains, trees, or clouds that are then filled in using water-based markers applied in smooth lines of colour. For some, the untraditional use of colour is liberating and they can't wait to start. For others, it involves a certain amount of risk-taking and uncertainty, so I encourage discussion among peers as they deliberate their choices and brave, vivid examples are displayed for all to see. Once students have settled into the absorbing task of filling in the sections, soft classical or new age music facilitates their concentration—an instrumental version of "O Canada" also suits perfectly.

Assessment

An important part of my job is to design lessons so that students experience success. This includes identifying the skills and concepts I intend to teach, and making them clear to students right from the start. To more objectively assess their work, whether written or visual, I use a rubric that outlines the skills and concepts that students are expected to demonstrate. Students use the rubric as a checklist to monitor their progress, and I use it to assess their use of the identified skills and concepts.

Another assessment tool is our weekly art journals—a regular part of our classroom routine that enriches my assessment of students' understanding. First, we add new words to our cumulative Art Journal Vocabulary list that is displayed permanently in a prominent location. Students then write about what we did and record their thoughts about the art lesson. Because they are writing with purpose and the entries are based on something they have just done or experienced, I find the writing they produce is confident, well-organized, and descriptive. It is also a great way for me to learn about the connections they have made, the concepts they have internalized, and their thoughts and opinions about what we are doing. Art-journal writing in my classroom seems effortless—expectations are clear, the topic is fresh and familiar, and the stress moves from "I don't know what to write about" to "How can I write well to tell about this?"

Adaptations

After students have completed the initial guided lesson to create a Ted Harrison–style landscape, I try to allow for further exploration by incorporating the technique back into other curriculum areas. For example, sometimes students write poems and create accompanying illustrations in the style of Ted Harrison, illustrate song lyrics, such as those for "I'd Like to Teach the World to Sing," and then project slide images of their artwork on the wall as they sing in unison at assemblies, and design postage stamps to depict the province or territory they have researched. I've also scanned students' artwork for use within HyperStudio software as a way of presenting their work along with creative writing or informational text in a multimedia format.

This lesson can also be adapted to other authors/illustrators. Eric Carle's stories are well-suited to early primary grades, and his technique of illustrating can be modified to accommodate young students working at painting, cutting, and pasting. I've introduced the concepts of relief sculpture and texture using Barbara Reid's stories and Plasticine illustrations, and rely on Chris Van Allsburg's engaging drawings and text in *The Mysteries of Harris Burdick* (1996) to inspire skilled sketching and creative writing with older students.

Reflections

Opportunities for integrating curriculum grow increasingly evident as my students and I develop our sense of interconnectedness through such experiences as the one presented here. Subjects and concepts that were once isolated units have become interwoven and any systematically imposed separateness becomes threatened. Specifically, I find art-related experiences contribute to students' positive outlook, enthusiasm, and the meaningfulness of their learning.

In this instance, integration resulted in student recollections that intermingle the poetry of Robert Service, the artwork of Ted Harrison, the geography of Canada, and the concept of free expression. I became aware of this several months later when our class was visiting a local art gallery and I went to gather up a young, headstrong student who had wandered from our tour. English was his second language, never spoken at home, and he was receiving extensive academic support within the grade 4 program. Knowing this added insight to our struggles with his disruptive behaviour, inattentiveness, and lack of task commitment. The young ESL student stood gazing wide-eyed at a painting. "Oh my gosh, Miss Jardine," he whispered, "it's a real Ted Harrison." He then turned and looked at me. "Remember, he's the guy who did the pictures in that book you showed us . . . that poem we read . . . with the midnight sun and the guy who died in the cold . . . and we maked pictures like him with all the different colours . . . remember?" he asked with genuine urgency. Yes, I remembered, and more importantly, so did he.

Young journalists in Enchant School use local newspapers as models to extend their writing skills and their knowledge of current events. Their unit activities help them realize how important literacy skills are to their being well-informed citizens.

"In this century, literacy is more than reading and writing—it is a person's ability to thoughtfully identify, gather, analyze and use information so that they can control the decisions they make in their lives" (Hansen, 2003). The development of the language arts in an integrated way is important in developing the literacy processes of children. Children do not learn language skills in isolation from each other. Although we separate the language arts to speak about them and to discuss the content and structure of each process, it is clear that children best learn their language in an integrated way. Ability as a writer is enhanced by ability as a reader, and proficiency in listening and viewing enhances ability to represent visually. Also, children can expand their capacity to listen as they learn music and to establish a greater understanding of their physical and emotional selves as they learn through drama and dance.

Integrating the Fine Arts

In addition to integrating the language arts, other forms of integration enhance a child's literacy development. Gardner's research on intelligence (Blythe & Gardner, 1990) suggests that we don't have one fixed intelligence, but at least seven separate ones (see Figure 10–1 on page 406). Gardner defines *intelligence* as our capacity to solve problems and create products that would be valued in a cultural setting. Four of the seven intelligences (verbal, visual, musical, and kinesthetic) parallel the fine arts areas of visual art, music, dance, and drama. The other intelligences are also connected to the language arts and the fine arts: logical, interpersonal, and intrapersonal.

Our ability to communicate effectively not only through language but also through visual art, music, dance, and drama is an indicator of our capabilities as an effective human being participating fully in our cultural setting. We want to develop

To Guide Your Reading

As you read this chapter, prepare to

Explain how to encourage children in the development of all of their intelligences

•

Identify some of the important reasons for integrating the fine arts with the language arts

•

Explain how to use children's literature to help children in the development of their visual artistic abilities

•

Describe strategies that will encourage the musical talents of children

•

Explain how to encourage drama and movement in the day-to-day language arts experiences of the classroom

Category	Likes, Needs, Is Good At . . .
Verbal "Word lovers"	Seeing and hearing words, talking and discussing, telling stories, reading and writing (e.g., poetry, literature), memorizing (e.g., places, names, facts), using or appreciating humour, using word play, doing word puzzles
Visual "Imagers"	Thinking in pictures and seeing spatial relationships, drawing, building, designing and creating, daydreaming and imagining, looking at pictures, watching movies, reading maps and charts, doing mazes and puzzles
Musical "Music lovers"	Singing, humming and listening to music, playing instruments, responding to music (e.g., likes to tap out rhythms), composing music, picking up sounds, remembering melodies, noticing pitches and rhythms, timbre
Interpersonal "People-people"	Lots of friends, joining groups, talking out or mediating and resolving conflicts, empathetic and understanding, sharing, comparing, relating, cooperating, interviewing others, leadership, and organizing
Intrapersonal "Loners"	Aware of inner self (e.g., feelings, intentions, goals), working alone, having own space and self-pacing, focuses on own feelings and dreams, pursuing own interests and goals, original thinking, self-reflecting
Logical "Reasoners"	Experimenting, asking questions, problem-solving, figuring out how things work, exploring abstract relationships and discovering patterns, categorizing and classifying, reasoning and using logic (inductive and deductive), math, playing logic games
Kinesthetic "Body movers"	Moving and using body to communicate, touching and using nonverbal communication (e.g., hands, face, gestures, hands-on learning), kinesthetic-tactile learning, sports, dancing, drama, and acting

Figure 10–1 Gardner's Seven Intelligences
Source: Gardner, 1993b.

these intelligences in our children primarily through the language arts; teaching them to be effective users of language in all its forms. We also want to enhance their abilities by integrating the skills they have learned in the language arts with the fine arts.

REASONS FOR INTEGRATING THE FINE ARTS WITH THE LANGUAGE ARTS

There are a number of reasons for integrating the fine arts with the language arts:

1. *The fine arts are fundamental components of all cultures and time periods.* In the same way that literature is a component of our collective memory, the other fine arts are also a part of our cultural legacy. It is through our stories, music, art, and drama that we define our cultural

heritage and allow our students the opportunity to bridge our culture with other cultures around the world. Our tradition in the language arts of providing students with the opportunity to read stories from different cultural traditions ought to expand to include the music, art, dance, and drama of these other cultures.

2. *The fine arts teach us that what we think or feel cannot be reduced to words.* As important as language is as an expression of who and what we are, it is equally important to remember that our feelings and emotions are often better communicated through the fine arts. We recognize the value of quality children's literature in part because of the visual art that the illustrator has created to enhance our experience of the story. It is this combination of story read or heard and story seen that creates the aesthetic experience we call literature.

3. *Students who engage in the fine arts have the opportunity to "be smart in different ways."* We run the risk as language arts teachers of placing too much emphasis on the role of language in learning in the sense that we often ignore the place and value of other expressive arts in the learning of children. McCarthy (1987) in her work with learning styles points out the value of experiential learning. It is important that children be given opportunities to experience their own learning in a variety of ways, moving beyond intellectual approaches to more intuitive, reflective, or hands-on approaches. McCarthy suggests that our approach is inexcusably narrow if we fail to recognize the diversity of learning styles in children.

4. *The fine arts develop the brain.* We need to find the balance in our teaching so that those entrusted to our care can develop all of their abilities. It is true that children need to develop their ability to think logically and analytically. They also need to learn to trust gifts from their senses and cultivate their intuitive abilities. Kolb (1984) explored the ways in which learners perceive and process information. Some of us transfer value from ourselves to what we experience. We validate what happens to us through our emotions and not with our intellect. Others think more rationally. We engage in directed thinking and arrange what happens and what we perceive into rational categories. Still others perceive consciously but don't assign value to what we sense. Rather, we are conscious but let the sensations happen without imposing control. More intuitive learners impose control on perceptions but in an unconscious way. These learners understand what they see and feel in a whole and complete way. It is important that we accommodate all learners in our approach to teaching the language arts. All the initiatives we undertake to integrate the fine arts with the language arts will enhance development of the whole learner.

5. *The fine arts provide avenues of achievement for students who might not be otherwise successful.* Allowing students the opportunity to demonstrate their abilities in a variety of ways ensures that students will find appropriate and relevant expressions for their abilities and interests. In teaching an integrated language arts unit on memory, for example, students were exposed to Steven Gammel's art through his illustrations of Mem Fox's story *Wilfrid Gordon McDonald Partridge* (1996). They also listened to the music of Shirley Eikhart and her song "Emily Remembers," and explored information books such as *A Kid's Guide to the Brain* (1994) by Sylvia Funston and Jay Ingram. Students were given choices in how they responded to the various artifacts. Some responded by visually representing in response to the music, others chose to write in response to the stories. Others gathered facts and wrote reports, sharing information with the class.

6. *The fine arts develop the values of perseverance and hard work.* "The self-discipline required to master an instrument or learn lines from a school play can transfer to academic learning" (Cornett & Smithrim, 2001).

7. ***The fine arts are a necessary part of life.*** The fine arts help students cultivate their abilities as thinkers and doers. They learn to focus through the fine arts on the broad pictures as well as minute details and learn to see and listen in different ways. They cultivate an aesthetic sense of the world and can then use that new insight to solve problems in other areas of their lives, in science and mathematics, in any area they choose.

8. ***There is a strong positive relationship between the fine arts and academic success.*** The fine arts are participatory. They engage students physically, emotionally, intellectually, and spiritually. They help children integrate their lives and, as such, offer tremendous potential for enhancing academic achievement.

9. ***The fine arts offer alternative forms of assessment and evaluation.*** Extensive use of portfolios as assessment tools in music, art, drama, and writing provides us with examples of effective ways of measuring growth and achievement beyond the traditional tests.

10. ***The National Symposium on Arts Education of Canada calls for arts education for all children.*** The symposium's vision is based on the following principles (Cornett & Smithrim, 2001):

    - That participation in the arts is a fundamental right of all citizens
    - That all Canadians should have access to quality arts education through publicly financed education programs
    - That arts education programs should be delivered by teachers who have the capacity to deliver quality programs
    - That communities should promote and support participation in the arts (Articipation)
    - That the arts are vital to life and learning

The Language Arts and Visual Art

"The most fundamental fact to be understood about art is that whatever it shows is presented as a symbol. A human figure carved in wood is never just a human figure, a painted apple is never just an apple. Images point to the nature of the human condition" (Arnheim, 1989, p. 26). Similarly, language carries meaning beyond the literal "facts" of a story and metaphor is more than a literary device. It is a conceptual framework by which we organize our experience. One of our goals as language arts teachers is to teach children to understand and appreciate the metaphors that guide the ways in which they view the world, and one of the important avenues to exploring metaphor in this sense is through art and stories.

A starting point to integrate art and language is through children's literature. In children's literature, artist and author work together to produce an integrated aesthetic work that children can experience on many levels. The artist represents the story in visual form, illuminating and expanding the words to create a work that is visually responsive to the text, thereby enhancing and elaborating its meaning. Children can begin exploring their own sense of visual representation through an introduction to the work of illustrators and through exposure to the vast collection of exemplary art in the literature they read and explore.

The books of Toronto artist, writer, and illustrator Barbara Reid are excellent examples of creative artistic ability. Reid's Plasticine artwork has won her many awards and readers around the world. In her book *The Party* (1997), children are invited to explore the many facets of attending a family reunion (see top of next page). The story captures all the fun of a family summer picnic—the games, food, family, and friends. The illustrations allow children to explore the story through their other senses, and often children will be seen touching Reid's illustrations, wanting the tactile experience of the Plasticine artwork as they visually explore the story.

"Want to play sharks?" Danny asks.
Yes we do!
"I'll be It. If I catch you,
then you're a shark too!"

The lawnchairs are lifeboats,
the grass is all water.
Kate leaps to the birdbath —
too late! Danny's got her.
We're all in the game at the party.

The same experience awaits readers in Reid's *Two by Two* (1992), a retelling of the story of Noah and the building and stocking of the ark (see below). Children enjoy the sensory experience of reliving the story as they explore the text and illustrations. *Two by Two* gives them the added experience of singing, "Who Built the Ark?" adding music to the sensory feast.

With hoot and squawk and squeak and bark,
The animals tumbled off the ark.

27

Cornett and Smithrim (2001) suggest that visual art needs to be experienced as a whole before it is broken down into its component parts, which means children need to view and make art first, so that a desire to want to know more is developed in them (p. 145). Through exposure to the literature written and illustrated for them, children learn about visual art elements and design concepts. Specifically, they learn about colour, line, shape, texture, form, pattern, space, contrast, light, composition, perspective, balance, and symmetry.

Having experienced Barbara Reid's books, students want to create art for themselves using Reid's techniques. Giving students those opportunities to work with clay and produce illustrations for their own stories helps them develop their artistic sensibilities and their awareness of how ideas and concepts can be visually represented. Regardless of the medium they use, students need to have many opportunities to express themselves in words and pictures. Teachers need to help them see that the goal is not perfect art, but meaning-making. Like the children in Vande Griek and Milelli's *The Art Room* (2002), who learn to express themselves when they paint with Emily Carr, all students need to know that their creative expressions are valued.

Students can learn a great deal by viewing the work of accomplished artists. Sharing books such as Elisa Gutierrez's *Picturescape* (2005), in which the main character goes on a field trip to an art gallery, is one way to introduce them to some of Canada's well-known artists—e.g., Emily Carr, William Kurelek, Tom Thompson, Alex Colville, Christopher Pratt, and David Blackwood. While sharing this wordless picture book and absorbing the illustrations, students can compose their own stories inspired by the art.

The Profile at the beginning of this chapter provides another example of an activity that combines language and art. Heidi Jardine-Stoddart helps her grade 4 class explore the artwork of Ted Harrison. Children enjoy the illustrations of Robert Service's poems, "The Cremation of Sam McGee" and "The Shooting of Dan McGrew." Ted Harrison's unique artistic style is one that children enjoy and often wish to emulate. As language arts teachers, we can support and extend our students in their artistic development by encouraging them in the study of Ted Harrison's painting style and in the replication of his style through their own stories and poetry. Students can also explore their visual artistic abilities using digital drawing programs such as Kid Pix or other paint-and-draw software.

Students can also develop their visual artistic talents through their own illustration of stories or poetry that they read. Writers who use particularly vivid and descriptive language can be the vehicles for this development. Natalie Babbitt's engaging novel *Tuck Everlasting* (1975) is an example of this quality of writing. Eleven-year-old Winnie Foster, one of the central characters in the story, meets a remarkable family, the Tucks, who live forever, frozen in time, sharing a secret that must be kept. Winnie discovers their secret and is taken by Mae Tuck and her two sons Jesse and Miles to their small cottage in the woods where she must be convinced not to reveal to anyone what she knows. Natalie Babbitt's description of the Tucks' house is particularly memorable as this part of the story unfolds.

> Winnie had grown up with order. She was used to it. Under the pitiless double assaults of her mother and grandmother, the cottage where she lived was always squeaking clean, mopped and swept and scoured into limp submission. There was no room for carelessness, no putting things off until later. The Foster women had made a fortress out of duty. Within it they were indomitable. And Winnie was in training.
>
> So she was unprepared for the homely little house beside the pond, unprepared for the gentle eddies of dust, the silver cobwebs, the mouse who lived—and welcome to him!—in a table drawer. There were only three rooms. The kitchen came first, with an open cabinet where dishes were stacked in perilous towers without the least regard for their varying dimensions. There was an enormous black stove, and a metal sink, and every surface, every wall, was piled and strewn and hung with everything imaginable, from onions to lanterns to wooden spoons to washtubs. And in a corner stood Tuck's forgotten shotgun.
>
> The parlor came next, where the furniture, loose and sloping with age, was set about helter-skelter. An ancient green-plush sofa lolled alone in the center, like yet another mossy, fallen log, facing a soot-streaked fireplace still deep in last winter's ashes. The table with the drawer that housed the mouse was pushed off, also alone, into a far corner, and three armchairs and an elderly rocker stood about aimlessly, like strangers at a party, ignoring each other.

Much can be done with the language in this description of the Tucks' cottage. Upper-elementary level students can be asked to choose their favourite phrases or sentences from this passage to help them appreciate the quality of the description, the use of simile and metaphor; the pure richness of the language. Children can be asked to illustrate this section of the story using their visual artistic skills to see how they would capture Babbitt's description through drawing or painting.

Meaningful integration of visual art with language arts means more than simply drawing something after reading or listening to a story. Cornett and Smithrim (2001) suggest that integration maintain the integrity of each area being integrated. A critical question when integrating is, "What did my students learn about all the areas being integrated?" In our example, "What did they learn about story, about describing, about metaphor as a tool in writing?" "What did they learning about drawing; about interpreting?" Cornett and Smithrim tell us that the classroom teacher doesn't necessarily have to know how to draw well to integrate visual art principles and practices, but the teacher needs a basic knowledge and skill level to use language and present examples of possibilities to students. They suggest the following guidelines to help students "do" art successfully:

- Teach how to use a variety of media, tools, and techniques—printing, collage, watercolour, chalk, tempura, original stencilling, mobiles, sculpting, rubbings, papier-mâché—and use different surfaces (e.g., fabric, wood).

- Use an *explore-practice-express* lesson sequence. Demonstrate ways to use materials and tools and give time to explore and experiment.

- Limit direction-giving.

- Similar to responding to writing, give more descriptive feedback than praise as students work.

- Create an atmosphere and expectation for appropriate behaviour. Art making should be a time for focus and concentration. Play music, without lyrics, or make a rule about quiet.

- Invite students to write or tell stories about their art or find music that goes with their art.

The Language Arts and Music

Most children enter school with some background in music. Because the introduction to music generally occurs in powerful social contexts like singing with friends, listening to the radio as the family travels, or singing in church, the result for most children is strong ties to styles and genres of music. Children whose parents sing to them and who participate musically through the family either via singing or learning to play a musical instrument are more likely to sing and play music well and have diverse tastes. According to Cornett and Smithrim,

> The elementary and middle school years need to be musically rich. Young children are more open to types of music—from classical to country—and it is what they hear the most that becomes what they like and value. The teaching implication is to take advantage of this openness to musical diversity by providing experiences with an eclectic range of styles, types, periods and cultural music experiences. Such variety sustains interest, engenders a flexibility of attitude, and builds respect for the diverse expressions of people. (p. 300)

As language arts teachers, we have a responsibility to integrate music with the language arts so that children make the connection between their spoken and written language and the language of music. As we explore musical notation and composition, we help children see how a different language, musical expression, can also enhance their understanding of the world around them. Teaching and composing songs as well as listening to curriculum-related music become a part of the language arts curriculum. The following strategies integrate music with the language arts:

- Teach songs from diverse cultures and for holidays (traditional ones and others that are part of themes or units).

- Help students learn songs that make up a cultural repertoire, including songs that make up their own cultural repertoire.

- Present songs and rhythmic activities for pure enjoyment.
- Use activities that support awareness of musical elements and concepts to help students use musical intelligence and develop musical vocabulary.
- Invite guests to play musical instruments, sing, or share about unique aspects of music.
- Involve students in making and playing instruments as a means of creative expression.
- Play a variety of types of music to stretch students' concepts of the familiar.
- Encourage musical responses to literature.
- Use music, vocal, or instrumental, as a way of introducing a piece of literature. Encourage students to see likenesses in theme.
- Listen to music and ask students to represent through drawings, drama, or dance what images it stimulates for them.
- Explore the rhythm of poetry through musical activities such as drumming.
- Sing with students to show the value of all voices.
- Share personal musical tastes and preferences as a way of celebrating diversity.
- Cooperate with the music specialist to integrate music throughout the curriculum.

The following activity is an example of how music and the language arts can be integrated in a grade 4 classroom. The children listen attentively to Ms. Lacey as she reads them Margot Fonteyn's retelling of *Swan Lake*, illustrated by Trina Schart Hyman (Fonteyn, 1989). Ms. Lacey also shares information about the author, Dame Margot Fonteyn, her illustrious career as a ballerina, and her particular interest in dancing the ballet *Swan Lake*. The children construct a plotline for the story and work in small groups to imagine the scenes for presenting this story as a ballet. What parts of the story would they include? They then listen to Tchaikovsky's musical score for the ballet, discovering the familiar parts of the story as it is told by the music. Students finish by comparing this version of *Swan Lake* with other versions, noting where the differences are in the various stories and speculating about the reasons for those differences. The children then listen to *Tchaikovsky Discovers America*, part of the Classical Kids Series on CD that combines dramatic stories and classical music to captivate, engage, and entertain them with the life and music of Pyotr Tchaikovsky.

This same class continues its musical explorations by listening to another of the stories of great composers presented in this series, *Beethoven Lives Upstairs*. Set in the autumn of 1822, Christoph writes letters to his uncle about the strange person who has rented the upstairs part of his house. He begins his first letter, "I hope you will remember me. It is Christoph, your nephew, who writes. As for the reasons, I will not keep you in suspense. I write, Uncle, because something terrible has happened. A madman has moved into our house." The "madman" in question is the eccentric Ludwig van Beethoven. Through reading the letters and listening to the story and music on the CD, children explore some of the aspects of Beethoven's life and his music. The children finish their exploration by listening to and learning to play "Ode to Joy," one of Beethoven's famous piano pieces, on simple keyboards.

The Language Arts and Drama

Drama integrates all of the arts (music, art, dance, and literature), so it has the potential to play a very significant role in language arts development. Drama enhances these other areas of the curriculum. Students can begin to explore characters and their relationships to one another and to areas such as social studies, science, and health. In the language arts and other subjects, creative drama can be used to help students make sense of the world around them.

Drama helps students enhance their oral language skills and bring congruence between word and action. It is a powerful means of self-expression through speaking and listening. Drama also develops social skills and assists students in appreciating and understanding group process. Drama is also a form of entertainment where students find enjoyment in the exploration of their worlds through representation.

Similar to the other arts, successful integration of drama into the language arts curriculum depends on the skill level of the teacher. Language arts teachers need a repertoire of strategies to teach students how to interact with each other and respond.

There is a difference between putting on rehearsed plays a few times a year and the daily use of drama in the language arts classroom. According to Cornett and Smithrim, drama in this sense

> . . . is participant driven and process centred with a teacher or leader guiding children through explorations of personal experiences, social issues or pieces of literature. In creative drama, children improvise action and dialogue and use drama elements to structure the process. They creatively use voice, body, and space to make others believe in a mood, idea or message and take on "pretend" roles to generate creative problem solutions. The purposes in creative drama are artistic, emotional, and academic. (2001, p. 213)

READERS THEATRE

A place to begin integrating drama in the language arts curriculum is with *readers theatre*, a language arts technique through which any piece of literature or other material is divided into parts, which are read orally. This technique enables children of varying levels of ability to participate in a group presentation. The children do not memorize their lines, but do practise them so that the reading is fluent and expressive. The use of voices, restrained gestures, and facial expression project the mood. Action or physical movement is merely suggested.

Children, regardless of their levels of competency, are grouped together and roles are assigned according to the abilities and interests of those participating. There are usually two kinds of speaking parts—narrator(s) and characters. Narrators are assigned the parts in the story that do not belong to characters. Large segments of narration may be divided among several narrators, thus allowing more children to participate in each performance. The narrator links the various segments together, providing what is necessary to the comprehension of the play. There are as many children involved in each presentation of readers theatre as there are characters and narrator roles.

One way to perform readers theatre is to have all the performers, each with a complete script in hand, stand in a row with backs to the audience. Each time a character speaks, she or he turns to face the audience, reads the part, then turns away from the audience until her or his turn comes up again.

Another suggestion for performance is to have the readers stand at strategic points in the classroom in order to focus the audience's attention on each speaker as the play unfolds. Readers theatre presentations may be enhanced by selective and limited use of scenery and costumes; the use of simple masks or makeup rather than full costumes; and the use of very simple props.

The richest source of material for readers theatre is literature from which a story or poem, in whole or in part, can be adapted. Any story with a range of characters and sufficient dialogue is suitable. Often, all that is required is the marking of the various parts in the text so that children see where their various parts are found. Often, folktales are rich sources of material for readers theatre. Verna Aardema's retelling of the African folktales *Why Mosquitoes Buzz in People's Ears* (1975) and *Who's in Rabbit's House?* (1977) are enjoyable to perform as readers theatre with both young and older children. Older students can also perform using their own writing. While adapting their writing, stories, or other types of work does not give children experience with the rich texts of celebrated literature, it does allow them to have valuable integrated language learning experiences.

Readers theatre offers a rich experience in both speaking and listening. The actors practise before any presentation and improve their fluency, accuracy, and phrasing. Readers theatre provides children of all reading abilities the opportunity to participate in a meaningful activity.

The focus in readers theatre is primarily on the speaking of the text and not on the performance. Children are given many opportunities to practise their reading and/or speaking voices as a prelude to developing other dramatic skills.

PLANNING DRAMAS

by Joe Norris

A range of drama activities can be used in exploring a story. In the story drama that follows, an entire text/story is explored through a number of drama activities. A story drama was chosen over different techniques with different texts to show how a number of activities can be sequenced together. But not all types of drama activities need to be this extensive, with an entire story being taught through drama. Often, one or two drama activities can be used to teach a particular concept in a unit of study. This comprehensive example is given to provide a strong taste of the flavours that can be experienced in using drama as a learning medium by linking drama techniques to a specific piece of literature. Consequently, a drama activity can be an isolated exercise that enhances a specific aspect of a lesson or a series of activities around a certain theme in a piece of literature. A few examples of isolated drama activities with language arts content and a discussion of some orientation to drama activities follow the story drama. Some teachers might wish to begin with these and other activities before embarking on an integrated story drama; however, the drama has many built-in orientation activities to assist the students in working in process drama. A list of books on drama in education appears in Figure 10–2. The list has been divided into two sections: books that focus on practical exercises and those that focus on the theoretical understandings. There is, however, often overlap between the two categories.

A STORY DRAMA

Students are gathered in a circle with the room darkened. For mood, the overhead projector is on, covered with a coloured transparency and aimed toward the ceiling. It will have been explained to the students that the circle is a place where everyone can see each other so that all may communicate face to face.

Students are seated comfortably in a circle on the floor as the visiting teacher/university drama instructor Joe Norris prepares to engage this group of students in a story drama.

Books on Drama in Education

More Practical

Boal, A. (1992). *Games for Actors and Non-Actors.* New York: Routledge.

Booth, D., & Lundy, C. (1985). *Improvisation: Learning Though Drama.* New York: Harcourt, Brace Jovanovich.

Goldberg, J. (1998). *Great Jobs for Theater Majors.* Chicago: VGM Career Horizons.

Heinig, R. (1988). *Creative Drama for the Classroom Teacher.* Englewood Cliffs, New Jersey: Prentice Hall.

Johnstone, K. (1992). *Impro: Improvisation and the Theatre.* New York: Routledge.

McCaslin, N. (2000). *Creative Drama in the Classroom and Beyond* (7th ed.). New York: Longman.

Morgan, N., & Saxton, J. (1987). *Teaching Drama: A Mind of Many Wonders.* Cheltenham, UK: Maple leaf Stanley Thornes.

Neelands, J. (1990). *Structuring Drama Work.* New York: Cambridge University Press. ❦

O'Neill, C., & Lambert, A. (1982). *Drama Structures.* London: Hutchinson.

Pallin, G. (2005). *Stage Management: The Essential Handbook.* Toronto: Playwrights Canada Press. ❦

Rump, N. (1996). *Puppets and Masks: Stagecraft and Storytelling.* Worcester, MA: Davis Publications.

Saldana, J. (1995). *Drama of Color.* Portsmouth, NH: Heinemann.

Schanker, H., & Ommanney, K. (1999). *The Stage and the School.* New York: Glencoe/McGraw-Hill.

Spolin, V. (1996). *Improvisation for the Theatre* (3rd ed.). Evanston, IL: Northwestern University Press.

Spolin, V. (1986). *Theatre Games for the Classroom: A Teacher's Handbook.* Evanston, IL: Northwestern University Press.

Tanner, F. A. (1982). *Basic Drama Projects* (6th ed.). Caldwell, ID: Clark Publishing Company.

Tarlington, C., & Verriour, P. (1991). *Role Drama.* Ontario: Pembroke. ❦

More Theoretical

Bolton, G. (1984). *Drama as Education: An Argument for Placing Drama at the Centre of the Curriculum.* Burnt Mill, Harlowe, Essex, UK: Longman.

Cameron, K., & Gillespie, P. (2000). *The Enjoyment of Theatre* (5th ed.). Needham Heights, MA: Allyn & Bacon.

Courtney, R. (1989). *Play, Drama, and Thought: The Intellectual Background to Dramatic Education.* New York: Simon & Pierre Pub. Co. Ltd.

Heathcote, D., & Bolton G. (1985). *Drama for Learning: Dorothy Heathcote's Mantle of the Expert Approach to Education.* Portsmouth, NH: Heinemann.

Hodgson, J. (1988). *The Uses of Drama: Acting as a Social and Educational Force.* London: Methuen.

Morgan, N., & Saxton, J. (1991). *Asking Better Questions.* Ontario: Pembroke. ❦

Stanislavski, K. (2003). *An Actor Prepares.* New York: Routledge.

Wagner, B. (1988). *Dorothy Heathcote: Drama as a Learning Medium.* London: Hutchinson.

Way, B. (1967). *Development though Drama.* London: Longman.

Figure 10–2 Books on Drama in Education

The teacher begins with a warm-up sometimes referred to as "The Thunderstorm":

- The teacher asks the student on the right to gently rub her/his hands together.
- Each student in turn rubs hands until everyone is rubbing and the sound is noticeable.
- The teacher then snaps his/her fingers and each student in turn changes from rubbing to snapping.
- The teacher then slaps his/her knees and again each student in turn changes to slapping.
- The teacher then pounds his/her feet, which again is cumulatively added.
- The sequence is then reversed, going from pounding feet to slapping knees to snapping fingers to rubbing hands to silence.

The teacher then explains that they have just performed their first play, *The Thunderstorm.* The lights come up, signalling the end of the activity, and a conversation unfolds supported by the teacher's questions. Students are asked how effective they thought the soundscape was. What were the key elements? How might it be refined? What type of mood was created? Were any specific feelings or memories elicited? What other sounds could we make that could add to the thunder-storm? How might this be used in the reading and writing of stories? How do movies use sound-scapes? After the conversation, which is often referred to as *debriefing*, students usually ask to do it again.

After the debriefing, the teacher says that the students will be collectively making a sound-scape of their own. The lights are once more dimmed with the teacher saying in a loud and rever-ent voice, "In the very earliest time . . ."

"We are going to go back in time, way back in time to the very earliest time. Back to a time before people walked on the earth. Let's go back to the time when the earth was just being made. Let's imagine what sounds could have been made during that time. Using our imaginations let's make a sound with either our bodies, like clapping our hands, or our voices like a 'Shhhhhhhhhhhhh' sound. First we will do them one at a time and then later we'll put them together. I will pass around this object (any suitable hand-held object can be used) and when you have it, it means that it is your turn."

The first time around, the teacher accepts what sounds students come up with.

The second time around, students are asked to find a different type of sound. If they made a voice sound, they are to make a body sound and vice versa.

The third time, the teacher enters the centre of the circle and claims that the students will become a "piano." The teacher points to a student who makes a sound, and then raises hands indi-cating volume for the sound and then lowers hands almost to the floor. Another student is chosen, then a third, for demonstration purposes.

The students are told that now they will make a soundscape of the very earliest time. But now they can choose any of the sounds that they heard and even make up new ones. It is explained that the class has brainstormed sounds and that using a sound invented by another is not stealing but a compliment because it was chosen to be included. Different people can repeat the same sound more than once.

The class is also told that they should listen carefully and make a sound that builds on the sound that came before it. In this way, as with *The Thunderstorm*, a story will be created.

Joe Norris helps students produce a soundscape.

Students close their eyes as they listen to Joe's directions for creating their own soundscapes.

The teacher begins by saying, "In the very earliest time . . ." and, by pointing to one student, then another and another, the soundscape emerges. The teacher will direct by raising and lowering hands to vary the volume and, at times, a whole section of students can be chosen rather than individuals. It runs for a minute or so and is ended with a fade or crescendo and the teacher saying, "In the very earliest time . . ."

The classroom lights are once more raised and the debriefing begins.

The students are asked to comment on the play they made about the very earliest time. Did any sounds evoke pictures? What where they? Was there a story in the sounds? What happened at the beginning, the end? What other ways could the story have gone? How could it have started or ended differently?

Following the second debriefing, the students are placed in small groups (no more than six) and asked to create their own soundscape. They are instructed to give each other their own ideas of what might have taken place "in the very earliest time" and then asked to make a composite of those ideas. They are informed that they should talk a little and try some. Over time they become aware that going through the spirals of doing and reflecting provides some great ideas that will not come from the talk, but through experimenting. The teacher may give a time limit for the work but this can be adjusted as groups pace themselves. The teacher then takes time to sit back and let them go.

Directions could include the following:

It doesn't have to be the creation of the world. It can include animals and people if you wish. What you need to do, however, is to make sure you tell a story of the very earliest time, but only using sounds. Remember to try to use ideas from each member of the group, and don't just talk it through, but try some ideas by doing them as well. You will present your soundscape to one another with the audience having their eyes shut. Think of where you might want your audience when you present.

When the appropriate time comes, the class is reassembled and the presentations begin. Each group can present in turn with all discussion saved to the last or discussion could occur after each presentation. The presentations take less time and the discussion provides more depth. The method chosen to use as an example here is a discussion after each presentation.

Students, in small groups, present their soundscapes to the rest of the class. Joe Norris engages class members in a discussion following each presentation.

This discussion can be a rich experience in learning for both the students and teacher. Since they now have a series of concrete experiences that can be expanded on, the classroom discussion will be relevant to these experiences. The teacher can make connections and introduce new concepts and vocabulary in the course of a natural conversation. The debriefing can help to make explicit the learning that took place in the doing.

At the same time, this can be a vulnerable time for students if the presentations are not framed properly. The teacher instructs the audience that this is not a "critiquing activity" but one that will show "works in progress" so we can witness many versions of "the very earliest time." The teacher also instructs them that this form of communication is divergent and that many possible interpretations can come from a presentation. The audience can, and will, come up with different meanings than the ones the originators planned. Rather than worry about which one is "right," the teacher has them accept all that are plausible. Students can evaluate their own participation using the checklist in Figure 10-3.

The following may be useful to students prior to the presentations and during the discussions:

- The teacher tells the students that the presentations they are about to see are meant to assist them in understanding the "very earliest time." They are works in progress and no one has time enough to refine them for formal presentations. Students are sharing them with one another so that they can better understand the story they are about to read. "Let's see what other meanings each presentation can give us."

- In the debriefing, the teacher asks the audience what they heard, what the sounds helped them to see, and what they think the story was about. The teacher focuses on the meanings elicited.

- The teacher discusses the sounds in terms of volume, rate, duration, and blending.

- The teacher asks what is different among the scenes presented, not which is better. This juxtaposition assists the students in understanding what choices lead to what results.

- The teacher may also ask the entire class what ideas came to them about what else could be added or changed in the piece. In this way, all presentations become co-authored.

Participation Checklist for: Name: _____

Category	Comment	5	4	3	2	1	0
Could my attendance be considered regular and punctual?							
Do I arrive in class mentally and physically prepared to participate fully?							
Am I able to maintain focus in class?							
Do I take risks to stretch myself?							
Do I challenge myself for improvement and try to overcome my resistances?							
Can my work in class be perceived as enthusiastic?							
Do I take the initiative and offer new directions?							
Am I flexible? Do I adapt to changes and try new things?							
Do I take responsibility for all class members and share my thoughts and ideas?							
Do I recognize myself as just one of the group? (don't monopolize)							
Do I accept feedback as an invitation to growth?							
Do I offer feedback in a constructive manner?							
Do I talk at, to, with people? at = 0, to = 3, with = 5							
Do I accept the diversity of others?							
Do I respond authentically, thoughtfully, spontaneously to others?							
Do I take the time to really listen and try to understand what others are saying?							
Do I try to address the negative feelings I may have for others or do I allow them to fester?							
Could I be considered a strong team member?							
Do I recognize the needs of the class and take the initiative to address them?							
Am I willing to put in that required "extra" that makes a group function effectively?							

5 = Excellent   0 = Poor

Personal Goals (use back):

Figure 10–3 Participation Checklist

Up to this point, students could have spent up to three hours on the first line of the poem that introduces the story. Some may consider this too much time, but for the first drama, it is laying down a foundation of skills that will provide a firm footing for what is to follow. This time spent could be done in one session or over a period of days. Again, each decision has its own set of advantages and disadvantages. The three-hour sequence can build its own momentum as each activity prepares students for the next. Some may believe this is too much time for one sitting and might spread it out. If so, additional warm-ups would be planned at the beginning of each segment.

If there is a period of time before the next activity, a collective repetition of the sound collage of "in the very earliest time" would be an appropriate warm-up.

The teacher asks the students to close their eyes, and proposes to read the poem "Magic Words," taken from a book called *Shaking the Pumpkin: Traditional Poetry of the Indian North Americas* (Rothenberg, 1986). The poem begins a story called "The Enchanted Caribou," and this is the story that the students will be studying through drama. The teacher asks the students to try and keep their eyes shut and see the story this time, as the last few exercises were focusing on the sounds. The teacher reads the poem:

Magic Words

In the very earliest time,

when both people and animals lived on earth,

a person could become an animal if he wanted to

and an animal could become a human being.

Sometimes they were people

and sometimes animals

and there was no difference.

All spoke the same language.

That was the time when words were like magic.

The human mind had mysterious powers.

A word spoken by chance

might have strange consequences.

It would suddenly come alive

and what people wanted to happen could happen—

all you had to do was say it.

Nobody could explain this:

That's the way it was.

For the debriefing, the teacher passes the chosen "turn object" around the circle, with each student taking a turn telling a thing or two of what he/she saw and/or felt. This is a time for the teacher to ask probing questions after each student's response. The focus is on visual details. For example:

Student:	I saw a person change into an animal.
Teacher:	What kind?
Student:	A bear.
Teacher:	Could you tell what kind of bear?
Student:	I think it was a black bear?
Teacher:	What about it made you think that?
Student:	I'm not sure. Its snout was as long as a grizzly but it was blackish. It could have been a cross between the two.

Teacher:	That's fine. When we use our imaginations, sometimes details get blurred. You invented a new type of bear for our story. How did it move?
Student:	. . .

After the debriefing, the teacher has the students walk aimlessly around the room and teaches them through side-coaching the game Atom. As they mill about, the teacher calls out a number requesting that they form groups of this size. Sometimes, this game is used as an elimination game, like musical chairs, but in this case there may be one group of a different size. The teacher does this about six times, then adds a task with the number. For example, "Atom five and form with your bodies the letter *H*, and freeze." This begins to move the students into tableau work. The teacher may use a few letters and numbers and insist on freezing. Then, she changes the letters and numbers to a situation or event. For instance, she says, "Atom six and create a hockey team on the ice" or "Atom five and create a classroom." She ends with "Atom four on family" that places the students into their new working groups and acts as a transition to the next task.

The teacher explains to the students that a *tableau* is a frozen picture or action that focuses the meaning of an event. It is not posed like a family portrait, but it is a frozen event in time. The students are asked to take their family units from the last Atom to create a scene of a family going on vacation in a car. They decide who will be the parents and the children and where will they be sitting and begin a conversation. As they work through the scene, the teacher says, "freeze," and then says, "picture one, remember it." The teacher continues taking pictures as groups work in parallel action. At the end, each group chooses one of the pictures taken or creates a composite of all the pictures to make a tableau of a family road trip.

Each group is given an opportunity to present. This time a different form of debriefing to extend the activity may be used. As each group freezes, the rest of the class wanders around as in an art gallery looking at the sculptures. They also freeze, and when tapped on the shoulder one at a time, the teacher asks them to comment in role on the piece of art before them. Another variation would be to have a member of the audience pair with a member of the sculpture and state what they think the inner thoughts of the tableau characters are.

The foregoing tableau activity could be considered another warm-up as the activities chosen do not directly relate to the topic of "The Enchanted Caribou." Warm-ups assist students to acquire the skills needed for the following activity. Some teachers may choose to sequence "warm-ups" differently, with them occurring in a series of orientation-to-drama lessons prior to the entire "Enchanted Caribou" activity. Others may prefer to make a warm-up a class in itself. Each approach has its own merits.

Returning to "The Enchanted Caribou," the teacher rereads the poem to the students as they follow with their own copies. In new groups of approximately five, they are asked to choose a phrase and make a tableau of it. An alternative might be to have the teacher prepare phrases on file cards and assign different phrases to different groups. Regardless, the teacher asks the students to move according to the phrase and freeze it, collecting picture ideas as they did with the family.

The teacher reminds the students that they should experiment and refine, not just talk about it. Time is needed for the groups to establish a working relationship and to plan, try something out, talk about the experiment, and redo.

Students create a tableau, or a frozen picture, in response to Joe Norris's suggestion to create a family portrait.

The presentations of these tableaux can take a number of different directions. Similar to the family tableaux, the students look over the tableau and make comments. The difference would be that the teacher rereads the poem and the students try to match a tableau with a tableau. Each spectator's response would be followed by a question from the teacher that would focus on details. "What part of the sculpture tells you that? Is it one detail in the sculpture of the entire piece? Could it also be another phrase? Which one? Why?" After the audience has its say, the sculpture thaws, and gives its phrase. The teacher mediates, trying to make connections between the sculpture and the audience's reactions.

A second alternative would be to have the students spread out in the poem's sequence around the room with the teacher reading the poem and drawing attention to the sculptures that the phrases highlight. If brought to a public presentation, a narrator could read through lines with the frozen groups saying theirs, while in tableau. A spotlight or overhead projector could pan from sculpture to sculpture. Again, the performance/theatre grows from the in-depth work of the classroom drama.

A typical way of proceeding after working with the poetic prologue of the story would be to read the entire story to the class. However, that is not the preferred direction in this drama. In order for the students to "live-through" the drama, the story should unfold as they live through it rather than through knowing the entire story beforehand. The story is broken into segments, with each segment having its own possible drama.

There is a natural break between what has come before and the next activity. The room requires a specific set-up, and it is best if students enter the room to the new environment. Lights could be changed, and it is important that the desks/tables are moved to the side. Scattered around the floor are various pieces of construction materials including odd bits of cloth, twigs, stones, paper, and pieces of yarn cut up into various lengths.

The students gather around the periphery of the room and are told that they are about to begin the story of "The Enchanted Caribou" and that they will be going to live the lives of some of the characters, the first being Tyya. They close their eyes and the teacher rereads the poem "Magic Words" and moves to page 4 of the story and reads that as well.

Page 4 defines Tyya as a young woman who walks along the beach collecting things from which to make dolls for children. The teacher explains to the students that the items scattered around are the things that they will find on their beach, and they will wander around looking for objects as Tyya did. The following is an example of a side-coaching script that a teacher prepares for this type of lesson. A reverent tone is suggested in its reading:

Today, we are all going to explore a bit of Tyya's character. I would like you to remain where you are with your eyes closed and listen to my voice. In this activity, my words will guide your actions. I would like you to imagine you are alone on a long beach made up of sand, rocks, and driftwood. The items scattered around the room are the objects on your beach. As beaches go, we would call this one rugged. Ignore those around you or imagine as they pass by you that they are the gulls mentioned in the story. It is important that you believe you are alone. You are on this beach for a purpose. On your side, you have a large bag made from animal hide and in it you are placing materials that you have found to make your dolls.

When I say "begin," open your eyes and start strolling the beach searching for materials. I have arranged a lot of things in the centre of the room, but don't grab quickly. Your bag is almost full, so you want to choose wisely. You have room for only seven more things and these seven things will probably help you make one full doll or another children's toy. Make your choices carefully. Remember that while Tyya was alone on the beach, you are in a drama and will need to share by leaving objects for others to take. Begin.

Take your time and look for things that you might like to use, as you will be making your doll or toy when you return from the beach. (Pause.) For Tyya, each object must have importance and a strong positive energy because she doesn't want to pass on any negative energy to the children. (Pause.) Look at the objects and imagine what they could become. Think of things that you might need and what you might make of them.

- The teacher side-coaches throughout this activity, making suggestions when needed.
- The teacher could play some Native drum music in the background.

When most have finished, the teacher gives a one-minute warning. Keeping the mood of the activity, the teacher asks the students to form a circle. Each student, as Tyya, chooses the object that he or she believes has the most magic (positive energy) and explains why the object was chosen and what it might be used for in the making of the doll/toy. The teacher asks each student follow-up questions based on their response, maintaining a reverent tone in the discussion.

When finished, the students are asked to find private spaces so that they can make their doll/toy. The teacher asks them to think about things that will become the magic of the doll when it is given to a child. The teacher asks them to imagine a specific child the doll will be given to and the joy it will bring. The teacher observes students' constructions and makes comments as they work, still keeping a reverent tone. The students are reminded that Tyya's work is important to her people and that the dolls/toys bring joy to the children.

When finished, the students bring their dolls to the centre of the room and wander around the room looking at each other's dolls as if they were in a museum or art gallery. Then, the students take their dolls and form a circle. In a ritual fashion, each student completes the following sentences:

My name is Tyya . . .
My doll's name (toy's name) is . . .
I wish that it brings . . . (joy, love, happiness, peace) . . . into a child's life.

The teacher reads pages 6 to 10 from "The Enchanted Caribou," which tell about Tyya being lost in a fog and how she meets a young man named Etosack, who assists her; the story tells how Etosack brings her back to his brothers' tent and how they chant and dance to the magic hunting song.

Hunting Chant (optional)

- The teacher reads pages 8 to 10 from "The Enchanted Caribou," stopping at the magic hunting song.
- The students are placed into groups of four to five.
- The teacher explains that while the book gives an example of a hunting chant, the students can make up their own version of the chant.
- The students brainstorm on the chalkboard both the content of the chant and what forms it might take. The teacher may introduce the term *ritual*.
- From page 13 of the book, the teacher shows the students the shadow picture of the dance and asks them how they might bring the frozen pictures to life. She asks them to include movement with the chant.
- The room may be lit with an overhead and coloured transparency.
- The teacher says, "We are going to hear each chant but as we do, let us make our bodies move so that they might cast shadows, like those in the picture." Focusing an overhead projector on the students may make stark shadows on the wall. (If a shadow screen is available, this can be used.)
- The teacher reads the last line of page 10 before the chant and has the chant recited by each group. After the last chant is read on page 12, the students lie down as if sleeping.
- The teacher pauses and then reads page 14, which tells of when the brothers leave to hunt and warn Tyya not to let anyone in. It also recounts how later that day a strange woman appears who tries to convince Tyya to let her in.

Students participate in a hunting chant and dance that they have created.

There are three powerful potential dramas here. The students could explore the concept of warnings as in parents discussing how they might protect their children. The second could be on making a convincing argument for not heeding the warning. The third could be to dramatize Tyya's decision to let or not let the shaman in. Each is briefly explained.

Warnings

- The students are placed in groups of four to five. The teacher asks them to talk about times when they have been given some kind of warning and discuss whether it was followed and why or why not.

- The students report back, but this time in role. They are parents who are invited to a town hall meeting. Some children are participating in dangerous behaviours and the town is thinking of strategies to stop the children from getting hurt. What kinds of warnings might work? Why?

Why not? The teacher is in role as the person who is collecting their opinions to bring to the mayor and guides the drama through this role.

- Depending on time, the teacher could stop the drama here and move into a discussion with the entire class on what characteristics make a warning effective or the class could proceed to the next activity.

- The students are placed into the same groups and come up with a few different warnings that they believe would be effective for Tyya.

- Each group provides warnings that the brothers could have given Tyya.

Convincing Arguments

- Similar to the warning activity, the same groups come up with counter arguments to support not heeding the warnings.

- The students report these to the entire class.

Decisions

- The teacher asks for two volunteers. One is to be Tyya and the other is to sculpt Tyya into what she might have felt like before making the decision to let or not let the shaman in.

- Once Tyya is sculpted, two more volunteers stand on either side of Tyya. One is the voice of "Reasons For ..." letting the shaman in and the other is "Reasons Against ..." Members of the class can decide on reasons for or against by adding other ideas.

- The two voices take Tyya's hands and create a tug of war and state the collected reasons one at a time.

- Tyya is then asked for her decision.

The teacher reads the remainder of the story in which we learn that the shaman does enter and turns Tyya into a white caribou. Etosack searches for her and in a dream he is told how to change her back. His people learn to respect the white caribou knowing that "a person could become an animal if he wanted to and an animal could become a human being," as the opening poem claims.

There are other potential drama opportunities present in the story; the above are ones that have been successfully used with elementary students. The story drama has provided some examples of a variety of the teaching techniques that can be used when working with a text. In addition, it shows the type of stance a teacher takes in planning and participating in the lessons and some of the theatrical conventions that can be used to translate and represent the text. Its aim is to give both a practical example and theoretical discussion on how a number of drama activities may be employed in working with a single text. These, however, have in no way exhausted the number of possible approaches that could be used with this and/or other literary texts.

More Approaches to Teaching Drama

The following section provides more approaches that a teacher may use with a text of his or her own choosing, whether it is a story drama or an isolated activity. These approaches are organized using Bolton's (1979) categorization of exercises, games, theatre, and drama for understanding. Bolton's system of categorizing drama activities has gone through many changes since it was first published, but it is still a useful schema for those beginning to use drama in their teaching. Many books that are listed in the resource bibliography have an extensive assortment of activities that teachers can adapt for their particular needs. Neelands (1990) is one of many that provide drama techniques and activities that can be used in teaching through drama, and Somers' (1994) Chapter 10 describes how to create a drama about the history of a community. These and others provide a range of material and the following descriptions are intended only as an introduction.

DRAMA EXERCISES

For Bolton, exercises may be (1) *directly experiential*, such as closing one's eyes and listening to the surrounding sounds; (2) *dramatic skill practice*, such as walking and talking in a specific way; (3) a *drama exercise* where students may be side-coached through an experience; (4) *games* that could be used to highlight a skill or understanding; and (5) a variety of *other art forms*, including the makings of songs and the drawing of a set. In the story drama, a variety of these exercises were used. An example of each is given and linked to a specific text and/or topic.

Directly Experiential. An example of a directly experiential activity would be listening to sounds that are being made within a room and/or outside of the room with one's eyes closed. This could be used to highlight a text that either focuses on sounds and/or the lack of sight. In these types of experiences, students are not in role but may later use the experience to inform a role. Having students visit a site like a hospital, zoo, or construction zone enhances the detail and belief in a drama that would follow. The same would be true of having them do what the characters would do, such as lifting and packing objects, cleaning scientific equipment, and sorting written material.

Dramatic Skill Practice. A dramatic skill practice is one that focuses on the acquisition of a skill that assists in an actual presentation of a drama. An exercise that focuses on the ability to project one's voice would be one such skill. Another is the "mirror" activity. It is one of the basic dramatic skill practices because it focuses on the actor's ability to be precise and to listen intently to the other actors. It is given in detail here as many other dramatic skills build on this one:

The students close their eyes and form a straight line according to height, without talking, by touching each other's heads ONLY. Once they are done this warm-up (it may take some time) they open their eyes and form groups of two with students of similar height. The teacher positions the groups around the room. The teacher instructs, "Find a space in the room where you can stand approximately one metre away from your partner, swing your arms and not touch another person." They decide who will be A and who will be B, and then the teacher chooses a student with whom he can demonstrate the task. The procedure is as follows:

- Look each other in the eyes.
- Put arms out horizontal to the ground.
- Find a distance whereby you can see the tips of your partner's fingers while looking into your partner's eyes.
- Then put arms in front with palms facing your partner's, bent upward.
- In the demonstration, the teacher is the leader and the student is the mirror.
- The teacher moves slowly, keeping the mirror in pace. The observers are asked to determine who is the mirror and who is the leader.
- The teacher explains that the speed of light is 300 000 kilometres per second, so no one should be able to tell who is sending or receiving. (This will be the degree of accuracy required when they do it.)

The students start and are side-coached with comments from the teacher regarding speed and accuracy. For this activity, accuracy should not be sacrificed for speed. After some time, the students in each group switch roles so that all experience being both the leader and the follower. Changing members of the groups is another option.

Students could present for one another and/or the activity can be debriefed with comments on precision, the ability to work as a team, and places where accuracy/precision are needed in life in general and in drama specifically. On one occasion, while working with a group of grade 6 students, the mirror exercise was extended by having all students line up against a wall and the teacher took a drink at the Malamute Saloon as might be imagined to have taken place in "The Shooting of Dan McGrew" (Service, 1988). The students followed the lead of the teacher who opened a bottle, poured a glass, and took a drink. Simultaneously, they all followed the leader. The students were then given role cards to provide more detail. As they drank in unison, they had to drink as a person who might have witnessed the shooting. The mirror activity assisted the students in warming-up to the lesson and in beginning to explore their assigned roles through physicalization.

Drama Exercise. A drama exercise is one in which students experience through their imaginations, most often in role. The following guided imagery activity takes students through a lost-in-the-wilderness experience and would be best used with upper-elementary students. Students should have experience with guided imagery and debriefing prior to undertaking the exercise below, as they will live through an experience of almost freezing to death. For a thorough discussion on guided imagery, see Norris (1995). This activity can be connected with any literary material that deals with the North, including "The Enchanted Caribou" (Cleaver, 1985) and "The Shooting of Dan McGrew" (Service, 1944). It is one that must be debriefed immediately following the activity in order to take the students back out of role. Side-coaching would proceed along these lines:

> I would like you to find a place where you can relax, a private space where you will feel free to let your mind wander and daydream.
>
> Once you find that space, close your eyes and go to the blank screen of your mind/imagination and let your mind drift. Forget about the worries of the day and relax as you listen to my voice.
>
> I am going to take you on a trip up north to the cold Arctic. You can use my words to assist you on your journey, but you may tune out whenever you wish. My words are here as a guide and you can use them as you see fit. Ready, keep your eyes closed, begin.
>
> We are going to try to explore the lived experience of one of the people we will be studying. Like we have mentioned before, if you do not feel comfortable with some of the experience, tune out. You be the guide to decide what experiences you want to live.

It is a cold day . . . a very cold day, and you feel the cold penetrating your outer clothing. You find yourself alone in the wilderness as you walk through deep snow to find shelter.

Feel the cold. Can you feel the wind biting at your exposed face? How about your ankles and wrists? Are they exposed? Try to feel the cold on your back as the wind catches you from behind.

Feel alone. You don't think you can make it to safety. You have been travelling for a very long time. Can you remember how long? You aren't sure you will make it to some form of civilization before your energy runs out.

Feel your body ache as it struggles forward. One foot up/down the other foot up/down; up/down; up/down; up/down. You continue until you think you cannot go any further and take one more step, up/down, then you fall face forward into the snow. You ask yourself, Is it worth it to continue? Maybe you should sleep here for a while.

With your last ounce of energy, you pull your head up and look around. What do you see? Are there any trees? Is there a storm in the air?

You want to give up . . . but . . . slowly you become aware of the smell of smoke . . . someone must be nearby. Pick yourself up with the last bit of energy that only hope can bring. Struggle to make it. You come to the top of a hill and see a village in the distance. Travel to the edge of the village and stand there celebrating its presence.

Take a step forward. You know that you are going to make it.

Games. Many types of games have a part to play in a drama classroom as they provide experiences that can occur in daily living. Used as warm-ups, they make strong connections to the material being studied.

"Yes, but . . ." could be considered one such game. The students are gathered around in a circle and the teacher starts with a comment like, "On my summer vacation, I went to Ottawa and spent a week there." Each person in line escalates the conversation by saying something like, "Yes, but when I went to Ottawa, I spent two weeks and saw the Parliament buildings." "Yes, but I saw the prime minister." "Yes, but I actually met the prime minister." The game continues and sets up a conversation regarding tall tales. This can be integrated with English and social studies by having the students tell tall tales (English) as voyageurs (social studies) who tell about their adventures.

Other Art Forms. At times, having students create other art forms assists them in making connections to both the subject material and the drama. Writing a song or dub poem, drawing people or settings, making props or building a set could be some examples of using other art forms. With the poem, "Magic Words," the students could colour the words, phrases, and lines and explain their choices. This is a form of translation that could then be used to further translate ideas into the spoken word. For example, colouring the text of a poem could suggest how to script it into a choral speech presentation.

DRAMATIC PLAYING (ROLE-PLAYING)

While the exercises can focus on the content of a text, the degree of role-playing is often minimal. Dramatic playing uses the natural make-believe activities that we all do. Courtney (1980) claims that we are all playwrights, as even adults pre-live many "what if" situations in their minds. With children, this is often made public and occurs with others. A drama classroom, although public, is an environment that is semi-structured by the teacher. A critical aspect of dramatic playing, however, is belief. While a certain amount of natural giddiness can be expected at first, the role must be played with integrity and dignity. Without these, the role play becomes frivolous and insignificant. Assisting students in building a character prior to the role play can help in achieving a commitment to the role, thereby making the drama significant. Asking autobiographical questions of the students' characters is one strategy, as are interviewing and hot seating in which other students ask questions of the characters.

Dramatic playing can be either text-based or improvisational. When text-based, there is less latitude in character development as the choices made need to be plausible with the text. Consequently, establishing the character encourages the students to delve deeper into the text. In an improvisation, there is a wider range of choices, but the constructed drama will still create its own plausible rules. Asking students to teach each other a game that they know and later adding a conflict would be an example of improvisational dramatic playing. Exploring the characters in Judy Blume's *The Pain and the Great One* (1984) would be working with a fixed text. Asking students as the "Pain" and the "Great One" to create an out-scene about a trip to the zoo would be a blending of the fixed text and improvisation.

Over time, the students will know what it means to act with belief and naturally avoid the frivolous. If drama is learning by doing and reflecting on the doing, then some of the insights must come from the drama. One can over-plan and constrain the work. Each drama teacher must consider how much background is needed before the drama begins.

THEATRE

Theatre is concerned with communicating to an audience, whereas drama focuses on the lived-experience of participants. Consequently, theatre moves into an entirely different realm of the psyche than drama; drama is a responsive act, whereas theatre is a deliberate one. It could be said that drama is the process, whereas theatre is the product. As in other subject areas, this raises the process/product debate. Some emphasize that the purpose of education is to produce and therefore focus on the product, while others focus more on the intrinsic value of the experience, recognizing that the students are the products of their own work. The stance taken here is that both approaches are complementary. Theatre can enhance understanding as it does encourage the students to look at the text differently. Consequently, it assists the students in their learning. But the students' learning is where its purpose lies, not in the products that students create. When moving to performance, a good foundation of process/drama activities strengthens the work.

In the drama, the students are not concerned with projection of voice, picturization of the scene, and making artistic decisions. In the staging of process work, a communication element is added. For example, through the drama the students may come to a better understanding of warnings and this would be an end in itself. Many of the activities undertaken in "The Enchanted Caribou" can be taken to performance, but often this is not the aim. With theatre it is. The poem could be performed as a choral speech and a class period devoted to making decisions on how the phrases would be said and by whom. Other students could decide how to sculpt a tableau to highlight some of the phrases in the text. The performance could continue with tableau as students read and speak the text. In this way, the students first understand the story; then they are ready to stage it. Both activities have educational merit.

DRAMA AND BUILDING UNDERSTANDING

There are many books that explain the theory and practice of drama for understanding, including books by Morgan and Saxton (1987), Neelands (1984, 1990), O'Neill (1995), and Wagner (1976, 1998). All agree that the major emphasis of the drama is on student understanding and learning. Through the "what if" of drama, participants have a quasi-experience of what it might be like to experience life as a different person or live in a different time or place. Since the drama expects a mental, emotional, and physical involvement, it uses an integrated approach.

A student writes a letter home as a character who witnessed the "Shooting of Dan McGrew" or participates in a town hall meeting to discuss ways to protect the children from their own risky behaviours—both take the students through language to a deep level of experience and understanding. Knowledge, then, is not something external to them but mediated by them. The story drama of "The Enchanted Caribou" was designed/planned to give students a lived-through understanding of some of the key elements of the text. Drama for understanding aims to provide students with rich experiences through which a greater understanding of the event, person, or concept can be found/created. As such, it is constructivist in approach.

PLANNING THE LESSONS

Planning story drama and dramatic activities for teaching unfold over time. "The Enchanted Caribou" emerged over many years of teaching various components to different groups. Sometimes an activity is taken from another drama and modified for use with this story. As teachers gradually become comfortable and knowledgeable with certain activities, they begin to see how they can be used elsewhere. The plans emerge naturally from the content being studied.

In the planning of successful drama in education activities, it is important to be continually cognizant that often there are major components to a lesson plan. Each lesson has (1) specific content (story, theme, issue) that is to be examined, (2) a dramatic processing activity to assist in the exploration, and often (3) a dramatic form into which the exploration will be translated. Students need to have a certain basic ability in these, or be taught these in the lesson to ensure they have a successful experience. An underemphasis of one of these may result in an unsuccessful drama experience.

For example, if a side-coached parallel action activity was planned in which all students were Little Red Riding Hood going to her grandmother's house to explore the issue of safety, the content would include the story in general and specific safety issues. The processes would be side-coaching and parallel action. If the students are unfamiliar with the processes, some latitude needs to be incorporated teaching them these skills through instructions, in the drama and during the debriefing. If some type of presentation like a tableau or creative movement were planned, that would become the form to be taught. Having the students freeze during the parallel action would be an example of using a process to assist in the exploration of form. Figure 10–4 provides an overview of how a teacher might brainstorm activities for planning drama lessons. Notice the importance of the language arts strands—reading, writing, listening, speaking, viewing, and visually representing—in drama.

The drama lesson involves working on three different levels simultaneously, with the teacher planning the process and choosing the forms that may best be used to teach language arts content. Each process and form explores the content differently, and this is the strength of drama in teaching and learning. It provides multiple lenses through which to make meaning of the world.

Although a drama activity can follow any format prescribed in a general teaching methods text in planning for drama, adding a script of side-coaching directions and questions for debriefing can greatly enhance the lesson. The side-coaching script enables the teacher to fine-tune instructions so that the students get the most out of the experience. A thorough list of questions helps the teacher draw out student ideas, and over time this list grows as the teacher uses questions

Content	Process	Form
Little Red Riding Hood Safety Taking care of the ill	Parallel action/side-coaching Debriefing Inner dialogue	Tableau Creative movement
The Shooting of Dan McGrew Surviving cold Revenge	Side-coaching/parallel action Mirror activity Writing in role Interview/interrogation	Choral speech

Figure 10–4 How a Teacher Might Brainstorm Drama Activities

that emerge from the debriefing for future lessons. Both the scripting of side-coaching and potential questions can be considered a warm-up for the teacher.

Finally, the lessons will pattern the spiral of doing and then reflecting on the doing. A plan may go through many spirals and many lessons before some sense of closure is reached. It is recommended that in the early stages, a teacher builds in more spirals for students who are new to drama. Later, as they become more proficient, students can be left on their own more often as the reflection will occur naturally in their work.

Planning for the drama can be an enjoyable activity. It is like script work as it creates an imaginary world of play. Also, like a script, a group of participants will act it out. Unlike a script, however, it will change as the participants live through it. In the teaching of drama, there are times when the plan is abandoned and the lesson takes on a life of its own. These can be rewarding times for the students and the teacher. The plan does its job when the students make it their own.

The Language Arts and Dance

The language arts are the primary vehicle for knowing and expressing ourselves in the world. Using our physical bodies as a form of expression either through sport, movement or dance allows us to engage a creative, non-rational part of our minds in our learning.

Twenty-five second-graders have gathered on the carpet in the reading area. Their teacher begins to share Ellen Stoll Walsh's picture storybook *Hop Jump* (1993) with them, a story about frogs who only know how to hop and jump until Betsy tries leaping, turning, and twisting like the leaves. "It's called dancing," she says. And soon most of the frogs join in. The children are invited to hop and jump like the frogs and then to leap and turn and twist like the leaves. Soon, they are all dancing with the frogs in the story.

The children then listen to the story *Rap a Tap Tap Here's Bojangles—Think of That* (2002) by Leo and Diane Dillon. The story shares the spirit and exuberance of the legendary dancer, Bill "Bojangles" Robinson. Written in verse, each page spread ends with "Rap a tap tap—think of that." The children are invited to tap out the rhythm with their hands and feet as the story is read again and again.

Through dance, children have the opportunity to respond to literature in a way that recognizes their internal need to use movement as a means of expression. Dance study and integration include ideas related to dance elements, creation and composition, presentation and performance, dance history, as well as dance genres and forms. As language arts teachers, we can build a repertoire of information and examples of various dance forms like ballet and jazz and about important dancers and choreographers. All of this can be integrated into the language arts curriculum where it is appropriate.

Cornett and Smithrim (2001) suggest starting small and growing from there. Teachers can start with a single lesson using one dance/movement tool to explore how we move, where, when, and to what effect. This might be a lesson connected to a story, a lesson on the shapes we can make with our bodies, or the use of warm-ups to shift the energy in a group. Providing children with carefully structured experiences that honour the medium and help them develop their own skills will allow for continued growth and development.

There is also a wealth of children's literature that lends itself to integrating dance and movement. For example, Byrd Baylor's *Sometimes I Dance Mountains* (1973) explores dance through a poetic text that can stimulate many movement explorations during or after the book has been read. In Ian Wallace's *Chin Chiang and the* Dragon's Dance (1984), a young boy gains the respect of his grandfather when he learns and performs the dragon's dance. And in Bill Martin and John Archambault's *Barn Dance!* (1988), the animals of the farm gather together with a skinny little boy to take part in a barn hoedown.

▪ Review

Integrating the fine arts with the language arts is important for the well-rounded intellectual, emotional, physical, and spiritual development of children. Many of our cultural traditions are rooted in the fine arts and students need the opportunities to explore our cultural heritage through visual art, music, drama, and dance. The fine arts also allow students to be successful in ways that allow them to engage a variety of intelligences. And success in the fine arts enhances overall academic achievement.

The development of children's visual artistic ability invites them to explore meaning at deeper symbolic levels and encourages them to expand their interpretations of text. Reading descriptive passages or stories and then interpreting them visually contributes to the child's writing ability as each learns to represent meaning in this expanded way.

Drama and dance give students a further opportunity to construct meaning, both individually and in groups using texts and movement. These activities require students to work together and to develop good cooperative learning skills.

▪ Extensions

1. Take a new piece of literature that you may wish to teach and use the examples given in the "The Language Arts and Drama" section to design one or two drama activities you might use to teach the piece. Make a list of the language arts, drama, and social skills that may be learned from the experience.

2. Find artists who illustrate children's books using different media. Plan visual art lessons that will allow children to explore the style and use the medium employed by these artists.

3. Using the types of presentations provided in the "The Language Arts and Drama" section, determine what types of experiential drama activities you might employ to enhance your students' sense of belief.

4. Invite children to include music to accompany oral renditions of stories or poems they have written. Explore a range of styles of music from modern to baroque.

5. Keep a log of the pre-lived dramas that you create in your mind. Use these to understand how people use drama to assist them in their daily lives.

6. Observe yourself over a period of time and determine your own threshold levels. Are there other personal thresholds that are not listed here?

chapter eleven

Putting It All Together

Procedure

Literature circles comprise a literacy strategy that engages my students in meaningful discussions of texts that they are reading together. The process is designed to be student-led, with each group of students responsible for determining how much will be read for each literature circles session, preparing for a discussion, and engaging in a discussion after each section of text is read. The strategy can be implemented across the grade levels; however, it has been my experience that it is better suited for the middle of grade 3 and up.

Literature circles help students develop a range of language arts skills and abilities, but my ultimate goal of literature circles is for students to engage in *grand conversations* about what they are reading. To support them in their early attempts, I provide role sheets to scaffold and structure their discussions. Many students need the structure of role sheets to learn how to engage in meaningful discussions. After a few rounds of literature circles using role sheets, my students then move toward peer-led discussions using their own response-log entries as discussion starters and supports.

> *"I model, model, model the process and then model some more! I also debrief with the students after every session and reinforce the positive."*

Cheryl Miles
Literacy Support Teacher
Fredericton, New Brunswick

I present my students with four main roles to assume when they engage in discussions. Initially, students rotate through the different roles for each group discussion, but as they become familiar and comfortable with the roles, all group members prepare journal responses that combine the four roles.

Discussion Leader Role

The discussion leader prepares three to five open-ended questions to initiate the discussion. These questions are based on the reading completed for the discussion

session. Effective discussion-leader questions might include the following:

- What would you do if you were a character? An event?
- What do you think will happen next?
- Did anything in this section surprise you?
- How did you feel when . . . ?
- What is your favourite part of this reading? Why?

Language Leader Role

The purpose of this role is to focus on the language of the text as well as to explore and extend vocabulary, word meaning, knowledge of the author's craft, and literary elements. During reading, my students use sticky notes to mark keywords, phrases, sentences, or paragraphs that they would like to explore with the group in the post-reading discussion session.

While reading a novel that used a lot of nautical terms, one group revealed that none of the members were familiar with such terminology. I directed this group to use other resources, such as a dictionary, to clarify meanings. Their small dilemma provided an opportunity for me to encourage these students to take responsibility for their own learning in a meaningful and purposeful way.

Summarizer Role

The purpose of this role is to develop summarizing skills. This requires the student(s) to write a brief overview of the reading to convey the main ideas and highlight the key points prior to the discussion. Summaries are shared and discussed with the group.

Artistic Role

This role provides opportunities for students to represent their understanding of a text creatively through art. The student(s) draw or sketch a picture or other graphic representation elicited by the reading. The representation can be a visual rendering of a character, a setting, an event, a map, a personal connection, and so on.

All Roles

Prior to the discussion session, all students in the group reflect on, and write about, their personal connections to the text. They share these with the group during discussion. Connections may include relating the text to another one or an author, to television shows or movies, to personal experiences similar to a character or event in the story, or to someone or something they know.

All roles need to be modelled repeatedly to the class before students can complete these roles in a group. I model, model, model the process and then model some more! I also debrief with the students after every session and reinforce the positive.

Group projects and presentations are prepared by each group following the reading and discussions. These projects and presentations provide each group of students with an opportunity to share their selected reading with the whole class and provide closure for the group. They take many different forms such as dramatizations of scenes, readers theatre presentations, dioramas, posters to advertise the text, book reviews, collages, interviews with a character, a poem based on the text, news broadcasts, puppet shows, board games, research on the time period, CD covers to advertise the book, etc.

Assessment

My role as teacher is to act as a facilitator for the groups and to sit in on the groups as an observer. I make observations on group cooperation, discussions, and the main components of literature circles and provide feedback to the class following each session. I also determine where the whole class would benefit from minilessons on particular topics and teach those lessons to the entire class during subsequent literature circles sessions. My assessment is based on rubrics, observation notes, anecdotal records, analysis of role sheets or response logs, and presentations. I also involve students in the assessment process through individual or group self-evaluations.

Adaptations

One of my main concerns is matching the text to the reader. My groups are heterogeneous in respect to both abilities and interests. I think it is important for students to have choice. And, over the year, I want to offer students the opportunity to explore different genres of literature. These factors make text selection somewhat complex, so I use *book talks* and *book ballots* to guide me.

I introduce the selections to the students through a book talk in order to tap into their prior knowledge and interests, then give them time to peruse the reading selections.

I provide each student with a book ballot on which to record their first, second, and third picks for their reading. I explain beforehand that it may not be possible to provide everyone with his or her first choice. When a particular reading selection appears to be very popular with the students, I try to offer it as a selection in a future round of literature circles. With this information, I then organize groups based on text selection.

When the self-selection (through the ballots) results in students choosing texts that are either too difficult for them to read or so easy they do not provide stimulation, I conference individually to guide those students to make another choice. Students sometimes select easier texts until they are confident and comfortable with the literature circles process. I allow this for a while and intervene only when it continues beyond what I judge is supportive of the student.

Reflections

My literature circles evolve over time. I do not begin the student-led discussions until all are comfortable with the four roles. Initial discussions are short, but I maintain faith that my students will increase the depth and sophistication of their discussions, and they do. With practice, their discussions gradually become grand conversations. In regard to other aspects of group interactions, I try to let students solve their own problems. I give them the responsibility and am surprised by how little I have to intervene.

After a round of literature circles is complete, I take a break and engage the students in other literacy activities. I have found that three to four rounds of literature circles are enough for the year. However, I have been pleasantly surprised when some students have asked for more!

As a teacher–consultant for blind and visually impaired students, Stephen Cripps works individually with children and with their teachers. He provides guidance in making curriculum materials and classroom practices appropriate for the special needs students. He frequently consults with teachers regarding the use of pictures with visually impaired children, explaining that large, well-defined pictures with basic details are better for low vision than those with many details as is often the case in digitalized pictures and graphs. He notes that children with reduced vision often have a base of experience significantly different from that of their peers. Internet and computer software can be very helpful in filling in some of the experiential gaps, ultimately making greater meaning construction possible.

Teachers face many challenges as they design their instructional programs. First and foremost, they consider their students, their instructional needs, and how to make the language arts programs meaningful for all students. In many Canadian classrooms, students represent a range of linguistic and cultural groups. Cultural diversity permeates classrooms. Teachers want to provide equal educational opportunities for all students, introduce cultural alternatives, and promote tolerance for and an appreciation of cultural diversity. One way to do those things is to include reading culturally diverse literature with students.

Culturally diverse literature is an important vehicle for helping students value cultural differences and recognize ethnic similarities. For example, the book *Hide and Sneak* (Kusugak, 1992) offers glimpses into the way of life in the Arctic, including its traditions and culture. *Celebrating Ramadan* (Hoyt-Goldsmith, 2001) describes and illustrates the annual Islamic customs of celebration. Mina's *Spring of Colors* (Gilmore, 2000) indicates what it is like to be an immigrant in Canadian society.

Next, teachers think about how to create a community of learners in their classrooms. It is widely recognized that language is learned through social interaction and that students learn from each other as well as from the teacher. Teachers know that collaborative learning doesn't just "happen" (Gambrell & Mazzoni, 1999). Teachers plan programs that facilitate development of a community of learners who support each other's learning and feel confident in taking risks to extend their understandings and experiences. It is a hallmark of learning communities that students and teachers

To Guide Your Reading

As you read this chapter, prepare to

Explain why teachers should include culturally diverse literature as part of the literature in the language arts program

•

Explain how teachers develop resource-based units, thematic units, and inquiry-based units

•

Explain the benefits to students of the readers and writers workshop approach to reading and writing

•

Explain how teachers set up readers and writers workshops

learn together in ways that acknowledge and respect that each is capable of making a unique contribution.

Teachers expend much time and energy to plan their language arts programs. They plan the block of time allocated specifically for language arts instruction and they also think about how the language arts are learned and used as tools for learning. They decide how to provide students with comprehensive instruction that incorporates the language arts across the curriculum. The three instructional frameworks introduced in Chapter 2 are resource-based units, thematic units, and inquiry-based units. Within these organizational frameworks, many teachers use readers and writers workshops to organize a large part of their instruction. Teachers use these frameworks to generally shape their programs and then make adaptations to meet the needs of their students.

Teachers often search for the "one best way" to design language arts instruction and to develop units, but there is no one best way. Instead, teachers must choose from thousands of books and other print and nonprint resources, activities, and assignments as they plan. As the decision makers about instruction, teachers depend upon well-grounded and respected research to guide their choices. Figure 11–1 shows ten research-based best practices (Gambrell & Mazzoni, 1999) to be included in well-designed language arts programs. Teachers incorporate these practices in resource-based, thematic, and inquiry-based units as well as in language activities across curriculum.

In this text, you've read about each of the six language arts, how they are learned, and many components of language arts instruction. In this chapter, you will see how teachers bring these together to create programs of instruction. You will be introduced to instructional frameworks for unit planning and steps to take in planning readers and writers workshops Teachers planning language arts programs are like jugglers who balance many and different sized balls with rhythm and agility, keeping all in the air. They give just the right amount of time and attention to each of the components to create programs that entice and meet the needs of all students. Teachers begin with frameworks for an instructional approach and then choose the literature, activities, and

1. Teach reading for authentic meaning-making literacy experiences: for pleasure, to be informed, and to perform a task.
2. Use high quality literature.
3. Integrate a comprehensive word study/phonics program into reading/writing instruction.
4. Use multiple texts that link and expand concepts.
5. Balance teacher-led and student-led discussions.
6. Build a whole-class community that emphasizes important concepts and builds background knowledge.
7. Work with students in small groups while other students read and write about what they have learned.
8. Give students plenty of time to read and write in class.
9. Give students direct instruction in decoding, as well as comprehension strategies that promote independent reading. Balance direct instruction, guided instruction, and independent learning.
10. Use a variety of assessment techniques.

Figure 11–1 Research-Based Best Practices
Source: Gambrell & Mazzoni, 1999 in *Best Practices in Literacy Instruction.* New York: The Guilford Press.

assignments based on their instructional goals and beliefs about how children learn. It is a complex task and one that benefits from experience.

As teachers gain experience developing units, they often go beyond the "What shall I do with this book?" or "What shall I teach in this unit?" questions to think about the choices they make as they plan instruction and teach (McGee & Tompkins, 1995). Teachers need to think about why students should choose many of the books they read and why skill and strategy instruction should be taught in context. Through this reflection, teachers realize how theories about how children learn, along with their instructional goals, provide the foundation for language arts instruction (Zarrillo, 1989).

Culturally Diverse Literature

Choosing resources is one of the most important components of planning language arts instruction. Teachers must choose a wide variety of resources, including fine quality and diverse literature. According to Canadian researchers Joyce Bainbridge and Sylvia Pantaleo (1999), "Multicultural literature depicts and explores the lives of individuals belonging to a wide range of groups" (p. 110). Culturally diverse literature is a vehicle for fostering cultural awareness and appreciation. It affirms the cultural identity of students of diverse backgrounds and develops all students' understanding of and appreciation for other cultures. Students explore and expand their cultural values and beliefs as they read culturally diverse literature (Rasinski & Padak, 1990). They vicariously experience other cultures, and these experiences influence the way they interact with people in our multicultural society (Bainbridge & Pantaleo, 1999).

CULTURALLY CONSCIOUS LITERATURE

Educators recommend selecting culturally diverse literature that is culturally conscious (Sims, 1982; Norton, 1999)—that is to say, literature that accurately reflects a group's culture, language, history, and values without perpetuating stereotypes. Such literature often deals with issues of prejudice, discrimination, and human dignity. According to Yokota (1993), these books should be rich in cultural details with authentic dialogue, and should present cultural issues in enough depth that readers can think and talk about them. Inclusion of cultural group members should be purposeful. They should be distinct individuals whose lives are rooted in the culture, never simply added to fulfill a quota.

Culturally diverse literature includes six types of literature, and each type offers a different perspective on the lives and contributions of each cultural group. The six types are

1. *Folktales and other traditional stories.* Traditional stories—including folktales, legends, and myths—are a part of every culture, and a wide variety of these stories are available for children. Cinderella stories, for example, come from many different cultures and include *Mufaro's Beautiful Daughters: An African Tale* (Steptoe, 1987); *Yeh-Shen: A Cinderella Story from China* (Louie, 1982) and *Bound* (Napoli, 2004), also from China; *The Egyptian Cinderella* (Climo, 1989); *The Rough Face Girl* (Martin, 1992), an Algonquian version; and *The Gift of the Crocodile: A Cinderella Story* (Sierra, 2000)

2. *Historical fiction.* These books describe the immigration of different cultural groups to North America, their assimilation into Canadian life, and the stories of young people in other places and other times. In *Nykola and Granny* (1989), Constance Horne tells the story of a young boy's emigration from the Ukraine to Western Canada at the turn of the century. Similarly, *Silver Threads* (1996), by Marsha Forchuk Skrypuch, also tells of people fleeing the Ukraine and their experiences as new Canadians at the beginning of the First World War. Skrypuch's *Nobody's Child* (2003) tells of orphans' attempts to survive the Armenian massacres 1915–1923. Deborah

Ellis, too, tells an orphan's story in her tale from Afghanistan, *Parvana's Journey* (2002). Marilynn Reynolds, another Canadian author, writes compassionately of bygone times on the prairies in *The Prairie Fire* (1999) as does Gillian Chan in *The Carved Box* (2001).

3. ***Contemporary realistic fiction.*** These contemporary stories focus on the experiences of culturally diverse people in Canada. *Mina Spring of Colors* (Gilmore, 2000) describes Mina's difficulties dealing with her recently arrived grandfather's Indian traditions as perceived by her Canadian classmates. Thomas King's *Medicine River* (King, 1997) and Jan Bourdeau Waboose's (2000) *Sky Sisters* help young readers to understand the First Nations' experience in Canadian society.

4. ***Biographies.*** These books detail the contributions of people from various cultural groups. Some biographies, such as *James McKay: A Métis Builder of Canada* (Grant, 1995), detail the lives of historical figures; others, such as *Terry Fox: His Story* (Scrivener, 2000), highlight contemporary persons.

5. ***Poetry.*** There are a few collections of poems, songs, and chants written by people of various cultural groups that are available for children. Some examples are *If You Could Wear My Sneakers* (Fitch, 1997*), Canadian Poems for Canadian Kids* (Hamilton, 2005), *Off to the Sweet Shores of Africa and Other Drum Rhymes* (Unobagha, 2000), and *The Trees Stand Shining: Poetry of the North American Indians* (Jones, 1993).

6. ***Informational books.*** Other books provide information about various cultures, including information about holidays and rituals, language, cooking, and the arts, as well as information about the country in which the culture originated. *The French* (Horton, 2000), from the *We Came to North America* series is a good example of such books. *Japan, the People*, from the *Lands, Peoples, and Culture Series* created by Bobbie Kalman (2001) is another example.

Culturally diverse literature must meet the criteria for good literature as well as for cultural consciousness. That is, books should depict culturally diverse groups in active, rather than passive,

Teachers include culturally conscious literature in the wide variety of books in their classroom libraries.

roles. One example is *Daniel's Story* (Matas, 1993), which depicts the terrible realities of the discrimination against Jewish people during the Second World War. The story is beautifully written, and the details are historically and culturally accurate.

Until recently, most books about Aboriginal peoples and other cultural groups have been written by European authors who, because of their own ethnicity, represent an "outside" viewpoint (Bishop, 1992b). An inside perspective is more likely to give an authentic view of what members of the cultural group believe to be true about themselves, while an outside perspective describes how others see that group's beliefs and behaviours. The difference in perspective means that there is a difference in what the authors say and how they say it, as well as a difference in their purpose for writing (Reimer, 1992). Some authors, however, do successfully write about another culture. Byrd Baylor and Paul Goble are notable examples. They have a sensitivity learned through research about and participation in different cultural groups. Today more people within each cultural group are writing about their own cultures and are providing more authentic "inside" viewpoints in culturally diverse literature.

There are many reasons to use culturally diverse literature in elementary and middle-school classrooms, whether students represent diverse cultures or not. First, students enjoy reading these stories, informational books, and poems; through reading they learn more about what it means to be human, and they discover that people of all cultural groups are real people with similar emotions, needs, and dreams. Bainbridge and Pantaleo (1999) indicate that through multicultural literature, students become aware of stereotyping and learn to recognize the contributions various cultural groups make to Canadian society.

Second, students learn about the wealth of diversity through culturally diverse books, and they develop sensitivity to and appreciation for people of other cultural groups (Walker-Dalhouse, 1992). Culturally diverse literature also challenges racial and ethnic stereotypes by providing an inside view of a culture.

Third, students broaden their knowledge of geography and learn different views of history through culturally diverse literature. They read about the countries that minority groups left as they immigrated to Canada, and they gain non-mainstream perspectives about historical events. For example, Joy Kogawa (1982) tells of her experiences of relocation and internment in the moving story of *Obasan*. Through reading and responding to culturally diverse books, students challenge traditional assumptions about the history of Canada, and gain a more balanced view of historical events and the contributions of people from various cultural groups. They learn that traditional historical accounts have emphasized the contributions of European immigrants, and particularly those made by men.

Fourth, culturally diverse literature raises issues of social injustice—prejudice, racism, discrimination, segregation, colonization, anti-Semitism, and genocide.

Using culturally diverse literature has additional benefits for students from various cultural and ethnic backgrounds. When students read books about their own cultural group, they develop pride in their cultural heritage and learn that their culture has made important contributions to Canada and to the rest of the world (Harris, 1992a, 1992b). In addition, students often become more interested in reading because they identify with the characters and events.

Literature Featuring Aboriginal Peoples. Many authors, especially Michael Arvaarluk Kusugak, C. J. Taylor, Leo Yerxa, Thomas King, Tomson Highway, and Paul Goble, have written sensitively about Aboriginal cultural topics. Some books about Aboriginal culture are retellings of traditional folktales, myths, and legends, such as *The Legend of the Indian Paintbrush* (de Paola, 1988) and *Iktomi and the Boulder* (Goble, 1988). Michael Arvaarluk Kusugak's book, co-written with Robert Munsch, *A Promise Is a Promise* (1988), is a traditional Inuit legend passed down to him by his grandmother. Tomson Highway's two children's books *Dragonfly Kites* (2002) and *Caribou Song* (2001), in particular, present beautifully written stories from Canada's north. The author says, "The beauty of Canada's north, the extraordinary beauty of the culture of the north, the beauty of language is an integral part of Canadian culture" (2003). *Dragonfly Kites* is a superbly written story about Joe and Cody, two young Cree brothers living in Northern Manitoba, who create stories and games from objects found around them in nature. *Caribou Song* tells the story of two Cree children who follow the caribou by dogsled with their family. A list of literature that features Aboriginal culture is presented in Figure 11–2. The themes in these books include passing traditions and stories to the next generation, mistreatment and injustice that Aboriginal peoples have suffered at the hands of Europeans and European Canadians, and a reverence for living things and the Earth. By presenting Aboriginal literature in the classroom, teachers show respect for Aboriginal culture, beliefs, spirituality, and traditions.

Ancona, G. (1993). *Powwow.* Orlando: Harcourt Brace. (M–U)

Archibald, J., Friesen, V., & Smith, J. (1993). *Courageous Spirits: Aboriginal Heroes of Our Children.* Penticton, BC: Theytus Books. (M–U) ✤

Ballantyne, A. (1991). *Wisakyjak and the New World.* Waterloo: Penumbra Press. (P) ✤

Bouchard, D. (1990). *The Elders Are Watching.* Tofino, BC: Eagle Dancer Enterprises. (M–U) ✤

Brooks, M. (1997). *The Bone Dance.* Toronto: Groundwood. (U) ✤

Bruchac, J. (1994). *The Great Ball Game.* New York: Dial. (P)

Cameron, A. (1991). *Raven and Snipe.* Madeira Park: Harbour Publishing. (P–M)

Cardinal, P. (1997). *The Cree People.* Edmonton: Duval House. (M–U) ✤

Clark, J. (1995). *The Dream Carvers.* Toronto: Viking. (M–U) ✤

George, J. C. (1972). *Julie of the Wolves.* New York: Harper & Row. (U) (Inuit)

George, J. C. (1997). *Arctic Son.* New York: Hyperion. (U)

Grant, A. (1995). *James McKay: A Métis Builder of Canada.* Winnipeg: Pemmican. (U) ✤

Highway, T. (2001). *Caribou Song.* Toronto: HarperCollins. (M–U) ✤

Highway, T. (2002). *Dragonfly Kites.* Toronto: HarperCollins. (P–M) ✤

Hoyt-Goldsmith, D. (1990). *Totem Pole.* New York: Holiday House. (M)

Hoyt-Goldsmith, D. (1992). *Arctic Hunter.* New York: Holiday House. (M)

Kalman, B. (1994). *Settler Sayings.* Niagara-on-the-Lake: Crabtree. (M) ✤

King, T. (1998). *Coyote Sings to the Moon.* Toronto: Groundwood. (M–U) ✤

Kusugak, M. (1990). *Baseball Bats for Christmas.* Toronto: Annick Press. (P) ✤

Locker, T. (1991). *The Land of Gray Wolf.* New York: Dial. (M–U)

Luenn, N. (1990). *Nessa's Fish.* New York: Atheneum. (P–M) (Inuit)

Martin, J. B. (2001). *The Lamp, The Ice, and the Boat Called Fish.* Boston: Houghton Mifflin. (M–U) (Inuit)

McLellan, J. (1991). *Nanabosho, Soaring Eagle and the Great Sturgeon.* Winnipeg: Pemmican Publications. (P–M) ✤

McLellan, J. (1993). *Nanabosho Dances.* Winnipeg: Pemmican. (P) ✤

Munsch, R., & Kusugak, M. (1988). *A Promise Is a Promise.* Toronto: Annick Press. (P) ✤

O'Dell, S., & Hall, E. (1992). *Thunder Rolling in the Mountains.* Boston: Houghton Mifflin. (U)

Paulsen, G. (1988). *Dogsong.* New York: Bradbury Press. (U)

Plain, F. (1994). *Grandfather Drum.* Winnipeg: Pemmican. (P) ✤

Richards, D. (1993). *Soldier Boys.* Saskatoon: Thistledown Press. (M–U) ✤

Schwartz, V. F. (2003). *Initiation.* Toronto: Fitzhenry & Whiteside. (U) ✤

Seattle, C. (1991). *Brother Eagle, Sister Sky.* New York: Dial. (P–M–U)

Speare, E. G. (1983). *The Sign of the Beaver.* Boston: Houghton Mifflin. (M–U)

Taylor, C. J. (2004). *Peace Walker: The Legend of Hiawatha and Tekanawita.* Toronto: Tundra Books. (M–U) ✤

Taylor, C. J. (1994). *Bones in the Basket.* Montreal: Tundra Books. (M–U) ✤

Taylor, H. (1997). *When Bear Stole the Chinook: A Siksika Tale.* New York: Farrrar Straus Gerioux. (P–M)

Walters, E. (1998). *The War of the Eagles.* Victoria: Orca. (U) ✤

Whetung, J. (1996). *The Vision Seeker.* Don Mills, ON: Stoddart Publishing. ((M–U) ✤

P = primary grades (K–2); M = middle grades (3–5); U = upper grades (6–8).

Figure 11–2 Literature Featuring Aboriginal Culture

Boraks-Nemetz, L. (1994). *The Old Brown Suitcase.* Brentwood Bay: Ben-Simon. (U) (Polish)

Czernecki, S., & Rhodes, T. (1994). *The Hummingbirds' Gift.* Winnipeg: Hyperion. (M–U) (Mexican) 🍁

Fairbridge, L. (1992). *In Such a Place.* Toronto: Doubleday. (U) (South Africa) 🍁

Freedman, J. (1991). *One Hand Clapping.* Toronto: Groundwood Books. (U) (Japanese) 🍁

Gilman, P. (1992). *Something from Nothing.* Toronto: North Winds Press. (P) (Jewish) 🍁

Horne, C. (1989). *Nykola and Granny.* Agincourt: Gage Educational Publishing. (M–U) (Ukrainian) 🍁

Jairam, P. B. (1991). *Golden Stories to Treasure.* Scarborough: Dharmik Books. (M) (Indian) 🍁

Kernaghan, E. (1995). *Dance of the Snow Dragon.* Saskatoon: Thistledown Press. (U) (Tibetan) 🍁

Khan, R. (1999). *Dahling, if You Luv Me, Would You Please, Please Smile.* Toronto: Stoddart Kids. (U) 🍁

Marineau, M. (1995). *Road to Chlifa.* Red Deer: Red Deer College Press. (U) (Lebanese) 🍁

Mollel, T. (1990). *The Orphan Boy.* Toronto: Oxford University Press. (P–M) (African) 🍁

Mollel, T. (1992). *A Promise to the Sun.* Toronto: Little, Brown & Company. (P) (African) 🍁

Oberman, S. (1994). *The Always Prayer Shawl.* Honesdale, PA: Boyd Mills Press. (M) (Jewish)

Walsh, A. (1994). *Shabash!* Victoria: Beach Holme Publishers. (P) (Sikh) 🍁

Yee, P. (1991). *Roses Sing on New Snow.* Toronto: Groundwood Books. (P) (Chinese) 🍁

P = primary grades (K–2); M = middle grades (3–5); U = upper grades (6–8).

Figure 11–3 Literature Featuring Diverse Cultural Groups

Literature Featuring Diverse Cultural Groups (Transcultural Literature). In addition to Aboriginal peoples, there are other underrepresented cultural groups in Canada, including Jewish, Chinese, Japanese, and African Canadians. The book *Struggle and Hope: The Story of Chinese Canadians* (Yee, 1996) explores events and experiences from Chinese Canadian history. Being the majority culture, Canadians descended from European heritage are sometimes ignored in discussions of cultural groups, but to ignore them denies the distinct cultures of many Canadians (Yokota, 1993).

Within the European-descended Canadian umbrella category are a variety of groups, including German, Italian, Swedish, and Russian peoples. Patricia Polacco's *Thunder Cake* (1990), the story of a Russian grandmother who calms her granddaughter's fear of thunderstorms by making a "thunder cake," is a popular book. Maggi's (2001) retelling of a Venezuelan indigenous legend in *The Great Canoe: A Karina Legend* is an important addition to multicultural literature. Figure 11–3 presents a list of books featuring diverse cultural groups.

TEACHING ABOUT CULTURAL DIVERSITY

Some teachers share culturally diverse literature with their students; others include multicultural components in their lessons and teach resource-based units, thematic units, and inquiry-based units to raise students' awareness of racism, inequality, and other social issues. We encourage teachers to include culturally diverse literature in their instructional units. According to Zarillo (1994), culturally diverse resource-based units and thematic units

- Celebrate cultural diversity in Canada
- Increase cultural understanding and respect
- Provide opportunities to use all six language arts
- Provide opportunities for students who are learning English to use language in meaningful ways
- Incorporate aesthetic reading and response-to-literature activities
- Use books that accurately portray cultural groups

Rasinski and Padak (1990) have identified four approaches for incorporating culturally diverse literature into resource-based, thematic, and inquiry-based units. These approaches are based on Banks's (1994b) multicultural curriculum model and differ in the extent to which cultural diversity becomes a central part of the curriculum.

1. **The contributions approach.** This approach focuses on lessons taught in connection with a holiday or other special occasions (Rasinski & Padak, 1990). The purpose of activities is to familiarize students with holidays, specific customs, or the contributions of important people, but these activities do not teach cultural values or challenge students to re-examine their beliefs. A week-long unit might focus on reading *Mina's Spring of Colors* (Gilmore, 2000), a story about Holi, the festival of colour, celebrated in India. The story is about a young girl named Mina, whose parents celebrate Holi in Canada. *How My Parents Learned to Eat* (Friedman, 1984) is a story about a sailor who courts a young Japanese woman after the Second World War. In the latter book, the young woman learns to eat with a knife and fork to surprise the sailor, and the sailor learns to eat with chopsticks to surprise the woman. This approach is an easy way to include cultural diversity in the curriculum, but students gain only a superficial understanding of cultural diversity.

2. **The additive approach.** In this second approach, lessons using culturally diverse literature are added to the existing curriculum (Rasinski & Padak, 1990). In a genre unit on folktales, for example, *Mufaro's Beautiful Daughters: An African Tale* (Steptoe, 1987), *Yeh-Shen: A Cinderella Story from China* (Louie, 1982), and *The Egyptian Cinderella* (Climo, 1989) might be added as transcultural versions of the Cinderella story. The teacher would choose to read these books because they are well written books and the students will enjoy them. This approach is similar to the contributions approach; information about cultural diversity is added to the curriculum, but not woven through it.

3. **The transformation approach.** Resource-based units, thematic units, and inquiry-based units are modified in this approach to promote the study of historical events and contemporary issues from the viewpoint of culturally diverse groups (Rasinski & Padak, 1990). Primary-grade students, for example, might read *A Promise Is a Promise* (Munsch & Kusugak, 1988), *Something from Nothing* (Gilman, 1992), or *Where Is Gah-Ning?* (Munsch, 1991) as part of a unit on families, and then talk about the common features of families from diverse cultural groups. Or, during a thematic unit on WWII, upper-grade students might read to learn about the Japanese Canadian viewpoint about the war and their unfair internment. These literature experiences and response activities allow students to see the interconnectedness of various ethnic groups within Canadian society and the ways that diverse cultural groups have shaped Canadian history.

4. **The social action approach.** In this fourth approach, students study important social issues and take action to solve problems through thematic units (Rasinski & Padak, 1990). Students read culturally diverse literature in order to gain an "inside" view on social issues. For example, students might study immigration and begin by reading to learn about modern-day refugees who risk their lives coming to Canada. Afterwards they can talk about their own attitudes toward immigrant groups, and they can research how and when their families came to Canada. The question "who belongs here?" might direct their study and lead them to find ways to encourage tolerance and assist with refugee programs in their community. In this approach, students read, do research, think deeply about social issues, and apply what they are learning in their own communities.

STRATEGIES FOR TEACHING CULTURALLY DIVERSE STUDENTS

1. Provide instructions in a written format, such as on a chart, overhead, or by using PowerPoint to support oral directions.

2. Encourage students to do some assignments using words in their first language.

3. Offer one-on-one and small group practice of the pronunciation of words.

4. Provide opportunities for students to work with a partner during language activities.

5. Provide opportunities for students to retell their understanding of a story.

6. Ask students to write some material in their first language and then work with a partner to translate it.

7. Show students how to use rebus symbols (pictures) in their writing.

8. Provide opportunities for students to find classmates who share their first language through well-researched school websites. Correspondence can be translated and shared with others.

9. Encourage students to listen to audio-taped stories and articles and discuss them with a partner.

10. Allow more time and structure for oral language activities such as role-playing or readers theatre.

Resource-Based Units

Teachers plan resource-based units featuring popular and award-winning stories for children and adolescents. In today's society, students are expected to engage effectively in many new literacies and technologies (Leu, 2000). It is therefore appropriate that resource-based units also include a variety of print and nonprint media and texts, such as newspapers, video, and the Internet. Some resource-based units feature a single book, either a picture book or a chapter book, while others feature sets of books for a genre unit or an author study unit. A novel study is but one example of a resource-based unit. Figure 11–4 on pages 444–445 presents a list of recommended trade books, genres, and authors and illustrators for resource-based units for kindergarten through grade 8. During these units, students move through the five stages of reading as they read and respond to stories, learn reading and writing skills and strategies, and engage in language arts activities.

For more about the stages of reading, see Chapter 4, "The Reading and Writing Processes," pages 129–140.

HOW TO DEVELOP A RESOURCE-BASED UNIT

Teachers develop a resource-based unit through an eight-step series of activities, beginning with choosing the literature and other resources for the unit, continuing to identify and schedule activities, and ending with deciding how to assess students' learning. Whether teachers are using trade books, anthology selections, videos, or the Internet, they develop a unit using these steps to meet the needs of their students. Canadian teachers also consult the provincial curriculum documents that describe the requirements for the grades and programs they are teaching. Effective teachers do not simply follow directions in commercially published teachers' manuals and planning guides. While they may consult such guides, they build their own programs to design instruction especially for the students whom they teach. Teachers need to make the plans themselves because they are the ones who best know their students, the resources they have available, the time available for the unit, the curriculum they want to teach, and the language arts activities they want to use.

The length of time involved in teaching a resource-based unit varies widely depending upon grade level and complexity of the resource. Usually resource-based units featuring a picture book are completed in one week, and units featuring a chapter book and other resources are completed in two, three, or four weeks. Genre and author units may last two, three, or four weeks. Only occasionally do teachers continue resource-based units beyond four weeks. Longer units risk losing students' interest in this particular book or, worse yet, their love of literature.

Step 1: Select the Literature. Teachers begin by selecting the reading material for the unit. The literature may be a story in a picture book format, a chapter book, or a story selected from a basal reading textbook. The reading materials should be high-quality literature and should often include culturally diverse selections. Sometimes teachers select several related stories—books representing the same genre, books written by the same author for an author study, or books illustrated by the same artist for an illustrator study. Teachers collect multiple copies of the book or books for

Trade Books	Genres	Authors and Illustrators
Primary Grades (K–2)		
Bogart, J. (1991). *Sarah Saw a Blue Macaw*. Markham, ON: Scholastic Canada. 🍁	Alphabet books	Jo Ellen Bogart 🍁
Brett, J. (1989). *The Mitten*. New York: Putnam.	Biographies	Jan Brett 🍁
Carle, E. (1969). *The Very Hungry Caterpillar*. New York: Viking.	Fairy tales	Eric Carle
Gilman, P. (1999). *Jillian Jiggs and the Secret Surprise*. Markham, ON: North Winds Press, Scholastic Canada. 🍁	Folk tales	Donald Crews
	Number books	Tomie de Paola
	Pattern stories	Dr. Seuss
		Lois Ehlert
Gregory, N. (2000). *Wild Girl and Gran*. Red Deer, AB: Red Deer Press. 🍁		Sheree Fitch 🍁
		Mem Fox
Henkes, K. (1991). *Chrysanthemum*. New York: Greenwillow.		Phoebe Gilman 🍁
Hutchins, P. (1968). *Rosie's Walk*. New York: Macmillan.		Georgia Graham 🍁
Jennings, S. (1993). *Sleep Tight, Mrs. Ming*. Toronto: Annick Press. 🍁		Tana Hoban
		Sharon Jennings 🍁
Lawson, J. (1996). *Whatever You Do, Don't Go Near That Canoe*. Richmond Hill, ON: Scholastic Canada. 🍁		Steven Kellogg
		Julie Lawson 🍁
Lionni, L. (1969). *Alexander and the Wind-up Mouse*. New York: Knopf.		James Marshall
		Bill Martin and John Archambault
Numeroff, L. (1985). *If You Give a Mouse a Cookie*. New York: Harper & Row.		Robert Munsch 🍁
Rylant, C. (1985). *The Relatives Came*. New York: Bradbury Press.		Barbara Reid 🍁
		Kathy Stinson 🍁
Vaage, C. (1995). *Bibi and the Bull*. Red Deer, AB: Red Deer College Press. 🍁		Werner Zimmerman 🍁
Middle Grades (3–5)		
Cleary, B. (1981). *Ramona Quimby, Age 8*. New York: Morrow.	Aboriginal legends and myths	Byrd Baylor
Coerr, E. (1977). *Sadako and the Thousand Paper Cranes*. New York: Putnam.	Biography	Beverly Cleary
	Contemporary realistic fiction	Karen Cushman
Cushman, K. (1995). *The Mid-wife's Apprentice*. New York: Harper Collins Children's Books.		Deborah Ellis 🍁
	Fables	Jean Fritz
Gardiner, J. R. (1980). *Stone Fox*. New York: Harper & Row.	Historical fiction	Paul Goble
Horvaff, P. (2002). *Everything on a Waffle*. Toronto: Groundwood Books. 🍁	Poetry	Eloise Greenfield
	Tall tales	Karen Hesse
Korman, G. (1981). *I Want to Go Home*. New York: Scholastic.	Wordplay books	Jean Little 🍁
Little, J. (2002). *Birdie, for Now*. Vancouver: Orca Book Publishers. 🍁		Patricia MacLachlan
		Ann Martin
Lowry, L. (1989). *Number the Stars*. Boston: Houghton Mifflin.		L. M. Montgomery 🍁
MacLachlan, P. (1985). *Sarah, Plain and Tall*. New York: Harper & Row.		Kit Pearson 🍁
		Patricia Polacco
Montgomery, L. M. (1908/1999). *Anne of Green Gables*. New York: Harper Festival.		Jack Prelutsky
		Cynthia Rylant
Naylor, P. R. (1991). *Shiloh*. New York: Macmillan.		William Steig
Paterson, K. (1977). *Bridge to Terabithia*. New York: Crowell.		Marvin Terban
Pearson, K. (2003). *The Guests of War Trilogy*. Toronto, ON: Puffin Books. 🍁		Chris Van Allsburg
		Eric Walters 🍁
Walters, E. (1997). *Trapped in Ice*. Toronto, ON: Puffin Books. 🍁		Budge Wilson 🍁
White, E. B. (1980). *Charlotte's Web*. New York: HarperCollins.		Jane Yolen
Ye, T-X. (2002). *White Lily*. Toronto: Doubleday Canada. 🍁		

(continued)

Figure 11–4 Recommended Trade Books, Genres, and Authors and Illustrators for Resource-Based Units

Upper Grades (6–8)

Babbitt, N. (1975). *Tuck Everlasting*. New York: Farrar, Straus & Giroux.

Bedard, M. (2001). *Stained Glass*. Toronto: Tundra Books. 🍁

Buffie, M. (1998). *Angels Turn Their Backs*. Toronto, ON: Kids Can Press. 🍁

Creech, S. (1997). *Chasing Redbird*. London: Macmillan Children's Books.

Ellis, S. (1994). *Out of the Blue*. Toronto, ON: Groundwood Books/Douglas & McIntyre. 🍁

Friesen, G. (2000). *Men of Stone*. Toronto, ON: Kids Can Press. 🍁

George, J. C. (1972). *Julie of the Wolves*. New York: Harper & Row.

Johnston, J. (2001). *In Spite of Killer Bees*. Toronto: Tundra Books. 🍁

Lawson, J. (1998). *Turns on a Dime*. Toronto, ON: Stoddart Kids. 🍁

Lowry, L. (1993). *The Giver*. Boston: Houghton Mifflin.

Matas, C. (1998). *Telling*. Toronto, ON: Key Porter Books Ltd. 🍁

Paulsen, G. (1987). *Hatchet*. New York: Viking.

Slade, A. (2001). *Dust*. New York: HarperCollins. 🍁

Toten, T. (2001). *The Game*. Red Deer, AB: Red Deer Press. 🍁

Voigt, C. (1982). *Dicey's Song*. New York: Atheneum.

Watts, I. (2000). *Remember Me*. Toronto, ON: Tundra Books. 🍁

Contemporary realistic fiction
Fantasy
Historical fiction
Myths
Poetry
Science fiction

Lloyd Alexander
Avi
Alison Baird
Sharon Creech
Paula Danziger
Sarah Ellis 🍁
Russell Freedman
Gayle Friesen 🍁
Virginia Hamilton
Anita Horrocks 🍁

Monica Hughes 🍁
David Macaulay
Carol Matas 🍁
Walter Dean Myers
Scott O'Dell
Kenneth Oppel 🍁
Katherine Paterson
Gary Paulsen 🍁
Richard Peck
J.K. Rowling
Jerry Spinelli
Cora Taylor 🍁
Yoshiko Uchida
Tim Wynne-Jones 🍁
Laurence Yep
Paul Zindel

Figure 11–4 Recommended Trade Books, Genres, and Authors and Illustrators for Resource-Based Units *(continued)*

the resource-based unit. When teachers use trade books, they have to collect class sets of the books for the unit. In some school districts, class sets of selected books are available for teachers. However, in other school districts, teachers have to request that administrators purchase multiple copies of books or buy them themselves through book clubs. When teachers use picture books, students can share books so only half as many books as students are needed.

Once the book (or books) is selected, teachers collect related resources for the unit. Related resources include the following:

- Other versions of the same story
- Other books written by the same author
- Other books illustrated by the same artist
- Books with the same theme
- Books with similar settings
- Books in the same genre
- Informational books on a related topic
- Poetry books on a related topic
- Audio tapes or videos of the story
- Webpages about the author or illustrator

Teachers collect one or two copies of ten, twenty, thirty, or more books as resources, which they add to the classroom library during the unit. These resources are placed on a special shelf or in a crate in the library centre. At the beginning of the unit, teachers do a book talk to introduce the resources, and then students look at them and read them during independent reading time.

Step 2: Develop a Unit Plan. Teachers read or reread the selected book or books and then think about the focus they will use for the unit. Sometimes teachers focus on an element of story structure, the historical setting, wordplay, the author or genre, or a concept or topic related to the book, such as weather or life in the desert.

After determining the focus, teachers think about which activities they will use at each of the five stages of the reading process. For each stage, teachers ask themselves these questions:

1. *Preparing*
   - What background knowledge do students need before reading?
   - What key concepts and vocabulary should I teach before reading?
   - How will I introduce the story and stimulate students' interest in reading?

2. *Reading*
   - How will students read this story?
   - What reading strategies and skills will I model or ask students to use?
   - How can I make it challenging for more capable readers, and accessible for less capable readers and students learning English as a second language?

3. *Responding*
   - Will students write in reading logs? How often?
   - Will students participate in grand conversations? How often?
   - What scenes from the book will students want or need to dramatize?

4. *Exploring*
   - What words might be added to the word wall?
   - What vocabulary activities might be used?
   - Will students reread the story?
   - What skill and strategy minilessons might be taught?
   - How can I focus students' attention on words and sentences in the book?
   - How will other resources be used?
   - What can I share about the author, illustrator, or genre?

5. *Extending*
   - What projects might students choose to pursue?
   - How will other resources be used?
   - How will students share projects?

Teachers often brainstorm ideas and jot notes on a chart divided into sections for each stage. Then they use the ideas they have brainstormed as they plan the unit. Usually, not all of the brainstormed ideas will be used. Rather, teachers select the most important ones according to their focus, student needs and interests, and the available time.

Step 3: Identify Language Arts Strategies and Skills (Curriculum) to Teach During the Unit. Teachers decide which strategies and skills to teach using the resources. Their choice is dependent on the students' observed needs, opportunities afforded by the book, and school district and provincial requirements. Sometimes teachers plan minilessons to directly teach skills and strategies,

For more information on language arts strategies, see Chapter 1, "Learning and the Language Arts," pages 34–40. Also, see the lists of minilesson topics in Chapters 3 to 11.

and at other times they plan to model how to use the skills and strategies as they read aloud, or to ask students to share how they use the skills and strategies during grand conversations.

Step 4: Locate Multimedia Materials and Internet Websites Related to the Unit. Teachers locate multimedia materials to use in the unit. Multimedia materials include film, CD-ROMs, and video versions of stories to view and compare with the book version; audio tapes of stories to use at listening centres; storyboards made from paperback versions of the story to sequence; and author information and interviews on video, audio tape, and the Internet. Teachers also plan how they will use computers for unit activities, especially writing and researching activities. Frequently, preparation includes book-marking relevant websites for teacher and student use. Teachers may also plan for use of other equipment such as cameras and recorders needed for unit projects.

Step 5: Incorporate Activities Representing All Six Language Arts. Teachers review the plans they are developing to make sure that students have opportunities to engage in listening, speaking, reading, writing, viewing, and visually representing activities during the unit. Of course, not all six language arts fit into every unit, but for most units they do. Figure 11–5 on page 448 lists many of the activities discussed in this book, according to the language art they illustrate.

For more information on the six language arts, see Chapter 1, "Learning and the Language Arts," pages 26–29.

Step 6: Coordinate Grouping Patterns with Activities. Teachers think about how to incorporate whole-class, small-group, buddy, and individual activities into their unit plans. It is important that students have opportunities to read and write independently as well as to work with small groups and to come together as a class. If the piece of literature that students are reading will be read together as a class, then students need opportunities to reread it with a buddy or independently, or to read related books independently. These grouping patterns should be alternated during various activities in the unit. Teachers often go back to their planning sheet and highlight activities with coloured markers according to grouping patterns.

Step 7: Create a Time Schedule. Teachers create a time schedule that allows students sufficient time to move through the five stages of the reading process and to complete the activities planned for the unit. Resource-based reading programs require large blocks of time, at least two hours in length, in which students read, listen, talk, and write about the literature they are reading.

Using this block of time, teachers complete weekly lesson plans, and the activities they include represent each of the five stages of the reading process. The stages are not clearly separated and they overlap, but preparing, reading, responding, exploring, and extending activities are included in the lesson plan.

Step 8: Plan for the Assessment of the Resource-Based Unit. Teachers collect information about students' processes in language learning as well as the products of their learning. The information they collect helps them design instruction. Students, too, participate in assessment of their own learning by reflecting on their processes and products. To help make assessment a manageable, consistent, and effective process, teachers often begin a unit by distributing unit folders. Students keep all work, reading logs, reading materials, and related materials in the folder. Periodically during the unit and again at the end, students turn in their completed folders for teachers to evaluate. Keeping all the materials together makes the unit easier for both students and teachers to manage and provides a picture of progress and achievements.

For more information on assessing students' learning in the language arts, see Chapter 2, "Teaching the Language Arts," pages 68–83.

Teachers also plan specific ways to document students' learning and assign grades. One form of record keeping is an assignment checklist. This sheet is developed with students and distributed at the beginning of the resource-based unit. Students keep track of their work during the unit and sometimes negotiate to change the sheet as the unit evolves. Students keep the lists in unit folders, and they mark off each item as it is completed. At the end of the unit, students turn in their completed assignment checklist and other completed work. An assignment

Listening
Listen to books at listening centres
Listen to teacher read aloud
Listen to classmates' comments during conversations about literature
Listen to choral readings and readers theatre performances
Listen to classmates retell stories
Listen to classmates read their books from the author's chair
Listen to oral reports and debates

Speaking
Participate in conversations about literature
Retell and tell stories
Do book talks
Present oral reports
Interview community members
Participate in debates
Talk with classmates about their rough drafts
Share projects and writings

Reading
Read stories, essays, informational books, and poems
Read books independently
Read books with a buddy
Participate in readers theatre and choral reading activities
Read words on the word wall
Proofread drafts of own and others' writing
Read books from the author's chair
Reread favourite stories or other text selections
Participate in a read-around
Read Internet-based websites

Writing
Write entries in reading logs and other journals
Do quickwrites
Write friendly letters, business letters, and letters to authors
Write stories, retellings of familiar stories, and innovations
Write scripts for readers theatre or other dramatic productions
Write "All about . . ." books, reports, and other books
Write poems
Write words and sentences on word walls, charts, and story quilts
Word-process lists, webs, stories, and reports

Viewing
View illustrated oral reports by peers or guest speakers
Sequence storyboards
Watch classmates dramatize and retell stories
Compare book and video versions of stories
View films, videos, CD-ROMs, or websites to collect background information related to unit topics
View films, CD-ROMs, videos, or websites about authors and illustrators
View posters and other projects classmates create

Visually Representing
Make diagrams about elements of story structure
Make puppets of story characters and present puppet shows, dramatizations, and role-plays of stories
Create posters, Venn diagrams, collages, graphs, and other charts
Make clusters during prewriting
Draw open-mind portraits
Create a diorama depicting an aspect from the story
Use clay or Plasticine to sculpt part of a story
Use clip art and available pictures to illustrate poems, stories, and other writing

Figure 11–5 Activities Illustrating the Six Language Arts

checklist for an upper-grade resource-based unit on the book *Dust* by Arthur Slade (2001), a fantasy set in rural Saskatchewan during the Great Depression of the 1930s, is presented in Figure 11–6. While this list does not include every activity students were involved in, it does list the activities and other assignments that the teacher holds students accountable for. Teachers also create and distribute rubrics showing the criteria on which assignments will be graded. Rubrics are also kept in the unit folders. For primary grades, the rubrics are simple and include few criteria easily understood by the children. In upper grades, the rubrics are more detailed. Students in upper grades often contribute to compilation of the rubrics. The checklist shown in Figure 11-6 includes a point system as a way of assigning value. Students complete the checklist on the left side of the sheet and add titles of books and other requested

---

Dust

Name _____

Student's Check		Teacher's Check

_____ 1. Read *Dust*.   _____

_____ 2. Write at least 10 entries in your reading log. Use a double-entry format with quotes and your connections. (20)   _____

_____ 3. Participate in small-group grand conversations.   _____

_____ 4. Create a story board. Chapter # _____ (10)   _____

_____ 5. Make an open-mind portrait of Robert with four mind pages. (10)   _____

_____ 6. Write an essay about the theme of the book. (10)   _____

_____ 7. Choose and analyze 10 words from the word wall according to prefix, root word, and suffix. (10)   _____

_____ 8. Read one book from the text set. Write a brief summary in your reading log and compare what you learned about fantasy with *Dust*. (10)

   Title _____
   Author _____   _____

_____ 9. Engage in a grand conversation about the book. (5)   _____

_____ 10. Create a project and share it with the class. (25)   _____

   Project _____
   Date shared _____

Total   _____

Figure 11–6 An Assignment Checklist for an Upper-Grade Resource-Based Unit on *Dust*

---

information. Teachers award points (up to the number listed in parentheses) on the lines on the right side of the sheet, and total the number of points on the bottom of the page. The points can be correlated with the criteria on the rubric. Then the total score can be translated into a letter grade or other type of grade.

Some teachers engage in an informal ninth step. When their unit plans are complete, they carefully rethink what they are expecting of students and how they will assist students in achieving those goals. They try to identify the aspects of the unit that are its strengths and those that are sources of possible difficulties. By taking time to identify these features in advance, they are better prepared to make decisions as the unit proceeds and the students engage in the planned activities.

A PRIMARY-GRADE RESOURCE-BASED UNIT ON THE MITTEN

Jan Brett's *The Mitten* (1989), a cumulative picture book story about a series of animals who climb into a mitten that a little boy has dropped in the snow on a cold winter day, is the featured selection in resource-based units taught in many primary-grade classrooms. A planning cluster for a resource-based unit on *The Mitten* is shown in Figure 11–7 on page 520. Teachers use the big book version of *The Mitten* to introduce the unit and to examine Brett's innovative use of borders. Students use the teacher's collection of stuffed animals and puppets representing the animals in

Word Wall

Nicki	grandmother
Baba	mitten
glove	mole
cozy	tunnelling along
snowshoe rabbit	big kickers
hedgehog	prickles
owl	commotion
swooped down	glinty talons
badger	diggers
fox	trotted
drowsy	muzzle
bear	lumbered by
swelled	stretched
meadow mouse	acorn
wriggled	bear's nose
whiskers	enormous sneeze
yarn	knitted
wool	sheep
Ukraine	borders

Word-Study Activities

- Word posters
- Word sorts
- Individual word cards
- Semantic feature analysis to compare animals

Maps and Globes

- Locate the Ukraine setting for this book on a map or globe.

Phonemic Awareness and Phonics

- Collect rhyming objects and pictures related to the story for students to match (e.g., mitten–kitten, fox–box, bear–hair–pear–chair, mouse–house).
- Have students "stretch" these words from the story: *mole, snow, owl, mouse, cozy, nose.*
- Focus on a consonant sound: /m/ for *mitten*, /y/ for *yarn*, or /n/ for *Nicki.*
- Teach the *r*-controlled vowel sound using *yarn.*
- Focus on a vowel sound: short *i* for *mitten*, long *o* for *snow.*

Illustration Techniques

- Examine Brett's use of borders in many of her books, and encourage students to create borders in the books they write.
- Also, note the side mitten panels with looking back and looking forward scenes on each page of *The Mitten.*

Compare Versions of the Story

Read these versions and make a chart to compare them with Brett's version:

Koopmans, L. (1990). *The Woodcutter's Mitten.* New York: Crocodile Books.

Tresselt, A. (1964). *The Mitten.* New York: Lothrop, Lee & Shepard.

Big Book

Introduce the story using the big book version of the book (published by Scholastic) and shared reading.

The Mitten

Research

- Research one of the animals— mole, rabbit, hedgehog, owl, badger, fox, bear, mouse— mentioned in the story and create a class book about the animal.
- Research sheep, wool, and yarn using these books:

Fowler, A. (1993). *Woolly Sheep and Hungry Goats.* Chicago: Childrens Press.

Mitgutsch, A. (1975). *From Sheep to Scarf.* Minneapolis: Carolrhoda.

Sequencing Activities

- Sequence events using story boards cut from two copies of the book, backed with cardboard and laminated.
- Dramatize the story with puppets or stuffed animals.
- Create a circle diagram of the story. Have students draw pictures of each event and post them in a circle, beginning and ending with the grandmother.

Other Books by Jan Brett

(1985). *Annie and the Wild Animals.* Boston: Houghton Mifflin.

(1987). *Goldilocks and the Three Bears.* New York: Putnam.

(1991). *Berlioz the Bear.* New York: Putnam.

(1991). *The Owl and the Pussycat.* New York: Putnam.

(1992). *Trouble With Trolls.* New York: Putnam.

(1994). *Town Mouse, Country Mouse.* New York: Putnam.

(1995). *Armadillo Rodeo.* New York: Putnam.

Writing Activities

- Write a reading log entry.
- Write a class collaboration retelling of the story.
- Create a found poem using words and phrases from the book.
- Write letters to the author.
- Create a story quilt with a mitten design on each square and a sentence about the book.

Other Activities

- Compare mittens and gloves.
- Examine types of yarn.
- Have a parent demonstrate how to knit a mitten.
- Experiment with stretching a mitten.

Figure 11–7 A Planning Cluster for a Primary-Grade Resource-Based Unit on *The Mitten*

the story—a mole, a rabbit, a hedgehog, an owl, a badger, a fox, a bear, and a mouse—as they retell the story. Students read the story several times—in small groups with the teacher, with partners, and independently. The teacher also reads aloud several other versions of the story, including *The Woodcutter's Mitten* (Koopmans, 1990) and *The Mitten* (Tresselt, 1964), and students make a chart to compare the versions. The teacher presents minilessons on phonemic awareness and phonics skills, creates a word wall, and involves students in word-study activities. Students participate in sequencing and writing activities, and learn about knitting from a parent volunteer. The teacher also sets out other books by Jan Brett and reads some of the books aloud to students. As their extension project, students divide into small groups to research one of the animals mentioned in the story. Grade 5 students work with the primary-grade students as they research the animals and share what they learn on large posters.

A MIDDLE-GRADE RESOURCE-BASED UNIT ON KIT PEARSON AND HER BOOKS

Students begin the unit by reading *Awake and Dreaming* (Pearson, 1996) together as a class. This Governor General's Award–winning book tells the story of a young girl named Theo, who lives with her too-young mother and leads a desperate life on and off the streets of Vancouver. After students read this book together, they read other books by Kit Pearson in small groups and independently. Teachers focus on strategies and skills, teaching both by modelling and through planned minilessons. Students keep reading logs in which they write after reading each of the books. They participate in a variety of visually representing activities, including making open-mind portraits of favourite characters, and learn about story structure. Many of Pearson's stories focus on theme, and students have opportunities to think deeply about the meanings of the stories. Students learn about Kit Pearson and they may choose to write letters to the author as a project. Students create a graph to determine their favourite book written by Kit Pearson and pursue group and individual projects. A planning cluster for this unit is presented in Figure 11–8 on page 452.

For more information on resource-based units, see Chapter 4, "The Reading and Writing Processes," pages 133–136 and 140–143. Also, see Chapter 6, "Reading and Writing Narrative Text," pages 242–247 and 272.

AN UPPER-GRADE RESOURCE-BASED UNIT ON *THE GIVER*

Upper-grade students spend three or four weeks reading, responding to, exploring, and extending their understanding of Lois Lowry's Newbery Medal book *The Giver* (1993). Lowry creates a "perfect" community in which the people are secure but regulated. Jonas, the main character, is chosen to be a leader in the community, but he rebels against the society and escapes. To introduce this book, teachers might connect the book to the 1982 Constitution Act and the Canadian Charter of Rights and Freedoms, or to Gary Ross's 1998 film *Pleasantville* (for older students), or discuss the problems in Canadian society today and ask students to devise a "perfect" society. Or, students might think about how their lives would be different in a world without colours, like Jonas's.

Students can read the story together as a class, in small groups with the teacher, or in literature study groups, with buddies or independently. Students come together to discuss the story in grand conversations and deal with the complex issues presented in the book in both small groups and whole-class discussions. They also write in reading journals. Teachers identify skills and strategies to model during reading and to teach in minilessons. Students write important words from the story on the word wall and engage in a variety of word-study activities. Students also learn about the author and examine the story structure in the book. After reading, they can do a choral reading, create a poster of the "perfect" society, compare Canadian society with the society described in the book, and create other projects. Figure 11–9 shows a planning cluster for *The Giver*. Only words from the first three chapters are listed in the cluster due to space limitations.

Author Study

Learn about Canadian author Kit Pearson at the Canadian Children's Book Centre website: **www.bookcentre.ca.**

Types of Reading

- Read books together as a class.
- Read books in small literature study groups.
- Read books with a partner.
- Read books individually.
- Listen to books read aloud at the listening centre.

Visually Representing Activities

- Create a graph with photocopies of the book covers of each of Pearson's books at the top of each column. Have students choose their favourite books and colour in a square in that column.
- Make a diorama using a shoebox to create a scene from one of Kit Pearson's books.
- Have students make open-mind portraits to examine characters from the books they are reading.

Strategies and Skills

- Focus on connecting to personal experiences, generalizing themes, and monitoring own reading strategies.
- Encourage students to use meaning-making skills such as summarizing, inferring, noting details, and predicting.

Talk and Drama

- Have students dress up as one of the characters from a book written by Kit Pearson and be interviewed by the class.
- Write an "I Am" poem from the viewpoint of one character and read it aloud to the class.
- Have a small group of students dramatize a scene from one of her books and tell why that scene was chosen.

Reading Logs

- Have students keep a double-entry journal by copying one or two quotes from a book and their connections or reactions to the quote.
- Have students write several journal entries as if they were one of the characters in a Kit Pearson book.
- Students can create a web of the characters encountered in a book, using lines to show how they are related to one another.

Story Structure

- Focus on the theme of the book. Ask students to identify the theme— friendship, family, fear— and then have them expand on the concept.
- Ask students to reflect on reasons Kit Pearson uses a backdrop of WW II for many of her books.

Kit Pearson and Her Books

Books by Kit Pearson

(1986). *The Daring Game*. Toronto: Viking Kestrel.
(1987). *A Handful of Time*. Toronto: Viking Kestrel.
(1989). *The Sky Is Falling*. Toronto: Penguin.
(1990). *The Singing Basket*. Toronto: Groundwood.
(1991). *Looking at the Moon*. Toronto: Viking.
(1993). *The Lights Go On Again*. Toronto: Viking.
(1996). *Awake and Dreaming*. Toronto: Viking.
(1998). *Sea to Sea: An Anthology of Canadian Stories*. New York: Viking.
(1999). *This Land: A Cross-Country Anthology of Canadian Fiction for Young Readers*. Toronto: Penguin.
(2003). *The Guests of War Trilogy*. Toronto: Penguin Publishers.

Word Wall

Awake and Dreaming

family	homeless
nightmare	irresponsible
mysterious	security
poverty	mother
fragile	responsibility
magical	hope
schools	yearning
the Kaldors	Sharon
hungry	Theo
streets	dancing
grim	Vancouver
custody	routine
safe	dream

Governor General's Award Ruth Schwartz Children's Book Award

Projects

- Have students work together as a class to select a social action or community project to participate in, such as volunteering at a soup kitchen, after reading *Awake and Dreaming* by Kit Pearson.
- Have students design their own individual projects about favourite books.
- Also, find information about this author in the book *Writing Stories, Making Pictures: Biographies of 150 Canadian Children's Authors and Illustrators* published by the Canadian Children's Book Centre.
- Have students make a poster with information about the author to display in the library centre next to the text set of books.

Figure 11–8 A Planning Cluster for a Middle-Grade Resource-Based Unit on Kit Pearson and Her Books

Introducing the Book

- Read the book when studying ancient civilizations and focus on the traits of a civilization.
- Discuss the problems in Canadian society, and ask students to create a "perfect" society.
- Create a world with no colours.
- Share objects from a book box including an apple, a bicycle, a sled, the number 19, a stuffed bear "comfort object," and a kaleidoscope of colours.

Story Structure Activities

- Create a set of story boards, one for each chapter, with a picture representing the chapter and a summarizing paragraph.
- Analyze the theme of the book.
- Create a plot diagram to graph the highs and lows of the book.
- Make an open-mind portrait with several "mind" pages to track Jonas's thinking through the book.
- Draw a setting map with the locations mentioned in the books.

Word Wall

Chapter 1	Chapter 2
Jonas	Gabriel
bicycle	broken rules
citizens	Elders
loudspeakers	The Receiver
obediently	assignment
Lily	volunteer hours
frightened	Hall of Records
released	recreation hours
punishment	comfort object
Asher	stuffed elephant
community	bear
palpable	
public apology	Chapter 3
rumpled tunic	pale eyes
apprehensive	birthmother
ritual	hippo
Nurturer	Labourers
gender	humiliation
family unit	hoarded
Ceremony of Twelve	bewilderment
	apple

Strategies and Skills

- Model monitoring and revising meaning strategies. Ask students to reflect on their use of strategies when reading.
- Focus on decoding longer words by peeling off affixes and breaking words into syllables. Some words from the first two chapters to use: *obediently, inconveniencing, distraught, apprehensive, sympathetically, bewilderment.*

Grand Conversations

Hold grand conversations after reading two, three, or four chapters. Begin grand conversations in small groups and then come together for a whole-class discussion.

Choral Reading

To celebrate colours, have students prepare and present choral readings of colour poems in Mary O'Neill's *Hailstones and Halibut Bones* (1989), published by Doubleday.

The Giver

Author Information

- Collect information about Lois Lowry, including "Newbery Acceptance" by Lois Lowry, published in the July/August 1994 issue of *Horn Book* (pp. 414–422).
- Write letters to the author.

Comparing Societies

Students read a book about Canadian society and compare it to the "perfect" society in *The giver.*

Downie, D. & Robertson, B. (eds.). (1987). *New Wind Has Wings: Poems from Canada.* New York: Oxford.

Elwin, R., & Paulse, M. (1990). *Asha's Mums.* Toronto: Women's Press.

Greenwood, B. (1994). *A Pioneer Story: The Daily Life of a Canadian Family in 1840.* Toronto: Kids Can Press.

Harrison, T. (1992). *O Canada.* Toronto: Kids Can Press.

Kenna, K. (1995). *A People Apart.* Toronto: Somerville House Publishing.

Littlechild, G. (1993). *This Land is My Land.* Emeryville, CA: Children's Book Press.

Pearson, K. (1999). *This Land: A Cross-Country Anthology of Canadian Fiction for Young Readers.* Toronto: Penguin.

Word-Study Activities

- Create word clusters.
- Sort a set of words.
- Play the duck game with a secret word of the day.
- Collect powerful sentences and write them on posters.

Reading Log

- Keep a simulated journal, written from Jonas's viewpoint after reading each chapter.
- Write a double-entry journal with quotes from the story in one column and personal connections or predictions in the other column.

Writing Projects

- Write a sequel.
- Write found poems, "I Am" poems, or other poems.
- Write an essay comparing Jonas's society with ours.
- Write a reaction to this quote: "The greatest freedom is the freedom of choice."

Figure 11–9 A Planning Cluster for an Upper-Grade Resource-Based Unit on *The Giver*

Thematic Units and Inquiry-Based Units

Thematic units and inquiry-based units are interdisciplinary units that integrate reading and writing with social studies, science, math, and other curricular areas (Altwerger & Flores, 1994; Gamberg, et al. 1988; Kucer, Silva, & Delgado-Larocco, 1995). Sometimes they primarily focus on one curricular area and at other times they extend across most or all subject areas. Topics for these extended thematic units are broad and encompass many possible directions for exploration, such as what it means to be Canadian, our changing environment, or people who have changed the lives of others.

For more information on thematic units, see Chapter 4, "The Reading and Writing Processes," pages 143–144 and 161. Also see Chapter 6, "Reading and Writing Narrative Text," pages 233 and 245–247.

Teachers usually involve students in planning the thematic units or inquiry-based units and identifying some of the questions they want to explore and activities that interest them. By being involved, student interest in and commitment to unit activities is heightened. In contrast to situations where students are asked to read chapters in content-area textbooks in order to answer the questions at the end of the chapter, or to read a particular selection from an anthology prepared for their grade, thematic unit activities engage students in authentic and meaningful learning activities. Textbooks might be used as a resource, but only as one of many available resources. Students explore topics that interest them and research answers to questions they have posed and are genuinely interested in answering. Students share their learning during and at the end of the unit and are assessed on what they have learned as well as the processes they used in learning and working together.

HOW TO DEVELOP A THEMATIC UNIT OR AN INQUIRY-BASED UNIT

The starting point for many Canadian teachers in planning a thematic or an inquiry-based unit, is the required curriculum for their province or program. When selecting topics, teachers consider the language arts requirements together with the requirements in other areas such as science, social studies, and the fine arts. They combine this information with their students' interests and the resources they have or can make available. Thematic and inquiry-based units provide the framework for integrated instruction, but make it possible for students to engage in diverse activities and achieve similar, but not identical outcomes. Teachers usually choose the general topic and then identify three or four key concepts that they want to develop through the unit. Other times, teachers help students ask their own questions to research and study. The goal of these units is not to teach a collection of facts, but to help students grapple with several big understandings (Tunnell & Ammon, 1993). For that reason, teachers choose themes that are broad general concepts and allow for multiple interpretations. Ten important considerations in developing a thematic or inquiry-based unit are as follows:

1. *Collect a set of stories, informational books, and poems.* Teachers collect stories, poems, informational books, magazines, newspaper articles, and reference books related to the theme or topic of study. The resources are placed in the special area for materials related to the theme in the classroom library. Teachers read aloud some books to students, some will be read independently, and others students will read together as shared or guided reading. These materials can also be used for minilessons—to teach students, for example, about reading strategies and expository text structures. Other books can be used as models or patterns for writing projects. Teachers also write the poems on charts to share with students or arrange a bulletin board display of the poems.

2. *Set up a listening centre.* Teachers select audio tapes or CDs to accompany stories or informational books. They can also create their own audio tapes so that absent students can catch up on a book being read aloud day by day, or to provide additional reading experiences for students who listen to an audio tape when they read or reread a story or informational book.

3. *Coordinate content-area textbook readings.* Teachers can teach thematic units or inquiry-based units without textbooks; however, when information is available in a literature or content-area textbook, it can be used. Upper-grade students, in particular, read and discuss concepts presented in textbooks or use them as a reference for further study.

4. *Locate multimedia materials.* Teachers plan the films, videos, CD-ROMs, websites, charts, timelines, maps, models, posters, and other multimedia materials to be used in the thematic unit. Students view films, videos, and book-marked websites to provide background knowledge about the theme, and other multimedia materials are used in teaching the key concepts. Multimedia materials can be viewed or displayed in the classroom, and students can make others during the thematic unit.

5. *Identify potential words for the word wall.* Teachers preview books and identify potential words for the word wall. This list of potential words is useful in planning vocabulary activities, but teachers do not simply use their word lists for the classroom word wall. Students and the teacher develop the classroom word wall together as they read and discuss the key concepts and other information related to the theme.

6. *Plan how students will use learning logs.* Teachers plan for students to keep learning logs in which students take notes, write questions, make observations, clarify their thinking, and write reactions to what they are learning during thematic units and inquiry-based units (Tompkins, 1994). They also write quickwrites and make clusters to explore what they are learning.

7. *Identify literacy skills and strategies to teach during the theme.* Teachers plan minilessons to teach literacy skills and strategies from curriculum documents, such as expository text structures, how to use an index, skimming and scanning, how to write an alphabet book, and interviewing techniques. Minilessons are taught using a whole–part–whole approach so that students can apply what they are learning in reading and writing activities.

8. *Plan talk and visually representing activities related to the theme.* Students use talk and visually representing to learn during the thematic unit or the inquiry-based unit and to demonstrate their learning (Erickson, 1988; Nelson, 1988; San Jose, 1988). Possible talk and visually representing activities are as follows:

   - Give oral, illustrated reports.
   - Interview someone with special expertise on the theme.
   - Participate in a debate related to the theme.
   - Create charts and diagrams to display information.
   - Role-play a historical event.
   - Assume the role of a historical figure.
   - Participate in a readers theatre presentation of a story or poem.
   - Tell or retell a story, biography, or event.
   - Use a puppet show to tell a story, biography, or event.
   - Write and perform a skit or play.

9. *Brainstorm possible projects students may create to extend their learning.* Teachers think about possible projects students may choose to develop to extend and personalize their learning during these units. This advance planning makes it possible for teachers to collect needed supplies and to have suggestions ready to offer to students who need assistance in choosing a project. Students work on projects independently or in small groups and then share the projects with the class at the end of the theme. Projects involve one or more of the six language arts. Some project suggestions are as follows:

   For more information on extending projects, see Chapter 4, "The Reading and Writing Processes," pages 140–144.

   - Read a biography related to the unit.
   - Create a poster to illustrate a key concept.
   - Write and mail a letter to get information related to the theme.
   - Write a story related to the theme.
   - Perform a readers theatre production, puppet show, or other dramatization.
   - Write a poem, song, or rap related to the theme.

- Write an "All about . . . " book or report about one of the key concepts.
- Create a commercial or advertisement related to the theme.
- Create a tabletop display or diorama about the theme.
- Create a web showing what questions the students want to research.

10. ***Plan for the assessment of the unit.*** Teachers consider how they will assess students' learning as they make plans for activities and assignments. In this way, teachers can explain to students how they will be assessed at the beginning of the unit, and check that their assessment will emphasize students' learning of the key concepts and important ideas. An assignment checklist for a thematic unit about money for primary-grade students is shown in Figure 11–10.

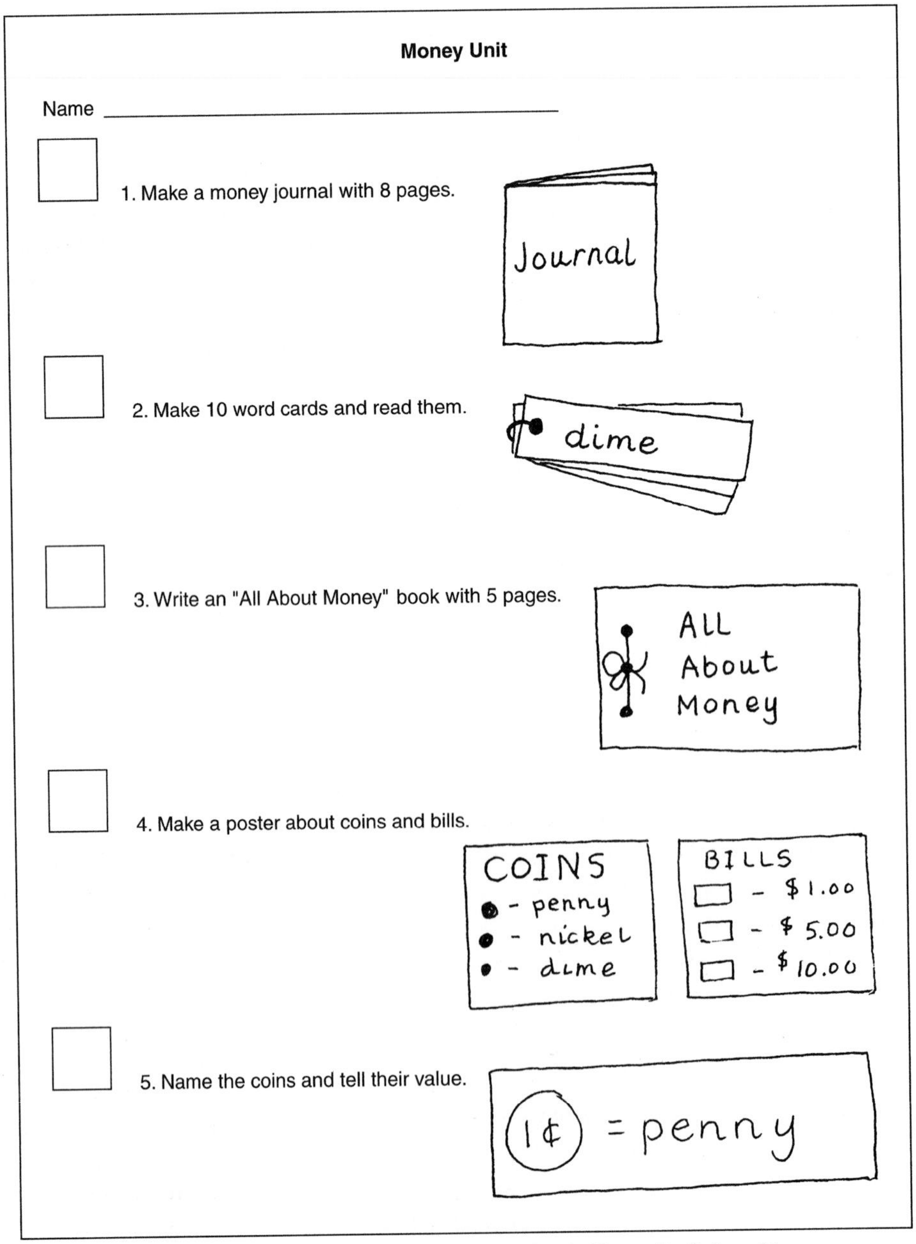

Money Unit

Name ______________________________

☐ 1. Make a money journal with 8 pages.

☐ 2. Make 10 word cards and read them.

☐ 3. Write an "All About Money" book with 5 pages.

☐ 4. Make a poster about coins and bills.

☐ 5. Name the coins and tell their value.

Figure 11–10 An Assignment Checklist for a Primary-Grade Thematic Unit on Money

Teachers consider the resources they have available, brainstorm possible activities, and then develop clusters to guide their planning. The goal in developing plans for a thematic unit or an inquiry-based unit is to consider a wide variety of resources that integrate listening, speaking, reading, writing, viewing, and visually representing with the content of the theme (Pappas, Kiefer, & Levstik, 1995).

A PRIMARY-GRADE THEMATIC UNIT ON MONEY

Teachers connect math, social studies, and the language arts in a thematic unit on money. Students read stories such as *Pigs Will Be Pigs* (Axelrod, 1994) and informational books including *The Story of Money* (Maestro, 1993) and *If You Made a Million* (Schwartz, 1989) as part of the unit. They learn to read money-related words, write in journals, make posters and charts about money, and write money story problems. Students investigate how people use money through field trips and literacy centres, examine money from other countries, and learn how early peoples bartered for goods and services, and used shells and beads for money. A planning cluster for a primary-grade thematic unit on money is presented in Figure 11–11 on page 458.

A MIDDLE-GRADE THEMATIC UNIT, "LITTLE THINGS GO TOGETHER TO MAKE LARGER ONES"

Middle-grade students enjoy the flexibility of integrated thematic units. Dynamic themes such as this one allow students and teachers to extend learning in directions of interest as the unit progresses. The unit begins with shared reading of *The Canada Geese Quilt* (Kinsey-Warnock, 1989). Quilt and puzzle motifs are employed to help students understand how each small piece of a whole is valued, significant, and necessary to create a meaningful whole. The primary language concepts and skills introduced and developed include components of stories, the components and processes of collaborative report writing, and the construction of picture books. While pursuing these major goals of the unit, teacher and students read a variety of literature and engage in activities in many curriculum areas to explore the theme from several perspectives. In one grade 5 class, the teacher heightened interest in the unit by adding the unit title to the quilt-bordered bulletin board word by word, day by day, during the week before she introduced *The Canada Geese Quilt*. Later in the unit, she involved the students in small group mathematical problem-solving that earned the winning teams pieces of a large floor puzzle showing a map of the world. Thematic units offer opportunities for meeting students' different needs and interests while at the same time they pursue common goals. A planning cluster for the middle-grade thematic unit, "Little Things Go Together to Make Larger Ones" is presented in Figure 11–12 on page 459.

AN UPPER-GRADE INQUIRY-BASED UNIT ON THE INDUSTRIAL REVOLUTION

As they study the Industrial Revolution, students learn social studies and science concepts and use the language arts as tools for learning. Teachers often use a K-W-L-S chart to begin the unit, allowing students to generate their own questions about a particular topic or issue. Students read stories set during the Industrial Revolution and read informational books and biographies to learn more about the historical period. Sometimes students form literature study groups to read *Lyddie* (Paterson, 1991) or another story set in this period. Students keep learning logs and post important words on the word wall. They research inventors and inventions of the period, and share what they learn in oral and written reports. Students participate in a variety of talk activities, including reports, debates, and dramatizations. They develop individual and class projects and share their individual projects with classmates at the end of the theme. Students often create a variety of visually representing activities, including timelines, posters, clusters, and Venn diagrams. They also make cubes to explore six dimensions of the Industrial Revolution; they describe, compare, analyze, associate, apply, and argue for or against industrialization. Figure 11–13 on page 460 presents a planning cluster for an upper-grade inquiry-based unit on the Industrial Revolution.

Stories

Axelrod, A. (1994). *Pigs Will Be Pigs.* New York: Four Winds Press.

Baylor, B. (1994). *The Table Where the Rich People Sit.* New York: Scribners.

Kimmel, E. (1990). *Four Dollars and Fifty Cents.* New York: Holiday House.

McPhail, D. (1990). *Pig Pig Gets a Job.* New York: Dutton.

Precek, K. W. (1989). *Penny in the Road.* New York: Macmillan.

Smith, M. (1994). *Argo, You Lucky Dog.* New York: Lothrop, Lee & Shepard.

Informational Books

Kain, C. (1993). *The Story of Money.* New York: Troll.

Leedy, L. (1992). *The Monster Money Book.* New York: Holiday.

Maestro, B. (1993). *The Story of Money.* New York: Clarion.

Schwartz, D. M. (1989). *If You Made a Million.* New York: Lothrop, Lee & Shepard.

Money Journal

- Have students keep a money journal in which they paste pictures of the coins and bills and write information about money.
- Write story problems about money. Students can use newspaper ads and coupons.

Literacy Centres

- Create a restaurant centre with menus, pads for taking orders, and a cash register.
- Set up a store (grocery store, toy store, shoe store, etc.) centre with objects with prices for students to "buy," play money, and a cash register.
- Create a bank centre so students can practise writing cheques and depositing and withdrawing money.

Visually Representing

- Make posters about each of the common Canadian coins and bills, and include information about the images on the front and back of each one.
- Create a display with examples of money from countries around the world.
- Make charts showing different coins that total 10¢, 25¢, 50¢, $1, $5, and $10.

Field Trips and Interviews

- Tour a bank and interview a teller to learn about that job.
- Take a walking field trip around the community and take photos of people using money.

Money

Writing Projects

- Write a class collaboration book about money, and have each child contribute one page to the book.
- Have children write individual books about things they would like to buy and how much the things cost.
- Have children write individual books about an amount of money, such as $1.00, and on each page draw a combination of coins and/or bills to equal that amount of money.
- Have students write riddles about money. The riddles can be compiled into a book. For example, "What is worth four quarters and has a picture of a loon on it? A $1.00 coin."

Timeline

- Create a timeline to document the history of money, beginning with bartering, the use of coins, introduction of paper money, Indian wampum, and money and credit cards used today.

Skills and Strategies

- Teach students how to write dollar ($) and cents (¢) symbols.
- Connect names of coins with their values (e.g., a dime is 10¢).

Word Wall

money	coins
bills	round and metal
paper money	penny
5 dollar bill	nickel
10 dollar bill	dime
20 dollar bill	quarter
50 dollar bill	half-dollar
100 dollar bill	trading
$ = dollar	barter
¢ = cents	salt
silver	shells
gold	blankets
Canadian mint	wampum
baht	bucks
pesos	serial numbers
pounds	landmarks
credit cards	rupee
banks	yen
money orders	francs
automated teller	cheques
machines	debit cards
loonie	bankrupt
toonie	

Figure 11–11 A Planning Cluster for a Primary-Grade Thematic Unit on Money

Word Wall

Canada geese	puzzle
migration	illustrator
population	author
immigrant	collage
emigrant	rhythm
children's rights	orchestra
increase	brass
decrease	woodwind
rights	strings
quilt block	royalty
binding	kingdom
pattern	generosity
tangram	collaborate
peace	assemble
piece	cooperate
border	ancestors
repeat	

Listening Activities

- Listen to audio version of *Peter and the Wolf.*
- Listen to audio version of *If You Could Wear My Sneakers*

Skills and Strategies

- Journal writing to extend learning
- Steps in picture book construction
- Connect literature to personal experiences
- Collaborative report writing organization
- Record information accurately from more than one source

Informational Books

Fitch, S. (1997). *If You Could Wear My Sneakers.* Toronto: Doubleday.

Johnston, T. (1985). *The Quilt Story.* New York: Putnam.

Jonas, A. (1984). *The Quilt.* New York: Greenwillow Books.

Martin, R. (2000). *The Twelve Months.* Don Mills, ON: Stoddart Kids.

Smith, D. J. (2002). *If the World Were a Village.* Toronto: Kids Can Press.

McGovern, A. (1968). *Stone Soup.* New York: Scholastic Inc.

Cross-Curricular Connections

- Math
  patterns and tangrams
  addition problem solving
- Physical Education
  cooperative and team games
- Art
  mixed media
  collage
- Music
  orchestra instruments and composition
- Social Studies
  mapping

Possible Interpretations of Theme

- Puzzles
- Quilts
- Children of the world
- Months of the year
- Countries of the world
- Collaborative report writing
- Construction of picture books

Little Things Go Together to Make Larger Ones

Stories

Bateson-Hill, M. (2001). *Shota and the Star Quilt.* Chicago: Zero to Ten Ltd.

Bourgeois, P.(2001). *Oma's Quilt.* Toronto, ON: Kids Can Press.

Brumbeau, J. (2004). *The Quiltmaker's Journey.* New York: Orchard Books.

Brumbeau, J.(2000). *The Quiltmaker's Gift.* New York: Orchard Books.

Coerr, E. (1986). *The Josefina Story Quilt.* New York: Harper & Row.

Kinsey-Warnock, N. (1989). *The Canada Geese Quilt.* New York: Cobblehill Books/Dutton

Lemieux, M. (1991). *Peter and the wolf.* Toronto: Kids Can Press.

Martin, R. (2000). *The Twelve Months.* Don Mills, ON: Stoddart Kids.

Talk Activities

- Discuss stories read in small groups.
- Have students tell the story their quilt block depicts.

Writing Projects

- Write learning journals to connect thematic learning across subject areas.
- Create picture books in small groups to emphasize cooperation.
- Write "If I were ..." or "If the world were ..." poems.

Visually Representing

- Make story quilts to retell literature read.
- Illustrate calendars to show months of the year.
- Create maps with family pictures showing countries of ancestors.

Extension Activities

- Write and publish a school or class newspaper.
- Make the title recipe after reading *Stone Soup* (McGovern, 1968).
- Read detective stories, adding clues to solve mysteries.

Figure 11–12 A Planning Cluster for a Middle-Grade Thematic Unit: "Little Things Go Together to Make Larger Ones"

Talk

- Have students give brief oral reports in which they describe an invention and explain how it benefitted people.
- Have students present brief talks based on compare–contrast, cause–effect, or problem–solution essays they have written.
- Have students dramatize scenes from the Industrial Revolution, including working conditions in factories, life in tenements, and the vast wealth of industrialists.
- Have students debate issues related to the Industrial Revolution, including whether the industrialization of North America was actually a "revolution" or whether industrialization has ultimately been more beneficial or harmful.

K-W-L Chart

Have students brainstorm what they already know about the Industrial Revolution at the beginning of the thematic unit and add questions to the middle column during the theme. At the end, finish the "L: What We Learned" section.

Stories

Collier, J. L. (1989). *The Winchesters.* New York: Avon.
McCully, E. A. (1996). *The Bobbin Girl.* New York: Dial.
Paterson, L. (1991). *Lyddie.* New York: Lodestar Books.
Skurzynshi, G. (1992). *Good-bye, Billy Radish.* New York: Bradbury Press.

Literature Study Groups

In small groups, students read and respond to *Lyddie* (Paterson, 1991) or another story set during the Industrial Revolution.

Industrial Revolution

Learning Logs

Have students take notes, write quickwrites, draw diagrams, and list important events on timelines in learning logs.

Informational Books

Clare, J. E. (1994). *Industrial Revolution.* San Diego: Gulliver.
Freedman, R. (1991). *The Wright Brothers: How They Invented the Airplane.* New York: Holiday House.
Freedman, R. (1994). *Kids at Work: Lewis Hine and the Crusade Against Child Labor.* New York: Clarion.

Haskins, J. (1991). *Outward Dreams: Black Inventors and Their Inventions.* New York: Walker.
Isherow, W. (1995). *The Triangle Factory Fire.* New York: Millbrook.
Langly, A. (1994). *The Industrial Revolution.* New York: Viking.
Macaulay, D. (1983). *Mill.* Boston: Houghton Mifflin.
Richards, N. (1984). *Dreamers and Doers: Inventors Who Changed the World.* New York: Atheneum.

Timelines, Lifelines, and Other Crafts

- Create timelines noting significant events of the Industrial Revolution.
- Draw a lifeline for an inventor.
- Make a Venn diagram comparing the domestic system and the industrial system.

Writing

- Create a class book comparing life for labourers, the middle class, and the wealthy during the Industrial Revolution.
- Make a cube, exploring six dimensions of the Industrial Revolution.
- Write compare–contrast, cause–effect, or problem–solution essays about events and outcomes of the Industrial Revolution.

Word Wall

standard of living	factory
manufacture	machines
middle class	upper class
labourers	unsanitary
working conditions	pollution
entrepreneurs	textiles
Industrial Revolution	guilds
industrialization	coal mining
capitalists	iron
domestic system	merchants
cottage industries	unskilled
apprentices	steel
mass production	inventions
steamships	banks
labour unions	telegraphs
working class	tenements
transportation	petroleum
rail network	clothing
transcontinental railroad	immigrants

Word-Study Activites

- Examine etymologies of words such as *textiles, factory, manufacturing, labourers, telegraph,* and *unsanitary.*
- Have students sort words related to textiles, transportation, communication, agriculture, and mining and minerals.

Figure 11–13 A Planning Cluster for an Upper-Grade Inquiry-Based Unit on the Industrial Revolution

Readers and Writers Workshops

Readers and writers workshops may be used in conjunction with a resource-based unit, a thematic unit, or an inquiry-based unit. Readers and writers workshops are a way of organizing instruction and learning. They offer opportunities for students themselves to make decisions about what to read and write and how to monitor their own processes within a predictable framework managed by teachers.

Nancie Atwell (1987, 1998) introduced readers workshop as an alternative to traditional reading instruction. In readers workshop, students read books that they choose themselves and respond to books through writing in reading logs and conferencing with teachers and classmates. This approach represents what we believe about how children learn and how literature can be used effectively in the classroom. Atwell developed readers workshop with her middle-school students, but it has been adapted and used successfully at every grade level, first through eighth (Bright, 2002; Hornsby, Sukarna, & Parry, 1986; McWhirter, 1990). There are several versions of readers workshop, but they usually contain these components: reading, responding, sharing, minilessons, and reading aloud to students.

Writers workshop is similar to readers workshop, except that the focus is on writing. Students write on topics that they choose themselves, and they assume ownership of their writing and learning (Atwell, 1987; Bright, 1995; Calkins, 1994; Graves, 1991; Hornsby et al., 1986). At the same time, the teacher's role changes from being a provider of knowledge to serving as a facilitator and guide. The classroom becomes a community of writers who write and share their writing. There is a spirit of pride and acceptance in the classroom.

Writers workshop is a 60- to 90-minute period scheduled each day (a typical writers workshop schedule is shown in Figure 11–14). During this time students are involved in three primary components: writing, sharing, and minilessons. The writing component involves students in all stages of the writing process, prewriting through publication. The sharing takes place in conferences with the teacher as well as with peers. Minilessons provide teacher-led instruction concerning the craft of writing and the procedures of writers workshop. Sometimes a fourth component, reading aloud to students, is added when reading and writing workshops are combined.

For more information about the writing process, see Chapter 4, "The Reading and Writing Processes," pp. 147–158.

ESTABLISHING A WORKSHOP ENVIRONMENT

Teachers begin to establish the workshop environment in their classroom from the first day of the school year by providing students with choices, time to read and write, and opportunities for

	Time	**Typical Activities**
Teacher Sharing	5–10 minutes	• reading aloud • sharing writing experiences
Minilesson	5–10 minutes	• teacher-directed instruction • focus on workshop procedures or writing technique
Writing	30–45 minutes	• students writing (all stages of writing process) • teacher conferencing with students
Sharing	10–15 minutes	• students sharing writing in process • students sharing published writing • sharing in small groups or whole class

Figure 11–14 Writers Workshop Schedule

response. Through their interactions with students, the respect they show to students, and the way they model reading and writing, teachers establish the classroom as a community of learners.

Teachers develop a schedule for readers and writers workshops with time allocated for each component, or they alternate between the two types of workshops. In their schedules, teachers allot as much time as possible for students to read and write. After developing the schedule, teachers post it in the classroom and talk with students about the activities and discuss their expectations with students. Teachers teach the workshop procedures and continue to model the procedures as students become comfortable with the routines. As students share what they are reading and writing at the end of workshop sessions, their enthusiasm grows and the benefits of the workshop approaches are reinforced.

Students keep two folders—one for readers workshop and one for writers workshop. In the readers workshop folder, students keep a list of books they have read, notes from minilessons, reading logs, and other materials. In the writers workshop folder, they keep all drafts and other compositions. They may also keep a list of all compositions, topics for future pieces, and notes from minilessons. They also keep language arts notebooks in which they jot down images, impressions, dialogue, and experiences that they can build upon for writing projects (Calkins, 1991).

Teachers use a workshop activity chart to monitor students' work on a daily basis. At the beginning of readers workshop, students or the teacher record what book (or chapter) they are reading, or if they are writing in a reading journal, sharing with their reading group, or working on an extended response project. For writers workshop, students identify the writing project they are involved in or the stage of the writing process they are at. A sample writers workshop chart is shown in Figure 11–15. Teachers can also use the chart to award weekly "effort" grades, to have students indicate their need to conference with the teacher, or to have students announce that they are ready to share the book they have read or publish their writing. Atwell (1987) calls this chart "the state of the class." Teachers can review students' progress and note which students need to meet with the

For more information on establishing a community of learners and a language-rich environment, see Chapter 2, "Teaching and the Language Arts," pages 63–65.

Writers Workshop Chart								
Names	Dates 10/18	10/19	10/20	10/21	10/22	10/25	10/26	10/27
Anthony	4 5	5	5	6	7	8	8	8 9
Brooke	2	2	2 3	2	2	4	5	6
Charles	8 9 1	3 1	1	2	2 3	4	5	6 7
Dina	6	6	6	7 8	8	9 1	1	2 3
Dustin	7 8	8	8	8	8	8	9 1	1
Eddie	2 3	2	2 4	5 6	8	9 1	1 2	2 3
Elizabeth	7	6	7	8	8	8	9	1 2
Elsa	2	3	4 5	5 6	6 7	8	8	9 1

Code:
1 = Prewrite
2 = Draft
3 = Conference
4 = Writers Group
5 = Revise
6 = Edit
7 = Conference
8 = Make Final Copy
9 = Publish

Figure 11–15 "State of the Class" Chart for Writers Workshop

teacher or receive additional attention. When students fill in the chart themselves, they develop responsibility for their actions and a stronger desire to accomplish tasks they set for themselves.

To monitor primary-grade students, teachers often use a pocket chart and have students place a card in their pocket, indicating whether they are reading or responding during readers workshop or at which stage of the writing process they are working during writers workshop.

Teachers take time during readers and writers workshops to observe students as they interact and work together in small groups. This gives teachers information about students' learning and their interactions with others during learning activities. Researchers who have observed in readers and writers workshop classrooms report that some students, even as young as first graders, are excluded from group activities because of gender, ethnicity, or socioeconomic status (Henkin, 1995; Lensmire, 1992). The socialization patterns in elementary classrooms seem to reflect society's. Henkin recommends that teachers be alert to the possibility that boys might only share books with other boys or that some students won't find anyone willing to be their editing partner. Teachers need to structure workshop groups to foster a classroom environment in which students treat each other equitably. If instances of exclusion or unfairness occur, they should be confronted directly. With teachers' guidance, and assistance in solving problems that arise, students working together in readers and writers workshops form supportive learning communities.

HOW TO SET UP A READERS WORKSHOP

Teachers move through a series of steps as they set up their classroom, prepare students to work independently in the classroom, and provide instruction. The steps in setting up a readers workshop are presented in the following Step by Step box.

Step by Step

Setting Up a Readers Workshop

1. **Collect books for readers workshop.** Students read all sorts of books during readers workshop, including stories, informational books, biographies, and poetry books. They also read magazines. Most of their reading materials are selected from the classroom or school library, but students also bring books from home and borrow books from the public library and classmates, pending the particular way the teacher chooses to implement readers workshop. Over the course of a school year, the teacher and students need to have available literally hundreds of books, including books written at a range of reading levels, in order to have appropriate books for all students. Primary teachers often worry about finding books that their emerging readers can handle independently. Alphabet and number books, pattern and predictable books, and books the teacher has read aloud several times are often the most accessible for kindergartners and grade 1 students. Primary-grade children often read and reread easy-to-read books.

    The teacher introduces students—especially reluctant readers—to the books to be read during workshop so that they can more effectively choose books to read independently. The best way to preview books is using a very brief book talk to interest students in the book. In book talks, the teacher tells students a little about the book, shows the cover, and perhaps reads the first paragraph or two (Prill, 1994/1995). The teacher also gives book talks to introduce new books, and students give book talks as they share books they have read with the class during the sharing part of readers workshop.

2. *Teach students readers workshop procedures.*   Students need to learn how to choose books, write responses to books they are reading, share books they have finished reading, and conference with the teacher, as well as other procedures related to readers workshop. Some of these procedures need to be taught before students begin readers workshop, and others can be introduced and reviewed as minilessons during readers workshop.

3. *Identify topics for minilessons.*   Minilessons are an important part of readers workshop because the workshop approach is more than reading practice. Instruction is important, and minilessons are the "teaching" step. The teacher presents minilessons on readers workshop procedures and on reading concepts, strategies, and skills. The teacher identifies topics for minilessons based on what students do during readers workshop, the questions students ask, and the skills and strategies that are expected to be introduced, practised, or reviewed at the grade level. The teacher uses examples from books students are reading, and students are often asked to reflect on their own reading processes. These minilessons can be taught to the whole class, small groups, or individual students, depending on which students need the instruction.

For more information on reading aloud to students, see Chapter 5, "Listening and Speaking in the Classroom," pages 178–180.

4. *Choose books to read aloud to students in conjunction with readers workshop.*   The teacher carefully chooses the books when a reading aloud component is included in readers workshop. The teacher may choose books that are more difficult than those which students can read independently, or ones that introduce students to a genre, an author, or a literary element. Sometimes the teacher reads the first book in a series aloud to students and then invites students to continue reading the sequels themselves. Whatever the reason, teachers choose books to read aloud for specific instructional purposes.

5. *Design a schedule for readers workshop.*   The teacher examines the daily and weekly schedules, considers all of the language arts activities in which students are involved, decides how much time is available for readers workshop, and allocates time to each of the readers workshop components. Some teachers make readers and writers workshops their entire language arts program. Others engage in workshop approach on a regular schedule such as two or three times a week, balancing with more teacher-directed lessons. They begin by reading aloud a book to the class, chapter by chapter, and talking about the book in a grand conversation. During this time, teachers focus on modelling reading strategies and talking about elements of story structure. Minilessons often follow and are related to teacher read-alouds. Next, students read self-selected books independently. The teacher conferences with small groups of students as they read and presents minilessons to small groups of students as needed. Then students spend 15 to 20 minutes writing in reading journals about their reading. Often teachers have students keep double-entry journals in which students record quotations from the story in one column and react to the quotations in the second column. Sharing is held during the last 15 minutes, sometimes in small groups and sometimes as a whole class. During sharing in small groups, students typically share their responses to the books they are reading. When sharing as a whole class, students do book talks about books they have finished reading or present extended response projects. Although schedules vary to meet the capabilities and needs of students, all schedules provide extended periods of time for uninterrupted reading.

6. *Plan for conferencing and monitoring.*   During readers workshop, students are reading and responding independently and the teacher must find ways to monitor students' progress. Many teachers keep individual records of reading achievements. They include what the student reads as well as anecdotal notes from observations and conferences. Teachers create conference schedules and meet with students individually and in small groups on a regular basis, usually once a week, to talk about their reading and their reading skills and strategies. They listen to students read excerpts aloud, and make plans for the next book. Teachers add the notes they make during these conferences to the folders they keep for each student.

VARIATIONS OF READERS WORKSHOP

In Canadian classrooms, teachers often integrate readers workshop into resource-based units, thematic units, or inquiry-based units. That is, workshop is an organizational approach to instruction and learning. In other instances, readers workshop is more of a stand-alone component of the language arts program. In one adaptation, students choose and read books from a special themed set of resources. Books may focus on a social studies or science theme such as the ocean or ancient Egypt, or the books may be written by one author or represent one genre, such as tall tales or time warp stories. In adaptations like this, readers workshop complements other language arts and curricular activities.

Other variations are referred to by other names. For example, another variation (discussed in detail at the beginning of this chapter) is literature circles (Daniels, 1994), also called *literature study groups* (Peterson & Eeds, 1990) and *book clubs* (Raphael & McMahon, 1994), in which students read in small groups. Students divide into small groups to read one of five or six related books. For example, grade 1 students might choose and read Barbara Reid stories in small groups, grade 3 students might read different versions of a fairy tale, such as "The Three Little Pigs," and grade 6 students might read survival stories such as Gary Paulsen's *Hatchet* (1987). A list of text-set suggestions for literature circles is presented in Figure 11–16 on page 466.

In a literature circle, small groups of students read a book (each with a copy of the same book) participate in one or more grand conversations in which they talk about the book and their reflections, and write in reading journals.

Teachers collect books for literature circles with five, six, or seven related titles and collect a few copies of each book. Then the teacher gives a book talk about each book, to introduce them to the students. One way to do this is to set each book on the chalk tray after the book talks and have students sign their names on the chalkboard above the book they want to read. Or, teachers can set the books on a table and place a sign-up sheet beside each book. Students take time to preview the books, and then select the book they want to read.

The books vary in length and difficulty to accommodate diversity among students, but students are not always placed in groups according to reading level. Students choose the books they want to read, and as they preview the books they consider how good a "fit" the book is and which one they find most interesting. Students can usually manage whatever book they choose because of support and assistance from their group or through determination. Once in a while, teachers counsel students to choose another book or provide an additional copy for reading with a tutor or at home to enable keeping pace with the literature circle group.

When students finish reading the book or the selected chapter, they engage in conversation to broaden and deepen their understanding. Sometimes teachers participate in the conversations and sometimes they don't. When the teachers are participants, they participate as fellow readers who share joys and difficulties, insights and speculations. They also help students develop literary insights by providing information, asking insightful questions, and guiding students to make comments. Eeds and Peterson (1991) advise that teachers need to listen carefully to what students say as they talk about a book, and label what students are talking about when appropriate.

Students talk about the characters, the plot, the theme—all the important issues in a story. They also make connections between the story and their own lives and the story and other stories they have read. They also notice literary language and read memorable passages aloud.

As students read and engage in grand conversations, the teacher circulates and meets with each group. During group meetings, the teacher may read along with students, read their reading

Primary Grades

Barbara Reid Stories
Reid, B. (1992). *Two by Two*. Richmond Hill, ON: North Winds Press. 🍁

Reid, B. (1997). *The Party*. Richmond Hill, ON: North Winds Press. 🍁

Reid, B. (1998). *Fun with Modeling Clay*. Toronto: Kids Can Press. 🍁

Reid, B. (2000). *The Golden Goose*. Markham, ON: North Winds Press. 🍁

Reid, B. (2003). *The Subway Mouse*. Markham, ON: North Winds Press. 🍁

Prairie Stories
Bannatyne-Cugnet, J. (2002). *Heartland: A Prairie Sampler*. Toronto: Tundra Books. 🍁

Bouchard, D. (1993). *If You're Not from the Prairie…* Vancouver: Raincoast Books. 🍁

Bouchard, D. (1996). *The Dust Bowl*. Vancouver: Raincoast Books. 🍁

Hundal, N. (1999). *Prairie Summer*. Toronto: Fitzhenry & Whiteside. 🍁

Reynolds, M. (1999). *The Prairie Fire*. Victoria: Orca Book Publishers. 🍁

Places in Canada
Carter, A. Laurel. (2003). *My Home Bay*. Red Deer, AB: Red Deer Press. 🍁

Graham, G. (1995). *Bibi and the Bull*. Red Deer, AB: Red Deer Press. 🍁

Hartry, N. (1997). *Hold on, McGinty!* Toronto: Doubleday Canada. 🍁

Kusugak, M. A. (1998). *Arctic Stories*. Willowdale, ON: Annick Press. 🍁

McFarlane, S. (1991). *Waiting for the Whales*. Victoria, BC: Orca Book Publishers. 🍁

Middle Grades

Carol Matas Stories
Matas, C. (1993). *Daniel's Story*. Toronto: Scholastic. 🍁

Matas, C. (1994). *After the War*. Toronto: Scholastic. 🍁

Matas, C. (1998). *Great Than Angels*. Toronto: Scholastic. 🍁

Matas, C. (1998). *Telling*. Toronto: Key Porter Books. 🍁

Matas, C. (2000). *Rebecca*. Toronto: Scholastic. 🍁

Boys' Stories
Doyle, B. (2003). *Boy O'Boy*. Toronto: Groundwood. 🍁

Scrimger, R. (1998). *The Nose from Jupiter*. Toronto: Tundra Books. 🍁

Trembath, D. (2000). *Frog Face and the Three Boys*. Victoria: Orca Book Publishers. 🍁

Walters, E. (1999). *Three-on-Three*. Vancouver: Orca Book Publishers. 🍁

Wynne-Jones, T. (2001). *Boy's Own: An Anthology of Canadian Fiction for Young Readers*. Toronto: Penguin. 🍁

Folktales
Arsenault, G. (2002). *Acadian Legends, Folktales, and Songs from Prince Edward Island* (S. Ross, Trans.). Charlottetown, PEI: Acorn Press. 🍁

Barton, B. (2003). *The Bear Says North: Tales from Northern Lands*. Toronto: Groundwood. 🍁

Jorisch, S. (2001). *As for the Princess? A Folktale from Quebec*. Toronto: Annick Press. 🍁

Scieszka, J. (1998). *Squids Will Be Squids: Fresh Morals, Beastly Fables*. Toronto: Viking (Penguin Books). 🍁

Yee, P. (1989). *Tales from Gold Mountain: Stories of the Chinese in the New World*. Toronto: Groundwood. 🍁

Upper Grades

Supernatural Stories
Baird, A. (2001). *The Witches of Willowmere*. Toronto: Penguin. 🍁

Buffie, M. (2000). *The Watcher*. Toronto: Kids Can Press. 🍁

Horrocks, A. (2000). *Topher*. Toronto: Stoddart Kids. 🍁

Lawrence, I. (1998). *The Wreckers*. New York: Delacorte Press. 🍁

Lewis, W. (2000). *Graveyard Girl: Stories*. Red Deer, AB: Red Deer Press. 🍁

Fitting in Stories
Brooks, K. (1999). *Being with Henry*. Toronto: Groundwood. 🍁

Brooks, K. (2002). *Lucas*. United Kingdom: The Chicken House. 🍁

Juby, S. (2000). *Alice, I Think*. Toronto: Harper Collins. 🍁

Kogawa, J. (1983). *Obasan*. Toronto: Penguin. 🍁

Toten, T. (2001). *The Game*. Red Deer, AB: Red Deer Press. 🍁

Beyond Borders
Bell, W. (1999). *Forbidden City*. Toronto: Doubleday. 🍁

Ellis, D. (2002). *Parvana's Journey*. Toronto: Groundwood Books. 🍁

Ellis, D. (2003). *Mud City*. Toronto: Doubleday Canada. 🍁

Pigott, P. (1995). *Hong Kong Rising: The History of a Remarkable Place*. Burnstown, ON: General Store Publishing House. 🍁

Ye, T-X., & Bell, W. (2003). *Throwaway Daughter*. Toronto: Doubleday Canada. 🍁

Figure 11–16 Text-Set Suggestions for Literature Circles

journal entries, or participate in grand conversations. While the teacher is meeting with one group, the other groups read independently or write in reading journals.

Students in literature circles often make only one journal entry when reading a picture book, but they make entries after reading every chapter or periodically when reading longer books. Sometimes they write their journal entries before discussing their reading and sometimes after. When they write before, their writing helps them clarify ideas to contribute to the conversation. When they write after, their entries often reflect what was heard in the grand conversation. Both help readers develop meaning. Writing in reading journals and talking about the book replace traditional workbook activities.

For years teachers have devoted 10, 20, or 30 minutes a day to silent reading in the classroom. Lyman Hunt (1970) called it Uninterrupted Sustained Silent Reading (USSR), McCracken and McCracken (1972) called it Sustained Silent Reading, and teachers have created their own acronyms, such as DEAR (Drop Everything and Read) Time. Students read self-selected library books during these practice periods. The idea behind these programs is that students need lots of reading practice in addition to reading instruction to become strategic, fluent readers. These programs were initially developed because research showed that students had few opportunities to transfer the skills and strategies they were learning to genuine reading activities and to read for sustained periods in school. Sustained reading has long been considered a way of increasing reading proficiency and sustaining an interest in reading that will lead to lifelong reading habits (Weaver, 1988). Guthrie (2003) explains that achievement in reading is a "by-product" of students' engagement. As they encounter and digest books, their competence in reading grows. Hence, the value of extended time for reading is clear, but it is important to note that these practice programs are not the same as readers workshop, because they lack instructional components.

HOW TO SET UP A WRITERS WORKSHOP

As teachers set up a writers workshop classroom, they collect writing supplies and resources as well as materials for making books their students will need. These include different kinds of paper—some lined and some unlined—and various writing instruments, including pencils, markers, and different-coloured pens and references such as dictionaries and thesauri. Bookmaking supplies include cardboard, contact paper, cloth and wallpaper for book covers, stencils, stamps, art supplies, and a saddleback stapler and other equipment for binding books. Teachers set up a bank of computers with word-processing programs and printers or arrange for students to have access to the school's computer lab. Teachers also encourage students to use the classroom library as a resource for information and ideas. Many times students' writing grows out of favourite books they have read.

Teachers also organize the classroom arrangement to facilitate working as a community of writers. Students sit at desks or tables arranged in small groups as they write. The teacher circulates around the classroom, conferencing briefly with students, and the classroom atmosphere is conducive to students writing independently, conversing quietly with other writers, moving around the classroom to collect materials, assisting classmates, or sharing ideas as needed in various stages of the writing process. There is a space for students to meet together in writing groups or with the teacher. Usually a table is available in that space, and this is where the teacher meets with individual students or small groups for conferences, proofreading, and minilessons.

In addition to collecting supplies and arranging the classroom, teachers need to prepare students for writers workshop and make plans for the instruction. In classrooms where workshop routines are well established and students are familiar with the writing process, students assume much of the responsibility for the smooth running of the workshop. The steps in setting up a writers workshop are presented in the following Step by Step box.

Step by Step

Setting Up a Writers Workshop

1. *Teach the stages of the writing process.*   Teachers often begin writers workshop by teaching or reviewing the five stages of the writing process, setting guidelines for writers workshop, and taking students through one writing activity together. In their discussion of the writing process and guidelines, teachers remind students that not all pieces of writing are taken through all stages, including publication. Rather, that they will make decisions as they engage in writing each piece. A set of guidelines for writers workshop that one grade 7 class developed is presented in Figure 11–17.

2. *Teach writers workshop procedures.*   Teachers need to explain how students will meet in groups to revise their writing, how to sign up for a conference with the teacher, how to proofread, how to use the publishing centre, and other procedures used in writers workshop.

3. *Identify topics for minilessons.*   As with readers workshop, teachers teach minilessons during writers workshop. The minilessons are on procedures related to writers workshop and writing

Ten Writers Workshop Rules

1. Keep everything in your writing folder.
2. Write rough drafts in pencil.
3. Double-space all rough drafts so you will have space to revise, and only write on one side of a page.
4. Revise in blue ink.
5. Edit in red ink.
6. Show your thinking and never erase except on the final copy.
7. Don't throw anything away—keep everything.
8. Date every piece of writing.
9. Keep a record of the compositions you write in your writing folder.
10. Work hard!

Figure 11–17 A Grade 7 Class's Guidelines for Writers Workshop

concepts, strategies, and skills that students can apply in their own writing. Some topics for minilessons come from teachers' observations of students as they write, questions students ask, and topics identified in grade-level curriculum guides.

For more information on the writing process, see Chapter 4, "The Reading and Writing Processes," pages 147–164.

Teachers also share information about authors and how they write during minilessons. In order for students to think of themselves as writers, they need to know what writers do. Each year there are more autobiographies written by authors. Popular Canadian author Sheree Fitch has written *Writing Maniac: How I Grew Up to be an Author and You Can Too* (2002), telling readers about her growth as a writer and showing students that writing well takes time and experience. Jean Little, author of *From Anna* (1991), has written an autobiography called *Little by Little: A Writer's Education* (1987) in which she reflects on her writing processes and why she writes about contemporary issues. Some of the other books in the "Meet the Author" series are *Firetalking*, by Patricia Polacco (1994), *Hau Kola/Hello Friend*, by Paul Goble (1994), and *Surprising Myself*, by Jean Fritz (1992). Films and videos about authors and illustrators are also available. For example, in the 27-minute video *Eric Carle: Picture Writer* (1993), Eric Carle demonstrates how he uses paint and collage to create the illustrations for his popular picture books.

4. *Design a writers workshop schedule*.   An important instructional decision that teachers make is how to organize their daily schedule and what portion of the language arts block to allocate to readers and writers workshops. In doing this, their priority is to provide students a block of time for uninterrupted writing. During writers workshop students move through the writing process as they write on self-selected or curriculum-related topics for 45 or 50 minutes. The teacher meets with small groups of students or individual students as they draft, revise, and edit their compositions during this writing time. Teachers use a 10- to 15-minute block of time, often prior to writing time, for giving minilessons on writers workshop procedures and writing concepts, strategies, and skills to the whole class. Other minilessons for small groups of students, or individual students are given as needed while other students write. Sharing is usually held during the last 15 minutes. (See the writers workshop schedule in Figure 11–14 on page 461.)

Other teachers coordinate writers workshop with resource-based, thematic, and inquiry-based units. For example, they may allocate the last hour of their language arts block for readers or writers workshop, and alternate readers workshop and writers workshop month by month, or grading period by grading period. Some teachers allocate time for writers workshop during the last week of a resource-based unit when students are developing a writing project. For example, in the resource-based unit on *The Mitten* discussed earlier in this chapter, primary-grade students use a writers workshop approach as they research one of the animals mentioned in the story and create posters to share what they learn.

5. *Plan for conferencing*.   Teachers conference with students as they write. Many teachers prefer moving around the classroom to meet with students rather than having the students come to a table to meet with the teacher. Too often a line forms as students wait to meet with the teacher, and students lose precious writing time. Some teachers move around the classroom in a regular pattern, meeting with one-fifth of the students each day. In this way they can conference with every student during the week.

Other teachers spend the first 15 to 20 minutes of writers workshop stopping briefly to check on ten or more students each day. Many use a zigzag pattern to get to all parts of the classroom each day. In primary classrooms, teachers often kneel down beside each student or carry their own stool to each student's desk. During the 1- or 2-minute conference, teachers ask students what they are writing, listen to students read a paragraph or two, and then ask what they plan to do next. Then these teachers use the remaining time during writers workshop to more formally conference with students who are revising and editing their compositions. Students often sign up for these conferences. The teachers make comments to find strengths, ask questions, and discover possibilities during these revising conferences. Some teachers like to read the pieces themselves, while others like to listen to students read their papers aloud.

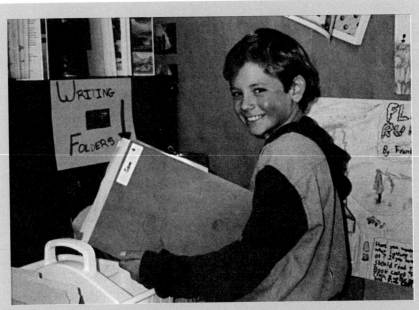

Teachers establish procedures, such as where to keep writing folders, in order for writers workshop to operate smoothly.

As they interact with students, teachers model the kinds of responses that students are learning to give to each other.

As students meet together to share their writing during revising and editing, they continue to develop their sense of community. They share their drafts with classmates in writers groups composed of four or five students. In some classrooms, teachers join in the writers groups whenever they can, but students normally run the groups themselves. They take turns reading their rough drafts to each other and listen as their classmates offer compliments and suggestions for revision. In contrast, students usually work with one partner to edit their writing, whether on paper or screen.

After proofreading their drafts with a classmate and then meeting with the teacher for a final editing, students make the final copy of their writings. Depending upon the facilities available, students usually want to print their writings on the computer so that their final copies will appear professional. Hence, the strong desirability noted in Chapter 9, "Words and the Language Tools to Use Them: Spelling, Grammar, and Handwriting," of students developing both fluent handwriting and keyboarding skills. Many times students compile their final copies to make books during writers workshop, but sometimes they attach their writing to artwork, make posters, write letters that are mailed, or perform scripts as skits or puppet shows. Not every piece is necessarily published, however. Sometimes students decide not to continue with a piece of writing. They file the piece in their writing folders and start something new.

6. *Include sharing.*   For the last 10 to 15 minutes of writers workshop, the class gathers together to share their writing, both work in progress and published pieces. Works in progress are often shared when writers seek peer assistance to help them overcome obstacles and move forward. Published pieces are shared to celebrate accomplishments. Younger students often sit in a circle or gather together on a rug for sharing time. If an author's chair is available, each student sits in the special chair to read his or her composition. After reading works in progress, authors ask for and classmates provide suggestions. When published pieces are read, classmates clap and offer compliments. They may also make other comments and suggestions, but the focus is on celebrating completed writing projects, not on revising the composition to make it better. Published pieces are often added to the classroom library, available for reading by classmates.

VARIATIONS OF WRITERS WORKSHOP

Sometimes teachers set up writers workshop for a limited period of time when their students are working on a project and need lengthy periods of time for writing. For example, as grade 3 students write weather reports after reading *Hurricane* (Weisner, 1990), or as upper-grade students write simulated journals or reports, they may participate in writers workshop for a week or two. During these project-oriented writers workshops, teachers sometimes teach minilessons on topics related to the assignment, but usually all of the writers workshop time is used for writing and then for sharing when students complete their projects.

Another variation is a combined readers–writers workshop. Teachers sometimes use this format when studying a literary genre. For example, students can read and write biographies, read and write tall tales or *pourquoi* tales, or read and write collections of letters or journals. Poetry, too, is sometimes experienced through combined workshops. After students learn about various poetic forms, and read and listen to many examples, they often choose to write poems during writers workshop.

Overall, readers and writers workshops offer teachers and students opportunities to engage in meaningful literacy activities for extended periods of time. Some teachers use readers and writers workshops as organizational frameworks for their entire language arts programs. However, many teachers use workshops to support and enhance their resource-based units, their thematic units, and their inquiry-based units. The teacher, as instructional decision-maker, chooses an organizational approach based on knowledge about and experience with students, resources, and curriculum.

For more information on reading and writing poetry, see Chapter 6, "Reading and Writing Narrative Text," pages 235–247 and 262–273.

 Review

Designing language arts instruction that reflects the theory and research about language and how students learn is an important responsibility. Choosing resources and approaches to instruction involves critical decision making. Among resources, teachers choose and use socially conscious, culturally diverse literature to help students learn about cultural groups in Canada and create a sense of belonging for all students. Culturally diverse literature is used as featured selections in resource-based units and included in classroom libraries for independent reading. In planning language arts programs, teachers consider students' interests and needs, curriculum requirements, and all language learning activities—those during language arts blocks and those associated with other subject areas such as social studies and science. They plan for broad, rich learning through resource-based, thematic, and inquiry-based units and engage students in authentic, meaningful reading and writing through reader and writer workshops.

The following key concepts are presented in this chapter:

1. Culturally diverse literature helps students understand the viewpoints of ethnically diverse groups and encourages greater appreciation of other cultures. Its use contributes to creating a sense of belonging in a learning community among students.

2. When teachers plan language arts programs, they consider students' interests and needs, required provincial or program curriculum, and available time and resources.

3. Three instructional frameworks are resource-based units, thematic units, and inquiry-based units.

4. Teachers can adapt and combine resource-based units, thematic units, and inquiry-based units to fit the needs of their students and their curriculum.

5. Plans for all units include the core components: focus and desired outcomes, learning activities, lists of resources, and plans for assessment of learning.

6. Students use all six language arts in all three units, often making cross-curriculum linkages with subject areas such as social studies, science, and the fine arts

7. Teachers should select high-quality print and nonprint resources, including culturally conscious literature, for inclusion in all three units. Textbooks may be used as one resource, but they should never be the only resource.

8. Readers and writers workshops are ways of organizing instruction that include reading, writing, minilessons, and sharing.

9. Readers and writers workshops are often used as ways of organizing a large part of a teacher's instruction and may be used in conjunction with resource-based units, thematic units, and inquiry-based units.

10. Teachers organize readers and writers workshops to give students blocks of uninterrupted time for reading and writing, preferably on a daily basis.

11. Teachers present minilessons on procedures, concepts, and strategies and skills.

12. In readers and writers workshops, students and teachers share responsibility for classroom management and student learning.

Extensions

1. Read a collection of culturally diverse books and create an annotated reading list or card file. Share one or more books from your collection with age-appropriate students. Include the students' responses in your annotation.

2. Plan a resource-based unit featuring a picture book or a chapter book. Draw a planning cluster and make a lesson plan. Incorporate activities involving all six language arts and create an assignment checklist.

3. Observe in a classroom using the readers and writers workshop approach. Write journal entries about your observations and note how the teacher manages the routine and conferences with students.

4. Plan a thematic unit incorporating the language arts and one or more areas of the curriculum. Draw a planning cluster and make a lesson plan. Compile a text set of ten or more books, including stories, informational books, and poems. Also design an assignment checklist.

5. Plan a minilesson to teach one writing technique to help students improve their writing. Employ at least one example from good quality literature to illustrate the author's use of the technique.

Appendix A Award-Winning Books for Children

Canadian Library Association Book of the Year for Children Award

The Book of the Year for Children Award has been given annually since 1947 by the Canadian Library Association (328 Frank Street, Ottawa, ON K2P 0X8, Canada) to outstanding children's books written in English. From 1954 through 1973, an award was also given to books written in French. All award-winning books were published during the preceding year and were written by a Canadian citizen.

2006 *The Crazy Man*, Pamela Porter (Groundwood).

2005 *Last Chance Bay*, Anne Laurel Carter (Penguin).

2004 *Boy O'Boy*, Brian Doyle, (Groundwood).

2003 *Hana's Suitcase*, Karen Levine (Second Story Press).

2002 *Orphan at My Door: The Home Child Diary of Victoria Cope*, Jean Little (Scholastic Canada Ltd.)

2001 *Wild Girl & Gran*, Nan Gregory (Red Deer Press).

2000 *Sunwing*, Kenneth Oppel (HarperCollins).

1999 *Stephen Fair*, Tim Wynne-Jones (Groundwood/Douglas & McIntyre).

1998 *Silverwing*, Kenneth Oppel (HarperCollins).

1997 *Uncle Ronald*, Brian Doyle (Groundwood).

1996 *The Tiny Kite of Eddie Wing*, Maxine Trottier (Stoddart).

1995 *Summer of the Mad Monk*, Cora Taylor (Douglas & McIntyre).

1994 *Some of the Kinder Planets*, Tim Wynne-Jones (Groundwood).

1993 *Ticket to Curlew*, Celia Barker Lottridge (Groundwood).

1992 *Eating between the Lines*, Kevin Major (Doubleday).

1991 *Redwork*, Michael Bedard (Lester & Orpen Dennys).

1990 *The Sky Is Falling*, Kit Pearson (Penguin).

1989 *Easy Avenue*, Brian Doyle (Groundwood/Douglas & McIntyre).

1988 *A Handful of Time*, Kit Pearson (Penguin).

1987 *Shadow in Hawthorn Bay*, Jane Lunn (Lester & Orpen Dennys).

1986 *Julie*, Cora Taylor (Western Producer Prairie Books).

1985 *Mama's Going to Buy You a Mockingbird*, by Jean Little (Penguin).

1984 *Sweetgrass*, Jan Hudson (Tree Frog Press).

1983 *Up to Low*, Brian Doyle (Groundwood/Douglas & McIntyre).

1982 *The Root Cellar*, Janet Lunn (Lester & Orpen Dennys).

1981 *The Violin Maker's Gift*, Donn Kushner (Macmillan).

1980 *River Runners*, James Houston (McClelland & Stewart).

1979 *Hold Fast*, Kevin Major (Clarke, Irwin).

1978 *Garbage Delight*, Dennis Lee (Macmillan).

1977 *Mouse Woman and the Vanished Princesses*, Christie Harris (McClelland & Stewart).

1976 *Jacob Two-Two Meets the Hooded Fang*, Mordecai Richler (McClelland & Stewart).

1975 *Alligator Pie*, Dennis Lee (Macmillan).

1974 *The Miraculous Hind*, Elizabeth Cleaver (Holt).

1973 *The Marrow of the World*, Ruth Nichols (Macmillan); *La petit sapin qui a poussé sur une étoile*, Simone Bussières (Laurentiennes).

1972 *Mary of Mile 18*, Ann Blades (Tundra). No French Award.

1971 *Cartier Discovers the St. Lawrence*, William Toye (Oxford); *La surprise de dame chenille*, Henriette Major (Centre de Psychologie et de Pédagogie).

1970 *Sally Go Round the Sun*, Edith Fowke (McClelland & Stewart); *La merveilleuse histoire de la naissance*, Lionel Gendron (Les Éditions de l'Homme).

1969 *And Tomorrow the Stars*, Kay Hill (Dodd). No French Award.

1968 *The White Archer*, James Houston (Academic); *Légendes indiennes du Canada*, Claude Melançon (Éditions du Jour).

1967 *Raven's Cry*, Christie Harris (McClelland & Stewart). No French Award.

1966 *Tikta Liktak*, James Houston (Longmans). (Published 1964.)

The Double Knights, James McNeil (Oxford). (Published 1965.)

Le chêne des tempetes, Andrée Maillet-Hobden (Fides). (Published 1964.)

Le wapiti, Monique Corriveau (Jeunesse). (Published 1965.)

1965 *Tales of Nanabozho*, Dorothy Reid (Oxford); *Le loup de noël*, Claude Aubry (Centre de Psychologie et de Pédagogie).

1964 *The Whale People*, Roderick Haig-Brown (Collins); *Ferie*, Cecile Chabot (Beuchemin).

1963 *The Incredible Journey*, Sheila Burnford (Little, Brown); *Drôle d'automne*, Paule Daveluy (Pelican).

1962 No English Award; *Les iles du roi Maha Maha II*, Claude Aubry (Pelican).

1961 *The St. Lawrence*, William Toye (Oxford); *Plantes vagabondes*, Marcelle Gauvreau (Centre de Psychologie et de Pédagogie).

1960 *The Golden Phoenix*, Marius Barbeau, retold by Michael Hornyansky (Oxford); *L'été enchanté*, Paule Daveluy (Atelier).

Newbery Medal Books

The Newbery Medal is named in honour of John Newbery (1713–1767), a British publisher and bookseller in the 1700s. Newbery is known as the "father of children's literature" because he was the first to propose publishing books specifically for children. The award is presented each year by the American Library Association to "the author of the most distinguished contribution to American literature for children" published during the preceding year. The award was first given in 1922 and is awarded annually. The winning book receives the Newbery Medal, and one or more runners-up are also recognized as "Honor" books.

2006 *Criss Cross*, Lynne Rae Perkins (Greenwillow Books/HarperCollins). **Honor Books:** *Whittington*, Alan Armstrong (Random House); *Hitler Youth: Growing Up in Hitler's Shadow*, Susan Campbell Bartoletti (Scholastic); *Princess Academy*, Shannon Hale (Bloomsbury Children's Books); *Show Way*, Jacqueline Woodson (G.P. Putnam's Sons).

2005 *Kira-Kira*, Cynthia Kadohata (Atheneum Books for Young Readers/Simon & Schuster). **Honor Books:** *Al Capone Does My Shirts*, Gennifer Choldenko (G.P. Putnam's Sons/a division of Penguin Young Readers Group); *The Voice that Challenged a Nation: Marian Anderson and the Struggle for Equal Rights*, Russell Freedman (Clarion Books/Houghton Mifflin); *Lizzie Bright and the Buckminster Boy*, Gary D. Schmidt (Clarion Books/Houghton Mifflin).

2004 *The Tale of Despereaux: Being the Story of a Mouse, a Princess, Some Soup, and a Spool of Thread*, Kate DiCamillo (Candlewick Press). **Honor books:** *Olive's Ocean*, Kevin Henkes (Greenwillow Books); *An American Plague: The True and Terrifying Story of the Yellow Fever Epidemic of 1793*, Jim Murphy (Clarion Books).

2003 *Crispin: The Cross of Lead*, Avi (Hyperion Books for Children). **Honor books:** *The House of Scorpion*, Nancy Farmer (Atheneum); *Pictures of Hollis Woods*, Patricia Reilly Giff (Random House/Wendy Lamb Books); *Hoot*, Carl Hiaasen (Knopf); *A Corner of the Universe*, Ann M. Martin (Scholastic); *Surviving the Applewhites*, Stephanie S. Tolan (HarperCollins).

2002 *A Single Shard*, Linda Sue Park (Clarion Books/Houghton Mifflin). **Honor books:** *Everything on a Waffle*, Polly Horvath (Farrar, Straus and Giroux); *Carver: A Life in Poems*, Marilyn Nelson (Front Street).

2001 *A Year Down Yonder*, Richard Peck (Dial Books for Young Readers). **Honor books:** *Because of Winn-Dixie*, Kate DiCamillo (Candlewick Press); *Hope Was Here*, Joan Bauer (G. P. Putnam's Sons); *Joey Pigza Loses Control*, Jack Gantos (Farrar, Straus and Giroux); *The Wanderer*, Sharon Creech (Joanna Cotler Books, HarperCollins).

2000 *Bud, Not Buddy*, Christopher Paul Curtis (Delacorte). **Honor books:** *Getting Near to Baby*, Audrey Couloumbis (Putnam); *Our Only May Amelia*, Jennifer L. Holm (HarperCollins); *26 Fairmount Avenue*, Tomie dePaola (Putnam).

1999 *Holes*, Louis Sachar (Frances Foster/Farrar, Straus and Giroux). **Honor books:** *A Long Way from Chicago*, Richard Peck (Dial).

1998 *Out of the Dust*, Karen Hesse (Scholastic). **Honor books:** *Ella Enchanted*, Gail Carson Levine (HarperCollins); *Lily's Crossing*, Patricia Reilly Giff (Delacorte); *Wringer*, Jerry Spinelli (HarperCollins).

1997 *View from Saturday*, E. L. Konigsburg (Atheneum). **Honor books:** *A Girl Named Disaster*, Nancy Farmer (Orchard); *Moorchild*, Eloise McGraw (McElderry); *The Thief*, Megan Whalen Turner (Greenwillow); *Belle Prater's Boy*, Ruth White (Farrar, Straus and Giroux).

1996 *The Midwife's Apprentice*, Karen Cushman (Clarion). **Honor books:** *What Jamie Saw*, Carolyn Coman (Front Street); *The Watsons Go to Birmingham—1963*, Christopher Paul Curtis (Delacorte); *Yolanda's Genius*, Carol Fenner (McElderry); *The Great Fire*, Jim Murphy (Scholastic).

1995 *Walk Two Moons*, Sharon Creech (HarperCollins). **Honor books:** *Catherine Called Birdy*, Karen Cushman (Clarion); *The Ear, the Eye and the Arm*, Nancy Farmer (Orchard).

1994 *The Giver*, Lois Lowry (Houghton Mifflin). **Honor books:** *Crazy Lady!*, Jane Leslie Conly (HarperCollins); *Dragon's Gate*, Laurence Yep (HarperCollins); *Eleanor Roosevelt: A Life of Discovery*, Russell Freedman (Clarion).

1993 *Missing May*, Cynthia Rylant (Orchard). **Honor books:** *The Dark-Thirty: Southern Tales of the Supernatural*, Patricia McKissack (Knopf); *Somewhere in the Darkness*, Walter Dean Myers (Scholastic); *What Hearts*, Bruce Books (HarperCollins).

1992 *Shiloh*, Phyllis Reynolds Naylor (Atheneum). **Honor books:** *Nothing but the Truth*, Avi (Orchard); *The Wright Brothers: How They Invented the Airplane*, Russell Freedman (Holiday).

1991 *Maniac Magee*, Jerry Spinelli (Little, Brown). **Honor book:** *The True Confessions of Charlotte Doyle*, Avi (Orchard).

1990 *Number the Stars*, Lois Lowry (Houghton Mifflin). **Honor books:** *Afternoon of the Elves*, Janet Taylor Lisel (Orchard); *Shabanu, Daughter of the Wind*, Susan Fisher Staples (Knopf); *The Winter Room*, Gary Paulsen (Orchard).

1989 *Joyful Noise: Poems for Two Voices*, Paul Fleishman (Harper & Row). **Honor books:** *In the Beginning*,

Virginia Hamilton (Harcourt Brace Jovanovich); *Scorpions*, Walter Dean Myers (Harper & Row).

1988 *Lincoln: A Photobiography*, Russell Freedman (Clarion). **Honor books:** *After the Rain*, Norma Fox Mazer (Morrow); *Hatchet*, Gary Paulsen (Bradbury).

1987 *The Whipping Boy*, Sid Fleischman (Greenwillow). **Honor books:** *A Fine White Dust*, Cynthia Rylant (Bradbury); *On My Honor*, Marion Dane Bauer (Clarion); *Volcano: The Eruption and Healing of Mount St. Helen's*, Patricia Lauber (Bradbury).

1986 *Sarah, Plain and Tall*, Patricia MacLachlan (Harper & Row). **Honor books:** *Commodore Perry in the Land of the Shogun*, Rhoda Blumberg (Lothrop, Lee & Shepard); *Dog Song*, Gary Paulsen (Bradbury).

1985 *The Hero and the Crown*, Robin McKinley (Greenwillow). **Honor books:** *Like Jake and Me*, Mavis Jukes (Alfred A. Knopf); *The Moves Make the Man*, Bruce Brooks (Harper & Row); *One-Eyed Cat*, Paula Fox (Bradbury).

1984 *Dear Mr. Henshaw*, Beverly Clearly (Morrow). **Honor books:** *The Sign of the Beaver*, Elizabeth George Speare (Houghton Mifflin); *A Solitary Blue*, Cynthia Voigt (Atheneum); *Sugaring Time*, Kathryn Lasky (Macmillan); *The Wish Giver*, Bill Brittain (Harper & Row).

1983 *Dicey's Song*, Cynthia Voigt (Atheneum). **Honor books:** *The Blue Sword*, Robin McKinley (Greenwillow); *Doctor DeSoto*, William Steig (Farrar, Straus and Giroux); *Graven Images*, Paul Fleischman (Harper & Row); *Homesick: My Own Story*, Jean Fritz (Putnam); *Sweet Whispers, Brother* Rush, Virginia Hamilton (Philomel).

1982 *A Visit to William Blake's Inn: Poems for Innocent and Experienced Travelers*, Nancy Willard (Harcourt Brace Jovanovich). **Honor books:** *Ramona Quimby, Age 8*, Beverly Clearly (Morrow); *Upon the Head of the Goat: A Childhood in Hungary, 1939–1944*, Aranka Siegal (Farrar, Straus and Giroux).

1981 *Jacob Have I loved*, Katherine Paterson (Crowell). **Honor books:** *The Fledgling*, Jane Langton (Harper & Row); *A Ring of Endless Light*, Madeleine L'Engle (Farrar, Straus and Giroux).

1980 *A Gathering of Days: A New England Girl's Journal, 1830–1832*, Joan W. Blos (Scribner). **Honor books:** *The Road from Home: The Story of an Armenian Girl*, David Kerdian (Greenwillow).

1979 *The Westing Game*, Ellen Raskin (Dutton). **Honor books:** *The Great Gilly Hopkins*, Katherine Paterson (Crowell).

1978 *Bridge to Terabithia*, Katherine Paterson (Crowell). **Honor books:** *Anpao: An American Indian Odyssey*, Jamake Highwater (Lippincott); *Ramona and Her Father*, Beverly Clearly (Morrow).

1977 *Roll of Thunder, Hear My Cry*, Mildred Taylor (Dial). **Honor books:** *Abel's Island*, William Steig (Farrar, Straus and Giroux); *A String in the Harp*, Nancy Bond (Atheneum).

1976 *The Grey King*, Susan Cooper (Atheneum). **Honor books:** *Dragonwings*, Laurence Yep (Harper & Row); *The Hundred Penny Box*, Sharon Bell Mathis (Viking).

1975 *M. C. Higgins, the Great*, Virginia Hamilton (Macmillan). **Honor books:** *Figgs and Phantoms*, Ellen Raskin (E. P. Dutton); *My Brother Sam Is Dead*, James Lincoln Collier and Christopher Collier (Four Winds); *The Perilous Guard*, Elizabeth Marie Pope (Houghton Mifflin); *Philip Hall Likes Me, I Reckon Maybe*, Bette Green (Dial).

1974 *The Slave Dancer*, Paula Fox (Bradbury). **Honor books:** *The Dark Is Rising*, Susan Cooper (Atheneum).

1973 *Julie of the Wolves*, Jean C. George (Harper & Row). **Honor books:** *Frog and Toad Together*, Arnold Lobel (Harper & Row); *The Upstairs Room*, Johanna Reiss (Crowell); *The Witches of Worm*, Zilpha Keatley Snyder (Atheneum).

1972 *Mrs. Frisby and the Rats of NIMH*, Robert C. O'Brien (Atheneum). **Honor books:** *Annie and the Old One*, Miska Miles (Atlantic-Little); *The Headless Cupid*, Zilpha Keatley Snyder (Atheneum); *Incident at Hawk's Hill*, Allan W. Eckert (Little, Brown); *The Planet of Junior Brown*, Virginia Hamilton (Macmillan); *The Tombs of Atuan*, Ursula K. Le Guin (Atheneum).

1971 *The Summer of the Swans*, Betsy Byars (Viking). **Honor books:** *Enchantress from the Stars*, Sylvia Louise Engdahl (Atheneum); *Kneeknock Rise*, Natalie Babbitt (Farrar, Straus and Giroux); *Sing Down the Moon*, Scott O'Dell (Houghton Mifflin).

1970 *Sounder*, William Armstrong (Harper & Row). **Honor books:** *Journey Outside*, Mary Q. Steele (Viking); *Our Eddie*, Sulamith Ish-Kishor (Pantheon); *The Many Ways of Seeing: An Introduction to the Pleasures of Art*, Janet Gaylord Moore (Harcourt Brace Jovanovich).

1969 *The High King*, Lloyd Alexander (Holt, Rinehart & Winston). **Honor books:** *To Be a Slave*, Julius Lester (Dial); *When Shlemiel Went to Warsaw and Other Stories*, Isaac Bashevis Singer (Farrar, Straus and Giroux).

1968 *From the Mixed-up Files of Mrs. Basil E. Frankweiler*, E. L. Konigsburg (Atheneum). **Honor books:** *The Black Pearl*, Scott O'Dell (Houghton Mifflin); *The Egypt Game*, Zilpha Keatley Snyder (Atheneum); *The Fearsome Inn*, Isaac Bashevis Singer (Scribner); *Jennifer, Hecate, Macbeth, William McKinley, and Me, Elizabeth*, E. L. Konigsburg (Atheneum).

1967 *Up a Road Slowly*, Irene Hunt (Follett). **Honor books:** *The Jazz Man*, Mary Hays Weik (Atheneum); *The King's Fifth*, Scott O'Dell (Houghton Mifflin); *Zlateh the Goat and Other Stories*, Isaac Bashevis Singer (Harper & Row).

1966 *I, Juan de Pareja*, Elizabeth Borton de Trevino (Farrar, Straus and Giroux). **Honor books:** *The Animal Family*, Randall Jarrell (Pantheon); *The Black Cauldron*, Lloyd Alexander (Holt, Rinehart & Winston); *The Noonday Friends*, Mary Stolz (Harper & Row).

1965 *Shadow of a Bull*, Maia Wojciechowska (Atheneum). **Honor books:** *Across Five Aprils*, Irene Hunt (Follett).

1964 *It's Like This, Cat*, Emily Neville (Harper & Row). **Honor books:** *The Loner*, Ester Wier (McKay); *Rascal*, Sterling North (E.P. Dutton).

1963 *A Wrinkle in Time*, Madeleine L'Engle (Farrar, Straus and Giroux). **Honor books:** *Thistle and Thyme: Tales and Legends from Scotland*, Sorche Nic Leodhas (Holt); *Men of Athens*, Olivia Coolidge (Houghton Mifflin).

1962 *The Bronze Bow*, Elizabeth George Speare (Houghton Mifflin). **Honor books:** *Frontier Living*, Edwin Tunis (World); *The Golden Goblet*, Eloise McCraw (Coward); *Belling the Tiger*, Mary Stolz (Harper & Row).

1961 *Island of the Blue Dolphins*, Scott O'Dell (Houghton Mifflin). **Honor books:** *America Moves Forward*, Gerald W. Johnson (Morrow); *Old Ramon*, Jack Schaefer (Houghton Mifflin); *The Cricket in Times Square*, George Selden (Farrar, Straus and Giroux).

1960 *Onion John*, Joseph Krumgold (Crowell). **Honor books:** *My Side of the Mountain*, Jean Craighead George (Dutton); *America Is Born*, Gerald W. Johnson (Morrow); *The Gammage Cup*, Carol Kendall (Harcourt Brace Jovanovich).

Books about Authors and Illustrators

ANTHOLOGIES

Canadian Children's Book Centre. (2000). *The storymakers: Illustrating children's books.* Markham, ON: Pembroke Publishers.

Canadian Children's Book Centre. (2000). *The storymakers: Writing children's books.* Markham, ON: Pembroke Publishers.

Collins, J. (1980, May). Giant problem or what is a kid's book anyway? *Canadian Materials.*

Department of Canadian Heritage—Publications Distribution Program. (1995). *Island treasures.* Victoria: Storyline Books.

Gertridge, A. (1994). *Meet Canadian authors and illustrators.* Richmond Hill, Ontario: Scholastic Canada.

Grant, J. (1989). *Kids' writers.* Markham, ON: Fitzhenry & Whiteside.

Heath, J. (1980). *Profiles in Canadian literature.* Toronto: Dundurn Press Ltd.

McClung, M. (1977). *Women in Canadian literature.* Markham, ON: Fitzhenry & Whiteside.

AUTHORS

Aardema, Verna Aardema, V. (1992). *A bookworm who hatched.* Katonah, NY: Richard C. Owen. (P–M)*

Andersen, Hans Christian Greene, C. (1991). *Hans Christian Andersen: Prince of storytellers.* Chicago: Children's Press. (P–M)

Asch, Frank Asch, F. (1997). *One man show.* Katonah, NY: Richard C. Owen. (P–M)

Blegvad, Erik Blegvad, E. (1979). *Self-portrait: Erik Blegvad.* Reading, MA: Addison-Wesley. (P–M–U)

Brown, Margaret Wise Brown, M. W. (1994). *The days before now.* New York: Simon & Schuster. (P–M); Greene, C. (1993). *Margaret Wise Brown: Author of Goodnight Moon.* Chicago: Children's Press. (P–M)

Bunting, Eve Bunting, E. (1995). *Once upon a time.* Katonah, NY: Richard C. Owen. (P–M)

Burnett, Frances Hodgson Carpenter, A. S., & Shirley, J. (1990). *Frances Hodgson Burnett: Beyond the secret garden.* Minneapolis: Lerner Books. (U)

Byars, Betsy Byars, B. (1991). *The moon and I.* New York: Messner. (M–U)

Carson, Rachel Wadsworth, G. (1991). *Rachel Carson: Voice for the earth.* Minneapolis: Lerner Books. (U)

Cleary, Beverly Cleary, B. (1988). *A girl from Yamhill: A memoir.* New York: Morrow. (M–U)

Cole, Joanna Cole, J. (1996). *On the bus with Joanna Cole.* Portsmouth, NH: Heinemann. (M–U)

Cowley, Joy Cowley, J. (1988). *Seventy kilometres from ice cream: A letter from Joy Cowley.* Katonah, NY: Richard C. Owen. (P)

Dahl, Roald Dahl, R. (1984). *Boy: Tales of childhood.* New York: Farrar, Straus and Giroux. (M–U)

dePaola, Tomie dePaola, T. (1989). *The art lesson.* New York: Putnam. (P)

Dillon, Leo and Diane Preiss, B. (1981). *The art of Leo and Diane Dillon.* New York: Ballantine. (M–U)

Dr. Seuss Weidt, M. N. (1994). *Oh, the places he went: A story about Dr. Seuss—Theodor Seuss Geisel.* Minneapolis: Carolrhoda. (M)

Duncan, Lois Duncan, L. (1982). *Chapters: My growth as a writer.* Boston: Little, Brown. (U)

Ehlert, Lois Ehlert, L. (1996). *Under my nose.* Katonah, NY: Richard C. Owen. (P–M)

Fritz, Jean Fritz, J. (1982). *Homesick: My own story.* New York: Putnam. (M–U); Fritz, J. (1992). *Surprising myself.* Katonah, NY: Richard C. Owen. (M)

Goble, Paul Goble, P. (1994). *Hau kola/Hello friend.* Katonah, NY: Richard C. Owen. (M)

Goodall, John Goodall, J. S. (1981). *Before the war, 1908–1939: An autobiography in pictures.* New York: Atheneum. (M–U)

Heller, Ruth Heller, R. (1996). *Fine lines.* Katonah, NY: Richard C. Owen. (P–M)

Henry, Marguerite Henry, M. (1980). *The illustrated Marguerite Henry.* Chicago: Rand McNally. (M–U)

Hinton, S. E. Daly, J. (1989). *Presenting S. E. Hinton.* Boston: Twayne. (U)

Hopkins, Lee Bennett Hopkins, L. B. (1992). *The writing bug.* Katonah, NY: Richard C. Owen. (M)

Howe, James Howe, J. (1994). *Playing with words.* Katonah, NY: Richard C. Owen. (M)

Hughes, Langston Cooper, F. (1994). *Coming home: From the life of Langston Hughes.* New York: Philomel. (M–U)

Hyman, Trina Schart Hyman, T. S. (1981). *Self-portrait: Trina Schart Hyman*. Reading, MA: Addison-Wesley. (P–M–U).

Kuskin, Karla Kuskin, K. (1995). *Thoughts, pictures, and words*. Katonah, NY: Richard C. Owen. (M)

Lester, Helen Lester, H. (1997). *Author: A true story*. Boston: Houghton Mifflin. (P–M)

Lewis, C. S. Lewis, C. S. (1985). *Letters to children*. New York: Macmillan. (M–U)

Little, Jean Little, J. (1987). *Little by Little: A writer's education*. Toronto: Penguin Canada. (M–U); Little, J. (1990). *Stars come out within*. Toronto: Penguin Canada. (M–U)

Lyon, George Ella Lyon, G. E. (1996). *A wordful child*. Katonah, NY: Richard C. Owen. (P–M)

Mahy, Margaret Mahy, M. (1995). *My mysterious world*. Katonah, NY: Richard C. Owen. (M)

McKissack, Patricia McKissack, P. (1997). *Can you imagine?* Katonah, NY: Richard C. Owen. (P–M)

McPhail, David McPhail, D. (1996). *In flight with David McPhail*. Portsmouth, NH: Heinemann. (P–M)

Meltzer, Milton Meltzer, M. (1988). *Starting from home: A writer's beginnings*. New York: Viking. (U)

Mohr, Nicholasa Mohr, N. (1994). *Nicholasa Mohr: Growing up inside the sanctuary of my imagination*. New York: Messner. (U)

Montgomery, Lucy Maude Gillen, M. (1978). *Lucy Maude Montgomery*. Markham, Ontario: Fitzhenry & Whiteside.

Naylor, Phyllis Naylor, P. R. (1978). *How I came to be a writer*. New York: Atheneum. (U)

Pallotta, Jerry Ryan, P. (1993). *Chasing the alphabet: The story of children's author Jerry Pallotta*. Boston: Shining Sea Press. (M)

Paulsen, Gary Paulsen, G. (1990). *Woodsong*. New York: Bradbury Press.

Peck, Richard Peck, R. (1991). *Anonymously yours*. New York: Messner. (U)

Peet, Bill Peet, B. (1989). *Bill Peet: An autobiography*. Boston: Houghton Mifflin. (M–U)

Polacco, Patricia Polacco, P. (1994). *Fire talking*. Katonah, NY: Richard C. Owen. (M)

Potter, Beatrix Aldis, D. (1969). *Nothing is impossible: The story of Beatrix Potter*. New York: Atheneum. (M); Collins, D. R. (1989). *The country artist: A story about Beatrix Potter*. Minneapolis: Carolrhoda. (M)

Rylant, Cynthia Rylant, C. (1992). *Best wishes*. Katonah, NY: Richard C. Owen. (P–M)

Singer, Isaac Bashevis Singer, I. B. (1969). *A day of pleasure: Stories of a boy growing up in Warsaw*. New York: Farrar, Straus and Giroux. (U)

Stevens, Janet Stevens, J. (1995). *From pictures to words: A book about making a book*. New York: Holiday House. (P–M)

Uchida, Yoshiko Uchida, U. (1991). *The invisible thread*. New York: Messner. (U)

Wilder, Laura Ingalls Blair, G. (1981). *Laura Ingalls Wilder*. New York: Putnam. (P–M); Greene, C.

(1990). *Laura Ingalls Wilder: Author of the Little House books*. Chicago: Children's Press. (P–M)

Yep, Laurence Yep, L. (1991). *The lost garden: A memoir*. New York: Messner. (U)

Yolen, Jane Yolen, J. (1992). *A letter from Phoenix Farm*. Katonah, NY: Richard C. Owen. (P–M–U)

Zemach, Margot Zemach, M. (1978). *Self-portrait: Margot Zemach*. Reading, MA: Addison-Wesley. (P–M–U)

*P = primary grades (K–2); M = middle grades (3–5); U = upper grades (6–8).

Individual Articles Profiling Authors and Illustrators

Adoff, Arnold White, M. L. (1988). Profile: Arnold Adoff. *Language Arts, 65*, 584–591.

Alexander, Lloyd Greenlaw, M. J. (1984). Profile: Lloyd Alexander. *Language Arts, 61*, 406–413; Tunnell, M. O. (1989). An interview with Lloyd Alexander. *The New Advocate, 2*, 83–96.

Anno, Mitsumasa Aoki, H. (1983). A conversation with Mitsumasa Anno. Horn Book Magazine, 59, 132–145; Swinger, A. K. (1987). Profile: Mitsumasa Anno's journey. *Language Arts, 64*, 762–766.

Baker, Keith Baker, K. (1993). "Have you ever been dead?" Questions and letters from children. *The Reading Teacher, 46*, 372–375.

Baylor, Byrd Bosma, B. (1987). Profile: Byrd Baylor. *Language Arts, 64*, 315–318.

Bourgeois, Paulette The Canadian Children's Book Centre. (1987, April). Meet the author: Paulette Bourgeois. *Children's Book News*.

Brett, Jan Raymond, A. (1992, April). Jan Brett: Making it look easy. *Teaching PreK–8, 22*, 38–40.

Brown, Marcia Brown, M. (1983). Caldecott Medal Acceptance. *Horn Book Magazine, 59*, 414–422.

Brown, Margaret Wise Hurd, C. (1983). Remembering Margaret Wise Brown. *Horn Book Magazine, 59*, 553– 560.

Browne, Anthony Marantz, S., & Marantz, K. (1985). An interview with Anthony Browne. *Horn Book Magazine, 61*, 696–704.

Bryan, Ashley Marantz, S., & Marantz, K. (1988). Interview with Ashley Bryan. *Horn Book Magazine, 64*, 173–179; Swinger, A. K. (1984). Profile: Ashley Bryan. *Language Arts, 61*, 305–311.

Buffie, Margaret Telgen, D. (Ed.). (1993). *Buffie, Margaret 1945–. Something about the Author*. Gale Research Company, Vol. 71.

Bunting, Eve Raymond, A. (October, 1986). Eve Bunting: From Ireland with love. *Teaching PreK–8, 17*, 38–40.

Byars, Betsy Robertson, I. (1980). Profile: Betsy Byars— Writer for today's child. *Language Arts, 57*, 328–334.

Carle, Eric Yolen, J. (1988). In the artist's studio: Eric Carle. *The New Advocate, 1*, 148–154.

Ciardi, John Odland, N. (1982). Profile: John Ciardi. *Language Arts, 59,* 872–876.

Cleary, Beverly Cleary, B. (1984). Newbery Medal acceptance. *Horn Book Magazine, 50,* 429–438; Reuter, D. (1984). Beverly Cleary, *Horn Book Magazine, 50,* 439–443.

Clifton, Lucille Sims, R. (1982). Profile: Lucille Clifton. *Language Arts, 59,* 160–167.

Collier, James and Christopher Raymond, A. (January, 1988). Meet James and Christopher Collier. *Teaching PreK–8, 18,* 35–38.

Conrad, Pam Raymond, A. (1990, November/December). Pam Conrad: She said to herself, "Now what?" *Teaching PreK–8, 21,* 38–40.

Creech, Sharon An interview with Sharon Creech, 1995 Newbery Medal winner. (1996). *The Reading Teacher, 49,* 380–382.

Degan, Bruce Elliot, I. (1991, October). Bruce Degan: Doing what he likes best. *Teaching PreK–8, 21,* 44–47.

Diaz, David Conversation with a winner—David Diaz talks about *Smoky Night.* (1996). *The Reading Teacher, 49,* 386–388.

Dillon, Leo and Diane Cummings, P. (1992). *Talking with artists* (pp. 22–29). New York: Bradbury Press.

Dr. Seuss Roth, R. (1989). On beyond zebra with Dr. Seuss. *The New Advocate, 2,* 213–226.

Egielski, Richard Cummings, P. (1992). *Talking with artists* (pp. 30–35). New York: Bradbury Press; Egielski, R. (1987). Caldecott Medal acceptance. *Horn Book Magazine, 63,* 433–435; Yorinks, A. (1987). Richard Egielski. *Horn Book Magazine, 63,* 436–438.

Ehlert, Lois Cummings, P. (1992). *Talking with artists* (pp. 36–41). New York: Bradbury Press.

Feelings, Tom Feelings, T. (1985). The artist at work: Technique and the artist's vision. *Horn Book Magazine, 61,* 685–695.

Fleischman, Sid Fleischman, P. (1987). Sid Fleischman. *Horn Book Magazine, 63,* 429–432; Fleischman, S. (1987). Newbery Medal acceptance. *Horn Book Magazine, 63,* 423–438; Johnson, E. R. (1982). Profile: Sid Fleischman. *Language Arts, 59,* 754–759.

Fox, Mem Manning, M., & Manning, G. (March, 1990). Mem Fox: Mem's the word in down under? *Teaching PreK–8, 20,* 29–31; Phelan, C. (1993, May). Talking with Mem Fox, *Book Links,* 29–32.

Freedman, Russell Dempsey, F. J. (1988). Russell Freedman. *Horn Book Magazine, 64,* 452–456; Freedman, R. (1988). Newbery Medal acceptance. *Horn Book Magazine, 64,* 444–451.

Fritz, Jean Ammon, R. (1983). Profile: Jean Fritz, *Language Arts, 60,* 365–369; Fritz, J. (1985). Turning history inside out. *Horn Book Magazine, 61,* 29–34; Heins, E. L. (1986). Presentation of the Laura Ingalls Wilder Medal. *Horn Book Magazine, 62,* 430–431.

Gay, Marie-Louise Olendorf, D. (Ed.). (1992). *Gay, Marie-Louise 1952–. Something About the Author.* Gale Research Company, Vol. 68.

Gerstein, Mordicai Yolen, J. (1990). In the artist's studio: Mordicai Gerstein. *The New Advocate, 3,* 25–28.

Giff, Patricia Reilly Raymond, A. (1987, April). Patricia Reilly Giff: A writer who believes in reading. *Teaching PreK–8, 17,* 34–37.

Gilman, Phoebe O'Reilly, G. (1993, June/July). Phoebe Gilman: Winner of the 1993 Ruth Schwartz award. *Canadian Bookseller.*

Gilson, Jamie Johnson, R. (1983). Profile: Jamie Gilson. *Language Arts, 60,* 661–667.

Goble, Paul Stott, J. C. (1984). Profile: Paul Goble. *Language Arts, 61,* 867–873.

Godrey, Martyn Godfrey, M. (1989, February). A book week journal: My visit to the rock. *Quill & Quire.*

Goffstein, M. B. Marantz, S., & Marantz, K. (1986). M. B. Goffstein: An interview. *Horn Book Magazine, 62,* 688–694; Shannon, G. (1983). Goffstein and friends. *Horn Book Magazine, 59,* 88–95.

Greenfield, Eloise Kiah, R. B. (1980). Profile: Eloise Greenfield. *Language Arts, 57,* 653–659.

Haley, Gail E. Haley, G. E. (1990). Of mermaids, myths, and meaning: A sea tale. *The New Advocate, 3,* 1–12.

Hamilton, Virginia Hamilton, V. (1986). Coretta Scott King Award acceptance. *Horn Book Magazine, 62,* 683–687; Garret, J. (1993, January). Virginia Hamilton: 1992 Andersen winner, *Book Links,* 22–25.

Henkes, Kevin Elliot, I. (1989, January). Meet Kevin Henkes: Young man on a roll. *Teaching PreK–8, 19,* 43–45.

Hoover, H. M. Porter, E. J. (1982). Profile: H. M. Hoover. *Language Arts, 59,* 609–613.

Howe, James Raymond, A. (1987, February). James Howe: Corn, ham and punster cheese. *Teaching PreK–8, 17,* 32–34.

Hughes, Monica Nakamura, J. (Ed.). (1991). *Monica Hughes 1925–. Something about the Author.* Gale Research Company, Vol. 11; Olendorf, D., & Telgen, D. (Eds.). (1993). *Hughes, Monica (Ince) 1925–. Something about the Author.* Gale Research Company, Vol. 70.

Hunter, Bernice Thurman Greenwood, B. (1989, Spring). Introducing Bernice Thurman Hunter. *CANSCAIP News.*

Hyman, Trina Schart Hyman, K. (1985). Trina Schart Hyman. *Horn Book Magazine, 61,* 422–425; Hyman, T. S. (1985). Caldecott Medal acceptance. *Horn Book Magazine, 61,* 410–421; Saul, W. (1988). Once-upon-a-time artist in the land of now: An interview with Trina Schart Hyman. *The New Advocate, 1,* 8–17; White, D. E. (1983). Profile: Trina Schart Hyman. *Language Arts, 60,* 782–792.

Jonas, Ann Marantz, S., & Marantz, K. (1987). Interview with Ann Jonas. *Horn Book Magazine, 63,* 308–313; Raymond, A. (1987, December). Ann Jonas: Reflections 1987. *Teaching PreK–8, 18,* 44–46.

Keats, Ezra Jack Lanes, S. G. (1984). Ezra Jack Keats: In memoriam. *Horn Book Magazine, 60,* 551–558; Pope, M., & Pope, L. (1990). Ezra Jack Keats: A childhood revisited. *The New Advocate, 3,* 13–24.

Kellogg, Steven Cummings, P. (1992). *Talking with artists* (pp. 54–59). New York: Bradbury Press.

Khalsa, Dayal Kaur Lyons, T. L. (1990). Dayal Kaur Khalsa. *Canadian Children's Literature, 59.*

Konigsburg, E. L. Jones, L. T. (1986). Profile: Elaine Konigsburg. *Language Arts, 63,* 177–184.

Lasky, Kathryn Lasky, K. (1990). The fiction of history: Or, what did Miss Kitty really do? *The New Advocate, 3,* 157–166.

Korman, Gordon Ferns, C. (1985). An interview with Gordon Korman. *Canadian Children's Literature, 38.*

Kovalski, Maryann Commire, A. (Ed.). (1990). *Kovalski, Maryann 1951–. Something about the Author.* Gale Research Company, Vol. 58.

Kropp, Paul Hancock, P. (1993). Introducing Paul Kropp. *CANSCAIP News,* Spring.

Lee, Dennis Ross, C., & Davies, C. B. (1984). Re-realizing Mother Goose: An interview with Dennis Lee on *Jelly Belly. Canadian Children's Literature, 33.*

L'Engle, Madeleine Raymond, A. (1991, May). Madeleine L'Engle: Getting the last laugh. *Teaching PreK–8, 21,* 34–36; Samuels, L. A. (1981). Profile: Madeleine L'Engle. *Language Arts, 58,* 704–712.

Lester, Julius Lester, J. (1988). The storyteller's voice: Reflections on the rewriting of Uncle Remus. *The New Advocate, 1,* 137–142.

Little, Jean (1989, December). An interview with Jean Little. *Grail: An Ecumenical Journal;* Olendorf, D. (Ed.). (1992). *Little, Jean 1932–. Something about the Author.* Gale Research Company, Vol. 68.

Livingston, Myra Cohn Porter, E. J. (1980). Profile: Myra Cohn Livingston. *Language Arts, 57,* 901–905.

Lobel, Anita Raymond, A. (1989, November/December). Anita Lobel: Up from the crossroad. *Teaching PreK–8, 20,* 52–55.

Lobel, Arnold Lobel, A. (1981). Caldecott Medal acceptance. *Horn Book Magazine, 57,* 400–404; Lobel, A. (1981). Arnold at home. *Horn Book Magazine, 57,* 405–410; White, D. E. (1988). Profile: Arnold Lobel. *Language Arts, 65,* 489–494.

Lowry, Lois Lowry, L. (1988). Rabble Starkey. *Horn Book Magazine, 64,* 29–31; Lowry, L. (1990). Number the stars: Lois Lowry's journey to the Newbery Award. *The Reading Teacher, 44,* 98–101; Raymond, A. (1987, October). "Anastasia," and then some. *Teaching PreK–8, 18,* 44–46; An interview with Lois Lowry, 1994 Newbery Medal winner. (1994–1995). *The Reading Teacher, 48,* 308–309.

Lunn, Janet Olendorf, D. (Ed.). (1992). *Lunn, Janet 1928–. Something about the Author.* Gale Research Company, Vol. 68.

Macaulay, David Ammon, R. (1982). Profile: David Macaulay. *Language Arts, 59,* 374–378.

Mackay, Claire Mackay, C. (1989). Real plums in imaginary cakes. *Canadian Children's Literature, 54.*

MacLachlan, Patricia Babbitt, N. (1986). Patricia MacLachlan: The biography. *Horn Book Magazine, 62,* 414–416; Courtney, A. (1985). Profile: Patricia MacLachlan. *Language Arts, 62,* 783–787; MacLachlan, P. (1986). Newbery Medal acceptance. *Horn Book Magazine, 62,* 407–413; MacLachlan,

R. (1986). A hypothetical dilemma. *Horn Book Magazine, 62,* 416–419; Raymond, A. (1989, May). Patricia MacLachlan: An advocate of "Bare boning." *Teaching PreK–8, 19,* 46–48.

Martchenko, Michael Commire, A. (Ed.). (1988). *Martchenko, Michael 1942–. Something about the Author.* Gale Research Company, Vol. 50.

Martin, Bill, Jr. Larrick, N. (1982). Profile: Bill Martin, Jr. *Language Arts, 59,* 490–494.

Mayer, Marianna Raymond, A. (1991, January). Marianna Mayer: Myths, legends, and folklore. *Teaching PreK–8, 21,* 42–44.

McCloskey, Robert Mandel, E. (1991, May). Make way for ducklings by Robert McCloskey. *Book Links,* 38–42.

McDermott, Gerald McDermott, G. (1988). Sky father, earth mother: An artist interprets myth. *The New Advocate, 1,* 1–7; White D. E. (1982). Profile: Gerald McDermott. *Language Arts, 59,* 273–279.

McKinley, Robin McKinley, R. (1985). Newbery Medal acceptance. *Horn Book Magazine, 61,* 395–405; Winding, T. (1985). Robin McKinley. *Horn Book Magazine, 61,* 406–409.

McKissack, Patricia Bishop, R. S. (1992). A conversation with Patricia McKissack. *Language Arts, 69,* 69–74.

Merriam, Eve Cox, S. T. (1989). A word or two with Eve Merriam: Talking about poetry. *The New Advocate, 2,* 139–150; Sloan, G. (1981). Profile: Eve Merriam. *Language Arts, 58,* 957–964.

Mikolaycak, Charles White, D. E. (1981). Profile: Charles Mikolaycak. *Language Arts, 58,* 850–857.

Mohr, Nicholasa Zarnowski, M. (1991). An interview with author Nicholasa Mohr. *The Reading Teacher, 45,* 100–107.

Montresor, Beni Raymond, A. (1990, April). Beni Montresor: Carmen, Cannes and Caldecott. *Teaching PreK–8, 20,* 31–33.

Moser, Barry Moser, B. (1987). Artist at work: Illustrating the classics. *Horn Book Magazine, 63,* 703–709; Moser, B. (1991). Family photographs, gathered fragments. *The New Advocate, 4,* 1–10.

Muller, Robin Greenwood, B. (1990). Introducing Robin Muller. *CANSCAIP News,* Spring.

Munsch, Robert Jenkinson, D. (1989). Profile: Robert Munsch, *Language Arts, 66,* 665–675.

Myers, Walter Dean Bishop, R. S. (1990). Profile: Walter Dean Myers. *Language Arts, 67,* 862–866.

Naylor, Phyllis Reynolds Naylor, P. R. (1992). The writing of *Shiloh. The Reading Teacher, 46,* 10–13.

Nutt, Ken Oppel, K. (1989, August). Ken Nutt (a.k.a Eric Beddows): Zooming to the top. *Quill & Quire.*

O'Dell, Scott Roop, P. (1984). Profile: Scott O'Dell. *Language Arts, 61,* 750–752.

Parker, Nancy Winslow Raymond, A. (1990, May). Nancy Winslow Parker: "I knew it would happen." *Teaching PreK–8, 20,* 34–36.

Paterson, Katherine Jones, L. T. (1981). Profile: Katherine Paterson. *Language Arts, 58,* 189–196; Namovic, G. I. (1981). Katherine Paterson. *Horn*

Book Magazine, 57, 394–399; Paterson, K. (1981). Newbery Medal acceptance. *Horn Book Magazine*, 57, 385–393.

Pearson, Kit Schwartz, E. (1990, Summer). Introducing Kit Pearson. *CANSCAIP News*.

Penrose, Gordon Olendorf, D. (Ed.). (1991). *Penrose, Gordon 1925– (Dr. Zed). Something About the Author*. Gale Research Company, Vol. 66.

Pinkney, Jerry Cummings, P. (1992). *Talking with artists* (pp. 60–65). New York: Bradbury Press.

Prelutsky, Jack Raymond, A. (1986, November/December). Jack Prelutsky . . . Man of many talents. *Teaching PreK–8*, 17, 38–42; Vardell, S. (1991). An interview with Jack Prelutsky. *The New Advocate*, 4, 101–112.

Provensen, Alice and Martin Provensen, A., & Provensen, M. (1984). Caldecott Medal acceptance. *Horn Book Magazine*, 50, 444–448; Willard, N. (1984). Alice and Martin Provensen. *Horn Book Magazine*, 50, 449–452.

Reid, Barbara Graitskell, S. (1989). An interview with Barbara Reid. *Canadian Children's Literature*, 56.

Rice, Eve Raymond, A. (1989, April). Meet Eve Rice: Author/artist/doctor (doctor?). *Teaching PreK–8*, 19, 40–42.

Rylant, Cynthia Silvey, A. (1987). An interview with Cynthia Rylant. *Horn Book Magazine*, 63, 695–702.

Say, Allen An interview with Allen Say, 1994 Caldecott Award winner. (1994–1995). *The Reading Teacher*, 48, 304–306.

Schoenherr, John Gauch, P. L. (1988). John Schoenherr. *Horn Book Magazine*, 64, 460–463; Schoenherr, J. (1988). Caldecott Medal acceptance. *Horn Book Magazine*, 64, 457–459.

Schwartz, Alvin Vardell, S. M. (1987). Profile: Alvin Schwartz. *Language Arts*, 64, 426–432.

Schwartz, Amy Cummings, P. (1992). *Talking with artists* (pp. 66–71). New York: Bradbury Press.

Scieszka, Jon Raymond, A. (1992, May). Jon Scieszka: Telling the true story. *Teaching PreK–8*, 22, 38–40.

Sendak, Maurice Sendak, M. (1983). Laura Ingalls Wilder Award acceptance. *Horn Book Magazine*, 59, 474–477.

Sewall, Marcia Sewall, M. (1988). The pilgrims of Plimoth. *Horn Book Magazine*, 64, 32–34.

Shulevitz, Uri Raymond, A. (1992, January). Uri Shulevitz: For children of all ages. *Teaching PreK–8*, 21, 38–40.

Smith, Lane Cummings, P. (1992). *Talking with artists* (pp. 72–77). New York: Bradbury Press.

Smucker, Barbara (Claassen) Nakamura, J. (Ed.). (1991). *Barbara (Claassen) Smucker 1915–. Something about the Author*. Gale Research Company, Vol. 11.

Soto, Gary Soto, G. (1992). Author for a day: Glitter and rainbows. *The Reading Teacher*, 46, 200–203.

Speare, Elizabeth George Hassler, P. J. (1993, May). The books of Elizabeth George Speare. *Book Links*, 14–20.

Spinelli, Jerry Spinelli, J. (1991). Capturing *Maniac Magee*. *The Reading Teacher*, 45, 174–177.

Steig, Bill Raymond, A. (1991, August/September). Jeanne and Bill Steig: It adds up to magic. *Teaching PreK–8*, 21, 52–54.

Steptoe, John Bradley, D. H. (1991). John Steptoe: Retrospective of an imagemaker. *The New Advocate*, 4, 11–24.

Tafuri, Nancy Raymond, A. (1987, January). Nancy Tafuri . . . Nature, picturebooks, and joy. *Teaching PreK–8*, 17, 34–36.

Taylor, Mildred D. Dussel, S. L. (1981). Profile: Mildred D. Taylor. *Language Arts*, 58, 599–604.

Taylor, Theodore Bagnall, N. (1980). Profile: Theodore Taylor: His models of self-reliance. *Language Arts*, 57, 86–91.

Uchida, Yoshiko Chang, C. E. S. (1984). Profile: Yoshiko Uchida. *Language Arts*, 61, 189–194.

Van Allsburg, Chris Cummings, P. (1992). *Talking with artists* (pp. 78–83). New York: Bradbury Press; Keifer, B. (1987). Profile: Chris Van Allsburg in three dimensions. *Language Arts*, 64, 664–671; Macaulay, D. (1986). Chris Van Allsburg. *Horn Book Magazine*, 62, 424–426; McKee, B. (1986). Van Allsburg: From a different perspective. *Horn Book Magazine*, 62, 556–571; Van Allsburg, C. (1982). Caldecott Medal acceptance. *Horn Book Magazine*, 58, 380–383; Van Allsburg, C. (1986). Caldecott Medal acceptance, *Horn Book Magazine*, 62, 420–424.

Voigt, Cynthia Kauffman, D. (1985). Profile: Cynthia Voigt. *Language Arts*, 62, 876–880; Voigt, C. (1983). Newbery Medal acceptance. *Horn Book Magazine*, 59, 401–409.

Waddell, Evelyn Margaret Commire, A. (Ed.). (1978). *Waddell, Evelyn Margaret 1918– (Lyn Cook). Something about the Author*. Gale Research Company, Vol. 10.

Wallace, Ian Commire, A. (Ed.). (1989). *Wallace, Ian 1950–. Something about the Author*. Gale Research Company, Vol. 56.

Weisner, David Cummings, P. (1992). *Talking with artists* (pp. 84–89). New York: Bradbury Press.

White, E. B. Hopkins, L. B. (1986). Profile: In memoriam: E. B. White. *Language Arts*, 63, 491–494; Newmeyer, P. F. (1985). The creation of E. B. White's *The Trumpet of the Swans*: The manuscripts. *Horn Book Magazine*, 61, 17–28; Newmeyer, P. F. (1987). E. B. White: Aspects of style. *Horn Book Magazine*, 63, 586–591.

Wiesner, David Caroff, S. F., & Moje, E. B. (1992–1993). A conversation with David Wiesner: 1992 Caldecott Medal winner. *The Reading Teacher*, 46, 284–289.

Willard, Nancy Lucas, B. (1982). Nancy Willard. *Horn Book Magazine*, 58, 374–379; Willard, N. (1982). Newbery Medal acceptance. *Horn Book Magazine*, 58, 369–373.

Williams, Vera B. Raymond A. (1988, October). Vera B. Williams: Postcards and peace vigils. *Teaching PreK–8*, 19, 40–42.

Wilson, Eric H. Commire, A. (Ed.). (1984). *Wilson, Eric H. 1940–. Something about the Author*. Gale Research Company, Vol. 34.

Worth, Valerie Hopkins, L. B. (1991). Profile: Valerie Worth. *Language Arts, 68,* 499–501.

Yolen, Jane White, D. E. (1983). Profile: Jane Yolen. *Language Arts, 60,* 652–660; Yolen, J. (1989). On silent wings: The making of *Owl Moon. The New Advocate, 2,* 199–212; Yolen, J. (1991). The route to story. *The New Advocate, 4,* 143–149; Yolen J. (1992). Past time: The writing of the picture book *Encounter. The New* Advocate, 5, 235–239.

Yorinks, Arthur Raymond, A. (1991, November/December). Arthur Yorinks: Talent in abundance. *Teaching PreK–8, 21,* 51–53.

Zalben, Jane Breskin Yolen, J. (1990). In the artist's studio: Jane Breskin Zalben. *The New Advocate, 3,* 175–178.

Audiovisual Materials Profiling Authors and Illustrators

Alexander, Lloyd *Meet the Newbery author: Lloyd Alexander* [sound filmstrip]. American School Publishers. (U)

Andersen, Hans Christian *Meet the author: Hans Christian Andersen* [sound filmstrip or video]. American School Publishers. (M)

Armstrong, William H. *Meet the Newbery author: William H. Armstrong* [sound filmstrip]. American School Publishers. (M–U)

Babbitt, Natalie *Meet the Newbery author: Natalie Babbitt* [sound filmstrip]. American School Publishers. (U)

Berenstain, Stan and Jan *Meet Stan and Jan Berenstain* [sound filmstrip]. American School Publishers. (P)

Blume, Judy *First choice: Authors and books—Judy Blume* [sound filmstrip]. Pied Piper. (M–U)

Brown, Marc *Meet Marc Brown* [video]. American School Publishers. (P–M)

Byars, Betsy *Meet the Newbery author: Betsy Byars* [sound filmstrip]. American School Publishers. (M–U)

Carle, Eric *Eric Carle: Picture writer* [video]. Philomel. (P–M)

Cherry, Lynne *Get to know Lynne Cherry* [video]. Harcourt Brace. (M)

Cleary, Beverly *First choice: Authors and books—Beverly Cleary* [sound filmstrip]. Pied Piper. (M); *Meet the Newbery author: Beverly Cleary* [sound filmstrip]. American School Publishers. (M)

Collier, James Lincoln and Christopher *Meet the Newbery authors: James Lincoln Collier and Christopher Collier* [sound filmstrip]. American School Publishers. (U)

Cooper, Susan *Meet the Newbery author: Susan Cooper* [sound filmstrip]. American School Publishers. (U)

Crews, Donald *Trumpet video visits Donald Crews* [video]. Trumpet Book Club. (P–M)

Dahl, Roald *The author's eye: Roald Dahl* [kit with video]. American School Publishers. (M–U)

Fleischman, Sid *First choice: Authors and books—Sid Fleischman* [sound filmstrip]. Pied Piper. (M–U)

Fritz, Jean *Homesick: My own story* [sound filmstrip]. American School Publishers. (M–U)

George, Jean Craighead *Meet the Newbery author: Jean Craighead George* [sound filmstrip]. American School Publishers. (U)

Giovanni, Nikki *First choice: Poets and poetry—Nikki Giovanni* [sound filmstrip]. Pied Piper. (M–U)

Greene, Bette *Meet the Newbery author: Bette Greene* [sound filmstrip]. American School Publishers. (M–U)

Haley, Gail E. *Tracing a legend: The story of the green man by Gail E. Haley* [sound filmstrip]. Weston Woods. (M); *Creating Jack and the bean tree: Tradition and technique* [sound filmstrip]. Weston Woods. (M)

Hamilton, Virginia *First choice: Authors and books—Virginia Hamilton* [sound filmstrip] Pied Piper. (U); *Meet the Newbery author: Virginia Hamilton* [sound filmstrip] American School Publishers. (U)

Henry, Marguerite *First choice: Authors and books—Marguerite Henry* [sound filmstrip]. Pied Piper. (M–U); *Meet the Newbery author: Marguerite Henry* [sound filmstrip]. American School Publishers. (M)

Highwater, Jamake *Meet the Newbery author: Jamake Highwater* [sound filmstrip]. American School Publishers. (M–U)

Keats, Ezra Jack *Ezra Jack Keats* [film]. Weston Woods. (P)

Kellogg, Steven *How a picture book is made* [video]. Weston Woods (P–M); *Trumpet video visits Steven Kellogg* [video]. Trumpet Book Club. (P–M)

Konigsburg, E. L. *First choice: Authors and books—E. L. Konigsburg* [sound filmstrip]. Pied Piper. (M–U)

Kuskin, Karla *First choice: Poets and poetry—Karla Kuskin* [sound filmstrip]. Pied Piper. (M–U); *Poetry explained by Karla Kuskin* [sound filmstrip]. Weston Woods. (M–U)

L'Engle, Madeleine *Meet the Newbery author: Madeleine L'Engle* [sound filmstrip]. American School Publishers. (U)

Livingston, Myra Cohn *First choice: Poets and poetry—Myra Cohn Livingston* [sound filmstrip]. Pied Piper. (M–U)

Lobel, Arnold *Meet the Newbery author: Arnold Lobel* [sound filmstrip]. American School Publishers. (P–M)

Macaulay, David *David Macaulay in his studio* [video]. Houghton Mifflin. (M–U)

McCloskey, Robert *Robert McCloskey* [film]. Weston Woods. (P–M)

McCord, David *First choice: Poets and poetry—David McCord* [sound filmstrip]. Pied Piper. (M–U)

McDermott, Gerald *Evolution of a graphic concept: The stonecutter* [sound filmstrip]. Weston Woods. (P–M)

Merriam, Eve *First choice: Poets and poetry—Eve Merriam* [sound filmstrip]. Pied Piper. (M–U)

Milne, A. A. *Meet the author: A. A. Milne (and Pooh)* [sound filmstrip or video]. American School Publishers. (P)

Most, B. *Get to know Bernard Most* [video]. Harcourt Brace. (P–M)

O'Dell, Scott *Meet the Newbery author: Scott O'Dell* [sound filmstrip]. American School Publishers. (U); *A visit with Scott O'Dell* [video]. Houghton Mifflin. (U)

Paterson, Katherine *The author's eye: Katherine Paterson* [kit with video]. American School Publishers. (M–U); *Meet the Newbery author: Katherine Paterson* [sound filmstrip]. American School Publishers. (M–U)

Paulsen, Gary *Trumpet video visits Gary Paulsen* [video]. Trumpet Book Club. (U)

Peet, Bill *Bill Peet in his studio* [video]. Houghton Mifflin. (M)

Pinkney, Jerry *Meet the Caldecott illustrator: Jerry Pinkney* [video]. American School Publishers. (P–M)

Potter, Beatrix *Beatrix Potter had a pet named Peter* [sound filmstrip or video]. American School Publishers. (P)

Rylant, Cynthia *Meet the Newbery author: Cynthia Rylant* [sound filmstrip or video]. American School Publishers. (M–U); *Meet the picture book author: Cynthia Rylant* [video]. American School Publishers. (P–M)

Sendak, Maurice *Sendak* [film]. Weston Woods. (P–M)

Seuss, Dr. *Who's Dr. Seuss? Meet Ted Geisel* [sound filmstrip]. American School Publishers. (P–M)

Singer, Issac Bashevis *Meet the Newbery author: Isaac Bashevis Singer* [sound filmstrip]. American School Publishers. (U)

Sobol, Donald J. *The case of the Model-A Ford and the man in the snorkel under the hood: Donald J. Sobol* [sound filmstrip]. American School Publishers. (M)

White, E. B. *Meet the Newbery author: E. B. White* [sound filmstrip]. American School Publishers. (M–U)

Wilder, Laura Ingalls *Meet the Newbery author: Laura Ingalls Wilder* [sound filmstrip]. American School Publishers. (M–U)

Willard, Nancy *Meet the Newbery author: Nancy Willard* [sound filmstrip]. American School Publishers. (M–U)

Yep, Laurence *Meet the Newbery author: Laurence Yep* [sound filmstrip]. American School Publishers. (U)

Zolotow, Charllotte *Charlotte Zolotow: The grower* [sound filmstrip]. American School Publishers. (P–M)

Appendix C Basic Grammar, Punctuation, and Syntax

Subject–Verb Agreement

The **subject** and the <u>**verb**</u> must agree in number: A singular subject needs a singular verb; a plural subject needs a plural verb. The **subject** tells what or whom the sentence is about and the <u>**verb**</u> describes what the subject does.

✗	✔	WHY?
The **list** of names <u>**were circulated**</u> to the staff.	The **list** of names <u>**was circulated**</u> to the staff.	The subject is **list**, not names. **List** is singular. Use the singular verb <u>**was circulated**</u>.
The **software** in the computers <u>**are**</u> the latest program.	The **software** in the computers <u>**is**</u> the latest program.	The subject is **software**, not computers. **Software** is singular. Use the singular verb <u>**is**</u>.
The **leaves** on the maple tree <u>**turns**</u> red in the fall.	The **leaves** on the maple tree <u>**turn**</u> red in the fall.	The subject is **leaves**, not maple tree. **Leaves** is plural. Use the plural verb <u>**turn**</u>.
The **books** on the shelf <u>**is gathering**</u> dust.	The **books** on the shelf <u>**are gathering**</u> dust.	The subject is **books**, not shelf. **Books** is plural. Use the plural verb <u>**are gathering**</u>.
TIP Ignore the words that come between the subject and the verb.		
The finance **committee** <u>**have approved**</u> a new budget.	The finance **committee** <u>**has approved**</u> a new budget.	The members of the group are acting as **one unit**, not as individuals. Use the singular verb <u>**has approved**</u>.
After four days of deliberation, the **jury** <u>**remains**</u> divided.	After four days of deliberation, the **jury** <u>**remain**</u> divided.	The members of the group are acting as **individuals**, not as one unit. Use the plural verb <u>**remain**</u>.
Everyone in the audience <u>**were moved**</u> by the performance.	**Everyone** in the audience <u>**was moved**</u> by the performance.	Use a singular verb after words such as **any, anybody, anyone, anything, each, every, everybody, everyone, everything, no one, nobody, nothing, somebody, someone, something**.
Only a **few** <u>**is staying**</u> to the end.	Only a few <u>**are staying**</u> to the end.	Use a plural verb after words such as **all, both, few, many, several, some**.

The Apostrophe (')

The apostrophe has two main functions: to show possession and to form contractions. Knowing when to use an apostrophe and whether to put it before or after the letter *s* is a key to avoiding a frequently made mistake in punctuation.

✕	✔	WHY?
The tire on **Terrys** bike has a puncture.	The tire on **Terry's** bike has a puncture.	**Terry** is singular. Add the **'s** to show the bike belongs to Terry.
James computer is loaded with state-of-the-art software.	**James's** computer is loaded with state-of-the-art software.	**James** is singular and ends in **s**. Add an **'s** to show possession if the word isn't awkward to pronounce.
Ulysses travels played a significant role in Greek mythology.	**Ulysses'** travels played a significant role in Greek mythology.	**Ulysses** is singular and ends in **'s**. Add only an **'** after the last **s** when the word is awkward to pronounce.
The **ladies** tennis match attracted a sell-out crowd.	The **ladies'** tennis match attracted a sell-out crowd.	**Ladies** is plural and ends in **s**. Add an **'** after the **s** to show possession.
They watched the **mens'** golf tournament on TV.	They watched the **men's** golf tournament on TV.	**Men** is plural and doesn't end in **s**. Add an **'s** to show possession.
Terry and Robin's cars were vandalized.	**Terry's and Robin's** cars were vandalized.	**Terry** and **Robin** are singular and separate: Each person has a car. Add an **'s** after each name to show possession.
Terry's, Lynn's, and Robin's apartment was painted before they moved in. They decided to rent two **video's** for the weekend.	**Terry, Lynn, and Robin's** apartment was painted before they moved in. They decided to rent two **videos** for the weekend.	**Terry, Lynn, and Robin** are one singular unit: They jointly possess the apartment. Add the **'s** after the last person's name to show possession. The **s** in **videos** is used to make a plural and not to show possession. Do not use the **'** to make the word plural.

Commonly Confused Words 1

Many words in the English language are frequently confused one for the other. The word pairs below are called **homonyms**—words that sound alike but have different meanings.

WORD	DEFINITION	EXAMPLE
ascent assent	the act of rising agreement or acceptance	The balloon's **ascent** was rapid. He gave his **assent** to the proposal.
bloc block	a group of people, companies, or countries with a common interest a solid piece (e.g., wood, ice); to obstruct	The members of the political party voted as a **bloc**. How quickly will the **block** of ice melt? Did the felled tree **block** the road?
canvas canvass	a strong, heavy cloth to solicit opinions or views	**Canvas** makes a good protective cover. She phoned residents to **canvass** their views.
check cheque	to verify; to restrain or impede; a bank draft (used in the U.S.) a bank draft (used in Canada, Britain)	**Check** your letter carefully for careless errors. The flood was held in **check** by sandbags along the shore. The Chicago office awaited the **check** from its New York affiliate. She cashed the **cheque** as soon as it arrived.
coarse course	rough or crude direction or action; part of a meal; a series of lessons	The book contained **coarse** language. The wind blew the sailboat off **course**. The five-**course** gourmet meal was a delight. Which language arts **course** are you enrolled in?
complement compliment	one of two things that go well together or suit each other to congratulate or to praise	Wine and food should **complement** each other. Please **compliment** the chef on a wonderful meal.
dependant dependent	one who relies on the support of another unable to do without	Are you a **dependant** of your parents? He was **dependent** on drugs to ease the pain.
flair flare	an instinct or knack for doing something well a bright flame or light	Her **flair** for photography earned wide recognition. He launched a **flare** to signal an emergency.
foreword forward	a preface or introduction in a book ahead or to advance	She wrote a **foreword** to her latest novel. They looked **forward** to their winter vacation.
forth fourth	to go forward, set out a number that follows third	They put **forth** some good ideas. It's her **fourth** attempt to beat the record.
hoard horde	to amass or collect; to overstock in scarce times a throng of people or a swarm of insects, animals	They put aside a **hoard** of food before winter's onset. A **horde** of invaders swept across the land.
it's its	a contraction of it is indicates possession	**It's** all over but the shouting. The dog wagged **its** tail when it saw me.
lean lien	not much fat; to rest against something a legal claim against property	She always purchased **lean** meat. **Lean** the board against the wall. A **lien** was issued against his car to cover the debt.
lightening lightning	brightening; reducing in weight a flash of bright light during a thunderstorm	The sky was **lightening** after the storm. Her mailbag began **lightening** after 15 minutes of deliveries. A flash of **lightning** illuminated the sky.

Commonly Confused Words 2

Many words in the English language are often confused one for the other. The word pairs below have similarities in spelling or in meaning.

WORD	DEFINITION	EXAMPLE
accept except	to receive; to agree to an action to exclude; not including	We **accept** courier parcels at the reception desk. I **accept** your offer of a free gift. She was **excepted** from the meeting. Everyone went to the movie **except** me.
affect effect	to influence; to move or touch, as in feelings a result or outcome	Computers **affect** the way we work. Her kindness **affected** him deeply. Staff cuts had a deep **effect** on morale.
aggravate irritate	to worsen something that already exists to annoy or to vex	You'll **aggravate** your injury if you exercise. You **irritate** me when you arrive late.
alternate alternative	a substitute way of doing things two or more options; a matter of choice	We found an **alternate** solution to the problem. We took the **alternative** route home. I had no **alternative** but to replace the broken lamp.
among between	involves more than two things or two persons involves only two things or two persons	**Among** all my discs, this one is my favourite. **Between** the two, I like this one better.
anyone any one	any kind of a person any single person or thing	**Anyone** can go to the dance. The ticket was valid for **any one** of the games.
assure ensure	to express certainty or confidence to make sure or to guarantee	Can you **assure** me that the rain will stop? Success at work helps to **ensure** promotion.
balance remainder	difference between a credit and a debt a small amount left over	The **balance** owing is seven dollars. I'll eat the **remainder** of the cookies tomorrow.
beside besides	by the side of in addition to	We picnicked **beside** the lake. **Besides** you, there will be five of us.
biannual biennial	twice a year once every two years	The craft show has become a popular **biannual** event. The **biennial** games are held on even-numbered years.
bring take	to come with something or someone to remove or carry something or someone elsewhere	Please **bring** some snacks for the party. Please **take** my coat to the dry cleaners.
can may	indicates a physical or mental ability to do something indicates permission	I **can** do anything better than you. You **may** borrow my car for a few hours.
client customer	uses professional services uses commercial services	The lawyer's office was filled with **clients**. **Customers** flocked to the clothing sale.
colleague partner	business associate legally constituted member of partnership	I consider my boss a good **colleague**. She joined the firm as a full **partner**.
continual continuous	repeated again and again over a period of time no break in the action or the process	Mowing the lawn is a **continual** activity. The well produced a **continuous** flow of oil.

Source: Copyright © 1999 from *The Write Guide* series, The Writing Edge, 35 Merton St. #1607, Toronto, ON, M4S 3G4.

Glossary

Accommodation: one of the two cognitive processes (see also *assimilation*) by which children learn concepts and add information to their cognitive structures (Piaget, 1969). Accommodation refers to new information or experience that disrupts the existing schemata by which children understand the world; how it is acted on, absorbed, or accommodated, and results in a different, more complex capacity to understand.

Aesthetic reading: reading for pleasure, for meaning-making, and for the deep personal engagement that connects the reader's life with the textual experience (Rosenblatt 1978, 1991).

Aesthetic response: involvement of the reader's personal, emotional, often empathetic (rather than cerebral) response to the imaginative and expressive qualities of language. See also *efferent response*.

Alphabetic principle: the one-to-one correspondence between phonemes (or sounds) and graphemes (or letters) so that each letter represents one sound. English is not a purely phonetic language, only approximately half its words being spelled phonetically.

Amelia Frances Howard Gibbon Award: given since 1971 by the Canadian Library Association, this award honours excellence in children's illustration in a book published in Canada. The award must go to a citizen or resident of Canada.

Assimilation: the cognitive process by which new information in the environment is integrated into existing schemata (Piaget, 1969). Students learn when their existing schemata are enlarged because of assimilated learning. See also *accommodation*.

Automaticity: the capacity to carry out a complex act effectively and without conscious awareness and control, while at the same time performing another non-automatic act. Thus, proficient readers who can identify words automatically can redirect their mental resources to other cognitive processes: e.g., aesthetic and emotional meaning-making, and analysis.

Basal readers: resources for teaching language arts concepts, strategies, and skills. (They are so-called because they were originally intended to provide the basis for reading-instruction programs.) They provide information about language arts topics and a sequence of topics, models, examples, and practice activities for each grade level.

Big books: enlarged picture books used in shared reading with emergent (usually primary-grade) readers.

Caldecott Medal: named for the British illustrator of children's books, Randolph Caldecott (1846–1886), and awarded annually since 1938 to the preceding year's "artist of the most distinguished American picture book for children." The winning book receives the Caldecott Medal, and one or more runners-up are also recognized as "Honor" books.

Canadian Library Award: given by the Canadian Library Association to recognize the year's most distinguished children's book by a Canadian citizen.

Canadian literature awards: See *Amelia Frances Howard Gibbon Award*; *Canadian Library Award*; *Children's Choice Awards*; and *Governor General's Literary Awards*.

Censorship: the authorized attempt to suppress printed matter, films, news, etc., on the grounds of obscenity or threat to security. It is also the impulse to prevent certain ideas and memories from emerging into consciousness. Informal censorship also occurs in the personal selection and rejection of material and the attempt to prevent access of others to that material.

Challenged books: texts that groups or individuals attempt to censor by having them removed from libraries, especially school libraries. School districts generally have procedures for dealing with challenges, and for deciding whether or not a book should be removed.

Chapter books: stories, beginners' novels, and informational books with few, if any, illustrations. They are written in chapter format, mainly for middle and upper-elementary readers, as they move from a reliance on illustrations to a focus on text.

Children's Choice Awards: awarded regionally in Canada (and at the state level in the United States) on the basis of students' votes, and highly regarded by authors and illustrators. The students' choices are selected from recent titles compiled by teachers and librarians. Awards include Manitoba Young Reader's Choice Award, given by the Manitoba School Library Audio Visual Association for the favourite Canadian book of Manitoba's young readers; the Red Cedar Book Award, given by the Young Readers' Choice Awards Society of BC for British Columbia schoolchildren's favourite fiction and non-fiction books; the Silver Birch Award, given by the Ontario Library Association for the best books chosen by Ontario students in grades 4 to 6; the Red Maple Award, also given by the Ontario Library Association for the best Canadian children's fiction chosen by Ontario students, grades 7, 8, and 9; the Ruth Schwartz Children's Book Award, given by the Ontario Arts Council and Canadian Booksellers Association for the best book selected by Ontario schoolchildren.

Children's literature: literature intended for young people. Children's literature, like all literature, has inherent imaginative and artistic qualities that offer pleasure and understanding. Literature has the power to evoke strong emotions, to engage the intellect, to express feelings, and act in beautiful language, and to allow the vicarious experience of different times, places, and characters. Language used with skill and artistry gives pleasure to readers of all ages, deepens their thinking and feeling, and encourages them to explore the nature of humankind at an appropriate level.

Clustering: a pre-writing strategy by which students gather and organize information and ideas. The topic is written at the centre of a web-like diagram; main ideas supporting the topic are drawn out from the centre like rays, with details added as information is gathered.

Constructivism: a learning theory showing how learners participate actively in their own learning. Piaget (1969) views learning as processes of assimilation and accommodation, with learners modifying their cognitive structures as they interact with and adapt to their environment. Because learners construct their own knowledge from personal experience (which arises from particulars of culture, home, and community), the meanings readers construct from the texts they negotiate will be as varied as their background experience.

Contemporary realistic fiction: fiction that offers an imaginative reflection of the concerns and dilemmas of contemporary life. Set in the world as we know it, and governed by natural laws as we understand them, contemporary realistic fiction is intended to provide a believable mirror of life. Fictional situations within a child's understanding encourage involvement and empathy, and provide a vision of the human condition. Believable characters who solve real problems suggest models for living in the contemporary world, and offer the opportunity for the safe exploration of human relations and varied cultures through the imagination.

Context cues: cues that assist children to construct their understanding of reading material in terms of what makes sense and seems "right." Prior knowledge offers a context for new information, while linguistic cues include syntactic (grammar or word order) and semantic (meaning) aspects of language.

Critical literacy: reading that goes beyond the *what* of written language to the *how* and *why*, and *so what?* It goes beyond the reader's competency and comprehension to require a capacity for reflective insight, to "read" the symbolism, the relations of power, the cultural influences, and the writer's craft in a philosophical and political context. Children who are encouraged to focus on craft and to reflect on their own responses (on how a book was written and how it affected them) develop active, critical, metacognitive reading strategies.

Cueing systems: four types of cues that organize language and make oral and written communication possible. The four cueing systems are the phonological (or sound) system of language; the syntactic (or structural) system of language; the semantic (or meaning) system of language; and the pragmatic (or social and cultural use) system of language.

Cultural literacy: a working familiarity with commonly held values, and with general knowledge from past cultures that have shaped and defined modern society.

Cursive writing: joining letters together to form a word in one continuous movement. Some controversy exists over the best time to lead children from manuscript to cursive writing.

DEAR (Drop Everything and Read): daily (silent) reading practice, in addition to regular reading instruction, in which students read self-selected library books. See also *USSR (Uninterrupted Sustained Silent Reading).*

Dialect: nonstandard, informal forms of a spoken language (in this case, Standard English) used by different social classes, cultural, ethnic, or regional groups. The style, or register, of Standard English is formal, and is used in textbooks, newspapers, most media, and schools. Each dialect is distinctive; it differs from Standard English in its phonology, syntax, and semantics, but is neither inferior nor substandard.

Dialogue: an interactive written or spoken conversation between or among any number of people. A dialogue is not a forum for "winning" (like a debate). Participants build on mutual trust and respect, acknowledge and support one another, offer ideas, encourage questioning, and create an opportunity for real communication.

Direct assessment: basing assessment on a sample of writing (rather than multiple-choice and short-answer questions as is the case in indirect assessment). Although judgment is unavoidably subjective, direct assessment is generally agreed to be the only way to assess the learning writer's ability authentically.

Direct instruction: instruction that offers systematic, planned lessons with explicit information. Not necessarily confined to skill-and-drill activities, direct instruction provides information and opportunities for students to apply what they are learning with guidance from the teacher. See also *indirect instruction.*

Discourse: a linguistics term that describes a continuous spoken or written discussion. It is also used to denote a topic area or thought system shaped by commonly held assumptions and aims (e.g., feminist discourse, capitalist discourse, patriarchal discourse, post-structural discourse).

DLTA (Directed Listening–Thinking Approach): an approach by which the teacher prepares the student(s) for active listening habits. The teacher prepares students for reading (provides necessary background information to stimulate interest, and encourages predictions and focus) and reads aloud, stopping periodically to discuss student perceptions and predictions. On completion, the teacher encourages students' reflection and expression of response to the literature, and connection to their own experience.

D'Nealian handwriting: an innovative manuscript and cursive handwriting program designed to increase legibility and to ease the transition from manuscript to cursive handwriting.

Drama, context for learning: a learning medium that offers a powerful form of communication, and can have a positive effect on students' oral language development and literacy learning. The experience of drama activities and role-playing can evoke an aesthetic response to literature, and build a deeper understanding of the lived experience of what others might have experienced, encouraging risk-taking, empathy, and creativity. Often divergent in nature, drama often results in an emergent curriculum with multiple meanings.

Dramatic forms: in the language arts, forms include storytelling, puppetry, choral speech, choric drama, readers theatre, dramatization, and story theatre. All of these dramatic forms require students to create or interpret meaning within the "as if" world of drama. The forms described in this text require language to express this meaning. Scripts, props, and movement are also used.

Efferent response: a response that occurs as the student reads to locate, observe, and remember information, and reads directions and explanations. Rosenblatt (1978) suggests a continuum of efferent and aesthetic responses to literature. Although readers often use both purposes simultaneously, one approach generally predominates.

Elkonin boxes: an aid to word segmentation; a difficult phonemic awareness activity for learners. The teacher shows an object, or picture of the object, and draws a series of boxes corresponding to the number of sounds heard in the word. Teacher or child moves a marker into each box as the sound is pronounced.

Emergent literacy: the concept that young children begin to learn to read and write very early in life through participating in real-life settings in which reading and writing are used, and through active involvement with literacy materials: e.g., social and cultural language learning such as children's readiness to listen to stories read aloud, to notice labels and signs, and to experiment with pencils. It has replaced the traditional reading readiness approach.

English as a second language (ESL): a course of study for students whose native language is not English (these students are referred to as *ESL students*). The needs of linguistically diverse students are best met if teachers value and support the students' proficiency in their native languages while they acquire English.

Expository writing: non-fiction, informational writing that invites both efferent (fact-finding) and aesthetic (personally pleasurable and expressive) reading, as children learn about their world. Expository texts of quality demonstrate accuracy (current and complete information) and organization (clear, logical, and readable). They are well designed (visually and aesthetically enhancing) and written in a lively, stimulating style that engages the reader's wonder and curiosity.

Expressive writing: one of three categories (with poetic writing and transactional writing) by which Britton et al. (1975) describe the functions of language. Expressive writing is used to muse and reflect, to record and explore the writer's feelings, mood, opinions, and preoccupations.

Family literacy programs: programs designed for families whose parents are non-fluent readers. Parents develop their own reading and writing competencies, learn how to support their children's reading, and participate with their children in reading and writing activities. Cultural differences are considered strengths to be built upon, not weaknesses (unlike the older "deficit" model).

Fantasy: a genre rooted in myth, legend, dreams, and subconscious archetypes. Well-written fantasy creates an imagined world (in which, for example, time travel, or extraterrestrial beings, or talking animals occur) that is made psychologically credible to the reader through its richly detailed setting, inner logic, and internal consistency, and because, like all good fiction, it poses important questions about the human condition. Fantasy includes such sub-genres as high fantasy (Ursula Le Guin's *A Wizard of Earthsea*, 1984), science fiction (Monica Hughes's *Keeper of the Isis Light*, 2000), time fantasy, (Kit Pearson's *Awake and Dreaming*, 1996; Julie Lawson's *White Jade Tiger*, 1993), and fantastic animal stories (E. B. White's *Charlotte's Web*, 1980).

Figurative language: language, conveyed by idioms and figures of speech, that is metaphorical, symbolic, and open to multiple interpretations. Children need to move beyond explicit, literal, dictionary meanings to understand how flexible, subtle, and expressive language can be.

Genre: the distinctive form of a category of literature (e.g., novel, poem, science fiction, biography) by which it is identified and classified (e.g., the form and function of an expository text differs from that of a folk tale).

Governor General's Literary Awards: an award that recognizes literary excellence in French and English in annual prizes for fiction, poetry, drama, non-fiction, children's literature text, children's literature illustration, and translation. The prizes are highly prestigious, accompanied by elaborate presentation ceremonies, and timed to coincide with the major book-buying season.

Grammar: the structural organization of English; the rules governing how words are combined into sentences. The term often replaces *syntax.* Where grammar has traditionally been taught prescriptively (dealing with "correct" and "incorrect" usage), it is more usually taught today in a functional and descriptive manner.

Grand conversations: book discussions and literature circles in which students explore interpretations and reflect on their feelings. The teacher serves primarily as a facilitator–participant, and the focus is on clarifying and deepening students' understanding.

Graphophonics: the print–sound relationship of text. The reader identifies graphic cues (letters, clusters, words) with speech sounds.

Great Vowel Shift: the striking change in the pronunciation of long vowels that took place toward the beginning of the Modern English (1500–present) period. For instance, the word *name* had two syllables and rhymed with *comma* during the Middle English period, but during the Great Vowel Shift, its pronunciation shifted to rhyme with *game* (Hook, 1975).

Guided reading: reading where the teacher and students (usually in small groups) read and talk their way through a text in a cycle of questioning, reading (aloud or silently), and discussion. This scaffolding enables students to develop and use reading strategies. Selections used for guided reading should be at the students' zone of proximal development.

Handwriting: See *cursive writing, D'Nealian handwriting,* and *manuscript handwriting.*

Heuristics: in educational instruction, a process of assisting learners to make educated guesses, and discover through exploration, rather than to learn simply by being told.

High fantasy: a sub-genre of fantasy often influenced by myths and legends, and is generally concerned with the conflict between good and evil. It is characteristically written in a tone of high seriousness, often in a heroic vein, and involves a quest or journey that accompanies the protagonist's moral growth and the achievement of some transcendent goal.

Historical fiction: fiction set within a specific past time and place, and written with attention to authenticity of setting and accurate representation of what is known to be factual. Events are shown, not in isolation, but as part of a historical continuity that gives meaning to the present time. Through understanding issues of the past, the reader is often given insight into contemporary problems.

Holistic scoring: evaluating writing as a whole, or as a single impression, rather than enumerating the components that give it its strengths and weaknesses. Holistic scoring accomplishes its evaluative function more quickly and consistently than conventional assessment. Consistency grows from the development of effective writing criteria and model anchor papers.

Hypermedia: computer software that organizes and links multimedia information (sound, graphics, text, video, animation) so that the user can retrieve and modify information in various forms, and move from one medium to another in a non-linear manner.

Hypertext: writing that is non-linear. Reading hypertext is an associative rather than a sequential act. Readers can control what they read and the sequence in which they read it, by selecting at random, or by choosing options or pathways.

Indirect instruction: instruction that occurs as teachers respond to students' on-the-spot needs, questions, and teachable moments, and by the skills and behaviours that teachers themselves are modelling. See also *direct instruction.*

Inner speech: a theory by Lev Vygotsky (1986), who noted children talking aloud to themselves while performing an activity or task to guide or direct their thinking. He concluded that language is a mechanism for thought and that children's egocentric speech ("self-talk") gradually becomes inner speech, whereby children talk to themselves mentally rather than orally. Children use both self-talk and inner speech to guide their learning.

Inquiry-based units: units for which students and teacher develop their own questions to read about, write about, and study. Inquiry-based units are often interdisciplinary, used in conjunction with science, social studies, and/or fine arts.

Instructional reading level: the reading level at which the student can read successfully with regular classroom support. Teachers use the percentage of words students can read correctly to determine if the reading material is too difficult, too easy, or appropriate for the student at this time. If the student reads 95 percent of the words correctly, the

book is easy, at the independent reading level for that child. If the student reads 90–94 percent correctly, the book is at the instructional reading level. If the student reads fewer than 90 percent of the words correctly, the book is too difficult, at the student's frustration level.

Integration: learning language in a way that is not separated from other subjects or fields of knowledge, but integrated with them, and integral to them. Language teachers promote authentic communication about issues active in their students' experience, whether from their homes, communities, or other subjects.

Invented spelling: unique, invented spellings created by young children as they begin to write, based on their knowledge of the phonological system. Young children use ingenious strategies (like letter names to spell words, e.g., *U* for *you*) that differ at each stage of their way to becoming conventional spellers. Teacher analysis of a child's invented spelling provides information about the individual's level of spelling development and suggests the appropriate type of instruction.

Literacy: once meant *knowing how to read;* it has expanded to connote the competence to carry out the complex tasks of reading and writing related to the work world and life outside school. Other kinds of literacy (computer literacy, visual literacy, critical literacy, cultural literacy) indicate other crucial modes of making meaning. Literacy, then, is not a prescription, or reading list, but rather a way to come to learn about the world and to participate more fully in society.

Literacy centres: learning stations in primary classrooms where students can work in small groups to practise skills and explore literacy concepts. Students might, for example, manipulate literacy materials, write group poems, compile charts, watch a video, or experiment with artistic techniques.

Mainstreaming: the integration of students with special needs into regular classrooms. Children with mild disabilities may be entirely integrated into the class, while those with more severe disabilities receive specialized instruction where necessary.

Manuscript handwriting: similar to the type style of primary-level textbooks. It is assumed to facilitate young children's introduction to reading and writing, the letters being easier to form and more legible than those of the cursive form.

Metacognition: the knowledge children acquire about their own cognitive processes. As children are able, for example, to reflect on their own literacy processes, and to understand which learning strategies are most effective for them, they become increasingly aware of what they know and don't know, and are able to regulate this knowledge to maximize learning.

Metafiction: a type of fiction—unlike realism, which attempts to create the illusion of a "real" world—that draws attention to its own fictionality. Metafiction shows how texts "mean" by such devices as narrators who directly address the reader; ironic or satirical parodies of other texts; mixtures of genres and discourses; and other experimentations.

Metalinguistic awareness: the capacity to use language to think and talk of language; to understand language as a formal code, that is, a system of communication. For example, two individuals in conversation discuss whether they understand one another's meaning. With children, metalinguistic awareness may refer to comprehension of such terms as *letter, word, sentence,* and *sound.*

Middle English (1100–1500): a period of tremendous change in the English language. For nearly three hundred years, following the Norman Conquest of England, French was the official language for government, law, poetry, and history, although the lower classes continued to speak English. By the end of the fourteenth century (the time of Chaucer's *Canterbury Tales*), English was restored. By then, a large portion of the Old English vocabulary had been lost, while Latin borrowings and thousands of French words were added to the language. Grammatical gender was lost, and word endings and plural forms changed, although some irregular verbs were retained (e.g., *sing, fly*) that still contribute to usage problems.

Minilessons: brief, direct-instruction lessons designed (within the larger context of the class process) to introduce, practise, or review a particular skill, concept, or strategy.

Miscues: reading errors. Teachers can categorize students' miscues according to the semantic, graphophonic, and syntactic cueing systems in order to examine what word-identification strategies students are using.

Modern English (1500–present): a period of the development of the English language characterized by the invention of the printing press, and expansion through trade, colonization, and trade. The printing press served to standardize spelling, while travel absorbed words from more than fifty languages. This period saw the Great Vowel Shift and changes in syntax, particularly the disappearance of the double negative, and standardization of comparatives and superlatives.

Morpheme: the smallest meaningful unit in language (e.g., *dog*; *play*). Word parts that change the meanings of words are also morphemes (*-s*; *-ing*). *Dog* is a free morpheme because it conveys meaning while standing alone; *-s* is a bound morpheme because it must be attached to a free morpheme to convey meaning.

Morphology: in linguistics, the study of the structure of words (as opposed to *syntax*, the study of the arrangement of words in the higher units of phrases, sentences, etc.). See also *morpheme*.

Multicultural literature: literature that meets criteria for good literature while also enriching and expanding the reader's cultural consciousness. Through access to diverse cultural contexts, mainstream students develop sensitivity to and appreciation for people of cultural groups other than their own; they expand their understanding of historical perspectives, often challenging traditional assumptions about the history of the dominant (especially North American) culture; and they raise issues of social justice, and are able to challenge racial and ethnic stereotypes. Non-mainstream students benefit from multicultural literature that makes the "insider" point of view visible in the social fabric. These students' reading is enriched when they find their own cultural experience and values acknowledged and respected; and when they find characters and events with whom they can identify.

Narrative: (1) the general term for a story or account of any event or experience, fact or fiction, long or short, detailed or simplified; and (2) the form that story takes. Narratives are frequently arranged according to cause and effect or chronology. The way people choose to tell a story often reveals their values and assumptions, and the way they make meaning. Teachers seek strategies to evoke and empower student narrative competency and expressiveness in all the language arts.

Native speaker ability: the ability to use language in various situations and for various purposes. In order to meet the needs of linguistically diverse students, teachers try to help students to develop a high level of proficiency in their native language as well as to add English as a second language.

Newbery Medal: a medal named in honour of John Newbery (1713–1767), the first English publisher of children's books, that has been given annually (since 1922) by the American Library Association's Association for Library Service to Children. The recipient is recognized as the author of the most distinguished book in children's literature published in the United States in the preceding year. The winning book receives the Newbery Medal, and one or more runners-up are also recognized as "Honor" books.

Old English (AD 450–1100): the first recorded period of the development of the English language. The English language began as a mingling of the dialects of the Angles, Saxons, and other Germanic tribes in Britain. Borrowed Viking and Roman words also made their way into the predominantly Germanic word stock. Old English spelling, structure, and pronunciation are significantly different from Modern English, and the language would not be understood by a Modern English speaker.

Performance-based assessment: a summative evaluation of a student's ability or knowledge based on performance or product. Performance-based learning is often seen as real-world performance defined by precise rubrics that define criteria for quality performance at various levels of achievement.

Persuasive writing: writing with a purpose. The writer supports, develops, and consistently maintains a position, with the intention of persuading the reader by logic, or through an appeal to the reader's character or emotions.

Phonemic awareness: children's basic understanding that speech is composed of a series of individual sounds, provides the foundation for phonics. The emphasis is on the sounds of spoken words, not on reading letters or pronouncing letter names. Developing phonemic awareness enables children to use sound–symbol correspondences to read and spell words. Phonemic awareness is a powerful predictor of later reading achievement.

Phonetic spelling: spelling by choosing letters on the basis of sound alone (e.g., *LIV* for *live*; *NE* for *knee*). Phonetic spelling is decipherable because it represents all the essential sound features in a word. Phonetic spellers are typically about six years old.

Phonics: the set of relationships between *phonology* (the sounds in speech) and *orthography* (the spelling patterns of written language). Phonics is a controversial topic; current thinking is that reading is a complex process, and that the phonological system works in conjunction with the semantic, syntactic, and pragmatic systems, not in isolation. Adams (1990) recommends that phonics instruction (sound– symbol correspondences; how to blend sounds to decode words; how to segment sounds to spell; useful phonics generalizations or "rules") should be systematic, intensive, and completed by the third grade.

Phonology: the study of sound patterns in language, and how they combine to create words and meaning.

Picture book: a short book (usually 32 pages, sometimes 24 or 48 pages) with pictures on every page or double-page set. Not to be confused with illustrated books (in which the illustrations are subordinate to the text), the art and text of picture books are equally important, and function like an interdependent double text to convey the book's content, theme, and meaning.

Poetic writing: one of three categories (with *expressive writing* and *transactional writing*) by which Britton et al. (1975) describe the functions of language. Poetic writing is created for aesthetic satisfaction and pleasure.

Polysemic: in linguistics, a word's ability to denote more than one meaning. Polysemic texts, with their multiple possible meanings, provide opportunities for accomplished readers to infer, interpret, and speculate.

Portfolios: systematic and meaningful collections of artifacts documenting students' language arts learning and development over a period of time, and reflecting their day-to-day learning in the language arts and across the curriculum. Students usually choose the items to place in their portfolios, within guidelines provided by the teacher; portfolios are therefore a useful vehicle for encouraging self-reflection, self-evaluation, and goal setting.

Pragmatics: one of the four cueing systems that make oral and written communication possible. Pragmatics deals with the social and cultural contexts of language use. People make meaning with different intentions and for different audiences, and their language varies accordingly (for example, in regional or cultural dialects; and in peer-group speech communities).

Predictable books: books characterized by (1) repetition (of words, sentences, rhymes); (2) cumulative sequence (elements are repeated and expanded in each episode); (3) rhyme and rhythm; (4) sequential patterns (like the alphabet or days of the week), which structure the text. Predictable books are often used in shared reading with young children, and offer a valuable tool to emergent readers because their repetition enables children to predict the next sentence or episode.

Quickwriting: a writing strategy used to brainstorm ideas, to focus on content rather than mechanics, and to encourage the student's natural writing voice. Students write on a topic continuously for five to ten minutes, letting their thoughts flow from mind to pen without focusing on mechanics or revision.

Reader-response: both a critical and a pedagogical approach to literature. Reader-response focuses on the reader's unadulterated, felt response to the text, the "web of feelings, sensations, images, ideas" (Rosenblatt, 1978) based on the reader's own prior experience, cultural history, knowledge of life, and experience of other texts. The focus is on the reader, not on the literary tradition, and the teacher's role is to provide instruction that can arouse, challenge, refine, and enlarge the reader's response to literature.

Readers theatre: a formal dramatic presentation of a script by a group of readers. In readers theatre, children approach literature through performance rather than discussion. Students usually prepare scripts from books they have read, rehearsing, interpreting, and performing them through voice and gesture, rather than through action.

Readers workshop: an alternative to traditional reading instruction that provides students with choices, time to read and write, and opportunities for response through conversation and writing. Students read books that they choose themselves, and respond to books through writing in reading logs and conferencing. Readers workshop usually includes reading, sharing, minilessons, and reading aloud to students.

Reading logs: logs in which students respond to stories and books they are reading, or that are being read to them. As they gain experience reading and responding to literature, students frequently move from retellings and summaries to personal and interpretive comments.

Reading readiness: a former approach to literacy instruction that assumed that there is a point in children's development when it is time to begin teaching them to read and write. Kindergarten children were "readied" for formal reading and writing instruction, which would begin in the first grade. This approach has now been largely replaced by the concept of *emergent literacy*.

Reading series: See *basal readers*.

Realism: See *contemporary realistic fiction* and *historical fiction*.

Resource-based units: units centred on a featured selection or several related books. Students work as a group (becoming a community of readers); read (independently, with a partner, or with the teacher); respond in reading logs and grand conversations; participate in minilessons on the unit's concept, strategy, or skill; and create projects to extend their reading. See also *grand conversations* and *minilessons*.

Rubrics: scoring guides to assess students' growth as writers. Rubrics may have several levels of assessment, with coherent and clearly articulated descriptors related to the domains of ideas, organization, language, and mechanics at each level. Clear criteria and specific expectations help students view writing less as a mystery, and more as a task that they can perform, and at which they can improve.

Scaffolding: support mechanisms that teachers, parents, or other more competent individuals provide to help children successfully perform a task within their zone of proximal development (Vygotsky, 1978; Bruner, 1986). Also see *zone of proximal development*.

Schemata (singular: *schema***):** the cognitive structure's conceptual filing system. Schemata are mental frameworks in which children and adults organize and store the information derived from their experiences. Learners invent new categories and personalize them according to their values, interests, and cultural history. See also *accommodation* and *assimilation*.

Semantic map (or *web***):** a diagram showing relationships among concepts; used to organize ideas, topics, and units of study. See also *clustering*.

Semantics: one of the four cueing systems that make communication possible, *semantics* is the meaning system of language. Vocabulary is the key component; children acquire vocabulary, not only learning new words, but, through a process of refinement, learning that words have both connotations and denotations (i.e., shades of meaning, several meanings, contextual meanings).

Skills: specific, automatic, or unconscious information-processing techniques, such as decoding and spelling, or reference and study skills. See also *strategy*.

SQ4R study strategy: a six-step technique in which students survey, question, read, recite, review, and reflect in order to read and remember information in a content-area reading assignment.

Standardized achievement tests: tests generally used to assess the achievement of individual students, and (like those used for university admission) to predict future performance and likelihood of success. Their value lies in offering teachers insight into their students within a wider context than the isolated classroom. However, their use is problematic for purposes other than individual assessment: for example, in certifying completion of a grade, evaluating teachers, accrediting schools, or validating the excellence of school systems.

Story map: a diagram or chart that helps students visualize structures and relationships in stories. Students add information, illustrations, and text from the story they are reading to enrich the story map, which may take the form of beginning–middle–end plot diagrams, character clusters (or theme, setting, genre clusters, etc.), Venn diagrams, plot profiles to chart tensions, and sociograms.

Storyboard: a sequential series of components used for ordering and other stage activities. A storyboard with picture-book text and illustrations cut out and individually affixed to cards can be examined in terms of illustrations and/or arranged sequentially. A more sophisticated video storyboard might have dialogue, setting, and shooting directions, each organized sequentially.

Strategy: an overall method, behaviour, plan, or scheme to enable task performance or problem-solving. One strategy can be used in various learning situations. Some thinking strategies that readers and writers use include the following: tapping prior knowledge; predicting; organizing ideas; visualizing; making connections; generalizing; and revising meaning. (*Skills*, on the other hand, are more specific automatic or unconscious information-processing techniques, such as decoding and spelling, or reference and study skills.)

SSR (Sustained Silent Reading): a daily period of silent reading in the classroom when children read self-selected books. See also *DEAR* and *USSR*.

Syntax: the structural organization of English; the grammar that regulates how words are combined into sentences. Also see *grammar*.

Thematic organization: the arrangement of learning matter around a central concept, author, or topic. Connecting compelling ideas to one another (within a field or across the curriculum) facilitates learning through its connection to the lives and experiences of students.

Thematic units: interdisciplinary units that integrate the language arts with social studies, science, math, and other curricular areas. Topics are broad and encompass many possibilities (e.g., civilization, inventions). Students use all the language arts as they investigate, solve problems, learn, and demonstrate their new learning.

Time fantasy: a sub-genre of science fiction in which parallel worlds running simultaneously to ours touch our primary world in magical places, allowing time travel back and forth. In addition, there are time-warp fantasies, in which a character from the present can go back in time, or vice-versa. As time shifts, its fluidity suggests thoughts of actions and consequences of the way we use time in our lives, and of time's relativity. See also *fantasy*.

Trade books: books published for children as literature (stories, informational books, poems), and not as educational texts. Books published as part of an educational program, and used in schools, are referred to as "textbooks."

Transactional theory: a theory based on the work of Louise Rosenblatt (1978), who posits that meaning comes from a transaction between reader and text in the specific context of the reader's background knowledge, experience, and world view. Also see *reader-response*.

Transactional writing: one of three categories (with expressive writing and poetic writing) by which Britton et al. (1975) describe the functions of language. Transactional writing is used to get things done, to accomplish a goal, to advise, persuade, or instruct.

Unit: a series of lessons planned around a curriculum text or theme, so that individual lessons work in consort with other lessons on a shared topic.

USSR (Uninterrupted Sustained Silent Reading): See *SSR* and *DEAR*.

Visual literacy: the capacity to "read" and visually decode the artifacts of society (not just the art of high culture), moving from close observation and concrete description, to inferences and generalizations, to creative reflection and insight.

Whole language: a philosophy about learning, language, and the nature of relationships between children and adults. Children are viewed as learning language through using it, making meaning in a personal, social, and cultural context. Practices associated with whole language include immersing children in a print-rich environment that includes quality literature, and basing assessments on their language use in the classroom.

Word walls: large sheets of paper, initially blank, hung on a classroom wall, on which students and teacher write down accumulative lists of interesting, confusing, and important words from books they are reading and from thematic unit concepts.

Writers workshop: similar to readers workshop, but with a writing focus, writers workshop includes writing, sharing, and minilessons.

Students write on topics they choose themselves, and assume ownership of their writing and learning. The teacher's role is that of facilitator to a community of writers.

Writing process: what students do as they think and write. The stages of the writing process are prewriting (gathering and organizing ideas); drafting (getting the ideas down on paper); revising (refining and clarifying ideas); editing (putting the writing in its final form, including mechanics and proofreading); and publishing (sharing with an appropriate audience). The stages are not necessarily linear, and in fact more frequently merge and recur cyclically.

Zone of proximal development: the range of tasks a child can perform with guidance from others but cannot yet perform independently. Vygotsky (1978) believed that children learn best when what they are attempting to learn is within this zone.

References

Professional References

Adams, M. J. (1990). *Beginning to read: Thinking and learning about print* (Executive Summary). Cambridge, MA: MIT Press.

Adams, M. J. (1994). *Beginning to read: Thinking and learning about print*. Cambridge, MA: MIT Press.

Allen, V. A. (1991). *Teaching bilingual and ESL children*. In J. Flood, J. M. Jensen, D. Lapp, & J. R. Squire (Eds.), *Handbook of research on teaching the English language artsarts* (pp. 356–364). Upper Saddle River, NJ: Prentice Hall/Merrill.

Altwerger, B., & Flores, B. (1994). Theme cycles: Creating communities of learners. *Primary Voices K–6, 2*, 2–6.

Alvermann, D. (2002). Preface. In D. Alvermann (Ed.). *Adolescents and literacies in a digital world*. New York: Peter Lang.

Alvermann, D., & Boothby, P. (1986). Children's transfer of graphic organizer instruction. *Reading Psychology, 7*(2), 87–100.

Anderson, K. F. (1985). The development of spelling ability and linguistic strategies. *The Reading Teacher, 39*, 140–147.

Anderson-Inman, L., & Horney, M. (1999). Electronic books: Reading and studying with supportive resources. *Reading Online*. Retrieved from http://www.readingonline.org/home.html.

Anderson-Inman, L., Horney, M. A., Chen, D. T., & Lewin, L. (1994). Hypertext literacy: Observations from the Electotext project. *Language Arts, 71*, 279–287.

Andrews, J., & Lupart, J. (1993). *The inclusive classroom: Educating exceptional children*. Scarborough, ON: Nelson.

Applebee, A. N. (1978). *The child's concept of story: Ages 2 to 17*. Chicago: University of Chicago Press.

Applebee, A. N., & Langer, J. A. (1983). Instructional scaffolding: Reading and writing and natural language activities. *Language Arts, 60*, 168–175.

Apseloff, M. (1979). Old wine in new bottles: Adult poetry for children. *Children's Literature in Education, 10*, 194–202.

Arnheim, R. (1989). *Thoughts on art education*. Santa Monica, CA: Getty Center for Education in the Arts.

Ashton-Warner, S. (1965). *Teacher*. New York: Simon & Schuster.

Askov, E., & Greff, K. N. (1975). Handwriting: Copying versus tracing as the most effective type of practice. *Journal of Educational Research, 69*, 96–98.

Atwell, N. (1987). *In the middle: Writing, reading, and learning with adolescents*. Portsmouth, NH: Heinemann.

Atwell, N. (1998). *In the middle: New understandings about writing, reading, and literature* (2nd ed.). Toronto: Irwin Publishing.

Au, K. (1992). Constructing the theme of a story. *Language Arts, 69*, 106–111.

Au, K. (1997). Literacy for all students: Ten steps toward making a difference. *The Reading Teacher, 51*(3), 186–194.

Baghban, M. J. M. (1984). *Our daughter learns to read and write: A case study from birth to three*. Newark, DE: International Reading Association.

Bainbridge, J., & Malicky, G. (2004). *Constructing meaning: Balancing elementary language arts* (2nd ed.). Toronto: Harcourt Canada.

Bainbridge, J., & Pantaleo, S. (1999). *Learning with literature in the Canadian elementary classroom*. Edmonton: University of Alberta Press.

Ball, E., & Blachman, B. (1991). Does phoneme segmentation training in kindergarten make a difference in early word recognition and developmental spelling? *Reading Research Quarterly, 26*, 49–86.

Banks, J. A. (1994a). *An introduction to multicultural education*. Boston: Allyn & Bacon.

Banks, J. A. (1994b). *Multiethnic education: Theory and practice* (3rd ed.). Boston: Allyn & Bacon.

Barbe, W. B., & Milone, M. N., Jr. (1980). *Why manuscript writing should come before cursive writing* (Zaner-Bloser Professional Pamphlet No. 11). Columbus, OH: Zaner-Bloser.

Barber, C. L. (1993). *The English language: A historical introduction*. Cambridge: Cambridge University Press.

Barone, D. (1990). The written responses of young children: Beyond comprehension to story understanding. *The New Advocate, 3*, 49–56.

Bartel, M. (2005). Some ideas about composition and design elements, principles, and visual effects. Retrieved from www.goshen.edu/art/ed/compose.htm April 27, 2006.

Baskwill, J., & Whitman, P. (1988). *Evaluation: Whole language, whole child*. New York: Scholastic.

Baugh, A. C., & Cable, T. (1978). *The history of the English language* (3rd ed.). Upper Saddle River, NJ: Prentice Hall.

Baumann, J. F. (1987). Direct instruction reconsidered. *Journal of Reading, 31*, 712–718.

Bear, D. R., Templeton, S., Invernizzi, M., & Johnston, F. (1996). *Words their way: Word study for phonics, vocabulary, and spelling instruction*. Upper Saddle River, NJ: Prentice Hall/Merrill.

Beck, I., McKeown, M. & Kucan, L. (2002). *Bringing words to life: Robust vocabulary instruction*. New York: The Guilford Press.

Beers, J. W., & Henderson, E. H. (1977). A study of developing orthographic concepts among first graders. *Research in the Teaching of English, 11*, 133–148.

Berninger, V. W. (1997). Treatment of handwriting problems in beginning writers: Transfer from handwriting to composition. *Journal of Educational Psychology, 89*, 652–666.

Berthoff, A. E. (1981). *The making of meaning*. Montclair, NJ: Boynton/Cook.

Bishop, R. S. (1992). Multicultural literature for children: Making informed choices. In V. J. Harris (Ed.), *Teaching multicultural literature in grades K–8* (pp. 37–54). Norwood, MA: Christopher-Gordon.

Bishop, R. S. (Ed.). (1994). *Kaleidoscope: A multicultural booklist for grades K–8*. Urbana, IL: National Council of Teachers of English.

Blachowicz, C., & Fisher, P. (1996). *Teaching vocabulary in all classrooms*. Upper Saddle River, NJ: Prentice Hall/Merrill.

Blachowicz, C. and Fisher.P. (2000). Vocabulary instruction. In M.L. Kamil, P.B. Mosenthal, P.D. Pearson and R. Barr (Eds.) *Handbook of Reading Research* (Vol. 3, pp. 503–523).

Blachowicz, C. L. Z., & Lee, J. J. (1991). Vocabulary development in the whole literacy classroom. *The Reading Teacher, 45,* 188–195.

Black, S. E. (1989). *Improving the written communication skills of upper elementary alternative education students by using a word processor.* ERIC document ED321256.

Blackburn, E. (1985). Stories never end. In J. Hansen, J. Newkirk, & D. Graves (Eds.), *Breaking ground: Teachers relate reading and writing in the elementary school* (pp. 3–13). Portsmouth, NH: Heinemann.

Blair-Larsen, S., & Held Williams, K. (Eds.) (1999). *The balanced reading program: Helping all students achieve success.* Newark, DE: International Reading Association.

Blanton, W. E., Wood, K. D., & Moorman, G. B. (1990). The role of purpose in reading instruction. *The Reading Teacher, 43,* 486–493.

Blythe, T., & Gardner, H. (1990). A school for all intelligences. *Educational Leadership, 47*(7), 33–36.

Bode, B. A. (1989). Dialogue journal writing. *The Reading Teacher, 42,* 568–571.

Bolton, G. (1979). *Towards a theory of drama in education.* Burnt Mill: Longman.

Bonin, S. (1988). Beyond storyland: Young writers can tell it other ways. In T. Newkirk & N. Atwell (Eds.), *Understanding writing* (2nd ed.) (pp. 47–51). Portsmouth, NH: Heinemann.

Booth, D., & Lundy, C. (1985). *Improvisation.* New York: Harcourt, Brace, Jovanovich.

Borgh, K., & Dickson, W. P. (1986). *The effect on children's writing of adding speech synthesis to a word processor.* ERIC document ED277007.

Bowser, J. (1993). Structuring the middle-school classroom for spoken language. *English Journal, 82,* 38–41.

Brailsford, A., & Coles, J. (2004). *Balanced literacy in action.* Markham, ON: Scholastic.

Bray, E. (1994). *Playbuilding: A guide for group creation of plays with young people.* Portsmouth, NH: Heinemann.

Brent, R., & Anderson, P. (1993). Developing children's classroom listening strategies. *The Reading Teacher, 47,* 122–126.

Bright, R. (1995). *Writing instruction in the intermediate grades: What is said, what is done, what is understood.* Newark, DE: International Reading Association.

Bright, R. (2002). *Write from the start: Writers workshop for the primary grades.* Winnipeg: Portage & Main Publishers.

Bright, R., McMullin, L., & Platt, D. (1999). *From your child's teacher.* Toronto: Fitzhenry & Whiteside.

Britton, J., Burgess, T., Martin, N., McLeod, A., & Rosen, H. (1975). *The development of writing abilities.* London: Macmillan.

Bromley, K. D. (1991). *Webbing with literature: Creating story maps with children's books.* Boston: Allyn & Bacon.

Bromley, K. D. (1996). *Webbing with literature: Creating story maps with children's books* (2nd ed.). Boston: Allyn & Bacon.

Brooks, C. K. (Ed.). (1985). *Tapping potential: English and language arts for the black learner.* Urbana, IL: National Council of Teachers of English.

Bruce, B. (2002). Diversity and critical social engagement: How changing technologies enable new modes of literacy in changing circumstances. In D. Alvermann (Ed.) *Adolescents and literacies in a digital world.* New York: Peter Lang.

Bruner, J. (1986). *Actual minds, possible worlds.* Cambridge, MA: Harvard University Press.

Buckingham, D. & Sefton-Green, J. (1998). In S. Howard (Ed.), *Wired up: young people and the electronic media* (pp. vii–ix). London: UCL Press.

Burbules, N. & Bruce, B. (1995, November). This is not a paper. *Educational Researcher, 24* (8), 12–18.

Burmark, L. (2002). Visual literacy: Learn to see, see to learn. Alexandria, VA: Association for Supervision and Curriculum Development.

Busink, R. (1997). Reading and phonological awareness: What we have learned and how we can use it. *Reading Research and Instruction, 36,* 199–215.

Butler, A., & Turbill, J. (1984). *Towards a reading-writing classroom.* Portsmouth, NH: Heinemann.

Button, K., Johnson, M. J., & Furgerson, P. (1996). Interactive writing in a primary classroom. *The Reading Teacher, 49,* 446–454.

Byron, K. (1986). *Drama in the English classroom.* New York: Methuen.

Cairney, T. (1990). Intertextuality: Infectious echoes from the past. *The Reading Teacher, 43,* 478–484.

Cairney, T. (1992). Fostering and building students' intertextual histories. *Language Arts, 69,* 502–507.

Calfee, R., & Patrick, C. (1995). *Teach our children well: Bringing K–12 education into the 21st century.* Stanford, CA: Stanford Alumni Association.

Calkins, L. M. (1980). When children want to punctuate: Basic skills belong in context. *Language Arts, 57,* 567–573.

Calkins, L. M. (1991). *Living between the lines.* Portsmouth, NH: Heinemann.

Calkins, L. M. (1994). *The art of teaching writing* (2nd ed.). Portsmouth, NH: Heinemann.

Cambourne, B., & Turbill, J. (1987). *Coping with chaos.* Rozelle, New South Wales, Australia: Primary English Teaching Association.

Cameron, L. (1998). A practitioner's reflections. *Orbit: Phonics in the Literacy Program, 28*(4), 10–15.

Cammack, D. (2002). Literacy, technology, and room of her own: Analyzing adolescent girls' online conversations from historical and technological perspectives. *Yearbook of the National Reading Conference, 51,* 129–141.

Carr, E., & Wixon, K. K. (1986). Guidelines for evaluating vocabulary instruction. *Journal of Reading, 29,* 588–595.

Caserta-Henry, C. (1996). Reading buddies: A first-grade intervention program. *The Reading Teacher, 49,* 500–503.

Caverly, D. C., & Orlando, V. P. (1991). Textbook study strategies. In D. C. Caverly & V. P. Orlando (Eds.), *Teaching reading and study strategies at the college level* (pp. 86–165). Newark, DE: International Reading Association.

Cazden, C. D. (1988). *Classroom discourse: The language of teaching and learning*. Portsmouth, NH: Heinemann.

Cecil, N. L. (1994). *For the love of language: Poetry for every learner*. Winnipeg: Peguis.

Chandler-Olcott, K., & Mahar, D. (2003). "Tech-savviness" meets multiliteracies: Exploring adolescent girls' technology-related literacy practices. *Reading Research Quarterly, 38*, 356–385.

Chapman, M. (2002). Phonemic awareness in perspective. *Canadian Children, 27*(2), 18–25.

Chapman, V., & Sopko, D. (2003). Developing strategic use of combined-text trade books. *The Reading Teacher, 57*, 236–239.

Cheng, L. R. (1987). *Assessing Asian language performance*. Rockville, MD: Aspen.

Cintorino, M. A. (1993). Getting together, getting along, getting to the business of teaching and learning. *English Journal, 82*, 23–32.

Clarke, J. D., Goode, T., & Neelands, J. (1997). *Lessons for the living: Drama in the transition years*. Markham: Mayfair.

Clay, M. M. (1967). The reading behavior of five-year-old children: A research report. *New Zealand Journal of Education Studies, 2*(1), 11–31.

Clay, M. M. (1985). *The early detection of reading difficulties* (3rd ed.). Portsmouth, NH: Heinemann.

Clay, M. M. (1991). *Becoming literate: The construction of inner control*. Portsmouth, NH: Heinemann.

Cleary, L. M. (1993). Hobbes: "I press rewind through the pictures in my head." In S. Hudson-Ross, L. M. Cleary, & M. Casey (Eds.), *Children's voices: Children talk about literacy* (pp. 136–143). Portsmouth, NH: Heinemann.

Clemmons, J., Lasse, L., Cooper, D., Areglado, N., & Dill, M. (1993). *Portfolios in the classroom: A teacher's sourcebook*. New York: Scholastic.

Clymer, T. (1996). The utility of phonic generalizations in the primary grades. *The Reading Teacher, 50*, 182–187.

Cochran-Smith, M. (1984). *The making of a reader*. Norwood, NJ: Ablex.

Cole, N. (1997). *The ETS gender study: How females and males perform in educational settings*. Princeton, NJ: Educational Testing Service.

Cooper, D. J., & Kiger, N. D. (2003). *Literacy: Helping children construct meaning* (5th ed.). Boston: Houghton Mifflin.

Copeland, J. S. (1993). *Speaking of poets: Interviews with poets who write for children and young adults*. Urbana, IL: National Council of Teachers of English.

Copeland, J. S., & Copeland, V. L. (1994). *Speaking of poets 2: Interviews with poets who write for children and young adults*. Urbana, IL: National Council of Teachers of English.

Corcoran, B. (1987). Teachers creating readers. In B. Corcoran & E. Evans (Eds.), *Readers, texts, teachers* (pp. 41–74). Upper Montclair, NJ: Boynton/Cook.

Cornett, C., & Smithrim, K. (2001). *The arts as meaning makers: Integrating literature and the arts throughout the curriculum* (Canadian ed.). Don Mills, ON: Prentice Hall.

Courtney, R. (1980). *The dramatic curriculum*. New York: Drama Book Specialists.

Cox, C., & Many, J. E. (1992). Toward an understanding of the aesthetic response to literature. *Language Arts, 69*, 28–33.

Crystal, D. (2001). *Language and the internet*. Cambridge: Cambridge University Press.

Cullinan, B. E. (1987). Inviting readers to literature. In B. E. Cullinan (Ed.), *Children's literature in the reading program* (pp. 2–14). Newark, DE: International Reading Association.

Cullinan, B. E., Jaggar, A., & Strickland, D. (1974). Oral language expansion in the primary grades. In B. Cullinan (Ed.), *Black dialects and reading*. Urbana, IL: National Council of Teachers of English.

Cullinan, B. E., Scala, M. C., & Schroder, V. C. (1995). *Three voices: An invitation to poetry across the curriculum*. York, ME: Stenhouse.

Cummins, J. (1989). *Empowering minority students*. Sacramento: California Association for Bilingual Education.

Cunningham, P. M. (1995). *Phonics they use: Words for reading and writing* (2nd ed.). New York: HarperCollins.

Cunningham, P. M., & Cunningham, J. W. (1992). Making words: Enhancing the invented spelling-decoding connection. *The Reading Teacher, 46*, 106–115.

Curry-Tash, M. (1998). The politics of teleliteracy and adbusting in the classroom. *English Journal, 87*(1), 43–48.

Dagenais, D., & Day, E. (1998). Classroom language experiences of trilingual children in French immersion. *The Canadian Modern Language Review/La Revue canadienne des langues vivantes, 54*(3), 376–393.

Dahl, K., & Farnan, N. (1998). *Children's writing: Perspectives from research*. Newark, DE: International Reading Association; and Chicago, IL: National Reading Conference.

Daniels, H. (1994). *Literature circles: Voice and choice in the student-centered classroom*. York, ME: Stenhouse.

D'Aoust, C. (1992). Portfolios: Process for students and teachers. In K. B. Yancy (Ed.), *Portfolios in the writing classroom* (pp. 39–48). Urbana, IL: National Council of Teachers of English.

de Beaugrande, R. (1980). *Text, discourse and process*. Norwood, NJ: Ablex.

De Fina, A. A. (1992). *Portfolio assessment: Getting started*. New York: Scholastic.

Dekker, M. M. (1991). Books, reading, and response: A teacher-researcher tells a story. *The New Advocate, 4*, 37–46.

Devine, T. G. (1978). Listening: What do we know after fifty years of research and theorizing? *Journal of Reading, 21* (January), 296–304.

Devine, T. G. (1981). *Teaching study skills: A guide for teachers*. Boston: Allyn & Bacon.

Devine, T. G. (1982). *Listening skills schoolwide: Activities and programs*. Urbana, IL: ERIC Clearinghouse on Reading and Communication Skills and the National Council of Teachers of English.

Dixon, J. (1967). *Growth through English*. Huddersfield, England: National Association for the Teaching of English.

Dixon-Krauss, L. (1996). *Vygotsky in the classroom: Mediated literacy instruction and assessment*. White Plains, NY: Longman.

D'Odorico, L., & Zammuner, V. (1993). The influence of using a word processor on children's story writing. *European Journal of Psychology of Education, 8*(1), 51–64.

Doll, E. (1941). The essentials of an inclusive concept of mental deficiency. *American Journal of Mental Deficiency, 46,* 214–219.

Downing, J. (1971–1972). Children's developing concepts of spoken and written language. *Journal of Reading Behavior, 4,* 1–19.

Downing, J., & Oliver, P. (1973–1974). The child's conception of "a word." *Reading Research Quarterly, 9,* 568–582.

Dreher, S. (2003). A novel idea: Reading aloud in a high school English classroom. *English Journal, 93,* 50–53.

Dressel, J. H. (1990). The effects of listening to and discussing different qualities of children's literature on the narrative writing of fifth graders. *Research in the Teaching of English, 24,* 397–414.

Duffelmeyer, F. (2002). Alphabet activities on the internet. *The Reading Teacher, 55*(7), 631–635.

Dunning, S., & Stafford, W. (1992). *Getting the knack: 20 poetry writing exercises.* Urbana, IL: National Council of Teachers of English.

Durkin, D. (1966). *Children who read early.* New York: Teachers College Press.

Durkin, D. (1989). *Curriculum reform: Teaching reading in kindergarten.* Technical Report No. 465. Urbana, IL: Center for the Study of Reading.

Durkin, D. (1993). *Teaching them to read* (6th ed.). New York: Allyn & Bacon.

Duthie, C. (1994). Nonfiction: A genre study for the primary classroom. *Language Arts, 71,* 588–595.

Duthie, C., & Zimet, E. K. (1992). Poetry is like directions for your imagination! *The Reading Teacher, 46,* 14–24.

Dweck, C. S. (1986). Motivational processes affecting learning. *American Psychologist, 41,* 1040–1048.

Dwyer, J. (Ed.). (1991). *A sea of talk.* Portsmouth, NH: Heinemann.

Dyson, A. H. (1984). "N spells my grandmama": Fostering early thinking about print. *The Reading Teacher, 38,* 262–271.

Dyson, A. H. (1985). Second graders sharing writing: The multiple social realities of a literacy event. *Written Communication, 2,* 189–215.

Dyson, A. H. (1986). The imaginary worlds of childhood: A multimedia presentation. *Language Arts, 63,* 799–808.

Dyson, A. H. (1993). *Social worlds of children learning to write in an urban primary school.* New York: Teachers College Press.

Eagleton, M. & Guinee, K. (2002). Strategies for supporting student Internet inquiry. *New England Reading Association Journal, 38* (2), 39–47.

Eeds, M., & Peterson, R. (1991). Teacher as curator: Learning to talk about literature. *The Reading Teacher, 45,* 118–126.

Eeds, M., & Peterson, R. (1995). What teachers need to know about the literary craft. In N. L. Roser & M. G. Martinez (Eds.), *Book talk and beyond: Children and teachers respond to literature* (pp. 10–23). Newark, DE: International Reading Association.

Eeds, M., & Wells, D. (1989). Grand conversations: An exploration of meaning construction in literature study groups. *Research in the Teaching of English, 23,* 4–29.

Ehri, L. (1993). How English orthography influences phonological knowledge as children learn to read and spell. In R. J. Scales (Ed.), *Literacy and language analysis* (pp. 21–43). Hillsdale, NJ: Erlbaum.

Egawa, K. (1990). Harnessing the power of language: First graders' literature engagement with Owl moon. *Language Arts, 67,* 582–588.

Erickson, K. L. (1988). Building castles in the classroom. *Language Arts, 65,* 14–19.

Ernst, K. (1993). *Picturing learning.* Portsmouth, NH: Heinemann.

Faigley, L., & Witte, S. (1981). Analyzing revision. *College Composition and Communication, 32,* 400–410.

Faltis, C. J. (1993). *Join fostering: Adapting teaching strategies for the multilingual classroom.* Upper Saddle River, NJ: Prentice Hall/Merrill.

Farr, R., & Tone, B. (1994). *Portfolio and performance assessment.* Orlando: Harcourt & Brace.

Farrell, E. (2006). *John Lennon: All I want is the truth.* New York: Viking.

Farrell, J. (2005). *Invisible allies: Microbes that shape our lives.* New York: Farrar, Straus and Giroux.

Farris, P. J. (1997). *Language Arts process, product, and assessment* (2nd. ed.). Madison, WI: Brown & Benchmark Publishers.

Fehring, H., & Green, P. (Eds.). (2001). *Critical literacy: A collection of articles from the Australian Literacy Educators Association.* Newark, DE: International Reading.

Fennessey, S. (1995). Living history through drama and literature. *The Reading Teacher, 49,* 16–19.

Fisher, B. (1991). *Joyful learning: A whole language kindergarten.* Portsmouth, NH: Heinemann.

Fisher, C. J., & Natarella, M. A. (1982). Young children's preferences in poetry: A national survey of first, second, and third graders. *Research in the Teaching of English, 16,* 339–354.

Fisher, D., Flood, J., Lapp, D., & Frey, N. (2004, September). Interactive read-alouds: Is there a common set of implementation practices? *The Reading Teacher, 58*(1), 8–17.

Fitzgerald, J. (1989). Enhancing two related thought processes: Revision in writing and critical thinking. *The Reading Teacher, 43,* 42–48.

Five, C. L. (1986). Fifth graders respond to a changed reading program. *Harvard Educational Review, 56,* 395–405.

Fleming, D. (2002). *Alphabet under construction.* New York: Henry Holt.

Flexner, S. B. (1993). *The Random House dictionary of the English language* (3rd ed.). New York: Random House.

Flood, J., Lapp, D., & Farnan, N. (1986). A reading-writing procedure that teaches expository paragraph structure. *The Reading Teacher, 39,* 556–562.

Flower, L., & Hayes, J. R. (1994). The cognition of discovery: Defining a rhetorical problem. In S. Perl (Ed.), *Landmark essays on writing process* (pp. 63–74). Davis, CA: Heragoras Press.

Foulke, E. (1968). Listening comprehension as a function of word rate. *Journal of Communication, 18,* 198–206.

Fountas, I. C., & Pinnell, G. S. (1996). *Guided reading: Good first teaching for all children.* Portsmouth, NH: Heinemann.

Fountas, I. C., & Pinnell, G. S. (2000). *Guiding readers and writers (grades 3–6).* Portsmouth, NH: Heinemann.

Fraser, I. S., & Hodson, L. M. (1978). Twenty-one kicks at the grammar horse. *English Journal, 67,* 49–53.

Freeman, D. E., & Freeman, Y. S. (1993). Strategies for promoting the primary languages of all students. *The Reading Teacher, 46*, 552–558.

Freeman, E. B. (1991). Informational books: Models for student report writing. *Language Arts, 68*, 470–473.

Freeman, E. B., & Person, D. G. (Eds.). (1992). *Using nonfiction trade books in the elementary classroom: From ants to zeppelins*. Urbana, IL: National Council of Teachers of English.

Freeman, Y. S., & Freeman, D. E. (1992). *Whole language for second language learners*. Portsmouth, NH: Heinemann.

Freire, P. (1970). *Pedagogy of the oppressed*. New York: Continuum.

Freire, P., & Macedo, D. (1987). *Literacy: Reading the word and the world*. South Hadley, MA: Bergin & Garvey Publishers.

Fulwiler, T. (1985). Research writing. In M. Schwartz (Ed.), *Writing for many roles* (pp. 207–230). Upper Montclair, NJ: Boynton/Cook.

Funston, S., & Ingram, J. (1994). *A Kid's Guide to the Brain*. Toronto: Greey de Pencier Books.

Furner, B. A. (1969). Recommended instructional procedures in a method emphasizing the perceptual-motor nature of learning in handwriting. *Elementary English, 46*, 1021–1030.

Gamberg, R., Kwak, W., Hutchings, M., & Altheim, J. (1988). *Learning and loving it: Theme studies in the classroom*. Toronto: Heinemann.

Gambrell, L. B. (1985). Dialogue journals: Reading-writing interaction. *The Reading Teacher, 38*, 512–515.

Gambrell, L B., & Mazzoni, 1999. In L. M. Morrow, L. B. Gambrell, & M. Pressley (Eds.), *Best Practices in Literacy Instruction*. New York: The Guilford Press.

Gardner, H. (1993a). *Frames of mind: The theory of multiple intelligences*. New York: Basic Books/HarperCollins.

Gardner, H. (1993b). *Multiple intelligences: The theory in practice*. New York: HarperCollins.

Gentry, J. R. (1981). Learning to spell developmentally. *The Reading Teacher, 34*, 378–381.

Gentry, J. R. (1982). Developmental spelling: Assessment. *Diagnostique, 8*, 52–61.

Gentry, J. R. (1987). *Spel . . . is a four-letter word*. Portsmouth, NH: Heinemann.

Gentry, J. R., & Gillet, J. W. (1993). *Teaching kids to spell*. Portsmouth, NH: Heinemann.

Gere, A. R., & Abbott, R. D. (1985). Talking about writing: The language of writing groups. *Research in the Teaching of English, 19*, 362–381.

Gibbons, P. (1991). *Learning to learn in a second language*. Portsmouth, NH: Heinemann.

Golden, J. M. (1984). Children's concept of story in reading and writing. *The Reading Teacher, 37*, 578–584.

Golden, J. M., Meiners, A., & Lewis, S. (1992). The growth of story meaning. *Language Arts, 69*, 22–27.

Golden, J. M. (2001). Reading in the dark: Using film as a tool in the English classroom. Urbana, IL: National Council of Teachers of English.

Goodman, K. S. (1969). Analysis of oral reading miscues: Applied psycholinguistics. *Reading Research Quarterly, 4*(1), 9–30.

Goodman, K. S. (1993). *Phonics phacts*. Portsmouth, NH: Heinemann.

Goodman, K. S., Goodman, Y. M., & Hood, W. J. (Eds.). (1989). *The whole language evaluation book*. Portsmouth, NH: Heinemann.

Goodman, K. S. (1994). Reading, writing, and written texts: A transactional socio-psycholinguistic view. In R. Ruddell, M. R. Ruddell, & H. Singer (Eds.), *Theoretical Models and Processes of Reading* (4th ed.). Newark, DE: International Reading Association.

Goodman, Y. M. (1978). Kid watching: An alternative to testing. *National Elementary Principals Journal, 57*, 41–45.

Gordon, C., Donnon, T. (2003). Early literacy: A success story. *Education Canada, 43*(3), 16–19.

Gough, P. (1972). One second of reading. In J. F. Kavanaugh & I. G. Mattingly (Eds.), *Language be ear and by eye: The relationships between speech and reading*. Cambridge, MA: MIT Press.

Gough, P. (1985). One second of reading: Postscript. In H. Singer & R. Ruddell (Eds.), *Theoretical Models and Processes of Reading* (3rd edition). Newark, DE: International Reading Association, 687–688.

Grabe, M., & Grabe, C. (1985). The microcomputer and the language experience approach. *The Reading Teacher, 38*, 508–511.

Grabe, M. & Grabe, C. (2001) *Integrated technology for meaningful learning* (2nd ed.). Boston: Houghton Mifflin.

Graham, S. (1992). Issues in handwriting instruction. *Focus on Exceptional Children, 25* (2), 1–14.

Graves, D. H. (1976). Let's get rid of the welfare mess in the teaching of writing. *Language Arts, 53*, 645–651.

Graves, D. H. (1983). *Writing: Teachers and children at work*. Portsmouth, NH: Heinemann.

Graves, D. H. (1989). *Experiment with fiction*. Portsmouth, NH: Heinemann.

Graves, D. H. (1991). *Build a literate classroom*. Portsmouth, NH: Heinemann.

Graves, D. H. (1992). *Explore poetry*. Portsmouth, NH: Heinemann.

Graves, D. H. (1994). *A fresh look at writing*. Portsmouth, NH: Heinemann.

Graves, D. H., & Hansen, J. (1983). The author's chair. *Language Arts, 60*, 176–183.

Graves, D. H., & Sunstein, B. S. (Eds.). (1992). *Portfolio portraits*. Portsmouth, NH: Heinemann.

Graves, M. (1985). *A word is a word . . . or is it?* Portsmouth, NH: Heinemann.

Green, D. H. (1989). Beyond books: Literature on the small screen. In M. K. Rudman (Ed.), *Children's literature: Resources for the classroom* (pp. 207–217). Norwood, MA: Christopher-Gordon.

Greenlee, M. E., Hiebert, E. H., Bridge, C. A., & Winograd, P. N. (1986). The effects of different audiences on young writers' letter writing. In J. A. Niles & R. V. Lalik (Eds.), *Solving problems in literacy: Learners, teachers, and researchers* (pp. 281–289). Rochester, NY: National Reading Conference.

Griffith, F., & Olson, M. (1992). Phonemic awareness helps beginning readers break the code. *The Reading Teacher, 45*, 516–523.

Groff, P. J. (1963). Who writes faster? *Education, 83*, 367–369.

Gurak, L. (2001). *Cyberliteracy: Navigating the internet with awareness*. New Haven: Yale University Press.

Hackney, C. (1993). *Handwriting: A way to self-expression.* Columbus, OH: Zaner-Bloser.

Hagood, M. C., Stevens, L. P., & Reinking, D. (2002). What do THEY have to teach us? Talkin' 'cross generations! In D. Alvermann (Ed.), *Adolescents and literacies in a digital world* (pp. 68–83). New York: Peter Lang.

Haley-James, S. M., & Hobson, C. D. (1980). Interviewing: A means of encouraging the drive to communicate. *Language Arts, 57,* 497–502.

Hall, N. (1998). Real literacy in a school setting: Five-year-olds take on the world. *The Reading Teacher, 52*(1), 8–17.

Halliday, M. A. K. (1978). *Language as social semiotic: The social interpretation of language and meaning.* Baltimore: University Park Press.

Hallows, J. (2002). Proven Techniques for Teaching Qwerty Keyboarding. Retrieved June 28 from www.cwu.edu/~setc/ldtech/keyboarding_techniques.html.

Hammerberg, D. (2001). Reading and writing "Hypertextually": Children's literature, technology, and early writing instruction. *Language Arts, 78*(3), 207–216.

Hammond, S. (1998). *Teacher's notes: Beethoven lives upstairs.* Pickering, ON: The Children's Group.

Hancock, M. R. (1992). Literature response journals: Insights beyond the printed page. *Language Arts, 61,* 141–150.

Hancock, M. R. (1993). Exploring and extending personal response through literature journals. *The Reading Teacher, 46,* 466–474.

Hanna, P. R., Hanna, J. S., Hodges, R. E., & Rudorf, E. H. (1966). *Phoneme-grapheme correspondences as cues to spelling improvement.* Washington, DC: US Government Printing Office.

Hansen, J. (1987). *When writers read.* Portsmouth, NH: Heinemann.

Hansen, J. (2003). The language arts interact. In J. Flood (Ed.), *Handbook of research on teaching the English language arts* (2nd ed.) (pp. 1026–1034). New Jersey: Lawrence Erlbaum Associates.

Harris, V. J. (1992a). Multiethnic children's literature. In K. D. Wood & A. Moss (Eds.), *Exploring literature in the classroom: Content and methods* (pp. 169–201). Norwood, MA: Christopher-Gordon.

Harris, V. J. (Ed.). (1992b). *Teaching multicultural literature in grades K–8.* Norwood, MA: Christopher-Gordon.

Harrison, S. (1981). Open letter from a left-handed teacher: Some sinistral ideas on the teaching of handwriting. *Teaching Exceptional Children, 13,* 116–120.

Harste, J. C. (1990). Jerry Harste speaks on reading and writing. *The Reading Teacher, 43,* 316–318.

Harste, J. C. (1993, April). Inquiry-based instruction. *Primary Voices K–6, 1,* 2–5.

Harste, J. C., Short, K. G., Burke, C. (1988). *Creating classrooms for authors: The reading-writing connection.* Portsmouth, NH: Heinemann.

Harste, J. C., Woodward, V. A., & Burke, C. L. (1984a). Examining our assumptions: A transactional view of literacy and learning. *Research in the Teaching of English, 18,* 84–108.

Harste, J. C., Woodward, V. A., & Burke, C. L. (1984b). *Language stories and literacy lessons.* Portsmouth, NH: Heinemann.

Harwayne, S. (1992). *Lasting impressions: Weaving literature into writing workshop.* Portsmouth, NH: Heinemann.

Hatfield, S. (1996). *Effective use of classroom computer stations across the curriculum.* ERIC Document Service No. ED396 704.

Hayden, R., & Kendrick, M. (2002). Understanding emergent literacy. In *Inter-provincial/territorial foundational training for family literacy.* Edmonton, AB: Centre for Family Literacy.

Head, M. H., & Readence, J. E. (1986). Anticipation guides: Meaning through prediction. In E. K. Dishner, T. W. Bean, J. E. Readence, & D. W. Moore (Eds.), *Reading in the content areas* (2nd ed.) (pp. 229–234). Dubuque, IA: Kendall/Hunt.

Heald-Taylor, G. (1987). How to use predictable books for K–2 language arts instruction. *The Reading Teacher, 40,* 656–661.

Heard, G. (1989). *For the good of the earth and sun: Teaching poetry.* Portsmouth, NH: Heinemann.

Heath, S. B. (1983a). Research currents: A lot of talk about nothing. *Language Arts, 60,* 999–1007.

Heath, S. B. (1983b). *Ways with words: Language, life, and work in communities and classrooms.* Cambridge: Cambridge University Press.

Heathcote, D., & Bolton, G. (1995). *Drama for learning: Dorothy Heathcote's mantle of the expert approach to education.* Portsmouth, NH: Heinemann.

Heinig, R. (1988). *Creative drama for the classroom teacher.* Englewood Cliffs, NJ: Prentice Hall.

Heinig, R. (1991). *Improvisation with favorite tales: Integrating drama into the reading/writing classroom.* Portsmouth, NH: Heinemann.

Henderson, E. H. (1980). Word knowledge and reading disability. In E. H. Henderson & J. W. Beers (Eds.), *Developmental and cognitive aspects of learning to spell: A reflection of word knowledge* (pp. 138–148). Newark, DE: International Reading Association.

Henderson, E. H. (1990). *Teaching Spelling* (2nd ed.). Boston: Houghton Mifflin.

Henkin, R. (1995). Insiders and outsiders in first-grade writing workshops: Gender and equity issues. *Language Arts, 72,* 429–434.

Henry, L. (2006). SEARCHing for an answer: The critical role of new literacies while reading on the Internet. *The Reading Teacher, 59* (7).

Hepler, S. (1991). Talking our way to literacy in the classroom community. *The New Advocate, 4,* 179–191.

Hickman, J. (1995). Not by chance. In N. L. Roser & M. G. Martinez (Eds.), *Book talk and beyond: Children and teachers respond to literature* (pp. 3–9). Newark, DE: International Reading Association.

Hidi, S., & Hildyard, A. (1983). The comparison of oral and written productions in two discourse modes. *Discourse Processes, 6,* 91–105.

Hiebert, E. (1989). A research-based writing program for students with high access to computers. *ACOT Report #2.* Cupertino, CA: Apple Computer, Inc.

Hildreth, G. (1960). Manuscript writing after sixty years. *Elementary English, 37,* 3–13.

Hillerich, R. L. (1977). Let's teach spelling—not phonetic misspelling. *Language Arts, 54,* 301–307.

Hipple, M. L. (1985). Journal writing in kindergarten. *Language Arts, 62,* 255–261.

Hirsch, E., & Niedermeyer, F. C. (1973). The effects of tracing prompts and discrimination training on kindergarten handwriting performance. *Journal of Educational Research, 67,* 81–83.

Hitchcock, M. E. (1989). *Elementary students' invented spellings at the correct stage of spelling development.* Unpublished doctoral dissertation, Norman, University of Oklahoma.

Holdaway, D. (1979). *The foundations of literacy.* Portsmouth, NH: Heinemann.

Hook, J. N. (1975). *History of the English language.* New York: Ronald Press.

Hopkins, L. B. (1987). *Pass the poetry, please!* New York: Harper & Row.

Horn, E. (1926). *A basic writing vocabulary.* Iowa City: University of Iowa Press.

Horn, E. (1957). Phonetics and spelling. *Elementary School Journal, 57,* 425–432.

Hornsby, D., Sukarna, D., & Parry, J. (1986). *Read on: A conference approach to reading.* Portsmouth, NH: Heinemann.

Howell, H. (1978). Write on, you sinistrals! *Language Arts, 55,* 852–856.

Hudson, B. A. (1980). Moving language around: Helping students become aware of language structure. *Language Arts, 57,* 614–620.

Hunt, L. C., Jr. (1970). The effect of self selection, interest and motivation upon independent, instructional and frustration levels. *The Reading Teacher, 24,* 416.

International Reading Association (IRA). (2003). *Integrating literacy and technology in the curriculum: A position statement of the International Reading Association.* Retrieved May 1, 2006 from www.reading.org/downloads/positions/ps1048_technology.pdf.

Jackson, A. D. (1971). A comparison of speed of legibility of manuscript and cursive handwriting of intermediate grade pupils. Unpublished doctoral dissertation, University of Arizona. *Dissertation Abstracts, 31,* 4384A.

Jackson, L. A., Tway, E., & Frager, A. (1987). Dear teacher, Johnny copied. *The Reading Teacher, 41,* 22–25.

Jalongo, M. R. (1991). Strategies for developing children's listening skills (*Phi Delta Kappan Fastback Series #314*). Bloomington, IN: Phi Delta Kappa Educational Foundation.

Jenkins, S., and Page, R. (2006). *Move!* Boston: Houghton Mifflin

Jobe R., & Dayton-Sakari, M. (1999). *Reluctant readers: Connecting students and books for successful reading experiences.* Markham, ON: Pembroke Publishers.

Johns, J. L., Van Leirsburg, P., & Davis, S. J. (1994). *Improving reading: A handbook of strategies.* Dubuque, IA: Kendall/Hunt.

Johnson, T. D., Langford, K. G., & Quorm, K. C. (1981). Characteristics of an effective spelling program. *Language Arts, 58,* 581–588.

Johnston, P., & Winograd, P. (1985). Passive failure in reading. *Journal of Reading Behavior, 17,* 279–301.

Juel, C. (1991). Beginning reading. In R. Barr, M. L. Kamil, P. Mosenthal, & P. D. Pearson (Eds.), *Handbook of reading research* (Vol. 2, pp. 759–788). New York: Longman.

Juel, C., Griffith, P. L., & Gough, P. B. (1986). Acquisition of literacy: A longitudinal study of children in first and second grade. *Journal of Educational Psychology, 78,* 243–255.

Kamil, M., & Lane, D. (1997). A classroom study of the efficacy of using information text for first grade reading instruction. Retrieved December 20, 2003, from www.stanford.edu/~mkamil/Aera97.htm.

Karchmer, R. (2001). The journey ahead: Thirteen teachers report how the Internet influences literacy and literacy instruction in their K–12 classrooms. *Reading Research Quarterly, 36*(4), 442–466.

Karelitz, E. B. (1993). *The author's chair and beyond: Language and literacy in a primary classroom.* Portsmouth, NH: Heinemann.

Kielburger, M., & Kielburger, C. (2002). *Take action! A guide to active citizenship.* New York: John Wiley & Sons.

King, L., & Stovall, D. (1992). *Classroom publishing.* Hillsboro, OR: Blue Heron.

King, M. (1985). Proofreading is not reading. *Teaching English in the two-year college, 12,* 108–112.

Kinzer, C., & Leu, D. Jr. (1997). The challenge of change: Exploring literacy and learning in electronic environments. *Language Arts, 74*(2), 126–136.

Kist, W. (2005). *New literacies in action: Teaching and learning in multiple media.* New York: Teachers College Press.

Klein, M. L. (1988). *Teaching reading comprehension and vocabulary: A guide for teachers.* Upper Saddle River, NJ: Prentice Hall/Merrill.

Klesius, J. P., Griffith, P. L., & Zielonka, P. (1991). A whole language and traditional instruction comparison: Overall effectiveness and development of the alphabetic principle. *Reading Research and Instruction, 30,* 47–61.

Kolb, D. (1984). *Experiential Learning.* New Jersey: Prentice-Hall.

Krashen, S. (1982). *Principles and practices of second language acquisition.* Oxford: Pergamon Press.

Krashen, S. (1998). Bridging inequity with books. *Educational Leadership, 55*(4), 18–22.

Kreeft, J. (1984). Dialogue writing—Bridge from talk to essay writing. *Language Arts, 61,* 141–150.

Krogness, M. M. (1987). Folklore: A matter of the heart and the heart of the matter. *Language Arts, 64,* 808– 818.

Kucer, S. B., Silva, C., & Delgado-Larocco, E. L. (1995). *Curricular conversations: Themes in multilingual and monolingual classrooms.* York, ME: Stenhouse.

Kuhl, D., & Dewitz, P. (1994). *The effect of handwriting style on alphabet recognition.* Paper presented at the Annual Meeting of the American Educational Research Association, New Orleans, LA.

Kutiper, K. (1985). *A survey of the poetry preferences of seventh, eighth, and ninth graders.* Unpublished doctoral dissertation, University of Houston.

Kutiper, K., & Wilson, P. (1993). Updating poetry preferences: A look at the poetry children really like. *The Reading Teacher, 47,* 28–35.

Labbo, L. D., & Teale, W. H. (1990). Cross-age reading: A strategy for helping poor readers. *The Reading Teacher, 43,* 362–369.

LaBerge, D., & Samuels, S. J. (1974). Toward a theory of automatic information processing in reading. *Cognitive Psychology, 6,* 293–323.

Laminack, L. L., & Wood, K. (1996). *Spelling in use: Looking closely at spelling in whole language classrooms*. Urbana, IL: National Council of Teachers of English.

Lane, B. (1993). *After the end: Teaching and learning creative revision*. Portsmouth, NH: Heinemann.

Langer, J. A. (1981). From theory to practice: A prereading plan. *Journal of Reading, 25*, 152–157.

Langer, J. A. (1985). Children's sense of genre. *Written Communication, 2*, 157–187.

Langer, J. A. (1986). *Children reading and writing: Structures and strategies*. Norwood, NJ: Ablex.

Langer, J. A (1995). *Envisioning literature: Literary understanding and literature instruction*. New York: Teachers College Press.

Langhorne, M., Dunham, J., Gross, J., & Rehmke, D. (1989). *Teaching with computers: A new menu for the '90s*. Phoenix, AZ: Oryx Press.

Lapp, D., Flood, J., & Lungren, L. (1995). Strategies for gaining access to the information superhighway: Off the side street and on to the main road. *The Reading Teacher, 48*, 432–436.

Lara, S. G. M. (1989). Reading placement for code-switchers. *The Reading Teacher, 42*, 278–282.

Larrick, N. (1991). *Let's do a poem! Introducing poetry to children*. New York: Delacorte.

Law, B., & Eckes, M. (1990). *The more than just surviving handbook: ESL for every classroom teacher*. Winnipeg: Peguis.

Lehr, S. S. (1991). *The child's developing sense of theme: Responses to literature*. New York: Teachers College Press.

Lensmire, T. (1992). *When children write*. New York: Teachers College Press.

Leu, D. (2000). Literacy and technology: Deictic consequences for literacy education in an information age. In M. K. Kamil, P. Mosenthal, P. D. Pearson, & R. Barr (Eds.), *Handbook of reading research: Volume III* (pp. 743–770). Mahwah, NJ: Erlbaum.

Leu, D. J. Jr., Karchner, R. A., & Leu, D. D. (1999). The Miss Rumphius effect: Envisions for literacy and learning that transform the internet. *Reading Online*. Retrieved from www.readingonline.org/home.html.

Leu, D. J. Jr, & Kinzer, C. K. (1999). *Effective literacy instruction* (4th ed.). Upper Saddle River, NJ: Prentice Hall/Merrill.

Leu, D. J. Jr., & Kinzer, C. K. (2000). The convergence of literacy instruction and networked technologies for information and communication. *Reading Research Quarterly, 35*, 108–127.

Leu, D. J., Jr & Leu, D. D. (1998). *Teaching with the Internet: Lessons from the classroom* (2nd ed.). Norwood, MA: Christopher-Gordon Publishers.

Lewis, R. B., Ashton, T. M., Haapa, B., Kieley, C. L., & Fielden, C. (1999). *Improving the writing skills of students with learning disabilities: Are word processors with spelling and grammar checkers useful?* ERIC Document Reproduction Service No. EJ594984.

Lindfors, J. W. (1987). *Children's language and learning* (2nd ed.). Upper Saddle River, NJ: Prentice Hall.

Lindsay, G. A., & McLennan, D. (1983). Lined paper: Its effects on the legibility and creativity of young children's writing. *British Journal of Educational Psychology, 53*, 364–368.

Loban, W. D. (1976). *Language development: Kindergarten through grade twelve (Research Report No. 18)*. Urbana, IL: National Council of Teachers of English.

Loban, W. D. (1963). *The language of elementary school children*. Champaign, IL: National Council of Teachers of English.

Logan, G. (1988). Automaticity, resources, and memory: Theoretical controversies and practical implications. *Human Factors, 30*, 583–598.

Lomax, R. G., & McGee, L. M. (1987). Young children's concepts about print and meaning: Toward a model of word reading acquisition. *Reading Research Quarterly, 22*, 237–256.

Lukens, R. J. (1995). *A critical handbook of children's literature* (5th ed.). New York: HarperCollins.

Lundberg, I., Frost, J., & Petersen, O. (1988). Effects of an extensive program for stimulating phonological awareness in preschool children. *Reading Research Quarterly, 23*, 263–284.

Lundsteen, S. W. (1979). *Listening: Its impact on reading and the other language arts* (Rev. ed.). Urbana, IL: National Council of Teachers of English.

Lutz, W. (1989). *Doublespeak*. New York: HarperCollins.

Lutz, W. (1991). Notes toward a description of doublespeak (Rev. ed.). In W. Gibson & W. Lutz (Eds.), *Doublespeak: A brief history, definition, and bibliography, with a list of award winners, 1974–1990* (Concept Paper No. 2). Urbana, IL: National Council of Teachers of English.

Mackenzie, T. (Ed.) (1992). *Readers' workshop—bridging literature and literacy: Stories from teachers and their classrooms*. Toronto: Irwin.

Macon, J. M., Bewell, D., & Vogt, M. E. (1991). *Responses to literature, Grades K–8*. Newark, DE: International Reading Association.

Mallon, T. (1984). *A book of one's own: People and their diaries*. New York: Ticknor & Fields.

Mandler, J. M., & Johnson, N. S. (1977). Remembrance of things parsed: Story structure and recall. *Cognitive Psychology, 9*, 111–115.

Manley, A., & O'Neill, C. (1997). *Dreamseekers: Creative approaches to the African American heritage*. Portsmouth, NH: Heinemann.

Many, J. E. (1991). The effects of stance and age level on children's literary responses. *Journal of Reading Behavior, 23*, 61–85.

Manzo, A. V. (1969). The ReQuest procedure. *Journal of Reading, 13*, 123–126.

Marcus, S. (1990). Computers in the language arts: From pioneers to settlers. *Language Arts, 67*, 519–524.

Marinelli, S. (1996). Integrated spelling in the classroom. *Primary Voices K–6, 4*, 11–15.

Marques, E. (1997). *100 jobs for kids and young adults: A self-improvement tool*. Toronto: WiseChild Press.

Martin, N., D'Arcy, P., Newton, B., & Parker, R. (1976). *Writing and learning across the curriculum*. London: Schools Council Publications.

Martinez, M. G., & Roser, N. L. (1985). Read it again: The value of repeated readings during storytime. *The Reading Teacher, 38*, 782–786.

Martinez, M. G., & Roser, N. L. (1995). The books make a difference in story talk. In N. L. Roser & M. G. Martinez (Eds.), *Book talk and beyond: Children and teachers respond to literature* (pp. 32–41). Newark, DE: International Reading Association.

Marzano, R. J., Pickering, D., & McTighe, J. (1993). *Assessing student outcomes: Performance assessment using the dimensions of learning model*. Alexandria, VA: Association for Supervision and Curriculum Development.

Maslin, J. E., & Nelson, M. E. (2002). Peering into the future: Students using technology to create literacy products. *The Reading Teacher, 55*(7), 628–631.

Mason, J, Herman, P. & Au, K (1991). Children's developing knowledge of words. In J. Flood et al. (Eds.), *Handbook of research on teaching the English language arts*. New York: MacMillan.

Matthew, K. (1996). The impact of CD-ROM storybooks on children's reading comprehension and reading attitude. *Journal of Educational Multimedia and Hypermedia, 5*(3–4), 379–394.

Matthew, K. (1997). A comparison of the influence of interactive CD-ROM storybooks and traditional print storybooks on reading comprehension. *Journal of Research on Computing in Education, 29*(3), 263–275.

McCarrier, A., Pinnell, G.S., & Fountas, I. (2000). *Interactive writing: How language and literacy come together, K–2*. Portsmouth: Heinemann.

McCarthy, B. (1987). *The 4MAT System: Teaching to Learning Styles*. Barrington, Illinois: EXCEL, Inc.

McCracken, R. A., & McCracken, M. J. (1972). *Reading is only the tiger's tail*. San Rafael, CA: Leswing Press.

McCusker, L., Hillinger, M., & Bias, R. (1981). Phonological recoding and reading. *Psychological Bulletin, 89*, 217–245.

McGee, L. M., & Richgels, D. J. (1985). Teaching expository text structure to elementary students. *The Reading Teacher, 38*, 739–748.

McGee, L. M., & Tompkins, G. E. (1995). Literature-based reading instruction: What's guiding the instruction? *Language Arts, 72*, 405–414.

McGrath, J. (1991, May). Books that transcend the barrier of strangeness: Making friends. *Canadian Magazine*, 153–160.

McKay, R., & Kendrick, M. (2001). Images of literacy: Youth children's drawing about reading and writing. *Canadian Journal of Research in Early Childhood Education, 8*(4), 7–22.

McKenzie, G. R. (1979). Data charts: A crutch for helping pupils organize reports. *Language Arts, 56*, 784–788.

McWhirter, A. M. (1990). Whole language in the middle school. *The Reading Teacher, 43*, 562–565.

Meyer, B. J., & Freedle, R. O. (1984). Effects of discourse type on recall. *American Educational Research Journal, 21*, 121–143.

Mills, H., O'Keefe, T., & Stephens, D. (1992). *Looking closely: Exploring the role of phonics in one whole language classroom*. Urbana, IL: National Council of Teachers of English.

Moffitt, A. S., & Wartella, E. (1992). A survey of leisure reading pursuits of female and male adolescents. *Reading Research and Instruction, 31*(2), 1–17.

Mohr, M. M. (1984). *Revision: The rhythm of meaning*. Upper Montclair, NJ: Boynton/Cook.

Montgomery, D., Karlan, G., & Coutinho, M. (2001). The effectiveness of word processor spell checker programs to produce target words for misspellings generated by students with learning disabilities. *Journal of Special Education, 16*(2), 27–41.

Morgan, N., & Saxton, J. (1987). *Teaching drama: A mind of many wonders*. London: Hutchinson.

Morgan, N., & Saxton, J. (1991). *Asking better questions*. Ontario: Pembroke.

Morrice, C., & Simmons, M. (1991). Beyond reading buddies: A whole language cross-age program. *The Reading Teacher, 44*, 572–578.

Morrow, L. M. (1989). Designing the classroom to promote literacy development. In D. S. Strickland & L. M. Morrow (Eds.), *Emerging literacy: Young children learn to read and write*. Newark, DE: International Reading Association.

Morrow, L. M. (1996). *Motivating reading and writing in diverse classrooms* (NCTE Research Report No. 28). Urbana, IL: National Council of Teachers of English.

Morrow, L. M. (2003). Motivating lifelong voluntary readers. In J. Flood, D. Lapp, J. R. Squire, & J. M. Jensen (Eds.), *Handbook of research on teaching the English language arts* (pp. 857–867). Mahwah, NJ: Erlbaum.

Morrow, L.M. (2005). *Literacy development in the early years: Helping children read and write* (5th ed.). Upper Saddle River, NJ: Pearson.

Murray, D. H. (1982). *Learning by teaching*. Montclair, NJ: Boynton/Cook.

Nagy, W. E. (1988). *Teaching vocabulary to improve reading comprehension*. Urbana, IL: ERIC Clearinghouse on Reading and Communication Skills and the National Council of Teachers of English and the International Reading Association.

Nagy, W. E., & Herman, P. (1985). Incidental vs. instructional approaches to increasing reading vocabulary. *Educational Perspectives, 23*, 16–21.

Nash, M. F. (1995). "Leading from behind": Dialogue response journals. In N. L. Roser & M. G. Martinez (Eds.), *Book talk and beyond: Children and teachers respond to literature* (pp. 217–225). Newark, DE: International Reading Association.

Nathan, R. (1987). I have a loose tooth and other unphotographic events: Tales from a first grade journal. In T. Fulwiler (Ed.), *The journal book* (pp. 187–192). Portsmouth, NH: Boynton/Cook.

Nathenson-Mejia, S. (1989). Writing in a second language: Negotiating meaning through invented spelling. *Language Arts, 66*, 516–526.

NCTE Elementary Section Steering Committee. (1996). Exploring language arts standards within a cycle of learning. *Language Arts, 73*, 10–13.

Neelands, J. (1984). *Making sense of drama*. London: Heinemann.

Neelands, J. (1990). *Structuring drama work*. New York: Cambridge University Press.

Neelands, J. (1992). *Learning through imagined experience*. London: Hodders.

Neelands, J. (1998). *Beginning drama: 11–14*. London: David Fulton.

Nelson, P. A. (1988). Drama, doorway to the past. *Language Arts, 65*, 20–25.

Newkirk, T. (2000). Misreading masculinity: speculations on the great gender gap in writing. *Language Arts, 77*(4), 177–184.

Newkirk, T., & McLure, P. (1992). *Listening in: Children talk about books (and other things)*. Portsmouth, NH: Heinemann.

Niles, O. S. (1974). Organization perceived. In H. L. Herber (Ed.), *Perspectives in reading: Developing study skills in secondary schools.* Newark, DE: International Reading Association.

Noguchi, R. R. (1991). *Grammar and the teaching of writing: Limits and possibilities.* Urbana, IL: National Council of Teachers of English.

Norris, J. (1995). Responsible guided-imagery. *Youth Theatre Journal, 7*(4), 4–9.

Norton, D. (1992). *The impact of literature-based reading.* New York: Merrill.

Noyce, R. M., & Christie, J. F. (1983). Effects of an integrated approach to grammar instruction on third graders' reading and writing. *Elementary School Journal, 84,* 63–69.

Nystrand, M., Gamoran, A., & Heck, M. J. (1993). Using small groups for response to and thinking about literature. *English Journal, 82,* 14–22.

Ogle, D. M. (1986). K-W-L: A teaching model that develops active reading of expository text. *The Reading Teacher, 39,* 564–570.

Ogle, D. M. (1989). The know, want to know, learn strategy. In K. D. Muth (Ed.), *Children's comprehension of text: Research into practice* (pp. 205–223). Newark, DE: International Reading Association.

Ohlhausen, M. M., & Jepsen, M. (1992). Lessons from Goldilocks: "Somebody's been choosing my books but I can make my own choices now!" *The New Advocate, 5,* 31–46.

Oldfather, P. (1995). Commentary: What's needed to maintain and extend motivation for literacy in the middle grades? *Journal of Reading, 38,* 420–422.

O'Neill, C. (1995). *Drama worlds.* Portsmouth, NH: Heinemann.

O'Neill, C., & Lambert, A. (1982). *Drama structures.* London: Hutchinson.

Opie, I., & Opie, P. (1959). *The lore and language of school children.* Oxford: Oxford University Press.

Outhred, L. (1987). To write or not to write: Does using a word processor assist reluctant writers? *Australia and New Zealand Journal of Developmental Disabilities, 13*(4), 2111–2117.

Owston, R., & Wideman, H. (1997). Word processors and children's writing in a high-computer-access setting. *Journal of Research on Computing in Education, 30*(2), 202–220.

Pahl, K., & Rowsell, J. (2005). *Literacy & education: Understanding the new literacies in the classroom.* London: Paul Chapman Publishing.

Palinscar, A. (1985). The unpacking of a multi-component, metacognitive training package. Paper presented at the Annual Meeting of the American Educational Research Association, Chicago, Ill.

Pallin, G. (2005). *Stage management: The essential handbook.* Toronto: Playwrights Canada Press.

Papandropoulou, I., & Sinclair, H. (1974). What is a word? Experimental study of children's ideas on grammar. *Human Development, 17,* 241–258.

Pappas, C. C. (1991). Fostering full access to literacy by including information books. *Language Arts, 68,* 449–462.

Pappas, C. C. (1993). Is narrative "primary"? Some insights from kindergartners' pretend readings of stories and information books. *Journal of Reading Behavior, 25,* 97–129.

Pappas, C. C., & Brown, E. (1987). Learning to read by reading: Learning how to extend the functional potential of language. *Research in the Teaching of English, 21,* 160–184.

Pappas, C. C., Kiefer, B. Z., & Levstik, L. S. (1995). *An integrated language perspective in the elementary school: Theory into action* (2nd ed.). New York: Longman.

Paris, S. G., & Jacobs, J. E. (1984). The benefits of informed instruction for children's reading awareness and comprehension skills. *Child Development, 55,* 2083–2093.

Paris, S. G., Wasik, B. A., & Turner, J. C. (1991). The development of strategic readers. In R. Barr, M. L. Kamil, P. B. Mosenthal, & P. D. Pearson (Eds.), *Handbook of reading research* (Vol. 2, pp. 609–640). New York: Longman.

Parry, J., & Hornsby, D. (1985). *Write on: A conference approach to writing.* Portsmouth, NH: Heinemann.

Pearson, P. D. (1993). Teaching and learning reading: A research perspective. *Language Arts, 70,* 502–511.

Pearson, P. D., & Fielding, L. (1991). Comprehension instruction. In R. Barr, M. L. Kamil, P. Mosenthal, & P. D. Pearson (Eds.), *Handbook of reading research,* Vol. II (pp. 815–860). White Plains, NY: Longman.

Pearson, P. D., & Fielding, L. (1982). Research update: Listening comprehension. *Language Arts, 59,* 617–629.

Perfetti, C., Beck, I., Bell, L., & Hughes, C. (1987). Phonemic knowledge and learning to read are reciprocal: A longitudinal study of first grade children. *Merrill-Palmer Quarterly, 33,* 283–319.

Perl, S. (1994). Understanding composing. In S. Perl (Ed.), *Landmark essays on writing process* (pp. 99–106). Davis, CA: Heragoras Press.

Peterson, L. (1991). Gender and the autobiographical essay: Research perspectives. *College Composition and Communication, 42*(2), 170–183.

Peterson, R., & Eeds, M. (1990). *Grand conversations: Literature groups in action.* New York: Scholastic.

Peterson, S. (2001). Teachers' perceptions of gender equity in writing assessment. *English Quarterly, 33* (1&2), 22–30.

Peyton, J. K., & Seyoum, M. (1989). The effect of teacher strategies on students' interactive writing: The case of dialogue journals. *Research in the Teaching of English, 23,* 310–334.

Piaget, J. (1969). *The psychology of intelligence.* NJ: Littlefield, Adams.

Piaget, J. (1975). *The development of thought: Equilibration of cognitive structures.* New York: Viking.

Pianfetti, E. S. (2001). Teachers and technology: Digital literacy through professional development. *Language Arts, 78,* 255–262.

Picciotto, L. P. (1992). *Evaluation: A team effort.* Toronto: Scholastic.

Picciotto, L. P. (1993). *Learning together: A whole year in a primary classroom.* Toronto: Scholastic.

Picciotto, L. P. (1996). *Student-led parent conferences.* New York, NY: Scholastic.

Piccolo, J. A. (1987). Expository text structures: Teaching and learning strategies. *The Reading Teacher, 40,* 838–847.

Pikulski, J. (1990). Informal reading inventories. *The Reading Teacher, 43,* 686–688.

Pinnell, G., Fried, M. D., & Estice, R. M. (1990). Reading Recovery: Learning how to make a difference. *The Reading Teacher, 43,* 282–295.

Pinnell, G. S., & Jaggar, A. M. (1991). Oral language: Speaking and listening in the classroom. In J. Flood, J. M. Jensen, D. Lapp, & J. R. Squire (Eds.), *Handbook of research on the teaching of the English language arts* (pp. 691–742). New York: Macmillan.

Piper, D. (1993). Students in the mainstream who face linguistic and cultural challenges. In J. Andrews & J. Lupart (Eds.), *The inclusive classroom: Educating exceptional children*. Scarborough, ON: Nelson.

Pitcher, E. G., & Prelinger, E. (1963). *Children tell stories: An analysis of fantasy*. New York: International Universities Press.

Pooley, R. C. (1974). *The teaching of English usage*. Urbana, IL: National Council of Teachers for English.

Porter, C., & Cleland, J. (1995). *The portfolio as a learning strategy*. Portsmouth, NH: Heinemann.

Postman, N. (1992). The disappearance of childhood. In N. Postman (Ed.), *Conscientious objections: Stirring up trouble about language, technology and education* (pp. 147–161). New York: Vintage.

Pressley, M. (1992). Encouraging mindful use of prior knowledge: Attempting to construct explanatory answers facilitates learning. *Educational Psychologist, 27*, 91–109.

Pressley, M. (1998). *Reading instruction that works: The case for balanced teaching*. New York: The Guilford Press.

Prill, P. (1994/1995). Helping children use the classroom library. *The Reading Teacher, 48*, 363–364.

Purcell Cone, P. (2000). Responding to children's literature through dance. *Teaching Elementary Physical Education, 11*(6), 11–15.

Queenan, M. (1986). Finding grain in the marble. *Language Arts, 63*, 666–673.

Rankin, P. R. (1926). The importance of listening ability. *English Journal, 17*, 623–640.

Raphael, T. E., Englert, C. S., & Kirschner, B. W. (1989). Acquisition of expository writing skills. In J. M. Mason (Ed.), *Reading and writing connections* (pp. 261–290). Boston: Allyn & Bacon.

Raphael, T. E., & McMahon, S. I. (1994). Book club: An alternative framework for reading instruction. *The Reading Teacher, 48*, 102–116.

Rasinski, T. V., & Padak, N. D. (1990). Multicultural learning through children's literature. *Language Arts, 67*, 576–580.

Read, C. (1975). *Children's categorization of speech sounds in English* (NCTE Research Report No. 17). Urbana, IL: National Council of Teachers of English.

Read, C. (1986). *Children's creative spelling*. London: Routledge & Kegan Paul.

Reed, B. (1992, November). Canadian history from cows to catalogues. *Canadian Review, 20*(6).

Reimer, K. M. (1992). Multiethnic literature: Holding fast to dreams. *Language Arts, 69*, 14–21.

Reinking, D. (1997). Me and my hypertext:) A multiple digression analysis of technology and literacy (sic). *The Reading Teacher, 50*(8), 626–643.

Reyes, M. de la Luz. (1991). A process approach to literacy using dialogue journals and literature logs with second language learners. *Research in the Teaching of English, 25*, 291–313.

Rhodes, L. K., & Dudley-Marling, C. (1988). *Readers and writers with a difference: A holistic approach to teaching learning disabled and remedial students*. Portsmouth, NH: Heinemann.

Rhodes, L. K., & Nathenson-Mejia, S. (1992). Anecdotal records: A powerful tool for ongoing literacy assessment. *The Reading Teacher, 45*, 502–511.

Richardson, J. S. (2000). *Read it aloud! Using literature in the secondary content classroom*. Newark, DE: International Reading Association.

Rico, G. L. (1983). *Writing the natural way*. Los Angeles: Tarcher.

Roberts, S. (2002). Taking a technological path to poetry writing. *The Reading Teacher, 55*(7), 678–687.

Robinson, F. P. (1946). *Effective study* (2nd ed.). New York: Harper & Row.

Rog, L. (2003). *Guided reading basics*. Markham, ON: Pembroke Publishers.

Roop, P. (1992). Nonfiction books in the primary classroom: Soaring with the swans. In E. B. Freeman & D. G. Person (Eds.), *Using nonfiction tradebooks in the elementary classroom: From ants to zeppelins* (pp. 106–112). Urbana, IL: National Council of Teachers of English.

Roop, P. (1995). Keep the reading lights burning. In M. Sorensen & B. Lehman (Eds.), *Teaching with children's books: Paths to literature-based instruction* (pp. 197–202). Urbana, IL: National Council of Teachers of English.

Rose, D. H., & Meyer, A. (1994). The role of technology in language arts instruction. *Language Arts, 71*, 290–294.

Rosenblatt, L. M. (1978). *The reader, the text, the poem: The transactional theory of the literary work*. Carbondale: Southern Illinois University Press.

Rosenblatt, L. M. (1983). *Literature as exploration* (4th ed.). New York: Modern Language Association.

Rosenblatt, L. M. (1985a). The transactional theory of the literary work: Implications for research. In C. R. Cooper (Ed.), *Researching response to literature and the teaching of literature* (pp. 33–53). Norwood, NJ: Ablex.

Rosenblatt, L. M. (1985b). Viewpoints: Transaction versus interaction—A terminological rescue operation. *Research in the Teaching of English, 19*, 98–107.

Rosenblatt, L. M. (1991). Literature—S.O.S.! *Language Arts, 68*, 444–448.

Routman, R. (1996). *Literacy at the crossroads: Crucial talk about reading, writing, and other teaching dilemmas*. Portsmouth, NH: Heinemann.

Rowsell, J. (2005). Literacy revisited. *Orbit, 36*(1). Retrieved September 20, 2006 from http://www.oise.utoronto/orbit/rowsell_editorial.html.

Rudasill, L. (1986). Advertising gimmicks: Teaching critical thinking. In J. Golub (Ed.), *Activities to promote critical thinking (Classroom practices in teaching English)* (pp. 127–129). Urbana, IL: National Council of Teachers of English.

Ruddell, M. R. (2001). *Teaching content reading and writing* (3rd ed.). New York: John Wiley & Sons.

Rumelhart, D. (1975). Notes on a schema for stories. In D. G. Bobrow (Ed.), *Representation and understanding: Studies in cognitive science* (pp. 99–135). New York: Academic Press.

Rumelhart, D. (1994). Toward an Interactive Model of Reading. In R. Ruddell and N. Unrau (Eds.) *Theoretical models and processes of reading* (5th ed.). Newark, DE: International Reading Association, 1149–1179.

Saldaña, J. (1995). *Drama of color.* Portsmouth, NH: Heinemann.

Sampson, M., Rasinski, T., & Sampson, M. (2003). *Total literacy: Reading, writing and learning.* Belmont, CA: Wadsworth/ Thomson Learning.

Samway, K. D., Whang, G., Cade, C., Gamil, M., Lubandina, M. A., & Phommachanh, K. (1991). Reading the skeleton, the heart, and the brain of a book: Students' perspectives on literature study circles. *The Reading Teacher, 45,* 196–205.

Scarcella, R. (1990). *Teaching language minority students in the multicultural classroom.* Upper Saddle River, NJ: Prentice Hall/ Merrill.

Scher, A., & Verrall, C. (1988). *100+ ideas for drama.* Portsmouth, NH: Heinemann.

Scher, A., & Verrall, C. (1989). *Another 100+ ideas for drama.* Portsmouth, NH: Heinemann.

Schickedanz, J. A. (1990). *Adam's righting revolutions: One child's literacy development from infancy through grade one.* Portsmouth, NH: Heinemann.

Schlosser., E. (2006). *Chew on this: Everything you don't want to know about fast food.* New York: Houghton Mifflin

Schmitt, M. C. (1990). A questionnaire to measure children's awareness of strategic reading processes. *The Reading Teacher, 43,* 454–461.

Schrader, C. T. (1990). *The word processor as a tool for developing young writers.* ERIC Document Reproduction Service No. ED321276.

Shafer, K. (1993). Talk in the middle: Two conversational skills for friendship. *English Journal, 82,* 53–55.

Shanahan, T. (1988). The reading–writing relationship: Seven instructional principles. *The Reading Teacher, 41,* 636–647.

Shanahan, T., & Knight, L. (1991). *Guidelines for judging and selecting language arts textbooks: A modest proposal (NCTE Concept Paper No. 1).* Urbana, IL: National Council of Teachers of English.

Sharp, V. (1999). *Computer education for teachers* (3rd ed.). Boston: McGraw-Hill.

Shefelbine, J. (1995). *Learning and using phonics in beginning reading* (Literacy research paper; volume 10). New York: Scholastic.

Shor, I. (2003). What is critical literacy? *Journal for Pedagogy, Pluralism & Practice.* Retrieved September 23, 2003, from www.lesley.edu/journals/jppp/4/shor.html.

Short, K., Kauffman, G., & Kahn, L. (2003). "I just *need* to draw": Responding to literature across multiple sign systems. *The Reading Teacher, 54*(2), 160–171.

Shuy, R. W. (1987). Research currents: Dialogue as the heart of learning. *Language Arts, 64,* 890–897.

Sidman, J. (2005). *Song of the water boatman and other pond poems.* Boston: Houghton Mifflin

Sipe, L. R. (2000). The construction of literacy understanding by first and second graders in oral response to picture storybook read-alouds. *Reading Research Quarterly, 35,* 252–275.

Sippola, A. E. (1995). K-W-L-S. *The Reading Teacher, 48*(1), 542–543.

Slaughter, H. (1988). Indirect and direct teaching in a whole language program. *The Reading Teacher, 41,* 30–34.

Slaughter, J. P. (1993). *Beyond storybooks: Young children and the shared book experience.* Newark, DE: International Reading Association.

Slavin, R. (1997). *Educational psychology* (5th ed.). Boston: Allyn & Bacon.

Smith, F. (1982). *Writing and the writer.* New York: Holt, Rinehart & Winston.

Smith, F. (1988). *Joining the literacy club: Further essays into education.* Portsmouth, NH: Heinemann.

Smith, N. J. (1985). The word processing approach to language experience. *The Reading Teacher, 38,* 556– 559.

Smith, P. L., & Tompkins, G. E. (1988). Structured notetaking: A strategy for content area readers. *Journal of Reading, 32,* 46–53.

Snider, V. (1997). The relationship between phonemic awareness and later reading achievement. *Journal of Educational Research, 90,* 203–211.

Snow, C., Burns, M., & Griffin, P. (2005). *Preventing reading difficulties in young children.* Washington, DC: National Academy Press.

Snow, C., Griffin, P., & Tabors, P. (2002). *The home-school study of language and literacy development.* Retrieved March 8, 2006 from http://www.gse.harvard.edu.

Somers, J. (1994). *Drama in the curriculum.* New York: Cassell.

Sommers, N. (1994). Revision strategies of student writers and experienced adult writers. In S. Perl (Ed.), *Landmark essays on writing process* (pp. 75–84). Davis, CA: Heragoras Press.

Sorenson, M. (1993). Teach each other: Connecting talking and writing. *English Journal, 82,* 42–47.

Sowers, S. (1985). The story and the "all about" book. In J. Hansen, T. Newkirk, & D. Graves (Eds.), *Breaking ground: Teachers relate reading and writing in the elementary school* (pp. 73–82). Portsmouth, NH: Heinemann.

Spangenberg-Urbschat, K., & Pritchard, R. (Eds.). (1994). *Kids come in all languages: Reading instruction for ESL students.* Newark, DE: International Reading Association.

Speaker, R. B., Jr., & Speaker, P. R. (1991). Sentence collecting: Authentic literacy events in the classroom. *Journal of Reading, 35,* 92–95.

Spolin, V. (1986). *Theatre games for the classroom: A teacher's handbook.* Evanston, IL: Northwestern University Press.

Standards for the English language arts. (1996). Urbana, IL: National Council of Teachers of English and the International Reading Association.

Stanovich, K. (1980). Toward an interactive-compensatory model of individual differences in the development of reading fluency. *Reading Research Quarterly, 16,* 37–71.

Stanovich, K. (1990). Concepts in developmental theories of reading skill: Cognitive resources, automaticity, and modularity. *Developmental Review, 10,* 72–100.

Stanovich, P. (1998). Shaping practice to fit the evidence. *Orbit, 28*(4), 37–42.

Staton, J. (1980). Writing and counseling: Using a dialogue journal. *Language Arts, 57,* 514–518.

Staton, J. (1987). The power of responding in dialogue journals. In T. Fulwiler (Ed.), *The journal book* (pp. 47–63). Portsmouth, NH: Boynton/Cook.

Stauffer, R. G. (1970). *The language experience approach to the teaching of reading.* New York: Harper & Row.

Stauffer, R. G. (1975). *Directing the reading–thinking process.* New York: Harper & Row.

Stein, N. L., & Glenn, C. G. (1979). An analysis of story comprehension in elementary school children. In R. O. Freedle (Ed.), *New directions in discourse processing* (pp. 53–120). Norwood, NJ: Ablex.

Steinbergh, J. W. (1993). Chandra: "To live a life of no secrecy." In S. Hudson-Ross, L. M. Cleary, & M. Casey (Eds.), *Children's voices: Children talk about literacy* (pp. 202–214). Portsmouth, NH: Heinemann.

Stewart, M. T. (2004). Early literacy in the climate of No Child Left Behind. *The Reading Teacher, 52*(1), 8–17.

Stewig, J. W. (1981). Choral speaking: Who has the time? Why take the time? *Childhood Education, 57,* 25–29.

Stires, S. (1991a). Thinking through the process: Self-evaluation in writing. In B. M. Power & R. Hubbard (Eds.), *The Heinemann reader: Literacy in process* (pp. 295–310). Portsmouth, NH: Heinemann.

Stires, S. (Ed.). (1991b). *With promise: Redefining reading and writing for "special" students.* Portsmouth, NH: Heinemann.

Sticht, T., & James, J. (1984). Listening and reading. In: P. D. Pearson (Ed.) *Handbook of Reading Research* (pp. 293–318). New York: Longmans.

Strong, W. (1996). *Writer's toolbox: A sentence-combining workshop.* New York: McGraw-Hill.

Sulzby, E. (1985a). Children's emergent reading of favorite storybooks: A developmental study. *Reading Research Quarterly, 20,* 458–481.

Sulzby, E. (1985b). Kindergartners as readers and writers. In M. Farr (Ed.), *Advances in writing research, Vol. 1: Children's early writing development* (pp. 127–199). Norwood, NJ: Ablex.

Sumara, D., & Walker, L. (1991). The teacher's role in whole language. *Language Arts, 68,* 276–285.

Swain, M. (1988). Manipulating and complementing content teaching to maximize second language learning. *TESL Canada Journal/Revue TESL du Canada, 6*(1), 68–83.

Tanner, F. A. (1982). *Basic drama projects* (6th ed.). Caldwell, ID: Clark Publishing Company.

Tanner, F. A. (1982). *Creative communication.* Caldwell, ID: Clark Publishing Company.

Tarlington, C., & Verriour, P. (1983). *Offstage: Elementary education through drama.* Toronto: Oxford University Press.

Tarlington, C., & Verriour, P. (1991). *Role drama.* Ontario: Pembroke.

Taylor, D. (1983). *Family literacy: Young children learning to read and write.* Exeter, NH: Heinemann.

Taylor, D. (1993). *From the child's point of view.* Portsmouth, NH: Heinemann.

Taylor, D., & Dorsey-Gaines, C. (1987). *Growing up literate: Learning from inner-city families.* Portsmouth, NH: Heinemann.

Taylor, K. K., & Kidder, E. B. (1988). The development of spelling skills: From first grade through eighth grade. *Written Communication, 5,* 222–244.

Taylor, P. (1998). *Redcoats and patriots: Reflective practice in drama and social studies.* Portsmouth, NH: Heinemann.

Teale, W. H. (1982). Toward a theory of how children learn to read and write. *Language Arts, 59,* 555–570.

Teale, W., Leu, D., Labbo, L., & Kinzer, C. (2002). The CTELL project: New ways technology can help educate tomorrow's reading teachers. *The Reading Teacher, 55*(7), 654–659.

Teale, W. H., & Sulzby, E. (1989). Emerging literacy: New perspectives. In D. S. Strickland & L. M. Morrow (Eds.), *Emerging literacy: Young children learn to read and write.* (pp. 1–15). Newark, DE: International Reading Association.

Temple, C., Nathan, R., Burris, N., & Temple, F. (1988). *The beginnings of writing.* Boston: Allyn & Bacon.

Templeton, S. (1979). Spelling first, sound later: The relationship between orthography and higher order phonological knowledge in older students. *Research in the Teaching of English, 13,* 255–265.

Templeton, S. (1980). Young children invent words: Developing concepts of "word-ness." *The Reading Teacher, 33,* 454–459.

Templeton, S., & Spivey, E. (1980). The concept of word in young children as a function of level of cognitive development. *Research in the Teaching of English, 14,* 265–278.

Terry, A. (1974). *Children's poetry preferences: A national survey of upper elementary grades (NCTE Research Report No. 16).* Urbana, IL: National Council of Teachers of English.

Thomas, S., & Oldfather, P. (1995). Enhancing student and teacher engagement in literacy learning: A shared inquiry approach. *The Reading Teacher, 49,* 192–202.

Thurber, D. N. (1987). *D'Nealian handwriting (Grades K–8).* Glenview, IL: Scott, Foresman.

Tiedt, I. (1970). Exploring poetry patterns. *Elementary English, 45,* 1082–1084.

Tierney, R. J. (1983). Writer–reader transactions: Defining the dimensions of negotiation. In P. L. Stock (Ed.), *Forum: Essays on theory and practice in the teaching of writing* (pp. 147–151). Upper Montclair, NJ: Boynton/Cook.

Tierney, R. J., & Pearson, P. D. (1983). Toward a composing model of reading. *Language Arts, 60,* 568–580.

Tierney, R. J., & Pearson, P. D. (1992). Learning to learn from text: A framework for improving classroom practice. In E. K. Dishner, T. W. Bean, J. E. Readence, & D. W. Moore (Eds.), *Reading in the content areas: Improving classroom instruction* (pp. 85–99). Dubuque, IA: Kendall-Hunt.

Tompkins, G. E. (1994). *Teaching writing: Balancing process and product* (2nd ed.). Upper Saddle River, NJ: Prentice Hall/Merrill.

Tompkins, G. E. (1995). Hear ye, hear ye, and learn the lesson well: Fifth graders read and write about the American Revolution. In M. Sorensen & B. Lehman (Eds.), *Teaching with children's books: Paths to literature-based instruction* (pp. 171–187). Urbana, IL: National Council of Teachers of English.

Tompkins, G. E., Friend, M., & Smith, P. L. (1987). Strategies for more effective listening. In C. R. Personke & D. D. Johnson (Eds.), *Language arts and the beginning teacher* (Chapter 3). Upper Saddle River, NJ: Prentice Hall.

Tompkins, G. E., & McGee, L. M. (1983). Launching nonstandard speakers into Standard English. *Language Arts, 60,* 463–469.

Tompkins, G. E., & McGee, L. M. (1993). *Teaching reading with literature: Case studies to action plans.* Upper Saddle River, NJ: Prentice Hall/Merrill.

Tompkins, G. E., Smith, P. L., & Hitchcock, M. E. (1987). *Elementary students' use of expository text structures in report writing.* Paper presented at the National Reading Conference, St. Petersburg Beach, FL.

Tompkins, G. E., & Webeler, M. B. (1983). What will happen next? Using predictable books with young children. *The Reading Teacher, 36*, 498–502.

Tompkins, G. E., & Yaden, D. B., Jr. (1986). *Answering students' questions about words.* Urbana, IL: ERIC Clearinghouse on Communication Skills and the National Council of Teachers of English.

Toohey, K. (1996). Learning English as a second language in kindergarten: A community of practice perspective. *The Canadian Modern Language Review/La Revue canadienne des langues vivantes, 52*(4), 549–576.

Trachtenburg, R., & Ferruggia, A. (1989). Big books from little voices: Reaching high risk beginning readers. *The Reading Teacher, 42*, 284–289.

Treiman, R. (1985). Phonemic analysis, spelling, and reading. In T. H. Carr (Ed.), *The development of reading skills* (pp. 5–18). San Francisco: Jossey-Bass.

Trelease, J. (1995). *The new read-aloud handbook* (4th ed.). New York: Penguin.

Trepanier-Street, M., Romatowski, J. & McNair, S. (1990). Children's responses to stereotypical and non-stereotypical story starters. *Journal of Research in Childhood Education, 5*(1), 60–72.

Troika, R. C. (1981). Synthesis of research on bilingual education. *Educational Leadership, 38*, 498–504.

True, J. (1979). Round robin reading is for the birds. *Language Arts, 56*, 918–921.

Tunmer, W., & Nesdale, A. (1985). Phonemic segmentation skill and beginning reading. *Journal of Educational Psychology, 77*, 417–427.

Tunnell, M. O., & Ammon, R. (Eds.). (1993). *The story of ourselves: Teaching history through children's literature.* Portsmouth, NH: Heinemann.

Tutolo, D. (1981). Critical listening/reading of advertisements. *Language Arts, 58*, 679–683.

Tway, E. (1980). How to find and encourage the nuggets in children's writing. *Language Arts, 57*, 299–304.

Typing Tutor. (n.d.). Sunburst Communications, 39 Washington Avenue, Pleasantville, NY 10570.

Urzua, C. (1980). Doing what comes naturally: Recent research in second language acquisition. In G. S. Pinnell (Ed.), *Discovering language with children* (pp. 33–38). Urbana, IL: National Council of Teachers of English.

Urzua, C. (1992). Faith in learners through literature studies. *Language Arts, 69*, 492–501.

Valencia, S. W., Pearson, P. D. (1986). New models of reading assessment. (ERIC Document Reproduction Service No. ED281167). Washington, DC: National Institute of Education.

Valencia, S. W., Hiebert, E. H., & Afflerbach, P. P. (1994). *Authentic reading assessment: Practices and possibilities.* Newark, DE: International Reading Association.

Valentine, S. L. (1986). Beginning poets dig for poems. *Language Arts, 63*, 246–252.

Vardell, S. M. (1991). A new "picture of the world": The NCTE Orbis Pictus Award for outstanding nonfiction for children. *Language Arts, 68*, 474–479.

Venezky, R. L. (1970). *The structure of English orthography.* The Hague: Mouton.

Vygotsky, L. S. (1978). *Mind in society.* Cambridge, MA: Harvard University Press.

Vygotsky, L. S. (1986). *Thought and language.* Cambridge, MA: MIT Press.

Wagner, B. J. (1976). *Dorothy Heathcote: Drama as a learning medium.* Washington, DC: National Education Association.

Wagner, B. J. (1983). The expanding circle of informal classroom drama. In B. A. Busching & J. I. Schwartz (Eds.), *Integrating the language arts in the elementary school* (pp. 155–163). Urbana, IL: National Council of Teachers of English.

Wagner, B. J. (1998). *Educational drama and language arts: What research shows.* Portsmouth, NH: Heinemann.

Walker-Dalhouse, D. (1992). Using African-American literature to increase ethnic understanding. *The Reading Teacher, 45*, 416–422.

Watts Pailliotet, A. (2000, July). Welcome to the new literacies department. *Reading Online, 4* (1). Available at www.readingonline.org/newliteracies/wattspailliotet1.

Watts-Taffe, S., Gwinn, C., Johnson, J., & Horn, M. (2003). Preparing preservice teachers to integrate technology with the elementary literacy program. *The Reading Teacher, 57*(2), 130–138.

Weaver, C. (1979). *Grammar for teachers: Perspectives and definitions.* Urbana, IL: National Council of Teachers of English.

Weaver, C. (1994a). *Reading process and practice: From socio-psycholinguistics to whole language* (2nd ed.). Portsmouth, NH: Heinemann.

Weaver, C. (Ed.). (1994b). *Success at last! Helping students with AD(H)D achieve their potential.* Portsmouth, NH: Heinemann.

Weaver, C. (1996). *Teaching grammar in context.* Portsmouth, NH: Heinemann.

Wells, G. (1986). *The meaning makers: Children learning language and using language to learn.* Portsmouth, NH: Heinemann.

Wells, G., & Chang-Wells, G. L. (1992). *Constructing knowledge together: Classrooms as centers of inquiry and literacy.* Portsmouth, NH: Heinemann.

Wepner, S., Valmont, W. & Thurlow, K. (Eds.). (2000). *Linking literacy and technology: A guide for K–8 classrooms.* Newark, DE: International Reading Association.

Werner, E. K. (1975). *A study of communication time.* Unpublished master's thesis, University of Maryland, College Park.

White, T. G., Sowell, J., & Yanagihara, A. (1989). Teaching elementary students to use word-part clues. *The Reading Teacher, 42*, 302–308.

Whitin, P. E. (1994). Opening potential: Visual response to literature. *Language Arts, 71*, 101–107.

Whitin, P. E. (1996a). Exploring visual response to literature. *Research in the Teaching of English, 30*, 114–140.

Whitin, P. E. (1996b). *Sketching stories, stretching minds.* Portsmouth, NH: Heinemann.

Wilde, S. (1993). *You kan red this! Spelling and punctuation for whole language classrooms, K–6.* Portsmouth, NH: Heinemann.

Wilen, W. W. (1986). *Questioning skills for teachers* (2nd ed.). Washington, DC: National Education Association.

Wilkinson, L. C. (1984). Research currents: Peer group talk in elementary school. *Language Arts, 61*, 164–169.

Wilt, M. E. (1950). A study of teacher awareness of listening as a factor in elementary education. *Journal of Educational Research, 43*, 626–636.

Winsor, P. J., & Pearson, P. D. (1992). *Children at risk: Their phonemic awareness development in holistic instruction. Technical Report No. 556,* Center for the Study of Reading, Champaign, Illinois.

Wittrock, M. C., & Alesandrini, K. (1990). Generation of summaries and analogies and analytic and holistic abilities. *American Research Journal, 27,* 489–502.

Wollman-Bonilla, J. E. (1989). Reading journals: Invitations to participate in literature. *The Reading Teacher, 43,* 112–120.

Wolvin, A. D., & Coakley, C. G. (1979). *Listening instruction* (TRIP Booklet). Urbana, IL: ERIC Clearinghouse on Reading and Communication Skills and the Speech Communication Association.

Wolvin, A. D., & Coakley, C. G. (1985). *Listening* (2nd ed.). Dubuque, IA: William C. Brown.

Wong-Fillmore, L. (1985). When does teacher talk work as input? In S. M. Gass & C. G. Madden (Eds.), *Input in second language acquisition* (pp. 17–50). Rowley, MA: Newbury House.

Woolland, B. (1993). *The Teaching of Drama in the Primary School.* New York: Longman.

Wright, C. D., & Wright, J. P. (1980). Handwriting: The effectiveness of copying from moving versus still models. *Journal of Educational Research, 74,* 95–98.

Wylie, R. E., & Durrell, D. D. (1970). Teaching vowels through phonograms. *Elementary English, 47,* 787–791.

Yaden, D. B., Jr. (1988). Understanding stories through repeated read-alouds: How many does it take? *The Reading Teacher, 41,* 556–560.

Yokota, J. (1993). Issues in selecting multicultural children's literature. *Language Arts, 70,* 156–167.

Yopp, H. K. (1988). The validity and reliability of phonemic awareness tests. *Reading Research Quarterly, 23,* 159–177.

Yopp, H. K. (1992). Developing phonemic awareness in young children. *The Reading Teacher, 45,* 696–703.

Yopp, H. K. (1995). Read-aloud books for developing phonemic awareness: An annotated bibliography. *The Reading Teacher, 48,* 538–542.

Yopp, H. K., & Yopp, R. H. (1996). *Literature-based reading activities* (2nd ed.). Boston: Allyn & Bacon.

Young, J., & Brozo, W. (2001). Boys will be boys, or will they? Literacy & masculinities. *Reading Research Quarterly, 36*(3), 316–325.

Zarrillo, J. (1989). Teachers' interpretations of literature-based reading. *The Reading Teacher, 43,* 22–28.

Zarrillo, J. (1994). *Multicultural literature, multicultural teaching: Units for the elementary grades.* Fort Worth, TX: Harcourt Brace.

Zatlokal, B. (1990, March). Coming soon to a school or library near you. *The Junior Canadian Magazine,* 53–54.

Zebroski, J. T. (1994). *Thinking through theory: Vygotskian perspectives on the teaching of writing.* Portsmouth, NH: Boynton/Cook.

Zutell, J. (1979). Spelling strategies of primary school children and their relationship to Piaget's concept of decentration. *Research in the Teaching of English, 13,* 69–79.

Children's Resources

Aardema, V. (1975). *Why mosquitoes buzz in people's ears: A West Africa tale.* New York: Dial Press.

Aardema, V. (1977). *Who's in rabbit's house: A Masai tale.* New York: Dial Press.

Abbett, L. (1996). *Freebies for kids.* Chicago: Contemporary Books.

Adelson, L. (1972). *Dandelions don't bite: The story of words.* New York: Pantheon.

Adler, D. A. (1990). *A picture book of Helen Keller.* New York: Holiday House.

Adler, D. A. (1995). *A picture book of Patrick Henry.* New York: Holiday House.

Adoff, A. (1995). *Street music: City poems.* New York: HarperCollins.

Agard, J. (1989). *The Calypso alphabet.* Illus. J. Bent. Toronto: Fitzhenry & Whiteside.

Agee, J. (1992). *Go hang a salami! I'm a lasagna hog! and other palindromes.* New York: Farrar, Straus & Giroux.

Ahlberg, J., & Ahlberg, A. (1986). *The jolly postman, or other people's letters.* Boston: Little, Brown.

Aker, D. (2005). *One on one.* Toronto: HarperCollins.

Allen, C. (1991). *The rug makers.* Orlando, FL: Steck-Vaughn.

Aliki. (1979). *Mummies made in Egypt.* New York: HarperCollins.

Aliki. (1983). *A medieval feast.* New York: Crowell.

Aliki. (1995). *Tabby: A story in pictures.* New York: HarperCollins.

Amon, A. (Sel.). (1981). *The earth is sore: Native Americans on nature.* New York: Atheneum.

Ancona, G. (1992). *Man and mustang.* New York: Macmillan.

Ancona, G. (1993). *Powwow.* Orlando: Harcourt Brace.

Andrews, J. (1985). *The very last first time.* Vancouver: Douglas & McIntyre.

Andrews, J. (1990). *The auction.* Toronto: Groundwood/Douglas & McIntyre.

Andrews, J. (1996). *Keri.* Toronto: Groundwood Books.

Andrews, W. (1994). *Protecting the ozone layer.* Toronto: Health Canada Ltd.

Andrews, W. (1995). *Understanding global warming.* Toronto: Health Canada Ltd.

Anno, M. (1982). *Anno's Britain.* New York: Philomel.

Anno, M. (1983). *Anno's U.S.A.* New York: Philomel.

Archambault, J., & Martin, B. Jr. (1994). *A beautiful feast for a big king cat.* New York: HarperCollins.

Arnold, C. (1993). *Dinosaurs all around: An artist's view of the prehistoric world.* New York: Clarion.

Arnosky, J. (1995). *I see animals hiding.* New York: Scholastic.

Arsenault, G. (2002). *Acadian legends, folktales, and songs from Prince Edward Island* (S. Ross, Trans.). Charlottetown, PEI: Acorn Press.

Avi. (1984). *The fighting ground.* New York: HarperCollins.

Avi. (1991). *Nothing but the truth.* New York: Orchard.

Avi. (2002). *Crispin: The cross of lead.* New York: Hyperion Books for Children.

Axelrod, A. (1994). *Pigs will be pigs.* New York: Four Winds Press.

Babbitt, N. (1975). *Tuck everlasting.* New York: Farrar, Straus & Giroux.

Badone, D. (1992). *Time detectives: Clues from our past.* Willowdale: Annick Press.

Bailey, L. (1992). *How come the best clues are always in the garbage?* Toronto: Kids Can Press.

Bailey, L. (1996). *How can a frozen detective stay hot on the trail?* Morton Grove, IL: Albert Whitman & Co.

Bailey, L. (2000). *Adventures in the Middle Ages*. Toronto: Kids Can Press.

Baird, A. (2001). *The witches of Willowmere*. Toronto: Penguin.

Baker, K. (1991). *Hide and snake*. Orlando: Harcourt Brace.

Ballantyne, A. (1991). *Wisakyjak and the new world*. Waterloo, ON: Penumbra Press.

Bancheck, L. (1978). *Snake in, snake out*. New York: Crowell.

Bannatyne-Cugnet, J. (1992). *A prairie alphabet*. Illus. Y. Moore. Montreal: Tundra Books.

Bannatyne-Cugnet, J. (1993). *Grandpa's alkali*. Red Deer, AB: Red Deer College Press.

Bannatyne-Cugnet, J. (1994). *A prairie year*. Montreal: Tundra Books.

Bannatyne-Cugnet, J. (2002). *Heartland: A Prairie Sampler*. Toronto: Tundra Books.

Barclay, J. (1998). *How cold was it?* Montreal, QC: Lobster Press.

Barker-Lottridge, C. (2002). *Berta: A remarkable dog*. Toronto: Groundwood.

Barnes, D. (2005). *My school is alive!* (Available at www.kidsgardening.com.)

Barnett, D. (1976). *Poundmaker*. Don Mills, ON: Fitzhenry & Whiteside.

Barnette M. (2003). *Dog days and dandelions*. New York: St. Martin's Press.

Baron, A. (1996). *Red fox dances*. Cambridge, MA: Candlewick.

Barracca, D., & Barracca, S. (1990). *The adventures of taxi dog*. New York: Dial.

Barrett, J. (1978). *Cloudy with a chance of meatballs*. New York: Atheneum.

Barrett, J. (1983). *A snake is totally tail*. New York: Atheneum.

Barton, B. (1982). *Airport*. New York: Harper & Row.

Barton, R. (2003). *The bear says north: Tales from northern lands*. Toronto: Groundwood.

Base, G. (1988). *Animalia*. Don Mills, ON: Stoddart.

Bates, C. (2001). *Shooting star*. (Sports Stories Series). Halifax, NS: James Lorimer & Co.

Bates, K. L. (1993). *America the beautiful*. New York: Atheneum.

Bauer, C. F. (Sel.). (1986). *Snowy day: Stories and poems*. New York: Lippincott.

Bayer, J. (1984). *A, my name is Alice*. New York: Dial.

Baylor, B (1973). *Sometimes I dance mountains*. New York: Scribner's.

Baylor, B. (1981). *Desert voices*. Illus. P. Parnall. New York: Scribner.

Beal, G. (1996). *The Kingfisher illustrated pocket thesaurus*. New York: Kingfisher.

Beattie, O., Geiger, J., & Tanaka, S. (1992). *Buried in ice*. Toronto: Madison Press Books.

Beatty, P. (1987). *Charley skedaddle*. New York: Morrow.

Beck, A. (2002). *Elliot gets stuck*. Toronto: Kids Can Press.

Bedard, M. (1990). *Redwork*. Toronto: Lester & Orpen Dennys.

Bedard, M. (2001). *Stained glass*. Toronto: Tundra Books.

Behn, H. (1964). *Cricket songs*. New York: Harcourt Brace Jovanovich.

Behn, H. (1971). *More cricket songs*. New York: Harcourt Brace Jovanovich.

Bell, W. (1999). *Forbidden city*. Toronto: Doubleday.

Bellamy, J. (1996). *The Webster's children's thesaurus*. New York: Barnes and Noble.

Beller, J. (1984). *A-B-Cing: An action alphabet*. New York: Crown.

Bellingham, B. (1985). *Storm child*. Toronto: James Lorimer and Co.

Bennett, J. (1985). *Teeny tiny*. New York: Putnam.

Bennett, J. (2000). *Jason Mason Middleton-Tap*. Vancouver: Raincoast.

Berenstain, S., & Berenstain, J. (1968). *Inside, outside, upside, down*. New York: Random House.

Berenstain, S., & Berenstain, J. (1971). *Bears in the night*. New York: Random House.

Berton, P. (1991). *The death of Isaac Brock: Adventures in Canadian history*. Toronto: McClelland & Stewart.

Beveridge, C. (2003). *Shadows of disaster*. Vancouver: Ronsdale Press.

Bial, R. (1996). *With needle and thread*. Boston, MA: Houghton Mifflin Co.

Blades, A. (1971). *Mary of mile 18*. Montreal: Tundra Books.

Blades, A. (1985). *By the sea: An alphabet book*. Toronto: Kids Can Press.

Blume, J. (1971). *Freckle juice*. New York: Dell.

Blume, J. (1972). *Tales of a fourth grade nothing*. New York: Dutton.

Blume, J. (1981). *The one in the middle is the green kangaroo*. New York: Dell.

Blume, J. (1984). *The pain and the great one*. New York: Dell.

Bogart, J. (1991). *Sarah saw a blue macaw*. Richmond Hill, ON: Scholastic Canada.

Bogart, J. (2001). *The night the stars flew*. Toronto: North Winds Press.

Bogart, J. (2002). *Capturing joy: The story of Maud Lewis*. Toronto: Tundra Books.

Bogart, J., & Reid, B. (1994). *Gifts*. Richmond Hill, ON: North Winds Press/Scholastic Canada.

Bollard, J. (1998). *Scholastic children's thesaurus*. Richmond Hill, ON: Scholastic.

Bondar, R. (1994). *Touching the earth*. Willowdale, ON: Firefly Books.

Bondar, B., & Bondar, R. (1993). *On the shuttle: Eight days in space*. Toronto: Greey de Pencier Books.

Bonsall, C. (1996). *Mine's the best*. New York: HarperCollins.

Booth, D. (Ed.) (1989). *Til all the stars have fallen: Canadian poems for children*. Illus. K. MacDonald Denton. Toronto: Kids Can Press.

Booth, D. (Ed.) (1990). *Voices on the wind: Poems for all seasons*. Illus. M. Lemieux. Toronto: Kids Can Press.

Booth, D. & Kovalski, M. (1993). *Doctor Knickerbocker*. Toronto: Kids Can Press.

Booth, D. & Reczuch, K. (1996). *The dust bowl*. Toronto: Kids Can Press.

Boraks-Nemetz, L. (1994). *The old brown suitcase*. Brentwood Bay: Ben-Simon.

Borden, D. (1983). *Yeah, I'm a little kid*. Toronto: Annick Press.

Bossley, M. M. (1996). *The perfect gymnast*. Toronto: James Lorimer.

Bouchard, D. (1990). *The elders are watching*. Tofino: Eagle Dancer Enterprises.

Bouchard, D. (1994). *The colours of British Columbia*. Vancouver: Raincoast Books.

Bouchard, D. (1995). *If you're not from the prairie . . .* New York: Atheneum.

Bouchard, D. (1996). *Voices from the wild: An animal sensgoria*. Vancouver: Raincoast Books.

Bouchard, D. (1997). *If Sarah will take me*. Victoria: Orca Book Publishers.

Bouchard, D. (1997). *Prairie born*. Victoria: Orca Books.

Bouchard, D. (1999). *A barnyard bestiary*. Victoria: Orca Books.

Bouchard, D., & Zhong-Yang, H. (1999). *The dragon new year*. Vancouver: Raincoast Books.

Bourgeois, P. (1986). *Franklin in the dark*. Toronto: Kids Can Press.

Bourgeois, P. (1987). *The amazing apple book*. Toronto: Kids Can Press.

Bourgeois, P. (1990). *The amazing dirt book*. Toronto: Kids Can Press.

Bourgeois, P. (1991). *Canadian fire fighters*. Toronto: Kids Can Press.

Bourgeois, P. (1991). *Canadian garbage collectors*. Toronto: Kids Can Press.

Bourgeois, P. (1991). *Canadian postal workers*. Toronto: Kids Can Press.

Bourgeois, P. (1992). *Canadian police officers*. Illus. K. LaFave. Toronto: Kids Can Press.

Bourgeois, P. (1993). *Franklin is bossy*. Toronto: Kids Can Press.

Bourgeois, P. (1994). *Franklin is messy*. Toronto: Kids Can Press.

Bourgeois, P. (1994). *The many hats of Mr. Minches*. Don Mills, ON: Stoddart.

Bourgeois, P. (1995). *Franklin plays the game*. Toronto: Kids Can Press.

Bourdeau Waboose, J. (2000). *Sky sisters*. Illus. B. Deines. Toronto: Kids Can Press.

Bowen, G. (1994). *Stranded at Plimoth plantation, 1626*. New York: HarperCollins.

Brailsford, A., & Coles, J. (2004). Balanced literacy in action. Markham, ON: Scholastic.

Brandis, M. (1985). *The quarter-pie window*. Erin, ON: Porcupine's Quill.

Brandis, M. (1996). *Rebellion: A novel of Upper Canada*. Illus. G. Brender. Erin, ON: Porcupine's Quill.

Brighton, C. (1987). *Galileo's treasure box*. New York: Walker.

Brooks, M. (2005). *Bone dance*. Scarborough, ON: Groundwood.

Bruchac, J. (1994). *The great ball game: A Muskogee story*. Illus. S. L. Roth. New York: Dial.

Brett, J. (1987). *Goldilocks and the three bears*. New York: Putnam.

Brett, J. (1989). *The mitten*. New York: Putnam.

Briggs, R. (1980). *The snowman*. Harmondsworth, UK: Puffin Books.

Brinckloe, J. (1985). *Fireflies!* New York: Aladdin.

Brooks, K. (2002). *Lucas*. United Kingdom: The Chicken House.

Brooks, M. (1999). *Being with Henry*. Toronto: Douglas & McIntyre.

Brown, M. (1983). *What do you call a dumb bunny? And other rabbit riddles, games, jokes, and cartoons*. Boston: Little, Brown.

Brown, M. (1984). *There's no place like home*. New York: Parents Magazine Press.

Browne, P. (1996). *A gaggle of geese: The collective names of the animal kingdom*. New York: Atheneum.

Browne, S. C., & D'Souza, M. (2001). *Marconi's secret*. Portugal Cove, NF: ESP Press.

Bruce, H. (1992). *Maud: The life of L. M. Montgomery*. Toronto: Seal.

Buchholz, K. (1995). *How the pinto got her colour*. Illus. A. Hanley. Winnipeg: Pemmican Publications.

Buchignani, W. (1994). *Tell no one who you are: The hidden childhood of Régine Miller*. Montreal: Tundra Books.

Buffie, M. (1998). *Angels turn their backs*. Toronto: Kids Can Press.

Buffie, M. (2000). *The watcher*. Toronto: Kids Can Press.

Bunting, E. (1984). *The man who could call down owls*. New York: Macmillan.

Bunting, E. (1988). *How many days to America? A Thanksgiving story*. New York: Clarion.

Bunting, E. (1990). *The wall*. New York: Clarion.

Bunting, E. (1991). *Fly away home*. New York: Clarion.

Bunting, E. (1994). *A day's work*. New York: Clarion.

Bunting, E. (1994a). *Flower garden*. San Diego: Harcourt Brace.

Bunting, E. (1994b). *Smoky night*. San Diego, CA: Harcourt Brace & Co.

Bunting, E. (1995). *Dandelions*. New York: Harcourt Brace.

Bunting, E. (1995). *Once upon a time*. Katowah, NY: Richard C. Owen.

Bunting, E. (1996). *The blue and the gray*. New York: Scholastic.

Burdett, L. (1997). *A midsummer night's dream*. Willowdale, ON: Firefly Books.

Burnett, F. H. (1911). *The secret garden*. Toronto: Copp Clark.

Burningham, J. (1985). *Opposites*. New York: Crown Books.

Burningham, J. (1986). *Cluck baa, jangle twang, slam bang, skip trip, sniff shout, wobble pop*. New York: Viking.

Burton, K. (1995). *One grey mouse*. Toronto: Kids Can Press.

Butler, G. (1995). *The Killik: A Newfoundland story*. Montreal: Tundra Books.

Byars, B. (1968). *The midnight fox*. New York: Viking.

Byars, B. (1970). *The summer of the swans*. New York: Viking.

Calmenson, S. (1994). *Merigold and grandma on the town*. New York: HarperCollins.

Cameron, A. (1985). *How the loon lost her voice*. Madeira Park, BC: Harbour Publishing.

Cameron, A. (1991). *Raven and snipe*. Madeira Park, NL: Harbour Publishing.

Canadian global almanac 2004. (2003). Toronto: John Wiley & Sons.

Canadian junior dictionary. (2000). Toronto: Gage Publishing Ltd.

Cardinal. P. (1997). *The Cree people*. Edmonton: Duval House.

Carle, E. (1969). *The very hungry caterpillar*. Cleveland: Collins-World.

Carle, E. (1973). *Have you seen my cat?* New York: Philomel.

Carle, E. (1984). *The very busy spider*. New York: Philomel.

Carle, E. (1986). *The grouchy ladybug*. New York: Harper & Row.

Carle, E. (1987a). *A house for hermit crab*. Saxonville, MA: Picture Book Studio.

Carle, E. (1987b). *The tiny seed*. Saxonville, MA: Picture Book Studio.

Carle, E. (1989). *Eric Carle's animals, animals*. New York: Philomel.

Carle, E. (1990). *The very quiet cricket*. New York: Philomel.

Carle, E. (1993). *Eric Carle: Picture writer*. MARC Records: Library video.com.

Carle, E. (1995). *The very lonely firefly*. New York: Philomel.

Carle, E. (1998). *Hello, red fox*. New York: Simon & Schuster.

Carney, M. (2002). *Where does a tiger-heron spend the night?* Toronto: Kids Can Press.

Carrick, C. (1989). *Aladdin and the wonderful lamp*. New York: Scholastic.

Carroll, L. (1992). *Lewis Carroll's Jabberwocky*. Illus. J. B. Zalben. Honesdale, PA: Wordsong.

Carter, A. Laurel. (2003). *My home bay*. Red Deer, AB: Red Deer Press.

Cartlidge, M. (1993). *Mouse's letters*. New York: Dutton.

Cartlidge, M. (1995). *Mouse's scrapbook*. New York: Dutton.

Casey, D. (1995). *Weather everywhere*. New York: Macmillan.

Cassedy, S. (1993). *Zoomrimes: Poems about things that go*. New York: HarperCollins.

Cauley, L. B. (1981). *Goldilocks and the three bears*. New York: Putnam.

Cauley, L. B. (1984). *The town mouse and the country mouse*. New York: Putnam.

Cauley, L. B. (1988). *The pancake boy*. New York: Putnam.

Cha, D. (1998). *Dia's story cloth*. New York: Lee & Low Books.

Chan, G. (2001). *The carved box*. Toronto: Kids Can Press.

Chan, H. (1996). *Ghost train*. Vancouver: Groundwood Books/ Douglas & McIntyre.

Chase, E., & Reid, B. (1984). *The new baby calf*. Toronto: Scholastic.

Chataway, C. (2002). *The perfect pet*. Toronto: Kids Can Press.

Cherry, L. (1992). *A river ran wild*. Orlando: Harcourt Brace.

Chester, J. (1995). *A for Antarctica*. New York: Tricycle.

Choi, S. N. (1991). *Year of impossible goodbyes*. Boston: Houghton Mifflin.

Citra, B. (1999). *Ellie's new home*. Victoria, BC: Orca Books.

Clark, J. (1995). *The dream carvers*. Toronto: Viking.

Clarke, B. (1990). *Amazing frogs and toads*. Don Mills, ON: Stoddart Publishing.

Classical Kids. (1991). *Mozart's magic fantasy: A journey through the magic flute* [CD]. Pickering, ON: The Children's Group.

Classical Kids. (1993). *Mr. Bach comes to call* [CD]. Pickering, ON: The Children's Group.

Classical Kids. (1993). *Vivaldi's ring of mystery* [CD]. Pickering, ON: The Children's Group.

Classical Kids. (1995). *Hallelujah Handel* [CD]. Pickering, ON: The Children's Group.

Classical Kids. (1998). *Mozart's magnificent voyage* [CD]. Pickering, ON: The Children's Group.

Classical Kids. (2000). *Daydreams & lullabies* [CD]. Pickering, ON: The Children's Group.

Classical Kids. (2000). *Tchaikovsky discovers America* [CD]. Pickering, ON: The Children's Group.

Cleary, B. (1981). *Ramona Quimby, age 8*. New York: Morrow.

Cleary, B. (1983). *Dear Mr. Henshaw*. New York: Morrow.

Cleaver, E. (1985). *The enchanted caribou*. Toronto: Oxford University Press.

Climo, S. (1989). *The Egyptian Cinderella*. New York: Crowell.

Cobb, M. (1995). *The quilt-block history of pioneer days*. Riverside, NJ: Millbrook Press.

Coerr, E. (1977). *Sadako and the thousand paper cranes*. New York: Putnam.

Coerr, E. (1986). *The Josefina story quilt*. New York: HarperTrophy.

Coerr, E. (1995). *Buffalo Bill and the pony express*. New York: HarperCollins.

Coffey, M. (1998). *A cat in a kayak*. Toronto: Annick Press.

Cohen, B. (1983). *Molly's pilgrim*. New York: Lothrop, Lee & Shepard.

Cohen, C. L. (1996). *Where's the fly?* New York: Greenwillow.

Cohen, L. (1995). *Dance me to the end of love*. New York: Welcome Enterprises.

Cole, H. (1995). *Jack's garden*. New York: Greenwillow.

Cole, J. (1981). *A snake's body*. New York: Morrow.

Cole, J. (1986). *Hungry, hungry sharks*. Chicago: Random House.

Cole, J. (1989). *The magic school bus inside the human body*. New York: Scholastic.

Cole, J. (1991). *My puppy is born*. New York: Morrow.

Cole, J. (1992). *The magic school bus on the ocean floor*. New York: Scholastic.

Cole, J. (1994). *The magic school bus in the time of the dinosaurs*. New York: Scholastic.

Cole, J. (1995). *The magic school bus inside a hurricane*. New York: Scholastic.

Cole, J. (1996). *On the bus with Joanna Cole: A creative auto-biography*. Portsmouth, NH: Heinemann.

Cole, J., & Calmenson, S. (1995). *Yours till banana splits: 201 auto-graph rhymes*. New York: Morrow.

Collis, H. (1987). *101 American English idioms*. Lincolnwood, IL: Passport.

Colman, P. (1994). *Toilets, bathtubs, sinks, and sewers: A history of the bathroom*. New York: Atheneum.

Colman, P. (1995). *Rosie the riveter: Women working on the home front in World War II*. New York: Crown.

Conrad, P. (1989). *The tub people*. New York: Harper & Row.

Conrad, P. (1991). *Pedro's journal: A voyage with Christopher Columbus, August 3, 1492–February 14, 1493*. Honedale, PA: Boyds Mills Press.

Conrad, P. (1995). *Animal lingo*. New York: HarperCollins.

Cook-Waldron, K. (1994). *A wilderness Passover*. Red Deer: Red Deer College Press.

Coombs, E. and Tanaka, S. (1991). *Mr. Dressup's things to make and do*. Don Mills, ON: Stoddart.

Cooper, F. (1996). *Mandela: From the life of the South African states-man*. New York: Philomel.

Coren, M. (1994). *The man who created Narnia: The story of C. S. Lewis.* Toronto: Lester Publishing.

Cowcher, H. (1990). *Antarctica.* New York: Farrar, Straus & Giroux.

Cox, J. A. (1980). *Put your foot in your mouth and other silly sayings.* New York: Random House.

Creech, S. (1997). *Chasing redbird.* London: Macmillan Children's Books.

Creech, S. (2000). *The wanderer.* London: Macmillan Children's Books.

Crews, D. (1980). *Truck.* New York: Greenwillow.

Crews, D. (1991). *Bigmama's.* New York: Greenwillow.

Crews, D. (1995). *Sail away.* New York: Greenwillow.

Crews, D. (2001). *Inside freight train.* New York: HarperCollins.

Crossley-Holland, K. (2002). *Arthur: At the crossing places.* New York: Arthur A. Levine.

Crossley-Holland, K. (2002). *Arthur: The seeing stone.* New York: Arthur A. Levine.

Cullinan, B. E. (Ed.). (1996). *A jar of tiny stars: Poems by NCTE award-winning poets.* Honesdale, PA: Boyds Mills Press.

Cumyn, A. (2002). *The secret life of Owen Skye.* Toronto: Douglas & McIntyre.

Cushman, K. (1994). *Catherine, called Birdy.* New York: HarperCollins.

Cushman, K. (1995). *The mid-wife's apprentice.* New York: HarperCollins Juvenile Books.

Cushman, K. (1996). *The ballad of Lucy Whipple.* New York: Clarion.

Czernecki, S., & Rhodes, T. (1994). *The hummingbirds' gift.* Winnipeg: Hyperion.

Dahl, R. (1961). *James and the giant peach.* New York: Knopf.

Dahl, R. (1964). *Charlie and the chocolate factory.* New York: Knopf.

Danziger, P. (1994). *Amber Brown is not a crayon.* New York: Putnam.

Davidge, B. (1990). *Mummer's song.* Toronto: Douglas & McIntyre.

Dawber, D. (1991). *My underwear's inside out: The care and feeding of younger poets.* Kingston: Quarry Press.

Dawber, D. (1997). *How do you wrestle a goldfish?* Nepean: Borealis Press.

Day, D. (1991). *Aska's animals.* Toronto: Doubleday.

Day, D. (1992). *Aska's birds.* Toronto: Doubleday.

Day, D. (1994). *Aska's sea creatures.* Toronto: Doubleday.

Day, D. (2002). *Edward the "crazy man."* Toronto: Annick Press.

de Gasztold, C. B. (1992). *Prayers from the ark.* New York: Viking.

Degen, B. (1983). *Jamberry.* New York: Harper & Row.

Degen, B. (1996). *Sailaway home.* New York: Scholastic.

Delton, J. (1992). *Lights, action, land-ho!* New York: Dell.

Demers, J. (1989). *One more dinosaur.* St. Petersburg, FL: Pages Publishing Group-Willowisp Press.

Denenberg, B. (1996). *When will this cruel war be over? The Civil War diary of Emma Simpson.* New York: Scholastic.

Denton, K. M. (1998). *A child's treasury of nursery rhymes.* Toronto: Kids Can Press.

dePaola, T. (1978). *Pancakes for breakfast.* New York: Harcourt Brace Jovanovich.

dePaola, T. (1985). *Hey diddle diddle and other Mother Goose rhymes.* New York: Putnam.

dePaola, T. (1988). *The legend of the Indian paintbrush.* New York: Putnam.

dePaola, T. (1988). *Tomie dePaola's book of poems.* New York: Putnam.

Derrickson, J. (2001). *Bomo and the beef snacks.* Markham, ON: North Winds Press.

Dewar, T. (1993). *Inside dinosaurs and other prehistoric creatures.* Richmond Hill, ON: Scholastic Canada.

Dewey, A. (1995). *The sky.* Seattle, WA: Green Tiger Press.

Di Camillo, K. (2000). *Because of Winn-Dixie.* Cambridge, MA: Candlewick.

Dickinson, E. (1978). *I'm nobody! Who are you? Poems of Emily Dickinson for children.* Owing Mills, MD: Stemmer House.

Dickinson, T. (1988). *Exploring the sky by day: the equinox guide to weather and the atmosphere.* Camden East, ON: Camden House.

Dickinson, T. (1989). *Exploring the night sky: The equinox astronomy guide for beginners.* Illus. J. Bianchi. Camden East, ON: Camden House.

Dillon, L. & Dillon, D. (2002). *Rap a tap tap here's Bojangles—think of that.* New York: Scholastic.

Dixon, N. (1995). *Kites.* Toronto: Kids Can Press.

Donnelly, J. (1991). *A wall of names: The story of the Vietnam Veterans Memorial.* New York: Random House.

Dooley, N. (1991). *Everybody cooks rice.* Minneapolis: Carolrhoda.

Downie, A., & Rawlyk, G. (1980). *A proper Acadian.* Toronto: Kids Can Press.

Downie, A., & Robertson, B. (Comp.). (1987). *The new wind has wings: Poems from Canada.* Toronto: Oxford University Press.

Doyle, B. (2001). *Mary Ann Alice.* Vancouver: Douglas & McIntyre.

Doyle, B. (2003). *Boy o'boy.* Toronto: Groundwood Books.

Duke, K. (1983). *Guinea pig ABC.* New York: Dutton.

Dunn, S. (1994). *Gimme a break, rattlesnake.* Don Mills, ON: Stoddart.

Dunning, S., Leuders, E., & Smith, H. (1967). *Reflections on a gift of watermelon pickle, and other modern verse.* New York: Lothrop, Lee & Shepard.

Earle, S. (2000). *Sea critters.* Washington: National Geographic Society.

Eastman, P. D. (1960). *Are you my mother?* New York: Random House.

Ebbitt-Cutler, M. (2002). *Breaking free: The story of William Kurelek.* Toronto: Tundra Books.

Ehlert, L. (1987). *Growing vegetable soup.* San Diego: Harcourt Brace Jovanovich.

Ehlert, L. (1989). *Color zoo.* New York: Lippincott.

Ehlert, L. (1990). *Feathers for lunch.* Orlando: Harcourt Brace.

Ehlert, L. (1994). *Eating the alphabet: Fruits and vegetables from A to Z.* San Diego: Harcourt Brace.

Ehlert, L. (1996). *Under my nose.* Katonah, NY: Richard C. Owen.

Eikhard, S. (1991). *Emily remembers.* Toronto: Shirley Eikhard Music Inc.

Elkin, B. (1983). *Money.* Chicago: Children's Press.

Ellis, D. (2000). *The breadwinner.* Vancouver: Douglas & McIntyre.

Ellis, D. (2002). *A company of fools.* Markham, ON: Fitzhenry & Whiteside.

Ellis, D. (2002). *Looking for X.* Toronto: Douglas & McIntyre.

Ellis, D. (2002). *Parvana's Journey.* Toronto: Douglas & McIntyre.

Ellis, D. (2003). *Mud city.* Toronto: Groundwood.

Ellis, D. (2003) *The several lives of Orphan Jack.* Toronto: Douglas & McIntyre.

Ellis, S. (1986). *The baby project.* Toronto: Groundwood.

Ellis, S. (1994). *Out of the blue.* Toronto: Groundwood.

Ellis, S. (2001). *A prairie as wide as the sea: An immigrant diary of Ivy Weatherall.*

Elwin, R., & Paulse, M. (1990). *Asha's mums.* Toronto: Women's Press.

Ernst, L. C. (1983). *Sam Johnson and the blue ribbon quilt.* New York: Mulberry Books.

Facklam, M. (1996). *Creepy, crawly caterpillars.* Boston: Little, Brown.

Fairbridge, L. (1992). *In such a place.* Toronto: Doubleday.

Fairbridge, L. (1995). *Stormbound.* Toronto: Doubleday.

Fakih, K. O. (1995). *Off the clock: A Lexicon of time words and expressions.* New York: Ticknor.

Farrell, J. (2005). *Invisible allies: Microbes that shape our lives.* Vancouver: Douglas & McIntyre.

Farris, K. (Ed.) (1991). *The Kids Can Press French & English word book.* Illus. L. Hendry. Toronto: Kids Can Press.

Farris, K. (Ed.). (1993). *The new kids' question and answer book: Questions kids ask about nature, science and the environment.* Toronto: Greey de Pencier.

Feder, J. (1995). *Table, chair, bear: A book in many languages.* New York: Ticknor.

Feelings, M. (1971). *Moja means one: Swahili counting book.* New York: Dial Books for Young Readers.

Feelings, M. (1974). *Jambo means hello: Swahili alphabet.* New York: Dial Books for Young Readers.

Fernandez, L., & Jacobson, R. (2000). *The magnificent piano recital.* Victoria: Orca Books.

Fisher, A. (1988). *The house of a mouse.* New York: Harper & Row.

Fitch, S. (1991). *Merry-go-day.* Toronto: Doubleday.

Fitch, S. (1992). *There were monkeys in my kitchen.* Toronto: Doubleday.

Fitch, S. (1995). *I am small.* Toronto: Doubleday.

Fitch, S. (1995). *Mabel Murple.* Toronto: Doubleday.

Fitch, S. (1997). *If you could wear my sneakers.* Toronto: Doubleday.

Fitch, S. (1997). *There's a mouse in my house.* Illus. L. Watts. Toronto: Doubleday.

Fitch, S. (1999). *If I were the moon.* Toronto: Doubleday.

Fitch, S. (2002). *Writing maniac: How I grew up to be a writer and you can too.* Portland, ME: Stenhouse Publishers.

Fitch, S. (2005). *The gravesavers.* Toronto: Doubleday.

Fitzhugh, L. (1964). *Harriet the spy.* New York: Harper & Row.

Fleischman, P. (1985). *I am phoenix: Poems for two voices.* New York: Harper & Row.

Fleischman, P. (1988). *Joyful noise: Poems for two voices.* New York: Harper & Row.

Fleischman, P. (1991). *Bull run.* New York: HarperCollins.

Fleming, D. (1994). *Barnyard banter.* New York: Henry Holt.

Fleming, D. (2002). *Alphabet under construction.* New York: Henry Holt.

Flournoy, V. (1985). *The patchwork quilt.* New York: Dial.

Foggo, C. (1997). *One thing that's true.* Toronto: Kids Can Press.

Fonteyn, M. (1989). *Swan Lake.* San Diego, CA: Harcourt, Brace, Jovanovich.

Ford, M. (1995). *Sunflower.* New York: Greenwillow.

Fowke, E. (1990). *Folklore of Canada: Tall tales, songs, stories, rhymes, jokes from every corner of Canada.* Toronto: McClelland & Stewart.

Fowler, A. (1990). *It's a good thing there are insects.* Chicago: Children's Press.

Fowler, A. (1992). *It could still be water.* Chicago: Children's Press.

Fox, H. (1986). *Hattie and the fox.* New York: Bradbury.

Fox, M. (1994). *Tough Boris.* San Diego: Harcourt, Brace, Jovanovich.

Fox, M. (1996). *Wilfrid Gordon McDonald Partridge.* Norwood, South Australia: Omnibus Books.

Francis, N. (1988). *Super flyers.* Illus. J. Bradford. Toronto: Kids Can Press.

Fraser, M. A. (1993). *Ten mile day and the building of the transcontinental railroad.* New York: Henry Holt.

Freedman, J. (1991). *One hand clapping.* Toronto: Groundwood.

Freedman, R. (1996). *The life and death of Crazy Horse.* New York: Holiday House.

Freeman, D. (1968). *Corduroy.* New York: Viking.

Freeman, D. (1972). *A pocket for Corduroy.* New York: Viking.

Free Stuff Editor, & Meadowbrook. (2002). *Free stuff for kids.* B. Hehner (Ed.). Don Mills, ON: Stoddart.

Friedman, I. R. (1984). *How my parents learned to eat.* Boston: Houghton Mifflin.

Friesen, G. (2000). *Men of stone.* Toronto: Kids Can Press.

Fritz, J. (1976). *Will you sign here, John Hancock?* New York: Coward-McCann.

Fritz, J. (1987). *Brady.* New York: Penguin.

Fritz, J. (1989). *The great little Madison.* New York: Putnam.

Fritz, J. (1992). *Surprising myself.* Katonah, NY: Richard C. Owen.

Froman, R. (1974). *Seeing things: A book of poems.* New York: Crowell.

Frost, R. (1982). *A swinger of birches: Poems of Robert Frost for young people.* Owing Mills, MD: Stemmer House.

Frost, R. (1988). *Birches.* Illus. E. Young. New York: Henry Holt.

Funston, S., & Ingram, J. (1994). *A kid's guide to the brain.* Toronto: Owl Books.

Gage Canadian dictionary (2000). Toronto: Gage Publishing Ltd.

Gage Canadian dictionary intermediate (1997). Toronto: Gage Publishing Ltd.

Gal, L., & Gal, R. (1997). *The parrot.* Toronto: Groundwood Books.

Galdone, P. (1970). *The three little pigs*. New York: Seabury.

Galdone, P. (1972). *The three bears*. New York: Houghton Mifflin.

Galdone, P. (1973a). *The little red hen*. New York: Seabury.

Galdone, P. (1973b). *The three billy goats Gruff*. New York: Seabury.

Galdone, P. (1975). *The gingerbread boy*. New York: Seabury.

Galdone, P. (1978). *Cinderella*. New York: McGraw-Hill.

Galdone, P. (1986). *Over in the meadow*. New York: Simon & Schuster.

Galloway, P. (1995). *Truly Grimm tales*. Toronto: Lester Publishing.

Gardiner, J. R. (1980). *Stone fox*. New York: Harper & Row.

Garg, A. (2002). *A word a day*. London: Wiley.

Gay, M.-L. (2002). *Stella, fairy of the forest*. Vancouver: Groundwood Books/Douglas & McIntyre.

Geisert, B. (1995). *Haystack*. Boston: Houghton Mifflin.

George, D. (1974). *My heart soars*. Saanichton, BC: Hancock House.

George, J. C. (1972). *Julie of the wolves*. New York: Harper & Row.

George, J. C. (1993). *Dear Rebecca, winter is here*. New York: HarperCollins. George, J. C. (1997). *Arctic son*. New York: Hyperion.

George, R. E. (1976). *Roald Dahl's Charlie and the chocolate factory*. New York: Knopf.

George, R. E. (1982). *Roald Dahl's James and the giant peach*. New York: Knopf.

Gertridge, A. (1994). *Meet Canadian authors and illustrators*. Richmond Hill, ON: Scholastic.

Ghent, N. (2003). *No small thing*. Toronto: HarperCollins.

Gibbons, G. (1984). *Fire! Fire!* New York: Harper & Row.

Gibbons, G. (1989). *Monarch butterfly*. New York: Holiday House.

Gibbons, G. (1990). *Weather words and what they mean*. New York: Holiday House.

Gibbons, G. (1991). *Surrounded by sea: Life on a New England fishing island*. Boston: Little, Brown.

Gibbons, G. (1992). *Spiders*. New York: Holiday House.

Gibbons, G. (1995). *Knights in shining armor*. Boston: Little, Brown.

Giblin, J. C. (1990). *The riddle of the Rosetta stone: Key to ancient Egypt*. New York: Crowell.

Giff, P. R. (1984). *The beast in Ms. Rooney's room*. New York: Dell.

Giff, P. R. (1995). *Ronald Morgan goes to camp*. New York: Viking.

Gilman, P. (1985). *Jillian Jiggs*. Richmond Hill: Scholastic.

Gilman, P. (1990). *Grandma and the pirates*. Richmond Hill: Scholastic Canada.

Gilman, P. (1992). *Something from nothing*. Toronto: North Winds Press.

Gilman, P. (1994). *Jillian Jiggs to the rescue*. Richmond Hill: Scholastic Canada.

Gilman, P. (1999). *Jillian Jiggs and the secret surprise*. Richmond Hill, ON: North Winds Press/Scholastic Canada.

Gilmore, R. (2000). *Mina's spring of colors*. Markham, ON: Fitzhenry & Whiteside.

Gilson, J. (1985). *Hello, my name is scrambled eggs*. New York: Morrow.

Glaser, I. J. (1995). *Dreams of glory: Poems starring girls*. New York: Atheneum.

Goble, P. (1988). *Iktomi and the boulder*. New York: Orchard.

Goble, P. (1994). *Hau kola/Hello friend*. Katonah, NY: Richard C. Owen.

Godfrey. M. (1992). *Is it ok if this monster stays for lunch?* Toronto: Oxford University Press.

Godkin, C. (1995). *Ladybug garden*. Markham, Ontario: Fitzhenry and Whiteside.

Godkin, C. (1995). *What about ladybugs?* New York: Sierra.

Goldstein, B. S. (Sel.). (1989). *Bear in mind: A book of bear poems*. New York: Puffin.

Goldstein, B. S. (Ed.). (1992*). Inner chimes: Poems on poetry*. Honesdale, PA: Wordsong.

Goldstein, B. S. (Sel.). (1992). *What's on the menu?* New York: Viking.

Golenbock, P. (1990). *Teammates*. San Diego: Harcourt Brace Jovanovich.

Golick, M. (1995). *Wacky word games*. Markham: Pembroke Publishers.

Goodall, J. S. (1986). *The story of a castle*. New York: Macmillan.

Graham, G. (1995). *Bibi and the bull*. Red Deer, AB: Red Deer Press.

Graham, G. (1998). *The strongest man this side of Cremona*. Red Deer, AB: Northern Lights/Red Deer College Press.

Graham, J. B. (1994). *Splish splash: Poems*. New York: Ticknor.

Graham-Barber, L. (1995). *A chartreuse leotard in a magenta limousine: And other words named after people and places*. New York: Hyperion.

Grahame, K. (1961). *The wind in the willows*. New York: Scribner.

Granfield, L. (1995). *In Flanders fields: The story of the poem by John McCrae*. Illus. J. Wilson. Toronto: Lester Publishing.

Grant, A. (1995). *James McKay: A Métis builder of Canada*. Winnipeg: Pemmican.

Gray, N. (1988). *A country far away*. New York: Orchard.

Greenfeld, H. (1978). *Sumer is icumen in: Our ever-changing language*. New York: Crown Books.

Greenfield, E. (1988). *Nathaniel talking*. New York: Black Butterfly Children's Books.

Greenfield, E. (1988). *Under the Sunday tree*. New York: Harper & Row.

Greenfield, E. (1991). *Night on Neighborhood Street*. New York: Dial.

Greenwood, B. (1989). *Jeanne Sauvé*. Markham: Fitzhenry & Whiteside.

Greenwood, B. (1995). *A pioneer story: The daily life of a pioneer family in 1840*. Illus. H. Collins. Ticknor & Fields.

Greenwood, B., & McKim, A. (1987). *Her special vision: A biography of Jean Little*. Toronto: Irwin Publishing.

Gregory, K. (1996). *The winter of red snow: The Revolutionary War diary of Abigail Jane Stewart*. New York: Scholastic.

Gregory, N. (2000). *Wild girl and gran*. Red Deer, AB: Red Deer College Press.

Gregory, N., & Lightburn, R. (1995). *How Smudge came*. Red Deer, AB: Red Deer College Press/Northern Lights Books.

Gryski, C. (1985). *Cat's cradle, owl's eyes: A book of string games*. Illus. T. Sankey. Toronto: Kids Can Press.

Gryski, C. (1993). *Boondoggle: Making bracelets with plastic lace.* Toronto: Kids Can Press.

Gryski, C. (1994). *Hands on, thumbs up.* Toronto: Kids Can Press.

Gryski, C. (1995). *Favourite string games.* Toronto: Kids Can Press.

Guarino, D. (1989). *Is your mama a llama?* New York: Scholastic.

Guback, G. (1994). *Luka's quilt.* New York: Greenwillow.

Guiberson, B. Z. (1991). *Cactus hotel.* New York: Henry Holt.

Gwynne, F. (1970). *The king who rained.* New York: Windmill Books.

Gwynne, F. (1976). *A chocolate moose for dinner.* New York: Windmill Books.

Gwynne, F. (1980*). The sixteen hand horse.* New York: Prentice Hall.

Gwynne, F. (1988). *A little pigeon toad.* New York: Simon & Schuster.

Hadley, E., & Hadley, T. (1983). *Legends of the sun and moon.* Cambridge: Cambridge University Press.

Hague, M. (1985). *Aesop's fables.* New York: Holt, Rinehart & Winston.

Hall, R. (1985). *Sniglets for kids.* Yellow Springs, OH: Antioch.

Hall, K., & Eisenberg, L. (1992). *Spacey riddles.* New York: Dial.

Hamilton, J. (Ed.) (2005). *Canadian poems for Canadian kids.* Vancouver: Subway Books.

Hamilton, V. (1968). *The house of Dies Drear.* New York: Macmillan.

Hamilton, V. (1992). *Drylongso.* Orlando: Harcourt Brace.

Hamilton, V. (2000). *The girl who spun gold.* New York: Scholastic.

Hampton, W. (2001). *Meltdown: A race against nuclear disaster at Three Mile Island: A reporter's story.* Cambridge, MA: Candlewick.

Hanson, J. (1972). *Homographic homophones. Fly and fly and other words that look and sound the same but are as different in meaning as bat and bat.* Minneapolis: Lerner.

Harcourt Brace Canadian dictionary for students. (1998). Toronto: Harcourt Canada.

The Harcourt Brace student thesaurus. (1991). San Diego: Harcourt Brace.

Harlow, J. (2000). *Star in the storm.* Toronto: Aladdin Paperbacks.

Harper, P. (2002). *Snow bear.* New York: Scholastic.

Harrison, J. (1994). *Dear bear.* Minneapolis: Carolrhoda.

Harrison, T. (1982). *A northern alphabet.* Montreal, PQ: Tundra Books.

Harrison, T. (1997). *Don't dig so deep, Nicholas!* Toronto: Owl Books.

Harrison, T. (2002). *O Canada.* Toronto: Kids Can Press.

Harter, P. (1994). *Shadow play: Night haiku.* New York: Simon & Schuster.

Hartman, G. (1991). *As the crow flies: A first book of maps.* New York: Bradbury Press.

Hartman, V. (1992). *Westward ho ho ho! Jokes from the wild west.* New York: Viking.

Hartry, N. (1997). *Hold on, McGinty!* Toronto: Doubleday.

Harvey, A. (Sel.). (1992). *Shades of green.* New York: Greenwillow.

Harvey, B. (1987). *Immigrant girl: Becky of Eldridge Street.* New York: Holiday House.

Harvey, B. (1988). *Cassie's journey: Going west in the 1860s.* New York: Holiday House.

Haworth-Attard, B. (2002). *Irish chain.* Toronto: HarperTrophy Canada.

Hazen, B. S. (1979). *Last, first, middle and nick: All about names.* Englewood Cliffs, NJ: Prentice-Hall.

Heard, G. (2003). *Creatures of the earth, sea, and sky: Animal poems.* Honesdale, PA: Boyds-Mill Press.

Hehner, B. (Ed.). (1994). *Free stuff for kids.* Don Mills, ON: Stoddart.

Heidbreder, R. (1999). *Python play and other recipes for fun.* Don Mills, ON: Stoddart.

Heiligman, D. (1996). *From caterpillar to butterfly.* New York: HarperCollins.

Heisel, S. E. (1993). *Wrapped in a riddle.* Boston: Houghton Mifflin.

Heller, R. (1983). *The reason for a flower.* New York: Putnam.

Heller, R. (1985). *How to hide a butterfly and other insects.* New York: Grosset & Dunlap.

Heller, R. (1987). *A cache of jewels and other collective nouns.* New York: Grosset & Dunlap.

Heller, R. (1988). *Kites sail high: A book about verbs.* New York: Grosset & Dunlap.

Heller, R. (1989). *Many luscious lollipops: A book about adjectives.* New York: Grosset & Dunlap.

Heller, R. (1990). *Merry-go-round: A book about nouns.* New York: Grosset & Dunlap.

Heller, R. (1995). *Behind the mask: A book of prepositions.* New York: Grosset & Dunlap.

Heller, R. (1998). *Up, up and away: A book about adverbs.* New York: Puffin.

Helmer, M. (2002). *Three barnyard tales: The little red hen; The ugly duckling; Chicken little (Once-upon-a-time series).* Toronto: Kids Can Press.

Hepworth, C. (1992). *Antics! An alphabetical anthology.* New York: Putnam.

Henkes, K. (1991). *Chrysanthemum.* New York: Greenwillow.

Henkes, K. (1996). *Lilly's purple plastic purse.* New York: Greenwillow.

Henkes, K. (2004). *Kitten's first full moon.* Toronto: HarperCollins.

Hesse, K. (1992). *Letters from Rifka.* New York: Holt.

Hesse, K. (1997). *Out of the dust.* New York: Scholastic.

Hickman, P. (1985). *Bugwise.* Toronto: Kids Can Press.

Hickman, P. (1988). *Birdwise.* Illus. J. Shore. Toronto: Kids Can Press.

Hickman, P. (1996). *The Kids Canadian tree book.* Illus. H. Collins. Toronto: Kids Can Press.

Highway, T. (2001). *Caribou song.* Illus. B. Deines. Toronto: HarperCollins.

Highway, T. (2002). *Dragonfly kites.* Illus. B. Deines. Toronto: HarperCollins.

Hill, E. (1980). *Where's Spot?* New York: Putnam.

Hill, K. (1978). *More Glooscap stories.* Toronto: McClelland & Stewart.

Hill, S. (Ed.). (1990). *Free stuff for kids.* Don Mills, ON: Stoddart.

Hirschi, R. (1992). *Desert.* New York: Bantam.

Hoban, T. (1973). *Over, under, and through and other spatial concepts*. New York: Macmillan.

Hoban, T. (1975). *Dig, drill, dump, fill*. New York: Greenwillow.

Hoban, T. (1981). *A children's zoo*. New York: Greenwillow.

Hoban, T. (1981). *More than one*. New York: Greenwillow.

Hoban, T. (1987). *26 letters and 99 cents*. New York: Greenwillow.

Hoban, T. (1991). *All about where*. New York: Greenwillow.

Hoban, T. (2000). *Cubes, cones, cylinders, spheres*. New York: Greenwillow.

Hopkins, L. B. (1984). *Surprises*. New York: Harper & Row.

Hopkins, L. B. (Sel.). (1985). *Munching: Poems about eating*. Boston: Little, Brown.

Hopkins, L. B. (Sel.). (1987). *Click, rumble, roar: Poems about machines*. New York: Crowell.

Hopkins, L. B. (1987). *Dinosaurs*. San Diego: Harcourt Brace Jovanovich.

Hopkins, L. B. (Sel.). (1991). *On the farm*. Boston: Little, Brown.

Hopkins, L. B. (Sel.). (1992). *To the zoo: Animal poems*. Boston: Little, Brown.

Hopkins, L. B. (1992). *Questions: Poems*. New York: HarperCollins.

Hopkins, L. B. (Sel.). (1993). *Extra innings: Baseball poems*. San Diego: Harcourt Brace.

Hopkins, L. B. (1994). *Weather*. New York: HarperCollins.

Hopkins, L. B. (1995). *Blast off! Poems about space*. New York: HarperCollins.

Hopkinson, D. (1993). *Sweet Clara and the freedom quilt*. New York: Knopf.

Horrocks, A. (1996). *Breath of a ghost*. Don Mills, ON: Stoddart.

Horrocks, A. (1998). *What they don't know*. Don Mills, ON: Stoddart Publishing.

Horrocks, A. (2000). *Topher*. Don Mills, ON: Stoddart Kids.

Horvaff, P. (2002). *Everything on a waffle*. Toronto: Groundwood Books.

Houston, J. (1967). *The white archer: An Eskimo legend*. Toronto: Longman.

Howard, E. F. (1991). *Aunt Flossie's hats (and crab cakes later)*. New York: Clarion.

Howarth, S. (1993). *The Middle Ages*. New York: Viking.

Howe, D., & Howe, J. (1979). *Bunnicula: A rabbit-tale of mystery*. New York: Atheneum.

Howe, J. (1982). *Howliday Inn*. New York: Atheneum.

Howe, J. (1983). *The celery stalks at midnight*. New York: Atheneum.

Howe, J. (1987). *Nighty-nightmare*. New York: Atheneum.

Howe, J. (1989). *The fright before Christmas*. New York: Atheneum.

Howe, J. (1989). *Scared silly*. New York: Atheneum.

Howe, J. (1990). *Hot fudge*. New York: Atheneum.

Howe, J. (1992). *Return to Howliday Inn*. New York: Atheneum.

Howe, J. (1995). *Knights*. New York: Orchard.

Hoyt, E. (1991). *Meeting the whales*. Camden East: Camden House.

Hoyt-Goldsmith, D. (1990). *Totem pole*. New York: Holiday House.

Hoyt-Goldsmith, D. (1992). *Arctic hunter*. New York: Holiday House.

Hoyt-Goldsmith, D. (2001). *Celebrating Ramadan*. New York: Holiday House.

Hubbard, W. (1990). *C is for curious: An ABC book of feelings*. San Francisco: Chronicle Books.

Hudson, J. (1984). *Sweetgrass*. Edmonton: Tree Frog Press.

Hughes, M. (1992). *The crystal drop*. Toronto: HarperCollins.

Hughes, M. (2000). *Keeper of the isis light*. Toronto: Bt Bound.

Hughes, M. (2001). *Jan's awesome party*. (First Novels Series). Halifax, NS: Formac Publishing.

Hume, S. E., & Milelli, P. (1997). *Rainbow Bay*. Vancouver: Raincoast Books.

Hundal, N. (1999). *Melted star journey*. Toronto: HarperCollins.

Hundal, N. (1999). *Prairie summer*. Toronto: Fitzhenry & Whiteside.

Hundal, N. (2001). *Number 21*. Toronto: Fitzhenry & Whiteside.

Hunt, I. (1987). *Across five Aprils*. New York: Berkley.

Hunt, J. (1989). *Illuminations*. New York: Bradbury.

Hunter, B. (1981). *That scatterbrain booky*. Toronto: Scholastic.

Huser, G. (2003) *Stitches*. Toronto: Douglas & McIntyre.

Hutchins, P. (1968). *Rosie's walk*. New York: Macmillan.

Hutchins, P. (1972). *Good-night, Owl!* New York: Macmillan.

Hutchins, P. (1976). *Don't forget the bacon!* New York: Mulberry.

Hutchins, P. (1986). *The doorbell rang*. New York: Morrow.

Hutchins, P. (1987). *Rosie's walk* (big book edition). New York: Scholastic.

Hutchins, P. (2002). *We're going on a picnic*. New York: HarperCollins.

Hyman, T. S. (1983). *Little Red Riding Hood*. New York: Holiday House.

Iglotiorte, J. (1994). *An Inuk boy becomes a hunter*. Halifax: Nimbus Publishing.

Ingram, J. (1992). *Real live science: Top scientists present amazing activities any kid can do*. Toronto: Maple Tree Press.

Interview with Tomson Highway. (n.d.). Retrieved March 10, 2004, from www.playwrightsworkshop.org/tomsonint.html.

Irvine, J. (1992). *How to make super pop-ups*. Illus. L. Hendry. Toronto: Kids Can Press.

Isaacs, A. (1994). *Swamp angel*. New York: Dutton.

Jaehyun Park, J. (2002). *The tiger and the dried persimmon*. Groundwood Books.

Jairam, P. B. (1991). *Golden stories to treasure*. Scarborough: Dharmik Books.

James, E., & Barkin, C. (1993). *Sincerely yours: How to write great letters*. New York: Clarion.

Janeczko, P. B. (Sel.). (1984). *Strings: A gathering of family poems*. New York: Bradbury Press.

Janeczko, P. B. (Sel.). (1993). *Looking for your name: A collection of contemporary poems*. New York: Orchard Books.

Janeczko, P. B. (1994). *Poetry from A to Z: A guide for young writers*. New York: Bradbury.

Janeczko, P. B. (1995). *Wherever home begins: 100 contemporary poems*. New York: Orchard/Jackson.

Jeffers, S. (1991). *Brother eagle, sister sky: A message from Chief Seattle*. New York: Dial.

Jenkins, P. (1991). *Flip book animation: And other ways to make cartoons move.* Toronto: Kids Can Press.

Jenkins, S., & Page, R. (2006). *Move!* Boston: Houghton Mifflin.

Jennings, S. (1993). *Sleep tight, Mrs. Ming.* Toronto: Annick Press.

Jeram, A. (1995). *Contrary Mary.* Cambridge, MA: Candlewick.

Johnson, C. (1965). *Harold and the purple crayon.* New York: Harper & Row.

Johnson, S. A. (1995). *Raptor rescue! An eagle flies free.* New York: Dutton.

Johnston, J. (1994). *Adam and Eve and pinch me.* Toronto: Lester Publishing.

Johnston, J. (2001). *In spite of killer bees.* Toronto: Tundra Books.

Johnston, S. (1995). *Alphabet city.* Toronto: Penguin.

Johnston, T. (1985). *The quilt story.* New York: Putnam.

Johnston, T. (1994). *Amber on the mountain.* New York: Dial.

Jonas, A. (1984). *The quilt.* New York: Greenwillow.

Jonas, A. (1990). *Aardvarks disembark.* New York: Greenwillow.

Jones, H. (1993). *The trees stand shining: Poetry of the North American Indians.* New York: Dial.

Jorisch, S. (2001). *As for the princess? A folktale from Quebec.* Toronto: Annick Press.

Juby, S. (2000). *Alice, I think.* Toronto: HarperCollins.

The junior encyclopedia of Canada (1990). Edmonton: Hurtig Publishers.

Kalan, R. (1995). *Jump, frog, jump.* New York: HarperTrophy.

Kaner, E. (1995). *Towers and tunnels.* Toronto: Kids Can Press.

Kaye, C. B. (1985). *Word works: Why the alphabet is a kid's best friend.* Boston: Little, Brown.

Keats, E. J. (1972). *Over in the meadow.* New York: Scholastic.

Keir, B. (1990). *Diary of a honeybee.* Auckland: Shortland Publications.

Keith, A. N. (1982). *Three came home.* Toronto: McClelland and Stewart.

Kellogg, S. (1973). *The island of the Skog.* New York: Dial.

Kellogg, S. (1987). *Aster Aardvark's alphabet adventures.* New York: Morrow.

Kenna, K. (1995). *A people apart.* Toronto: Somerville House.

Kennedy, X. J. (1985). *The forgetful wishing well: Poems for young people.* New York: McElderry Books.

Kennedy, X. J., & Kennedy, D. M. (1982). *Knock at a star: A child's introduction to poetry.* Boston: Little, Brown.

Kenny, C. (Ed.) (1999). *The Kids Can Press French & English phrase book.* Ill. by L. Hendry. Toronto: Kids Can Press.

Kernaghan, E. (1995). *Dance of the snow dragon.* Saskatoon: Thistledown Press.

Khan, R. (1999). *Dahling, if you luv me, would you please, please smile.* Don Mills, ON: Stoddart Kids.

King, T. (1995). *Medicine River.* Toronto: Penguin.

King, T. (1998). *Coyote sings to the moon.* Toronto: Groundwood.

Kingsley, C. (2001). *Ten little puppies.* Toronto: Fitzhenry & Whiteside.

Kinsey-Warnock, N. (1992). *The Canada geese quilt.* New York: Yearling.

Kissinger, K. (1994). *All the colours we are.* St. Paul, MN: Redleaf Press.

Kitagawa, M. (1986). *This is my own: Letter to Wes and other writings on Japanese Canadians, 1941–1948.* Vancouver: Talonbooks.

Klausner, J. (1990). *Talk about words: How words travel and change.* New York: Thomas Crowell.

Knight, A. S. (1993). *The way west: Journal of a pioneer woman.* New York: Simon & Schuster.

Knight, M. B. (1993). *Who belongs here? An American story.* Gardiner, ME: Tulbury House.

Koch, K. (1980). *Wishes, lies, and dreams.* New York: Vintage.

Koch, K. (1990). *Rose, where did you get that red?* New York: Vintage.

Kogawa, J. (1982). *Obasan.* Boston: D. R. Godine.

Kogawa, J. (1986). *Naomi's Road.* Toronto: Oxford University Press.

Konigsburg, E. L. (1983). *From the mixed-up files of Mrs. Basil E. Frankweiler.* New York: Atheneum.

Konigsburg, E. L. (1996). *The view from Saturday.* New York: Atheneum.

Koopmans, L. (1990). *The woodcutter's mitten.* New York: Crocodile Books.

Korman, G. (1981). *I want to go home.* New York: Scholastic.

Kouhi, E. (1993). *North country spring.* Waterloo, ON: Penumbra Press.

Kovalski, M. (1987). *The wheels on the bus.* Boston: Little, Brown.

Kovalski, M. (1992). *Take me out to the ballgame.* Toronto: North Winds Press.

Kraske, R. (1975). *The story of the dictionary.* New York: Harcourt Brace Jovanovich.

Krebs, L., & Cairns, J. (2003). *We all went on safari: A counting journey through Tanzania.* Barefoot Books.

Krensky, S. (1994). *Lionel in the winter.* New York: Dial.

Kurelek. W. (1973). *A prairie boy's winter.* Montreal: Tundra Books.

Kurelek. W. (1975). *A prairie boy's summer.* Montreal: Tundra Books.

Kuskin, K. (1980). *Dogs and dragons, trees and dreams.* New York: Harper & Row.

Kusugak, M. A. (1990). *Baseball bats for Christmas.* Toronto: Annick Press.

Kusugak, M. A. (1992). *Hide and sneak.* Toronto: Annick Press.

Kusugak, M. A. (1998). *Arctic stories.* Willowdale, ON: Annick Press.

Laker, J. (1976). *Merry ever after.* New York: Viking.

Langen, A., & Droop, C. (1994). *Letters from Felix: A little rabbit on a world tour.* New York: Abbeville Press.

Langstaff, J. (1974). *Oh, a-hunting we will go.* New York: Atheneum.

Langston, L. (2003). *Lesia's Dream.* Toronto: HarperTrophy.

Lansky, B. (1996). *Free stuff for kids.* New York: Simon & Schuster.

Larrick, N. (1988). *Cats are cats.* Illus. E. Young. New York: Philomel.

Larrick, N. (Sel.). (1990). *Mice are nice.* New York: Philomel.

Lasker, J. (1976). *Merry ever after: The story of two medieval weddings.* New York: Viking.

Lasky, K. (1983). *Sugaring time.* New York: Macmillan.

Lasky, K. (1996). *A journey to the new world: The diary of Remember Patience Whipple*. New York: Scholastic.

Lasky, K. (1996). *Surtsey: The newest place on earth*. New York: Hyperion.

Lauber, P. (1990). *How we learned the earth is round*. New York: Crowell.

Lauber, P. (1995). *Who eats what? Food chains and food webs*. New York: HarperCollins.

Lawrence, I. (1998). *The wreckers*. New York: Delacorte Press.

Lawrence, R. D. (1990). *Wolves*. Toronto: Key Porter.

Lawson, J. (1992). *A morning to polish and keep*. Red Deer, AB: Red Deer College Press.

Lawson, J. (1993). *White jade tiger*. Vancouver: Beach Holme.

Lawson, J. (1996). *Whatever you do, don't go near that canoe*. Richmond Hill, ON: Scholastic Canada.

Lawson, J. (1998). *Turns on a dime*. Don Mills, ON: Stoddart Kids.

Lawson, J. (2003) *Arizona Charlie and the Klondike Kid*. Victoria: Orca Books.

Lawson, J. *Arizona Charlie and the Klondike Kid*. (2003). Victoria: Orca Books.

Lear, E. (1983). *An Edward Lear alphabet*. New York: Mulberry Books.

Lear, E. (1986). *The Owl and the Pussycat*. Illus. L. B. Cauley. New York: Putnam.

Lear, E. (1995). *Daffy down dillies: Silly limericks by Edward Lear*. Honesdale, PA: Wordsong.

Lear, E. (1995). *There was an old man . . . a collection of limericks*. Illus. M. Lemieux. Toronto: Kids Can Press.

Leblanc, L. (1990). *That's enough, Maddie!* Halifax: Formac Publishing.

Leblanc, L. (1992). *Maddie in goal*. Halifax: Formac Publishing.

Leblanc, L. (1993). *Maddie goes to Paris*. Halifax: Formac Publishing.

Leblanc, L. (1993). *Maddie wants music*. Halifax: Formac Publishing.

Lee, D. (1974). *Alligator pie*. Toronto: Macmillan.

Lee, D. (1977). *Garbage delight*. Toronto: Macmillan.

Lee, D. (1983). *Jelly belly*. Toronto: Macmillan.

Lee, D. (1991). *The ice cream store*. Toronto: HarperCollins.

Lee, D. (1993). *Ping and pong*. Toronto: HarperCollins.

Lee, D. (2000). *Bubblegum delicious: Poems*. Toronto: Key Porter Books.

Lee, D. (2001). *The cat and the wizard*. Toronto: Key Porter Books.

LeFord, B. (1995). *A blue butterfly: A story about Claude Monet*. New York: Doubleday.

Lemieux, M. (1999). *Stormy night*. Toronto: Kids Can Press.

L'Engle, M. (1962). *A wrinkle in time*. New York: Farrar, Straus & Giroux.

Lester, H. (1988). *Tacky the penguin*. Boston: Houghton Mifflin.

Lesynski, L. (1999). *Dirty dog boogie*. Toronto: Annick Press.

Lesynski, L. (2001). *Nothing beats a pizza*. Toronto: Annick Press.

Lesynski, L. (2004). *Zigzag: Zoems for zindergarten*. Toronto: Annick Press.

Levine, E. (1986). *. . . If you traveled west in a covered wagon*. New York: Scholastic.

Levine, G. (1996). *Ella enchanted*. Toronto: HarperCollins.

Lewis, C. S. (1950). *The lion, the witch and the wardrobe*. New York: Macmillan.

Lewis, J. P. (1995). *Black swan/white crow*. New York: Atheneum.

Lewis, J. P. (1996). *Riddle-icious*. New York: Knopf.

Lewis, R. (Ed.). (1965). *In a spring garden*. New York: Dial.

Lewis, W. (2000). *Graveyard girl: Stories*. Red Deer, AB: Red Deer Press.

Lewison, W. C. (1992). *"Buzz," Said the bee*. New York: Scholastic.

Lillie, P. (1993). *Everything has a place*. New York: Greenwillow.

Lind, J. (1989). *Gathie Falk*. Vancouver: Douglas & McIntyre.

Lind, J. (1989). *Mary and Christopher Pratt*. Vancouver: Douglas & McIntyre.

Lionni, L. (1961). *On my beach there are many pebbles*. London: Mulberry Books.

Lionni, L. (1963). *Swimmy*. New York: Random House.

Lionni, L. (1969). *Alexander and the wind-up mouse*. New York: Pantheon.

Lionni, L. (1985). *Frederick's fables*. New York: Pantheon.

Little, J. (1984). *Mama's going to buy you a mockingbird*. Toronto: Puffin Books.

Little, J. (1987). *Little by little: A writer's education*. New York: Viking Kestrel.

Little, J. (1990). *Stars come out within*. Markham: Penguin Books.

Little, J. (1991). *From Anna*. New York: HarperCollins Juvenile Books.

Little, J. (1991). *Jess was the brave one*. Toronto: Viking.

Little, J. (2001). *Orphan at my door: The home child diary of Victoria Cape*. (Dear Canada Series). Toronto: Scholastic Canada.

Little, J. (2002). *Birdie, for now*. Vancouver: Orca Books.

Littlechild, G. (1993). *This land is my land*. Emeryville, CA: Children's Book Press.

Litzinger, R. (1993). *The old woman and her pig*. New York: Harcourt, Brace, Jovanovich.

Livingston, M. C. (Sel.). (1984). *Sky songs*. New York: Holiday House.

Livingston, M. C. (1985). *Celebrations*. New York: Holiday House.

Livingston, M. C. (1986). *Earth songs*. New York: Holiday House.

Livingston, M. C. (Sel.). (1986). *Sea Songs*. New York: Holiday House.

Livingston, M. C. (Sel.). (1987). *New Year's poems*. New York: Holiday House.

Livingston, M. C. (Sel.). (1988). *Space songs*. New York: Holiday House.

Livingston, M. C. (Sel.). (1990). *If the owl calls again: A collection of owl poems*. New York: McElderry Books.

Livingston, M. C. (Sel.). (1991). *Lots of limericks*. New York: McElderry Books.

Livingston, M. C. (Sel.). (1992). *If you ever meet a whale*. New York: Holiday House.

Livingston, M. C. (Sel.). (1993). *Roll along: Poems on wheels*. New York: McElderry.

Llewellyn, C. (1995). *Truck*. New York: Dorling Kindersley.

Lobel, A. (1970). *Frog and Toad are friends*. New York: Harper & Row.

Lobel, A. (1972). *Frog and Toad together.* New York: Harper & Row.

Lobel, A. (1972). *Mouse tales.* New York: Harper & Row.

Lobel, A. (1977). *Mouse soup.* New York: Harper & Row.

Lobel, A. (1980). *Fables.* New York: Harper & Row.

Lobel, A. (1983). *The book of pigericks: Pig limericks.* New York: Harper & Row.

Lobel, A. (1990). *Alison's zinnia.* New York: Greenwillow.

Locker, T. (1991). *The land of Gray Wolf.* New York: Dial.

Long, W. (1995). *Celebrating excellence: Canadian women athletes.* Vancouver: Polestar.

Longfellow, H. W. (1990). *Paul Revere's ride.* New York: Dutton.

Lottridge, C. (Ed.) (1994). *Mother Goose: A Canadian sampler.* Toronto: Groundwood.

Lottridge, C. (1992). *Ticket to curlew.* Toronto: Groundwood.

Lottridge, C. B. (1986). *One watermelon seed.* Illus. K. P. Kau. Toronto: Oxford University Press.

Loughead, D. (1998). *All I need and other poems for kids.* Etobicoke: Moonstruck Press.

Louie, A. (1982). *Yeh-Shen: A Cinderella story from China.* New York: Philomel.

Lowell, S. (1992). *The three little javelinas.* Flagstaff, AZ: Northland.

Lowry, L. (1979). *Anastasia Krupnik.* Boston: Houghton Mifflin.

Lowry, L. (1989). *Number the stars.* Boston: Houghton Mifflin.

Lowry, L. (1993). *The giver.* Boston: Houghton Mifflin.

Luenn, N. (1990). *Nessa's fish.* New York: Atheneum.

Lunn, J. (1988). *Amos's sweater.* Vancouver: Douglas & McIntyre.

Lunn, J., & Gal, L. (1979). *Twelve dancing princesses.* Toronto: Methuen.

Lunn, J., & Moore, C. (1992). *The story of Canada.* Illus. A. Daniel. Toronto: Lester Publishing.

Lyon, G. E. (1989). *Together.* New York: Orchard.

Macaulay, D. (1977). *Castle.* Boston: Houghton Mifflin.

Macaulay, D. (1990). *Black and white.* Boston: Houghton Mifflin.

MacCarthy, P. (1991). *Herds of words.* New York: Dial.

Mackay, C. (1987). *Paycheques and picket lines: All about unions in Canada.* Illus. E. Parker. Toronto: Kids Can Press.

Mackay, C. (1994). *Touching all the bases: Baseball for kids of all ages.* Richmond Hill: Scholastic Canada.

MacLachlan, P. (1985). *Sarah, plain and tall.* New York: Harper & Row.

MacLachlan, P. (1994). *Skylark.* New York: HarperCollins.

Maestro, B. (1992). *How do apples grow?* New York: HarperCollins.

Maestro, B. (1993). *The story of money.* New York: Clarion.

Maestro, B., & Maestro, G. (1979). *On the go: A book of adjectives.* New York: Crown.

Maestro, B., & Maestro, G. (1985). *Camping out.* New York: Crown.

Maestro, B., & Maestro, G. (1989). *Taxi: A book of city words.* New York: Clarion.

Maestro, G. (1984). *What's a frank Frank? Tasty homograph riddles.* New York: Clarion Books.

Maggi, M. E., & Calderon, G. (2001). *The great canoe: A Karina legend* (E. Amado, Trans.). Toronto: Douglas & McIntyre.

Magnuson, W. (1989). *Canadian English idioms: Sayings and expressions.* Calgary: Prairie House Books.

Major, K. (2000). *Eh? To zed: A Canadian AbeCedarium.* Red Deer, AB: Red Deer Press.

Major, K. (2003). *Ann and Seamus.* Toronto: Groundwood Books.

The making-a-book activity book. (n.d.). Based on the 1988 Vancouver Art Gallery exhibition, "Once upon a time" sponsored by Placer Dome Inc., Vancouver: Douglas & McIntyre Ltd.

Manson, A. (1995). *Just like new.* Illus. K. Reczuch. Toronto: Groundwood Books/Douglas & McIntyre.

Marineau, M. (1995). *Road to Chlifa.* Red Deer, AB: Red Deer College Press.

Markle, S. (1993). *Outside and inside trees.* New York: Bradbury Press.

Marshall, I. (1989). *The Beothuk of Newfoundland.* St. John's: Breakwater Books.

Martin, B., Jr. (1970). *Monday, Monday, I like Monday.* New York: Holt, Rinehart & Winston.

Martin, B., Jr. (1983). *Brown bear, brown bear, what do you see?* New York: Holt, Rinehart & Winston.

Martin, B., Jr. (1992). *Polar bear, polar bear, what do you hear?* New York: Holt, Rinehart & Winston.

Martin, B., Jr., & Archambault, J. (1985). *The ghost-eye tree.* New York: Holt, Rinehart & Winston.

Martin, B., Jr., & Archambault, J. (1986). *White Dynamite and Curly Kidd.* New York: Henry Holt.

Martin, B., Jr., & Archambault, J. (1988). *Barn dance!* New York: Henry Holt.

Martin, J. B. (1998). *Snowflake Bentley.* Boston: Houghton Mifflin.

Martin, F. (1992). *The rough face girl.* New York: Putnam.

Marzollo, J., & Marzollo, C. (1987). *Jed and the space bandits.* New York: Dial.

Matas, C. (1991). *The race.* Toronto: HarperCollins.

Matas, C. (1993). *Daniel's story.* Markham, ON: Scholastic Canada.

Matas, C. (1994). *After the war.* Toronto: Scholastic.

Matas, C. (1995). *The primrose path.* Winnipeg: Blizzard Publishing.

Matas, C. (1998). *Greater than angels.* Toronto: Scholastic.

Matas, C. (1998). *Telling.* Toronto: Key Porter Books.

Matas, C. (2000). *Rebecca.* Toronto: Scholastic.

May, E. (1991). *Claiming the future.* Markham: Pembroke.

Mayer, M. (1974). *Frog goes to dinner.* New York: Dial.

Mayer, M. (1978). *Beauty and the beast.* New York: Macmillan.

Mayer, M. (1987). *The Pied Piper of Hamelin.* New York: Macmillan.

Mayer, M. (1987). *The ugly duckling.* New York: Macmillan.

Maynard, C. (1995). *Airplane.* New York: Dorling Kindersley.

McArthur, W. and Ursell, G. (Eds.). (1989). *Jumbo gumbo: Songs, poems and stories for children.* Regina: Couteau Books.

McCabe, N. (1990). *Laurie Graham.* Markham: Fitzhenry & Whiteside.

McCloskey, R. (1969). *Make way for ducklings*. New York: Viking.

McCord, D. (1974). *One at a time*. Boston: Little, Brown.

McCormick, R. (2002). *Plants and art activities*. St. Catharines, ON: Crabtree Publishing.

McCrum, R., Cran, I., & MacNeil, R. (1986). *The story of English*. New York: Viking Press.

McCully, E. A. (1984). *Picnic*. New York: Harper & Row.

McCurdy, M. (Ed.). (1994). *Escape from slavery: The boyhood of Frederick Douglass in his own words*. New York: Knopf.

McFadden, F. (1990). *Wayne Gretzky*. Markham: Fitzhenry & Whiteside.

McFarlane, S. (1994). *Eagle dreams*. Victoria: Orca Books.

McFarlane, S. (1995). *Tides of change*. Victoria: Orca Books.

McFarlane, S., & Lightburn, R. (1998). *Waiting for the whales*. Victoria, BC: Orca Books.

McGowan, M. (2003). *Newton and the Giant*. Toronto: HarperCollins.

McGraw, S. (1991). *Papier-maché for kids*. Toronto: Firefly Books.

McGugan, J. (1994). *Josepha: A prairie boy's story*. Red Deer, AB: Red Deer College Press.

McIlwain, J. (1994). *The DK children's illustrated dictionary*. London: Dorling Kindersley.

McKissack, P. C. (1986). *Flossie and the fox*. New York: Dial.

McKissack, P. C. (1988). *Mirandy and Brother Wind*. New York: Knopf.

McKissack, P. C. (1997). *A picture of freedom: The diary of Clotee, a slave girl*. New York: Scholastic.

McKissack, P. C., & McKissack, F. (1995). *Red-tail angels: The story of the Tuskegee airmen of World War II*. New York: Walker.

McLellan, J. (1991). *Nanabosho, Soaring Eagle and the great sturgeon*. Winnipeg: Pemmican Publications.

McLellan, J. (1993). *Nanabosho dances*. Winnipeg: Pemmican Publications.

McMillan, B. (1989). *Super, super, superwords*. New York: Lothrop, Lee & Shepard.

McMillan, B. (1990). *One sun: A book of terse verse*. New York: Holiday House.

McMillan, B. (1995). *Summer ice: Life along the Antarctic peninsula*. Boston: Houghton Mifflin.

McNeil, F. (Ed.). (1990). *Do whales jump at night? Poems for kids*. Toronto: Douglas & McIntyre.

McPhail, D. (1987). *First flight*. Boston: Little, Brown.

Mead, A. (1995). *Junebug*. New York: Farrar, Straus & Giroux.

Meltzer, M. (1984). *A book about names*. New York: Crowell.

Merriam, E. (1992). *Fighting words*. New York: Morrow.

Merriam, E. (1966). *It doesn't always have to rhyme*. New York: Atheneum.

Merritt, S. E. (1993). *Her story: Women from Canada's past*. St. Catharines, ON: Vanwell Publishing.

Micucci, C. (1995). *The life and times of the honeybee*. New York: Ticknor.

Middleton, J. E. (1990). *The Huron carol*. Toronto: Lester & Orpen Dennys.

Miles, M. (1971). *Annie and the Old One*. New York: Little, Brown.

Mills, J. (1995). *The stonehook schooner*. Toronto: Key Porter Kids.

Mills, L. (1991). *The rag coat*. Boston: Little, Brown.

Milne, A. A. (1956). *The house at Pooh Corner*. New York: Dutton.

Moak, A. (2002). *A big city ABC*. Toronto: Tundra Books.

Mochizuki, K. (1993). *Baseball saved us*. New York: Lee & Lothrop.

Mollel, T. (1990). *The orphan boy*. Don Mills, ON: Oxford University Press.

Mollel, T. (1992). *A promise to the sun*. Toronto: Little, Brown.

Montgomery, L. M. (1999). *Anne of Green Gables*. New York: HarperFestival. (Original work published 1908.)

Moore, C. (1995). *The night before Christmas*. New York: North-South.

Moore, C. (1998). *A visit from St. Nicholas*. Illus. K. Fernandes. Toronto: Doubleday.

Morimoto, J. (1987). *My Hiroshima*. New York: Puffin.

Morpurgo, M. (1995). *Arthur, High King of Britain*. San Diego: Harcourt Brace.

Morris, N. (1996). *Oceans*. New York: Crabtree Publishing.

Morrison, L. (1985). *The break dance kids: Poems of sport, motion, and locomotion*. New York: Lothrop, Lee & Shepard.

Morrison. L. (1995). *Slam dunk: Basketball poems*. New York: Hyperion.

Mortillaro N. (2005). *Sun and storms: Canadian summer weather*. Toronto: Scholastic.

Morton, D. (1974). *The Queen vs Louis Riel*. Toronto: University of Toronto Press.

Moses, A. (1992). *If I were an ant*. Illus. T. Dunnington. Chicago: Children's Press.

Moss, L. (1995). *Zin! Zin! Zin! A violin*. New York: Simon & Schuster.

Most, B. (1991). *A dinosaur named after me*. Orlando, FL: Harcourt Brace.

Most, B. (1992). *Zoodles*. San Diego: Harcourt Brace Jovanovich.

Mowat, F. (1995). *Born naked*. (n.p.): Mariner Books.

Muller, R. (1992). *Hickory, dickory, dock*. Richmond Hill, ON: North Winds Press.

Muller, R. (1993). *Row, row, row your boat*. Richmond Hill, ON: North Winds Press.

Munsch, R. (1980). *The paper bag princess*. Willowdale, ON: Annick Press.

Munsch, R. (1985). *Mortimer*. Toronto: Annick Press.

Munsch, R. (1991). *Where is Gah-Ning?* Toronto: Annick Press.

Munsch, R. (1992). *Purple, green, yellow*. Toronto: Annick Press.

Munsch, R., & Kusugak, M. (1988). *A promise is a promise*. Toronto: Annick Press.

My first Canadian Oxford dictionary. (2003). Don Mills, ON: Oxford University Press.

My first Canadian Oxford thesaurus (2003). Don Mills, ON: Oxford University Press.

My first thesaurus (1989). Scarborough, ON: Nelson.

Myers, W. D. (1988). *Scorpions*. New York: Harper & Row.

National Geographic. (1996). *Creatures of long ago: dinosaurs*. Los Angeles: The National Geographic Society.

Napoli, D. (2004). *Bound*. New York: Atheneum.

Naylor, P. R. (1991). *Shiloh*. New York: Atheneum.

Neaman, E. (1992). *Folk rhymes from around the world*. Vancouver: Pacific Educational Press.

Neering, R. (1977). *Louis Riel*. Don Mills, ON: Fitzhenry & Whiteside.

Neering, R. (1990). *Pioneers: Canadian lives series*. Markham, ON: Fitzhenry and Whiteside.

Neitzel, S. (1989). *The jacket that I wear in the snow*. New York: Greenwillow Books.

Nelson Canadian dictionary of the English language. (1993). Toronto: Nelson.

Ness, E. (1966). *Sam, bangs, and moonshine*. New York: Holt, Rinehart & Winston.

Neumeier, M., & Glasser, B. (1985). *Action alphabet*. New York: Greenwillow.

New, W. (1998). *Vanilla gorilla: Poems*. Vancouver: Ronsdale Press.

Newman, F. (1980). *Round slice of moon and other poems for Canadian kids*. Toronto: Scholastic.

Newton, P. (1990). *The stonecutter*. New York: Putnam.

Nichol, B. (1993). *Beethoven lives upstairs*. Toronto: Lester Publishing.

Nichol, B. (1997). *Biscuits in the cupboard*. Don Mills, ON: Stoddart Kids.

Nickel, B. (1999). *From the top of a grain elevator*. Vancouver: Beach Holme.

Nixon, J. L. (1987). *A family apart*. New York: Bantam Books.

Noble, T. H. (1980). *The day Jimmy's boa ate the wash*. New York: Dial.

Nolan, H. (1995). *How much, how many, how far, how heavy, how long, how tall is 1000?* Toronto: Kids Can Press.

Northey, L. (2002). *I'm a hop hop hoppity frog*. Don Mills, ON: Stoddart Kids.

Noyes, A. (1981). *The highwayman*. Illus. C. Keeping. Oxford: Oxford University Press.

Numeroff, L. J. (1985). *If you give a mouse a cookie*. New York: Harper & Row.

Numeroff, L. J. (1991). *If you give a moose a muffin*. New York: HarperCollins.

Numeroff, L. J. (1993). *Dogs don't wear sneakers*. New York: Simon & Schuster.

Numeroff, L. J. (1995). *Chimps don't wear glasses*. New York: Simon & Schuster.

Obed, E. B. (1988). *Borrowed black*. St John's: Breakwater Books.

Obed, E. B. (1990). *Wind in my pocket*. St John's: Breakwater Books.

Oberman, S. (1994). *The always prayer shawl*. Honesdale, PA: Boyd Mills Press.

Obligado, L. (1983). *Faint frogs feeling feverish and other terrifically tantalizing tongue twisters*. New York: Puffin.

O'Brien, R. C. (1971). *Mrs. Frisby and the rats of NIMH*. New York: Atheneum.

O'Dell, S. (1960). *Island of the blue dolphins*. Boston: Houghton Mifflin.

O'Dell, S. (1976). *The 290*. Boston: Houghton Mifflin.

O'Dell, S., & Hall, E. (1992). *Thunder rolling in the mountains*. Boston: Houghton Mifflin.

O'Huigan, S. (1983). *Scary poems for rotten kids*. Toronto: Black Moss Press.

O'Huigan, S. (1983). *Well, you can imagine*. Windsor: Black Moss Press.

O'Neill, M. (1989). *Hailstones and halibut bones: Adventures in color*. Garden City, NJ: Doubleday.

Ontario Science Centre (1988). *How sport works*. Illus. P. Cupples. Toronto: Kids Can Press.

Onyefulu, I. (1993). *A is for Africa*. Toronto: Penguin Books.

Oppel, K. (1997). *Silverwing*. Toronto: HarperCollins.

Oppel, K. (1999). *Sunwing*. Toronto: HarperCollins.

Oppel, K. (2002). *Firewing*. Toronto: HarperCollins.

Osborne, M. P. (1992). *Dinosaurs before dark*. New York: Scholastic.

Pallotta, J. (1988). *The flower alphabet book*. Watertown, MA: Charlesbridge.

Pallotta, J. (1990). *The frog alphabet book: And other awesome amphibians*. Watertown, MA: Charlesbridge.

Pallotta, J. (1991). *The underwater alphabet book*. Watertown, MA: Charlesbridge.

Pallotta, J. (1994). *The desert alphabet book*. Watertown, MA: Charlesbridge.

Palmer, S. (2000). *A little alphabet book*. London: Oxford University Press.

Parish, P. (1963). *Amelia Bedelia*. New York: Harper & Row.

Parker, N. W., & Wright, J. R. (1990). *Frogs, toads, lizards, and salamanders*. New York: Greenwillow.

Parnwell, E., & Grennan, M. (1996). *The Canadian Oxford picture dictionary* (monolingual edition). Toronto: Oxford University Press.

Parrish, T. (2002). *The grouchy grammarian*. London: Wiley.

Parry, C. (Ed.). (1991). *Zoomerang a boomerang*. Toronto: Kids Can Press.

Parry, C. (1994). *Eleanora's diary*. Richmond Hill: Scholastic Canada.

Partridge, E. (2005). *John Lennon: All I want is the truth*. New York: Viking.

Paterson, K. (1987). *Bridge to Terabithia*. New York: HarperTrophy.

Paterson, K. (1991). *Lyddie*. New York: Viking.

Paterson, K. (1994). *Flip-flop girl*. New York: Lodestar.

Paul, A. (1996). *Eight hands round: A patchwork alphabet*. New York: HarperTrophy.

Paulsen, G. (1987). *Hatchet*. New York: Bradbury Press.

Paulsen, G. (1988). *Dogsong*. New York: Bradbury Press.

Paulsen, G. (1993). *Nightjohn*. New York: Delacorte.

Paulsen, G. (2000). *The beet fields: Memories of a sixteenth summer*. New York: Random House.

Pearson, K. (1986). *The daring game*. Toronto: Viking Kestrel.

Pearson, K. (1987). *A handful of time*. Toronto: Viking Kestrel.

Pearson, K. (1989). *The sky is falling*. Toronto: Penguin.

Pearson, K. (1990). *The singing basket*. Toronto: Groundwood Books.

Pearson, K. (1991). *Looking at the moon*. Toronto: Viking.

Pearson, K. (1993). *The lights go on again*. Toronto: Viking.

Pearson, K. (1996). *Awake and dreaming*. Toronto: Viking.

Pearson, K. (1998). *Sea to sea: An anthology of Canadian stories*. New York: Viking.

Pearson, K. (1999). *This land: A cross-country anthology of Canadian fiction for young readers*. Toronto: Penguin.

Pearson, K. (2003). *The guests of war trilogy*. Toronto: Penguin.

Peek, M. (1985). *Mary wore her red dress*. New York: Clarion.

Penrose, G. (1992). *More science surprises from Dr. Zed*. Toronto: Greey de Pencier Books.

Perl, L. (1988). *Don't sing before breakfast, don't sing in the moonlight*. New York: Random House.

Perlman, J. (1993). *The tender tale of Cinderella Penguin: A classic tale retold*. Montreal: National Film Board of Canada.

Perry, S. (1995). *If*. Malibu, CA: J. P. Getty Museum and Children's Library Press.

Pfister, M. (1992). *The rainbow fish*. New York: North-South Books.

Pigott, P. (1995). *Hong Kong rising: The history of a remarkable place*. Burnstown, ON: General Store Publishing House.

Pilling, A. (1990). *Before I go to sleep*. Toronto: Kids Can Press.

Pinkney, A. (1993). *Seven candles for Kwanzaa*. New York: Dial.

Pinkney, A. D. (1994). *Dear Benjamin Banneker*. San Diego: Gulliver/Harcourt Brace.

Pitseolak (1989). *Pitseolak pictures out of my life*. Edited from tape recorded interviews by Dorothy Eber. Toronto: Oxford University Press.

Pizer, V. (1981). *Take my word for it*. New York: Dodd, Mead.

Plain, F. (1994). *Grandfather drum*. Winnipeg: Pemmican.

Polacco, P. (1988). *Rechenka's eggs*. New York: Philomel.

Polacco, P. (1990). *Thunder cake*. New York: Philomel.

Polacco, P. (1993). *The keeping quilt*. New York: Simon & Schuster.

Polacco, P. (1994). *Firetalking*. Katonah, NY: Richard C. Owen.

Polacco, P. (1994). *Pink and Say*. New York: Philomel.

Pomerantz, C. (1982). *If I had a paka: Poems in 11 languages*. New York: Greenwillow.

Pomerantz, C. (1993). *The outside dog*. New York: HarperCollins.

Potter, B. (1902). *The tale of Peter Rabbit*. New York: Warne.

Potter, B. (1995). *Dear Peter Rabbit*. New York: Warne.

Poulsen, D. (1996). *Billy and the bearman*. Toronto: Napoleon Publishing.

Prelutsky, J. (1977). *It's Halloween*. New York: Greenwillow.

Prelutsky, J. (1982). *The baby uggs are hatching*. New York: Mulberry.

Prelutsky, J. (Sel.). (1983). *The Random House book of poetry for children*. New York: Random House.

Prelutsky, J. (1984). *It's snowing! It's snowing!* New York: Greenwillow.

Prelutsky, J. (1984). *The new kid on the block*. New York: Greenwillow.

Prelutsky, J. (1988). *Tyrannosaurus was a beast*. New York: Greenwillow.

Prelutsky, J. (1989). *Poems of A. Nonny Mouse*. New York: Knopf.

Prelutsky, J. (1990). *Something big has been here*. New York: Greenwillow.

Prelutsky, J. (1993). *The dragons are singing tonight*. New York: Greenwillow.

Prelutsky, J. (1993). *A. Nonny Mouse writes again!* New York: Knopf.

Prelutsky, J. (1996). *A pizza the size of the sun*. New York: Greenwillow.

Prelutsky, J. (2001). *For laughing out loud: Poems to tickle your funny bone*. New York: Knopf Books for Young Readers.

Priest, R. (1994). *The ballad of the blue bonnet*. Toronto: Groundwood.

Pryor, B. (1987). *The house on Maple Street*. New York: Morrow.

Rabbi, N. S. (1994). *Casey over there*. San Diego: Harcourt Brace.

Rae, J. (1998). *Dog tales*. Vancouver: Whitecap Books.

Raffi, (1988). *Wheels on the bus*. New York: Crown Publishers.

Ransome, A. (1968). *The fool of the world and the flying ship*. New York: Farrar, Straus & Giroux.

Rathmann, P. (1995). *Officer Buckle and Gloria*. New York: Putnam.

Rauzon, M. J. (1993). *Horns, antlers, fangs, and tusks*. New York: Lothrop, Lee & Shepard.

Reczuch, K., & Manson, A. (1995). *Just like new*. Toronto: Groundwood Books.

Rees, E. (1995). *Fast Freddie Frog and other tongue twister rhymes*. Honesdale, PA: Wordsong.

Reid, B. (1987). *Sing a song of Mother Goose*. Richmond Hill: North Winds Press.

Reid, B. (1991). *Zoe's rainy day*. Toronto: HarperCollins.

Reid, B. (1991). *Zoe's snowy day*. Toronto: HarperCollins.

Reid, B. (1991). *Zoe's sunny day*. Toronto: HarperCollins.

Reid, B. (1991). *Zoe's windy day*. Toronto: HarperCollins.

Reid, B. (1992). *Two by two*. Toronto: Scholastic Canada.

Reid, B. (1997). *The party*. Toronto: Scholastic.

Reid, B. (1998). *Fun with modeling clay*. Toronto: Kids Can Press.

Reid, B. (2000). *The golden goose*. Markham, ON: North Winds Press.

Reid, B. (2003). *The subway mouse*. Toronto: Scholastic Canada.

Reiser, L. (1992). *Any kind of dog*. New York: Greenwillow.

Reynolds, M. (1999). *The prairie fire*. Victoria: Orca Book Publishers.

Richards, D. (1993). *Soldier boys*. Saskatoon: Thistledown Press.

Ringgold, F. (1996). *Tar Beach*. New York: Crown.

Ringgold, F. (1992). *Aunt Harriet's underground railroad in the sky*. New York: Crown.

Ripley, C. (1991). *Two dozen dinosaurs: A first book of dinosaurs facts, mysteries, games and fun*. Toronto: Greey de Pencier Books.

Robb, L. (1995). *Snuffles and snouts*. New York: Dial.

Robertson, J. (1991). *Sea witches*. Toronto: Oxford University Press.

Rockwell, A. (1984). *Trucks*. New York: Dutton.

Roget's student thesaurus (Rev. ed.). (1994). New York: HarperCollins.

Rohmann, E. (2002). *My friend rabbit*. Brookfield, CT: Roaring Book Press.

Roop, P. (1996). *The buffalo jump*. Flagstaff, AZ: Rising Moon.

Roop, P., & Roop, C. (1990). *I Columbus: My journal 1492–1493*. New York: Walker.

Roop, P., & Roop, C. (1993). *Off the map: The journals of Lewis and Clark*. New York: Walker.

Rosen, M. (1989). *We're going on a bear hunt*. New York: Macmillan.

Roth, S. L. (1992). *Marco Polo: His notebook*. New York: Doubleday.

Rothenberg, J. (1986). *Shaking the pumpkin: Traditional poetry of the Indian North Americas*. New York: A. Van der Marck Editions.

Rotner, S. (1995). *Wheels around*. Boston: Houghton Mifflin.

Rotner, S. (1996). *Action alphabet*. New York: Atheneum.

Rowland, D. (1991). *Little Red Riding Hood/The wolf's tale*. New York: Birch Lane Press.

Rowling, J. K. (1998). *Harry Potter and the sorcerer's stone*. New York: Scholastic.

Rubin, S. (2001). *Steven Spielberg: Crazy for movies*. New York: Abrams.

Ruurs, M. (2001). *A Pacific alphabet*. Toronto: Whitecap Books.

Ryder, J. (1989). *Where butterflies grow*. New York: Lodestar.

Rylant, C. (1985). *The relatives came*. New York: Bradbury Press.

Rylant, C. (1988). *All I see*. New York: Orchard.

Rylant, C. (1995). *Mr. Putter and Tabby pick the pears*. Orlando, FL: Harcourt Brace.

Sadiq, N. (1985). *Camels can make you homesick*. Toronto: James Lorimer and Co.

San Souci, R. (1998). *Cendrillon: A Caribbean Cinderella*. New York: Simon and Schuster Books for Young Readers.

Sanders, E. (1995). *What's your name? From Ariel to Zoe*. New York: Holiday.

Sarnoff, J., & Ruffins, R. (1981). *Words: A book about the origins of everyday words and phrases*. New York: Scribner.

Savan, B. (1991). *Earthcycles and ecosystems*. Toronto: Kids Can Press.

Say, A. (1993). *Grandfather's journey*. Boston: Houghton Mifflin.

Scargill, M. (1977). *A short history of Canadian English*. Victoria, BC: Sono Nis Press.

Schlosser, E., & Wilson, C. (2006). *Chew on this: Everything you don't want to know about fast food*. New York: Houghton Mifflin.

Schneider, R. M. (1995). *Add it, dip it, fix it: A book of verbs*. Boston: Houghton Mifflin.

Scholastic children's dictionary. (1996). New York: Scholastic.

Schwartz, A. (1973). *Tomfoolery: Trickery and foolery with words*. Philadelphia: Lippincott.

Schwartz, A. (1982). *The cat's elbow and other secret languages*. New York: Farrar, Straus & Giroux.

Schwartz, A. (1982). *There is a carrot in my ear and other noodle tales*. New York: Harper & Row.

Schwartz, A. (1984). *In a dark, dark room*. New York: Scholastic.

Schwartz, A. (1992). *Busy buzzing bumblebees and other tongue twisters*. New York: HarperCollins.

Schwartz, D. M. (1989). *If you made a million*. New York: Lothrop, Lee & Shepard.

Schwartz, D. M. (1994). *How much is a million?* New York: Morrow.

Schwartz, V. F. (2003). *Initiation*. Toronto: Fitzhenry & Whiteside.

Scieszka, J. (1989). *The true story of the 3 little pigs!* New York: Viking.

Scieszka, J. (1991). *The time warp trio: The not-so-jolly-roger*. New York: Penguin Books.

Scieszka, J. (1998). *Squids will be squids: Fresh morals, beastly fables*. Toronto: Viking (Penguin Books).

Scott, A. H. (1990). *One good horse: A cowpuncher's counting book*. New York: Greenwillow.

Scott, R. (1991). *The student editors guide to words*. Toronto: Gage Educational Publishing.

Scrimger, R. (1998). *The nose from Jupiter*. Toronto: Tundra Books.

Scrimger, R. (2002). *Princess Bun Bun*. Toronto: Tundra Books.

Scrivener, L. (2000). *Terry Fox: His story*. Toronto: McClelland & Stewart.

Seattle, C. (1991). *Brother Eagle, Sister Sky*. New York: Dial.

Sendak, M. (1962). *Chicken soup with rice*. New York: Harper & Row.

Sendak, M. (1963). *Where the wild things are*. New York: Harper & Row.

Sendak, M. (1975). *Seven little monsters*. New York: Harper & Row.

Service, R. (1944). *The complete poems of Robert Service*. New York: The Blakiston Company.

Service, R. (1986). *The Cremation of Sam McGee*. Illus. T. Harrison. Toronto: Kids Can Press.

Service, R. (1988). *The Shooting of Dan McGrew*. Illus. T. Harrison. Toronto: Kids Can Press.

Seuss, Dr. (1963). *Hop on pop*. New York: Random House.

Seuss, Dr. (1965). *Fox in socks*. New York: Random House.

Seuss, Dr. (1979). *Oh say can you say?* New York: Beginner Books.

Seuss, Dr. (1985). *The cat in the hat*. New York: Random House.

Seuss, Dr. (1988). *Green eggs and ham*. New York: Random House.

Sewall, M. (1995). *Thunder from the clear sky*. New York: Atheneum.

Shannon, C. (1996). *Spring: A haiku story*. New York: Greenwillow.

Shannon, M. (1994). *Gawain and the Green Knight*. New York: Putnam.

Sharmat, M. W. (1972). *Nate the Great*. New York: Dell.

Sharmat, M. W. (1995). *Nate the Great and the tardy tortoise*. New York: Dell.

Shaw, N. (1992). *Sheep out to eat*. Boston: Houghton Mifflin.

Shea, P. D. (1995). *The whispering cloth: A refugee's story*. Honesdale, PA: Boyds Mills Press.

Sheidlower, J. (1998). *Jesse's word of the day*. New York: Random House.

Shemie, B. (1989). *House of snow, skin and bones—native dwellings: The far north*. Montreal: Tundra Books.

Sherman, I. (1980). *Walking talking words*. New York: Harcourt Brace Jovanovich.

Shiefman, V. (1981). *M is for move*. New York: Dutton.

Showers, P. (1985). *What happens to a hamburger?* New York: Harper & Row.

Sidman, J. (2005). *Song of the water boatman and other pond poems*. Boston: Houghton Mifflin.

Siebert, D. (1984). *Truck song*. New York: Harper & Row.

Siebert, D. (1988). *Mojave*. New York: HarperCollins.

Sierra, J. (2000). *The gift of the crocodile: A Cinderella story*. New York: Simon and Schuster Books for Young Readers.

Silsbe, B. (2001). *A tree is just a tree?* Vancouver: Raincoast.

Silverman, E. (1994). *Don't fidget a feather!* New York: Simon & Schuster.

Silverstein, S. (1974). *Where the sidewalk ends*. New York: Harper & Row.

Silverstein, S. (1981). *A light in the attic*. New York: Harper & Row.

Silverstein, S. (1996). *Falling up*. New York: HarperCollins.

Simmie, L. (1986). *An armadillo is not a pillow*. Saskatoon: Western Producer Prairie Books.

Simon, S. (1989). *Whales*. New York: Crowell.

Simon, S. (1990). *Oceans*. New York: Morrow Junior Books.

Simon, S. (1992). *Wolves*. New York: HarperCollins.

Simon, S. (1993). *Mercury*. New York: Morrow.

Simon, S. (2002). *Under the Ice: A Canadian museum of nature book*. Toronto: Kids Can Press.

Singer, M. (1995). *A wasp is not a bee*. New York: Holt.

Skrypuch, M. F. (1996). *Silver threads*. Toronto: Viking.

Skrypuch, M. F. (2001). *Hope's war*. Toronto: Boardwalk Books.

Skrypuch, M. F. (2003). *Nobody's child*. Toronto: Dundurn Press.

Slade, A. (2001). *Dust*. Toronto: HarperCollins.

Smith, D. J., & Armstrong, S. (2002). *If the world were a village: A book about the world's people*. Toronto: Kids Can Press.

Smith, J. (1988). *The show-and-tell war*. New York: Harper & Row.

Smith, J. (1991). *But no elephants*. New York: Parents Magazine Press.

Smith, M. (1991). *A snake mistake*. New York: HarperCollins.

Smith, W. J., & Ra, C. (1992). *Behind the king's kitchen: A roster of rhyming riddles*. Honesdale, PA: Wordsong.

Smucker, B. (1977). *Underground to Canada*. New York: Irwin and Co. Ltd.

Smucker, B. (1995). *Selina and the bear paw quilt*. Illus. J. Wilson. Toronto: Lester Publishing.

Sorel, N. (1970). *Word people*. New York: American Heritage.

Sorenson, L. (1995). *Canada: The land*. Vero Beach, FL: Rourke Book Co.

Soto, G. (1992). *Neighborhood odes*. Orlando: Harcourt Brace.

Soto, G. (1993). *Too many tamales*. New York: Putnam.

Soto, G. (1995). *Canto familiar*. Orlando: Harcourt Brace.

Soto, G. (1995). *Chato's kitchen*. New York: Putnam.

Souhami, J. (1996). *Old MacDonald*. New York: Orchard.

Souza, D. M. (1994). *Northern lights*. Minneapolis: Carolrhoda.

Spalding, A. (1995). *Finders keepers*. Victoria, BC: Beach Holme Publishers.

Speare, E. G. (1958). *The witch of Blackbird Pond*. Boston: Houghton Mifflin.

Speare, E. G. (1983). *The sign of the beaver*. Boston: Houghton Mifflin.

Sperling, S. (1979). *Poplollies and bellibones: A celebration of lost words*. New York: Penguin.

Sperry, A. (1968). *Call it courage*. New York: Macmillan.

Spier, P. (1971). *Gobble growl grunt*. New York: Doubleday.

Spier, P. (1972). *Crash! Bang! Boom!* New York: Doubleday.

Spinelli, J. (1990). *Maniac Magee*. Boston: Little, Brown.

Stanley, D. (1983). *The conversation club*. New York: Macmillan.

Stanley, D., & Vennema, P. (1994). *Cleopatra*. New York: Morrow Junior Books.

Staunton, T. (2001). *Great play, Morgan*. (First Novels Series). Halifax, NS: Formac Publishing.

Steckler, A. (1981). *101 more words and how they began*. Garden City, NY: Doubleday.

Steele, P. (1995). *Castles*. New York: Kingfisher.

Steig, W. (1992). *Alpha beta chowder*. New York: HarperCollins.

Steig, W. (1969). *Sylvester and the magic pebble*. New York: Simon & Schuster.

Steig, W. (1971). *Amos and Boris*. New York: Farrar, Straus & Giroux.

Steig, W. (1982). *Doctor De Soto*. New York: Farrar, Straus & Giroux.

Steig, W. (1986). *Brave Irene*. New York: Farrar, Straus & Giroux.

Steltzer, U. (1995). *Building an igloo*. New York: Holt.

Steptoe, J. (1987). *Mufaro's beautiful daughters: An African tale*. New York: Lothrop, Lee & Shepard.

Sterne, N. (1979). *Tyrannosaurus wrecks: A book of dinosaur riddles*. New York: Crowell.

Stevens, J. (1987). *The three billy goats Gruff*. San Diego: Harcourt Brace Jovanovich.

Stevenson, J. (1995). *Sweet corn: Poems*. New York: Greenwillow.

Stevenson, R. L. (1985). *Happy thought: Poems for children*. Illus. V. Gad. Toronto: Midway Publications.

Steward, S. (2003). *Raven Quest*. Toronto: Scholastic.

Stinson, K. (1982). *Red is best*. Toronto: Annick Press.

Stinson, K. (1983). *Big or little*. Illus. R. Baird Lewis. Toronto: Annick Press.

Stinson, K. (1985). *Those green things*. Toronto: Annick Press.

Stinson, K. (1986). *The bare naked book*. Illus. H. Collins. Toronto: Annick Press.

Stinson, K. (1991). *Who is sleeping in Aunty's bed?* Toronto: Oxford University Press.

Sullivan, C. (1993). *Cowboys*. New York: Rizzoli.

Surat, M. M. (1983). *Angel child, dragon child*. Milwaukee: Raintree.

Suzuki, D. (1988). *Looking at weather*. Don Mills, ON: Stoddart.

Suzuki, D. (1994). *If we could see the air*. Don Mills, ON: Stoddart.

Swamp, Chief J. (1995). *Giving thanks: A Native American good morning message*. New York: Lee & Low.

Swede, G. (1991). *I want to lasso time*. Toronto: Simon & Pierre.

Takashima, S. (1971). *A child in prison camp*. New York: William Morrow and Company.

Tanaka, S. (1996). *I was there: On board the Titanic*. Toronto: Scholastic.

Tanaka, S. (1999). *Secrets of the mummies: Uncovering the bodies of ancient Egyptians*. Richmond Hill, ON: Scholastic Canada.

Tanaka, S. (2000). *The buried city of Pompeii: What it was like when Vesuvius exploded*. New York: Hyperion Press.

Taylor, B. (1992). *Desert life*. New York: Dorling Kindersley.

Taylor, C. (1985). *Julie*. Saskatoon: Western Producer Prairie Books.

Taylor, C. (1987). *The doll*. Saskatoon: Western Producer Prairie Books.

Taylor, C. (1992). *Little Water and the gift of the animals: A Seneca legend*. Montreal: Tundra Books.

Taylor, C. (1994). *Summer of the mad monk*. Toronto: Greystone Books/Douglas & McIntyre.

Taylor, C. (1997). *Vanishing act*. Red Deer, AB: Red Deer College Press.

Taylor, C. J. (1994). *Bones in the basket*. Montreal: Tundra Books.

Taylor, C. J. (1997). *The secret of the white buffalo*. Montreal: Tundra Books.

Taylor, M. D. (1976). *Roll of thunder, hear my cry*. New York: Dial.

Taylor, M. D. (1987). *The gold Cadillac*. New York: Dial.

Terban, M. (1983). *In a pickle and other funny idioms*. New York: Clarion books.

Terban, M. (1984). *I think I thought and other tricky verbs*. New York: Clarion.

Terban, M. (1985). *Too hot to hoot: Funny palindrome riddles*. New York: Clarion.

Terban, M. (1986). *Your foot's on my feet! and other tricky nouns*. New York: Clarion.

Terban, M. (1988). *Guppies in tuxedos: Funny eponyms*. New York: Clarion.

Terban, M. (1989). *Superdupers! Really funny real words*. New York: Clarion.

Terban, M. (1990). *Punching the clock: Funny action idioms*. New York: Clarion Books.

Terban, M. (1991). *Hey, hay! A wagonful of funny homonym riddles*. New York: Clarion Books.

Terban, M. (1992). *Funny you should ask: How to make up jokes and riddles with wordplay*. New York: Clarion.

Terban, M. (1993). *It figures! Fun figures of speech*. New York: Clarion.

Terban, M. (1995). *Time to rhyme: A rhyming dictionary*. Honesdale, PA: Wordsong.

Terkel, S. (1975). *Working*. New York: Avon.

Thayer, E. L. (1988). *Casey at the bat: A ballad of the republic, sung in the year 1888*. Illus. P. Polacco. New York: Putnam.

Thomas, D. (1997). *Fern Hill*. Illus. M. Kimber. Red Deer: Red Deer College Press.

Thomas, L. (1988). *What's it? Gadgets, objects, machines and more*. Toronto: Greey de Pencier.

Thomas, S. M. (1995). *Putting the world to sleep*. Boston: Houghton Mifflin.

Thompson, J., & Macintosh, B. (1996). *A pirate's life for me!* Watertown: Charlesbridge.

Thomson, P. (1995). *Katie Henio: Navajo sheep herder*. New York: Cobblehill.

Thornhill, J. (1988). *Wildlife ABC: A nature alphabet*. Toronto: Greey de Pencier Books.

Thurman, M. (1992). *Fun-tastic collages*. Markham: Pembroke Publishers.

Tolhurst, M. (1990). *Somebody and the three Blairs*. New York: Orchard Books.

Tolowa, M. (1995). *The orphan boy*. Don Mills, ON: Stoddart.

Torres, L. (1993). *Subway sparrow*. New York: Farrar, Straus & Giroux.

Toten, T. (2001). *The game*. Red Deer, AB: Red Deer College Press.

Tregebov, R. (1993). *The big storm*. New York: Hyperion.

Trembath, D. (2000). *Frog face and the three boys*. Victoria: Orca Books.

Tresselt, A. (1964). *The mitten*. New York: Lothrop, Lee & Shepard.

Tryon, L. (1994). *Albert's Thanksgiving*. New York: Atheneum.

Turkle, B. (1976). *Deep in the forest*. New York: Dutton.

Turner, A. (1987). *Nettie's trip south*. New York: Macmillan.

Tynes, M. (1991). *Save the world for me*. East Lawrencetown: Pottersfield Press.

Uchida, Y. (1971). *Journey to Topaz*. Berkeley: Creative Arts Book Company.

Uchida, Y. (1993). *The bracelet*. New York: Philomel.

Unobagha, U. (2000). *Off to the sweet shores of Africa*. San Francisco: Chronicle Books.

Vaage, C. (1995). *Bibi and the bull*. Red Deer, AB: Red Deer College Press.

Vaes, A. (1994). *Reynard the fox*. New York: Turner.

Van Allsburg, C. (1979). *The garden of Abdul Gasazi*. Boston: Houghton Mifflin.

Van Allsburg, C. (1981). *Jumanji*. Boston: Houghton Mifflin.

Van Allsburg, C. (1983). *The wreck of the zephyr*. Boston: Houghton Miffilin.

Van Allsburg, C. (1985). *The polar express*. Boston: Houghton Mifflin.

Van Allsburg, C. (1986). *The stranger*. Boston: Houghton Mifflin.

Van Allsburg, C. (1987). *The Z was zapped*. Boston: Houghton Mifflin.

Van Allsburg, C. (1993). *The sweetest fig*. Boston: Houghton Mifflin.

Van Allsburg, C. (1995). *Bad day at Riverbend*. Boston: Houghton Mifflin.

Van Allsburg, C. (1996). *The mysteries of Harris Burdick* (Portfolio ed.). Boston: Houghton Mifflin.

Vande Griek, S., & Milelli, P. (2002). *The art room*. Toronto: Groundwood Books.

Van Leeuwen, J. (1995). *Oliver and Amanda and the big snow.* New York: Dial.

Vaughan, M. (1990). *Clouds.* Auckland: Shortland Publications.

Viorst, J. (1977). *Alexander and the terrible, horrible, no good, very bad day.* New York: Atheneum.

Viorst, J. (1981). *If I were in charge of the world and other worries.* New York: Atheneum.

Voigt, C. (1982). *Dicey's song.* New York: Atheneum.

Waber, B. (1972). *Ira sleeps over.* Boston: Houghton Mifflin.

Waber, B. (1995). *Do you see a mouse?* Boston: Houghton Mifflin.

Waboose, J. B., & Deines, B. (2000). *SkySisters.* Toronto: Kids Can Press.

Wadsworth, G. (1995). *Giant sequoia trees.* Minneapolis: Lerner.

Waggoner, K. (1995). *Partners.* New York: Simon & Schuster.

Wakan, N. (1993). *Haiku—one breath poetry.* Vancouver: Pacific Rim Publishers.

Wallace, I. (1984). *Chin Chiang and the dragon's dance.* Toronto: Groundwood Books.

Walsh, A. (1994). *Shabash!* Victoria: Beach Holme Publishers.

Walsh, A. (2001). *Heroes of Isle aux Morts.* Toronto: Tundra Books.

Walsh, E. S. (1993). *Hop jump.* New York: Harcourt Brace and Company.

Walters, E. (1997). *Trapped in ice.* Toronto: Puffin Books.
Walters, E. (1998). *The war of the eagles.* Vancouver: Orca Books.

Walters, E. (1999). *Three-on-three.* Vancouver: Orca Books.

Walters, E. (2003). *Run.* Toronto: Viking.

Walton, R. (1995). *What to do when a bug climbs in your mouth: And other poems to drive you buggy.* New York: Lothrop & Lee.

Ward, K. (1989). *Twelve kids one cow.* Toronto: Kids Can Press.

Waters, K. (1989). *Sarah Morton's day: A day in the life of a pilgrim girl.* New York: Scholastic.

Waterton, B. (1978). *A salmon for Simon.* Vancouver: Douglas & McIntyre.

Watts, B. (1987). *Ladybug.* Morristown, NJ: Silver Burdett.

Watts, B. (1991). *Frog.* New York: Lodestar.

Watts, I. (2000). *Remember me.* Toronto: Tundra Books.

Weber-Pillwax, C. (1989). *Billy's world.* Edmonton: Reid More Books.

Weisner, D. (1990). *Hurricane.* New York: Clarion.

Weisner, D. (1991). *Tuesday.* New York: Clarion.

Weiss, A. E. (1980). *What's that you said? How words change.* New York: Harcourt Brace Jovanovich.

Weiss, N. (1987). *If you're happy and you know it.* New York: Greenwillow.

Weiss, N. (1989). *Where does the brown bear go?* New York: Viking.

West, C. (1996). *"I don't care!" said the bear.* Cambridge, MA: Candlewick.

Westcott, N. B. (1980). *I know an old lady who swallowed a fly.* Boston: Little, Brown.

Westcott, N. B. (1988). *The lady with the alligator purse.* Boston: Little, Brown.

Westcott, N. B. (1989). *Skip to my Lou.* Boston: Little, Brown.

Westcott, N. B. (1990). *There's a hole in the bucket.* New York: HarperCollins.

Westcott, N. B. (1994). *Never take a pig to lunch: And other poems about the fun of eating.* New York: Orchard.

Whelan, G. (1992). *Bringing the farmhouse home.* Riverside, NJ: Simon & Schuster.

White, E. B. (1952/1980). *Charlotte's web.* New York: HarperCollins.

Wideman, R. (1989). *David Suzuki.* Markham: Fitzhenry & Whiteside.

Wiebe, R. (1992). *Chinook Christmas.* Red Deer, AB: Red Deer College Press.

Wilder, L. I. (1953). *Little house on the prairie.* Illus. G. Williams. New York: Scholastic.

Wilder, L. I. (1971). *The long winter.* New York: Harper & Row.

Wildsmith, B. (1968). *Fishes.* New York: Franklin Watts.

Wilkins, C. (1989). *Old Mrs. Schmatterbung and other friends.* Toronto: McClelland & Stewart.

Winter, J. (1988). *Follow the drinking gourd.* New York: Knopf.

Wittels, H., & Greisman, J. (1985). *A first thesaurus.* Racine, WI: Western.

Wolfe, F. (2001). *Where I live.* Toronto: Tundra Books.

Wolk, A. (1980). *Everyday words from names of people and places.* New York: Elsevier/Nelson.

Wong, J. S. (1994). *Good luck gold and other poems.* New York: McElderry Books.

Wynne-Jones, T. (1992). *Zoom upstream.* Toronto: Groundwood Books.

Wynne-Jones, T. (1995). *The maestro.* Toronto: Groundwood Books.

Wynne-Jones, T. (2000). *The boy in the burning house.* Toronto: Groundwood Books.

Wynne-Jones, T. (2001). *Boy's own: An anthology of Canadian fiction for young readers.* Toronto: Penguin.

Wynne-Jones, T. (2003). *Ned Mouse breaks away.* Toronto: Groundwood.

Ye, T.-X. (2002). *White lily.* Toronto: Doubleday.

Ye, T.-X., & Bell, W. (2003). *Throwaway daughter.* Toronto: Doubleday.

Yee, P. (1989). *Tales from Gold Mountain: Stories of the Chinese in the new world.* Toronto: Groundwood.

Yee, P. (1996). *Ghost train.* Vancouver: Douglas & McIntyre.

Yee, P. (1996). *Struggle and hope: The story of Chinese Canadians.* Toronto: Umbrella Press.

Yerxa, L. (1993). *Last leaf, first snowflake to fall.* Vancouver: Douglas & McIntyre.

Yolen, J. (1980). *Commander Toad in space.* New York: Coward McCann.

Yolen, J. (1986). *The sleeping beauty.* New York: Knopf.

Yolen, J. (1987). *Owl moon.* New York: Philomel.

Yolen, J. (1990). *Bird watch: A book of poetry.* New York: Philomel.

Yolen, J. (1990). *Dinosaur dances.* New York: Putnam.

Yolen, J. (1992). *Encounter.* Orlando: Harcourt Brace.

Yolen, J. (1993). *Weather report: Poems*. Honesdale, PA: Wordsong.

Yolen, J. (1993). *Welcome to the green house*. New York: Putnam.

Yolen, J. (1994). *Here there be unicorns*. San Diego: Harcourt Brace.

Yolen, J. (1995). *Water music: Poems for children*. Honesdale, PA: Wordsong.

Yolen, J. (1996). *Sacred places*. New York: Harcourt Brace.

Yolen, J. (1997). *Owl moon*. New York: Philomel Books.

Young, E. (1979). *The lion and the mouse*. New York: Putnam.

Zalben, J. B. (1992). *Lewis Carroll's Jabberwocky*. Honesdale, PA: Boyds Mills Press.

Zeman, L. (1999). *Sinbad: From the tales of the thousand and one nights*. Montreal: Tundra Books.

Zelinsky, P. O. (1986). *Rumpelstiltskin*. New York: Dutton.

Zemach, M. (1983). *The little red hen*. New York: Farrar, Straus & Giroux.

Zhang, S. N. (1993). *A little tiger in the Chinese night: An autobiography in art*. Montreal: Tundra Books.

Ziefert, H. (1983). *Small potatoes club*. New York: Dell.

Ziefert, H. (1986). *A new coat for Anna*. New York: Knopf.

Ziefert, H. (1991). *Bob and Shirley: A tale of two lobsters*. New York: HarperCollins.

Ziegler, S. (1988). *A visit to the airport*. Chicago: Children's Press.

Zimmermann, H. (1990). *Alphonse knows—the colour of spring*. Toronto: Oxford University Press.

Zoehfeld, K. W. (1995). *How mountains are made*. New York: HarperCollins.

Zwicky, J. (1992). *Lyric philosophy*. Toronto: University of Toronto Press.

Author Index

Subject Index

Credits